I0836708

Painted by Chappel. Engraved by W. Wellstood.

GENERAL TAYLOR AT MONTEREY.

From the original picture in the possession of the Publishers.

Johnson, Fry & Cº Publishers, N.Y.

HISTORY
OF THE
UNITED STATES

VOL 3

Painted by | DEATH OF GENERAL PIKE. | Alonzo Chappel

NEW YORK,
JOHNSON, FRY & COMPANY,
27 BEEKMAN STREET.

HISTORY

OF THE

UNITED STATES.

FROM

THE EARLIEST PERIOD

TO

THE ADMINISTRATION OF JAMES BUCHANAN.

BY

J. A. SPENCER, D. D.,

MEMBER OF THE NEW YORK HISTORICAL SOCIETY, MEMBRE DE LA SOCIÉTÉ ORIENTALE DE FRANCE,
AUTHOR OF "EGYPT AND THE HOLY LAND," ETC., ETC., ETC.

Illustrated with highly Finished Steel Engravings,

FROM ORIGINAL PICTURES BY LEUTZE, WEIR, POWELL, CHAPPEL, AND OTHER AMERICAN ARTISTS.

IN THREE VOLUMES.

VOLUME III.

New York:

JOHNSON, FRY AND COMPANY,

27 BEEKMAN STREET.

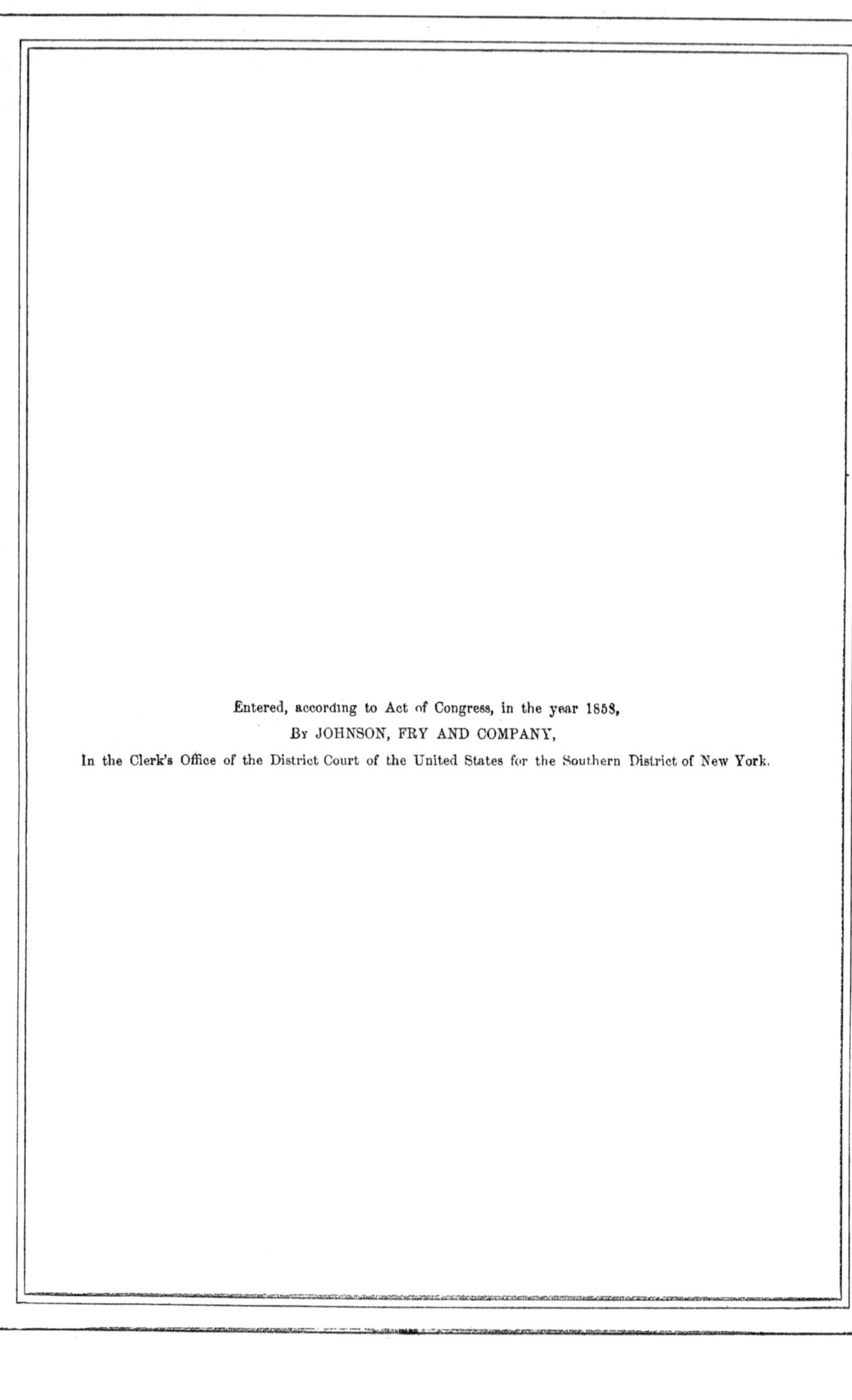

CONTENTS OF VOL. III.

BOOK FIFTH.

FROM THE INAUGURATION OF THOMAS JEFFERSON TO THE CLOSE OF THE SECOND WAR WITH ENGLAND.

CHAPTER I.

1801-1802.

OPENING YEAR OF THE NEW ADMINISTRATION.

CHAPTER II.

1802-1803.

THE ACQUISITION OF LOUISIANA.

CHAPTER III.

1803-1805.

PROGRESS OF EVENTS DURING 1803, 1804, AND 1805.

CHAPTER IV.

1805-1807.

TWO YEARS OF JEFFERSON'S SECOND TERM.

CHAPTER V.

1807-1809.

CLOSE OF JEFFERSON'S PRESIDENCY.

CHAPTER VI.

1809-1811.

THE TWO YEARS PRECEDING THE WAR.

CHAPTER VII.

1811-1812.

OPENING OF THE WAR.

CHAPTER VIII.

1812.

OPERATIONS OF THE YEAR 1812.

CHAPTER IX.

1812-1813.

PROGRESS OF THE WAR DURING 1813.

CHAPTER X.

1813.

CONCLUSION OF THE CAMPAIGN OF 1813.

CHAPTER XI.

1814.

OPERATIONS IN THE NORTH DURING 1814.

CHAPTER XII.

1814.

THE INVASION OF WASHINGTON.

CHAPTER XIII.

1814, 1815.

THE END OF THE WAR.

BOOK SIXTH.

FROM THE RETURN OF PEACE IN 1815, TO THE END OF J. Q. ADAMS'S ADMINISTRATION.

CHAPTER I.

1815–1817.

CLOSE OF MADISON'S PRESIDENCY.

CHAPTER II.

1817–1819.

MONROE'S FIRST TWO YEARS.

CHAPTER III.

1819-1822.

PROGRESS OF AFFAIRS DURING 1819-1822.

CHAPTER IV.

1822-1825.

END OF MONROE'S ADMINISTRATION.

CHAPTER V.

1825-1829.

JOHN QUINCY ADAMS'S ADMINISTRATION.

BOOK SEVENTH.

FROM THE INAUGURATION OF ANDREW JACKSON TO THE ADMINISTRATION OF JAMES BUCHANAN.

CHAPTER I.

1829-1832.

JACKSON'S ADMINISTRATION: FIRST THREE YEARS.

CHAPTER II.

1832-1837.

JACKSON'S ADMINISTRATION CONCLUDED.

CHAPTER III.

1837-1841.

VAN BUREN'S ADMINISTRATION.

CHAPTER IV.

1841–1845.

HARRISON'S AND TYLER'S ADMINISTRATION.

CHAPTER V.

1845–1847.

POLK'S ADMINISTRATION: TWO YEARS.

CHAPTER VI.

1847–1849.

POLK'S ADMINISTRATION, CONCLUDED.

CHAPTER VII.

1849–1850.

TAYLOR AND FILLMORE'S ADMINISTRATION.

CHAPTER VIII.

1853–1857.

FRANKLIN PIERCE'S ADMINISTRATION.

CHAPTER IX.

1857.

OPENING OF BUCHANAN'S ADMINISTRATION.

Book Fifth.

FROM THE

INAUGURATION OF THOMAS JEFFERSON

TO THE

CLOSE OF THE SECOND WAR WITH ENGLAND.

1801—1815.

HISTORY

OF THE

UNITED STATES OF AMERICA.

CHAPTER I.

1801-1802.

OPENING YEAR OF THE NEW ADMINISTRATION.

Inaugural Address of Thomas Jefferson — His cabinet appointments — Letter to John Dickinson — The question of removals from office a perplexing one — Jefferson's views on the subject, in letters to Monroe, Gerry, and Lincoln — Case of the New Haven collector — The judges appointed by John Adams — Answers to Macon's queries — R. R. Livingston minister to France — The navy — The demands of the pasha of Tripoli — Commodore Dale and the American squadron in the Mediterranean — The opening of the seventh Congress — Jefferson sends a message instead of delivering a speech — The message — Mr. Tucker's remarks on it — Measures for economy and reform — Revision of the judiciary act — Jefferson's views on the subject — Bill for repeal of the act brought into Congress — Long and earnest debate — Memorial against the repeal — Views of the federalists — The bill passed — Not wholly approved by the party — Subsequent arrangements as to the courts — Repeal of laws establishing internal taxes — Mr. Jefferson and Mr. Tucker quoted on this point — Other acts of the session — Congress adjourns in May, 1802.

On Wednesday, the 4th day of March, 1801, the Senate of the United States assembled in their chamber, and Aaron Burr took the oath of office as vice-president. Soon after, Thomas Jefferson, attended by the heads of
1801. the departments, the marshal of the district, his officers, and other gentlemen, came into the Senate chamber, and took his seat in that chair of which he had himself been the occupant for the preceding four years. On his right, Burr was seated; and on his left, John Marshall, the chief justice of the United States. After a short pause, Jefferson arose and addressed the audience in the following terms:

"*Friends and Fellow-Citizens;*

"Called upon to undertake the duties of the first executive office of our country, I avail myself of the presence of that portion of my fellow-citizens which is here assembled, to express my grateful thanks for the favor with which they have been pleased to look towards me, to declare a sincere consciousness, that the task is above my talents, and that I approach it with those anxious and awful presentiments, which the greatness of the charge, and the weakness of my powers, so justly inspire. A rising nation, spread over a wide and fruitful land, traversing all the seas with the rich productions of their industry, engaged in commerce with nations who feel power and forget right, advancing rapidly to destinies beyond the reach of mortal eye; when I contemplate these transcendent objects, and see the honor, the happiness, and the hopes of this beloved country committed to the issue and the auspices of this day, I shrink from the contemplation, and humble myself before the magnitude of the undertaking. Utterly, indeed, should I despair, did not the presence of many, whom I here see, remind me, that, in the other high authorities provided by our Constitution, I shall find resources of wisdom, of virtue, and of zeal, on which to rely under all difficulties. To you, then, gentlemen, who are charged with the sovereign functions of legislation, and to those associated with you, I look with encouragement for that guidance and support which may enable us to steer with safety the vessel in which we are all embarked, amidst the conflicting elements of a troubled world.

"During the contest of opinion through which we have passed, the animation of discussions and of exertions has sometimes worn an aspect which might impose on strangers unused to think freely, and 1801. to speak and to write what they think; but this being now decided by the voice of the nation, announced according to the rules of the Constitution, all will of course arrange themselves under the will of the law, and unite in common efforts for the common good. All too will bear in mind this sacred principle, that though the will of the majority is in all cases to prevail, that will, to be rightful, must be reasonable; that the minority possess their equal rights, which equal laws must protect, and to violate which would be oppression. Let us then, fellow-citizens, unite with one heart and one mind, let us restore to social intercourse, that harmony and affection without which, liberty, and even life itself, are but dreary things. And let us reflect, that having banished from our land that religious intolerance under which mankind so long bled and suffered, we have yet gained little, if we countenance a political intolerance, as despotic as wicked, and capable of as bitter and bloody persecutions. During the throes and convulsions of the ancient world, during the agonizing spasms of infuriated man, seeking through blood and slaughter his long-lost liberty, it was not wonderful that the agitation of the billows should reach even this distant and peaceful shore; that this should be more felt and feared by some, and less by others; and should divide opinions as to measures of safety; but every difference of opinion is not a difference of principle. We have called by different names brethren of the same principle. We are all republicans; we are all federalists. If there be any among us who would wish to dissolve this Union, or to change its republican form, let them stand undisturbed as monuments of the safety with which error of opinion may be tolerated, where reason is left free to combat it. I know, indeed, that some honest men fear that a republican government cannot be strong; that this government is not strong enough. But would the honest patriot, in the full tide of successful experiment, abandon a government which has so far kept us free and firm, on the theoretic and visionary fear, that this government, the world's best hope, may, by possibility, want energy to preserve itself? I trust not. I believe this, on the contrary, the strongest government on earth. I believe it the only one, where every man, at the call of the law, would fly to the standard of the law, and would meet invasions of the public order as his own personal concern. Sometimes it is said, that man cannot be trusted with the government of himself. Can he then be trusted with the government of others? Or, have we found angels in the form of kings, to govern him? Let history answer this question.

"Let us, then, with courage and confidence, pursue our own federal and republican principles; our attachment to union and representative government. Kindly separated by nature and a wide ocean from the exterminating havoc of one quarter of the globe; too high-minded to endure the degradations of the others; possessing a chosen country, with room enough for our descendants to the thousandth and thousandth generation; entertaining a due sense of our equal right to the use of our own faculties, to the acquisitions of our own industry, to honor and confidence from our fellow-citizens, resulting not from birth, but from our actions and their sense of them; enlightened by a benign religion, professed indeed and practised in various forms, yet all of them inculcating honesty, truth, temperance, gratitude, and the love of man; acknowledging and adoring an overruling Providence, which, by all its dispensations, proves that it delights in the happiness of man here, and his greater happiness hereafter; with all these blessings, what more is necessary to make us a happy and prosperous people? Still one thing more, fellow-citizens, a wise and frugal government, which shall restrain men from injuring one another, shall leave them otherwise free to regulate their own pursuits of industry and improvement, and shall not take from the mouth of labor the bread it has earned. This is the sum of good government; and this is necessary to close the circle of our felicities.

"About to enter, fellow-citizens, on the exercise of duties which comprehend every thing dear and valuable to you, it is proper you should understand what I deem the essential principles of our government, and consequently, those which ought to shape its administration. I will compress them within the narrowest compass they will bear, stating the general principle, but not all its limitations. Equal and exact justice to all men, of whatever state or persuasion, religious or political; peace, commerce, and honest friendship with all nations, entangling alliances with none; the support of the state governments in all their rights, as the most competent administrations for our domestic concerns, and the surest bulwarks against anti-republican tendencies; the preservation of the general government in its whole constitutional vigor, as the sheet-anchor of our peace at home, and safety abroad; a jealous care of the right of election by the people, a mild and safe corrective of abuses which are lopped by the sword of revolution where peaceable remedies are unprovided; absolute acquiescence in the decisions of the majority, the vital principle of republics, from which there is no appeal but to force, the vital principle and immediate parent of despotism; a well-disciplined militia, our best reliance in peace, and for the first moments of war, till regulars may relieve them; the supremacy of the civil over the military authority; economy in the public expense, that labor may be lightly burdened; the honest payment of our debts and sacred preservation of the public faith; encouragement of agriculture, and of commerce as its handmaid; the diffusion of information, and arraignment of all abuses at the bar of public reason; freedom of religion; freedom of the press; and freedom of person, under the protection of the *habeas corpus;* and trial by juries impartially selected. These principles form the bright constellation which has gone before us, and guided our steps through an age of revolution and reformation. The wisdom of our sages, and blood of our heroes, have been devoted to their attainment: they should be the creed of our political faith, the text of civic instruction, the touchstone by which to try the services of those we trust; and should we wander from them in moments of error or of alarm, let us hasten to retrace our steps, and to regain the road which alone leads to peace, liberty, and safety.

"I repair, then, fellow-citizens, to the post you have assigned me. With experience enough in subordinate offices to have seen the difficulties of this, the greatest of all, I have learned to expect that it will rarely fall to the lot of imperfect man, to retire from this station with the reputation and the favor which bring him into it. Without pretensions to that high confidence you reposed in our first and greatest revolutionary character, whose pre-eminent services had entitled him to the first place in his country's love, and destined for him the fairest page in the volume of faithful history, I ask so much confidence only as may give firmness and effect to the legal administration of your affairs. I shall often go wrong through defect of judgment. When right, I shall often be thought wrong by those whose positions will not command a view of the whole ground. I ask your indulgence for my own errors, which will never be intentional; and your support against the errors of others, who may condemn what they would not, if seen in all its parts. The approbation im-

1801.

plied by your suffrage, is a great consolation to me for the past; and my future solicitude will be, to retain the good opinion of those who have bestowed it in advance, to conciliate that of others, by doing them all the good in my power, and to be instrumental to the happiness and freedom of all.

"Relying then on the patronage of your good-will, I advance with obedience to the work, ready to retire from it whenever you become sensible how much better choices it is in your power to make. And may that Infinite Power which rules the destinies of the universe, lead our councils to what is best, and give them a favorable issue for your prosperity."

The oath of office was then administered by the chief justice; and Thomas Jefferson, the third president of the United States, and now, in the fifty-eighth year of his age, retired from the Senate-chamber with high hopes and sanguine expectations of the successful prosecution of his responsible and important duties. His Inaugural Address has been very highly lauded on the one hand, and quite as severely criticised on the other. The impartial reader must judge for himself of its merits; it will repay a careful examination. Mr. Tucker says of it; "On the style, it may be remarked, that though it is somewhat ambitious and rhetorical for a state paper, it does no discredit to the pains which had been evidently bestowed on it, and some of the principles it contained were expressed with a sententious and felicitous brevity, which made so lively an impression on the public mind, that they acquired and yet retain the currency of popular maxims."

The next day, with the consent of the Senate, the president appointed James Madison secretary of state; Henry Dearborn, of Massachusetts, secretary of war; and Levi Lincoln, of the same state, attorney-general. The secretaries of the treasury and of the navy, Samuel Dexter and Benjamin Stoddert, who had been appointed by John Adams, were continued in office a short time; but in May, Albert Gallatin was placed over the treasury; and in July, Robert Smith, of Maryland, received the secretaryship of the navy, which Livingston, chancellor of New York, had first refused. Gideon Granger, a Connecticut republican, was at the same time appointed postmaster-general,* in place of Habersham of Georgia. And these nominations did not receive the confirmation of the Senate till the 26th of January, 1802.

Two days after his inauguration, Jefferson wrote to John Dickinson with the utmost apparent fervor and exultation. The pleasure of reading his letter, he tells him, "was like the joy we expect in the mansions of the blessed, when, received with the embraces of our forefathers, we shall be welcomed with their blessing as having done our part not unworthily of them. The storm through which we have passed has been tremendous indeed. The tough sides of our Argosie have been thoroughly tried. Her strength

1801.

---

* The postmaster-general was not made a member of the cabinet until the administration of Andrew Jackson.

has stood the waves into which she was steered with a view to sink her. We shall put her on the republican tack, and she will now show, by the beauty of her motion, the skill of her builders. Figure apart, our fellow-citizens have been led, hoodwinked, from their principles, by a most extraordinary combination of circumstances. But the band is removed; and they now see for themselves. I hope to see shortly a perfect consolidation; to effect which, nothing shall be wanting on my part, short of the abandonment of the principles of the Revolution. A just and solid republican government maintained here, will be a standing monument and example for the aim and imitation of the people of other countries; and I join with you in the hope and belief that they will see from our example, that a free government is of all others the most energetic."

The new president, immediately on his entrance upon office, found himself in a perplexing position. The party who had placed him in his coveted chair had got the idea, that they were entitled to the rewards of exertion, and that all the patronage of the government was to be bestowed upon them exclusively. The present holders of office,—most of them, by the way, having been appointed by Washington,—were of course, to be removed, and the many friends and supporters of the new dynasty were to be put in their places. The democracy were clamorous for the spoils; the federalists were anxiously waiting the result which the president and dominant party had reached on this question. Indiscriminate removals, it was felt, would be unwise, and very bad policy: while at the same time, it was perfectly certain, that nothing short of a very large excision would suffice to quiet the eager expectants for office and power. Mr. Hale, noticing the fact that it was but natural that Jefferson and the men who elected him, should wish that their friends should have a fair share in the offices under government, states what is worth remembering in our political history: "He set the first example of a president removing men from office because their political opinions differed from his own." It is worth remembering, too, that "by the frequent exercise of the power of removal for this cause alone, more strength must be given to the national government, and especially to the executive—that branch which freemen should watch with most jealousy—than by the most latitudinarian construction of the Constitution which any federalist was ever disposed to give to it.*

Writing to James Monroe, on the 7th of March, the president thus speaks: "I suspect that an incorrect idea of my views has got abroad. I am in hopes my Inaugural Address will in some measure set this to rights, as it will present the leading objects to be conciliation, and adherence to sound principle. This I know is impracticable with the leaders of the late faction, whom I abandon as incurables, and will never turn an inch out of my way to reconcile them. But with the main body of the federalists, I believe it

* Hale's "*History of the United States*," vol. ii., p. 140.

very practicable. . . . These people (I always exclude their leaders) are now aggregated with us; they look with a certain degree of affection and confidence to the administration, ready to become attached to it, *if it avoids in the outset, acts which might revolt and throw them off*. To give time for perfect consolidation seems prudent. I have firmly refused to follow the counsels of those who have desired the giving offices to some of their leaders, in order to reconcile. I have given, and will give, only to republicans, under existing circumstances. But I believe, with others, that deprivations of office, if made on the ground of political principles alone, would revolt our new converts, and give a body to leaders who now stand alone. Some I know must be made. They must be as few as possible, done gradually, and bottomed on some malversation or inherent disqualification. Where we shall draw the line between retaining all, and none, is not yet settled, and will not be till we get our administration together; and perhaps, even then we shall proceed *à tâtons*, balancing our measures according to the impression we perceive them to make."

To Mr. Giles, under date of the 23d of March, Jefferson avowed his determination, 1. To remove all who had been appointed by Mr. Adams after the election was known. 2. All who had been guilty of misconduct: 3. Not to remove those who merely differed from the republican party, except the attorneys and marshals of the federal courts.

The importance of this point, and the manner in which the present administration set the example, which has been only too faithfully copied ever since, demands the reader's thoughtful consideration. An extract or two more from Jefferson's letters will help to elucidate his views and the course he adopted.

"I was not deluded," he writes to Elbridge Gerry,* "by the eulogiums of the public papers in the first moments of change. If they could have continued to get all the loaves and fishes, that is, if I would have gone over to them, they would have continued to eulogize. But I well knew that the moment that such removals should take place, as the justice of the preceding administration ought to have executed, their hue and cry would be set up, and they would take their old stand. I shall disregard that also. Mr. Adams's last appointments, when he knew he was naming counsellors and aids for me, and not for himself, I set aside as far as depends on me. Officers who have been guilty of gross abuses of office, such as marshals packing juries,

1801.

* Notwithstanding the tone of Mr. Jefferson's remarks in his Inaugural, upon the "benign religion" which the American people, as a people, professed and were guided by, he occupies a considerable portion of his letter to Gerry in drawing out a sneering comparison between the printers of newspapers and the clergy. The former find it to their interest to keep up and create party noise and disturbance: equally so, he asserts of the latter. "The mild and simple principles of the Christian philosophy would produce too much calm, too much regularity of good, to extract from its disciples a support for a numerous priesthood, were they not to sophisticate it, ramify it, split it into hairs, and twist its texts, until they cover the divine morality of its Author with mysteries, and require a priesthood to explain them." See Tucker's "*Life of Jefferson*," vol. ii., p. 98.

etc., I shall now remove, as my predecessor ought in justice to have done. The instances will be few, and governed by strict rule, and not party passion. The right of opinion shall suffer no invasion from me. Those who have acted well have nothing to fear, however they may have differed from me in opinion: those who have done ill, however, have nothing to hope; nor shall I fail to do justice lest it should be ascribed to that difference of opinion."

In another letter, he writes to Levi Lincoln: "We are proceeding gradually in the regeneration of offices, and introducing republicans to some share in them. I do not know that it will be pushed further than was settled before you went away, except as to Essex men. I must ask you to make out a list of those in office in yours and the neighboring states, and to furnish me with it. . . . I understand that Jackson is a very determined one, though in private life amiable and honorable. But amiable monarchists are not safe subjects of republican confidence. What will be the effect of his removal? How should it be timed? Who his successor? What place can General Lyman properly occupy?"

1801.

To the "bitter remonstrance" of the merchants of New Haven, who felt it hard that an effective officer, of unsullied character, should be displaced in behalf of an old man, who was so dim-sighted that he could scarcely sign his own name, Jefferson replied at length. One paragraph contains the following:—"I lament sincerely that unessential differences of opinion should ever have been deemed sufficient to interdict half the society from the rights and the blessings of self-government, to proscribe them as unworthy of every trust. It would have been to me a circumstance of great relief, had I found a moderate participation of office in the hands of the majority. I would gladly have left to time and accident, to raise them to their just share. But their total exclusion calls for prompter corrections. I shall correct the procedure; but that done, return with joy to that state of things, when the only question concerning a candidate shall be, Is he honest? Is he capable? Is he faithful to the Constitution?"

The judges recently appointed under the new judiciary act, (see vol. ii., p. 513,) were, as we have seen above, marked by Jefferson for removal. "Between the 13th of February and the 4th of March," says the author of the "Familiar Letters," "all the judges were appointed by Mr. Adams, and the commissions issued. The individuals selected for these offices were men of high standing, and worthy of all confidence. But the popular cry was set up, and the measure vehemently condemned by all the Jeffersonian party. The judges were called 'the midnight judges of John Adams,' in allusion to the supposed time of appointment, at the close of his official duties. He said that he regarded (though one can hardly credit that he did so) all Mr. Adams's appointments after the 14th of February, while the House of Representatives were balloting for president,) as absolutely void. This must be understood to mean, that though

1801.

Mr. Adams was *constitutionally* president up to the midnight hour of the 3d of March; yet he ought to have submitted his will to that of his successor, and should have refrained from carrying an act of Congress into effect, which might not conform to that will. On the same principle, Mr. Jefferson withheld the commissions of certain magistrates, whom Mr. Adams had appointed, in the District of Columbia. The commissions were made out and ready for delivery, but Mr. Jefferson ordered them to be suppressed.

1801.

One of these magistrates, Mr. Marbury, applied to the Supreme Court for a writ of *mandamus* to Mr. Madison, the new secretary of state, to deliver his commission. But after an able investigation of constitutional law, the court did not grant the motion. Mr. Jefferson found a commission, duly made out and signed by Mr. Adams, appointing a gentleman district judge in Rhode Island; this commission he suppressed, and appointed one 'in whom he could confide.'"

Under date of May 14th, Nathaniel Macon, of North Carolina, obtained from the president, the following answers to some queries of his, in respect of certain matters not touched upon in the Inaugural Address.

"Levees are done away with.

"The first communication to the next Congress will be, like all subsequent ones, by message, to which no answer will be expected.

"The diplomatic establishment in Europe will be reduced to three ministers.

"The compensation to collectors depends on you, and not on me.

"The army is undergoing a chaste reformation.

"The navy will be reduced to the legal establishment by the last of this month.

"Agencies in every department will be revised.

"We shall push you to the uttermost in economizing.

"A very early recommendation had been given to the postmaster-general to employ no printer, foreigner, or revolutionary tory, in any of his offices. This department is still untouched.

"The arrival of Mr. Gallatin, yesterday, completed the organization of our administration."

One of the first acts of Jefferson's administration was, to send Mr. Dawson, a member of Congress, as a special messenger to France, with the treaty lately concluded with that nation, duly ratified, (see vol. ii., p. 504.) He took occasion at the same time, under date of March 18th, to send to the notorious Thomas Paine, "assurances of his high esteem, and affectionate attachment," and to offer to this "reviler both of General Washington and of the Christian religion," a passage home in the United States sloop of war Maryland. As might have been expected, the opposition availed itself of this conduct of the president to bestow upon him some sharp and bitter censure.* In this letter to Paine, the president also stated, that he had appointed Robert R. Liv-

1801.

* For the letter to Paine, and Mr. Tucker's remarks upon Jefferson's conduct, see "*Life of Jefferson*," vol. ii., pp. 94–96.

ingston, chancellor of New York, minister-plenipotentiary to France. He was not, however, to take his departure from the United States until intelligence should be received of the ratification of the Convention. Livingston, we may here mention, sailed for France in the autumn of the present year.

The party which had just taken the reins of power, had, as we have seen, no great love for the navy; and in accordance with Mr. Jefferson's wishes, a law had been passed for its reduction, the sale and dismantling of the ships, etc. The impudent demand, however, of the pasha of Tripoli, forced the president to avail himself of the naval arm; and accordingly, in May, Commodore Dale was ordered to the Mediterranean with a squadron of three frigates, and a sloop of war, to act as occasion might require. It appears, that Yussuf Caramalli, pasha of Tripoli, having dispossessed his brother Hamet, held that dependency of the Porte; and hearing, in 1800, of the gifts made to Algiers and Tunis, resolved to have his full share of the spoils of the rising nation, and to number amongst his tributaries also, the youthful Republic of the west. Just at this time, too, the other Barbary states were in a very quarrelsome mood with America. Algiers complained that the tribute was in arrear. Tunis found fault with the quality of the goods sent; certain planks and oars were too short; and guns of a particular description were greatly wanted. Morocco also had intimated a general disgust at the increasing marine of the new naval power, which had as yet brought no good to it. Yussuf accordingly charged the American government with unfairness, in bestowing upon him no more than some paltry gratuities, whilst Tunis had so much more, and Algiers had even received a frigate. And he told the consul that he would wait for six months for a present in money, and if it did not arrive by that time, would declare war against the United States. He was as good as his word too; for no money having come by the day he had designated, on May the 14th, 1801, the flag-staff of the American consulate was cut down, and the declaration of war was fully made. "Thus our concessions to one nest of pirates, in 1795, preferred as an alternative to completing and sending out the six frigates that had been conditionally authorized by the act of Congress of the year before, to impose by force of arms, our own terms, naturally provoked and encouraged the cupidity and insolence of another."

Commodore Dale arrived at Gibraltar on the 1st of July, and found the Tripolitan admiral lying in the harbor with a frigate of twenty-six and a brig of sixteen guns. **1801.** Notwithstanding the admiral's assurances of peace, Dale thought it best to leave one of his ships to watch them. Another vessel he sent along the northern shore to act as convoy to the American trade; and with the other two appearing before Algiers and Tunis, allayed most of the resentment affected by those powers, by the mere sight of his broadside. Soon afterwards the little Enterprise, a twelve-gun schooner, under command of Lieutenant Sterrett, making for Malta, fell in with a polacre-rigged Tripolitan ship of fourteen guns, and in a running combat of three hours, which was twice renewed by the pirates after they had struck, completely disabled her, killing or wounding fifty of her crew, without the loss of a single man. The instructions of the American commander not permitting him to carry the vessel in, he proceeded to dismantle her. "Her armament was thrown overboard, and she was stripped of every thing but one old sail and a single spar that were left to enable her to reach port. After attending to the wounded, (the whole crew was but eighty, and only thirty were found living after the fight,) the prize was abandoned, and it is understood that a long time elapsed before she got in. When her unfortunate Rais appeared in Tripoli, even his wounds did not avail him. He was placed on a jackass, paraded through the streets, and received the bastinado." It will readily be conceived, that the Tripolitan pirates had little encouragement to meet American vessels of war in future; and we find that, from this date, they entertained a very salutary terror of those who were as able as they were willing to give their enemies such effectual castigation.*

Dale did not maintain a very rigid blockade, but kept a most vigilant watch against the attacks of Tunis and Algiers as well; visiting various ports, and convoying the merchantmen of the United States whenever requisite. The two Tripolitans at Gibraltar were rendered perfectly useless to the pasha, and although the dey solicited passports for their crews, his request was denied. At the end of November, in accordance with his instructions, the gallant commodore returned, with his own ship and the Enterprise, leaving the Philadelphia and the Essex to look after the interests of the Union in that quarter.

On the 6th of November, the president addressed a circular to the heads of the departments, in which was unfolded his plan of proceeding; and sketching the practice of Washington's administration, in contrast with that of John Adams, he signified his purpose of acting upon his former chief's scheme, until experience should suggest any improvements. Professing his "unlimited, unqualified, and unabated" confidence in his ministers, not one of whom could he change to his better satisfaction, "if he had the universe to choose from;" he distinctly disavowed his intention of suffering the government to be "parcelled out," "among four independent heads," as in his opinion, had been the case with his immediate predecessor. It will be seen, as we proceed, that Thomas Jefferson was as good as his word in regard to these matters.

1801.

The seventh Congress commenced its session, in the city of Washington, on Monday, the 7th of December. Both in the Senate and in the House, the democratic party had a clear working majority, and accordingly, Abraham Baldwin was elected president *pro tempore* of the Senate, and Nathaniel Macon, speaker of the House. Bayard,

* See "*Cooper's Naval History*," vol. i., p. 200.

the federalist candidate for speaker, received only twenty-six votes; not half those which were given for Macon.

Jefferson, as we have seen above, determined to adopt a different mode of communicating with Congress from that adopted by Washington and Adams. He thought the speeches and answers of the two Houses, savored too much of the forms of royalty; and so he prepared a message instead of a speech, which he sent with an explanatory letter, to the president of the Senate and the speaker of the House. This plan, we may mention, has been followed by Jefferson's successors.* The message was in the following terms.

"*Fellow-Citizens of the Senate and House of Representatives:*

"It is a circumstance of sincere gratification to me, that on meeting the great council of our nation, I am able to announce to them, on grounds of reasonable certainty, that the wars and troubles which have for so many years afflicted our sister nations have at length come to an end, and that the communications of peace and commerce are once more opening among them. While we devoutly return thanks to the beneficent Being who has been pleased to breathe into them the spirit of conciliation and forgiveness, we are bound with peculiar gratitude to be thankful to him that our own peace has been preserved through so perilous a season, and ourselves permitted quietly to cultivate the earth and to practise and improve those arts which tend to increase our comforts. The assurances, indeed, of friendly disposition, received from all the powers with whom we have principal relations, had inspired a confidence that our peace with them would not have been disturbed. But a cessation of the irregularities which had affected the commerce of neutral nations, and of the irritations and injuries produced by them, cannot but add to this confidence; and strengthens, at the same time, the hope, that wrongs committed on unoffending friends, under a pressure of circumstances, will now be reviewed with candor, and will be considered as founding just claims of retribution for the past and new assurance for the future.

"Among our Indian neighbors, also, a spirit of peace and friendship generally prevails; and I am happy to inform you that the continued efforts to introduce among them the implements and

* "It was one of Mr. Jefferson's reforms. The former way of assembling the two Houses to hear an address in person from the president, returning an answer to it, the two Houses going in form to present their answer, and the intervention of repeated committees to arrange the details of these ceremonious meetings, being considered too close an imitation of the royal mode of opening a British parliament. Some of the democratic friends of Mr. Jefferson doubted whether this change was a reform in that part of it which dispensed with the answer to the president. Their view of it was, that the answer to the speech or message, afforded a regular occasion for speaking to the state of the Union, and to all the topics presented; which speaking, losing its regular vent, would afterwards break out irregularly, in the discussion of particular measures, and to the interruption of the business on hand. Experience has developed that irregularity and another—that of speaking to the message, on the motions to refer particular clauses of it to appropriate committees; thereby delaying the reference; and in one instance, during Mr. Fillmore's administration, preventing the reference during the entire session." Benton's "*Abridgement of the Debates of Congress*," vol. ii., p. 541.

the practice of husbandry, and of the household arts, have not been without success; that they are becoming more and more sensible of the superiority of this dependence for clothing and subsistence over the precarious resources of hunting and fishing; and already we are able to announce, that instead of that constant diminution of their numbers, produced by their wars and their wants, some of them begin to experience an increase of population.

"To this state of general peace with which we have been blessed, one only exception exists. Tripoli, the least considerable of the Barbary states, had come forward with demands unfounded either in right or in compact, and had permitted itself to denounce war, on our failure to comply before a given day. The style of the demand admitted but one answer. I sent a small squadron of frigates into the Mediterranean, with assurances to that power of our sincere desire to remain in peace, but with orders to protect our commerce against the threatened attack. The measure was seasonable and salutary. The bey had already declared war in form. His cruisers were out. Two had arrived at Gibraltar. Our commerce in the Mediterranean was blockaded and that of the Atlantic in peril. The arrival of our squadron dispelled the danger. One of the Tripolitan cruisers having fallen in with and engaged the small schooner Enterprise, commanded by Lieutenant Sterrett, which had gone as a tender to our larger vessels, was captured, after a heavy slaughter of her men, without the loss of a single one on our part. The bravery exhibited by our citizens on that element, will, I trust, be a testimony to the world that it is not the want of that virtue which makes us seek their peace, but a conscientious desire to direct the energies of our nation to the multiplication of the human race, and not to its destruction. Unauthorized by the Constitution, without the sanction of Congress, to go beyond the line of defence, the vessel being disabled from committing further hostilities was liberated with its crew. The legislature will doubtless consider whether, by authorizing measures of offence also, they will place our force on an equal footing with that of its adversaries. I communicate all material information on this subject, that in the exercise of the important function confided by the Constitution to the legislature exclusively, their judgment may form itself on a knowledge and consideration of every circumstance of weight.

"I wish I could say that our situation with all the other Barbary states was entirely satisfactory. Discovering that some delays had taken place in the performance of certain articles stipulated by us, I thought it my duty, by immediate measures for fulfilling them, to vindicate to ourselves the right of considering the effect of departure from stipulation on their side. From the papers which will be laid before you, you will be enabled to judge whether our treaties are regarded by them as fixing at all the measure of their demands, or as guarding from the exercise of force our vessels within their power; and to consider how far it will be safe and expedient to leave our affairs with them in their present posture.

"I lay before you the result of the census lately taken of our inhabitants, to a conformity with which we are to reduce the ensuing rates of representation and taxation. You will perceive that the increase of numbers during the last ten years, proceeding in geometrical ratio, promises a duplication in little more than twenty-two years. We contemplate this rapid growth and the prospect it holds up to us, not with a view to the injuries it may enable us to do to others in some future day, but to the settlement of the extensive country still remaining vacant within our limits, to the multiplication of men susceptible of happiness, educated in the love of order, habituated to self-government, and valuing its blessings above all price.

"Other circumstances, combined with the increase of numbers, have produced an augmentation of revenue arising from consumption, in a ratio far beyond that of population alone, and though the changes of foreign relations now taking place so desirably for the world may for a season affect this branch of revenue, yet weighing all probabilities of expense, as well as of income, there is reasonable ground of confidence, that we may now safely dispense with all the internal taxes, comprehending excises, stamps, auctions, licenses, carriages, and refined sugars, to which the postage on newspapers may be added, to facilitate the progress of information, and that the remaining sources of revenue will be sufficient to provide for the support of government, to pay the interest of the public debts, and to discharge the principals in shorter periods than the laws or the general expectation had contemplated. War, indeed, and untoward events, may change this prospect of things and call for expenses which the imposts could not meet; but sound principles will not justify our taxing the industry of our fellow-citizens to accumulate treasure for wars to happen we know not when, and which might not perhaps happen but from the temptations offered by that treasure.

"These views, however, of reducing our burdens, are formed on the expectation that a sensible, and at the same time a salutary reduction, may take place in our habitual expenditures. For this purpose, those of the civil government, the army, and navy, will need revisal.

"When we consider that this government is charged with the external and mutual relations only of these states; that the states themselves have the principal care of our persons, our property, and our reputation, constituting the great field of human concerns; we may well doubt whether our organization is not too complicated, too expensive; whether offices and officers have not been multiplied unnecessarily, and sometimes injuriously to the service they were meant to promote. I will cause to be laid before you an essay toward a statement of those who, under public employment of various kinds, draw money from the treasury or from our citizens. Time has not permitted a perfect enumeration, the ramifications of office being too multiplied and remote to be completely traced in a first trial. Among those who are dependent on executive discretion, I have begun the reduction of what was deemed necessary. The expenses of diplomatic agency have been considerably diminished. The inspectors of internal revenue, who were found to obstruct the accountability of the institution, have been discontinued. Several agencies created by executive authority, on salaries fixed by that also, have been suppressed, and I should suggest the expediency of regulating that power by law, so as to subject its exercises to legislative inspection and sanction. Other reformations of the same kind will be pursued with that caution which is requisite in removing useless things, not to injure what is retained. But the great mass of public offices is established by law, and, therefore, by law alone can be abolished. Should the legislature think it expedient to pass this roll in review, and try all its parts by the test of public utility, they may be assured of every aid and light which executive information can yield. Considering the general tendency to multiply offices and dependencies, and to increase expense to the ultimate term of burden which the citizen can bear, it behooves us to avail ourselves of every occasion which presents itself for taking off the surcharge; that it never may be seen here that, after leaving to labor the smallest portion of its earnings on which it can subsist, government shall itself consume the residue of what it was instituted to guard.

"In our care too of the public contributions intrusted to our direction, it would be prudent to multiply barriers against their dissipation, by appropriating specific sums to every specific purpose susceptible of definition; by disallowing all applications of money varying from the appropriation in object or transcending it in amount; by reducing the undefined field of contingencies, and thereby circumscribing discretionary powers over money; and by bringing back to a single department all accountabilities for money where the examination may be prompt, efficacious, and uniform.

"An account of the receipts and expenditures of the last year, as prepared by the secretary of the treasury, will as usual be laid before you. The success which has attended the late sales of the public lands shows, that with attention they may be made an important source of receipt. Among the payments, those made in discharge of the principal and interest of the national debt will show that the public faith has been exactly maintained. To these will be added an estimate of appropriations necessary for the ensuing year. This last will of course be effected by such modifications of the systems of expense as you shall think proper to adopt.

"A statement has been formed by the secretary of war, on mature consideration, of all the posts and stations where garrisons will be expedient, and of the number of men requisite for each garrison. The whole amount is considerably short of the present military establishment. For the surplus no particular use can be pointed out. For defence against invasion their number is as nothing; nor is it conceived needful or safe that a standing army should be kept up in time of peace for that purpose. Uncertain as we must ever be of the particular point in our circumference where an enemy may choose to invade us, the only force which can be ready at every point and competent to oppose them, is the body of neighboring citizens as formed into a militia. On these, collected from the parts most convenient, in numbers proportioned to the invading foe, it is best to rely, not only to meet the first attack, but if it threatens to be permanent, to maintain the defence until regulars may be engaged to relieve them. These considerations render it important that we should, at every session, continue to amend the defects which from time to time show themselves in the laws for regulating the militia, until they are sufficiently perfect. Nor should we now or at any time separate, until we can say we have done every thing for the militia which we could do were an enemy at our door.

"The provisions of military stores on hand will be laid before you, that you may judge of the additions still requisite.

"With respect to the extent to which our naval preparations should be carried, some difference of opinion may be expected to appear; but just attention to the circumstances of every part of the Union will doubtless reconcile all. A small force will probably continue to be wanted for actual service in the Mediterranean. Whatever annual sum beyond that you may think proper to appropriate to naval preparations, would perhaps be better employed in providing those articles which may be kept without waste or consumption, and be in readiness when any exigence calls them into use. Progress has been made, as will appear by papers now communicated, in providing materials for seventy-four gun ships, as directed by law.

"How far the authority given by the legislature for procuring and establishing sites for naval purposes has been perfectly understood and pursued in the execution, admits of some doubt. A statement of the expenses already incurred on that subject shall be laid before you. I have in certain cases suspended or slackened these expenditures, that the legislature might determine whether so many yards are necessary as have been contemplated. The works at this place are among those permitted to go on; and five of the seven frigates directed to be laid up have been brought and laid up here, where, besides the safety of their position, they are under the eye of the executive administration, as well as of its agents, and where yourselves also will be guided by your own view in the legislative provisions respecting them which may from time to time be necessary. They are preserved in such condition, as well the vessels as whatever belongs to them, as to be at all times ready for sea on a short warning. Two others are yet to be laid up so soon as they shall have received the repairs requisite to put them also into sound condition. As a superintending officer will be necessary at each yard, his duties and emoluments, hitherto fixed by the executive, will be a more proper subject for legislation. A communication will also be made of our progress in the execution of the law respecting the vessels directed to be sold.

"The fortifications of our harbors, more or less advanced, present considerations of great difficulty. While some of them are on a scale sufficiently proportioned to the advantages of their position, to the efficacy of their protection, and the importance of the points within it, others are so extensive, will cost so much in their first erection, so much in their maintenance, and require such a force to garrison them, as to make it questionable what is best now to be done. A statement of those commenced or projected, of the expenses already incurred, and estimates of their future cost, so far as can be foreseen, shall be laid before you, that you may be enabled to judge whether any attention is necessary in the laws respecting this subject.

1801.

"Agriculture, manufactures, commerce, and navigation, the four pillars of our prosperity, are the most thriving when left most free to individual enterprise. Protection from casual embarrassments, however, may sometimes be seasonably interposed. If in the course of your observations or inquiries they should appear to need any aid within the limits of our constitutional powers, your sense of their importance is a sufficient assurance they will occupy your attention. We cannot, indeed, but all feel an anxious solicitude for the difficulties under which our carrying trade will soon be placed. How far it can be relieved, otherwise than by time, is a subject of important consideration.

"The judiciary system of the United States, and especially that portion of it recently erected, will of course present itself to the contemplation of Congress; and that they may be able to judge of the proportion which the institution bears to the business it has to perform, I have caused to be procured from the several states, and now lay before Congress, an exact statement of all the causes decided since the first establishment of the courts, and of those which were depending when additional courts and judges were brought in to their aid.

"And while on the judiciary organization, it will be worthy your consideration, whether the protection of the inestimable institution of juries has been extended to all the cases involving the security of our persons and property. Their impartial selection also being essential to their value, we ought further to consider, whether that is sufficiently secured in those states where they are named by a marshal depending on executive will, or designated by the court or by officers dependent on them.

"I cannot omit recommending a revisal of the laws on the subject of naturalization. Considering the ordinary chances of human life, a denial of citizenship under a residence of fourteen years is a denial to a great proportion of those who ask it, and controls a policy pursued from their first settlement by many of these states, and still believed of consequence to their prosperity. And shall we refuse the unhappy fugitives from distress that hospitality which the savages of the wilderness extended to our fathers arriving in this land? Shall oppressed humanity find no asylum on this globe? The Constitution, indeed, has wisely provided that, for admission to certain offices of important trust, a residence shall be required sufficient to develop character and design. But might not the general character and capabilities of a citizen be safely communicated to every one manifesting a *bonâ fide* purpose of embarking his life and fortunes permanently with us? with restrictions, perhaps, to guard against the fraudulent usurpation of our flag; an abuse which brings so much embarrassment and loss on the genuine citizen, and so much danger to the nation of being involved in war, that no endeavor should be spared to detect and suppress it.

"These, fellow-citizens, are the matters respecting the state of the nation which I have thought of importance to be submitted to your consideration at this time. Some others of less moment, or not yet ready for communication, will be the subject of separate messages. I am happy in this opportunity of committing the arduous affairs of our government to the collected wisdom of the Union. Nothing shall be wanting on my part to inform, as far as in my power, the legislative judgment, nor to carry that judgment into faithful execution. The prudence and temperance of your discussions will promote, within your own walls, that conciliation which so much befriends rational conclusion; and by its example will encourage among our constituents that progress of opinion which is tending to unite them in object and in will. That all should be satisfied with any one order of things is not to be expected, but I indulge the pleasing persuasion that the great body of our citizens will cordially concur in honest and disinterested efforts, which have for their object to preserve the general and state governments in their constitutional form and equilibrium; to maintain peace abroad, and order and obedience to the laws at home; to establish principles and practices of administration favorable to the security of liberty and property; and to reduce expenses to what is necessary for the useful purposes of government."

The message of the head of the republican party was, according to Mr. Tucker, violently assailed by the federalists. "The points deemed most exceptionable, or at least most vulnerable to attack, were the reduction of the revenue, the army, and navy, the revision of the judicial system, and the proposed facility to naturalization; all of which they attributed either to false or visionary notions of government, or to an unprincipled sacrifice of the best interests of the nation to popular prejudices. The very mode of communication, which has since received the sanction of general usage, and which is in accordance with the universal practice in the states, did not escape censure; that was arraigned as proceeding from an overweening desire of popularity, and a covert design to cast an invidious shade on the character of General Washington and Mr. Adams.

"All these measures were the more unacceptable, because, if they had a fortunate issue, they would be at once a practical rebuke on their own course when in power, and a triumphant vindication of that of the republicans. The best talents of the party were, therefore, put in requisition, to bring them into discredit with the people, and to show that, so far as they were able to reduce the taxes, and yet make good the public engagements, they were indebted to the schemes of finance introduced by their predecessors, and which they had invariably opposed. The general expressions of philanthropy which occasionally found a place in the message, were sneered at as an offering to a spurious philosophy then in vogue; and disaster and ruin were confidently predicted to the nation for committing the reins to those who had neither the skill nor firmness to guide them. . . . . Mr. Jefferson had, however, the consolation of knowing that his course, so obnoxious to his adversaries, was approved by his friends, who constituted a great majority of the American people; and, confident that it was adapted to the solid interests of the nation, as well as suited to its ruling tastes, he trusted to time to justify him in the eyes of the fairer portion even of his opponents."* His biographer is confident, that Jefferson was not disappointed in this expectation. The reader will be better able to judge when he has reached the close of the third president's career.

The party now in power determined to carry their plans of reform and economy into execution as speedily as possible. The first measure of importance introduced by them into Congress, was that for the revision (as it was called,) of the federal judiciary. **1801.** From some cause or other, Mr. Jefferson entertained no liking for the arrangements which established the supreme judicial tribunal to decide the great questions which would come before it for adjudication; and, as we have noted, he took it very ill of John Adams and the federal party, that they had enacted certain laws on this subject and appointed men to fill the chairs in the courts of the United States. Writing, on the 19th of December, to John Dickinson, Jefferson states, amongst other things, bearing upon his policy;—"My great anxiety at present is, to avail ourselves of our ascendency to establish good principles and good practices; to fortify republicanism behind as many barriers as possible, that the outworks may give time to rally and save the citadel, should that be again in danger. On *their* part *they have retired into the judiciary* as a stronghold. There, the remains of federalism are to be preserved and fed from the treasury; and from that battery all the works of republicanism are to be beaten down and erased. By a fraudulent use of the Constitution, which has made judges *irremovable*, they have multiplied useless judges merely to strengthen their phalanx."

A bill to repeal the law respecting the circuit courts, under which those who were designated as "midnight judges" had been appointed, was accordingly brought in, early in January, and warmly debated in both Houses of Congress. The president had, as he

* Tucker's "*Life of Jefferson*," vol. ii., pp. 108–9.

intimated in his message, obtained from every state an account of the whole number of causes tried since the institution of the national government, under an impression, it would seem—an idea which the federalists ridiculed—that the number of the suits was the measure of the utility and necessity of the existing organization.

James A. Bayard was the chief speaker against the repeal, in the House of Representatives; and William B. Giles led the debate on the other side. In the Senate, Gouverneur Morris and Stevens T. Mason were the principal advocates of federal and republican views on this subject.* The arguments in favor of the repeal most relied on, were, that the new courts were useless, and that there was no constitutional objection to abolishing them. And the ground taken in opposition by the federalists was, that Congress had not the power to deprive the judges of their stations by the indirect course of repealing the law under which they had been appointed.

1801.

Some members of the bar at Philadelphia, republicans too, memorialized Congress, reciting the great inconveniences sustained under the old law "by the court, the bar, and the suitors;"—the evils arising from the want of "opportunity for reflection and repose" experienced by the judges when "constantly engaged in traversing the states;" and from the circumstance that they were called to preside in states, "the laws, usages, and practices of which were essentially different from those in which they were educated;"—the honorable character of the recently appointed judges;—the increased confidence of the public in the courts:—and after stating that "the inevitable consequences of the late system were embarrassment, uncertainty, and delay," declared, that "the abolition of the court will probably be attended with great public inconvenience."

The federalists did not fully believe that their antagonists would dare to repeal this law; and should the republicans attack it, they expected, as Mr. Tucker says, that "it would afford them abundant materials to bring their adversaries into discredit with the people; who would thus have their eyes opened, and see that those who had been advocates for a strict interpretation of the Constitution, could be ultra-latitudinarian in construing it, when it suited their purpose. So confident were they of the advantage they would have over their opponents in this argument, that they actually wished the latter would carry their purpose into execution. They, at all events, hoped they would attempt it, as whether they succeeded or failed, it would furnish them with the same fruitful theme of party reproach, and of making eloquent appeals in behalf of the violated Constitution."*

* For the long and able speeches of these gentlemen, see Williston's "*Eloquence of the United States*," vol. ii., pp. 82–285.

* Mr. Justice Story has well enumerated the reasons for the tenure of office, determined by the Constitution, for the members of the judiciary. To render that branch of the government a safeguard against the encroachments of party spirit and the tyranny of

After an earnest and protracted debate, which continued for sixteen days, the repeal was effected by a vote in the House, of fifty-nine to thirty-two. In the Senate, the republican party obtained the repeal by only a single vote.* It is admitted by Mr. Tucker, whose words we have quoted above—although it might be much more strongly stated—that "the course taken by the majority of the legislature, in the repeal of the judiciary act, did not receive the unanimous support of the republican party. To those who regarded the independence of the judges as a cardinal principle in free governments, the repeal appeared to be contrary to the spirit and meaning of the Constitution; as,
1802. if the judges could be deprived of their offices by the abolition of the courts, the provision in the Constitution, by which they were to hold them *during good behavior*, was rendered nugatory; and the judiciary were virtually rendered dependent on the legislature. Nor were there wanting moderate men in the republican ranks who believed the repeal of this law to be as clear an infraction of the Constitution as the sedition law had been. The number of these was, however, too small to produce effect; and their disapprobation, together with the louder voice of the opposition, was drowned in the popular huzzas, which were everywhere heard for the new administration."

The judiciary bill having been repealed, it was needful to rearrange the operations of the supreme court, upon which the whole of the judicial labors of the United States were now thrown. And another bill was passed, dividing the states, with the exception of Maine and the region beyond the mountains, into six circuits, in each of which one judge, with the assistance of a district judge, held courts, half-yearly; and the terms of the supreme court were made but one in each year;—instead of the original arrangement, of which we have given an account in a previous chapter (see vol. ii., p. 278.)

The president was laudably anxious to obtain a repeal of the internal taxes of every kind. On this subject he thus writes to Mr. Dickinson, in the letter before quoted: "You will, perhaps, have been alarmed, as some have been, at the proposition to abolish the whole of the internal taxes. But it is perfectly safe. They are under a million of dollars, and we can economize the government two or three millions a year. The impost alone gives us ten

---

faction; to secure the people against the intentional, as well as the unintentional, usurpations of the executive and legislative departments; to confer upon it the weight requisite for the fulfilment of its function under the Constitution, of acting at once as complement and as check to the other two branches; it was needful that the judiciary should be independent,—holding office *during good behavior;* for otherwise, the judges would soon be rendered odious, not because they did wrong, but because they refused to do wrong; and would become more dependent upon the appointing power, and secure nothing, but their own places, and the approbation of those who valued, because they knew the use of them; and in no other way could there be any practical restraint upon the acts of the government, or any practical enforcement of the rights of the citizens. In view of the action on the subject of the judiciary in several of the states, the student of history may well ponder the importance of its being independent of the changes and chances of popular elections, and party expediency and policy.

* See Benton's "*Abridgement of the Debates of Congress,*" vol. ii., pp. 545–565; and pp. 596–639.

or eleven millions annually, increasing at a compound ratio of six and two-thirds per cent. *per annum*, and consequently doubling in two years. But leaving that increase for contingencies, the present amount will support the government, pay the interest of the public debt, and discharge the principal in fifteen years. If the increase proceeds, and no contingencies demand it, it will pay off the principal in a shorter time. Exactly one half of the public debt, to wit, thirty-seven millions of dollars, is owned in the United States. That capital then will be set afloat, to be employed in rescuing our commerce from the hands of foreigners, or in agriculture, canals, bridges, or other useful enterprises. By suppressing at once the whole internal taxes, we abolish three-fourths of the offices now existing and spread over the land." For Mr. Tucker's statements on the subject of the public debt, and the wishes of the president in regard to its total extinction, we must refer the reader to his Life of Jefferson. The pages in which he speaks to these points are worthy careful consideration.*

Amongst the other more important acts of this session, we may enumerate—one for the reapportionment of Representatives, according to the result of the census of the preceding year, the ratio being continued at one Representative for thirty-three thousand inhabitants; one for determining the extent of the peace establishment, in respect of the army, and also for the regulation and maintenance of peace on the frontiers; one abolishing the internal taxes; and one for the redemption of the public debt, by the yearly appropriation of $7,300,000 to the sinking fund. But, as a late writer remarks: "the act now passed to provide for the redemption of the public debt, was only nominal in its operations; new loans were effected, and the reduction of the debt by the act was only in theory, as the appropriations for expenses for 1802, were more than equal to the receipts of the previous year."

1802.

In April of this year, Ohio, which had been under a territorial government for several years, was admitted into the Union. A convention at Chillicothe, in November, settled a constitution for the new state. The number of its inhabitants was about fifty thousand.

On the 3d of May, the first session of the seventh Congress was brought to its close. It was a long and busy session, and its career is the more noticeable inasmuch as the republican party were now able to carry the measures which they deemed advisable, confident of the support and encouragement of the executive in regard to the various points at issue between them and the federal party.

* We may mention here, that the value of the exports of the United States was upwards of $93,000,000. The tonnage of the United States was upwards of 900,000. The amount of duties received was upwards of $20,000,000; and of drawbacks paid by the states, nearly $8,000,000.

CHAPTER II.

1802–1803.

THE ACQUISITION OF LOUISIANA.

Louisiana ceded to France in 1800 — Excitement in the United States on the subject — Jefferson's letter to Livingston — The Americans prohibited from New Orleans as a place of deposit — Great agitation in the west — Meeting of Congress in December — President's message — Action in Congress — Resolution calling for papers — Resolutions adopted by the House — Jefferson's opinion as to the object of the federalists — Monroe appointed minister plenipotentiary to France — Letter to Monroe — Great changes in affairs from apparently trivial causes — Napoleon's purpose in sending a military colony to Louisiana — How altered — Sudden and propitious turn in the tide of events — The American envoys — Letter from the president to De Nemours in Paris — Motions in Congress for calling out troops — Money voted — Livingston's labors in Paris — Arrival of Monroe — Rapid progress of negotiations — Final arrangements — England's acquiescence in this sale — Substance of the treaty — Importance of this transaction — Jefferson's gratulations — His views as to the course to be pursued in Congress — Letter to Breckenridge — Tucker's opinions — The treaty ratified in October — Jefferson's letter to Lincoln on the constitutional question — Complaints of Spain — Meeting of Congress in October — The message — Movements in the House — Large majority in favor of the treaty — Purchase money voted — Claiborne and Wilkinson American commissioners — Monette's account of the final transfer, in December, to the United States — Views of the federalists as given by Dr. Sullivan — J. Q. Adams on this whole subject.

BY a secret treaty, in the year 1800, Spain had ceded the province of Louisiana to France. So soon as this fact became known in the United States, which was in the spring of 1802, it excited immediate anxiety and alarm. For the possession of the port of New Orleans, and the right to the navigation of the Mississippi, were indispensable to the prosperity, and even the quiet of the great west. It was perceived, too, at once, that the substitution of France for Spain, in a position so vitally momentous to the United States, could not be regarded with indifference, and that some steps must speedily be taken in respect to the existing condition of affairs. Collision would be certain to occur at no distant day, if the question should not be amicably settled in the mean time; and so lively and general were the apprehensions of the power and activity of France, that, it is believed, the American people would have been willing to incur the certain evils of war at once, rather than run the risk of the dangers which they apprehended. It was well for our country and her interests, that by a remarkable and wholly unlooked-for change of policy on the part of Napoleon, Mr. Jefferson was enabled to avail himself of the opening to settle this disputed question.

1802.

On the 18th of April, 1802, the president wrote a long letter to Mr. Livingston in Paris, on the subject of the cession of Louisiana to France, in which, with his usual perspicacity, he pointed out the new attitude which

France would henceforth assume towards the United States; and he enlarged upon the inevitable consequences that must ensue, should France persist in what would appear to be her present policy, viz., an alliance between the United States and Great Britain. "Every eye in the United States," he says, in concluding his letter, "is now fixed on the affairs of Louisiana. Perhaps nothing since the Revolutionary War, has produced more uneasy sensations through the body of the nation, and in spite of our temporary bickerings with France, she still has a strong hold on our affections.*

At a later date, in a letter to the same gentleman, the president adverted to the fact, that the French government acted in a way which plainly showed their feelings to be decidedly unfriendly. Cautioning Livingston as to the line of conduct to be pursued, so as not to commit the country in the disputes between France and England, he directed him to "give all his communications to the French government a very mild, complaisant, and even friendly connection, but always independent."

1802.

On the 16th of October, Morales, the Spanish intendant of the province of Louisiana, issued a proclamation, prohibiting the Americans from further use of New Orleans as a place of deposit. This measure produced great excitement throughout the west. The governor of Kentucky wrote to the president, on the 30th of November, informing him of the alarm and agitation in that state; and on the 1st of December the legislature memorialized Congress on the subject. These circumstances added to Mr. Jefferson's desire to obtain the cession of New Orleans to the United States.

The second session of the seventh Congress commenced some days later than usual, no quorum being present on the 6th of December. On the 15th the president sent in his message, which was chiefly occupied with the relations of the Union with other nations. It also referred to the dealings of the state of Georgia with the Indians; and to Indian affairs in other parts of the long western border line. It congratulated them on the prosperous state of the federal finances, and suggested one of the president's schemes about the navy. Opening with congratulations, and remarking, "with special satisfaction, those pleasing circumstances which, under the smiles of Providence, result from the skill, industry, and order of our citizens, managing their own affairs, in their own way, and for their own use; unembarrassed by too much regulation, unoppressed by fiscal exactions;"—it closed in a

1802.

* Mr. Jefferson was excessively annoyed by the abuse heaped upon him by a fellow named Callender, who, from abusing his opponents, turned upon Jefferson himself, and poured out upon him the full measure of his vindictive fury, because the president would not bestow upon him the postmastership of Richmond. "You will have seen by our newspapers," Jefferson wrote to Livingston, "that, with the aid of a lying renegadó from republicanism, the federalists have opened all their sluices of calumny. They say, we lied them out of power, and openly avow they will do the same by us. But it was not lies, or arguments, on our part which dethroned them, but their own foolish acts, alien laws, taxes, extravagances, and heresies." Tucker's "*Life of Jefferson*," vol. ii., pp. 119 121.

similar vein, with an enumeration of "the land-marks by which we are to guide ourselves in all our proceedings," amongst which is specified as one,—"to keep in all things within the pale of our constitutional powers, and cherish the federal Union, as the only rock of safety." The message met with some sharp criticism from the federalists, and the president's ideas on the subject of dry docks for the navy, afforded a fine opportunity to indulge in ridicule and witticism.

It was, however, the closing of the port of New Orleans that engrossed the minds of all men; and they looked, with natural anxiety, to Congress for some elucidation of the affair. On the 17th of December, the House of Representatives called on the president for information on the subject of the supposed violation, on the part of Spain, of the twenty-second article of the treaty of 1795. On the 22d, the fact that the Mississippi was virtually closed to American trade, was formally notified to Congress, by the president, in reply.

On the 5th of January, Mr. Griswold, of Connecticut, moved, that the president be called upon to lay before the House such official documents as he possessed, announcing the cession of Louisiana to France; together with a report explaining the stipulations, circumstances, and conditions, under which the province was to be given up; "with the usual reservation," adds
1803. Mr. Tucker, "as to what the president should think it improper to communicate. This resolution, being deemed by the republican party likely to embarrass the pending negotiation, and probably it was so intended by its supporters, was opposed, and finally rejected. Mr. Griswold, at the same time, offered other resolutions, asserting the right of the people of the United States to the navigation of the Mississippi, its recent obstruction by Spain, and proposing an inquiry into the measures proper to be taken for the maintenance of this right. The majority refused to consider the resolutions, but afterwards agreed *with closed doors* to the following substitute," (7th January.)

"*Resolved*,—That this House receive, with great sensibility, the information of a disposition in certain officers of the Spanish government, at New Orleans, to obstruct the navigation of the River Mississippi, as secured to the United States by the most solemn stipulations:—

"That, adhering to that humane and wise policy, which ought ever to characterize a free people, and by which the United States have always preferred to be governed; willing, at the same time, to ascribe this breach of compact to the unauthorized misconduct of certain individuals, rather than to a want of good faith on the part of His Catholic Majesty; and relying, with perfect confidence, on the vigilance and wisdom of the executive, they will wait the issue of such measures as that department of the government shall have pursued, for asserting the rights and vindicating the injuries of the United States;—holding it to be their duty, at the same time, to express their unalterable determination to maintain the boundaries, and the rights of navigation and commerce, through the River Mississippi, as established by existing treaties."*

Mr. Jefferson, whose suspicions of the federalists were never at rest, seemed to think, that the object of the opposition was, to force the country into a war with Spain, "in order to derange our finances," or if that could not be done, "to attach the western country to them, as their best friends, and thus get again into power." Which latter supposition may have some show of reason; although other and nobler motives, we think, might account for their actions in the matter. With a view of carrying his pacific policy into effect, the president, on the 10th of January, appointed Mr. Monroe (whose term of office, as Governor of Virginia, had recently ended) minister plenipotentiary to France, to act with Mr. Livingston, in the purchase of New Orleans and the Floridas; for, as he observed, in writing to Monroe upon the appointment, "the measures previously pursued by the administration being *invisible*, did not satisfy the minds of the western people; consequently, something *sensible* had become necessary."

1803.

The president was very earnest in urging Mr. Monroe to accept this appointment. "On the event of this mission," he wrote, "depend the future destinies of this republic. If we cannot, by a purchase of the country, insure to ourselves a course of perpetual peace, and friendship with all nations, then as war cannot be distant, [as the rupture of the peace of Amiens soon showed,] it behoves us immediately to be preparing for that course, without, however, hastening it; and it may be necessary (on your failure on the continent) to cross the channel. We shall get entangled in European politics, and, figuring more, be much less happy and prosperous. This can only be prevented by a successful issue to your present mission."

There can be no doubt, that Napoleon purposed to take possession of Louisiana, and one part of the fleet which he despatched under Le Clerc to reduce St. Domingo, was destined for this service. And there can be as little doubt, that had that object been accomplished, before the end of the next year, it would have been conquered by Great Britain; and the whole course of subsequent history must have been quite different from what it was.

How singular are the changes produced in the history of the world by what seem to be very slight and insufficient causes! The military colony of twenty thousand men was on the eve of embarkation, and Napoleon had resolved to make this colony, in the centre of the western hemisphere, the stand for a lever to wield at his pleasure the destinies of the globe. A petty squabble with England about the Island of Malta, deranged his plans, and he formed another resolve, viz., to rival his great prototype, Julius Cæsar, by the invasion and conquest of England. In order to do this, he could not spare his veterans to run the risk of a voyage across the Atlantic; for England was

* Tucker's "*Life of Jefferson*," vol. ii., p. 125.

mistress of the seas, and would certainly have wrested Louisiana from him without fail. Napoleon therefore abandoned his projects of conquest and glory in America, and, as money was in demand to enable him to carry forward his vast schemes of ambition and dominion, he suddenly resolved to offer the colony of Louisiana for sale to the United States.

"Never in the fortunes of mankind," as John Quincy Adams forcibly says, "was there a more sudden, complete, and propitious turn in the tide of events than this change in the purposes of Napoleon proved to the administration of Mr. Jefferson. The wrangling altercation with Spain for the navigation of the Mississippi, had been adjusted during the administration of Washington, by a treaty which had conceded to them the right, and stipulated to make the enjoyment effective, of deposit at New Orleans. In repurchasing

1803.

from Spain the colony of Louisiana, Napoleon, to disencumber himself from the burden of this stipulation, and to hold in his hand a rod over the western section of the Union, had compelled the dastardly and imbecile monarch of Spain to commit an act of perfidy, by withdrawing from the people of the United States this stipulated right of deposit, before delivering the possession of the colony to France. The great artery of the commerce of the Union was thus choked in its circulation. The sentiment of surprise, of alarm, of indignation, was instantaneous and universal among the people, (as has been pointed out on a previous page.) The hardy and enterprizing settlers of the western country could hardly be restrained from pouring down the swelling floods of their population, to take possession of New Orleans itself by the immediate exercise of the rights of *war*. A war with Spain must have been immediately followed by a war with France; which, however just the cause of the United States would have been, must necessarily give a direction to public affairs adverse to the whole system of Mr. Jefferson's policy, and in all probability, prove fatal to the success of his administration. Instigations to immediate war were at once attempted in Congress (p. 35,) and were strongly countenanced by the excited temper of the people."*

The president, as we have noted on a previous page, appointed Mr. Monroe minister plenipotentiary to France. With him he joined Mr. Livingston, already on the ground, and they both were commissioned to treat with Spain as well as France, remonstrating against the withdrawal of the right of deposit, and proposing anew the purchase of the Island of New Orleans. Besides the two envoys, ordinary and extraordinary, Mr. Jefferson relied on the good offices of M. Dupont de Nemours, whose residence in America, and whose standing in his own country, gave him peculiar advantages for acting as a mediator in a case that required some delicacy of treatment; and upon the issue of which so much hung. To this gentleman he addressed a letter, in which he endeavored to possess him with the opinions which he thought might be

* Adams's "*Life of James Madison*," pp. 81–82.

most serviceable to the United States, in respect of the object he had in view; —and, like a good merchant, undervaluing the tract of land he had set his heart upon, he spoke of the Floridas, excepting the portion already granted, as a barren sand. He also was careful to exaggerate the possibility, nay, the certainty of the loss of the alliance of the United States, should France take possession of the only outlet for the produce of the great valley of the west.

In Congress, later in the session, other motions were presented respecting this important business; for the western states began to show symptoms of increasing impatience, under so serious a restriction to their trade as the interdiction of the right of deposit at New Orleans. Mr. Ross of Pennsylvania, in the Senate, proposed, on the 14th of February, that the president should call out some fifty thousand militia, and occupy New Orleans*, and that

1803. $5,000,000 should be appropriated to that retaliatory measure. But Mr. Breckenridge of Kentucky, was more successful in his resolutions, raising the numbers of the militia, or of volunteers, to eighty thousand, but not defining the work they should be set to do, nor appropriating any specific sum of money, as the service was contingent merely. The president also asked and obtained an appropriation of $2,000,000, under the head of "foreign intercourse," as the commencement of a fund for effecting the purchase of New Orleans and the Floridas.

Napoleon had paid but slight attention to the memorial which Mr. Livingston presented on learning the fact of the retrocession of Louisiana to France. The sudden change, however, in his plans, led him to look favorably upon Livingston's representations; and so, most unexpectedly, he offered to the United States not New Orleans only, but the whole of Louisiana, for the sum of fifty millions of francs.

The Marquis de Marbois was the agent with whom Livingston had to treat, and Talleyrand was superintendent of the negotiation. At first, it seemed to the American ambassador a mere artifice to gain time; and he had no authority to do more than treat for the indemnity which was claimed in behalf of the American citizens, whose vessels had been taken or plundered by the French privateers, before and during the war under John Adams's administration. He ventured, however, lest he should be throwing away a fair opportunity of serving his country, to offer thirty millions of francs, and to sink the claims for indemnity.

Matters were in this condition when Monroe arrived. He left the United States in March, and reached Paris on the 12th of April, where he found Mr. Livingston so persuaded of the want of good faith in the French government, that he hoped to hear from his coadjutor, that possession had been taken of New Orleans. "Only force,"

* For the debate, in the Senate, on "the Mississippi Question," see Benton's "*Abridgement of the Debates of Congress*," vol. ii., pp. 668–92. With regard to the "Yazoo claims," and their various connections, see Tucker's "*Life of Jefferson*," vol. ii., pp. 138–141.

he said, "can give us New Orleans. We must employ force. Let
1803.
us first get possession of the country, and negotiate afterwards."

After his first astonishment,—and well might he be astonished, when, asking for a town, a province was offered; when, asking for the freedom of a river, the river itself, and others as mighty, nay, a new sea-coast, was offered;—the negotiations proceeded all the more rapidly, because of this surprise. And beside that, the whole tone of the diplomacy of the statesmen of France was changed when Napoleon made himself the head of the government.

Perceiving that more was to be made of the vast extent of territory which was offered for sale to the United States than Napoleon had thought of asking, Marbois fixed the price at eighty millions of francs,—insisting, with truth, that for the United States, that sum even was very far below the real value of the province. And the American plenipotentiaries finally acquiesced in this demand, on condition that twenty millions out of the eighty should be assigned to the payment of what was due from France to citizens of the United States.

The treaty was concluded on the 30th of April, and the instruments were signed by the three ministers four days afterwards. On that occasion, Mr. Livingston, expressing his satisfaction, said,—"We have lived long, but this is the noblest work of our whole lives. The treaty which we have just signed has not been obtained by art, or dictated by force. Equally advantageous to the two contracting parties, it will change vast solitudes into flourishing districts. From this day the United
States take their place among 1803.
the powers of the first rank; the English lose all exclusive influence in the affairs of America."

Napoleon, on his side, was greatly pleased with the bargain. He had at first objected to the reduction of the eighty millions to sixty; but when reminded that he had named fifty, and had not expected to obtain even that, he said,—"True;—the negotiation does not leave me any thing to desire. Sixty millions for an occupation that will not, perhaps, last for a day! I wish France to enjoy this unexpected capital; and that it may be employed in works beneficial to her marine. This accession of territory strengthens forever the power of the United States; and I have given to England," he added, with characteristic sagacity, "a maritime rival that will, sooner or later, humble her pride."

England, under the influence of fears and jealousies, equally strong, on her side, was willing to acquiesce in this transfer of the province of Louisiana; and it is a curious fact in the history of this transaction, that the purchase money "was, in the midst of a raging war, with the knowledge and assent of the British government, furnished by English bankers, to be expended in preparations for the conquest of England by invasion!"

At the very time that hostilities broke out afresh, in May, 1803, between France and Great Britain, Napoleon, presuming that no delay in the ratification of the treaty could take place at

Washington, ratified the cession of Louisiana to the United States. He was desirous of leaving no ground for considering the country as a French colony; so that if any attempt were made upon it by Great Britain, it might embroil her with America.

The treaty, which had just been concluded, first of all set forth the claims of France to the territory, by the cession of Spain, and formally renounced them in favor of the United States; but stipulated for the security of the inhabitants in their persons, property, (the forty thousand slaves being guaranteed as the property of their owners,) and religion; and also for their admission to the full rights of citizens of the Union.* It was further agreed, that the port of New Orleans should, for the next ensuing twelve years, be open to both French ships and Spanish, as freely as to American vessels; and that forever afterwards the former should be put on the footing of the most favored nations. One additional "convention" provided for the payment of the claims of American citizens before referred to; and another arranged the method of payment for the bargain; viz., three months after the delivery of the country to the American authorities, the sixty millions of francs, reckoned to be equal to $11,250,000, were to be paid to France in six *per cent.* stock of the United States; the interest of which was to be payable in Europe, and the stock itself, after fifteen years, redeemable to the amount of not less than $3,000,000 yearly, or in three equal annual instalments. The principal, if France thought proper to sell the stock, was to be disposed of so as to conduce most to the credit of the American funds.

"Thus closed these negotiations," says Mr. Gayarré, who has related them at large, and with great fulness of detail, "which eventuated in the most important treaty, perhaps, ever signed in the nineteenth century, if it be judged by its consequences to the United States and to the rest of the world. Among those consequences were the extension of the area of freedom, an immense accretion to the physical and moral power of the great American Republic, and the subsequent acquisition of the Floridas, Texas, California, and other portions of the Mexican territory. Other results, of at least equal magnitude, may be clearly foreseen, and it may be permitted to the pride of patriotism, to hope for the realization of Bonaparte's prevision, 'that the day may come when the cession of Louisiana to the United States, shall render the Americans too powerful for the continent of Europe.'"*

1803.

We can imagine the strong feelings of gratulation which filled the mind of the president in view of what had just been accomplished by Messrs. Livingston and Monroe. Writing, in July, to General Gates, he says, "I accept with

* The population amounted to some 80,000, including above 40,000 slaves.

* Gayarrés "*History of Louisiana: Spanish Domination*," pp. 450–526. See also the Appendix to the same volume, for the treaty and conventions between the United States and the French Republic, pp. 640–49.

pleasure, and with pleasure reciprocate, your congratulations on the acquisition of Louisiana: for it is a subject of mutual congratulation, as it interests every man of the nation. The territory acquired, as it includes all the waters of the Missouri and Mississippi, has more than doubled the area of the United States, and the new part is not inferior to the old, in soil, climate, productions, and important communications. If our legislature dispose of it with the wisdom we have a right to expect, they may make it the means of tempting all our Indians on the east side of the Mississippi to remove to the west; and of condensing instead of scattering, our population." One of which predictions certainly has been verified; but the other is entirely contradicted by the result.

The president was not, however, without serious misgivings as to the constitutional aspect of this important question; and he was well aware that the course he had adopted would be subjected to severe scrutiny by the opponents of his administration. Writing to Mr. Breckenridge, of Kentucky, in August, he gives expression to his views and opinions quite at large: "The treaty," he says, "must of course be laid before both Houses, because both have important functions to exercise respecting it. They, I presume, will see their duty to their country in ratifying and paying for it, so as to secure a good, which would otherwise, probably, be never again in their power. But I suppose they must then appeal to *the nation*, for an additional article to the Constitution, approving and confirming an act, which the nation had not previously authorized.

"The Constitution has made no provision for our holding foreign territory, still less for our incorporating foreign nations into our Union. The executive, in seizing the fugitive occurrence, which so much advances the good of this country, *have done an act beyond the Constitution.* The legislature, in casting behind them metaphysical subtleties, and risking themselves like faithful servants, must ratify and pay for it, and throw themselves on their country, for doing for them, unauthorized, what we know they would have done for themselves, had they been in a situation to do it. It is the case of a guardian, investing the money of his ward in purchasing an adjacent territory; and saying to him when of age,—I did this for your good, I pretend to no right to bind you, you may disavow me, and I must get out of the scrape as I can; I thought it my duty to risk myself for you.* But we shall not be disowned by the

1803.

* Mr. Tucker's remarks on this letter deserve the reader's attention. "Yet," he says, "the act of indemnity, in other words, the amendment to the Constitution, never took place; and as the treaty received the sanction of every branch of the government, and the silent acquiescence of the nation, it would seem not to have been required. Yet Mr. Jefferson's doubts appear to rest on strong ground; for, assuredly, if the executive, with the sanction of the Senate, could constitutionally buy Louisiana of France, and stipulate to incorporate it into the Union; it might also have bought Mexico of Spain, and then the whole character of the people of the United States, their government, religion, laws, and institutions, might have been merged in that of a nation more populous than itself; which supposition is utterly inconsistent with the jealous limitations of power imposed by the Constitution." Tucker's "*Life of Jefferson*," vol. ii., p. 147.

nation; and the act of indemnity will confirm and not weaken the Constitution, by more strongly marking out its lines."

It having been arranged that the ratifications should be exchanged within six months of the conclusion of the treaty, the president called Congress together at as early a date as he could, in order that they might take such action as the case required. In his message of the 17th of October, he stated the fact of the purchase and the treaty, as briefly as possible, and informed the

1803. Representatives, that as soon as the instruments transferring the sovereignty of Louisiana to the United States, "had received the constitutional sanction of the Senate, they would, without delay, be communicated to them, for the exercise of their functions, as to those conditions which are within the powers vested by the Constitution in Congress."

The treaty was ratified by the Senate on the 20th of October, by twenty-four votes against seven; and as the French *chargé d'affaires* held in his hand the ratification of his government, they were immediately exchanged, and the treaty was just kept from being voided by the expiration of the time specified. On the 22d it was officially communicated to Congress, that they might provide for its execution; and on the same day, the injunction of secrecy as to the appropriation of the two millions of dollars placed in the hands of the executive, was taken off.

Mr. Jefferson, before the assembling of Congress, sketched for Mr. Lincoln, the attorney-general, such an amendment of the Constitution as he thought would be required in consequence of the purchase of Louisiana. At the same time, he very prudently remarked, "The less that is said about any constitutional difficulty, the better: and it will be desirable for Congress to do what is necessary *in silence*." In September, writing from Monticello to Colonel Nicholas, the president says; "Whatever Congress shall think it necessary to do, should be done with as little debate as possible, and particularly so far as respects the constitutional difficulty." And yet in the same letter he says; "When an instrument admits two constructions, the one safe, the other dangerous, the one precise, the other indefinite, I prefer that which is safe and precise. I had rather ask an enlargement of power from the nation, where it is found necessary, than assume it by a construction which would make our powers boundless. One peculiar security is in the possession of a written Constitution. Let us not make it blank paper by construction." He further adds; "I confess I think it important in the present case, to set an example against broad construction, by appealing for new power to the people. If, however, our friends shall think differently, certainly I shall acquiesce with satisfaction; confiding, that the good sense of our country will correct the evil of construction, when it shall produce ill effects."

The Spanish government, which had very unwillingly yielded Louisiana to France, made loud complaints against its sale to the United States; for in this transfer to the American republic, Spain saw clearly the rapid approach of that day, which she had feared so many years, when the United States on her border, would be all-powerful, and when it would be impossible for her to retain possession of her provinces. Some show of opposition was made in respect to giving up Louisiana, and from what we know of the state of things in France at this date, there is little doubt that the French government connived at, if not encouraged, these proceedings.

When the eighth Congress assembled, it was found that the republicans were
1803. largely in the majority, and Nathaniel Macon was elected speaker of the House without difficulty. In the president's message, above referred to, it was hopefully shown, that although the acquisition (if confirmed) would add thirteen millions to the public debt, as most of it was not payable until after fifteen years, when it was calculated the existing debt would be all discharged, no additional taxes would be required. And as this aspect of the business was the one that most of all concerned the Representatives, it will be worth while to see how they received the intelligence of the marvellous increase of territory, and how they thought it best to deal with it.

The federalists, as was expected, set their faces against the entire transaction. Griswold, who appears to have led the opposition, proposed, on the 24th of October, a resolution calling for papers, and this the supporters of the government most strenuously resisted. "Each party," says Mr. Tucker, "referring to the call for papers in 1795, relative to the British Treaty, charged the other with inconsistency as the two parties had now changed places as to this question." The administration party urged forcibly against the federalists, that they, only a short time before, were willing to rush into a war with Spain, for the purpose of getting possession of New Orleans,—"the key to the Mississippi," alone; but now, demurred about receiving it, when it was offered, with the Mississippi itself, and the whole land thereon, to the farthest ocean to boot, for a pacific "consideration;" and busied themselves in discovering a flaw in the title. The resolution was finally rejected by a very small majority.

Failing on that point, next day the attack was repeated from a new quarter,—the *unconstitutionality* of the acquisition; for the United States government had no power under the Constitution to acquire new territory, nor was it accordant with that instrument, to give to the ports of Louisiana such a preference over the other ports of the Union, as was secured by the admission of French and Spanish vessels on payment of the same duties as were paid by American ships. John Randolph, with characteristic zeal, argued on the side of the government, and Nicholson, of Maryland, urged, "that the right to acquire territory was incident to every sovereign nation; that the states confederately had this power after their independence, and having surrendered it, with the power to declare war and make treaties, to Congress, first under the Confederation, and afterwards under the **1803.**
Constitution, it now belonged to the federal government; that territory can

be acquired only by conquest or purchase; of which the first mode is given to Congress, in the power to make war, and the last to the president and Senate, in the power to make treaties; and lastly, that these powers are expressly taken from the states by the Constitution, and being essential to sovereignty, must exist somewhere."

In respect to this point, as also the other which was urged by the federalists, viz., the preference given to the ports of Louisiana over those of other states, Mr. Tucker candidly confesses, that "the republican party now found that the very strict construction of the Constitution, for which they had contended when in the opposition, was not suited to them when in the exercise of power; and which, if pushed to that extreme of nicety, which some affected, would often defeat the main purposes for which the Constitution was established." Eighty-nine, therefore, voted in favor of the general resolution for carrying the treaty into effect, against twenty-three opponents; and the resolutions for a provincial government over the ceded territory, and for providing the purchase money, were passed without a division.*

The Spanish authorities in Louisiana had made every preparation, in the spring of 1803, to deliver the province over to the French Republic; and the arrival of General Victor, the commissioner, was waited for with great interest. The general, however, did not make his appearance, and news came, that the province had been sold to the United States. Laussat was to act as commissioner to receive Louisiana from the Spaniards, and then to transfer it to the United States. As we have intimated above, Spain expressed much indignation at this proceeding, and if she could, she would have refused her acquiescence; but she had no alternative except submission; and so Laussat issued his proclamation on the 30th of November, informing the Louisianians of the great change which was on the eve of taking place in their political relations, and with considerable skill enlarging upon the new privileges which they were thus to acquire. To prevent the possibility of violence from the lower classes of the populace, respecting whom much alarm was felt after the withdrawal of the Spanish troops, and the evacuation of the military posts, a volunteer battalion of young Americans was enrolled, and placed under the command of Daniel Clarke, junior, the American consul. They were soon joined by numbers of French creoles, until they were more than three hundred strong; they were organized in detachments, and patrolled the city of New Orleans, and maintained guard in the forts night and day, until the 17th of December, when the American troops had arrived in the vicinity of the city.

1803.

William C. C. Claiborne, governor of the Mississippi Territory, and General James Wilkinson, had been appointed by the president the American commissioners; and Governor Claiborne was authorized to exercise provisionally all the civil authority pertaining to the

* See Benton's "*Abridgement of the Debates of Congress*," vol. iii., pp. 53–77.

former Spanish governor and intendant, for the preservation of order, and the protection of persons and property. On the 20th of December, possession was taken of the province: we quote from Monette an account of the ceremonies connected with this eventful day.

On Monday morning, at sunrise, the tri-colored flag was elevated to the summit of the flag-staff in the public square. At eleven o'clock, A. M., the militia paraded near it, and precisely at noon the commissioners of the United States, at the head of the American troops, entered the city. The regular troops formed on the opposite side of the square, facing the militia. At
1803. this time, the colonial-prefect, attended by his secretary, and a number of French citizens, advanced from his quarters to the City Hall, saluted as he approached by a discharge of artillery.

At the City Hall, a large concourse of the most respectable citizens awaited his approach. Here, in the presence of the assembled multitude, the prefect delivered to the American commissioners the keys of the city, emblematic of the formal delivery of the province. He then declared, that such of the inhabitants as desired to pass under the government of the United States, were absolved from their allegiance to the French Republic.

Governor Claiborne then arose, and offered to the people of Louisiana his congratulations on the auspicious event which had placed them beyond the reach of chance. He assured them, that the people of the United States received them as brothers, and would hasten to extend to them the benefits of the free institutions which had formed the basis of our unexampled prosperity; and that, in the mean time, they should be protected in their liberty, their property, and their religion; their agriculture should be encouraged, and their commerce favored.

The tri-colored flag of France slowly descended, meeting the rising flag of the United States at half-mast. After the pause of a few minutes, the flag of France descended to the ground, and the star-spangled banner rose to the summit of the flag-staff, saluted by the roar of artillery, and the joyful response of the American people, accompanied by a full band of martial music, to the air of "Hail, Columbia!" The windows, balconies, and corridors of the vicinity were crowded with ladies, brilliant beyond comparison, each with the American flag in miniature proudly waving over their heads. The formal delivery of the more remote posts, and their dependencies, took place during the following spring. Further on, we shall speak of the troubles with Spain, which grew out of this transfer of Louisiana.

Sullivan, writing in 1833, in respect to the purchase of the new province, gives the views entertained by the federalists as to the president's course in this matter. "This diplomatic operation," he says, "has proved to be far more advantageous to the United States, than there was any ground even to hope for thirty years ago. The fears then entertained have disappeared in the changes which have occurred in the power and in the probable designs both of France and Spain, in relation to this country. And also, that whatever Mr. Jefferson's motives may have been, and however assuming to make this purchase, it was certainly better to have made it, and in whole, than to have had either a Spanish or French colony on the banks of the Mississippi. Thus Mr. Jefferson was so fortunate as to find, that an act which would have called for an impeachment under some circumstances, is now regarded as the most meritorious of his public life. It will be seen, hereafter, how well founded the apprehensions of Mr. Jefferson's opponents were. (Reference is here made to some futile attempt of Spain to impede the transfer.) With respect to the sum, (fifteen millions,) it was probably thrice as much as needed to have been given; because Bonaparte knew, at the time of the purchase, that, on renewal of the war, the whole country of Louisiana would be taken possession of by the British; and would consequently be lost both to France and Spain. . . . . . Notwithstanding it has proved, so far as can be now discerned, a useful measure, except in the amount it cost."

In concluding at this point, the narrative of the acquisition of Louisiana, it is worth while to observe, in the language of an eloquent statesman, that, "the renewal of the European war, and the partialities of Mr. Jefferson in favor of France, enabled him to accomplish an object which greatly enlarged the territories of the Union—which removed a most formidable source of future dissensions with France—which exceedingly strengthened the relative influence and power of the state and section of the Union, to which he himself belonged, and which in its consequences changed the character of the Confederacy itself. This operation, by far the greatest that has been accomplished by any administration under the Constitution, was consummated at the price of fifteen millions of dollars in money, and of *a direct, unqualified, admitted, violation of the Constitution of the United States.* According to the theory of Mr. Jefferson, as applied by him to the alien and sedition acts, it was absolutely null and void. It might have been nullified by the legislature of any one state in the Union, and if persisted in, would have warranted and justified a combination of states, and their secession from the Confederacy in resistance against it. That an amendment to the Constitution was necessary to legalize the annexation of Louisiana to the Union, was the opinion both of Mr. Jefferson and of Mr. Madison. They finally acquiesced, however, in the latitudinous construction of that instrument, which holds the treaty-making powers, together with an act Congress, sufficient for this operation. It was accordingly thus consummated by Mr. Jefferson, and has been sanctioned by the acquiescence of the people. Upwards of thirty years have passed away since this great change was effected. By a subsequent treaty with Spain, by virtue of the same powers and authority, the Floridas have been also annexed to the Union, and the boundaries of the United States have been extended from the Mississippi to the Pacific Ocean. There is now nothing in the

Constitution of the United States to inhibit their extension to the two polar circles from the Straits of Hudson to the Straits of Magellan. Whether this very capacity of enlargement of territory and multiplication of states by the constructive power of Congress, without check or control either by the states or by their people, will not finally terminate in the dissolution of the Union itself, time alone can determine. The credit of the acquisition of Louisiana, whether to be considered as a source of good or of evil, is perhaps due to Robert R. Livingston more than to any other man, but the merit of its accomplishment must ever remain as the great and imperishable memorial of the administration of Jefferson."*

* John Quincy Adams's "*Life of James Madison*," pp. 78, 79. See also Dr. J. W. Francis's able review of the life and services of Mr. Livingston, in an "*Address before the Philolexian Society of Columbia College*," 1831, in which he claims that "Chancellor Livingston was the prominent and efficient agent in this important negotiation."

CHAPTER III.

1803-1805.

PROGRESS OF EVENTS DURING 1803, 1804, AND 1805.

Mr. Jefferson's interest in western explorations—Lewis and Clarke's expedition to the mouth of the Columbia River—Second session of the seventh Congress—The president recommends the repeal of discriminating duties—Griswold's inquiry into the management of the treasury—The eighth Congress—Amendment to the Constitution respecting election of president and vice-president—Warmly opposed—Finally carried—Bankrupt law repealed—Jefferson's views as to the United States Bank—Mr. Tucker's statements—Judge Pickering tried and removed—Articles of impeachment against Judge Chase—Work of the session—Land acquired from Delaware Indians—Naval affairs in the Mediterranean—Truxtun's resignation—Commodore Morris removed on charge of inactivity in the service—Preble appointed to the command of the squadron—Loss of the Philadelphia—Destruction of this ship by Decatur in the harbor of Tripoli—Preble bombards Tripoli—Recalled—The disaster of the Intrepid—Loss of Somers, and others—Barron in command—Exploits of Eaton and Hamet Caramalli—Peace concluded—Terms of it—Popularity of the administration—Presidential contest—Burr dropped—Clinton the candidate for vice-president—Contest for governorship of New York—Burr's rage against Hamilton—Determines on revenge—Pushes a quarrel upon Hamilton—The challenge and its fatal result—Hamilton's death—Sullivan's remarks on the personal appearance of Hamilton and Burr—Congress opens in November—The president's message—Trial of Judge Chase—Acquitted—Disappointment of the dominant party—Laws enacted—The election and its results—Tucker's statements at the close of Thomas Jefferson's first term of service.

THE extent, boundaries, physical aspect, and resources of Louisiana being alike unknown, it became important for the government of the United States to take measures for examining into these important particulars at as early a day as practicable. Mr. Jefferson had, for a number of years, been interested in the exploration of the country west of the Mississippi. "He had, when in France, recommended it to Ledyard, after he was disappointed in his project of engaging in the fur trade, on the northwest coast of America; and in 1792, he proposed to the American Philosophical Society to effect the same object by subscription. 1803. It was actually undertaken by Michaux, the well known botanist, under the auspices of the society; but after proceeding as far as Kentucky, his purpose was countermanded by the French minister in the United States; for he, as we are informed, did not confine himself to geographical and scientific matters, but engaged in the political agitations and schemes in addition.

On the 18th of January, 1803, the president sent a confidential message to Congress, containing a recommendation on this subject, in consequence of which, an appropriation was made for defraying the expense of an exploring expedition overland to the Pacific. Mr. Jefferson, as his biographer says, "considered that the United States would be justly subject to the reproach of the scientific world, if they longer delayed to obtain more accurate geographical knowledge of the western wilderness,—a country highly interesting in itself, and which their people were destined one day to overspread. He was perhaps yet further stimulated to obtain a more accurate knowledge of the country, because he had a hope of obtaining it, sooner or later, from France." "In looking about for a fit person to conduct this enterprise, no one presented himself to his mind possessed of so many of the requisite qualifications as Captain Meriwether Lewis, who, reared in his neighborhood, had been long known to him, and had for nearly two years acted as his private secretary. His character is thus faithfully sketched by Mr. Jefferson, in a memoir of his life, prepared for the posthumous narrative of the expedition: 'Of courage undaunted; possessing a firmness and perseverance of purpose, which nothing but impossibilities could divert from its direction; careful as a father of those committed to his charge, yet steady in the maintenance of order and discipline; intimate with the Indian character, customs and principles; habituated to the hunting 1803. life; guarded, by exact observation of the vegetables and animals of his own country, against losing time in the description of objects already possessed; honest, disinterested, liberal, of sound understanding, and a fidelity to truth so scrupulous, that whatever he should report would be as certain as if seen by ourselves.'"

The judgment displayed in this selection, was justified by the event. The exploring party, exclusive of a small escort as far as the Mandans, consisted of twenty-eight individuals, carefully selected, exclusive of Captain Lewis and Captain Jonathan Clarke, who was second in command. This gentleman was the brother of George Rogers Clarke, and partook of his capacity to endure hardship and brave dangers, as well as his practical good sense. With his own hand the president prepared a set of instructions for Captain Lewis, which seem to embrace every object of importance which might demand his attention.

A passage or two from these "Instructions" will serve to display the spirit under which Jefferson wished the party to proceed on its interesting work.

"In all your intercourse with the natives, treat them in the most friendly and conciliatory manner which their own conduct will admit; allay all jealousies, as to the object of your journey; satisfy them of its innocence; make them acquainted with the position, extent, character, peaceable and commercial dispositions of the United States; of our wish to be neighborly, friendly, and useful to them, and of our dispositions to a commercial intercourse with them; confer with them on the points most convenient as mutual emporiums, and the articles of most desirable interchange, for them and for us. . . . Carry with you some matter of the kine-pox; inform those of them with whom you may be, of its efficacy as a preservative from the small-pox, and instruct and encourage them in the use of it. This may be especially done wherever you winter." "To your own discretion must be left the degree of danger you may risk, and the point at which you should decline; only saying, we wish you to err on the side of your safety, and to bring back your party safe, even if it be with less information."*

The larger part of the year was spent in making preparations for the expedition, and it was thought best that it should not enter the Missouri till the spring. About the middle of May, 1804, the party left the banks of the Mississippi. We may mention in the present connection, that the journey of this brave-hearted band, from the mouth of the Missouri, by the Columbia to the Pacific Ocean, and back, occupied them for twenty-eight months and ten days; and they richly merited the eulogy of the president, which we find in his message at the opening of Congress, in December, 1806. "They have traced the Missouri nearly to its source, descended the Columbia to the Pacific Ocean, ascertained with accuracy the geography of that interesting communication across our continent, learnt the character of the country, of its commerce and inhabitants; and it is but justice to say, that Messrs. Lewis and Clarke, and their brave companions have, by this arduous service, *deserved well of their country!*"

During the second session of the seventh Congress, few acts of general interest were passed. The most important was a law (February 17th) to prevent the importation of negroes, mulattoes, or other persons of color, (not being natives, citizens, or seamen, of the United States, or seamen, natives of countries beyond the Cape of Good Hope,) into any part of the United States, within a state which had prohibited, by law, the admission of any such negro, or person of color; under penalty of one thousand dollars,
and the forfeiture of the vessel **1803.**
in which such person was imported. The time had not then arrived when the importation of slaves was prohibited by the Constitution, and this law

* Lacepede, writing to Jefferson on this topic, seems almost to have caught a glimpse of the wonderful developments of the future: "If your nation," he says, "can establish an easy communication by rivers, canals, and short portages, between New York (for example) and a city that must be built at the mouth of the Columbia, *what a route for the commerce of Europe, Asia, and America!*"

was passed in conformity to the laws of certain states which had been passed to prohibit the importation of slaves.*

An amendment to the Constitution was proposed and debated in committee of the whole, but not having obtained the majority of two-thirds, was laid over till the following year. The object was, to prevent the recurrence of such a contingency as occurred at the last election of president and vice-president.

The president's recommendation to repeal the discriminating duties, did not, as Mr. Tucker states, receive the approbation of Congress. The merchants of New York and Philadelphia petitioned against this repeal, and the subject, although debated, was never acted upon. The petitioners, says the same writer, "had tried the effect of mutual burdens on the trade between them and foreign nations, but they had not made the experiment of mutual exemption; and supposing the discriminations to be equal, it is not easy to see, why the advantage to American vessels of a lower tonnage duty at home, would not be counterbalanced by the disadvantage of a higher duty abroad, in every voyage outward and homeward. In truth, all these discriminations, which operate as a bounty on some by the exclusion of others, are hurtful to the whole mercantile interest, and operate to lessen the amount of trade, by requiring a greater capital to carry it on, by narrowing the sphere of competition, and by lessening the total amount of imports and exports. We may, therefore, fairly infer, that whenever nations shall clearly see their interests, and be content to pursue them without jealousy or other bias, they will act on the principle recommended by Mr. Jefferson."*

Mr. Griswold, of Connecticut, made a party movement in order to bring suspicion upon the man- 1803.
agement of the treasury. He proposed an inquiry, when the session had almost reached its close, into the appropriation of the whole of the $7,300,000 to the discharge of the public debt, by the commissioners of the sinking fund; suggesting that it had not all been so applied. But this recrimination met with no better success than it deserved; Gallatin replied to the inquiries so fully, so clearly, and so promptly, as to gain a new triumph for the administration, out of what had been designed to involve them in perplexity, if not to cover them with shame. On the 3d of March, the seventh Congress reached its termination, and the attention of the people was bestowed upon the elections which went on during the summer.

On a previous page (p. 43) we have mentioned the opening of the eighth Congress, in October, 1803. At an early day of this session, an amendment to the Constitution (spoken of above) was proposed, relative to the election of president and vice-president, so as to designate the person voted for as presi-

* See Benton's "*Abridgement of the Debates of Congress*," vol. ii., pp. 725, 742.

* Tucker's "*Life of Jefferson*," vol. ii., p. 134. The biographer of the third president takes occasion also to point out "the small game" which the republican party were after, in decrying and attempting to destroy the mint, at this time. See p. 137.

dent or as vice-president, instead of the existing article, which required the electors to vote for two persons for these offices, of whom the one who had the highest number of votes was to be president.* This amendment, according to Mr. Tucker, "was vehemently opposed in both Houses by the opposition, but was finally carried by the requisite vote of two-thirds in both Houses. The change was opposed on the ground that it would, by means of party intrigue, favor the election of a vice-president who would be unfit to discharge the office of president; that the election by the House of Representatives might not be expected to be of frequent recurrence, and when it was, if they should choose the person who was least fit, it would be a salutary warning to both parties, to bestow their votes, in all cases, on persons properly qualified; that a change of the Constitution was, of itself, an evil, and was likely to prevent the veneration, which time, and time alone, confers; and that it was better to submit to a partial evil, than risk one yet greater in an untried experiment."

Notwithstanding the efforts of the opposition, the amendment was carried, and during the year 1804, it was ratified by the legislatures of three-fourths of the states, as required by the Constitution. Only Massachusetts, Connecticut, and Delaware, refused assent to the change. On the 25th of September, the secretary of state gave public notice of this amendment having been duly adopted and ratified.*

The president had never looked with favor upon the bankrupt law, which was enacted during one of the last years of Mr. Adams's administration; and it was at his instance, and with his hearty concurrence, that the law was repealed by Congress. "As this law authorized a majority of the creditors to discharge a bankrupt trader from all his preceding debts, it was regarded by many of the other classes of men, as an invidious privilege to the mercantile community; especially in the southern states, where the agricultural pursuits are predominant; and **1804.** as it was found, that by the power of making discriminations in favor of some creditors, and in fact of making surreptitious creditors, there was no difficulty in general, in obtaining the sanction of the requisite majority for the debtor's discharge, the law was condemned as affording but too much encouragement to fraud, waste, and a rash spirit of adventure." On this account, it was not regarded with favor by a large portion of the people, while, at the same time, those engaged in commercial pursuits, strongly urged that some law of the kind was absolutely necessary to a nation as extensively engaged as are the United States, in trade and commerce. The repeal was carried in the House, by a vote of ninety-nine to thirteen.

It will be recollected by the reader, that the anti-federalists had vehemently

---

* For the speeches in the Senate, December 2, 1803, of Uriah Tracy against, and of John Taylor, in favor of this amendment to the Constitution, see Williston's "*Eloquence of the United States*," vol. ii., pp. 320–63. See also Benton's "*Abridgement of the Debates of Congress*," vol. iii., pp. 30–37; 57–60.

* For this amendment, see vol. ii., pp. 236, 37.

opposed the creation of the Bank of the United States, respecting which, we have already given a full account in our second volume, (pp. 295-302.) Mr. Jefferson's sentiments accorded fully with those of the party whose leader he now was; and his antagonism to this institution was none the less active since his accession to the chief-magistracy. In writing to Mr. Gallatin, he expresses himself as firmly convinced that the Bank of the United States is an institution "most deadly hostile to the principles and forms of the Constitution." This he undertakes to demonstrate thus: "That it is hostile we know, 1. From a knowledge of the principles of the persons composing the body of directors in every bank, principal or branch; and those of most of the stockholders. 2. From their opposition to the measures and principles of the government, and to the election of those friendly to them: and, 3. From the sentiments of the newspapers they support. Now, while we are strong," he goes on to say, "it is the greatest duty we owe to the safety of our Constitution, to bring this powerful enemy to a perfect subordination under its authorities. The first measure would be, to reduce them to an equal footing only with other banks, as to the favors of the government. But in order to be able to meet a general combination of the banks against us in a critical emergency, could we not make a beginning towards an independent use of our own money? towards holding our own deposits in all the banks where it is received, and letting the treasurer give his draft or note for payment at any particular place, which, in a well-conducted government, ought to have as much credit as any private draft, or bank note, or bill, and would give us the same facilities which we derive from the banks?" Very likely, as Mr. Tucker suggests, Andrew Jackson availed himself of this hint at a later day, when he had resolved upon his course with respect to the last Bank of the United States.

In regard to the dangers arising from the existence of a national bank, we think that the president's biographer speaks with as much truth as candor. His sentiments, considering his political views, are worthy of note. "The public danger from such an institution," he says, "on which Mr. Jefferson's hostility rested yet more than on its supposed unconstitutionality, appears to have been egregiously overrated by him. The power of so wealthy a corporation, using all its money in loans, and able by its high credit, so to multiply its money, would indeed be formidable if it were possessed of a monopoly; but as its privileges were shared with other banks, and as those created by the states were everywhere equal or superior in wealth to the branches of the United States Bank, its power of doing mischief is almost neutralized, while that of rendering facilities to commerce remains. It would seem to furnish a conclusive argument against the imagined extent of their power, that it was not sufficient, in 1811, to preserve its own existence; and that its successor, with far more ample means and resources, and directed, according to its enemies, with an unexampled unity and energy of purpose to this single object, has not been a whit more capable of self-preservation."*

Just at the close of the session, in March, 1803, the House of Representatives sent a message to the Senate, impeaching John Pickering, judge of the district court for the district of New Hampshire, of high crimes and misdemeanors. The principal charge
1803. against him was, that he was habitually intoxicated, and in various other ways unfit for his high position. On the trial, which took place at this session of Congress, the charges were proved, and he was removed from his office.

Articles of impeachment were also ordered by the House to be preferred against Judge Chase, of Maryland, one of the justices of the supreme court of the United States, a man of considerable eloquence and power, and not easily daunted by any attack upon his judicial character and standing. Judge Peters, of the district court of Pennsylvania, was also noted for impeachment by the House, who seemed determined that the judiciary should undergo a thorough examination and purgation, so far as it was possible. A committee was appointed to draw up the articles in proper form, but the whole matter was postponed to the next session, when it was expected that there would be less difficulty in carrying out the designs of the House.†

On the 27th of March, 1804, Congress adjourned, after a long and active session. Beside the points we have already noted, we may mention, that the salaries of the principal officers of government were increased; additional duties were imposed on imports, 1804.
to defray the expenses of naval operations in the Mediterranean ; a naturalization law was passed, which required a residence of five years instead of fourteen; and two separate governments were established in the newly acquired territory of Louisiana, to be organized as the president might deem expedient.*

During the present year, (1804,) the Delaware Indians relinquished to the United States their title to an extensive tract east of the Mississippi, between the Wabash and Ohio, for which they were to receive annuities in animals and implements for agriculture, and in other necessaries. This was an important acquisition, not only for its extent and fertility, but because, by its commanding the Ohio for three hundred miles, and nearly half that distance the Wabash, the produce of the settled country could be safely conveyed down those rivers, and, with the cession recently made by the Kaskaskias, (1803,)

* Tucker's "*Life of Jefferson*," vol. ii., p. 159.

† See Benton's "*Abridgement of the Debates of Congress*," vol. iii., pp. 88–125.

* The claims connected with the "Yazoo purchase" furnished at the time, material for controversy and debate. Mr. Tucker gives an abstract of the arguments on both sides of the question, stating that the subject was finally postponed on the 10th of March, after several votes, which showed an almost equal strength of parties, by a vote of fifty-nine to forty-nine.—"*Life of Jefferson*," vol. ii., p. 162. See also Garland's "*Life of John Randolph*," vol. i., pp. 66, 199–205. According to this writer, "a more detestable, impudent, and dangerous villainy is not to be found on record."

it nearly consolidated the possessions of the United States north of the Ohio, from Lake Erie to the Mississippi. The Piankashaws, having some claim to the country ceded by the Delawares, were quieted by a fair purchase.

Resuming our account of naval affairs, (see p. 21,) we find that, early in 1802, Congress enacted laws which obviated the president's scruples, and fully authorized the capture and condemnation of any Tripolitan vessels that might be found. A relief squadron of five vessels, (Lieutenant Sterret's brave little Enterprise being one of them,) rated in all at a hundred and fifty-two guns, was dispatched under Commodore Morris to the Mediterranean. They left, however, at different dates, the last not before September; but the force in that sea had been increased by the Boston, under the eccentric Captain M'Niel, and by several smaller vessels, which had been got ready, and sent off as rapidly as was possible. The command of the squadron was, in the first instance, offered to Truxtun, and accepted by him, but, a question having arisen about allowing him a captain in the flag-ship, he resigned. "It is said that Commodore Truxtun did not intend to resign his commission in the navy, in 1802, but simply the command of the squadron to which he had been appointed. The construction put upon his communication by the department, however, was opposed to this idea, and he consequently retired to private life."

Into the particulars in regard to the operations of the American vessels under Commodore Morris, we need not here enter. During the latter part of 1802, and the autumn of 1803, Chauncey, Rodgers, Porter, and others, sustained the reputation of their countrymen for bravery and skill, and numerous successes were attained over flotillas of gunboats and pirate vessels. As well as he was able, also, the commodore maintained the blockade, convoyed American ships, and kept the rest of Barbary in order. **1803.** But the armament was not provided with guns of sufficient calibre for the bombardment of Tripoli, which was the only argument that the pasha was at all inclined to listen to. And, after his return, in November, Commodore Morris was called before a court of inquiry, and being pronounced wanting in diligence and activity in the duties assigned to him, was dismissed the service, in March, 1804.

Mr. Cooper naturally and properly condemns the course pursued on this occasion, and says, that "There can be little question that the act of the executive in this instance, was precipitate and wrong." With the disregard of the feelings of those who have adopted the profession of arms, that civilians are too commonly chargeable withal, and with their incapacity of discerning the difference between removing a country postmaster, or collector of port dues, and dismissing a military or naval officer, the president seems to have acted in a manner far from generous towards Morris, who, whatever errors in judgment he may have committed, was never charged with want of zeal or courage. "His dismissal from the navy has usually been deemed a high-handed political measure, rather than a military condemnation." The removal of Truxtun and Morris, with the resignation of Dale, and the death of Barry, reduced the number of captains to nine, the number named in the law for the reduction of the navy.

Carried on as it had been, this Tripolitan war promised to be indefinitely protracted; accordingly, a fresh squadron was dispatched, vessel by vessel, as they were ready for sea, under Commodore Preble. It consisted of the Constitution, a forty-four gun ship, the old Philadelphia, which was rated as a thirty-eight, two sixteen-gun brigs, and three twelve-gun schooners, including the gallant little Enterprise. At the outset of this new stage of the

1803.

affair, some trouble and detention arose from the capture of a vessel belonging to Morocco; but it was happily and promptly adjusted by Preble, before he entered the Mediterranean, in October, 1803.

Signalized by some of the most daring and brilliant exploits with which the records of the American navy are adorned, this period of the war was, nevertheless, on the whole, very disastrous. Chasing a Tripolitan vessel within the shoal-waters that protect the harbor of Tripoli, on the 31st of October, the Philadelphia struck upon a reef, and Bainbridge and his whole crew, amounting to three hundred and fifteen souls, were captured. The vessel thus lost to the United States, was subsequently got off the rocks by the enemy, and was moored off Tripoli, about a quarter of a mile from the pasha's castle.

Preble and his coadjutors determined, at an early day, that the Philadelphia should not be suffered to remain in the enemy's hands. Accordingly, Decatur having offered his services, they were accepted for the gallant enterprise of boarding and destroying the ship as she lay in the harbor of Tripoli. The Philadelphia had forty guns mounted, double-shotted, and ready for firing, and the whole force by land and sea, belonging to the enemy, was in readiness for efficient service; and yet Decatur, with a little ketch of sixty tons, mounting four small guns, and having a crew of seventy-five souls, undertook the capture and destruction of the frigate. After one unsuccessful effort to enter the harbor, in consequence of a severe gale, on the evening of the 9th of February, Decatur was enabled, on the 15th, in his ketch, the Intrepid,

1804.

to test his own and his countrymen's ability to carry out the gallant undertaking on which they had perilled their lives. The cool deliberation, the steady nerve, the unflinching gallantry, the entire success of Decatur and his men, are fully narrated by Mr. Cooper, in his "Naval History," and by Mr. Mackenzie, in his "Life of Decatur." The Philadelphia was set on fire; the brave band of assailants, without loss or injury, abandoned the burning ship; and slowly but exultingly, by the aid of their sweeps, withdrew from the scene of danger and of triumph. "Hull, spars, and rigging, were now enveloped in flames. As the metal of the Philadelphia's guns became heated, they were discharged in succession from both sides, serving as a brilliant salvo in honor of the victory, and not harmless for the Tripolitans, as her starboard battery was fired directly into the town. The town itself, the castles, the minarets of the mosques, and the shipping in the harbor, were all brought into distinct view by the splendor of the conflagration. It served also to reveal to the enemy the cause of their disaster in the little Intrepid, as she slowly withdrew from the harbor. The shot of the shipping and castle fell thickly around her, throwing up columns of spray, which the brilliant light converted into a new ornament of the scene. Only one shot took effect, and that passed through her topgallant sail. Three hearty American cheers were now given, in mingled triumph and derision. The cables of the Philadelphia having burned off, she drifted on the rocks, near the western entrance of the harbor; and then the whole spectacle, so full of moral sublimity, considering the means by which it had been effected, and of material grandeur, had its appropriate termination in the final catastrophe of her explosion."*

Preble, in his official report, did full justice to the gallantry and ability of Decatur, and by general consent, he was rewarded with immediate elevation to the rank of a captain in the navy, and was presented with a splendid sword, as a national testimony to his merit, and as an incentive to noble deeds in others.

The administration seems to have become sensible of the importance of increasing the force in the Mediterranean, and it was accordingly determined to send out reinforcements. During the latter part of the summer of 1804, Preble, five successive times, with the help of some gunboats and bomb vessels, belonging to the king of Naples, attempted the bombardment of the town of Tripoli. **1804.** The fact that they, as well as some attacks in boats upon the gunboats and shipping in the harbor, and the blockade, failed to secure the end contemplated, seems sufficient to show that the naval armament of the United States was not yet put on such a footing as was proper for a nation, that must of necessity be largely a commercial one.*

Although keenly disappointed at the news of his recall before he had been allowed to finish the war with Tripoli, Preble lost none of his zealous activity while waiting for his successor. Early in September of this year, he tried a new mode of annoyance, which ended more fatally to the Americans than any other attempt in the war. He fitted up the ketch, Intrepid, by which Decatur had achieved his feat against the Philadelphia, as a huge "infernal machine." And manning it with volunteers, Captain Somers being at the head, after taking the best precautions for securing a safe retreat to the crew, sent it into the harbor on the night of the 4th of September. It was watched with the most intense concern; and before

* Mackenzie's "*Life of Stephen Decatur*," p. 79.

* On the 3d of August, in one of these attacks by gunboats, Decatur engaged hand to hand with a Tripolitan officer, and would have been slain but for the noble self-devotion of a young man named Reuben James, who saved Decatur from the fatal blow by interposing his own head at this most critical moment. See Mackenzie's "*Life of Decatur*," pp. 89–93.

it had reached the point that was determined, the frightful explosion was beheld; but though signals were made, and boat parties sent out, no sign of the retreating crew was perceived; nor was one seen when daylight broke. Not only had the scheme failed in its direct object, it had wrought most lamentable harm for the projectors of it. It was afterwards found that the scorched and mangled corpses of Somers, Wadsworth, Israel, and their courageous followers had every one been picked up; Bainbridge (who was a prisoner all this time, and had once been wounded by the rebound of a shot from the Americans in their bombardments) was allowed to see, but could not identify any of them. How the explosion occurred no one could certainly tell, but it seemed probable that the magazines were fired
1804. by the shot of the enemy, who seeing the strange vessel drifting along in silence and darkness, and suspecting every movement of the Americans, discharged their guns with both grape and round shot, in every direction that they thought it possible an attack might be made upon them. No dead Turks were seen, and therefore the ketch had not been boarded; and it was not likely that any of her crew, through terror or rashness, had applied the match.*

On the 10th of September, Commodore Barron arrived, in the President, to take command of the Mediterranean squadron; and Preble, now relieved from his harassing position, returned, early in 1805, to the United States, where he and the gallant officers and men under him, received the thanks of Congress and of the country, for their noble efforts to sustain the reputation and establish the rights of Americans. The squadron under Barron consisted of two forty-fours, two thirty-eights, one thirty-two, two sixteens, and three twelves. And with these vessels the blockade was continued, although it could not be said that any hope was entertained of forcing an accommodation by that means; for new uneasiness had been showed by the other despots of Barbary, and it was necessary to detach part of the squadron, to look out near Gibraltar for cruisers from
Morocco. Nor would peace 1804.
have been secured so early, had not a movement by land been carried forward which materially aided the course of operations on the sea.

It will be remembered, that Yussuf Caramalli had obtained the throne by deposing his brother Hamet. "The latter," as Mr. Cooper states, "had escaped from the regency, and after passing a wandering life, had taken refuge among the Mamelukes of Egypt. It had often been suggested by the American agents, that the deposed prince might be made useful in carrying on the war against the usurper, and, at different times, several projects to that effect had been entertained, though never with any results. At length Mr. Eaton, the consul at Tunis, who had been a captain in the army, interested himself in the enterprise; and coming to America, so far

* See Sabine's "*Life of Edward Preble*," pp. 99–103. Mr. Cooper also enters fully into the question respecting the fate of Somers and his companions. See his "*Naval History*," vol. i., pp. 252–59.

prevailed on the government to lend itself to his views, as to obtain a species of indirect support. And Commodore Barron was directed to co-operate with Mr. Eaton, as far as he might deem it discreet."

Returning with Barron's squadron, in 1804, Eaton ascertained where the expelled pasha was to be found; and proceeded, in November, to Egypt, in the Argus, where the viceroy received them with favor, and gave permission to the prince of Tripoli to leave the country unmolested, although he had been fighting with the discontented Mamelukes against the government.

Early in 1805, Hamet "separated himself from the Mamelukes, and, attended by about forty followers, repaired to a point about twelve leagues to the westward of the old port of Alexandria. Here he was soon joined by Mr. Eaton, at the head of a small host of adventurers, whom he had obtained in Egypt. This party was composed of all nations, though Mr. Eaton expressed his belief, at the time, that had he possessed the means of subsistence, he might have marched a body of thirty thousand men against Tripoli, the reigning pasha having forced so many of his subjects into banishment. Soon after the junction agreed upon, Mr. Eaton, who now assumed the title of general, marched in the direction of Derne, taking the route across the desert of Barca."

With unflinching courage and dogged perseverance, Eaton and his allies pressed forward, and at the beginning of April, 1805, reached the coast in the vicinity of Derne. Having opened communications with the Argus, the Hornet, and the Nautilus, which had appeared on the coast, and obtained a field-piece, some stores and muskets, and the assistance of a few marines, the attack began,—the vessels standing close in and assisting.

The governor of Derne replied to Hamet's summons to surrender, in the terse but expressive oriental phrase, "Your head or mine!" He had a battery of eight or nine guns fronting the sea; and some eight hundred regular soldiers; with breastworks hastily run up, and loops cut for musketry in the houses, on the side he expected the attack. But more than one quarter of the town was in favor of the besiegers; and he had to repress mutiny within, as well as to resist assaults from without.

It did not require a very long time to silence the battery, so well did the vessels station themselves; and as soon as that was accomplished, Eaton's force stormed it, and for the first time the star-spangled banner waved over a fortress in the old world, captured by the bravery of the sons of the new world. This was on the 27th of April, 1805. As for the enemy, they had fled with so much precipitation, that they left their guns loaded and even primed; and they were immediately turned against the town. On the opposite side, Hamet, with a small cavalry force, had effected a lodgment; and so, being put between two fires, after this sharp encounter of two hours, the place submitted. "In this affair, only fourteen of the assailants were kill- **1805.**
ed and wounded, General Eaton being

among the latter. The attack was made by about twelve hundred men; while the place was supposed to be defended by three or four thousand. One or two attempts were made by the Tripolitans to regain possession, but they were easily repulsed, and, on one occasion, with some loss. The deposed pasha remained in possession of the town, and his authority was partially recognized in the province."

Commodore Barron declined assisting Eaton with further supplies and reinforcements, alleging that, as Hamet was in possession of the second province of the regency, "if he had the influence that he pretended to, he ought to be able to effect his object by means of the ordinary co-operation of the squadron." Next month, Barron, who was in very ill health, gave up the command to Commodore Rodgers; and negotiations for peace were commenced in earnest, Mr. Lear having arrived off Tripoli, for that purpose, in the Essex. After the usual intrigues, delays, and prevarications, a treaty was signed on the 3d of June. By it, no tribute was to be paid in future, but $60,000 were given by America, for the ransom of the prisoners remaining, after exchanging the Tripolitans in her power, man for man.

In several weighty respects it is not easy to approve of the terms of this peace with Tripoli, and under all the circumstances, it seems almost certain that better terms might have been obtained. How far Mr. Lear was compelled by his instructions we are unable to state; but the treaty was approved and ratified. Hamet, who was cast off with as little ceremony as he had been taken up, obtained only the liberation of his wife and children by Yussuf; and both he, and especially Mr. Eaton, considered themselves unhandsomely used and much injured by the treaty.* While, however, as Mr. Cooper says, "many condemned it as unwise, all rejoiced that it was the means of restoring so many brave men to their country. It is no more than liberal, moreover, to believe, that the situation of these unfortunate officers and men had a deep influence in inducing the government to forego abstract considerations, with a view to their relief."†

There being a prospect of speedy war with Tunis, which regency did not as yet understand the force and energy of the Americans, Commodore Rodgers, on the 1st of August, anchored in Tunis Bay, prepared to enforce, if necessary, the rights of his country. Literally, under the muzzles of his guns, Rodgers carried on a spirited negotiation, and his highness, the bey, soon found that the state of things was marvellously changed within a few years. His bravado now was ridiculous and contemptible; and affairs were promptly settled to the satisfaction of one of the parties at least. The bey having expressed a wish to send an ambassador to the United States, Decatur,

1805.

* Hamet afterwards came to the United States with a few of his followers, and applied to Congress for pecuniary relief. Some $2,400 were voted for this purpose, which only partially satisfied the exiled pasha. The legislature of Massachusetts granted to General Eaton ten thousand acres of land, as an expression of their high estimate of his heroism and patriotic services in behalf of his country's interests.

† Cooper's "*Naval History*," vol. i., pp. 261–66.

in September, sailed with an officer on such a mission, who was in due time landed in Washington. We may mention here, that though the Tunisian ambassador ventured to ask for the formerly-paid tribute, it was explicitly refused; and the bey, wiser by experience, deemed it inexpedient to take any hostile steps in consequence. A small squadron was kept up in the Mediterranean, in order to warn the Barbary powers against the venturing to renew their attacks upon American commerce.

Turning our attention to home affairs, we find, according to the biographer of Mr. Jefferson, that the administration at this date was at "the meridian of its popularity, and an unexampled quiet reigned over the land." The federal party seemed to have become virtually extinct, and the republicans carried every thing before them. This peaceful state of things, however, was delusive to a large extent, and "even then causes were at work which greatly agitated the last years of his administration, both in its domestic and foreign relations."

1804.

In preparing for the presidential contest, now near at hand, the members of Congress met in caucus, and agreed, as a matter of course, upon Thomas Jefferson for re-election. Aaron Burr, disliked and distrusted by those whom he had served so efficiently, had lost the confidence of the republican party, and they dropped him without scruple. George Clinton, governor of New York, an undoubted republican, and one who had always gone with Jefferson, was the man whom the majority of this caucus fixed upon as the candidate of the party. Breckenridge, Lincoln, Langdon, Granger, and M'Clay, were the others voted for, but by minorities varying from twenty in number to but one, and therefore indicating personal partialities rather than political confidence.

Burr, finding himself totally rejected by the republicans, as far as the vice-presidency was concerned, and being in such a condition that he could not well afford to be out of public office altogether, determined to become a candidate for governor of New York, the post which Clinton was about to vacate; on the other hand, the dominant party in the state had set up first Chancellor Lansing, who declined the contest almost as soon as he had accepted it; and then in his place Morgan Lewis, a man of very respectable qualifications, who was supported by the great families, and willing to be their representative.

The proceedings during this election were of a more than usually acrimonious character. Lewis was supported by the great mass of the democratic party, Burr by a section of that party, consisting chiefly of the younger and more ardent, or less scrupulous members of it. Many of the federalists also sided with Burr, just as on former occasions. Thus both parties were split; for Hamilton, and those who looked up to him as their political leader, opposed them with the utmost ardor. Hamilton, indeed, could do no otherwise, knowing Burr so well as he did, and so heartily distrusting him, (see vol. ii., p. 514.) The most atrocious libels were daily circulated by the press; and every means resorted to that animosity and party spirit could devise, to destroy the credit of the candidates by those opposed to them. Burr failed in this attempt to provide a haven for himself, when he should be driven from the chair of the Senate; and knowing well by whose instrumentality mainly it had been accomplished, he resolved to soothe his furious disappointment, by shedding the life-blood of the man whom he feared and hated beyond the power of any language adequately to express.

When such a man as Aaron Burr was, wanted a pretext for a certain course, it was not difficult to find one. Accordingly, he made choice of a libellous publication, such as the press had teemed with during the fierce political contest, and in June, engaged the services of his intimate friend, Judge Van Ness, to aid him in carrying out his fell design. It appears that Dr. Charles D. Cooper wrote a letter to a public journal some time previously, in which he stated, that Hamilton had characterized Burr as "a dangerous man," and one "not to be trusted with the reins of government," adding moreover, that he could "detail *a still more despicable opinion which General Hamilton has expressed of Mr. Burr.*" On the 17th of June, Burr sent a letter to Hamilton demanding "a prompt and unqualified acknowledgment or denial of the use of any expressions which would warrant the assertions of Mr. Cooper." Three days afterwards, Hamilton wrote a lengthy reply, in which he discussed the question of being held responsible for the *inferences* which persons might feel disposed to draw from his language and conduct, and expressed himself ready to avow or disavow promptly any precise or definite opinion which it might be charged that he had uttered of any gentleman. It was not such an answer, we think, as Hamilton ought to have sent to such a person as Aaron Burr, for he must have known at the very outset, that Burr was only seeking an occasion of quarrel with him, which might be pushed to a deadly encounter. It would have been far better to have said openly, what was true and well known, that he *did* look upon Burr as a dangerous, unscrupulous man, unfitted to be trusted with the affairs of state, and unworthy the confidence of the people, and then to have left the result to any legal process which Burr might see fit to invoke. But Hamilton did not do this, and his murderous opponent quickly saw his advantage in the matter. He immediately dispatched a curt, unceremonious note, insisting upon "a definite reply" to his demand. Van Ness pressed the subject upon Hamilton, who declined replying to this note, and left Burr to pursue the course he judged proper. This was just what he wished. He now had an opportunity to gratify his ardent longing for revenge.

1804.

On the 25th of June, the challenge was ready, and Van Ness called upon Hamilton to deliver it. Sincerely anxious to avoid this result, Hamilton attempted further negotiation through Judge Pendleton, his friend for the occasion; but it was all in vain. Burr had determined to kill him, if possible, and so he urged on matters in the most offensive and insulting manner.

1804. Some delay occurred, because Hamilton wished to discharge certain duties to his clients, and also to arrange his affairs in view of what he seemed to have a prevision must be the fatal termination of the encounter. He prepared his will, and wrote out his views as to this expected meeting, declaring himself as abhorring the shocking practice of duelling, yet, strangely insisting that he must violate his sacred principles of right and duty, and meet Burr, in order to be murdered. Fatal inconsistency! Unhappy yielding to the base and barbarous notions of honor too prevalent then and since! Hamilton's will, and the documents above referred to, are painfully interesting and instructive; and how strange it seems, that with his clear, piercing intellect, and with his sincere desire to be a Christian, and live and die as a Christian should live and die, he should have been so blinded as to consent for a moment to violate the laws of God as well as of man, by going to be shot at by Aaron Burr! Had Washington lived, we may well believe that he would not have found it difficult to convince Hamilton, that he needed not to commit an act so unworthy of him in order to establish his claims to the possession of courage and truth and uprightness. But Washington, who, when once he was tried in this way, treated the challenge with the scorn and contempt it deserved, had now gone to his rest; and Hamilton was unable to draw back from the doom impending over him.

On Wednesday, the 11th of July, the parties met at seven o'clock in the morning, at Weehawken, on the Jersey shore, opposite New York. The preliminaries being arranged, Burr and Hamilton were placed at ten paces distant, the one perfectly accomplished in the use of the duellist's pistol, the other hardly at all so, and already determined in his own mind not 1804.
to fire. Burr, eager for blood, discharged his pistol the instant the word was given; Hamilton, mortally wounded, aimlessly drew the trigger of his pistol, and fell heavily on his face. Burr, uninjured, and his companion in crime, Van Ness, immediately departed; and Dr. Hosack, Pendleton, and the boatmen who had conveyed Hamilton to the field of death, bore him back again to lie in agony untold—for his wife and seven children shared in that mortal stroke—till the next day, in his friend Bayard's house, and then to die. The consolations of religion were administered to him by Dr. Mason and Bishop Moore, and at two o'clock in the afternoon of Thursday, the 12th of July, he passed away to his final account. On Saturday, he was buried with military honors, by the Society of the Cincinnati, and attended to the grave by a vast concourse of mourners. Gouverneur Morris delivered an impressive funeral oration, from a stage erected in front of Trinity Church; and the eloquence of the pulpit, the bar, and the press, throughout the country, were expended in fitting orations, discourses, and eulogiums. Since the death of Washington, no blow so severe as this had fallen upon our country, and not

too strongly did Fisher Ames declare, that "his soul stiffened with despair when he thought what Hamilton would have been," remembering what he was when this sad calamity came upon him.*

Speaking of the personal appearance of Hamilton and Burr, Dr. Sullivan, whose interesting work we have several times referred to, gives some valuable reminiscences, which are worth quoting. He is recording his impressions of the men some ten years before the duel. "Hamilton," he says, "was under middle size, thin in person, but remarkably erect and dignified in his deportment. His hair was turned back from his forehead, powdered, and collected in a club behind. His complexion was exceedingly fair, and varying from this only by the almost feminine rosiness of his cheeks. His might be considered, as to figure and color, an uncommonly handsome face. When at rest, it had rather a severe and thoughtful expression; but when engaged in conversation it easily assumed an attractive smile. He was capable of inspiring the most affectionate attachment; but he could make those whom he opposed fear and hate him cordially. He was capable of intense and effectual application, as is abundantly proved by his public labors. But he had a rapidity and clearness of perception, in which he may not have been equalled. One who knew his habits of study, said of him, that when he had a serious object to accomplish, his practice was to reflect on it previously; and when he had gone through this labor, he retired to sleep, without regard to the hour of the night; and having slept six or seven hours, he rose, and having taken strong coffee, seated himself at his table, where he would remain six, seven, or eight hours, and the product of his rapid pen required little correction for the press. He was among the few alike excellent, whether in speaking or in writing. In private and friendly intercourse he is said to have been exceedingly amiable, and to have been affectionately beloved."

"Aaron Burr," says the same writer, "was at this time (December, 1795) probably about Hamilton's age. He had attained to celebrity as a lawyer at the same bar. He was about the same stature as Hamilton, and a thin man, but differently formed. His motions in walking were not, like Hamilton's, erect, but a little stooping, and far from graceful. His face was short and broad; his black eyes uncommonly piercing; his manner gentle and seductive. But he had also a calmness and sedateness, when these suited his purpose, and an eminent authority of manner, when the occasion called for this. He was said to have presided with great dignity in the Senate, and especially at the trial of Judge Chase. Though eminent as a lawyer, he was said not to be a man of distinguished

* As for Burr, conscious that he was regarded as an assassin, he fled first to Philadelphia, and then to the south, whence he addressed letters of characteristic *nonchalance* to his daughter; whilst a jury in New Jersey indicted him for murder, and another in New York brought against him a bill, which threatened him with disfranchisement, and incapacitation from the service of the public for twenty years. For a severe and scathing review of the life and career of Aaron Burr, from the pen of the Rev. Dr. F. L. Hawks, see the "*New York Review*," for January, 1838.

eloquence, nor of luxuriant mind. His speeches were short and to the purpose."

On the 5th of November, the second session of the eighth Congress was begun, and the president's message was read in the House, on the 8th of November. It congratulated our countrymen, as "a people who sincerely desired the happiness and prosperity of other nations," and who "justly calculated that their own well-being was advanced by that of the nations with which they had intercourse," and on the fact that the war in Europe had not extended more widely, nor become more destructive. It treated principally of the foreign relations of the Union; of the arrangements respecting Louisiana, the dealings recently commenced with the Indians, and treaties concluded with some of their tribes and awaiting the constitutional sanctions; of the gunboat scheme;* and of the revenue. In respect to this last subject, the president remarked; "It is also ascertained that the revenue, accrued during the last year, exceeds that of the preceding; and the probable receipts of the ensuing year may safely be relied on as sufficient, with the sum in the treasury,† to meet all the current demands of the year, to discharge upwards of three millions and a half of the engagements incurred under the British and French conventions, and to advance, in the further redemption of the funded debt, as rapidly as had been contemplated."

1804.

The message was concluded in the following terms: "In the discharge of the great duties confided to you by our country, you will take a broader view of the field of legislation:—whether the great interests of agriculture, manufactures, commerce, or navigation, can, within the pale of your constitutional powers, be aided in any of their relations? Whether laws are provided in all cases where they are wanting? Whether those provided are exactly what they should be? Whether any abuses take place in their administration, or in that of the public revenue? Whether the organization of the public agents, or of the public force, is perfect in all its parts? In fine, whether any thing can be done to advance the general good?—are questions within the limits of your functions, which will necessarily occupy your attention. In these and all other matters, which you in your wisdom may propose for the good of our country, you may count with assurance on my hearty co-operation and faithful execution."

The republican majority in Congress was now so considerable that "freedom of debate" was nearly impossible; every affair of importance being determined by the supporters of the administration in private caucus, before it was brought under the notice of the legislature. The consequence of such a procedure was, necessarily, that Congress was more largely influenced by party considerations and party pledges,

* For Mr. Tucker's remarks on this much ridiculed plan for defending the harbors of the country and protecting commerce, see his "*Life of Jefferson*," vol. ii., pp. 174-76. The subject will come up again in a subsequent chapter.

† The receipts in the treasury for the year, had been $11,500,000, from which $3,600,000 had been paid in discharge of the debt.

DECATUR'S CONFLICT WITH THE ALGERINE AT TRIPOLI.

"REUBEN JAMES INTERPOSING HIS HEAD TO SAVE THE LIFE OF HIS COMMANDER"

Johnson, Fry & Co. Publishers, New York.

than by the force of sound reason and sober discussion.

Early in December, according to the vote of the preceding session, the House proceeded to prepare articles of impeachment against Samuel Chase, one of the judges of the supreme
1804. court, and to the appointment of managers to conduct the business on its behalf, before the Senate. The articles of impeachment were eight in number; and they charged the accused with "arbitrary, oppressive, and unjust" conduct in the trial of John Fries; with several breaches of the law at the trial of Callender; with "manifest injustice, partiality, and intemperance;" with addressing to the Grand Jury, in May, 1803, "an intemperate and inflammatory political harangue;" etc. John Randolph and five others were appointed as managers.

On the 10th of December, they proceeded to the trial, and on the 2d of January, Judge Chase appeared at the bar of the Senate, and asked to be allowed to the first day of the next term to put in his answer. The request was refused, and he was required to
1805. answer the charges on the 4th of February, by a vote of twenty-two to eight. The Senate assembled on that day; and the accused judge addressed the court in answer to the articles exhibited against him. A replication in form was made to his answer, and on the 7th, the Senate proceeded to the trial. From that time until the 20th, the court was engaged in the examination of witnesses; and on that day the argument was opened by Messrs. Early and two others on the part of the managers. They were replied to by Messrs. Hopkinson, Martin, and others, the counsel for the accused, and Messrs. Rodney, Nicholson and Randolph, the other managers, closed the argument on the 27th of February.

The trial excited intense interest through the country, and it was confidently expected that the accused would be convicted. Burr, though under indictment for the murder of Hamilton, presided at the trial with a dignity and confidence becoming a better man; and much disappointment was shown by the dominant party that the defence was conducted with ability quite superior to that displayed by the prosecution. On Friday, the 1st of March, the court decided on the articles *seriatim*, and each member answered to each charge separately. Upon the first article of the impeachment sixteen pronounced him *guilty*, while eighteen said 1805.
not guilty; on the second, there were ten of the former, against twenty-four of the latter; on the third and fourth, the numbers on the first article were exactly reversed; on the fifth, he was unanimously acquitted; only four condemned him under the sixth article, and thirty declared him innocent; the vote on the seventh was the same as that on the second; and on the eighth, nineteen voted *guilty*, against but fifteen voting *not guilty*.

The result was, in consequence, an acquittal; and Burr,—to the delight of the federalists, and the chagrin of his own party, who had disowned him, summed up the whole in these words:—"There not being a constitutional majority on any one article, it becomes my duty to pronounce, that Samuel Chase, Esquire, is acquitted on the articles of impeachment exhibited against him by the House of Representatives."*

The keen disappointment at this unlooked-for result was manifested on more than one occasion. On the very afternoon of the day on which Judge Chase was acquitted, John Randolph, by resolution, proposed an amendment to the Constitution; by which, any federal judge should be removed on the joint address of both Houses of Congress, and the resolution was carried by a vote of sixty-eight to thirty-three. Mr. Tucker points out several other instances in which the republican majority displayed its chagrin at this acquittal and their own defeat in the matter of the judiciary.

During the present session of Congress, laws were passed for the purpose of preventing the hostile and predatory acts of persons on board of foreign vessels in the harbors and ports of the United States; and for regulating the clearance of armed American merchant vessels. The other subjects which principally engaged the attention of Congress, were, the acts providing for the government of the territory of New Orleans, and the District of Columbia. An amendatory act respecting the Yazoo claims was debated for several days, and finally passed by a small majority.†

During the autumn of 1804, the elections for president and vice-president were held, and the manifest superiority of the republican strength was plainly demonstrated. Mr. Jefferson for president, and George Clinton for vice-president, received all the votes of New Hampshire, Vermont, Massachusetts, Rhode Island, New York, New Jersey, Pennsylvania, Virginia, the two Carolinas, Georgia, Tennessee, Kentucky, and Ohio, with nine out of the eleven given by Maryland; in all, one hundred and sixty-two votes. On the other side, Charles Cotesworth Pinckney, and Rufus King, the federalist candidates, received only the votes of Connecticut and Delaware, with two from Maryland: in all no more than fourteen.*

On the 3d of March, the eighth Congress closed its career, and the first term of Mr. Jefferson's service reached its conclusion. His biographer, with admiring zeal, sums up the labors of the president, during the past four years, in the following words:

1805. "With this session, closed Mr. Jefferson's first presidential term, in which time he had, by a steady course

* Mr. Benton has given this trial quite at large, taken from the report prepared at the time by two competent short-hand writers: "*Abridgement of the Debates of Congress*," vol. iii., pp. 173–284.

† See Benton's "*Abridgement of the Debates of Congress*," vol. iii., pp. 315–38.

* The president remarks upon this result, in a letter to Volney, in February, 1805. "A word now," he says, "on our political state. The two parties which prevailed with so much violence when you were here, are almost wholly melted into one. At the late presidential election, I have received one hundred and sixty-two votes against fourteen only. . . Though the people in mass have joined us, their leaders had committed themselves too far to retract. Pride keeps them hostile: they brood over their angry passions, and give them vent in the newspapers which they maintain. They still make as much noise as if they were the whole nation. Unfortunately, these being the mercantile papers, published chiefly in the seaports, are the only ones which find their way to Europe, and make very false impressions there."

of economy, reduced the public debt more than twelve millions, though he had at the same time lessened the taxes, and a host of revenue officers; had doubled the area of the United States, averted the dangers of war both with France and Spain, chastised the Tripolitans and made war with Algiers and Tunis; extinguished the title to a large and valuable tract of Indian lands, and promoted civilization among them. For thus promoting the national prosperity, he was rewarded by the national favor, notwithstanding the unceasing virulence with which he had been assailed, as was evinced by the fact that he received a greater number of votes at the present election than in that of 1801.*"

* Tucker's "*Life of Jefferson,*" vol. ii., p. 180. John Randolph is still more enthusiastic in his admiration. See his life, by Garland, vol. i., p. 198.

CHAPTER IV.

1805-1807.

TWO YEARS OF JEFFERSON'S SECOND TERM.

The president's second inaugural address — His position and prospects — The ninth Congress — The president's message — Confidential message respecting Spanish affairs — Course pursued by Spain — Pinckney and Monroe envoys to Spain — Unsuccessful in their mission — Action in Congress — Resolution appropriating money for the president to use as he wished — Debate in the House — Armstrong and Bowdoin sent as envoys — Imminence of war with Spain — The administration charged with paying the $2,000,000 appropriation into the coffers of Napoleon — Mr. Tucker's reply — Relations with England unsatisfactory — Vessels of the United States seized and condemned — Carrying trade broken up — American seamen impressed by British officers — Remarks of the president in his message — Course pursued by Congress — Views of the parties — Criminations and recriminations — The question of the right of Congress to appropriate money for internal improvements — What was done in Congress — Proposal to lay a tax upon slaves imported into the United States — Further attempt respecting the judiciary — State of parties in the House — Discussion as to the successor of Jefferson in the presidential chair — Madison and Monroe prominent — John Randolph's course — Mr. Jefferson's letters and views — Aaron Burr and his schemes — Course adopted by the president — His proclamation — Opening of Congress — The message — Daring attempt to suspend the *habeas corpus* act — The conspiracy of Burr — His trial — The details — Burr escapes conviction — Remarks on his career.

ON the 4th of March, 1805, it was the pleasing duty of Thomas Jefferson again to address his fellow-citizens, before entering upon the duties and responsibilities of his second term of service as president of the United States. In style and language the second Inaugural address is hardly equal to the first; yet it evinces the powers of mind, and the political sentiments of its author, clearly and forcibly. He was now in his sixty-second year, and his well weighed words are worthy the reader's careful examination. 1805. We regret that our limits do not admit of their being quoted in full in this place.

Having thus, as he deemed it right

and proper, entered into a vindication of his administration, and congratulated the people on the prospects of peaceful and harmonious counsels and acts in the future, the president took again the oath of office, and entered with high hopes upon the duties of his lofty position. In the interval between the inauguration and the meeting of Congress, he sought relief from public cares and toils, in attending to his plantations and his slaves; and in the circle of his private friends, and family, whom he could assemble at Monticello. In October, he returned to Washington; "and perhaps," says his biographer, "he never felt so forcibly the transition from rural quiet, and the pure pleasures of domestic intercourse, to the feverish anxieties of the statesman, as on the present occasion. His course, during the first four years that he had held the helm, had been singularly prosperous; and if he had not always met with a smooth sea, he had been able to continue his course over it by the strong gale of his popularity; but from this time he met with adverse winds and opposing currents which greatly impaired the comfort of the voyage, and in some degree its success."*

1805.

The ninth Congress commenced its first session on the 2d of December. The republicans were decidedly in the majority, yet not so much so, as might have been supposed from the large vote by which Jefferson was placed a second time in the presidential chair. Indications were not wanting of a tendency to discord in the dominant party. The republicans from the south favored Varnum of Massachusetts, as a candidate for the speakership, in opposition to Macon, and the appointment of the latter was not secured, except by a very slender majority, and at the third ballot. The federalists hoped to secure a man of their own stamp, John Cotton Smith, in consequence of this variance, but were not strong enough to accomplish their aim.

1805.

The next day, the president sent in his message. It commenced with a passage respecting the "health laws," suggested by "the affliction of two of our cities, under the fatal fever, which in latter times has occasionally visited our shores;" and next it expatiated upon the unfriendly aspect of the relations of the Union with various foreign states, especially with Spain. The treaties formed, or being negotiated with several of "our Indian neighbors," and the progress they were making towards civilization, were properly noted. The expedition of Lewis and Clarke was adverted to; and a large addition to the number of gun-boats was suggested. The receipts for the year had been upwards of $13,000,000, from which $2,000,000 had been paid under the British treaty and convention, and $4,000,000 of the debt, leaving a balance of $5,000,000 in the treasury. Various recommendations were made in regard to the organization of the militia, the navy, etc.; and the message closed with a renewed and "public assurance, that he would exert his best endeavors to administer faithfully the executive department, and would zeal-

* Tucker's "*Life of Jefferson*," vol. ii., p. 184.

ously co-operate with Congress in every measure which might tend to secure the liberty, property, and personal safety of our fellow-citizens, and to consolidate the republican forms and principles of our government."

Three days afterwards the president sent a confidential message to Congress, on the subject of our relations with Spain, and the serious nature
1805. of the existing controversy with that power. This message was referred to a select committee, of which John Randolph was chairman; and by the proceedings which took place, as Mr. Tucker states, "it soon appeared that Mr. Randolph was no longer to be numbered amongst the supporters of the administration."

Spain, as we have before stated, (p. 42,) was very indignant at the manner in which she was used by Napoleon in regard to Louisiana; and she determined to throw every obstacle possible in the way of a peaceful settlement of the question with the United States, as to the boundaries of the newly acquired province. "The original claim of France had been from the Perdido East to the Rio Bravo West of the Mississippi. Mobile had been originally a French settlement, and all West Florida was as distinctly within the claim of France, as the mouth of the Mississippi first discovered by La Salle. Such was the understanding of the American plenipotentiaries and of Congress, who accordingly authorized the president to establish a collection district, on the shores, waters, and inlets of the Bay and River Mobile, and of rivers both east and west of the same. But Spain on her part reduced the province of Louisiana to little more than the Island of New Orleans. She assumed an attitude menacing immediate war; refused to ratify a convention made under the eye of her own government at Madrid, for indemnifying citizens of the United States, plundered under her authority during the preceding war; harassed and ransomed the citizens of the Union and their property on the waters of Mobile; and marched military forces to the borders of the Sabine, where they were met by troops of the United States, with whom a conflict was spared only by a temporary military convention between the respective commanders."*

In this juncture of affairs, James Monroe was directed to proceed from London to join Mr. Pinckney at Madrid, in order to procure the ratification of the former convention, and to come to an understanding with Spain as to the boundaries of Louisiana. "After nearly five months of fruitless endeavors," as the message states, "to bring them to some definite and satisfactory result, our ministers ended the conferences without having been able to obtain indemnity for spoliation of any description, or any satisfaction as to the boundaries of 1805.
Louisiana, other than a declaration that we had no right eastward of the Iberville, and that our line to the west was one which would have left us but a string of land on that bank of the River Mississippi."

Monroe had conveyed to the Spanish

* J. Q. Adams's "*Life of James Monroe*," p. 259.

court an offer to take the Rio Colorado as the western limit of the purchase, and to give up the demands for spoliations, etc., in exchange for the coveted territory east of the Mississippi; but his proposition was promptly rejected. The president was far from pleased with the manner in which Napoleon behaved as to this subject. "The conduct of France," he said in the message, "and the part she may take in the misunderstanding between the United States and Spain, are too important to be unconsidered. She was prompt and decided in her declarations, that our demands on Spain for French spoliations carried into Spanish ports, were included in the settlement between the United States and France. She took at once the ground that she had acquired no right from Spain, and had meant to deliver us none, eastward of the Iberville; her silence as to the western boundary leaving us to infer, her opinion *might* be against Spain in that quarter." The American envoys found that the Spanish government was entirely impracticable, and there seems no reason to doubt that war was contemplated against the United States. Mr. Monroe, after his fruitless labors, returned in the summer of 1805, to London; and the boundary question was left unsettled for the present.

The select committee, of which Mr. Randolph was chairman, made a report on the 3d of January, 1806, in which it was declared, that the aggressions of
1806. Spain afforded ample cause of war, but, as peace was on every account desirable for the United States, the hope was expressed that Spain would not proceed to extremities, but would honorably fulfil her engagements. Yet, in consequence of the insulting character of Spanish proceedings, the committee submitted a resolution, "that such a number of troops as the president should deem sufficient to protect the southern frontier from insult, should be immediately raised." This was not what Mr. Jefferson wished: his desire, as privately intimated, was for money, not troops. War was very repugnant to his views, and he thought much more could be accomplished with money than by fighting about Louisiana and Florida. Randolph sturdily opposed every thing of the sort, as derogatory to the dignity and independence of our country, and not unlike putting ourselves under *tribute* whenever France, or any other European nation saw fit to exact it.

On the same day, a resolution was offered by Mr. Bidwell, of Massachusetts, in accordance with the wishes of Mr. Jefferson, "that an appropriation be made for the purpose of defraying any extraordinary expenses that might be incurred in the intercourse
between the United States and 1806.
foreign nations, to be applied under the direction of the president." In the debate that followed, which was with closed doors, the two compliant members of the committee, Messrs. Bidwell and Varnum, seconded by others less dogged and self-asserting than Randolph, to whom they hinted the president's real desire, contrived to effect all that was required. And after a fortnight's debate in Congress, the wished-for $2,000,000 were appropriated to meet "extraordinary expenses of for-

eign intercourse," the Senate being informed, by a communication sent with the bill, but forming no part of it, that it was to enable the president to purchase the Spanish territories east of the Mississippi, that the appropriation was made. Randolph, scouting with all the impulsiveness of his nature, this having a "*double* set of opinions and principles, the one ostensible, to go upon the journals and before the public, the other the efficient and real motives to action," subsequently spoke of the conclusion of the fortnight's discussion most characteristically thus,—"the doors were closed, and the minority, whose motives were impeached, and whose motives were almost denounced, were voted down *without debate*."*

Congress having decided, as Mr. Tucker remarks, "on making the appropriation of two millions for the purchase of Florida, (although it is worth remembering, the resolution spoke only of "extraordinary expenses of foreign intercourse,") the president determined upon a last effort to effect an amicable settlement, at Paris, of all matters of dispute with Spain. He appointed General Armstrong of New York, and Mr. Bowdoin of Massachusetts, joint commissioners for that purpose, and proposed to add Colonel Wilson C. Nicholas of Virginia, as a third. But on that gentleman's declining the mission, the whole was left to the management of the two first." We may mention, in this connection, that, probably nothing but the destruction of the Spanish navy at Trafalgar, October 21st, 1805, prevented a war between Spain and the United States. General Wilkinson was actually ordered to meet hostilities by hostilities, so pressing and menacing were the Spanish advances in the south, and so little had been effected by negotiations. In fact, nothing of moment was accomplished during Mr. Jefferson's administration; for the American envoys at Paris, ere long were irreconcileably at variance, and the progress of negotiation was virtually at a complete standstill.

In regard to the $2,000,000 voted for the president to use at his discretion, it was charged directly upon the administration, that, as France wanted money and must have it, this pretty sum went into Napoleon's coffers, the United States ship Hornet having carried it out to the American ministers at Paris, for this very purpose. Mr. Tucker speaking of this matter says, in reply to the charge, "After Congress made the appropriation of two millions for the purchase of Florida, it was deemed of sufficient importance to despatch the Hornet sloop-of-war, to communicate the fact to the American ministers at Paris, and to furnish them with the means of paying the money forthwith; which was by enabling them to draw on funds in Holland placed there to discharge the foreign debt. These facts gave some color to the imputation which Mr. Jefferson's enemies had thrown out in the newspapers, that the two millions were meant to bribe France to compel Spain to make a cession of

* For a more full account of this whole matter, with extracts from Randolph's keen and caustic remarks in the House, see Garland's "*Life of John Randolph*," vol. i., pp. 213–228. See also, Tucker's "*Life of Jefferson*," vol. ii., pp. 187–196.

the Floridas; and that the Hornet actually carried out the money. The calumny, bold as it was when first propagated, has been so improved of late as to assert, not only that the two millions were carried in specie to France, but were actually paid to Bonaparte, without any consideration whatever; though the Hornet did not carry out a dollar, but only letters of credit, to be used if wanted for the purchase of Florida; and no part of which was used, as a reference to the treasury accounts would show, if the fact had not been established by a subsequent investigation in Congress."*

In the course of the vast and deadly struggle between Napoleon, now aspiring to universal dominion, and England, the most formidable of his enemies and supreme on the ocean, the policy adopted by the mistress of the seas, was vexatious and unjust in the extreme to neutral nations. The United States, profiting by the position of affairs in Europe, had greatly enlarged their commerce, and were reaping a rich harvest from the present golden opportunity. But Great Britain looked with no favorable eye upon these advantages which neutrals enjoyed from commercial intercourse with France and

1805. her allies; and she determined to interpose her power in order to put a stop to all trade of the kind, and to substitute a forced commerce between her own subjects and their enemies. For two years or more she had suffered neutral navigation to have the benefit of principles in the law of nations, formerly recognized by herself in the correspondence between Mr. King and Lord Hawkesbury, shortly before the close of the preceding war. But now, "suddenly, as if by a concerted signal, throughout the world of waters which encompass the globe, our hardy and peaceful, though intrepid mariners, found themselves arrested in their career of industry and skill; seized by British cruisers; their vessels and cargoes conducted into British ports, and by the spontaneous and sympathetic illumination of British courts of vice-admiralty, adjudicated to the captors, because they were engaged in a trade with the enemies of Britain, to which they had not usually been admitted in time of peace. Mr. Monroe had scarcely reached London, when he received a report from the consul of the United States, at that place, announcing that about twenty of their vessels had, within a few weeks, been brought into the British ports on the channel, and that by the condemnation of more than one of them, the admiralty court had settled *the principle*."*

It was not only with respect to the carrying trade, however, that serious difficulties existed between our country and England. There was another and a very galling one to Americans, which England pressed or relaxed as she saw fit; it was what John Quincy Adams forcibly calls the claim to the "right of man-stealing from the vessels of the United States." Officers of the British navy boarded American ships, and, down to the beardless midshipmen,

* Tucker's "*Life of Jefferson*," vol. ii., p. 210.

* J. Q. Adams's "*Life of James Monroe*," p. 264.

seized upon any seaman whom they chose to take for a British subject. In this high-handed manner, not less than three thousand American sailors had been forced to serve in the British navy. No independent nation could possibly submit to such outrages; and the United States uniformly protested against the course adopted by England, and denied totally any and every claim of right to impress seamen from their vessels, or within their jurisdiction.

In the president's message, at the opening of Congress, he had stated, that "the aspect of our foreign relations" had much changed. The coasts were infested and the harbors watched by private armed vessels; our ships were captured in the very act of entering our ports, and plundered at sea: their crews were taken out, maltreated, and abandoned. It had therefore been found necessary to equip a force to cruise within our own seas, and bring in the offenders for trial as pirates. Notwithstanding this highly suggestive fact, he persisted in recommending his pet scheme of defence by gunboats, and declared that it was desirable to "have a competent number of gunboats; and the number, to be competent, must be considerable." In order to stimulate the zeal of Congress, the president sent a special message, on the 17th of January, 1806, relating both to the interruption of the neutral trade, and to the impressment of the seamen; from which it appeared, that Mr. Madison at Washington, and Mr. Monroe at London, had been in communication with the ministers of Great Britain upon these questions.

Congress perceived the difficulty in the position of affairs; committees attempted to deal with it, but vainly; and it was proposed, in a committee of the whole, to suspend all importation from Great Britain, until "equitable and satisfactory arrangements were made." Then came other resolutions, retaliatory in intention, for the annoyances of the navigation laws, and other parts of the British maritime code. Others proceeded still further; certain articles should be declared contraband, as far as importation from England was concerned; no intercourse should be carried on with any European colonies, unless the Americans had a fair share in the trade; all intercourse with Great Britain should cease. In the end, by a large majority, Congress voted, in April, to prohibit certain articles of British growth or manufacture, after the 15th of the following November. Intercourse with revolted Hayti was strictly forbidden. The sum of $150,000 was appropriated for fortifying the ports and harbors, and $250,000 for building gunboats.

1806.

In the debates in the House, Randolph and others of the republicans, looking upon Napoleon, who had now mounted the imperial throne, as the enemy to free government and national independence, were disposed to pursue a more conciliatory and respectful course towards England. The federalists voted with these, not only because they agreed in opinion respecting the purposes of the emperor Napoleon, but also because they deemed the ground taken by the administration against British interference with the neutral trade to be unsound. Fisher Ames, in one of his letters at this date, expresses himself very strongly: "There was a time when infatuation in favor of France was a popular malady. If that time has so far passed over that men can either think or feel as Americans ought, it must be apparent, that Bonaparte wants but little, and is enraged that he so long wants that little, to be the world's master. Yet at this awful crisis, when the British navy alone prevents his final success, we of the United States come forward, with an ostentation of hostility to England, to annoy her with non-intercourse laws. Are we determined to leave nothing to chance, but to volunteer our industry in forging our chains?"

The republicans, on their side, charged upon the federalists, a desire to push matters to the point of war with France and Spain, and alliance with Great Britain. But these retorted, that the administration submitted tamely to insults from Spain, fawned upon Napoleon, and sought to provoke a quarrel with England. As a late English writer phrases it, "there truly was something almost sublime in the audacity with which Jefferson, without an army, without a navy even, (for he had broken it up and sold it,) with nothing at his back but a flotilla of gunboats, lectured the mistress of the seas upon 'maritime laws,' spoke of neutral *rights*, and encouraged his adherents to begin a war of commercial (more correctly, *anti*-commercial) enactments, as if by the prestige of the old war, he could carry every thing before him—*there*."

During the present session of Congress, the other important measures discussed and passed upon, were of a domestic character. Two of these require notice; more especially, as connected with questions which have agitated the whole country on various occasions. The first related to the constitutional rights possessed by Congress, in respect to appropriations of public money for promoting internal improvements. **1806.** It is evident, at a glance, that there are many and cogent arguments on both sides of this question; and it will probably ever remain open to discussion, from a constitutional point of view, although current practice may be regarded as having virtually, at least, settled the whole matter. On the 24th of March, an act was passed by a vote of sixty-six to fifty, for the construction of a national road from Cumberland, in Maryland, to the state of Ohio. "It was opposed," says Mr. Tucker, "altogether on the constitutional ground that the power of making roads was not given to Congress. But to obviate this objection, the consent of the states, through whose territories the road was to pass, (Maryland, Virginia, and Ohio,) was first required. Yet if Congress had not the power of making roads, as was contended, the consent of these states could not give it. This question continued to be long afterwards a subject of controversy between those who were severally disposed to a strict and a literal construction of the Constitution. But perhaps the strongest arguments against the power, are to be found in the mischiefs likely to arise from its inexpediency; by its being a source of local jealousy and heart-burning; by its presenting the means of wasting the national resources in expensive and improvident undertakings; by its great extension of the influence of the federal government; and by its furnishing the means of bribing and influencing individual states, with the money of the whole."*

Not only was this bill, appropriating $30,000 of the public money to this service, signed by Jefferson; but bills were also approved, appropriating $6,000 to the construction of a road from Nashville in Tennessee, to Natchez in Mississippi; $6,400 to a road from the frontier of Georgia, on the route from Athens to New Orleans; and $6,000 more to a road from the Mississippi River to the Ohio

The second question referred to above as keenly debated during this session, was that which related to the imposing a tax of ten dollars on each slave imported into the United States. South Carolina, finding the western market still open, and highly profitable, was carrying on the slave-trade with great energy, and it was impossible (according to the Constitution) to forbid this traffic, before 1808. The Representatives from this state retorted upon their northern opponents, by ascribing to the ship-owners of Rhode Island the having provided the means for carrying on this detestable commerce. If we may credit the statements of southern men, **1806.** most of the slaveholding members looked forward with great satisfaction to the time when Congress could, constitutionally, prevent the further importation of slaves; yet, as they averred, they were extremely unwilling to see any legislation on the subject by those who had no common interest or feeling with them concerning it. The truth probably was, that it was not legislation in respect to slavery in the abstract, that roused fierce and determined opposition to the proposed tax, but it was the having this species of property, as they termed it, treated as all other property was treated, and taxed like other luxuries imported from abroad. "After several propositions to reject or postpone the bill," Mr. Tucker informs us, "which failed by a vote of two-thirds of the House, it was, on the third reading, recommitted, and though afterwards reported with amendments, it was found so unpalatable to a large portion of the House, that it was never finally acted on."

The proposition which had been made at the preceding session, (see p. 66,) in respect to the removal of the federal judges by the president, whenever a joint application should be presented by both Houses of Congress, was renewed at the present session, but without success; and the question was not pressed by friends or foes, in the doubtful position in which it seemed to be placed at the time.

On the 21st of April, the first session of the ninth Congress was ended, and though it was not unusually long, it was one of the most animated and contentious which had occurred in **1806.** the career of the national legislature. "The House of Representatives," we are told by Mr. Jefferson's biographer, "manifestly consisted of

* Tucker's "*Life of Jefferson*," vol. ii., p. 199.

three parties; as, besides the two known divisions of republicans and federalists, there was a schism of the former, who differed from the administration on some leading points of foreign policy, and who, while they voted with the federalists on these questions, and on some collateral points, so as to show diminished confidence and good feeling towards the executive, took especial care not to be considered by the nation as being merged in the federal party, not only by their general declarations, but by their votes on all questions not involving the policy of the administration, on which occasions they concurred with the republicans. This party consisted principally of members from the Virginia delegation, and were all personally intimate with Mr. Randolph. The same party afterwards received a great accession of strength in Virginia, by bringing forward Mr. Monroe as a candidate for the presidency, in opposition to Mr. Madison; and it was not until the reconciliation of these gentlemen, by the good offices of Mr. Jefferson, that its ranks were broken as a party, and that some of the scattered fragments united with the federalists, in opposition to the war, and all the leading measures of the administration which preceded it."

This subject of "the succession," had, some years previously, occupied the anxious attention of John Adams, and he had made his wife the confidant of his hopes and his fears, when Washington was about to retire from public life. Similar anxieties, we find, now began to produce their effect upon the friends of such as were thought of favorably for filling the presidential chair. And it must be confessed, that, in this particular, a government whose head is dependent upon popular election every few years, labors under serious difficulties and embarrassments. For, as we shall see, the further on we get in our narrative, it has not, except very rarely, been the best and fittest men who have been designated for the presidency; nor even the best men of the dominant party; but unhappily, the men whom the party have judged it most probable that they could elect to this high office.

Mr. Jefferson appears to have all along assumed, that his friend and secretary of state, James Madison, was to be his successor; and perhaps there was not a person at that time in the United States to whom, personally, more citizens would have been disposed to give their confidence, as the chief magistrate of the nation. John Randolph, however, who had taken a strong dislike to the president and his purposes and wishes, determined to urge Mr. Monroe to aspire after "the succession."* He, as well as Madison, was a son of that state familiarly known as "the Old Dominion," and as Virginia

1806.

seemed to look upon herself as the quarter whence the presidents were to be chosen, the claims of Monroe appeared to be quite as reasonable and proper as those of Madison. Randolph warmly urged Monroe to return from England, where he was residing at this time as ambassador; and Jefferson was

* For the reasons which led Randolph to oppose the elevation of Madison, see Garland's "*Life of John Randolph*," vol. i., pp. 276–79.

afterwards charged, by Monroe's friends, with throwing impediments in his way of leaving Europe, for the purpose of keeping the field clear for his own candidate. Whatever may have been done in secret, publicly the president preserved a very fair appearance of neutrality in regard to the claims of his two friends; he did warn Monroe against reliance upon Randolph, but, according to his biographer's statement, "he abstained from any active measures in favor of either, and discharged the very delicate duties of friendship to the rivals, with scrupulous fidelity; as was afterwards *virtually* acknowledged by both."

From Mr. Jefferson's letters about this time, we learn, that the cares and responsibilities of office did not grow lighter, as he became more accustomed to them; and that he smarted more than ever under the attacks of opponents like Randolph in Congress, and the press. "That there is only one minister who is not opposed to me," he wrote to Duane, "is totally unfounded. There never was a more harmonious, a more cordial administration, nor even a moment when it has been otherwise." "That there is an ostensible cabinet, and a concealed one, a public profession, and a concealed counteraction, is false. That I have denounced republicans by the epithet of Jacobins, and declared that I would appoint none but those called Moderates of both parties, and that I have avowed, or entertain, any predilection for those called the third party, or *quids*, is in every tittle of it false. Our situation is difficult, and whatever we do is liable to the criticisms of those who wish to represent it awry. If we recommend measures in a public message, it may be said that members are not sent here to obey the mandates of the president, or to register the edicts of a sovereign. If we express opinions in conversation, we have then our Charles Jenkinsons and back-door counsellors. If we say nothing, 'we have no opinions, no plans, no cabinet.' In truth, it is the fable of the old man, his son, and the ass, over again."

Writing to Mr. Gallatin, in October, after adverting to various attempts to produce jealousy and dissension among the members of the administration, he assures him of his undiminished confidence and esteem. He adds: "I make the declaration, that no doubts or jealousies, which often beget the
facts they fear, may find a mo- 1806
ment's harbor in either of our minds. Our administration, now drawing to a close, I have a sublime pleasure in believing will be distinguished as much by having placed itself above all the passions which could disturb its harmony, as by the great operations by which it will have advanced the well-being of the nation."

And yet, notwithstanding Mr. Jefferson's "sublime pleasure" on this point, it was not long afterwards that he expressed himself in a very different strain. Writing to his old friend John Dickinson, under date of January 13th, he closes his letter in the following words:
"I have tired you, my friend, 1807.
with a long letter. But your tedium will end in a few lines more. Mine has yet two years to endure. I

am tired of an office where I can do no more good than many others who would be glad to be employed in it. To myself personally, it brings nothing but unceasing drudgery, and daily loss of friends. Every office becoming vacant, every appointment made, *me donne un ingrat, et cent ennemis*. My only consolation is in the belief that my fellow-citizens at large, give me credit for good intentions. I will certainly endeavor to merit the continuance of the good-will which follows well-intended actions, and their approbation will be the dearest reward I can carry into retirement."

The projects of Aaron Burr occupied a considerable share of public attention during the summer and autumn of 1806. This ambitious, but unprincipled man, cast off by the party which had placed him in the vice-president's chair,
1805. and looked upon with horror and deep indignation by a community which remembered that the blood of Hamilton was yet wet upon his hands, turned away in rage and disappointment from his native region, and sought in the great valley of the Mississippi some adventure adequate to his ability and his ambition. Schemes of conquest, and elevation to the height of political power, seem to have filled his mind; and we can well believe that Burr would let no scruples interfere with carrying out his plans. What these were, it is not easy, perhaps not possible, to say; indeed, it is quite probable, that he himself had no clear conception of what he purposed doing, but, like many another unprincipled adventurer, meant to be governed a good deal by circumstances and opportunities. Rumors ere long reached the north and east, that he was planning and organizing some vast expedition, the precise object of which no one could tell. Whether it was his design to make war on the Spanish province of Mexico; whether, knowing the discontents which existed in the west, he hoped to be able to separate this portion of the country from the Union; or whether, in the ruined condition of his fortunes, he hoped to repair them by some bold movement which promised a golden return; all was matter of conjecture; while, at the same time, there was none who doubted for a moment that he was equal to any undertaking, any desperate adventure, whether of foreign aggression or domestic treason.

Mr. Jefferson, whose dislike of Aaron Burr was intensely strong, lost 1806.
no time in endeavoring to ascertain the plans and purposes of his late rival before the people of the United States. He sent a confidential agent to the west, to get information and to take measures for bringing the guilty to punishment. He ordered the United States troops from the Sabine to New Orleans, and took every precaution to defeat any expedition which might be intended against Mexico. Having been informed that Burr purposed to plunder the bank at New Orleans, before invading the province of Mexico, Mr. Jefferson, on the 27th of November, issued a proclamation, cautioning all citizens against joining in Burr's enterprise, and orders were issued at the same time to the different points on the Ohio and Mississippi, to seize on the boats and

stores, and arrest the persons engaged in the expedition.

Congress assembled on the 1st of December, while this proclamation was fresh in the minds of all, and while tidings were daily looked for of revolt and outrage in the west and south. The next day, the president sent his message to Congress.* The first part treated entirely of "foreign relations," and whilst speaking of them he noticed "the criminal attempt of certain private individuals, to decide for their country the question of peace or war, by commencing active and unauthorized hostilities," which he had "by proclamation, as well as by special orders, promptly and efficaciously appeased." In allusion to Burr and his expedition, he further says: "In a country whose Constitution is derived from the will of the people, directly expressed by their free suffrages; where the principal executive functionaries, and those of the legislature, are renewed by them at short periods; where, under the character of juries, they exercise in person the greatest portion of the judiciary powers; where the laws are consequently so framed and administered as to bear with equal weight and favor on all, restraining no man in the pursuits of honest industry, and securing to every one the property which that acquires; it would not be supposed that any safeguards could be needed against insurrection or enterprise, on the public peace or authority. The laws, however, aware that these should not be trusted to moral restraints only, have wisely provided punishment for these crimes when committed. But would it not be salutary to give also the means of preventing their commission? Where an enterprise is meditated by private individuals against a foreign nation, in amity with the United States, powers of prevention, to a certain extent, are given by the laws; would they not be as reasonable and useful, where the enterprise preparing is against the United States? While adverting to this branch of law, it is proper to observe, that in enterprises meditated against foreign nations, the ordinary process of binding to the observance of the peace and good behavior, could it be extended to acts done out of the jurisdiction of the United States, would be effectual in some cases, where the offender is able to keep out of sight every indication of his purpose, which could draw on him the exercise of the powers now given by law."

1806.

The president also spoke in high terms of the success of Lewis and Clarke's expedition, and asked for moderate appropriations with reference to exploring some of the principal rivers in the valley of the Mississippi. In view of the near approach of the time when the slave-trade was to be abolished, his language was: "I congratulate you, fellow-citizens, on the approach of the period at which you may interpose your authority, constitutionally, to withdraw the citizens of the United States from all further participation in those violations of hu- 1806.

* The distinguished Henry Clay made his entrance into the Senate this session, and at an early day took an active part in advocating and defending plans and projects for internal improvements.

man rights, which have been so long continued on the unoffending inhabitants of Africa, and which the morality, the reputation, and the best interests of our country, have long been eager to proscribe. Although no law you may pass can take prohibitory effect till the first day of the year 1808, yet the intervening period is not too long to prevent, by timely notices, expeditions which cannot be completed before that day." The prosperous state of the finances was pointed out;* the employment of the surplus revenue on internal improvements was spoken of; and a "constitutional enumeration of federal powers" was suggested. After expressing some doubts as to the prospect of peace with foreign powers, the president concluded with various recommendations, looking to the event, whatever it might be, especially the fortifying exposed places and organizing the militia so as to render it promptly effective.

The next day, the president informed Congress that negotiations were in progress with the British government, and recommended a temporary suspension of the non-importation act. In accordance with this recommendation, a bill was passed authorizing the president to suspend this act at his discretion, to the second Monday in the succeeding December.

On the 16th of January, Congress called upon the president for information respecting Burr's movements, and the steps taken by the administration to counteract his treasonable projects. On the 22d, Mr. Jefferson responded to this call in a long and carefully written message, giving an account of what had transpired in relation to Burr's undertakings, and the measures which had been adopted by the authorities in the emergency. The president having stated in this message, that one of the persons arrested by General Wilkinson had been liberated by *habeas corpus*, the Senate, on the next day, with singularly hot haste, passed a bill, "suspending the writ of *habeas corpus* for three months," and immediately communicated it to the House, in confidence, with a request for their speedy concurrence. Messrs. Giles, J. Q. Adams, and Smith, were the committee who advised and carried through this piece of legislation; and the Senate of the United States, usually held to be the conservative portion of the legislature, asked the House of Representatives to agree to place the liberty of the citizens of the entire Union in the hands of Thomas Jefferson, because Aaron Burr, "with about ten boats, navigated by about six hands each, without any military appearance" had passed down the Ohio, determined to overthrow and destroy the government of this great Republic, and to build up for himself, an empire upon its ruins!

1807.

The message of the Senate was received on the 26th of January, and it met in the House the fate it deservedly merited. The House refused to keep the proceedings secret, and on the very first reading of the bill it was rejected by a majority of one hundred and thir-

* The receipts into the treasury to the last of September, amounted to $15,000,000 of which $2,700,000 had been paid on account of the claims under the Louisiana convention, and more than $5,000,000 on account of the debt, exclusive of interest.

teen against nineteen, a singular contrast to the unanimity with which it had been passed by the Senate, both Houses being agreed in their devotion to republican doctrines. Mr. Tucker, endeavoring to make the best of the matter, states that, "in truth, the bill passed the Senate in a moment of surprise, under the belief that it was necessary to prevent the escape of public offenders; and it affords a good practical illustration of the propriety of the rule which forbids hasty enactments."* The House resented the attempt so warmly, that a series of resolutions, directing the introduction of a bill "more effectually to secure the privilege of the writ of *habeas corpus* to persons in custody of the United States," was, at a later period of the session, rejected by a majority of two only.

Into the particulars respecting "Burr's conspiracy," we need not enter. He had purchased some boats on the Ohio, and was building others, and was also engaging men to navigate them, and accompany him on some enterprise down that river. Avowedly, his intention was to found a settlement at Washita, in Louisiana; but his known audacity and fondness for intrigue, the extent

1806. and nature of the preparations he was making, his broken character and fortunes, and what appeared to be intimations of a widely different object, incautiously given by some of his associates, led to the suspicion, if not belief, as we have intimated above, that he hoped either to seize upon New Orleans, and to erect as much of the valley of the Mississippi as he could acquire into an independent government; or to invade Mexico, and enrich himself by land piracy, and a foray into that wealthy colony of Spain.

At Natchez, whilst on his way to New Orleans, he was cited to appear before the supreme court of the Mississippi Territory. But his projects, whatever they were, had been enveloped in such a web of secrecy, that it was found impossible to obtain evidence sufficient to convict him, and he was discharged. Soon afterwards, however, hearing that several persons, who were under suspicion of being his accomplices, had been arrested at New Orleans and other places, he privately left Natchez, but was apprehended on the River Tombigbee, and was conveyed as a prisoner to Richmond, on the 26th of March, 1807. The next day, he was arrested there by the marshal, on the charge of fitting out an expedition against the territories of Spain, and after an examination by Chief Justice Marshall, was admitted to bail, in the sum of $10,000.

The pernicious effects of party spirit were strikingly exemplified in connection with the trial of Aaron Burr. "It became a favorite object with the federal party," says Mr. Tucker, "to obtain Burr's acquittal, and even to maintain his innocence, for the sake of thwarting the measures of the executive, and of proving the president vindictive and tyrannical. The other side felt the indignation which the schemes imputed to Burr would naturally excite, heightened by the desire of counteracting

* "*Life of Jefferson,*" vol. ii., p. 218. See also Benton's "*Abridgement of the Debates of Congress,*" vol. iii., pp. 504–15; 520–42.

their adversaries." As for the president himself, his biographer's exculpatory statements are more severe in condemnation of his course than any thing which was adduced by his most violent opponents. "Mr. Jefferson," he says, "could neither be blind nor insensible to this misplaced zeal or its cause, and it produced a reaction in his bosom, to which, however natural, and excusable in the great bulk of his party, it is to be wished that he had been superior. He felt so much anxiety to frustrate what he seemed to regard as an unprincipled determination in the federalists to screen a state criminal, and a party bias in the judges, merely because that criminal was now his enemy, that he kept up a regular correspondence with the United States Attorney, Mr. Hay, concerning the prosecution, and gave his counsel freely throughout its whole progress. There is indeed, much connected with this project and its prosecution, on which we cannot look back without regret, and even mortification."*

The trial began on the 22d of May, in the circuit court at Richmond, before Judges Marshall and Griffin. John Baker, Benjamin Botts, John Wickham, Edmund Randolph, and Luther Martin, and at a subsequent day Charles Lee,

1807. appeared as counsel for Burr; and to oppose them were Cæsar A. Rodney, (attorney-general in the place of Breckenridge, since the beginning of the year,) George Hay, (with whom Jefferson corresponded so sedulously,) Alexander M'Rae, and William Wirt. Burr also chose to act as his own counsel in the case, and his keen and subtle intellect was constantly exercised in directing and guiding the defence.

Much delay occurred in the selection of a grand jury. It was not easy to find impartial men qualified for that function; and after all, it is questionable, whether some of the jurors were not prepossessed with the belief in the prisoner's guilt. For a whole month the examination of witnesses in the preliminary trial proceeded, and time was wasted in interlocutory motions, discussions concerning the evidence that should go to the grand jury, the competency of the court to summon the president of the United States, as well as to compel the production of papers, and similar schemes for delaying and wearying out the jury and the court.

The case of Dr. Erick Bollman, and Samuel Swartwout, who had been arrested and committed to prison on a charge of treason in being concerned in Burr's conspiracy, had come up in February preceding, on which occasion the chief justice delivered his opinion upon the construction of the law of treason as defined by the Constitution. On the 21st of February, the prisoners were discharged from custody. Bollman, having been called on as a witness on the part of the United States, Mr. Hay, in open court, and by order of the president, tendered him a pardon, which he indignantly refused, asserting his innocence of any act requiring a pardon.

* Tucker's "*Life of Jefferson*," vol. ii., p. 230. As an offset to the president's course, Mr. Tucker mentions "the indecorum" on the part of the chief justice, in dining with a large party, where Burr himself was one of the guests.

Mr. Jefferson, we are sorry to say, was disposed to make very short work with poor Dr. Bollman. Writing to Mr. Hay, he says: "You ask what is to be done if Bollman finally rejects his pardon, and the judge decides it to have no effect? Move to commit him immediately for treason or misdemeanor, as you think the evidence will support; let the court decide where he shall be sent for trial; and on application I will have the marshal aided in his transportation, with the executive means." On the conviction of Burr, Hay was instructed to have a host more, "whose agency has been so prominent as to mark them as proper objects of punishment," committed; but, "as to obscure offenders, and repenting ones, let them lie for consideration." He further tells his correspondent that he has found up a new witness, whose evidence might tend to prove that "the most clamorous defenders of Burr, are all his accomplices;" and to fix upon Luther Martin "misprision of treason at least," and so to "put down that unprincipled and impudent federal bulldog." "Shall we move to commit Luther Martin as *particeps criminis* with Burr?" he asks; and in a P. S., "Will you send me a half dozen blank subpœnas?"* Truly, the publication of Mr. Jefferson's correspondence places him in a very strange position for the president of the United States to occupy.

The grand jury, on the 23d and 24th of June, pronounced Burr, with Herman Blennerhasset, General Dayton, and Smith, guilty of high treason and misdemeanor. Burr was then committed to prison, but on the representation of his counsel, that the prisoner's health was likely to be affected by confinement in the jail, and that his counsel could not have free communication with him there, the court allowed him to be removed to the public house he had previously occupied, and to be placed under a guard. This and other indulgences granted him, says Mr. Tucker, gave great scandal, at the time, to most of the republican party. On the other hand, Mr. Davis, Burr's friend and biographer, states, that "a description of the outrages and cruelty which he endured, would fill volumes;" but so far as appears, they were not particularly hard to bear, especially the luxuries of the table, the society of his daughter, etc.

Burr was put on his trial on the 3d of August, the court having adjourned to that day. From the 5th to the 16th, it was engaged in obtaining a jury, (no easy task, for "party feelings had taken so strong a hold, that almost every person called seemed to have made up his mind, from rumors and newspaper statements,") and discussing points of law. On the 17th, the treason case was opened; and the examination of the witnesses called by the government commenced. **1807.**

The charges against him were, that he had excited insurrection, rebellion, and war, on the 10th of December, 1806, at Blennerhasset's Island, in Virginia; and that he had also traitorously

* Mr. Martin repaid the president's denunciations with interest. It is related of him, that it was one of his common expressions when stigmatizing any person with the strongest terms of opprobrium, to say that he was "as great a scoundrel as Tom Jefferson."

intended to take possession of the city of New Orleans, with force and arms. To all which Burr pleaded "not guilty." The line of defence adopted by Burr's counsel was, the overthrowing of the evidence of Wilkinson, Eaton, and Truxtun. The first of these had received a letter from Burr, in cipher, which had been sent to the president as conclusive of the prisoner's guilt; and the two latter were ready to testify to Burr's determination to assassinate Mr. Jefferson, corrupt the navy, and overthrow Congress. There can be no doubt, we think, that Burr entertained some designs of the nature of those he stood charged with; but Wilkinson's testimony was looked upon as rather suspicious, for the letter in cipher was *altered* by him before the translation, which he swore to as correct, was made; and Mr. Eaton and Commodore Truxtun could only serve to prove an *intention* on the part of Burr to commit acts of treason against the United States. The prosecutors found it extremely difficult to make the overt acts they were able to establish, look like "the levying of war" against the government of the country. It could not be proved that, if the alleged overt act did take place, Burr was present and had part in it, for he happened to be hundreds of miles away, in another state, at the time specified. And Marshall, in his opinion, delivered on the 31st of August, submitted to the jury that, whether or not the assembling of the men in Blennerhasset's Island were the "levying of war," the presence of Burr, being nowhere alleged, except in the indictment, the overt act was not proved by so much as a single witness, and consequently, all other testimony was irrelevant.

The next day, Hay stated, that he must leave the case with the jury; and a verdict was after a short time returned, which, though objected to by Burr as informal, was allowed to stand, and was in fact, Not guilty. The indictments against Burr's alleged associates in his treason, were thereupon relinquished; and Burr's second trial came on.

The jury was impanelled on the 9th of September; the substance of the charge being, that the accused was guilty of a misdemeanor, in setting on foot a military enterprise against a foreign power, with whom the United States were at peace. After the prosecution had examined some of their witnesses, and the court had decided that the testimony of others was not relevant, Hay moved that the jury should be discharged. But Burr, who was fully sensible of the advantage he had gained, insisted upon a verdict: and as the court agreed that the jury could not be discharged without the consent of the accused, and that they must give a verdict, they retired, and soon returned and pronounced him "Not guilty."

This was on the 15th of September; but the whole matter was once more examined, and in the course of it, (so Burr wrote to his daughter,) Wilkinson "acknowledged, very modestly, that he had made certain alterations in the letter received from me, by erasures, etc., and then swore it to be a true copy." And the issue was a committal of Burr and Blennerhasset for trial in the District of Ohio, upon the old charges. They gave bail for their appearance, and were set at liberty; but after all, they were never tried, having forfeited their recognizances. The other trials all came to naught; only one of the so-called conspirators was brought in guilty, and he only of a misdemeanor.

Although the chief justice had recommitted Burr, Mr. Hay advised that all further prosecution be desisted from, as not likely to attain the end of convicting the guilty. No one doubted that Burr was, to a greater or less extent, a criminal; and the conduct and decision of the chief justice was severely commented upon by those who thought that he was bound to accomplish a very different result from that to which the trial was brought.* Burr soon
1807. after sailed for England, and his name and character were consigned to infamy. "An exile from his country, he wandered in poverty, a stranger in other lands; and when at last he returned to his own, it was to encounter the harder calamity of being treated as a stranger among his own countrymen. With the recklessness produced by a present which had no comfort, and a future which promised no hope, he surrendered himself without shame to the grovelling propensities which had formed his first step on the road to ruin, until at last, overcome by disease, in the decay of a worn-out body, and the imbecility of a much abased mind, he lay a shattered wreck of humanity, just entering upon eternity, with not enough of *man* left about him to make a Christian of. Ruined in fortune, and rotten in reputation, thus passed from the busy scene one who might have been a glorious actor in it; and when he was laid in the grave, decency congratulated itself that a nuisance was removed, and good men were glad that God had seen fit to deliver society from the contaminating contact of a festering mass of moral putrefaction.*

* "Why did you not tell Judge Marshall that the people of America demanded a conviction?" was the question put to Mr. Wirt after the trial. "Tell *him* that!" was the reply, "I would as soon have gone to Herschel, and told him that the people of America insisted that the moon had horns as a reason why he should draw her with them."

* See the "*New York Review*," for January, 1838, p. 212. The reader will find it useful to compare this scathing review of Burr's life and career, with the life of the same prominent actor in our political history, by Mr. Matthew L. Davis.

CHAPTER V.

1807-1809.

CLOSE OF JEFFERSON'S PRESIDENCY.

Mr. Jefferson's gunboat system — His message on the subject — Boats ordered to be built — Law respecting the abolition of the slave-trade — State of relations with England — Napoleon's "continental system" — England's "Orders in Council" — Treaty with England concluded by Monroe and Pinckney — The president refuses to submit it to the Senate — Censured for his course — Attempted renewal of negotiations — Assault on the Chesapeake by the Leopard — The president's proclamation on the subject — The result — Congress meets in October, 1807 — Substance of the president's message — Action of the House — Embargo recommended and passed in December, 1807 — Denounced by the federalists — Views and policy of France — "Orders in Council" of November 11th, 1807. — Napoleon's "Milan Decree" — Effects upon the commerce of the United States — Mr. Rose sent as minister to Washington — Accomplishes nothing — Papers sent in by the president to Congress — Report of the committee — Action of Congress — Discussion as to who should succeed Jefferson — Madison and Clinton the republican, C. C. Pinckney and King the federalist candidates — The embargo question and results — Mr. Tucker's remarks — Efforts of ministers at London and Paris — Congress meets in November, 1808 — The president's last message — Its contents — Results of the election — The debates, reports, etc., respecting the embargo — The enforcing act — The embargo repealed — J. Q. Adams's statements as to movements in New England against the Union — End of Mr. Jefferson's administration — Address of legislature of Virginia to him — Mr. Jefferson's true position in our history. Appendix to Chapter V. John Quincy Adams's remarks on Jefferson's administration.

Notwithstanding Mr. Jefferson's popularity, and the decided majority which the republicans possessed in Congress, there was a strong disposition manifested not to accede further to his favorite scheme of increasing the gunboats; and early in the year 1807, a resolution was passed calling on him for information as to the efficacy of gunboats in protecting harbors, together with the number wanted for the several ports.

1807.

We have, on a previous page (see p. 64,) referred to Mr. Tucker's defence of the plan proposed by the president. He has said all, probably, that can be said on that side of the question; but, as is evident, with very partial success. The gunboat scheme, as we are told, "was vehemently assailed by the president's adversaries, (1803,) in every form of argument and ridicule, and was triumphantly adduced as a further proof that he was not a practical statesman. The officers of the navy were believed to be, with scarcely an exception, opposed to the system of gunboats; especially those who were assigned to this service; partly because it was found to be personally very uncomfortable, and yet more perhaps, because the power they wielded was so inferior, and their command so insignificant, compared with that to which they had been familiarized. It was like compelling a proud man to give up a fine, richly caparisoned charger, for a pair of panniers and a donkey.

To stem the current of public opinion, which, so far as it was manifested, set so strong against these gunboats, and to turn it in their favor, Mr. Jefferson prevailed on Paine, who had, since his return, been addressing the people of the United States on various topics through the newspapers, to become their advocate. He set about it with his wonted self-confidence, and real talent in enforcing his views, and proceeded to show that a gun from a gunboat would do the same execution as from a seventy-four, and cost no more, perhaps less; but that a ship, carrying seventy-four guns, could bring only one half to bear upon the enemy at once; whereas, if they were distributed among seventy-four boats, they would all be equally effective at once. In spite of this logic, the public, pinning its faith on experienced men, remained incredulous; and when, soon afterwards, many of the new marine were driven ashore in a tempest, or were otherwise destroyed, no one seemed to regard their loss as a misfortune, and the officers of the navy did not affect to conceal their satisfaction; nor has any attempt been since made to replace them."

Having been called upon, as above stated, to furnish some proof of the efficacy of gunboats in protecting the harbors of the country, the president, on the 10th of February, sent a message to Congress on this subject. He stated, that the proposed mode of defence combined, 1. Land batteries, furnished with heavy cannon. 2. Movable artillery. 3. Floating batteries. 4. Gunboats to oppose an enemy at his entrance, and to co-operate with the batteries for his expulsion; that professional men in the army and navy favored the plan; and that gunboats are in general use among maritime nations for the purposes of defence, in proof of which several examples are cited. The president further stated, that two hundred gunboats would be required for the various harbors; that some of these would be of a size large enough to go out to sea if required: that seventy-three were already built or building, and the remaining one hundred and twenty-seven would cost from $500,000 to $600,000. Suggesting that only a few of these would be needed in times of peace, and that it was altogether a very economical arrangement, he concluded his message in the following terms: "It must be superfluous to observe, that this species of naval armament is proposed merely for defensive operations: that it can have but little effect towards protecting our commerce in the open seas, even on our coast; and still less can it become an excitement to engage in offensive maritime war, towards which it would furnish no means."*

1805.

An appropriation was subsequently made, by a vote of sixty-eight to thirty-six, of $150,000, for the purpose of building thirty gunboats. At the next Congress, in December, a law was passed

* Sullivan, who represents the views of the federalists, speaking of the gunboats, says, they "were fit for nothing but to destroy the lives of those who attempted to navigate them. A small boat with one great gun mounted in its bows, was well adapted to roll over in a heavy sea; and so it proved on actual experiment, and Mr. Jefferson's gunboats have long been abandoned; and even he seems to have been convinced of the folly of the invention."

which authorized the construction of one hundred and eighty-eight gunboats, in addition to those already built; which would raise the total number of vessels of this description in the navy, to two hundred and fifty-seven.* "This was the development of the much-condemned 'gunboat system,' which," as Mr. Cooper justly remarks, "for a short time, threatened destruction to the pride, discipline, tone, and even morals of the service. There can be no question, that, in certain circumstances, vessels of this nature may be particularly useful; but these circumstances are of rare occurrence, as they are almost always connected with attacks on towns and harbors. As the policy is now abandoned, it is unnecessary to point out the details by which it is rendered particularly unsuitable to this country; though there is one governing principle that may be mentioned, which, of itself, demonstrates its unfitness. The American coast has an extent of near two thousand miles, and to protect it by means of gunboats, even admitting the practicability of the method, must involve an expenditure sufficient to create a movable force in ships, that would not only answer all the same purposes of defence, but which would possess the additional advantage of acting, at need, offensively. In other words, it was entailing on the country the cost of an efficient marine, without enjoying its advantages."†

In accordance with the recommendation in the president's message, (see p. 79,) Congress during the present session, passed a law prohibiting the African slave-trade, after the 1st of January, 1808, under very severe penalties. **1807.** The debate was protracted to an unusual length, and gave rise to great and unwonted excitement among the members. There was a very general disposition in favor of the prohibition, but in regard to the details great contrarieties of opinion existed. Early in March, the debate was brought to a close, and the substance of the law as passed, was briefly as follows: a fine of $20,000, with forfeiture of the vessel, forbade the regular trade; and one of $5,000, with forfeiture of the vessel likewise, forbade the engaging in the traffic casually. Importation and sale was to be punished by fine, not below $1,000 nor above $10,000, and imprisonment varying between five and ten years. A fine of $800 was to be laid on the purchaser, who should know that the slave was imported contrary to this act. The states severally were to dispose of such slaves. And to prevent contraband trade, by means of the coasting vessels, it was enacted, that each coaster should have entered in its papers full descriptions of all slaves on board for transport, under penalty of heavy fine and forfeiture. Other regulations tended in the same direction, but the question of slavery itself was left untouched. It deserves, however, to be noted here, as a matter of justice to our country, that this action of Congress was in advance of that taken by any other nation in the civilized world, and that, though we may be reproached

* See Benton's "*Abridgement of the Debates of Congress*," vol. iii., pp. 625–40.

† Cooper's "*Naval History*," vol. ii., pp. 23–24.

with the continuance of slavery in our southern states, nevertheless, the United States, in 1820, were the first to declare the slave-trade to be piracy, and punishable accordingly.

Congress also repealed the tax on salt, continued the Mediterranean fund, and made a liberal compensation to Captains Lewis and Clarke and their companions, in donations of lands for their services in the Pacific enterprise. "The votes in both Houses," according to Mr. Tucker, "showed, that if the president had lost a small number of his former supporters, he had the undiminished confidence and attachment of the rest, constituting the great body of the republican party." On the 3d of March, the ninth Congress closed its second session.

1807.

It deserves to be put on record here, that Robert Fulton, in the summer of the year 1807, demonstrated to his countrymen and the world, the practicability of propelling vessels by the agency of steam. Some three or four years previously, he had, in conjunction with Chancellor Livingston, American minister to France, made a successful experiment with a boat built by him on the Seine. On returning to the United States, in 1806, Fulton constructed the "Clermont," which was launched from a ship-yard in New York, in the spring of 1807, and prepared for use in August of the same year. Despite the defects and difficulties, despite the sneers of the incredulous and the contemptuous disregard of the self-opinionated and conceited, Fulton persevered, and the Clermont made her first voyage from New York to Albany in thirty-two hours, and returned again in thirty hours. "In the midst of the most prolific creations of American industry," says Professor Renwick, "the services rendered by Fulton are, at length, admitted to be superior to those of any other, with the sole exception of Whitney. This rank is now awarded to him, not only by the tardy justice of his own countrymen, but by the almost universal suffrage of the whole civilized world, the bonds of whose union are daily drawn closer and closer, by an invention which, however long sought and nearly attained by others, was at last introduced into use by his talent and perseverance."*

The death of Mr. Fox, in September, 1806, brought about a change in the British government which was far from favorable to the views and policy of the United States. The president had counted upon the good offices of Mr. Fox towards settling existing difficulties and effecting a commercial treaty on more advantageous terms than those of Mr. Jay's treaty. Mr. Canning now became the head of the British ministry, and the president, early in February, deemed it advisable to furnish Mr. Monroe and his colleague at London, with more explicit instructions on the subject of impressments, neutral commerce, blockades, the India trade, and indemnification. On the point of impressments, they were directed to enter into no treaty which did not secure the American citizen against any and every exercise of this odious claim of Great Britain. The dispatches were,

* Renwick's "*Life of Robert Fulton*," p. 208.

however, too late; for on the 31st of December, 1806, a treaty was concluded between the American envoys and the British commissioners appointed to treat with them.

Previously to this, the deadly struggle between England and France had led to measures which seemed calculated to force the United States from their position of neutrality. Ever since the annihilation of the navies of Spain and France by the decisive victory at Trafalgar, Great Britain had strenuously exerted her gigantic powers to retain in her own hands solely, the trade of Europe. In May, 1806, she had declared the whole coast of Europe, from the Elbe in Germany, to Brest in France, (about a thousand miles of sea-coast,) to be in a state of blockade, which subjected American vessels attempting to enter the continental ports, to capture and condemnation.* Napoleon, on his part, having by his deadly blows, at Austerlitz and Jena, laid the continental powers prostrate, perceived no way of securing and extending his conquests, especially against the one nation that had successfully resisted his might, except that which he entitled the "Continental System," the first effort to realize which was the renowned "Berlin Decree," issued on the 21st of November, 1806.

From the terms of this decree, it was evident that the neutral trade of America would be affected, (to the full extent of Napoleon's power to enforce so prodigious an edict,) quite as injuriously as it had been by the imperious maxims of Great Britain. And although Armstrong, the American minister at Paris, obtained from the French minister of marine and colonies, what seemed to be an express statement, that the terms of the treaty of 1800 would still determine the relations of France to American commerce, it was too evident that Mr. Jefferson's view, that the flag should cover the goods, would not be allowed in the internecine warfare that the emperor of France was now waging with England.

1806.

The treaty just concluded, consisted of twenty-six articles; by which the permanent and unexpired provisions of Mr. Jay's treaty were confirmed, and the same stipulations made respecting the East India trade, rights of neutrals and belligerents, the appointment of consuls, the surrender of criminals, the equalization of duties, and the regulation of privateers. In addition to these conditions, it was agreed that the United States should have a circuitous trade with colonies of nations at war with Britain, during the existing hostilities; that the limits of maritime jurisdiction were extended to five miles from the coast; that care should be taken of the shipwrecked of each nation; that advantages in trade or navigation granted by either party to any nation, should

* "Of the excitement and agitation raised in our country by this inroad upon the laws of nations, and upon neutral commerce, an adequate idea can now scarcely be conceived. The complaints, the remonstrances, the appeals for protections to Congress, from the plundered merchants, rung throughout the Union. A fire spreading from Portland to New Orleans would have scarcely been more destructive. Memorial upon memorial, from all the cities of the land, loaded the tables of the legislative halls, with the cry of distress and the call upon the national arm for defence, restitution, and indemnity."—J. Q. Adams's "*Life of James Monroe*," p. 266.

be conferred upon the other; and that all laws relating to the African slave-trade should be communicated to each other.

Smaller advantages for the United States, than those secured by Mr. Jay's treaty, were proposed respecting the India trade, and illegal captures; but in several important particulars, this treaty was more favorable than the former one. There was an amicable spirit evinced by the article in which Britain consented to the trade of the United States with her enemies' colonies, for a time and under certain restrictions. And the concession made by Britain, who had the power to enforce the regulations regarding commerce, was far greater than that of the American commissioners, who merely gave up, in part, a claim which they had never been able to enforce. And there was an omission noted concerning provisions, which the United States agreed might be stopped as contraband, whilst Great Britain consented to waive the forfeiture, and to indemnify the neutrals for stopping them. On the subject of impressment, the British commissioners refused to give any satisfactory assurances; yet the American envoys, under all the circumstances, deemed it most advisable to put their names to the treaty, which they did as above stated. News of the "Berlin Decree"* having reached London before the treaty was completed, a note was addressed to the American ministers, in which was reserved to Great Britain the right to adopt countervailing regulations, in case Napoleon should execute that decree and neutrals submit to it.

The day before the close of the session of Congress, the president received from Mr. Erskine, the English minister at Washington, a copy of the treaty, and "it fell so far short of what he conceived to be the just claims of the United States, as well as of his instructions, that he decided at once on not submitting it to the Senate, but to try the effect of further negotiation. Besides other objections, there were two that were insuperable. These were, that the treaty contained no provision whatever on the subject of impressment; and because it was accompanied with a note from the British ministers, by which the British government reserved to itself the right of releasing itself from the stipulations in favor of neutral rights, if the United States submitted to the Berlin Decree, or other invasions of those rights by France."* **1807.**

This procedure on the part of the president, was looked upon as rather high-handed, and gave rise to much excitement in the United States. The commercial classes condemned the rejection of the treaty, which was deemed so much the better for their interests than Mr. Jay's, as the times were more troubled, and the indications of a friendly spirit to America more desirable in England. The federalists loudly complained of the unconstitutionality

* Early in January, 1807, only a few days after the conclusion of this negotiation, an "order in council" was issued by the British in reply to Napoleon's "Berlin Decree," and all coast trade with France was prohibited.

* Tucker's "*Life of Jefferson*," vol. ii., p. 224.

of the course chosen by the president. He had done that of his own motion, they said, which only with the Senate's concurrence he was competent to do. "Was this honest or wise in Mr. Jefferson?" they exclaimed; "Does it, or not, show that he was resolved, the parade of negotiation notwithstanding, to keep open the means of contention with Great Britain? And was not his motive to contribute to the universal dominion of Napoleon in Europe, including prostrate England? And was it wise for a *republic* to extinguish, if it could, the only power that then stood between the hopes of liberty and one universal despotism?" But the republicans stood by the president manfully, and justified his course as eminently wise and fitting in the emergency; for, they urged, had the treaty been ratified, on the condition which was affixed to it, it would have pledged the United States to such a co-operation with Great Britain against France, as must have ended in hostilities with the one and alliance with the other. Mr. Jefferson liked England too little to be concerned in any movement of that kind.

1807.

The course adopted by the president and his party was regarded by the British government as indicating an unfriendly spirit, and there is little doubt that it hastened the progress of international difficulties. The American envoys complained of the manner in which their labors were received, and expressed their opinion freely, that the treaty was decidedly advantageous to the United States. They were, however, instructed to renew negotiations with the English ministry, in order to obtain terms more in accordance with those desired by the president; and Mr. Madison, in March, wrote to them, explaining more fully the ground they were to take on the several points at issue. Towards the close of July, they attempted to open anew the negotiation, in a note addressed to Mr. Canning; but the difficulties connected with the attack on the Chesapeake suspended the correspondence for a considerable time. On the 22d of October, Mr. Canning answered the note of Messrs. Monroe and Pinckney, in which he stated that their proposal "for proceeding to negotiate anew, upon the basis of a treaty already solemnly concluded and signed, is wholly inadmissible."*

The British naval officers, on the coast of America, seem to have partaken largely of the unfriendly state of feeling which had been on the increase for some time past, and they were ready to go much beyond the instructions of their government, and to commit acts in violation of the well-understood rights and privileges of neutral nations. The outrage committed on the Chesapeake illustrates this fact very forcibly. This vessel was about to proceed to join the Mediterranean squadron, and on the 23d of June got to sea. She had been preceded by

1807.

* Mr. Monroe, finding that nothing further could be effected at the present juncture, returned to the United States in the latter part of the year 1807, leaving Mr. Pinckney in charge of his country's interests at the English court. This latter gentleman, after long-continued but fruitless labors, left England in February, 1811, and returned home.

one of the British cruisers, the Leopard, a fifty-gun ship; she herself being rated as a thirty-eight, but carrying forty-four guns. Outside the Capes of Virginia, and when about six or eight miles from land, the Leopard came up on her weather-quarter, and hailing, informed Commodore Barron that she had dispatches for him. The officer who came from the Leopard, however, only presented Vice-admiral Berkeley's circular order, and demanded several enumerated deserters. A conference of above half an hour ensued, the American officer standing upon his general orders, and the British lieutenant endeavoring to carry his point, apparently by the mere prestige of the superior force of his vessel. At length he returned to the Leopard, without obtaining the men; and without any definite understanding with Commodore Barron respecting the next step.

Not dreaming of a resort to violence, the Chesapeake was in every respect unprepared for action; the Leopard, on the other hand, had made her arrangements for attack, and waited only the word of command. Observing this, Barron and Captain Gordon endeavored hastily to get the gun-deck clear, and ordered the men to their quarters. As soon as the English vessel's boat had returned, the captain hailed the Chesapeake again; and on receiving Barron's reply, that he did not understand the hail, a shot was fired ahead of the Chesapeake, and in a few seconds followed by a whole broadside. The confusion on board the American vessel was increased tenfold by this; the Leopard hailed again and again; the Chesapeake returning no answer, but vainly striving to get her batteries into fighting order; and for about a quarter of an hour the Leopard poured a heavy fire into her unresisting antagonist,* doing great execution. Barron repeatedly desired that one gun at least might be fired, and finding it impossible, ordered the colors to be hauled down; just as one of the lieutenants, with a coal, which he took with his fingers from the galley, contrived to discharge a gun from the second division of the ship.

Commodore Barron "immediately sent a boat on board the Leopard, to say that the ship was at the disposal of the English captain, when the latter directed his officers to muster the American crew. The three men claimed to be deserters from the Melampus, and one that had run from the Halifax sloop-of-war, were carried away." And as the English captain declined to take charge of the vessel, she returned immediately to Hampton Roads.

1807.

Three of the Chesapeake's men were killed, and eighteen wounded; the commodore being amongst the latter; and the injuries done to hull, masts, and rigging were very great. The single ball fired from her, hulled the Leopard, but did no further harm. The four men

* More than a year before, on the 25th of April, 1806, the British ship Leander had fired upon a coasting vessel, near Sandy Hook, killing one of her crew; and drawing from the president a proclamation forbidding the entrance of that vessel, and two others with her, into the waters of the United States, and calling for the apprehension of the Leander's captain. This had excited a very bitter feeling against the British cruisers; but the outrage upon the Chesapeake raised the spirit of most of the nation to the highest pitch of indignation.

taken from the Chesapeake were tried at Halifax, and the deserter from the sloop was hung; the others were reprieved, on condition of entering the British service.

The news of this unprovoked assault having reached the president, he issued a proclamation, on the 2d of July, "in which," says Mr. Tucker, "after reciting the outrage, he interdicts all armed vessels bearing commissions from Great Britain from the harbors and waters of the United States, and forbids all supplies to them and all intercourse with them on pain of the law; and all officers, civil and military, were called upon to aid in executing these orders. There was an exception in favor of vessels in distress, or conveying dispatches. The indignation excited by this invasion of national rights, which was heightened, no doubt, by the feeble resistance made by the Chesapeake, pervaded every part of the community; and in city, town, and country, there were meetings expressing their keen resentment; tendering their support to the government, in all measures of retribution; and in the mean time, discontinuing every sort of intercourse with British ships of war. On this question all parties cordially co-operated without distinction; and the country, as Mr. Jefferson properly observed, had never been in such a state since the battle of Lexington."*

Commodore Barron was tried by a court-martial, and suspended for five years, without pay or emoluments. Captains Gordon and Hall were privately reprimanded; and the gunner of the Chesapeake was cashiered. On the other hand, the British government lost no time in disavowing the act of their over-zealous officials. Berkeley was recalled from the North American station; the captain of the Leopard was never afterwards employed; two of the negroes, taken as deserters from the Melampus, and claimed as citizens of the United States, were given up; the other (who was a South American by birth) had died. Little effect, however, was produced by these attempts at conciliation, and had the government been in other hands than those of Mr. Jefferson, a declaration of war not improbably would immediately have ensued.*

The critical position of the foreign relations of our country induced the president to summon Congress at an earlier period than usual. Accordingly, the members assembled on the 25th of October, and the message was sent in on the following day. **1807.** After adverting to circumstances seriously threatening the peace of the country, which occasioned that early summons of the legislature, he spoke of the injuries and depredations which had led to the extraordinary mission to London. He next noticed, briefly, the treaty which had been signed; representing it as signed by his commissioners, under a sort of protest, that they were acting against the instructions of their government, and his consequent rejection of the treaty. He next adverts

* Tucker's "*Life of Jefferson*," vol. ii., pp. 236–7.

* For a more full account of the attack on the Chesapeake, with the circumstances, etc., see Cooper's "*Naval History*," vol. ii., pp. 12–22.

to the attempt made to renew negotiations, by his orders, and that whilst he was hoping for some good result, the frigate Chesapeake was attacked, as we have seen, by order of the British admiral. He further mentioned the measures he had taken; and said that those aggressions of the British were continued by their ships remaining in the American waters, by habitual violations of their jurisdiction, and by putting to death one of the four men taken from the Chesapeake. He informed them that England had interdicted all trade by neutrals between ports not in amity with her, by which, as she was at war with nearly every nation on the Atlantic and Mediterranean, our vessels were compelled either to sacrifice their cargoes at the first port, or return home without a market. Of the relations with Spain, the president spoke as if that kingdom were not a mere appanage of France, but was acting independently in having issued a decree similar to the Berlin decree of November 21st, 1806. Overlooking entirely the unsettled relations with France, and the depredations committed by her, he added,— "with the other nations of Europe our harmony has been uninterrupted, and commerce and friendly intercourse have been maintained on their usual footing." So he recommended gunboats, and militia for manning them; and spoke of what had been done for replenishing the magazines with military stores.

The paragraph respecting Burr and his trial is worth quoting: "I informed
1807. Congress," he says, "at their last session, of the enterprises against the public peace, which were believed to be in preparation by Aaron Burr, and his associates, of the measures taken to defeat them, and to bring the offenders to justice. Their enterprises were happily defeated by the patriotic exertions of the militia, wherever called into action, by the fidelity of the army, and energy of the commander-in-chief in promptly arranging the difficulties presenting themselves on the Sabine, repairing to meet those arising on the Mississippi, and dissipating, before their explosion, plots engendering there. I shall think it my duty to lay before you the proceedings, and the evidence publicly exhibited on the arraignment of the principal offenders before the circuit court of Virginia. You will be enabled to judge whether the defect was in the testimony, in the law, or in the administration of the law; and wherever it shall be found, the legislature alone can apply or originate the remedy. The framers of our Constitution certainly supposed they had guarded, as well their government against destruction by treason, as their citizens against oppression, under pretence of it; and if these ends are not attained, it is of importance to inquire by what means more effectual they may be secured."

The message closed with stating, that the revenue during the preceding year, had amounted to nearly $16,000,000, which, with the money previously in the treasury, had been sufficient to discharge more than $4,000,000 of the debt, besides defraying the current expenses of the government. A part of the balance, it was suggested, might well be applied to the purposes of national defence, especially in the then doubtful position of our foreign relations.

The House, by means of a committee who reported on the 17th of November, responded temperately to much of the president's exhortations; and deemed the further protection of the ports and harbors most needful. They also denounced the stay of the British squadron in the American waters, after Jefferson's proclamation, as a flagrant violation of their jurisdiction. Their feeling was, however, rapidly warming; for news came of the seizure of the Danish fleet by Great Britain,—which made a much deeper impression upon them than the increased rapacity of the French, in enforcing the menaces of the "Berlin Decree." How greatly both the "continental system" of Napoleon, and the British "order in council" interfered with and restricted American commerce, has already been intimated; and notwithstanding the president's declaration of there being twenty thousand seamen afloat, it must be manifest, that in such a state of insecurity, the most valuable branches of foreign trade would be quite cut off.

1807.

On the 18th of December, a confidential message was sent to both Houses, showing "the great and increasing dangers" to the shipping, seamen, and merchandise of the United States at sea, in consequence of the hotter rage of the war, and recommending, in consequence of the great importance of keeping in safety, these essential resources, "an inhibition of the departure of our vessels from the ports of the United States."

With this message was transmitted a proclamation of the king of England, dated October 16th, 1807, which required all British seamen in foreign service to return home, and the official interpretation of the emperor of France, on the 18th of September, 1807, respecting the Berlin decree; wherein it was declared, that all neutral vessels were to be captured when proceeding to and from England. Beside what was furnished by these documents, Mr. Tucker states, that the president had a stronger motive for recommending the laying an embargo, for he "had received information through an authentic private channel, that the British ministry had issued an order against neutral commerce, in retaliation of the Berlin decree; which information was confirmed by a ministerial English newspaper received at the same time."

The subject was immediately entered upon by the House, and the president's wishes were speedily gratified. A bill laying an embargo was passed on the 22d of December, at eleven o'clock at night, by a vote of eighty-two to forty-four. A similar bill had been hurried through the Senate in a single day, by a vote of twenty-two to six; and all American vessels were thenceforward prohibited from sailing for foreign ports, all foreign vessels from taking out cargoes, and all coasting vessels were required to give bonds to land their cargoes in the United States.

1806.

The embargo was violently denounced by the federalists and such of the democratic party as were dissatisfied with the course pursued by Mr. Jefferson; and there was by no means a general disposition to acquiesce in a measure which bore so heavily as this upon the prosperity of the country. It was asserted, and with great show of reason, by the federalists, that the embargo would not and could not produce the desired result of compelling the belligerents to rescind their orders in council and their decrees; for, however important the trade with the United States might be considered to England and France, it was not to be presumed that either of those nations was to be forced in this way to change its determination. The resources of England and France were too great and too varied to be very seriously affected by a suspension of even the whole of American commerce. They had both resolved, that America should not be permitted to remain neutral, and they meant, if possible, to drive her to side with one or the other of the contending powers. Indeed, as Mr. Cooper says, rather dryly, "with a foreign trade that employed 700,000 tons of American shipping alone, Congress passed a law declaring an unlimited embargo, for all the purposes of foreign commerce, on every port in the Union; *anticipating a large portion of the injuries that might be expected from an open enemy, by inflicting them itself!*"*

* The supposition has also been thrown out that the embargo was intended to operate adversely to Great Britain, by the exasperation it must needs create, in that very section of the Union which was most amicably disposed towards England, for she was represented as the originator of the imperious necessity for putting a stop to their lucrative trade; rather than by any immediate effect it could have upon her commerce. Subsequent events seem to have imparted a degree of probability to this supposition.

It was also asserted by the opponents of the measure, that this policy was, in truth, in accordance with the real wishes and expectations of Napoleon. He had predicted, in October, the laying this embargo, and his course was a good deal influenced by his considering America as virtually leagued with him in the contest against England. His minister Champagny, in January, 1808, writes: "War exists, in fact, between England and the United States; and his majesty considers it as declared from the day in which England published her decrees. In that persuasion, his majesty, ready to consider the United States as associated with the cause of all the powers, who have to defend themselves against England, has not taken any definitive measures towards the American vessels which may have been brought into our ports. He has ordered that they should remain sequestered, until a decision may be had thereon, according to the dispositions which shall have been expressed by the the government of the United States." This letter was communicated to Congress by the president, in the latter part of March, 1808. Some months later, Mr. Jefferson, in a confidential letter to Mr. Armstrong at Paris, wrote: "Bonaparte does not wish us to go to war with England; knowing that we have not ships sufficient to carry on such a war. And to submit to pay England the tribute on our commerce, which she demanded by her orders in council, would be to aid her in the war against France, and would give the emperor just ground to declare war on us."

England, in this deadly struggle with

the emperor of France, showed no disposition to yield in the slightest degree. On the 11th of November, "Orders in Council" were issued in retaliation for Napoleon's "Berlin Decree."* By these orders, all neutral trade was prohibited with the ports of France and her allies, or of any country at war with Great Britain, and with all other European ports from which the British flag was excluded, unless such trade should be carried on through her ports, under her licenses, and paying duties to her exchequer. Napoleon, on the other hand, fulminated his "Milan Decree," on the 17th of December, and seized upon this pretext to complete his system of blockade and confiscation, by which he hoped effectually to cut off the commercial and financial resources of Great Britain. By this decree it was declared, that every vessel which should submit to be searched by a British ship of war, or which should touch at a British port, or should pay any impost whatever to the British government, should be *denationalized*, and subject to seizure and condemnation. "The two great belligerent powers thus mutually rivalled each other in the work of destroying the commerce of the only remaining neutral state their indiscriminate violence had left out of the circle of hostility. In vain were the justice and policy of the British orders in council of November arraigned in parliament by Lord Erskine and other members of the late ministry, who had themselves furnished the precedent and the pattern of that measure in the orders issued in the preceding January, on the same pretext of retaliating the Berlin decree. In vain was the wanton attack on Copenhagen assailed by them as subversive of the sacred principles of morality, of public law, and of the soundest maxims of national policy. All other considerations were merged in the apparent necessity of resisting the portentous power of the French emperor, who, after the victory of Friedland, and the peace of Tilsit, wielded the entire resources of the European continent, and directed them to the avowed purpose of subverting the British empire."*

1807.

It was at the close of the year 1807, that the British government dispatched Mr. Rose as a special minister to the United States, to adjust the difficulty which had arisen out of the assault on the frigate Chesapeake. On arriving at Washington, he addressed Mr.

* "By these acts of England and France, professing to be acts of retaliation, and not at all in a spirit of hostility to the United States, the neutral commerce of America was entirely destroyed. Not a vessel could sail to Europe or to England, to the vast colonial regions of North and South America, and the East and West Indies, without being subject to capture and condemnation. The trade of the whole world, in fact, was interdicted and could not be carried on without the risk of forfeiture. Both belligerents, however, had distinctly intimated, that if the United States would side with them, every advantage should be given to their commerce. But this is what they did not intend to do. They did not mean to surrender all the advantages they had hitherto enjoyed from their neutral position if it could be avoided. To side with England was war with France; with France, was war with England. Mr. Jefferson was not prepared for either alternative. What was to be done? Commerce, left thus exposed, must be ground into powder between the upper and nether millstone, and be scattered as chaff before the winds of heaven."—Garland's "*Life of John Randolph*," vol. i., p. 265.

* Wheaton's "*Life of William Pinkney*," p. 17.

Madison, the secretary of state, and informed him of the instructions by which he was to be guided in the matter in hand. Mr. Rose having required, that the president's proclamation, interdicting British vessels of war from
1808. the harbors of the United States, should be withdrawn before he could enter on the subject of reparation; and the president, on the other hand, having declined doing this, and having insisted upon bringing into review other cases of aggression and even the whole question of impressment itself, the further progress of negotiation was broken off. Mr. Rose, about the end of March, 1808, re-embarked for England, in the same frigate which had brought him out.

The result to which this attempt on the part of the British government arrived, excited afresh the political animosities of the two parties. The republicans maintained that the president had done right in every respect, and that the settlement of this dispute would have been of no real consequence in the then position of affairs. The federalists, on the other hand, charged upon the president and his party the adopting the present course out of hatred to England, and from a desire to further the wishes and views of France. From what we know of Mr. Jefferson's predilections, it is not at all unlikely, that the federalists had some ground for the charges of undue partiality towards France on the part of the great leader of the republicans in the United States.

On the 2d of February, 1808, the president communicated copies of the orders in council of November 11th, 1807, "as a further proof of the increasing dangers to our navigation and commerce, which led to the provident measures of the act of the present session, laying an embargo on our own vessels." On the 26th of February, he communicated to Congress, "letters 1808.
recently received from our ministers at Paris and London," but "not to be published." The "Milan Decree" was sent on the 17th of March, with a brief matter-of-fact message. Five days later he sent another message "relative to England and France," and on the same day a second message, "with documents, exhibiting a complete view of our differences with Great Britain and France; a long catalogue of letters, acts, copies of treaties, instructions, extracts, etc., selected with apparent impartiality, yet to the keen eyes of political opponents, seeming to disclose the bias of the president towards France. At the close of the message, he requests that the correspondence which, a month before, he desired to be kept confidential, should now be published, in order to remove unfounded suspicions against the government. Other messages were sent on the 30th of March and on the 1st and 2d of April.

The committee to whom these various documents were referred, made a report on the 16th of April, in which they gave a review of the injuries sustained by the United States from the course adopted by the belligerents. They held it to be the duty of Congress to interpose, and they recommended several expedients in the present emergency. They also recommended the continuance of the embargo, and the placing the power of suspending it, in the hands of the president, until the next session of Congress. A law was accordingly passed, authorizing Mr. Jefferson to suspend the embargo act, in the event of a peace between the contending powers, or, "if such changes in their measures affecting neutral commerce took place," as might "render that of the United States sufficiently safe." Mr. Tucker tells us, that "this law was passed because some hope was then entertained that a peace between France and England would be effected by the intervention of Austria. An intimation had been given by Napoleon, that France would not require England to renounce her maritime principles, nor would France renounce hers, but the question might be passed over in silence."*

The embargo question, in its various perplexing ramifications, occupied the attention of Congress, to a large extent, during most of the session, which was brought to a close on the 25th of April. Notwithstanding the engrossing nature of the subjects above referred to, Congress found time during the session, to enter upon an examination of the charges which John Randolph brought forward against General Wilkinson, the principal witness relied on for the conviction of Aaron Burr. There was also, we may add, an attempt to expel John Smith,† one of the Ohio Senators, on the ground that he had been involved in Burr's conspiracy; which failed, in April, because not quite two-thirds of the Senate were willing to vote for his expulsion.

Part of the session was taken up with complaints against the hall of the House of Representatives, in which acoustical science had been so sadly ignored, that the oratory of the members seemed to fail entirely of producing its desired effect. Complaints were heard too, against the city of Washington; and a proposal, which was supported by a considerable number, was brought forward, to remove the sittings of the legislature and the head-quarters of the government to Philadelphia again, until Washington should be a city of some consequence, and afford some of the advantages which were looked for in the national capital.

1808.

The most interesting question now agitated throughout the Union, was the coming presidential election. Who should be put forward as the candidate of the republican party? Would Mr. Jefferson stand for a third time? Should Madison or Monroe succeed him? Jefferson declared his fixed determination to retire, when pressed to violate his own long-ago avowed sentiments concerning the re-eligibility of the president. But he did not thereby escape his share in the troubles of the canvass.

James Monroe, as above stated, had returned from England, and, as was inevitable, a coolness sprang up between him and Madison, whom he regarded as a rival, and as having received unfair advantages for the approaching contest from their common

* Tucker's "*Life of Jefferson*," vol. ii., p. 265.

† For the debate on the case of John Smith, see Benton's "*Abridgement of the Debates of Congress*," vol. iii., pp. 554–606. Mr. Smith, in consequence of the vote (nineteen to ten) sent in his resignation to the governor of Ohio. With regard to General Wilkinson's affairs, see same vol., pp. 642–58, 663–74.

friend and leader. Personal influence, and the influence of adherents, newspaper articles, and all the approved appliances for such warfare, were brought into requisition; and caucus meetings for nominating the candidates of the party were held without any scruples whatever.

The most important of these meetings was one attended by nearly a hundred Senators and Representatives of the democratic party, John Quincy Adams, who had now quite deserted his former principles, being amongst them. Eighty-three votes were given in favor of Madison, and only three each for Monroe and George Clinton, for the presidency; and for the latter, seventy-nine votes were given for the vice-presidency; Madison and Clinton were therefore announced as the candidates by the party. On the same night, two caucuses were held by members of the Assembly of Virginia, at Richmond; one by the friends of Monroe, in the Capitol, the other by the supporters of Madison, in a hotel. One hundred and thirty-four at the latter meeting voted for Madison, without an opposing voice; but at the former, out of fifty-seven, ten voted for Madison.

In this state of things, it was plain that Monroe had no present chance of success; but this consideration hardly satisfied his wishes, nor did two letters written to him with that manifest intent, entirely reconcile him to the loss of the high honor almost within his reach. His friends, unaffected by the array in favor of his opponent, carried on their canvass with untiring zeal. And Clinton, until warned by a hint that another candidate for the vice-presidency might be put in his place by the party, if he did not withdraw from the competition for the higher office, persevered in his hopeless attempt to be the successor of Jefferson.*

As for the federalists, they were as much divided as a party could be, which had no chance of success. They did, indeed, propose General C. C. Pinckney and Rufus King as their candidates; but in many parts they relied rather on the chance of embarrassing the election, by voting for one or other of the unpopular candidates of the republicans, than on any expectation of being able to place any of their own men in offices of power and trust.

Congress, as we have stated, adjourned on the 25th of April; and during the summer the country was kept in a constant ferment by the preparations for the change in the person of the president, and by the measures which were as surely the forerunners of war, as negotiations, and amicable interventions, and arbitrations, are presages of the conclusion of hostilities.

1808.

* The third president, as above stated, though urged to do otherwise, refused to be a candidate for a second re-election. "Never," said he, "did a prisoner, released from his chains, feel such relief as I shall on shaking off the shackles of power. Nature intended me for the tranquil pursuits of science, by rendering them my supreme delight. But the enormities of the times in which I have lived have forced me to take a part in resisting them, and to commit myself on the boisterous ocean of political passions. I thank God for the opportunity of retiring from them without censure, and carrying with me the most consoling proofs of public approbation. I leave every thing in the hands of men so able to take care of them, that if we are destined to meet misfortunes, it will be because no human wisdom could avert them."

And then came the election; but before the issue was certainly known, the closing session of Congress had begun.

As the effects of the embargo began to be felt more seriously, the strength and earnestness of complaints against it rose higher and louder; and the federalists took occasion to note as consequences of it, such lamentable things as "vindictive prosecutions," "the multiplications of spies and informers," "a tyranny of officers, great and small, which would hardly have been endured in Algiers," "smuggling," and the mere mockery of justice, in trials arising out of embargo bonds. At the same time foreign trade began to find its way through the British colonies, and the coasting trade was carried on by means of wagons! And, deprived of occupation, numbers of seamen, native Americans as well as Britons in the American merchant-service, made their way through Canada to England, and to the means of obtaining a livelihood.

Our limits do not admit of details respecting the acts, supplementary, suspensory, and explanatory, by which the embargo was made more rigid, or alleviated, as occasion seemed to require: or respecting the violence of the debates in Congress, and the duels which arose out of expressions which appeared to apply to persons, rather than to principles, or politics. An examination into the particulars,* and the various steps taken by the president and the ruling party, will well repay the student who has the time and the patience to enter fully into the questions at issue.

All the evils produced by the embargo were, of course, aggravated as time wore away, without bringing any change in the policy of the administration. Mr. Tucker, in his remarks on this point, states, that "the inconvenience felt by the people of the United States from their own remedy was extreme, and put their patriotism and firmness to a severe test. Dependent as we were on foreign markets for the sale of our redundant products, now that we were not permitted to export them, they fell to half their wonted price, and even less. To many of the producers they did not repay the cost of production. The supply of foreign merchandise, too, which habit had made necessary, and of which there was no domestic supply, or an insufficient one, being cut off, its price rose proportionally high; and thus the expenses of the agricultural classes increased, in the same proportion that their means of defraying them diminished. It bore still harder on the sailors and ship owners, who were thrown entirely out of employment, and here the pressure was most severely felt in the states that were most addicted to navigation, for while it deprived the agricultural states of foreign merchandise, it deprived the navigating states of the means of making a livelihood. It is true, it operated as a bounty on manufactures, by making them scarcer and dearer; but this at first benefited but a small proportion of the community, both because men cannot suddenly

1808.

* For the debate in the House, during the month of April, on the suspension of the embargo, see Benton's "*Abridgement of the Debates of Congress*," vol. iii., pp. 678–707.

change their habits, and because, for many of the most essential manufactures, we had, as yet, neither the skill nor the materials; and years of privation were to be endured before this could be supplied. It is true also, that the embargo was of great temporary advantage in preserving the vast amount of American property then afloat on the ocean from the licensed freebooters of England and France, until the country could decide on its course of policy and provide for it."

The biographer of the president further points out how the embargo act bore with great severity upon England as well as the United States, and as each country was aware of the suffering and injury of the other, it became in fact, "a trial between the two nations who could suffer longest. In this contest, however, we lay under a disadvantage, which did not seem to be fully appreciated, either by the government or the people; for, in the first place, we deprived Great Britain of the trade of only one nation, while we deprived ourselves of the trade of all; and in the next, in consequence of the trade remaining to Great Britain, she was able to find substitutes for the articles formerly furnished her by the United States, but we deprived ourselves of the means of finding substitutes for theirs. Thus, our adversaries

1808. could procure cotton from Brazil, Egypt and the East Indies; tobacco from South America; naval stores from Sweden; lumber from Nova Scotia; grain from the Baltic, though at a greater cost: but we, exporting nothing, were unable to import the woolens, linens, silks, hardware, and pottery, to which we were accustomed, and which we had not yet learnt to make."

In this way the embargo was permanently injurious to the commerce of the United States; and as trade, when shut out from its accustomed outlets will create new channels for itself, so it happened to a considerable extent in the instance of the West Indies; consequently, as Mr. Tucker concludes, "if the effect of the embargo, as a measure of coercion, or as a means of appealing to the interests of Great Britain, was doubtful, it was clearly the most injurious expedient as a mere question of profit and loss." The merchants, it was urged, were the best judges of the question where their interests were concerned; if they chose to run the risk of capture on the sea, they should not have been cut off from the chances of profitable trade. In fine, all that could be said in defence of the embargo was, that it was better to endure the evils of it than to go to war, for it was hoped that the belligerents would abandon their lawless pretensions; if they did not, war was the final result. Mr. Jefferson's words are to this effect: writing to Levi Lincoln, in March, 1808, he says: "The embargo appears to be approved, even by the federalists of every quarter except yours. The alternative was between that and war, and in fact it is the last card we have to play, short of war. But if peace does not take place in Europe, and if France and England will not consent to withdraw the operation of their decrees and orders from us, when Congress shall meet in December, they will have to consider at what point of time the embargo, continued, becomes a greater evil than war." To the same effect, he wrote to Charles Pinckney; and to Dr. Leib, in the following June.*

The American minister at Paris endeavored, by repeated remonstrances, to effect a change in the unjust course pursued by France in respect to American commerce; but to no purpose. Mr. Pinckney also, at London, proposed to Mr. Canning the rescinding the orders in council, on condition that the embargo should be raised. The British minister rejected the overture, and took occasion in his letters to Mr. Pinckney to indulge in witty sarcasms, not particularly calculated to please or to profit those whom they were intended to reach.

In accordance with a resolution of the preceding session, Congress assembled on the 7th of November. The president's message was sent in on the following day; it is a long and able document, and it is worthy of careful examination, in consequence of its being the last occasion on which Thomas Jefferson was called upon to address the national legislature as the president of the United States. The message is mainly important in respect to the foreign relations of the country, growing out of the injustice and outrage of the belligerents upon neutral commerce, and the operation of the embargo. The president's language is laudatory of the course thus far pursued, and he commends to Congress the question of such further steps as may

1808.

be necessary in the then position of affairs, being confident that "whatever alternative may be chosen, it will be maintained with all the fortitude and patriotism which the crisis ought to inspire." The message also refers to the Chesapeake affair, and to fortifications and gunboats, and administered to the paralyzed commerce of the country the consolation, such as it was, that some of the capital which had been so profitably invested in mercantile ventures was beginning to be applied to internal manufactures and improvements; and that "little doubt remained that the establishments formed and forming, would, under the auspices of cheaper materials and subsistence, the freedom of labor from taxation with us, and of protecting duties and prohibitions, become permanent."

With respect to the Indians, the president stated, that "the public peace had been steadily maintained," and that there were such signs of advancing civilization as that it was already debated amongst the Cherokees, whether or not "to solicit the citizenship of the United States." He stated, that on Congress must rest the securing of a uniform condition of defensive preparation amongst the states; "the interest which they so deeply feel in their own and their country's security will present this as among the most important objects of their deliberation." Of the finances he was able to offer a flourishing account,—$2,300,000 paid out of the principal of the debt, since the last report, and nearly $14,000,000 in the treasury. Respecting which, and also respecting the accumulated surplus, he was in the

* Tucker's "*Life of Jefferson*," vol. ii., p. 268.

habit of looking forward to, he asked,—"Shall it lie unproductive in the public vaults? Shall the revenue be reduced? Or, shall it not rather be appropriated to the improvements of roads, canals, rivers, education, and other great foundations of prosperity and union, under the powers which Congress may already possess, or such amendment of the Constitution, as may be approved by the states? While uncertain of the course of things, the time may be advantageously employed in obtaining the powers necessary for a system of improvement, should that be thought best."

Availing himself of this "last occasion" of addressing the national legislature, after soliciting their indulgence for his errors, and expressing his gratitude for their confidence, he said,—"Looking forward with anxiety to their future destinies, I trust that in their steady character, unshaken by difficulties, in their love of liberty, obedience to law, and support of the public authorities, I see a sure guarantee
1808. of the permanence of our republic; and retiring from the charge of their affairs, I carry with me the consolation of a firm persuasion that Heaven has in store for our beloved country long ages to come of prosperity and happiness."

The election for president and vice-president resulted in large majorities for the republican candidates. Mr. Madison received the entire votes of Vermont, New Jersey, Pennsylvania, Virginia, South Carolina, Georgia, Kentucky, Tennessee, and Ohio; and also thirteen votes from New York, nine from Maryland, and eleven from North Carolina; a hundred and twenty-two in all, out of one hundred and seventy-six. Pinckney received all the votes of New Hampshire, Massachusetts, Rhode Island, Connecticut, and Delaware, with two from Maryland, and three from North Carolina; making a total of forty-seven. Clinton received six from New York; and Monroe wisely did not proceed to the last stage in the contest. James Madison was therefore chosen president. George Clinton was also chosen vice-president again; all the electors of New Jersey, Pennsylvania, Virginia, South Carolina, Georgia, Tennessee, and Kentucky, voting for him; with thirteen from New York, nine from Maryland, and eleven from North Carolina; in all a hundred and thirteen. While for Rufus King, the same who had supported Pinckney voted, forty-seven in all; and Vermont and Ohio gave their nine votes to Langdon; and three of Clinton's supporters for the presidency in New York, voted for Madison as vice-president, and the other three for Monroe; and there was one vote lost by a vacancy amongst the electors of Kentucky.

At this last session of Congress under Thomas Jefferson's administration, the principal interest centred in the debates, reports, and conclusions, concerning the embargo. In substance, this memorable enactment was a failure. Neither belligerent had been influenced by it to a change of policy. Neither "Decrees," nor "Orders," had been repealed. France had made no offer of a sacrifice for America's interests. Great Britain still swayed the sceptre of the seas, invincible. The United States were the poorer by some "fifty millions of exports,"—"the treble of what war would cost us," as Mr. Jefferson himself admitted the night before he vacated his seat in the Capitol. By smuggling, by permits from the governors of the states, by ballast licenses from the president, the embargo was customarily evaded. Safe and prosperous voyages made by the ballast-licensed ships had demonstrated the futility of the great pretext at home, for laying on the embargo. The justly boasted surplus was being wasted by the inevitable defalcation in the revenue. The men of highest mark in the country were opposed to the continuance of it; and in favor of it were seen the party leaders under Jefferson, and the southerners, who approved it because it crippled their "natural enemies," the men of the eastern states. It had inflamed the internal animosities of the Union. It had not won a solitary ally. And it had rendered war with England almost a necessity.

1808.

Towards the close of November, a committee of the House reported on the foreign relations of the Union, and submitted three resolutions for consideration: 1st. That the United States cannot, without a sacrifice of their rights, honor, and independence, submit to the late edicts of England and France. 2d. That it is expedient to prohibit the admission of either the ships or merchandise of those belligerents into the ports of the United States. 3d. That the country ought to be immediately placed in a state of defence.

"At every corner of this great city," exclaimed Mr. Josiah Quincy, in the House, November 28th, in a speech on the first resolution, "we meet some gentlemen of the majority, wringing their hands and exclaiming—'What shall we do? Nothing but embargo will save us. Remove it, and what shall we do?' Sir, it is not for me, an humble and uninfluential individual, at an awful distance from the predominant influences, to suggest plans of government. But to my eye, the path of duty is as distinct as the milky way; all studded with living sapphires; glowing with cumulating light. It is the path of active preparation; of dignified energy. It is the path of 1776. It consists, not in abandoning our rights, but in supporting them, as they exist, and where they exist—on the ocean, as well as on the land. It consists, in taking the nature of things, as the measure of the rights of your citizens; not the orders and decrees of imperious foreigners. Give what protection you can. Take no counsel of fear. Your strength will increase with the trial, and prove greater than you are now aware. But I shall be told, 'this may lead to war.' I ask, 'are we now at peace?' Certainly not, unless retiring from insult be peace; unless shrinking under the lash be peace. The surest way to prevent war is not to fear it. The idea, that nothing on earth is so dreadful as war, is inculcated too studiously among us. Disgrace is worse. Abandonment of essential rights is worse."

1808.

These resolutions were warmly discussed in the House: the first two passed by a large vote, the last unanimously. In the Senate, a motion was made by Mr. Hillhouse to repeal the embargo act, and was ably advocated by the mover and others. It was opposed by Mr. Giles and the republican Senators with much earnestness.

"Mr. President," said Mr. Giles, November 24th, "the eyes of the world are now turned upon us: if we sub-
1808. mit to these indignities and aggressions, Great Britain herself would despise us; she would consider us as an outcast amongst nations; she would not own us for her offspring; France would despise us; all the world would despise us: and what is infinitely worse, we should be compelled to despise ourselves! If we resist, we shall command the respect of our enemies, the sympathies of the world, and the noble approbation of our own consciences. Mr. President, our fate is in our own hands; let us have union, and we have nothing to fear. So highly do I prize union, at this awful moment, that I would prefer any one measure of resistance, with union, to any measure of resistance, with division. Let us then, sir, banish all personal feelings; let us present to our enemies the formidable front of an indissoluble band of brothers: nothing else is necessary to our success. Unequal as the contest may seem, favored as we are, by our situation, and under the blessing of a beneficent Providence, who has never lost sight of these United States in times of difficulty and trial, I have the most perfect confidence, that if we prove true to ourselves, we shall triumph over our enemies."

On the 2d of December, the question was taken on the resolution, and it was lost by a vote of twenty-five against six. In accordance with the third resolution of the House, noted above, $475,000 were appropriated to fortifications, principally at New York; four frigates were ordered to be got in readiness for actual service; nearly four thousand seamen were directed to be enlisted in addition to those already in the service, and additions were also made to the marine corps.

While, however, the Senate voted so strongly against the policy of repealing the embargo act, the greater part even of the friends of the administration had no expectation that it would be continued many months longer. Some thought it ought to be repealed in the spring; some, that it should be prolonged to the 1st of June, and a few, to the 1st of September; but none were desirous of extending it further. Looking forward then to the change of policy, various expedients connected with the repeal were proposed; but they were all postponed on the 10th of February, by a vote of sixty-five to fifty-five. "In the mean while the embargo was pressing with increased severity on every class of the community, whether producers or consumers; and this pressure, joined to the political opposition in the federal party, drove the people of New England, where that party was most numerous, and where the embargo was most felt, to a point of disaffection which had never before been witnessed in the United States. Many, therefore, entertained strong hopes that some course would be taken during 1809.
the present session, by which the industry and enterprise of the country would be again put into activity,

its vessels be once more suffered to venture on the ocean, and perhaps be permitted to arm in their own defence, if not to make reprisals. Indeed there was no one who did not admit that war would be preferable to the continuance of the embargo beyond a time not very distant ; and every day was adding to the number of those who believed that time already arrived."*

It was early in January that an act for enforcing the provisions of the embargo was passed, an act which, as Mr. Tucker says, armed the executive with new powers; and these powers, so much at variance with the spirit of our institutions, and the general lenity of the laws, afforded further materials for exciting popular odium against the administration, which was then charged with being as ambitious of arbitrary power at home, as it was submissive to the will of Napoleon abroad. The administration, continues the president's biographer, "and the majority who supported it, were, before Congress rose, turned from their purpose of trying the embargo a few months longer, from fear of the growing disaffection of the New England states, which they had reason to believe was producing consequences, not only subversive of the authority of the laws, but dangerous to the continuance of the Union. It has appeared by subsequent disclosures, that in the month of February, Mr. John Quincy Adams, who had supported the administration in the embargo and other measures of policy, ever since the affair of the Chesapeake, and who, finding his course was not approved by the legislature of Massachusetts, had resigned his office of Senator, made to the president the following communication;—that from information received by him, and which might be relied on, it was the determination of the ruling party in Massachusetts, and even New England, if the embargo was persisted in, no longer to submit to it, but to separate themselves from the Union, at least until the existing obstacles of foreign commerce were removed; that the plan was already digested, and that such was the pressure of the embargo on the community, that they would be supported by the people. He further said, that a secret agent of Great Britain was then in New England, by whose intrigues every aid would be proffered by that government to carry a project into execution, which would at once render the restrictions on the commerce between the United States and Great Britain nugatory, and all future opposition unavailing.* The danger thus threatening the Union was deemed paramount to all other considerations, and the president, with his cabinet, concluded that it would be better to modify their interdiction of commerce in such a way, that while employment

* Tucker's "*Life of Jefferson*," vol. ii., p. 285.

* In regard to Mr. Adams's accuracy on the point in question, a good deal of doubt has been expressed, and prominent members of the federal party have positively denied that there was ever any intention in New England to attempt the dissolution of the Union. On the contrary, they charge Mr. Adams with having taken the course he did, in order to gain the favor of the democratic party, and they point to his having soon after been sent on a foreign mission as a proof of the correctness of their views respecting him and his motives.

was afforded to American vessels, Great Britain and France should still feel the loss of American commerce."

Acting on this view of the matter, Congress passed a law for repealing the embargo after the 4th of March, as to all nations except France and Great Britain, and interdicting with them all commercial intercourse whatever, whether by exporting or importing, either directly or circuitously. This measure has always since been known under the name of the non-intercourse law. It passed on the 27th of February, by eighty-one votes to forty.

1809.

With the 3d of March, 1809, the administration of Thomas Jefferson reached its close, and the tenth Congress terminated its second session.* Mr. Tucker indulges himself in several eulogistic paragraphs respecting the administration of the third president, its wisdom, its ability, its success, etc., and he quotes in full the address which was presented to Mr. Jefferson by the legislature of Virginia, on the 6th of February, in testimony of their esteem and approbation. A brief extract or two from this address may not be inappropriate in concluding our narrative of Mr. Jefferson's public life.

After recording the "points of his administration, which the historian would not fail to seize, to expand, and to teach posterity to dwell upon with delight," as they believed, the address proceeds:—

"In the principles on which you have administered the government, we see only the continuation and maturity of the same virtues and abilities, which drew upon you in your youth the resentment of Dunmore. From the first brilliant and happy moment of your resistance to foreign tyranny, until the present day, we mark with pleasure and with gratitude the same uniform, consistent character, the same warm and devoted attachment to liberty and the republic, the same Roman love of your country, her rights, her peace, her honor, her prosperity.

"How blessed will be the retirement into which you are about to go! How deservedly blessed will it be! For you carry with you the richest of all rewards, the recollection of a life well spent in the service of your country, and proofs the most decisive, of the love, the gratitude, the veneration, of your countrymen.*

"That your retirement may be as

* For some remarks on Mr. Jefferson's administration, now just at its eventful close, see Appendix at the end of the present chapter. The reader who wishes to look at the third president's character from the point of view of those who do not admire or respect him, may also consult with advantage a caustic review of the life and character of Thomas Jefferson, in the "*New York Review*" for March, 1837, pp. 5–58.

* As an offset to these laudatory expressions, we may quote from the report of a committee of the legislature of Massachusetts, made in January, 1809, in which the state of the country at the time is depicted in the following terms: "Our agriculture is discouraged; the fisheries abandoned; navigation forbidden: our commerce at home restrained, if not annihilated; our commerce abroad cut off; our navy sold, dismantled, or degraded to the service of cutters or gunboats; the revenue extinguished; the cause of justice interrupted; the military power exalted above the civil, and by setting up a standard of political faith, unknown to the Constitution, the nation is weakened by internal animosities and divisions, at the moment when it is unnecessarily and improvidently exposed to war with Great Britain, France, and Spain."

happy as your life has been virtuous and useful; that our youth may see in the blissful close of your days, an additional inducement to form themselves on your model, is the devout and earnest prayer of your fellow-citizens who compose the General Assembly of Virginia."

Our own opinion of Mr. Jefferson's character as a man and as the head of the ruling party in the United States, might be set forth at large, were it at all needful on the present occasion; but, in truth, it is not. If, as we believe, our narrative of his public life and career is just, impartial, candid, and sufficiently full in respect to details, there is plainly little need, at our hands, of a formal delineation of his character and conduct. His acts will justify or condemn him, as they have all along in the judgment of the people; and his acts will prove incontestably, that he was either a high-minded, patriotic statesman and ruler, or an unscrupulous partisan and seeker after popular applause. Let the reader judge for himself, after carefully weighing the facts which are on record, and the principles which the third president avowed in his writings.

Thomas Jefferson must always fill a large space in our country's annals, whether it be for good or for evil. It is the duty of Americans to *study* his life and character, and to note well the effect produced by his opinions and principles upon our countrymen. If he were not the profound statesman and large-hearted patriot which his admirers claimed him to be, he was undoubtedly in possession of vast influence, and wielded it with consummate skill, for eight eventful years. If he were not a mere party leader, as his enemies openly and constantly asserted, it is undeniable that he never lost sight of the interests and the advancement of the party at whose head he was placed. Men have differed, widely differed, men will continue to differ, in their judgments respecting Thomas Jefferson and his claims to honor and respect. Let the youthful student weigh well what we have here laid before him, and what he will find in the authorities referred to in the course of our narrative; and let him judge soberly and fearlessly, as is the birthright no less than the bounden duty of every American.

APPENDIX TO CHAPTER V.

JOHN QUINCY ADAMS'S REMARKS ON JEFFERSON'S ADMINISTRATION.

IN the first wars of the French Revolution, Great Britain had begun by straining the claim of belligerent, as against neutral rights, beyond all the theories of international jurisprudence, and even beyond her own ordinary practice. There is in all war a conflict between the belligerent and the neutral right, which can in its nature be settled only by convention. And in addition to all the ordinary asperities of dissension between the nation at war and the nation at peace, she had asserted a right of man-stealing from the vessels of the United States. The claim of right was to take by force all sea-faring men, her own subjects, wherever they were found by her naval officers, to serve their king in his wars. And under color of this tyrant's right, her naval officers, down to the most beardless midshipman, actually took from the American merchant vessels which they visited, any seaman whom they chose to take for a British subject. After the treaty of November, 1794, she had relaxed all her pretensions against the neutral rights, and had gradually abandoned the practice of impressment till she was on the point of renouncing it by a formal treaty stipulation.

At the renewal of the war, after the peace of Amiens, it was at first urged with much respect for the rights of neutrality, but the practice of impressment was soon renewed with aggravated severity, and the commerce of neutral nations with the colonies of the adverse belligerent was wholly interdicted on the pretence of justification, because it had been forbidden by the enemy herself in the time of peace. This pretension had been first raised by Great Britain in the seven years' war, but she had been overawed by the armed neutrality from maintaining it in the war of the American Revolution. In the midst of this war with Napoleon, she suddenly reasserted the principle, and by a secret order in council, swept the ocean of nearly the whole mass of neutral commerce. Her war with France spread itself all over Europe, successively involving Spain, Italy, the Netherlands, Prussia, Austria, Russia, Denmark and Sweden. Not a single neutral power remained in Europe—and Great Britain, after annihilating at Trafalgar, the united naval power of France and Spain, ruling thenceforth with undisputed dominion upon the ocean, conceived the project of engrossing even the commerce with her enemy by intercepting all neutral navigation. These measures were met by corresponding acts of violence, and sophistical principles of national law, promulgated by Napoleon, rising to the summit of his greatness, and preparing his downfall by the abuse of his elevation.

Through this fiery ordeal the administration of Mr. Jefferson was to pass, and the severest of its tests were to be applied to Mr. Madison. His correspondence with the ministers of Great Britain, France, and Spain, and with the ministers of the United States to those nations during the remainder of Mr. Jefferson's administration, constitute the most important and most valuable materials of its history. His examination of the British doctrines relating to neutral trade, will hereafter be considered a standard treatise on the law of nations; not inferior to the works of any writer upon those subjects since the days of Grotius, and every way worthy of the author of Publius and Helvidius. There is indeed, in all the diplomatic papers of American statesmen, justly celebrated as they have been, nothing superior to this dissertation, which was not strictly official. It was composed amid the duties of the department of state, never more arduous than at that time—in the summer of 1806. It was published inofficially, and a copy of it was laid on the table of each member of Congress at the commencement of the session in December, 1806.

The controversies of conflicting neutral and belligerent rights, continued through the whole of Mr. Jefferson's administration, during the latter part of which they were verging rapidly to war. He had carried the policy of peace perhaps to an extreme. His system of defence by commercial restrictions, dry-docks, gun-boats, and embargoes, was stretched to its last hair's breadth of endurance. Far be it from me, my fellow-citizens, to speak of this system or its motives with disrespect. If there be a duty, binding in chains more adamantine than all the rest the conscience of a chief magistrate of this Union, it is that of preserving peace with all mankind—peace with the other nations of the earth—peace among the several states of this Union—peace in the hearts and temper of our own people. Yet must a president of the United States never cease to feel that his charge is to maintain the rights, the interests, and the honor, no less than the peace of his country—nor will he be permitted to forget that peace must be the offspring of two concurring wills; that to seek peace is not always to ensure it. He must remember too, that a reliance upon the operation of measures, from their effect on the *interests*, however clear and unequivocal, of nations, cannot be safe against a counter current of their passions. That nations, like individuals, sacrifice their peace to their pride, to their hatred, to their envy, to their jealousy, and even to the craft, which the cunning of hackneyed politicians not unfrequently mistakes for policy. That nations, like individuals, have sometimes the misfortune of losing their senses, and that lunatic communities, which cannot be confined in hospitals, must be resisted in arms, as a single maniac is sometimes restored to reason by the scourge. That national madness is infectious, and that a paroxysm of it in one people, especially when generated by the Furies that preside over war, produces a counter paroxysm in the adverse party. Such is the melancholy condition, as yet, of associated man. And while in the wise but mysterious dispensations of an overruling Providence, man shall so continue, the peace of every nation must depend not alone upon its own will, but upon that concurrently with the will of all others.

And such was the condition of the two mightiest nations of the earth during the administration of Mr. Jefferson. Frantic; in fits of mutual hatred, envy, and jealousy against each other; meditating mutual invasion and conquest; and forcing the other nations of the four quarters of the globe to the alternative of joining them as allies or encountering them as foes. Mr. Jefferson met them with moral philosophy and commercial restrictions, with dry-docks and gun-boats—with non-intercourses, and embargoes, till *the American nation were told that they could not be kicked into a war*, and till they were taunted by a British statesman in the imperial parliament of England, with their five fir frigates and their striped bunting.

Mr. Jefferson pursued his policy of peace till it brought the nation to the borders of internal war. An embargo of fourteen months' duration was at last reluctantly abandoned by him, when it had ceased to be obeyed by the people, and state courts were ready to pronounce it unconstitutional. A non-intercourse was then substituted in its place, and the helm of state passed from the hands of Mr. Jefferson to those of Mr. Madison, precisely at the moment of this perturbation of earth and sea threatened with war from abroad and at home, but with the principle definitely settled, that in our in tercoursewith foreign nations, reason, justice, and commercial restrictions require live-oak hearts and iron or brazen mouths to speak, that they may be distinctly heard, or attentively listened to, by the distant ears of foreigners, whether French or British, monarchial or republican.

James Madison

From the original Portrait by Gilbert Stuart

Martin, Johnson & Co. Publishers, N.Y.

CHAPTER VI.

1809–1811.

THE TWO YEARS PRECEDING THE WAR.

The Inauguration of James Madison — Inaugural Address of the fourth president — The new cabinet — Position of affairs on Madison's accession — Conduct of England and France — Mr. Erskine's negotiations and their results — Opening of Congress — The president's message — The British government refuses to sanction Mr. Erskine's acts — Irritation and excitement — Views of the federalists — Mr. Jackson appointed minister from England — His course — Congress meet — President's message quoted — Resolutions of the Senate — Acts of the House — The manufactures of the Union — Report on conduct of General Wilkinson — The Rambouillet decree — Napoleon's announcement of the revocation of his decrees — British government refuse to rescind the orders in council — Intercourse with France renewed — Occupancy of West Florida — Congress meet in December, 1810 — The president's message — Debate in the House on the petition of the territory of Orleans to be admitted as a state — Quincy's speech — Question as to the renewal of the charter of the Bank of the United States — Debate on the subject — The result — Debate on the non-intercourse act — Feeling in the navy towards England — Affair of the President and the Little Belt — The United States and two British ships — Mr. Foster appointed minister from England — His correspondence with the secretary of state—Meeting of Congress looked for with anxiety — Troubles in the cabinet — Monroe appointed secretary of state — The Indians in the north-west — Tecumseh's plans — General Harrison's movements — The battle of Tippecanoe — Severe and bloody contest — Its result.

ON the 4th day of March, 1809, a goodly company assembled in the capitol at Washington, to witness the inauguration of James Madison as fourth president of the United States. Mr. Jefferson was there, as were also many members of Congress, the foreign ministers, and a crowd of citizens. Mr. Madison was clad in a plain suit of black, entirely of American manufacture, and modestly, yet in a dignified manner, went through the important ceremonies of the day. His inaugural address, though brief, was not deficient in energy and ability; and it met with general approbation. As on previous occasions, we give the address in full.

"*Friends and Fellow-Citizens:*

"Unwilling to depart from examples of the most revered authority, I avail myself of the occasion now presented, to express the profound impression made on me by the call of my country to the station, to the duties of which I am about to pledge myself by the most solemn of sanctions. So distinguished a mark of confidence, proceeding from the deliberate and tranquil suffrage of a free and virtuous nation, would, under any circumstances, have commanded my gratitude and devotion, as well as filled me with an awful sense of the trust to be assumed. Under the various circumstances which give peculiar solemnity to the existing period, I feel, that both the honor and the responsibility allotted to me are inexpressibly enhanced.

"The present situation of the world

is indeed without a parallel; and that of our country full of difficulties.
1809.
The pressure of these too, is the more severely felt, because they have fallen upon us at a moment, when national prosperity being at a height not before attained, the contrast resulting from this change has been rendered the more striking. Under the benign influence of our republican institutions, and the maintenance of peace with all nations, whilst so many of them were engaged in bloody and wasteful wars, the fruits of a just policy were enjoyed in an unrivalled growth of our faculties and resources. Proofs of this were seen in the improvements of agriculture; in the successful enterprises of commerce; in the progress of manufactures and useful arts; in the increase of the public revenue, and the use made of it in reducing the public debt; and in the valuable works and establishments everywhere multiplying over the face of our land.

"It is a precious reflection, that the transition from this prosperous condition of our country, to the scene which has for some time been distressing us, is not chargeable on any unwarrantable views, nor, as I trust, on any involuntary errors in the public councils. Indulging no passions which trespass on the rights or the repose of other nations, it has been the true glory of the United States to cultivate peace, by observing justice, and to entitle themselves to the respect of the nations at war, by fulfilling their neutral obligations with the most scrupulous impartiality. If there be candor in the world, the truth of these assertions will not be questioned. Posterity at least will do justice to them.

"This unexceptionable course could not avail against the injustice and violence of the belligerent powers. In their rage against each other, or impelled by more direct motives, principles of retaliation have been introduced, equally contrary to universal reason and acknowledged law. How long their arbitrary edicts will be continued, in spite of the demonstrations, that not even a pretext for them has been given by the United States,
and of the fair and liberal at- 1809.
tempts to induce a revocation of them, cannot be anticipated. Assuring myself, that under every vicissitude, the determined spirit and united councils of the nation will be safeguards to its honor, and its essential interests, I repair to the post assigned me, with no other discouragement than what springs from my own inadequacy to its high duties. If I do not sink under the weight of this deep conviction, it is because I find some support in a consciousness of the purposes, and a confidence in the principles which I bring with me into this arduous service.

"To cherish peace and friendly intercourse with all nations having correspondent dispositions; to maintain sincere neutrality towards belligerent nations; to prefer, in all cases, amicable discussions and reasonable accommodation of differences, to a decision of them by an appeal to arms; to exclude foreign intrigues and foreign partialities, so degrading to all countries and so baneful to free ones: to foster a spirit of independence, too just to invade the rights of others, too proud to surrender our own, too liberal to indulge unworthy prejudices ourselves, and too elevated not to look down upon them in others; to hold the union of the states as the basis of their peace and happiness; to support the Constitution, which is the cement of the Union, as well in its limitations as in its authorities; to respect the rights and authorities reserved to the states and to the people, as equally incorporated with and essential to the success of the general system; to avoid the slightest interference with the rights of conscience or the functions of religion, so wisely exempted from civil jurisdiction; to preserve, in their full energy, the other salutary provisions in behalf of private and personal rights, and of the freedom of the press; to observe economy in public expenditures; to liberate the public resources by an honorable discharge of the public debts; to keep within the requisite limits a standing military force, always remembering, that an armed and trained militia is the firmest bulwark of republics, that without standing armies their liberty can never be in danger, nor, with large ones, safe; to promote, by authorized means, improvements friendly to agriculture, to manufactures, and to external as well as internal commerce; to favor, in like manner, the advancement of science and the diffusion of information, as the best aliment to true liberty; to carry on the benevolent plans which have been so meritoriously applied to the conversion of our aboriginal neighbors, from the degradation and wretchedness of savage life, to a participation of the improvements of which the human mind and manners are susceptible in a civilized state:—as far as sentiments and intentions such as these can aid the fulfilment of my duty, they will be a resource which cannot fail me.

"It is my good fortune, moreover, to have the path in which I am to tread, lighted by examples of illustrious services, successfully rendered in the most trying difficulties, by those who have marched before me. Of those of my immediate predecessor, it might least become me here to speak; I may, however, be pardoned for not suppressing the sympathy with which my heart is full, in the rich reward he enjoys in the benedictions of a beloved country, gratefully bestowed for exalted talents, zealously devoted, through a long career, to the advancement **1809.**
of its highest interests and happiness. But the source to which I look for the aids, which alone can supply my deficiencies, is in the well-tried intelligence and virtue of my fellow-citizens, and in the counsels of those representing them in the other departments associated in the care of the national interests. In these my confidence will, under every difficulty, be placed, next to that which we have all been encouraged to feel in the guardianship and guidance of that Almighty Being, whose power regulates the destiny of nations, whose blessings have been so conspicuously dispensed to this rising republic, and to whom we are bound to address our devout gratitude for the past, as well as our fervent supplications and best hopes for the future."

The oath of office was then administered to James Madison by Chief Justice Marshall, and the fourth president of the United States, warmly congratulated by a large circle of friends and political supporters, entered upon his responsible duties, not without hope that his administration might be prosperous and conducive to the best interests of the people of the United States.*

Immediately after his inauguration, the new president organized his cabinet. Robert Smith of Maryland, who had been secretary of the navy, was placed at the head of the department of state. Albert Gallatin retained the office of secretary of the treasury, and Cæsar A. Rodney that of attorney-general. William Eustis, of Massachusetts, was made secretary of war; Henry Dearborn being transferred to the collectorship of the port of Boston. Paul Hamilton, who had been governor of South Carolina, was selected as secretary of the navy, in place of Robert Smith. Gideon Granger was continued as postmaster-general, although, as the reader will remember, this officer formed no part of the cabinet at this date.

The accession of James Madison to power took place at a critical period in our country's history. The progress of events had been such under Jefferson's administration, that war with Great Britain seemed to be inevitable. Not only France, but the great rival of France, entertained very inadequate views of the spirit and energy of the people of the United States, if once thoroughly roused. Washington had deemed it more prudent to put up with some injustice and much unfairness, in the then condition of affairs; and Jefferson, who was timid by nature, and well aware that he was not at all adapted for the executive chair in time of war, had allowed matters to arrive at such a pass, that it began to be thought that Americans had no spirit whatever, were mere mercenary traffickers, and would submit to any indignities, sooner than enter upon measures of self-defence at the expense of their trade and money-getting opportunities. England had never been satisfied with the result of the Revolutionary War. She had ever since acted in an overbearing, offensive, and unhandsome style towards the growing republic of the west; and she had put forth claims and assertions, which it was impossible for any free people to submit to and retain its self-respect. And France, under the grasping ambition of Napoleon, wished to treat the United States as a sort of ward of hers, as one bound to be subservient, and deeply impressed with sentiments of gratitude and admiration for past favors and present smiles of approval.

1809.

The country, it is true, was in no fitting condition to go to war. Mr. Jefferson's policy had nearly destroyed the navy, and preparations for defence against invasion were scandalously insufficient. War would be carried on

* Sullivan speaks of Madison as "a man of small stature and grave appearance," and says: "he had a calm expression, a penetrating blue eye, and looked like a thinking man. He was dressed in black; bald on the top of his head; powdered; of rather protuberant person in front; small lower limbs; slow and grave in speech."

under every disadvantage, as respected finances, and the means of efficiently repelling attack. Yet, despite all these and kindred considerations, the people of the United States, as a people, were not at all unwilling then, any more than they have ever been since, to resort to arms in defence of their rights. The insolent assumptions of both England and France were borne with for a longer time than was, perhaps, called for; but when it began to be plainly seen, that these assumptions would not be removed without resort to battle, Americans were not long in letting it be understood, that they were not unready for the fight. It was impossible, not to say absurd, to suppose that this great nation of ours could subsist in a species of vassalage to England or France; and if neither of these powers could be induced to do us justice by peaceable means, why then we must assert our rights, and maintain our rights, by force of arms. There are crises in the history of nations, when there is no help for it; they must fight, or tamely submit to whatever superior force and haughty superciliousness may choose to prescribe. Such a crisis was fast approaching, when James Madison assumed the reins of government; and though war did not break out immediately, it was becoming evident to many, that war must come before long. We shall endeavor to narrate succinctly the several steps which led to the second war with Great Britain, from a careful consideration of which the reader will be able to judge for himself of the merits of the question, at one time hotly disputed, viz., respecting the necessity, the justice, and the policy of this war.

Congress, it will be remembered, just before its adjournment, (see p. 109,) determined upon the measure of refusing all commercial intercourse with both Great Britain and France. At the same time, it was declared, "that the president of the United States should be authorized, in case either France or Great Britain should so revoke or modify her edicts, as that they should cease to violate the neutral commerce of the United States, to declare the same by proclamation, after which the trade of the United States might be renewed with the government so doing."

1809.

Mr. David M. Erskine was the British minister at Washington at this date; and negotiations were carried on with great activity with a view (apparently) to the arrangement of the difficulties which had arisen between the two governments. Erskine, though not a very able diplomatist, was, nevertheless, sincerely desirous of effecting an accommodation; and he had received such assurances from Messrs. Smith, Gallatin, and Madison himself, before his inauguration as president, that he fully expected to be successful. In private conversations, we are told, Mr. Gallatin had even contrasted the dispositions of the retiring president and his successor; showing, that whilst the one had a leaning in favor of France the other was most inclined to the alliance of Great Britain. And the ambassador had, along with Gallatin, concerted some general scheme by which he persuaded himself all the trouble and suspicion pressing now so heavily on both countries would be removed.

On the 17th of April, Mr. Erskine addressed a letter to the secretary of state, in which he announced, that he had received instructions from Mr. Canning on the subjects then under discussion between the two nations. Considerable latitude was allowed to Erskine, and more than one course was pointed out to the United States, as satisfactory to the British government. But certain conditions were imperatively required, which it was supposed were due to the honor of Britain, without infringing upon that justly claimed by America.

Generally, the proposals were; ships of war of both belligerents to be equally excluded from the American waters; disavowal of the orders issued by Admiral Berkeley; (but no other mark of displeasure than the recall to be asked;) the restoration of the men taken from the Chesapeake, and also, a proper provision for the families left by the men killed on board her, by the attack of the Leopard; disavowal by the American government of the purpose to infringe the British rights, na-
1809. tional or personal, throughout the whole of that affair; deserters, who were British-born, to be surrendered when claimed; the recall of the "orders in council," if the retaliatory acts of the United States government were rescinded in favor of Great Britain, but not in favor of France; if the colonial trade which was prohibited in time of peace, were not attempted in war time; and if Britain might enforce these conditions, when violated, in the usual way.

The result of the interviews and correspondence between Mr. Erskine and the secretary of state, appeared in the form of the adoption of a suggestion made by the British government, to the effect, that, "a proclamation for the renewal of the intercourse with Great Britain" should be issued by the president, his majesty being "willing to withdraw his orders in council,"—and also purposing to send to the United States, "an envoy extraordinary, invested with full powers to conclude a treaty on all the points of the relations between the two countries." On the 19th of April, accordingly,—so rapidly was the negotiation conducted—the proclamation appeared, announcing the intended withdrawal of the offensive "orders," on the 10th of the following June, and the renewal of the trade with Great Britain, on the same day.

The news of this arrangement, as we may well believe, was received throughout the Union with the highest degree of gratification; and the general exultation furnished decisive evidence of the strong desire of all classes of persons to be at peace with Great Britain. Fresh activity was roused at once, and American vessels, in unusually large numbers, gladly ventured forth to avail themselves of renewed commercial intercourse with England.

The eleventh Congress, which had been summoned for a special session, in consequence of the critical position of the foreign relations of the country, assembled on the 22d of May.
The federal strength was a **1809.**
little increased by the late elections; yet the republicans found no difficulty

in placing Varnum in the speaker's chair.

Mr. Madison sent in his message the next day, and took occasion, at the very opening of it, "to communicate the commencement of a favorable change" in the foreign relations of the United States. Having mentioned the negotiations carried on with Mr. Erskine, the president further remarked: "While I take pleasure in doing justice to the councils of his Britannic Majesty, which, no longer adhering to the policy which made an abandonment by France of her decrees a prerequisite to a revocation of the British orders, have substituted the amicable course which has issued thus happily; I cannot do less than refer to the proposal heretofore made on the part of the United States, embracing a restoration of the suspended commerce, as a proof of the spirit of accommodation, which has at no time been intermitted, and to the result which now calls for our congratulations, as corroborating the principles by which the public councils have been guided, during a period of the most trying embarrassments. The discontinuance of the British orders, as they respect the United States, having been thus arranged, a communication of the event has been forwarded in one of our public vessels, to our minister-plenipotentiary at Paris, with instructions to avail himself of the important addition thereby made to the considerations which press on the justice of the French government a revocation of its decrees, or such a modification of them as that they shall cease to violate the neutral commerce of the United States. The revision of our commercial laws, proper to adapt them to the arrangement which has taken place with Great Britain, will doubtless engage the early attention of Congress."

The president also informed Congress that, under the brightening prospect of affairs, he had reduced the gunboat armament, except at New Orleans, to the condition it was to be in during peace, and had discharged the militia; and he suggested the propriety of modifying the laws respecting the army and navy establishments. The fortification of the sea-coast was in progress, he said, but more money was wanted to accomplish it. The protection and encouragement of "the several branches of manufacture which had been recently instituted or extended by the laudable exertions of our citizens," was recommended. It was a matter of just gratulation that "the whole of the eight per cent. stock remaining due by the United States," had been "reimbursed," and that above $9,500,000 had been in the treasury on the first of the preceding month. The falling off of the revenue from "the suspension of exports, and the consequent decrease of importations," was gently touched upon, and a hopeful anticipation of the following year indulged in. Nothing but "matters particularly urgent" were spoken of, and both "fidelity and alacrity" in co-operating with the Houses "for the welfare and happiness of our country" pledged to them.

No material alterations were made in the laws, nor any measures of particular importance adopted, during this extraordinary session, which lasted only five weeks, and was closed on the 20th of June. John Randolph and the section of the party which agreed with him, manifested considerable discontent, and opposed the policy of the administration in various ways; but the general expectation of returning peace and prosperity seemed, on the whole, to have produced a soothing effect upon the deliberations and action of Congress.

The British government was not at all pleased with the conduct of its minister at Washington, and peremptorily refused to carry into effect the arrangement agreed upon by Mr. Erskine and the secretary of state. It was charged upon Mr. Erskine, that he had exceeded his instructions, and had done so knowingly, and in contravention of the policy of the British government. The news of this unlooked for result reached America soon after the adjournment of Congress, and Mr. Erskine was compelled to discharge the unpleasant duty of announcing that his government did not approve of his conduct in the recent negotiations. The president thereupon had no alternative. He issued another proclamation, August 10th, declaring the act of non-intercourse to be revived and in full effect. Mr. Erskine soon after returned to England.

It is hardly possible to imagine the irritating effect upon the community produced by this sudden dashing of the hopes and expectations of commercial advantages. "Free trade and sailor's rights!" was an exclamation heard on every hand; the impressment of our seamen, and the violations of our flag, were discussed and denounced vehemently at public gatherings; and while the aged sires gave utterance to their indignant sense of wrong and outrage, the younger men stood by in silence, their eyes flashing with responsive fire, and their hearts glowing with manly patriotism. Had the president then come forward boldly, and put the contest with Great Britain to the issue of the sword, there can be no doubt that the war would have met with popular favor and support. But Mr. Madison was too cautious and peace-loving, to hasten matters and precipitate the crisis which was evidently not far distant; and whatever judgment may be pronounced upon his policy, it is but right and just to give the due meed of praise to the purity of his motives.

The federalists, who had rejoiced in the prospects of renewed intercourse with England, and had boasted of the evidently friendly dispositions of that country towards the United States, were greatly vexed at this sudden change in international relations; and they ventured to charge upon the administration insincerity, and a determination not to adjust the difficulties between the two nations. Mr. Dwight expresses the federalist view very strongly: "Mr. Madison had just entered upon the office of president of the United States. Mr. Jefferson had left the government surrounded with difficulties and embarrassments. The foreign commerce of the country, under the system of embargo and non-intercourse, was destroyed, and all the various branches of domestic industry — agricultural, mercantile, and mechanical —were in a state of deep depression

1809.

or stagnation; and the community were becoming very uneasy under privations, which were not only unnecessary, but extremely injurious and oppressive. Under such circumstances, it was a stroke of good policy in him, at his entrance upon the duties of chief magistrate, to excite popular feeling in favor of his administration, and nothing would be more likely to produce such an effect, than the adoption of measures which would relieve the nation from the multiplied evils of the restrictive policy. And it required no extraordinary degree of foresight to discern, that if such an arrangement as was contemplated with Mr. Erskine should be accomplished, it would be cordially welcomed throughout the country, and render the new chief magistrate universally popular. At the same time, if the arrangement should be rejected by the British government, whatever the cause for refusing to ratify it might be, it could hardly fail to raise a spirit of resentment in the United States, of a proportionate extent with the gratification which the adjustment had excited."* It is, perhaps, hardly necessary to say, that the republicans scouted this charge as both unjust and without any solid foundation. At the same time, a number of the supporters of the administration held the view, that the policy of the executive was too lukewarm and too conciliatory towards England, and, as we have said above, war at that date would have met with general approbation.

Early in October, Mr. Jackson arrived in the United States as successor to Mr. Erskine. He was a diplomatist of some standing, and had served recently in the mission at Denmark, the result of which had been the seizure of its entire fleet by Great Britain, (September, 1807;) and he appeared to have come to America with rather exaggerated notions of his own importance, and with a disposition to act superciliously towards the government. At first, there were several personal interviews between Mr. Jackson and Mr. Smith, the secretary of state; but the latter soon afterwards sent the British envoy word, that all "further discussions" were to be in "the written form." Mr. Jackson protested against this course of procedure, and it speedily became evident, from the tone and temper of the correspondence, that no favorable result was to be expected. Both sides were vexed and disappointed; and when Mr. Jackson insinuated, that there was a sort of collusion between the American government and Mr. Erskine, it was determined at once that no further intercourse could be held with a minister who had thus insulted the executive of the United States. An account of Mr. Jackson's course was transmitted to the British government, and not long after he was recalled; though it was evident that his conduct was not disapproved at home.

1809.

Our limits do not admit of dwelling upon the aggravation of political excitement, the criminations and recriminations, the personal affronts offered to Mr. Jackson, the unwarrantable procedure on his part in addressing a cir-

* "*History of the Hartford Convention,*" pp. 109, 110.

cular letter to the British consuls in the United States, vindicating his course in the recent negotiation; they are well worthy the student's consideration, not so much for their intrinsic importance, as because of their connection with the progress of the disputes with England which resulted in the war of 1812.

On the 29th of November, a week earlier than usual, Congress assembled according to adjournment. The next day the president sent in his message, which is worth noticing, as it exhibits the great change which a few months had brought about in the condition and prospects of the country. Having mentioned the failure of the negotiation with Mr. Erskine, and the course pursued by his successor, the president went on to say: "The correspondence between the department of state and this minister will show, how unessentially the features presented in

1809.

its commencement have been varied in its progress. It will show also, that, forgetting the respect due to all governments, he did not refrain from imputations on this, which required that no further communications should be received from him. And it would indicate a want of confidence, due to a government which so well understands and exacts what it becomes foreign ministers to show it, not to infer that the misconduct of its own representative will be viewed in the same light in which it has been regarded here."

"With France, the other belligerent," continued Mr. Madison, "whose trespasses on our commercial rights have long been the subject of our just remonstrances, the posture of our relations does not correspond with the measures taken on the part of the United States, to effect a favorable change." And again;—"By some of the other belligerents, although professing just and amicable dispositions, injuries materially affecting our commerce have not been duly controlled or repressed. In these cases, the interpositions deemed proper on our part have not been omitted. But it well deserves the consideration of the legislature, how far both the safety and the honor of the American flag may be consulted, by adequate provisions against that collusive prostitution of it by individuals, unworthy of the American name, which has so much favored the real or pretended suspicions, under which the honest commerce of their fellow-citizens has suffered."

The president also called the attention of Congress to the state of the national defences; recommended the "giving to our militia, the great bulwark of our security, and resource of our power, an organization the best adapted to eventual situations, for which the United States ought to be prepared;" assured the House that no loan had been found necessary, but that a deficiency in the revenue for the ensuing year was to be expected; and concluded his message with words of encouragement and congratulation: "In the midst of the wrongs and vexations experienced from external causes, there is much room for congratulation on the prosperity and happiness flowing from our situation at home. The blessing of health has never been more universal. The fruits of the seasons, though in particular articles and districts short of their usual redundancy, are more than sufficient for our wants and our comforts. The face of our country everywhere presents the evidence of laudable enterprise, of extensive capital, and of durable improvement. In a cultivation of the materials, and the extension of useful manufactures, more especially in the general application of household fabrics, we behold a rapid diminution of our dependence on foreign supplies. Nor is it unworthy of reflection, that this revolution in our pursuits and habits is in no slight degree a consequence of the impolitic and arbitrary edicts, by which the contending nations, in endeavoring, each of them, to obstruct our trade with the other, have so far abridged our means of procuring the productions and manufactures of which our own are now taking the place. Recollecting always, that for every advantage which may contribute to distinguish our lot from that to which others are doomed by the unhappy spirit of the times, we are indebted to that Divine Providence whose goodness has been so remarkably extended to this rising nation, it becomes us to cherish a devout gratitude, and to implore from the same Omnipotent source, a blessing on the consultations and measures about to be undertaken for the welfare of our beloved country."

In the Senate, a series of resolutions offered by Mr. Giles were passed with much unanimity, and the course of the administration in respect to the British negotiation, was approved in strong terms. The House took up the question, and after sharp debate, continued for more than three weeks, agreed to the resolutions by a vote of seventy-two to forty-one. The offending British envoy, as we have said, was soon after recalled, but his conduct met with no censure at home, and no apology was offered to the American government.

Mr. Macon, in behalf of the committee of foreign relations, reported a bill which prohibited all British and French vessels from entering any port of the United States, and the importation of goods from either country, unless brought directly from England or France; and which also provided for the discontinuance of these prohibitions whenever those nations ceased to violate neutral commerce. The Senate disagreed to this bill when it was sent up to that body by the House, and as neither branch was willing to give way, the bill was lost. Subsequently, the Senate concurred with the House in providing that, in case either Great Britain or France should, before the 3d of March, 1811, revoke its edicts in violation of the rights of neutrals, the president should, by proclamation, declare the facts; and if the other nation did not, within three months thereafter, pursue a like course, the act interdicting commercial intercourse was to be revived against such nation.

Few acts of general importance were passed. The law for detaching a hundred thousand men from the militia was continued; and there were acts passed for taking the third census; and for the creation of a loan for the payment of the public debt. Mr. Randolph proved himself very active in examining into financial and economical questions; and an attempt was made to fasten upon Mr. Gallatin, the secretary of the treasury, charges of corruption in the department over which he presided with signal ability. Towards the close of the session, Mr. Gallatin, under 1810. instructions from the House, presented a detailed report of the extent and condition of the domestic manufactures of the United States.*

We may mention in this connection, as of general interest, that the total value of the manufactures of the Union was estimated at $127,700,000. Nearly $39,500,000 of this sum consisted of textile goods, of cotton, silk, wool, flax, and hemp. Manufactures of hides and skins were valued at nearly $18,000,000; distilled and fermented liquors of all kinds, at above $16,500,000; manufactures of iron, at above $14,250,000; with above $6,000,000 worth of instruments and machinery. The articles manufactured from raw materials produced in the country, were in excess of the home demand, and were exported to a small amount yearly; as were one or two articles, such as cards for dressing wool and cotton, and cut-nails, which were made by means of machines invented by Americans. In another large class of manufactures, such as textile goods, hats, ropes, ironware, glass, liquors fermented and distilled, etc., the home supply was gradually approximating the amount of the demand, and the quantity required by importation was continually decreasing. This was especially the case with cotton, linen, and woolen goods, which had been much more attended to since the European war had enhanced both the prices, and the trouble of procuring them from Great Britain and France.

Of the varied proposals, arising from the discussion on the report presented by Mr. Gallatin, no one was adopted; the opposing interests of the different parts of the Union insuring the rejection of some, whilst, in respect of others, no practical scheme, suited to the circumstances of the country, could be devised. A plan respecting the Bank of the United States, whose charter was about to expire, was partially debated, and then postponed to the succeeding session of Congress. On the last day of the session, the select committee reported respecting the conduct of General Wilkinson in connection with the schemes of Aaron Burr and the Spanish possessions in the south. The subject was post- 1810. poned until the next session; and on the 1st of May, after sitting more than five months, and accomplishing almost nothing towards sustaining the honor and the rights of the nation, Congress adjourned.

Napoleon had resented the non-intercourse act of March, 1809, and his reply to the measures of Congress, and the representations addressed to him through General Armstrong, was a new decree, dated at Rambouillet, on the 23d of March, 1810, aimed especially at American commerce. Nearly a hundred and fifty vessels, belonging to citizens of the United States, which had

* For Henry Clay's active and zealous efforts in behalf of American industry, and his labors towards establishing "the American System," as it is called, we must refer to his biography, where he receives the due meed of praise.

been captured by French ships, and were waiting trial, were condemned at one swoop, and the proceeds of the sale of them ordered to be placed to a particular account in the imperial treasury. And at the same time every American vessel entering any port in the possession of France, was declared confiscated.

After this outrage, which was taken very meekly by the American government, Napoleon thought it better not to push matters in a wrong direction; and so, skilfully availing himself of the terms of the conditions on which the non-intercourse act was suspended, he announced to the government of the United States, early in August, the recall of the "decrees" of Berlin and Milan, on the 1st of November following, provided that the British "orders in council" should also be revoked, or the United States should "cause their rights to be respected by the English." His minister, the Duke de Cadore, in his communication to General Armstrong, also indulged himself in language which it is hard to tell whether it is more ridiculous or insolent. "It is," he said, "with the most particular satisfaction, sir, that I make known to you this determination of the emperor. His majesty loves the Americans. Their prosperity and their commerce are within the scope of his policy. The independence of America is one of the principal titles of glory to France. Since that epoch, the emperor is pleased in aggrandizing the United States; and under all circumstances, that which can contribute to the independence, to the prosperity, and the liberty of the Americans, the emperor will consider as conformable with the interests of his empire."

1810.

Mr. Pinkney, immediately on being informed of the declared revocation of the Berlin and Milan decrees, endeavored to induce the British government, to follow the example of France. But, influenced by pique as much as by principle, it refused to accept any thing short of an unconditional and immediate revocation of those "decrees." In vain did Mr. Pinkney press the subject, and offer full proof of his assertions: reply was evaded; and the American minister, after long and fruitless efforts, deemed it incumbent on him to put an end to his mission. He accordingly had his audience of leave on the 28th of February, 1811, and soon after returned to the United States.

The president, confiding in Napoleon's assurance on the subject of the "decrees," issued, on the 2d of November, a proclamation, declaring that intercourse with France was thenceforth renewed; and on the 10th, Great Britain, still holding out in her refusal to rescind the orders in council, the president issued another proclamation interdicting all commercial intercourse with England. We are sorry to say, that subsequent events served to prove that Napoleon had not acted ingenuously in this matter; and early in the following year, he declared that the decrees of Berlin and Milan were the fundamental laws of the empire. Official notice was also given, that no remuneration or redress was to be expected for the extensive plundering of American ships by French armed vessels.

A new element, meanwhile, was added to the present perplexed condition of affairs, by the president's authorizing Governor Claiborne 1810. to take possession of the Baton Rouge District, and to annex it to the Territory of Orleans. This was done in consequence of the inhabitants of West Florida having, in September, declared themselves independent of Spain, and proposed to be annexed to the United States. The government preferred the course which was adopted, leaving the title to be settled by negotiation. It can be no matter of surprise, that England, now the ally of Spain against France, took this procedure on the part of the United States with very ill grace, and looked upon it as, in part, a blow aimed at herself. And we can believe, that she endeavored to carry out her policy towards the United States with fresh alacrity and zeal, and that the annoying, insulting and outrageous conduct of the commanders of her ships of war stationed before the principal harbors of the United States, met with her entire approbation.

Congress assembled on the 5th of December, and the president sent in his second annual message on the same 1810. day. The state and condition of the foreign relations of the Union occupied the principal share of the president's attention in this able paper. He informed Congress of the result of the measures thus far, in regard to England and France; spoke of the depredations upon our commerce by licentious cruisers under the Danish flag; and set forth briefly the reasons which induced him to take possession of the territory west of the Perdido.

The country generally, Mr. Madison stated, gave evidence of substantial and increasing prosperity. "To a thriving agriculture," he went on to say, "and the improvements related to it, is added a highly interesting extension of useful manufactures, the combined product of professional occupations and of household industry. Such indeed is the experience of economy, as well as of policy, in these substitutes for supplies heretofore obtained by foreign commerce, that, in a national view, the change is justly regarded as, of itself, more than a recompense for those privations and losses, resulting from foreign injustice, which furnished the general impulse required for its accomplishment. How far it may be expedient to guard the infancy of this improvement in the distribution of labor, by regulations of the commercial tariff, is a subject which cannot fail to suggest itself to your patriotic reflections."

The establishment of a national university was also recommended, "by the consideration, that the additional instruction emanating from it would contribute not less to strengthen the foundations, than to adorn the structure of our free and happy system of government. Among the commercial abuses," continued the president, "still committed under the American flag, and leaving in force my former reference to that subject, it appears that American citizens are instrumental in carrying on a traffic in enslaved Africans, equally in violation of the laws of humanity, and in defiance of those of their own country. The same just and benevolent motives which produced the interdiction in force against this criminal conduct, will doubtless be felt by Congress, in devising further means of suppressing the evil."

Fortifications, the armories, the militia, the corps of engineers, and the military academy, were next spoken of. It was stated, that a lesser loan than was authorized had been contracted for the payment of three millions and three-quarters of the public debt, and that after meeting all the current expenses of the government, including the interest on the debt, there was a balance of two millions of dollars expected in the treasury. And for other matters the heads of departments were referred to, and supplementary communications were promised.

The occupancy of West Florida gave rise to earnest debate in Congress; and when the inhabitants of the Territory of Orleans petitioned to be admitted as a state into the Union, the federalists most strenuously resisted the measure on constitutional grounds. Josiah Quincy took the lead in the House against the admission, and on

1811. the 14th of January, delivered an able exposition of the views of New England against the preponderating influence which the formation of new southern states would give to that portion of the confederacy, and avowed sentiments and views which startled the members as much by their boldness as their cogency. "I am compelled to declare it as my deliberate opinion," said Mr. Quincy, "that, if this bill passes, the bonds of this Union are virtually dissolved: that the states, which compose it are free from their moral obligations; and that as it will be the right of all, so it will be the duty of some to prepare, definitely, for a separation: amicably, if they can, violently, if they must."

The speech of Mr. Quincy was long and forcibly argued: at its close, he thus expressed himself, in terms which the reader will look upon with interest in view of what the progress of events during forty years since has brought to pass: "New states are intended to be formed beyond the Mississippi. There is no limit to men's imaginations on this subject, short of California and Columbia River. When I said that the bill would justify a revolution and would produce it, I spoke of its principles and its practical consequences. To this principle and those consequences, I would call the attention of this House and nation. If it be about to introduce a condition of things absolutely insupportable, it becomes wise and honest men to anticipate the evil; and to warn and prepare the people against the event. I have no hesitation on the subject. The extension of this principle to the states contemplated beyond the Mississippi, cannot, will not, and ought not to be borne. And the sooner the people contemplate the unavoidable result, the better; the more likely that convulsions may be prevented; the more hope that the evils may be palliated or removed. . . I oppose this bill from no animosity to the people of New Orleans; but from the deep conviction, that it contains a principle incompatible with the liberties and safety of my country. I have no concealment of my opinion. The bill, if it passes, is a death-blow to the Constitution. It may, afterwards, linger; but lingering, its fate will, at no very distant period, be consummated."

Despite Mr. Quincy's urgency and vaticinations of evil, the bill finally passed by a large majority.

The most important subject which came before Congress during the present session, was that which related to the renewal of the charter of the Bank of the United States. The 4th of March, 1811, was the limit of its charter, and the stockholders and friends of the corporation, labored earnestly for an extension of its existence. Mr. Gallatin, secretary of the treasury, on being applied to by the committee of the Senate, presented an able report, in which he showed conclusively, that, as a bank, its affairs "had been wisely and skilfully managed." The capital stock of the bank was $10,000,000; it held $8,500,000 of deposits, some placed in its hands by government, more by private individuals; and it had issued $4,500,000 of notes. On the other hand, $18,030,000 were owing to it, mainly *good* debts we may suppose; in its vaults were stored up $5,000,000 of specie; and its buildings and the land they stood on had cost them something less than $500,000, and were worth at least that. So that there was "a balance for contingencies" of above $500,000 dollars. The secretary proposed, not only to renew the charter, but that its capital should ultimately be increased to $30,000,000. And he specified certain conditions, which he thought should be attached to the renewal, for he admitted that there were weighty "objections" to the continuance of the institution, under its existing charter.

1811.

Early in January, the select committee of the House, Mr. Burwell, of Virginia, being chairman, reported a bill for the renewal of the charter. On the 16th, the bill was taken up in committee of the whole, and a long and animated debate ensued. Burwell, Macon, Porter, and others, opposed, Fiske, Key, Garland, etc., advocated the renewal. The speeches were able on both sides; and the motion of Mr. Burwell, to strike out the first section, prevailed by a vote of fifty-nine to forty-six. On the 24th, the whole subject was indefinitely postponed by a vote of sixty-five to sixty-four.

1811.

The committee of the Senate, Mr. Crawford, of Virginia, being chairman, introduced a bill, on the 5th of February, for the renewal of the charter. An animated debate sprang up on a motion made by Mr. Anderson, of Tennessee, to strike out the first section. Mr. Crawford ably defended the constitutionality and expediency of the measure, and indignantly repelled the charge of apostasy made against him by the other democratic Senators. He was warmly supported by Richard Brent, of Virginia, and John Pope, of Kentucky, belonging to the same party; and by James Lloyd and Timothy Pickering, of Massachusetts, and John Taylor, of South Carolina. In opposition to the renewal of the charter, Henry Clay distinguished himself, as did also Messrs. Giles and Samuel Smith. The question was taken on the 20th of February, and resulted in a tie vote, of seventeen to seventeen; Messrs. Lloyd, Pickering, and Brent voting, in opposition to the instructions of the legislatures of Massachusetts and Virginia, in favor of the bill. The Senate being thus equally divided, the vice-president, George Clinton, alleging, as the ground of his course, the want of power in Congress to establish a national bank, gave the casting vote for striking out the first section of the bill.

This result was brought about in a measure, by strong party feeling. A violent prejudice existed in the public mind against the bank, and with many it was sufficient to condemn it, that it had originally been chartered by the federalists. The press was vigorous and unmeasured in its assaults, **1811.** and fearful abuse was heaped upon the democratic members of Congress who favored the continuance of the bank. "The influence of state banks was also," as Pitkin observes, "brought to bear on the great question then before Congress; and when it is considered, that the number of those banks had, at that time, increased to nearly ninety, located in most of the states, with a capital of more than $50,000,000, their influence could have had no inconsiderable weight. With this union of ideas and interests against the bank, it is not strange that the charter granting it should be suffered to expire."

Mr. Gallatin, in his response to the call of the Senate committee, had stated, that unless the charter were renewed, government must resort to the state banks, and that he could but prefer for its monetary transactions, such a currency as a national bank alone could supply, to that supplied by local banks, whose credit could not be general, and whose notes might in consequence vary in worth in different parts of the Union. And Mr. Fiske, of New York, in advocating the renewal of the charter, urged, with much force, that trouble would certainly arise out of any attempt to use the state banks for the purposes of the government. The revenue collected in each state must be given to one bank in that state or divided amongst them all. "If one is selected, all the rest become jealous and dissatisfied, and exert their capital and influence against the favorite bank, and its patron the government. This will awaken a spirit of faction as yet unknown. If all are gratified, the government must then open separate accounts with all the different banks in the country, to the number of fifty or sixty, and new companies will be formed to divide the business and share the profits. Indeed, if this course is adopted, there will be no end to the scenes of speculation and intrigue!"

Argument and entreaty were alike equally vain. Not even a temporary extension of the bank's existence was allowed; and after a fruitless effort to obtain a charter from **1811** the legislature of Pennsylvania, the struggle was given up, and the affairs of the bank were placed in the hands of trustees in order to bring them to a final settlement.

During the month of February, an obstinate and fiery debate arose and was kept up on the non-intercourse act, in which various measures were proposed against Great Britain and France. The sittings were often protracted beyond midnight, and not only the members of Congress, but the whole country took a deep interest in the result. The vacillating and insidious course of the French government, and the persistency of England in enforcing her lawless edicts and regulations against the commerce of the United States, kept alive the irritation and excitement in the community, and greatly aggravated the violence of party assaults and recriminations. As having reference to the appeal to arms, which many saw clearly must be made soon, the president was authorized to negotiate a loan of $5,000,000; and it was felt quite generally, that all further expedients would prove inefficient.

On the 27th of February, Mr. Joel Barlow was appointed minister to France, in place of General Armstrong, who had been recalled at his own request. In England, the interests of our country were entrusted to Jonathan Russell, as *chargé d'affaires*, Mr. Pinkney, as above stated, having returned to the United States. Both these gentlemen labored diligently, but, we are sorry to say, with very little success in endeavoring to obtain justice and right from the governments to which they were accredited.*

Congress terminated its busy session on the 3d of March, 1811; and great and well founded anxiety was felt in every direction, as to what next should be done in the then position of affairs.

Soon after, a rencontre happened on the water, which roused the feelings of the people to a high pitch of patriotism and eagerness for battle with England. Ever since the disgraceful attack on the Chesapeake, the officers of the navy seem to have longed for an opportunity of wiping out what **1811.** they considered the stigma on the service by that affair, and the whole maritime force of the nation was kept at home. The English, says Cooper, "increased their cruisers on the American coast, in proportion as the Americans themselves did, though their vessels no longer lay off the harbors, impressing men and detaining ships. It was seldom that a British cruiser was now seen near the land, the government probably cautioning its commanders to avoid unnecessary exhibitions of this sort, with a view to prevent collisions. Still they were numerous; cruised at no great distance: and by keeping up constant communications between Bermuda and Halifax, may be said to have intercepted nearly every ship that passed from one hemisphere to the other."

It was early in May, when word was brought to Commodore Rodgers, on board the President, forty-four, **1811.** that a man had been impressed from an American brig by an English vessel of war, off Sandy Hook. The President was promptly put in readiness to inquire into the facts, and on the 16th of May, at noon, made a sail, about six leagues from the land, to the southward of New York. It was soon

* The third census of the United States gave the following result: number of free whites, 5,862,073; number of slaves, 1,191,364; all others, except Indians not taxed, 186,377; making a total population of 7,239,814.

perceived, by the squareness of her yards and the symmetry of her build, that she was a vessel of war; and the American frigate stood for her, with the intention to get within hail. At two, P. M., the President set her broad pennant and ensign. The stranger now made several signals, but finding they were not answered, he wore and stood to southward. Chase was given directly, and between seven and eight in the evening, the President, bringing up on the weather bow of the stranger, hailed, "What ship is that?" The English vessel, which had the appearance of a small frigate, did not answer, but hailed in return. After a short pause, a second hail was given, when the strange vessel fired a gun, which entered the main-mast of the President. Of course this led to firing in return, and the comparative strength of the two ships was speedily tested. The President's antagonist was crippled very soon, and then condescended to answer the hail which was renewed. "Satisfied that his late opponent was disabled, and having no desire to do more than was already accomplished, Commodore Rodgers gave the name of his own ship, wore round, and running a short distance to leeward, he hauled by the wind again, with a view to remain nigh the English vessel during the night. The president kept lights displayed, in order to let her late antagonist know her position, and wore several times to remain near her." At the dawn of day, the President sent a boat, with the first lieutenant, to offer services, if any were required. The stranger proved to be his Britannic majesty's ship, Little Belt, eighteen, Captain Bingham. She had suffered severely, thirty-one being killed and wounded; the President, on the other hand, had received no injury, and only one of the crew, a boy, was wounded. The Little Belt declining all assistance, the ships parted company, and returned to their respective harbors.

Mr. Cooper enlarges upon this occurrence, its merits, the feeling which was aroused, etc. The English asserted that the President was the aggressor; but it seems to us clearly established, that the Little Belt fired first, and persisted in the unequal contest. Captain Bingham's account was generally accredited in England, and it served to increase the ill-feeling that was already very strong. At home, Commodore Rodgers was sharply censured by a considerable party, and his reputation suffered, from this cause, no doubt, very serious injury.*

Our naval historian relates another incident which is worth quoting here, as illustrating the state of feeling in the service at the time. "Not long after the meeting between the President and the Little Belt, **1811.** the United States, forty-four, bearing the broad pennant of Commodore Decatur, fell in with the Eurydice and Atalanta, British ships, off New York; and while the commanders were hailing, one of the seamen of the former vessel, (United States,) in carelessly

* Cooper's "*Naval History*," vol. ii., pp. 26–35. Mr. C. discusses quite fully the "general principles" involved in the case of the President and the Little Belt. His remarks are well worthy examination.

handling the lanyard of his lock, fired a gun.* The reader will learn in this fact, the high state of preparation that then prevailed in an American man-of-war; the lock having been cocked, and every thing in perfect readiness to commence an action at a moment's notice. Happily both parties were cool and discreet, and proper explanations having been made, the English commander was entirely satisfied that no insult or assault was intended."

Mr. Foster, the newly appointed British minister, arrived in the United States, in June, and speedily entered upon his duties. Long and important correspondence ensued, in which it was evident that Great Britain was not yet prepared to recede from the stand she had taken, and deal justly and rightly with America. Reparation was offered for the attack on the Chesapeake, by which the act was to be formally disavowed, the men taken from the ship were to be restored again, and pecuniary provision was to be made for the families of the killed or wounded. After some delay, the proposal was agreed to. But with respect to the vital questions which sprang out of the orders in council, and the claim to impressment, Mr. Foster was not at liberty, even if disposed, to afford satisfaction. These odious and insulting orders and claims continued to be enforced, and the nation was rapidly verging to the point of armed resistance against England. Dispatches from abroad showed, that not less than twenty-six vessels had been condemned in the court of admiralty, and that others were about to share the same fate. All the evils of war nearly, had already fallen upon the United States; while England was enjoying the advantages of war, without the cost. In fact, as it was estimated, her cruisers had captured nine hundred American vessels, since the year 1803. "She had, at this epoch," as Mr. Dallas forcibly states in his Exposition, "impressed from the crews of American merchant vessels, peaceably navigating the high seas, not less than six thousand mariners, who claimed to be citizens of the United States, and who were denied all opportunity to verify their claims. She had seized and confiscated the commercial property of American citizens to an incalculable amount. She had united in the enormities of France to declare a great proportion of the terraqueous globe in a state of blockade; chasing the American merchant flag effectually from the ocean. She had contemptuously disregarded the neutrality of the American territory, and the jurisdiction of the American laws, within the waters and harbors of the United States. She was enjoying the emoluments of a surreptitious trade, stained with every species of fraud and corruption, which gave to the belligerent powers the advantages of peace while the neutral powers were involved in the evils of war. She had, in short, usurped and exercised on the water, a tyranny similar to that which her great antagonist had usurped and

* This, says Mr. Cooper, was the excuse of the man. Commodore Decatur believed that the gun was fired intentionally by its captain, with a view to bring on an engagement. So strong was the feeling of the seamen of the day, that such an occurrence is highly probable.

exercised upon the land. And amidst all these proofs of ambition and avarice, she demanded that the victims of her usurpations and her violence should revere her as the sole defender of the rights and liberties of mankind."*

It may well be believed, that in such a state of affairs, the exasperated people looked with anxious concern to the approaching session of Congress, and the clamor for war was increased in every part of the Union, with the exception perhaps of the larger part of New England. Mr. Madison
1811.
was indisposed to extreme measures, and his cabinet were somewhat at variance with each other. Mr. Smith and Mr. Gallatin did not harmonize, and the president preferred to part with the former, who resigned, and James Monroe took the post of secretary of state, in November. William Pinkney also, soon after, succeeded Rodney as attorney-general.

In addition to the causes already pointed out as leading to difficulties with Great Britain, there were others which tended to the same result. The British government, from the position of Canada, and the facilities which it enjoyed in consequence, paid much attention to the enlisting the Indian tribes in favor of the quarrel which it was urging forward with the United States; and there is every reason to conclude, that British emissaries were actively engaged in fomenting dissensions and complaints which existed among the Indians in the north-west. The rapid progress of the white men's settlements, the narrowing of the hunting-grounds, the introduction of the white men's spirituous liquors, and the like, had led to serious troubles on various occasions, and the tribes in the north-west had frequently been concerned in robbing and murdering the settlers in the vicinity.

General Harrison, governor of the Territory of Indiana, had made, in 1809, a purchase of valuable land from the Miami Indians on the Wabash River. The sale of this tract gave great offence to Tecumseh, a Shawnee chief, whose ambition led him to aspire to the leadership of the western tribes, and whose superior abilities fitted him for that task which the noted Pontiac (vol. i., p. 250) had striven, fifty years previously, to accomplish; we mean, a confederacy and organized union of the Indians to repel the further advances of the white men. In August, 1810, Tecumseh and his warriors met General Harrison in council at Vincennes, which resulted in nothing but increased excitement and a determination on the part of Tecumseh and his twin-brother, the prophet, a crafty impostor, to proceed to extremities.

In the spring of 1811, the frontier inhabitants became seriously alarmed at the prospect of Indian outrages, which seemed to be on the in- **1811.**
crease; and at their solicitation, General Harrison resolved to move towards the prophet's town, at the junction of the Tippecanoe and Wabash Rivers, with a body of Kentucky and

* Dallas's "*Exposition of the Causes and Character of the Late War with Great Britain*," pp. 47, 48. This ably written tract is now rarely to be met with: it was printed at Philadelphia, in April, 1815; 8vo., pp. 82.

Indiana militia, and the fourth United States regiment, under Colonel Boyd, to demand satisfaction of the Indians, and to put a stop to their threatened hostilities. His expedition was made early in November. On his approach within a few miles of the prophet's town, the principal chiefs came out with offers of peace and submission, and requested Harrison to encamp for the night; but, as he suspected, this was only a treacherous artifice. At four in the morning, the camp was furiously assailed, and a bloody contest ensued, the Indians were however repulsed. The loss on the part of the Americans was sixty-two killed, and one hundred and twenty-six wounded; a still greater number fell on the side of the red men. In fact, this was one of the most desperate and hardly contested battles ever fought with the Indians. Tecumseh was not present, and the prophet occupied himself in conjurations on an eminence not far off, but out of danger. Harrison, having destroyed the prophet's town, and established forts, returned to Vincennes, and received high praise for his successful conduct of the expedition.*

* See Brackenridge's "*History of the Late War*," pp. 22–26; and Drake's "*History and Biography of the Indians of North America*," pp. 616–20.

CHAPTER VII.

1811–1812.

OPENING OF THE WAR.

Assembling of Congress on the 4th of November — Henry Clay elected speaker — The president's message — Abstract of its contents — Warlike measures resolved upon by the majority — Report and resolutions of the committee on foreign relations — The debate on the resolutions — The position of the president not agreeable — Determination of the ruling party — Burning of the theatre in Richmond, Virginia — Questions relating to the financial condition of the country in respect to war — Measures adopted — The "Henry plot" — Russell's dispatches from London — Embargo laid for ninety days — Other bills of a warlike tendency — Louisiana admitted as a state into the Union — Death of George Clinton, the vice-president — Foreign affairs — Barlow's labors in France — Troubles in England — Foster's letter to Monroe — The crisis reached — Madison's war message, in full — Report of committee of foreign relations on the message — Substance of the report — Debate carried on with closed doors — Bill passed in the House and the Senate — Approved by the president — The act declaring war — The president's proclamation — Address of the minority in Congress to their constituents — Other acts of Congress — Ratio of representation — Close of the long session — Proclamation of the president appointing a day of fasting and prayer. Appendix to Chapter VII. Address of the minority in Congress to their constituents.

In consequence of the unsettled and critical condition of our foreign relations, the president, by proclamation, in July, summoned Congress a month earlier than usual; and, on the 4th of November that body assembled in the city of Washington, ready to enter earnestly upon the important duties entrusted to their charge. The elections had resulted decidedly in favor of the administration, and the democratic party felt itself strong enough to venture upon more energetic measures than had as yet been deemed prudent. Henry Clay, who now made his first appearance in the House, and was an ardent supporter of the republican views, was elected speaker by a large vote over Mr. Bibb, whom the more moderate men of the party desired to have placed in the chair.

1811.

On the following day, the president sent in his third annual message, in which he entered quite at large into the important questions at that time agitating the nation. He expressed himself disappointed at the course pursued by the British government, who, not crediting the revocation of Napoleon's decrees, had refused to rescind the orders in council, and had pressed with additional severity the enforcement of these odious regulations. He further spoke of "the unfriendly spirit" evinced by the British authorities, who had threatened "measures of retaliation" for the continuance of the non-importation act, and declared, that "indemnity and redress for other wrongs have continued to be withheld, and our coasts and the mouths of our harbors have again witnessed scenes not less derogatory to the dearest of our national rights than vexatious to the regular course of our trade." The affair of the President and the Little Belt appropriately followed this statement.

With respect to France, the president said: "The justice and fairness which had been evinced on the part of the United States towards France, both before and since the revocation of her decrees, authorized an expectation that her government would have followed up that measure by all such others as were due to our reasonable claims, as well as dictated by its amicable professions. No proof, however, is yet given of an intention to repair the other wrongs done to the United States; and particularly to restore the great amount of American property seized and condemned under edicts, which, though not affecting our neutral relations, and therefore not entering into questions between the United States and other belligerents, were nevertheless founded in such unjust principles, that the reparation ought to have been prompt and ample. In addition to this and other demands of strict right, on that nation, the United States have much reason to be dissatisfied with the rigorous and unexpected restrictions, to which their trade with the French dominions has been subjected; and which, if not discontinued, will require at least corresponding restrictions on importations from France into the United States."

1811.

With the other powers of Europe, the relations of the United States continued on a friendly footing.

In speaking of the "ominous indications" which required the executive to take measures for providing for the general security, the president informed Congress of the progress of the coast defences, and the putting of part of the gunboats, the navy, the regulars, and the militia, into active use; the latter in Indiana chiefly, on account of the menacing combination of the Indians there under Tecumseh and the prophet.

Urging upon the national legislature "the duty of putting the United States into an armor and an attitude demanded by the crisis and corresponding to the national spirit and expectations," he recommended adequate provisions in men, ships, and all the materials of warlike preparations, and for appropriations suitable to the emergency. Laws to regulate the mercantile marine, and suppress smuggling, were also called for. The finances were said to be in a favorable condition. The receipts during the year had been over $13,500,000, which had enabled the government to meet its current liabilities, including interest; and to cancel more than $5,000,000 of the public debt. In conclusion, he assured the Houses of his "deep sense of the crisis," and his confidence in a happy issue from it, by the co-operation of their faithful zeal, and "the blessing of Heaven on our beloved country, and on all the means that may be employed in vindicating its rights and advancing its welfare."

1811.

The calm and deliberate tone of the president's message fell short of meeting the excited state of temper and disposition of the majority in Congress; and the democratic members, from the south and west especially, determined to lay aside inactivity and indecision, and to adopt warlike measures towards England.

Early in December, the committee on foreign relations, through Mr. Peter B. Porter, their chairman, brought in their report upon the president's message. The report was clear and decided in its views of the position of affairs and the action required at the hands of Congress. Six resolutions were recommended: 1st. To fill up the ranks of the present military establishment by the aid of a bounty. 2d. To raise an additional force of ten thousand men by the like means. 3d. To authorize the president to accept the services of fifty thousand volunteers. 4th. To give like authority to order out such detachments of militia as the public service may require. 5th. To cause the public vessels not now in service to be fitted out immediately. 6th. To permit merchant ships, owned and navigated wholly by American citizens, to arm in self-defence.

1811.

A long and earnest debate sprang up upon these resolutions, in which Randolph, Calhoun, R. M. Johnson, Macon, and others, took an active part. The first five were adopted by large majorities, and the sixth was laid upon the table; thus evidencing that war was expected, if not called for, by most of the people of the United States.* Similar strong feeling was exhibited in the Senate, in discussing the measures ne-

* As a matter worthy of record, we may mention here, that on the 30th of December, both Houses of Congress resolved to wear mourning for a month, in order to testify their deep sympathy with the people of Richmond, Virginia, in consequence of the sad calamity that had fallen upon them on the 26th inst. On that evening, the theatre, being very full of spectators, took fire, and in the panic which ensued nearly seventy lives were lost. Among those thus suddenly removed out of this world, were, Mr. Smith, the governor of Virginia, Mr. Venable, formerly a member of the House, and a number of other persons of distinction. The Monumental (Episcopal) Church was erected on the site, and an inscription on the monument briefly but forcibly tells the tale of the fearful blow which then fell upon the city of Richmond.

cessary under the existing state of affairs. Mr. Foster, the British minister, addressed Mr. Monroe, on the 17th of December, defending the course of his government; to which communication an answer was returned, by the secretary of state, on the 14th of January, 1812, and the conviction was expressed, that it was impossible to see any thing in the conduct of England "but a determined hostility to the rights and interests of the United States."

The position of the president was far from agreeable. He was, as we have previously intimated, constitutionally averse to war, and neither by ability nor experience well adapted to be at the head of affairs in times of commotion and excitement such as war would produce. His cabinet were not agreed with him on the expediency of hostilities, at that date and in view of all the circumstances: and no one of them seems to have been fitted for the onerous duties which would devolve upon them in the event of war. The policy of the party had always been opposed to the navy and the efficiency of the army; and no preparation had been made to enter upon a contest with a nation so powerful in both navy and army as Great Britain. The finances were in no condition to meet the expenses of war; taxes were odious, and it would be ruinous to the party to propose them; the presidential election was approaching, and Mr. Madison desired to follow in the steps of his predecessor and be re-elected to office; and so, as we have said, his position was far from agreeable, and seemed to grow, day by day, more and more perplexed and uncomfortable. While he was hesitating and holding back about the war, he was waited upon by some of the more ardent democrats, who significantly assured him, that he must make up his mind on this point, or that the party would be very likely to supersede him by elevating De Witt Clinton to the presidential chair. Mr. Madison gave way, and consented to accede to the wishes of the war party, and to endeavor to carry forward the struggle with energy and success.

The question whence the means were to be derived for carrying on the war was one of no little difficulty. Mr. Gallatin, though not favoring the war at that time, was nevertheless called upon to devise the means of providing the sinews of war. In view of the circumstances in which the United States were then placed, it was far from easy to see a clear way of raising any sum beyond what was requisite for the ordinary expenses of government. But here was the army, increased by the enlistment of twenty thousand men, to find money for; here were fifty thousand volunteers, or as many within that limit as could be obtained, to be equipped and supported; here was a share in the cost of furnishing and organizing a hundred thousand militiamen: here were the commissioning of the existing frigates, and the building of others; not to mention Mr. Jefferson's gunboats, and the fortifications at the various ports and harbors; and it was all to be done at once, for the navy had been sold out nearly, the army had substantially been disbanded, and there was hardly any financial expedient practicable, except increased duties on imports.

Mr. Gallatin, on the 10th of January, 1812, sent in a reply to the application for information on the part of the committee of ways and means, in which he expressed his opinion, that in case of war, the imposts would not yield more than $2,500,000. The duties on tonnage, merchandise, etc., he estimated at $6,000,000, leaving a deficiency of $3,600,000 to meet the expenditures of 1813. An annual loan, he thought, of $10,000,000 would be required during the war, and to meet the interest on this, the deficiency in the revenue, he recommended the raising $3,000,000 by a direct tax and $2,000,000 by indirect taxes, such as licenses, excise, stamps, etc. He concluded that there would probably be no difficulty in effecting the loans suggested, and recommended that they be made irredeemable for ten years.

1812.

Towards the close of February, the House acted upon this subject, and a loan of $11,000,000* was determined upon by a vote of ninety-two to twenty-nine. As the loan did not fill up very rapidly, we may mention, that the issue of $5,000,000 of treasury notes was directed, and the impost was doubled. There was no other security for notes or loans, than the surplus of the $8,000,000 a year theretofore pledged, by way of sinking-fund, to redeem the national debt, then amounting to $55,000,000. And these, as Ingersoll states, "were the only acts of the war-declaring Congress for invigorating the money-sinew of war."

Early in March, the president sent a communication to Congress, which created a decided sensation throughout the United States. Several documents accompanied this communication, the object of which was to prove, that, in February, 1809, while the British government was making amicable professions and engaged in pacific negotiations, the governor-general of Canada, Sir James Craig, was engaged, by means of a secret agent, John Henry, in an insidious and dishonorable effort to effect, if possible, a disruption of the Union, and the formation of an eastern confederacy in political connection with Great Britain. Henry entered actively upon this service; proceeded to Boston; made many and various attempts to accomplish his purpose; and wrote a number of letters to Sir James Craig on the subject; but he does not appear to have accomplished any thing, even with the most disaffected and rabid opponents of the administration. Henry, having vainly sought remuneration for his services from the British government, at home, came to the United States, in December, 1811, where, in February, 1812, he made an arrangement with the president to disclose his whole proceeding, with the

* "The incongruity between appropriations and provision for them by taxation was such, that without a cent to be raised by taxes, more than fifteen millions of dollars were appropriated for the army, and nearly two million seven hundred thousand for the navy, when the income by customs, for 1811, did not exceed thirteen millions, and that of 1812 was only about nine millions and a half. All modern wars are carried on in part by loans, but loans secured by taxes. Our war was to be sustained by borrowed money without taxes, at any rate until after the presidential election." Ingersoll's "*History of the Second War*," vol. i., p. 70.

letters, etc., for the comfortable sum of $50,000, paid to him out of the contingent fund. The British government, through its minister, most positively denied any complicity in this contemptible matter. Henry made off with his money as quickly as possible, and the federalists treated with indignant scorn charges coming from such a quarter.* Nevertheless, it is not to be concealed, that the "Henry affair" aroused to a still higher extent the exasperated feelings of the ruling party against England, who was deemed capable of any depth of treachery against the United States.

Mr. Jonathan Russell, who had, in November, 1811, been transferred to London, as *chargé d'affaires* for the United States, addressed a letter to Mr. Monroe, under date of the 14th of February, in which he stated, that no evidence could be discovered of an intention on the part of the British government to repeal the orders in

1812. council. On the 4th of March Mr. Russell wrote again to the secretary of state, and, giving the substance of some important discussions in parliament, he closed his dispatch in these words: "I no longer entertain a hope that we can honorably avoid war."

On the 1st of April, the president recommended the laying an embargo on all vessels then in port or thereafter arriving. Mr. Madison had named sixty days as the time during which the embargo should last; but the Senate extended it to ninety days, and the House concurred, on the 3d of April, by a small majority, notwithstanding the vehement opposition of John Randolph and Josiah Quincy. Although the president had gone thus far, he was not entirely without hope, that the last resort might still be avoided; for it was well known that Great Britain did not desire war any more than did the United States. But the ruling spirits of the party had made up their minds that the honor of the country demanded war, and that the domineering and insulting conduct of England could no longer be endured. Clay, Calhoun, Porter, and Lowndes, in the House; Giles, Campbell, and the western members, in the Senate, advocated this course with an array of eloquence and talent that bore down every opponent; and the president was compelled to go with them, as we have above stated, or lose all chance of re-election.

The embargo was soon after followed by a bill prohibiting, under heavy penalties, the exportation of specie and every kind of merchandise, domestic or foreign, during the ninety days of the embargo. In the course of the month of April, various other measures of a warlike tendency were adopted, such as acts organizing a corps of artificers, further provision for the corps of engineers, etc. And, early in May, on the receipt of several petitions, principally from New York, Congress debated the expediency of repealing the embargo.

Louisiana, on the 8th of April, was admitted into the Union, and took her

* See Dwight's "*History of the Hartford Convention*," pp. 195–212. Mr. Ingersoll also has some remarks on this point which are worth consulting. See his "*History of the Second War*," vol. ii., pp. 219-222.

place among the states at this interesting crisis in public affairs. About a fortnight later, the vice-president, George Clinton, at a ripe old age, was removed from this earthly scene, just as the storm of war was about to burst upon the country which he had served so long and ably. William H. Crawford, who had previously been chosen president of the Senate *pro tempore*, now took the vacant chair, and devoted his superior abilities to the discharge of his increased duties.

1812.

Turning our attention to the position of affairs in Europe, we find that Napoleon was pursuing his usual course towards the United States, of an entire disregard for fairness and honorable dealing. Mr. Barlow, the American minister to France, could obtain no satisfaction, and labored in vain to accomplish something for the interests of his country. The emperor would make no promise respecting redress of injuries to American commerce, nor was he willing to agree to discontinue them in the future. On the eve of setting out on his memorable invasion of Russia, he very curtly disposed of Mr. Barlow's importunities, and showed how little he cared for his "American prefect," as the federalists sneeringly termed Mr. Madison. Mr. Barlow, on the 1st of May, pressed the Duke of Bassano for an authentic act declaring the revocation of the decrees, in order that the British government might no longer have even a pretence for not revoking the orders in council; when, to his astonishment, the French minister sent him the emperor's decree, bearing date April 28th, 1811, by which the decrees of Berlin and Milan were definitively considered as not having existed, in regard to American vessels, from the 1st of the foregoing November. Barlow forwarded a copy of this decree to Mr. Russell, at London, for the purpose of putting the matter right in that quarter, and bringing the injurious orders in council to an end.

The merchants and manufacturers of England were suffering severely from being deprived of the usual market in America, and a powerful effort was made in parliament, by the Marquis of Lansdowne and Henry Brougham, to obtain the repeal of the orders in council. The nation was pressed to the earth by enormous taxation, to carry on the long and exhausting war with Napoleon; the operatives were out of employment and in deep distress; riots and disturbances occurred in the manufacturing districts; the great American market, worth, as Mr. Brougham stated, all other foreign markets put together, was closed to England; and yet the ministry resisted stoutly the demand of the people, and persisted, to the last moment, in refusing the revocation of the orders. On the 23d of June, however, when it was of no avail, the British government revoked its odious and injurious regulations, by means of which it had so deeply wounded the feelings of Americans and trampled upon their just rights and immunities. The tardy act of revocation was too late: America had buckled on her armor for the fight.

1812.

On the 30th of May, Mr. Foster, the British minister, addressed a long letter to Mr. Monroe, in which he reviewed the existing controversy, and, in substance, announced, that England would not recede from the ground she had assumed. "Great Britain feels, that to relinquish her just measures of self-defence and retaliation, would be to surrender the best means of her own preservation and rights; and with them the rights of other nations, so long as France maintains and acts upon such principles" as are set forth in the doctrines promulgated by the government of Napoleon. And he expressed the assurance, not very well timed, that the prince regent earnestly desired to restore harmony between the two countries, but of course on terms which were thought proper for so great a monarchy as that of Great Britain.

Matters had now reached their crisis: something beside talking must now be resorted to; and the president resolved upon his course.

On the 1st of June, Mr. Madison transmitted to Congress a confidential message, which, as it presents clearly and forcibly the various grounds on which war was held to be necessary under the existing state of affairs, we deem of sufficient importance to quote in full in this place.

1812.

"*To the Senate and House of Representatives of the United States:*

"I communicate to Congress certain documents, being a continuation of those heretofore laid before them, on the subject of our affairs with Great Britain.

"Without going back beyond the renewal in 1803, of the war in which Great Britain is engaged, and omitting unrepaired wrongs of inferior magnitude, the conduct of her government presents a series of acts hostile to the United States as an independent and neutral nation.

"British cruisers have been in the continual practice of violating the American flag on the great highway of nations, and of seizing and carrying off persons sailing under it; not in the exercise of a belligerent right, founded on the law of nations, against an enemy, but of a municipal prerogative over British subjects. British jurisdiction is thus extended to neutral vessels, in a situation where no laws can operate but the law of nations and the laws of the country to which the vessels belong; and a self-redress is assumed, which, if British subjects were wrongfully detained and alone concerned, is that substitution of force, for a resort to the responsible sovereign, which falls within the definition of war. Could the seizure of British subjects in such cases be regarded as within the exercise of a belligerent right, the acknowledged laws of war, which forbid an article of captured property to be adjudged without a regular investigation before a competent tribunal, would imperiously demand the fairest trial, where the sacred rights of persons were at issue. In place of such a trial, these rights are subjected to the will of every petty commander.

"The practice, hence, is so far from affecting British subjects alone, that, under the pretext of searching for these, thousands of American citizens, under the safeguard of public law, and of their national flag, have been torn from their country and every thing dear to them; have been dragged on board ships of war of a foreign nation, and exposed, under the severities of their discipline, to be exiled to the most distant and deadly climes, to risk their lives in the battles of their oppressors, and to be the melancholy instruments of taking away those of their own brethren.

"Against this crying enormity, which Great Britain would be so prompt to avenge if committed against herself, the United States have in vain exhausted remonstrances and expostulations. And that no proof might be wanting of their conciliatory dispositions, and no pretext left for a continuance of the practice, the British government was formally assured of the readiness of the United States to enter into arrangements such as could not be rejected, if the recovery of British subjects were the real and sole object. The communication passed without effect.

"British cruisers have been in the practice also, of violating the rights and the peace of our coasts. They hover over and harass our departing commerce. To the most insulting pretensions they have added the most lawless proceedings in our very harbors; and have wantonly spilt American blood within the sanctuary of our territorial jurisdiction. The principles and rules enforced by that nation, when a neutral nation, against armed vessels or belligerents hovering near her coasts, and disturbing her commerce, are well known. When called on, nevertheless, by the United States, to punish the greater offences committed by her own vessels, her government has bestowed on their commanders additional marks of honor and confidence.

"Under pretended blockades, without the presence of an adequate force, and sometimes without the practicability of applying one, our commerce has been plundered in every sea; the great staples of our country have been cut off from their legitimate markets; and a destructive blow aimed at our agricultural and maritime interests. In aggravation of these predatory measures, they have been considered as in force from the dates of their notification; a retrospective effect being thus added, as has been done in other important cases, to the unlawfulness of the course pursued. And to render the outrage the more signal, these mock blockades have been reiterated and enforced in the face of official communications from the British government, declaring, as the true definition of a legal blockade, 'that particular ports must be actually invested, and previous warning given to vessels bound to them not to enter.'

"Not content with these occasional expedients for laying waste our neutral trade, the cabinet of Great Britain resorted, at length, to the sweeping system of blockades, under the name of orders in council, which has been moulded and managed as might best suit its political views, its commercial jealousies, or the avidity of British cruisers.

"To our remonstrances against the complicated and transcendent injustice of this innovation, the first reply was, that the orders were reluctantly adopted by Great Britain as a necessary retaliation on the decrees of her enemy proclaiming a general blockade of the British isles, at a time when the naval force of that enemy dared not to issue from his own ports. She was reminded without effect, that her own prior blockades, unsupported by an adequate naval force, actually applied and continued, were a bar to this plea; that executed edicts against millions of our property could not be retaliation on edicts, confessedly impossible to be executed; that retaliation, to be just, should fall on the party setting the guilty example, not on an innocent party, which was not even chargeable with an acquiescence in it.

"When deprived of this flimsy veil for a prohibition of our trade with her enemy, by the repeal of his prohibition of our trade with Great Britain, her cabinet, instead of a corresponding repeal, or practical discontinuance of its orders, formally avowed a determination to persist in them against the United States, until the markets of her enemy should be laid open to British products; thus asserting an obligation on a neutral power to require one belligerent to encourage, by its internal regulations, the trade of another belligerent: contradicting her own practice towards all nations, in peace as well as in war; and betraying the insincerity of those professions which inculcated a belief that, having resorted to her orders with regret, she was anxious to find an occasion for putting an end to them.

"Abandoning still more all respect for the neutral rights of the United States, and for its own consistency, the British government now demands as prerequisites to a repeal of its orders, as they relate to the United States, that a formality should be observed in the repeal of the French decrees nowise necessary to their termination, nor exemplified by British usage; and that the French repeal, besides including that portion of the decrees which operates within a territorial jurisdiction, as well as that which operates on the high seas against the commerce of the United States, should not be a single special repeal in relation to the United States, but should be extended to whatever other neutral nations, unconnected with them, may be affected by those decrees. And as an additional insult, they are called on for a formal disavowal of conditions and pretensions advanced by the French government, for which the United States are so far from having made themselves responsible, that, in official explanations, which have been published to the world, and in a correspondence of the American minister at London with the British minister for foreign affairs, such a responsibility was explicitly and emphatically disclaimed.

"It has become, indeed, sufficiently certain, that the commerce of the United States is to be sacrificed, not as interfering with the belligerent rights of Great Britain, — not as supplying the wants of her enemies, which she herself supplies; but as interfering with the monopoly which she covets for her own commerce and navigation. She carries on a war against the lawful commerce of a friend, that she may the better carry on a commerce with an enemy — a commerce, polluted by the forgeries and perjuries which are, for the most part, the only passports by which it can succeed.

"Anxious to make every experiment short of the last resort of injured nations, the United States have withheld from Great Britain, under successive modifications, the benefits of a free intercourse with their market, the loss of which could not but outweigh the profits accruing from her restrictions of our commerce with other nations. And to entitle these experiments to their more favorable consideration, they were so framed as to enable her to place her adversary under the exclusive operation of them. To these appeals her government has been equally inflexible, as if willing to make sacrifices of every sort rather than yield to the claims of justice, or renounce the errors of a false pride. Nay, so far were the attempts carried to overcome the attachment of the British cabinet to its unjust edicts, that it received every encouragement within the competency of the executive branch of our government, to expect that a repeal of them would be followed by a war between the United States and France, unless the French edicts should also be repealed. Even this communication, although silencing forever the plea of a disposition in the United States to acquiesce in these edicts, originally the sole plea of them, received no attention.

"If no other proof existed of a predetermination of the British government against a repeal of its orders, it might be found in the correspondence of the minister-plenipotentiary of the United States at London, and the British secretary for foreign affairs, in 1810, on the question whether the blockade of May, 1806, was considered as in force, or as not in force. It had been ascertained that the French government, which urged this blockade as the ground of its Berlin decree, was willing, in the event of its removal, to repeal that decree; which being followed by alternate repeals of the other offensive edicts, might abolish the whole system on both sides. This inviting opportunity for accomplishing an object so important to the United States, and professed so often to be the desire of both the belligerents, was made known to the British government. As that government admits that an actual application of an adequate force is necessary to the existence of a legal blockade, and it was notorious, that, if such a force had ever been applied, its long discontinuance had annulled the blockade in question, there could be no sufficient objection on the part of Great Britain to a formal revocation of it; and no imaginable objection to a declaration of the fact that the blockade did not exist. The declaration would have been consistent with her avowed principles of blockade, and would have enabled the United States to demand from France the pledged repeal of her decrees; either with success, in which case the way would have been opened for a general repeal of the belligerent edicts; or without success, in which case the United States would be justified in turning their measures exclusively against France. The British government would, however, neither rescind the blockade, nor declare its non-existence; nor permit its non-existence to be inferred and affirmed by the American plenipotentiary. On the contrary, by representing the blockade to be comprehended in the orders in council, the United States were compelled so to regard it in their subsequent proceedings.

"There was a period when a favorable change in the policy of the British cabinet was justly considered as established. The minister-plenipotentiary of his Britannic majesty here, proposed an adjustment of the differences more immediately endangering the harmony of the two countries. The proposition was accepted with a promptitude and cordiality corresponding with the invariable professions of this government. A foundation appeared to be laid for a sincere and lasting reconciliation. The prospect, however, quickly vanished. The whole proceeding was disavowed by the British government, without any explanations which could at that time repress the belief, that the disavowal proceeded from a spirit of hostility to the commercial rights and prosperity of the United States. And it has since come into proof, that at the very moment when the public minister was holding the language of friendship, and inspiring confidence in the sincerity of the negotiation with which he was charged, a secret agent of his government was employed in intrigues, having for their object a subversion of our government, and a dismemberment of our happy Union.

"In reviewing the conduct of Great Britain towards the United States, our attention is necessarily drawn to the warfare just renewed by the savages on one of our extensive frontiers; a warfare which is known to spare neither age nor sex, and to be distinguished by features peculiarly shocking to humanity. It is difficult to account for the activity and combinations which have for some time been developing themselves among tribes in constant intercourse with British traders and garrisons, without connecting their hostility with that influence; and without recollecting the authenticated examples of such interpositions heretofore furnished by the officers and agents of that government.

"Such is the spectacle of injuries and indignities which have been heaped on our country; and such the crisis which its unexampled forbearance and conciliatory efforts have not been able to avert. It might at least have been expected, that an enlightened nation, if less urged by moral obligations, or invited by friendly dispositions on the part of the United States, would have found in its true interest alone a sufficient motive to respect their rights and their tranquillity on the high seas; that an enlarged policy would have favored that free and general circulation of commerce, in which the British nation is at all times interested, and which in times of war is the best alleviation of its calamities to herself, as well as the other belligerents; and more especially that the British cabinet would not, for the sake of a precarious and surreptitious intercourse with hostile markets, have persevered in a course of measures which necessarily put at hazard the invaluable market of a great and growing country, disposed to cultivate the mutual advantages of an active commerce.

"Other counsels have prevailed. Our moderation and conciliation have had no other effect than to encourage perseverance, and to enlarge pretensions. We behold our seafaring citizens still the daily victims of lawless violence committed on the great and common highway of nations, even within sight of the country which owes them protection. We behold our vessels, freighted with the products of our soil and industry, or returning with the honest proceeds of them, wrested from their lawful destinations, confiscated by prize courts, no longer the organs of public law, but the instruments of arbitrary edicts, and their unfortunate crews dispersed and lost, or forced or inveigled in British ports into British fleets; whilst arguments are employed, in support of these aggressions, which have no foundation but in a principle equally supporting a claim to regulate our external commerce in all cases whatsoever.

"We behold, in fine, on the side of Great Britain, a state of war against the United States; on the side of the United States, a state of peace towards Great Britain.

"Whether the United States shall continue passive under these progressive usurpations, and these accumulating wrongs, or, opposing force to force in defence of their natural rights, shall commit a just cause into the hands of the Almighty disposer of events, avoiding all connections which might entangle it in the contests or views of other powers, and preserving a constant readiness to concur in an honorable re-establishment of peace and friendship, is a solemn question, which the Constitution wisely confides to the legislative department of the government. In recommending it to their early deliberations, I am happy in the assurance that the decision will be worthy the enlightened and patriotic councils of a virtuous, a free, and a powerful nation.

"Having presented this view of the relations of the United States with Great Britain, and of the solemn alternative growing out of them, I proceed to remark, that the communications last made to Congress on the subject of our relations with France will have shown, that since the revocation of her decrees, as they violated the neutral rights of the United States, her government has authorized illegal captures by its privateers and public ships, and that other outrages have been practised on our vessels and our citizens. It will have been seen also, that no indemnity had been provided, or satisfactorily pledged, for the extensive spoliations committed under the violent and retrospective orders of the French government against the property of our citizens seized within the jurisdiction of France. I abstain, at this time, from recommending to the consideration of Congress definitive measures with respect to that nation, in the expectation, that the result of unclosed discussions between our minister-plenipotentiary at Paris and the French government, will speedily enable Congress to decide, with greater advantage, on the course due to the rights, the interests, and the honor of our country.

"JAMES MADISON."

This long and forcibly written document was immediately referred, in the House, to the committee on foreign relations, who entered upon its consideration with great promptitude and energy.

1812. On the 3d of June, the committee reported, through Mr. Calhoun, their chairman, setting forth the reasons and causes for war with Great Britain. We regret that the length of this able paper prevents our giving it in full upon our pages: in substance, it declared, that the encroachments and insults of England had been already borne with much too long, and that the impressment of our seamen, the British doctrine and system of blockade, the persistence in the orders of council, the exciting the Indians to hostilities and the like, absolutely demanded that the United States should seek redress by an appeal to arms, so that the world might know, that "we have not only inherited the liberty our fathers gave us, but also the will and power to maintain it."

Congress, during its deliberations on the subject of war, sat with closed doors; and notwithstanding the force and urgency of the committee's report, and the able advocacy of many of the members of the House, it was for a time doubtful, whether a majority would agree to an immediate declaration of war: the federalists warmly opposed it, and a portion of the democratic members agreed with them in opinion and action on this point. The bill was, however, carried in the House, on the 4th of June, by a vote of seventy-nine to forty-nine. It was immediately sent to the Senate, where it met with very strong opposition, and the debate was carried on hotly and energetically for nearly two weeks. On the 17th of June, having undergone some amendments, the bill passed in the Senate by a vote of nineteen to thirteen.* The next day, the House having agreed to the amendments, the bill was sent to the president, who immediately signified his approval.

The act declaring war against Great Britain, was terse and briefly expressed. It was drawn up by Mr. Pinkney, the attorney-general, and was in the following terms:—

"An act declaring war between the United Kingdom of Great Britain and Ireland, and the dependencies thereof, and the United States of America and their territories.

"Be it enacted, etc. That WAR be, and the same is hereby declared to exist between the United Kingdom of Great Britain and Ireland, and the dependencies thereof, and the United States of America and their territories; and that the president of the United States be and is hereby authorized to use the whole land and naval force of the United States to carry the same into effect, and to issue to 1812. private armed vessels of the United States commissions or letters of marque and general reprisal, in such form as he shall think proper, and under the seal of the United States, against the ves-

* Of the seventy-nine members of the House who voted for the declaration of war, forty-six resided south, and thirty-three north of the Delaware; of the nineteen Senators who voted for the war, fourteen resided south and five north of the Delaware. New England opposed the war; Massachusetts, (including Maine) New Hampshire, Rhode Island, and Connecticut, with a large part of New York, and the majority of New Jersey, deprecated hostilities; the west and south, with the large central states of Virginia and Pennsylvania, warmly supported the declaration; Vermont was the only New England state in favor of the war.

sels, goods, and effects of the government of the same United Kingdom of Great Britain and Ireland, and the subjects thereof."

On the 19th of June, the president issued his proclamation, announcing the fact that war now existed, and calling upon the authorities, and upon all good citizens, to sustain their country in the measures just adopted to secure her rights and privileges.

Directly after the act declaring war had been passed by Congress, the federalist members of the House determined to publish an address to their constituents on this subject. A long and able review of the war measures was accordingly prepared and issued, in which were given many, and, as they were deemed, very cogent reasons for opposing war at that date. For some extracts from this address, see Appendix at the end of the present chapter.

Congress, on the 26th of June, passed an act respecting letters of marque, prizes, and prize goods; and it was confidently expected, from the activity and enterprise of our countrymen, that they would be able to inflict very serious injury upon the commerce of the enemy. A number of other acts were passed by Congress during the session, among which may be noted, that which related to the apportionment of members of the House of Representatives, in accordance with the third census. After a good deal of debate and difference between the House and the Senate, the ratio finally adopted was thirty-five thousand; by which the number of members of the House was increased from one hundred and forty-two to one hundred and eighty-three. As a fitting termination to its labors, Congress, by a resolution, requested the president to recommend to the people the observance of a day of fasting and prayer, in view of the position of public affairs, and the need of divine assistance and support amid the many trials to which they were now especially exposed. On the 6th of July, this long and unusually protracted session of the national legislature was brought to its close.*

1812.

On the 9th of July, the president issued his proclamation, recommending the third Thursday in August to be set apart as "a day of public humiliation and prayer, to be observed by the people of the United States, in offering up supplications to Almighty God for the safety and welfare of the states, his blessing on their arms, and the speedy restoration of peace." It is worthy of note, as evidencing the convictions of the majority of Americans on the subject of God's providential guidance and direction in human affairs, that this day was very generally observed throughout nearly the whole country.

* John Adams, writing to a friend on the very day Congress adjourned, gave his opinion as to the declaration of war in plain terms: "It was with surprise that I hear it pronounced, not only by newspapers, but by persons in authority, ecclesiastical and civil, and political and military, that it is an unjust and unnecessary war, that the declaration of it was altogether unexpected, etc. How it is possible that a rational, a social, or a moral creature can say that the war is unjust, is to me utterly incomprehensible. How it can be said to be unnecessary is very mysterious. I have thought it both just and necessary for five or six years. How it can be said to be unexpected, is another wonder; I have expected it for more than five-and-twenty years, and have had great reason to be thankful that it has been postponed so long."

APPENDIX TO CHAPTER VII.

ADDRESS OF THE MINORITY IN CONGRESS.

The undersigned, Members of the House of Representatives, to their respective constituents.

A republic has for its basis the capacity and right of the people to govern themselves. A main principle of a representative republic is the responsibility of the representatives to their constituents. Freedom and publicity of debate are essential to the preservation of such forms of government. Every arbitrary abridgement of the right of speech in representatives, is a direct infringement of the liberty of the people. Every unnecessary concealment of their proceedings an approximation towards tyranny. When, by systematic rules, a majority takes to itself the right, at its pleasure, of limiting speech, or denying it altogether; when secret sessions multiply, and in proportion to the importance of questions, is the studious concealment of debate, a people may be assured that, such practices continuing, their freedom is but short-lived.

Reflections, such as these, have been forced upon the attention of the undersigned, members of the House of Representatives of the United States, by the events of the present session of Congress. They have witnessed a principle, adopted as the law of the House, by which, under a novel application of the previous question, a power is assumed by the majority to deny the privilege of speech, at any stage, and under any circumstances of debate. And recently, by an unprecedented assumption, the right to give reasons for an original motion, has been made to depend upon the will of the majority.

Principles more hostile than these to the existence of representative liberty, cannot easily be conceived. It is not, however, on these accounts, weighty as they are, that the undersigned have undertaken this address. A subject of higher and more immediate importance impels them to the present duty.

The momentous question of war with Great Britain is decided. On this topic, so vital to your interests, the right of public debate, in the face of the world, and especially of their constituents, has been denied to your Representatives. They have been called into secret sessions, on this most interesting of all your public relations, although the circumstances of the time and of the nation, afforded no one reason for secrecy, unless it be found in the apprehension of the effect of public debate on public opinion; or of public opinion on the result of the vote.

Except the message of the President of the United States, which is now before the public, nothing confidential was communicated. That message contained no fact not previously known. No one reason for war was intimated but such as was of a nature public and notorious. The intention to wage war and invade Canada, had been long since openly avowed. The object of hostile menace had been ostentatiously announced. The inadequacy of both our army and navy for successful invasion, and the insufficiency of the fortifications for the security of our seaboard, were everywhere known. Yet the doors of Congress were shut upon the people. They have been carefully kept in ignorance of the progress of measures, until the purposes of the administration were consummated, and the fate of the country sealed. In a situation so extraordinary, the undersigned have deemed it their duty, by no act of theirs to sanction a proceeding so novel and arbitrary. On the contrary, they made every attempt in their power to attain publicity for their proceedings. All such attempts were vain. When this momentous subject was stated, as for debate, they demanded that the doors should be opened.

This being refused, they declined discussion; being perfectly convinced, from indications too plain to be misunderstood, that, in the House, all argument with closed doors was hopeless; and that any act, giving implied validity to so flagrant an abuse of power, would be little less than treachery to the essential rights of a free people. In the situation, to which the undersigned have thus been reduced, they are compelled, reluctantly, to resort to this public declaration of such views of the state and relations of the country, as determined their judgment and vote upon the question of war. A measure of this kind has appeared to the undersigned to be more imperiously demanded, by the circumstance of a message and manifesto being prepared, and circulated at public expense, in which the causes for war were enumerated, and the motives for it concentrated, in a manner suited to agitate and influence the public mind. In executing this task, it will be the study of the undersigned to reconcile the great duty they owe to the people, with that constitutional respect, which is due to the administrators of public concerns.

In commencing this view of our affairs, the undersigned would fail in duty to themselves, did they refrain from recurring to the course, in relation to public measures, which they adopted and have undeviatingly pursued from the commencement of this long and eventful session; in which they deliberately sacrificed every minor consideration, to what they deemed the best interest of the country.

For a succession of years the undersigned have from principle disapproved a series of restrictions upon commerce, according to their estimation, inefficient as respected foreign nations, and injurious chiefly to ourselves. Success in the system had become identified with the pride, the character, and the hope of our cabinet. As is natural with men who have a great stake on the success of a favorite theory, pertinacity seemed to increase as its hopelessness became apparent. As the inefficiency of this system could not be admitted by its advocates, without insuring its abandonment, ill success was carefully attributed to the influence of opposition.

To this cause the people were taught to charge its successive failures, and not to its intrinsic imbecility. In this state of things, the undersigned deemed it proper to take away all apology for adherence to this oppressive system. They were desirous, at a period so critical in public affairs, as far as was consistent with the independence of opinion, to contribute to the restoration of harmony in the public councils, and concord among the people. And if any advantage could be thus obtained in our foreign relations, the undersigned, being engaged in no purpose of personal or party advancement, would rejoice in such an occurrence.

The course of public measures, also, at the opening of the session, gave hope that an enlarged and enlightened system of defence, with provision for security of our maritime rights, was about to be commenced; a purpose which, wherever found, they deemed it their duty to foster, by giving, to any system of measures, thus comprehensive, as unobstructed a course as was consistent with their general sense of public duty. After a course of policy thus liberal and conciliatory, it was cause of regret, that a communication should have been purchased by an unprecedented expenditure of secret-service money; and used by the chief magistrate, to disseminate suspicion and jealousy, and excite resentment among the citizens, by suggesting imputations against a portion of them, as unmerited by their patriotism, as unwarranted by evidence.

It has always been the opinion of the undersigned, that a system of peace was the policy which most comported with the character, condition, and interest of the United States; that their remoteness from the theatre of contest, in Europe, was their peculiar felicity; and that nothing but a necessity absolutely imperious, should induce them to enter as parties into wars, in which every consideration of virtue and policy seems to be forgotten, under the overbearing sway of rapacity and ambition. There is a new era in human affairs. The European world is convulsed. The advantages of our situation are peculiar. "Why quit our own to stand upon foreign ground? Why, by interweaving our destiny with that of any part of Europe, entangle our peace and prosperity in the toils of European ambition, rivalship, interest, humor, or caprice?"

In addition to the many moral and prudential considerations which should deter thoughtful men from hastening into the perils of such a war, there were some peculiar to the United States, resulting from the texture of the goverment, in no small degree experimental, composed of powerful and independent sovereignties, associated in relations some of which are critical as well as novel, why they should not be hastily precipitated into situations calculated to put to trial the strength of the moral bond by which they are united. Of all states, that of war is most likely to call into activity the passions which are hostile and dangerous to such a form of government. Time is yet important to our country, to settle and mature its recent institutions. Above all, it appeared to the undersigned, from signs not to be mistaken, that if we entered upon this war, we did it as a divided people; not only from a sense of the inadequacy of our means to success, but from moral and political objections of great weight and general influence.

It appears to the undersigned, that the wrongs of which the United States have to complain, although in some aspects very grievous to our interests, and in many humiliating to our pride, were yet of a nature which, in the present state of the world, either would not justify war, or which war would not remedy. Thus, for instance, the hovering of British vessels on our coasts, and the occasional insults to our ports, imperiously demanded such a systematic application of harbor and seacoast defence, as would repel such aggressions, but in no light can they be considered as making a resort to war, at the present time, on the part of the United States, either necessary or expedient. So also, with respect to the Indian war, of the origin of which but very imperfect information has as yet been given to the public. Without any express act of Congress, an expedition was, last year, set on foot, and prosecuted into the Indian territory, which had been relinquished by treaty, on the part of the United States. And now we are told about the agency of British traders, as to Indian hostilities. It deserves consideration, whether there has been such provident attention, as would have been proper to remove any cause of complaint, either real or imaginary, which the Indians might allege, and to secure their friendship. With all the sympathy and anxiety excited by the state of that frontier, important as it may be to apply adequate means of protection against the Indians, how is it safely insured by a declaration of war, which adds the British to the number of enemies?

As "a decent respect for the opinions of mankind" has not induced the two Houses of Congress to concur in declaring the reasons, or motives, for their enacting a declaration of war, the undersigned and the public are left to search, elsewhere, for causes either real or ostensible. If we are to consider the President of the United States, and the committee of the House of Representatives on foreign relations, as speaking on this solemn occasion for Congress, the United States have three principal topics of complaint against Great Britain,—impressment; blockades; and orders in council.

. . . .

After a lengthened consideration of these topics, from the federalist point of view, the Address of the Minority concludes in the following terms:

A nation, like the United States, happy in its great local relations; removed from the bloody theatre of Europe; with a maritime border opening vast fields for enterprise; with territorial possessions exceeding every real want; its firesides safe; its altars undefiled; from invasion nothing to fear; from acquisition nothing to hope; how shall such a nation look to heaven for its smiles, while throwing away, as though they were worthless, all the blessings and joys which peace and such a distinguished lot include? With what prayers can it address the Most High, when it prepares to pour forth its youthful rage upon a neighboring people, from whose strength it has nothing to dread, from whose devastation it has nothing to gain?

If our ills were of a nature that war would remedy, if war would compensate any of our losses, or remove any of our complaints, there might be some alleviation of the suffering in the charm of the prospect. But how will war upon the land protect commerce upon the ocean? What balm has Canada for wounded honor? How are our mariners benefited by a war which exposes those who are free, without promising release to those who are impressed?

But it is said that war is demanded by honor. Is national honor a principle which thirsts after vengeance, and is appeased only by blood, which, trampling on the hopes of man, and spurning the law of God, untaught by what is past, and careless of what is to come, precipitates itself into any folly or madness to gratify a selfish vanity, or to satiate some unhallowed rage? If honor demands a war with England, what opiate lulls that honor to sleep over the wrongs done us by France? On land, robberies, seizures, imprisonments, by French authority; at sea, pillage, sinkings, burnings, under French orders. These are notorious. Are they unfelt because they are French? Is any alleviation to be found in the correspondence and humiliations of the present minister-plenipotentiary of the United States, at the French court? In his communications to our government, as before the public, where is the cause for now selecting France as the friend of our country, and England as the enemy?

If no illusions of personal feeling, and no solicitude for elevation of place, should be permitted to misguide the public councils; if it is, indeed, honorable for the true statesman to consult the public welfare, to provide, in truth, for the public defence, and impose no yoke of bondage; ought the government of this country, with full knowledge of the wrongs inflicted by the French, to aid the French cause by engaging in war against the enemy of France? To supply the waste of such a war, and to meet the appropriations of millions extraordinary for the war expenditures, must our fellow-citizens, throughout the Union, be doomed to sustain the burden of war-taxes in various forms of direct and indirect imposition? For official information respecting the millions deemed requisite for charges of the war, for like information respecting the nature and amount of taxes deemed requisite for drawing those millions from the community, it is here sufficient to refer to estimates and reports made by the secretary of the treasury, and the committee of ways and means, and to the body of resolutions passed in March last, in the House of Representatives.

It would be some relief to our anxiety, if amends were likely to be made for the weakness and wildness of the project, by the prudence of the preparation. But in no aspect of this anomalous affair can we trace the great and distinctive properties of wisdom. There is seen a headlong rushing into difficulties, with little calculation about the means. and little concern about the consequences. With a navy comparatively nominal, we are about to enter into the lists against the greatest marine on the globe. With a commerce, unprotected and spread over every ocean, we propose to make profit by privateering, and for this endanger the wealth of which we are honest proprietors. An invasion is threatened of the colonies of a power, which, without putting a new ship into commission, or taking another soldier into pay, can spread alarm or desolation along the extensive range of our seaboard. The resources of our country, in their natural state, great beyond our wants or our hopes, are impaired by the effect of artificial restraints. Before adequate fortifications are prepared for domestic defence, before men or money are provided for a war of attack, why hasten into the midst of that awful contest, which is laying waste Europe? It cannot be concealed, that to engage in the present war against England, is to place ourselves on the side of France; and exposes us to the vassalage of states, serving under the banners of the French emperor.

The undersigned cannot refrain from asking, what are the United States to gain by this war? Will the gratification of some privateersmen compensate the nation for that sweep of our legitimate commerce, by the extended marine of our enemy, which this desperate act invites? Will Canada compensate the middle states for New-York; or the western states for New-Orleans? Let us not be deceived. A war of invasion may invite a retort of invasion. When we visit the peaceable and, as to us, innocent colonies of Great Britian with the horrors of war, can we be assured that our own coast will not be visited with like horrors?

At a crisis of the world such as the present, and under impressions such as these, the undersigned could not consider the war in which the United States have, in secret, been precipitated, as necessary, or required by any moral duty, or any political expediency.

(Signed,)

GEORGE SULLIVAN,	LEWIS B. STURGES,
MARTIN CHITTENDEN,	BENJAMIN TALLMADGE,
ABIJAH BIGELOW,	H. BLEECKER,
ELIJAH BRIGHAM,	JAMES EMOTT,
WILLIAM ELY,	ASA FITCH,
JOSIAH QUINCY,	THOMAS R. GOLD,
WILLIAM REED,	JAMES MILNOR,
SAMUEL TAGGART,	H. M. RIDGELY,
LABAN WHEATON,	C. GOLDSBOROUGH,
LEONARD WHITE,	PHILIP B. KEY,
RICHARD JACKSON, Jun.,	PHILIP STUART,
ELISHA R. POTTER,	JOHN BAKER,
EPAPHRODITUS CHAMPION,	JAMES BRECKENRIDGE,
JOHN DAVENPORT, Jun.,	JOS. LEWIS, Jun.,
LYMAN LAW,	THOMAS WILSON,
JONA. O. MOSELY,	A. M'BRYDE,
TIMOTHY PITKIN, Jun.,	JOS. PEARSON.

CHAPTER VIII.

1812.

OPERATIONS OF THE YEAR 1812.

Position of the country at the declaration of war — Advantages and disadvantages — State of feeling in New England — Pulpit harangues — State of feeling in the middle and southern states — Riot in Baltimore — Enthusiasm in the west — Appointment of officers for the army — Difficulties in the way — Canada to be invaded — General Hull's force — Sets out for Detroit — Delay in informing him of the declaration of war — Enters Canada — His proclamation — His strange inactivity and vacillation — Fall of Mackinaw — Hull retreats to Detroit — British activity — Captain Brush's company — Vanhorne defeated — Miller at Maguaga — Captain Heald evacuates Chicago — Expedition of Cass and M'Arthur — The British advance — Hull's surrender — Amazement and indignation of the country — Hull tried and condemned — Gallantry of the navy — The celebrated chase of the Constitution by a British squadron — The Constitution captures the Guerriere — Exultation and pride of the country — Victory of the Wasp over the Frolic — Effects of the American gunnery — Decatur in the United States captures the Macedonian — The Constitution takes the Java — Volunteer efforts in the north-west — Harrison in command — General Hopkins on the Wabash — Captain Zachary Taylor at Fort Harrison — Other expeditions in the west — Van Rensselaer at Lewiston — Determines to attack Queenstown — Exploits of Captain Wool — The battle — Disgraceful conduct of the militia on the American shore — The British victorious at the last — General Smyth's vainglorious attempt — Its result — Other efforts to do something — General Dearborn and his course — Absurd and vexatious conclusion — Estimate of the campaign of 1812.

THUS was our country a second time in arms against England. Angered, smarting under a sense of long-continued outrage and wrong; conscious of ability to assert their just rights, the larger portion of the United States threw down the gauntlet, and resolved to hazard their all in defence of their liberties and their claim to independence among the nations of the earth.

1812.

In many respects, our country was more favorably situate than at the commencement of the Revolutionary War. The population had considerably more than doubled. National resources had been largely developped. A settled government was in effective operation. National pride had grown and increased. Americans deemed themselves the equals of the oldest and haughtiest nations of the old world. And however absurd it might have seemed, on a calm review of the relative power and position of England and the United States, for the latter to venture single-handed upon the deadly struggle, Americans did not hesitate: with a sort of self-reliant audacity, they counted themselves a host, and deemed no odds sufficient to fright them from the tented field and the bloody conflict.

There was unquestionably zeal and spirit enough in our countrymen for this emergency. There was courage enough, strong hands and stout hearts enough; but, it must be confessed, there was no adequate preparation for the contest with so powerful an enemy as England. Neither in men, nor in officers; neither in the executive, nor his cabinet; neither in the financial provisions, nor in regard to the nature and character of the war, was there the proper foresight, the just conception, the needful training, the fitting ability for the vigorous and successful prosecution of hostilities against the neighboring colonies of England by land, or her vast and terrible array of ships of war on the sea. The haughty mistress of the ocean had her thousand floating castles, which proudly bore aloft the royal flag; and innumerable cruisers and privateers were ready in every sea to pounce upon the defenceless American commerce; while the entire naval force of the United States, in ordinary or in building, was only eight frigates and twelve sloops!*

But even this disparity of force, this confessedly insufficient preparation for war in nearly every respect, was not

1812. the worst feature in the then position of affairs. The rage of party feelings; the discords and bitter feuds of democrats and federalists; the lack of unanimity and concord in meeting the foe,—were serious and dreadful obstacles in the way of those who had brought about the declaration of war and were determined to carry it on at all hazards. Boston, so illustrious in the Revolutionary struggle, now scouted and denounced the second war against England, and the flags of her shipping were hoisted at half-mast when the news came to her, in token of mourning and humiliation. All New England resounded with the bitterest denunciations of the executive and the war party. The state legislatures, the merchants, the lawyers, the wealth and the talent of this portion of our country fiercely arrayed themselves against the administration and its measures; and many of the New England ministers, who thought themselves called upon to be guides in politics as well as religion, indulged in a style and violence of invective which has no parallel elsewhere in history. A specimen or two of their diatribes may not improperly be here quoted.

"It is a war," exclaimed one ardent beater of the "drum ecclesiastic," "unexampled in history; proclaimed on the most frivolous and groundless pretences; let no consideration whatever deter my brethren, at all times and in all places, from execrating the present war. Mr. Madison has declared it, let Mr. Madison carry it on. If you do not wish to become the slaves of those who are slaves, and are themselves the slaves of French slaves, you must cut the connection, or so far alter the Constitution as to secure yourselves a share in the government. The Union has been long since virtually dissolved, and it is high time that this part of the disunited states should take care of itself."

* In 1812, says Mr. Cooper, the navy of Great Britain nominally contained a thousand and sixty sail, of which between seven and eight hundred were efficient cruising vessels, and the state of things was such in Europe, that she was able to send as many ships as she thought necessary against the Americans. The navy—if we may use the term—of the United States, according to the same authority, consisted of but seventeen cruising vessels on the ocean, of which nine were of a class less than frigates.—See Cooper's "*Naval History*," vol. ii., p. 40.

"Should the English now be at liberty to send all their armies and all their ships to America," cried another, "and in one day burn every city from Maine to Georgia, your condescending rulers would play on their harps, while they gazed on the tremendous conflagration." And again, even more furiously shouted a third, "What sooty slave in all the Ancient Dominion more obsequiously watched the eye of his master, and flew to the indulgence of his desires more servilely, than those same masters have waited, and watched, and obeyed, the orders of the great Napoleon?" "How will the supporters of this anti-Christian warfare endure their sentence—endure their own reflections—endure the fire that forever burns—the worm which never dies—the hosannas of heaven, while the smoke of their torments ascends forever and ever?"* No wonder if, under such harangues as these must have been, New England arrayed herself against the war, and did every thing in her power to oppose and harass the administration.†

In the middle and southern states, there was greater diversity of sentiment on this subject. Some, if not many, disapproved of the war; but the majority undoubtedly were in favor of prosecuting it with vigor and energy. The strong feeling of those who supported the views of the war party was manifested, in one case, in a very violent and scandalous manner. It appears that at Baltimore, there was a newspaper, called "The Federal Gazette," the editor of which, not only ardently advocated the views of his party, but also indulged in very free strictures upon the administration and its course in regard to the war. This was on the 20th of June: the same evening, his office was mobbed, and his whole establishment destroyed. Some weeks afterwards, Hanson, the editor, endeavored to re-establish his paper, hoping that the law would protect him and his property; but fearing renewed assaults, he fortified his house, and aided by Generals Henry Lee and Lingan, Revolutionary officers, he determined to resist aggression by force. On the 27th of July, the mob again attacked Hanson's establishment; blood was shed; and the occupants of the house were persuaded by the mayor, as the only means of saving their lives, to surrender and go to jail, to answer charges against them. The next night the jail was broken open, and the prisoners shamefully abused and maltreated.

1812.

* See Ingersoll's "*History of the Second War*," vol. i., pp. 52–56.

† Mr. Dwight gives the correspondence between the authorities at Washington and the governor of Connecticut, in which are considered the grounds of the latter's refusal to allow the militia to leave the state. Mr. Dwight further says: "In July, 1812, the governor of Massachusetts issued a general order to the militia of that state, in which, after some preliminary remarks on the state of the country, and directing that the detachment of ten thousand men should be completed without delay,—it is added,—that as that body of men, being to be raised throughout the state, could not be assembled to repel a sudden invasion, and it would be extremely burdensome to keep them constantly in service, and if they were assembled they would not be adequate to the defence of the exposed points of a coast of several hundred miles in extent,—it was ordered, that the officers of the whole militia of the state hold themselves, and the militia under their command, in constant readiness to assemble and march to any part or parts of the state."—"*History of the Hartford Convention*," p. 269.

General Lingan died of the tortures he underwent; General Lee was lamed for life; and others escaped only by feigning to be dead. The city authorities plainly connived at these outrages, and the whole blame was thrown upon Hanson and his friends, for daring to defy "the democratic sentiment of Baltimore!"*

It was in the great west, however, that the war spirit prevailed over all opposition; and the stalwart denizens of that section of our country, were ready, to a man, to fight for the cause of liberty and equal rights. With them, enthusiasm and the love of country glowed in every bosom, and they were eager for the call to the battle-field.† Conscious of the dangers to which the frontier was exposed from savage incursions; fully persuaded that England was engaged in the mean and detestable occupation of inciting the Indians to murderous hostility; and with imaginations fired with the prospect of conquering Canada, and expelling the enemy from the continent; the people of the west entered heart and soul into the contest, and suffered not a doubt to enter their minds that victory would crown their patriotic efforts.

In looking back upon the zeal and spirit which animated our countrymen at this date, we may well give expression to the regret, that, not only was there very culpable negligence in the making proper preparation for the war, but also that the material out of which to choose officers of the higher grade was so scanty, and, for the most part, of so little value. Madison, as we have said, was utterly averse to war in any shape, and no one of his cabinet had either experience or ability to make up for his deficiencies. At first, he thought of appointing Henry Clay as commander-in-chief; but that eloquent Kentuckian was not acquainted with military science at all, and he was wanted in the House of Representatives. The president then sought among the survivors of the Revolution for a suitable head to the army, and Henry Dearborn, a major in the first war, and one of Mr. Jefferson's cabinet, was made commander-in-chief. With him were associated, as brigadier-generals, James Wilkinson, Wade Hampton, William Hull, and Joseph Bloomfield. The president also appointed Thomas Pinckney a major-general. In the case of these officers, it was soon after discovered, that age and long cessation from military toils and activity would seriously interfere with their being able to prosecute hostilities with vigor and reasonable prospect of success. Then too, although Congress had authorized the enlistment of twenty-five thousand men, it was found impossible to fill up the ranks from the few who felt any

* The reaction caused by this vile spirit of mobocracy, produced a change in the politics of Maryland.

† That distinguished federalist, John Jay, in reply to some inquiries on the subject of the war, expressed his views frankly and straightforwardly. (For John Adams's opinion, see p. 148.) Under date of July 28th, 1812, he wrote to a friend: "As the war has been *constitutionally* declared, the people are evidently bound to support it in the manner which *constitutional* laws do or shall prescribe. In my opinion, the declaration of war was neither necessary, nor expedient, nor seasonable; and I think that they who entertain this opinion do well in expressing it, both individually and collectively, on this very singular and important occasion."—"*Life of John Jay,*" vol. i., p. 445.

necessity of enlisting. The whole number of regulars at the opening of the war scarcely amounted to five thousand men, and these were scattered over a vast surface of country. The president was empowered to receive fifty thousand volunteers, and to call out one hundred thousand militia; but these, always unreliable, and though sometimes fighting with wonderful bravery, subject to sudden panics, were no match for the disciplined troops of the enemy, and would prove serviceable mainly in defending the sea-coast and the frontier. And, in addition to all this, several of the state authorities were not disposed to submit to the president's demand for the militia in the existing condition of things, as we shall see further on.

Some time before the declaration of war, the invasion of Canada had been determined upon. This was indeed the only aggressive movement which could be made, and very sanguine hopes of success were entertained by the administration; for, it was argued, if
1812. the United States had overcome England with a population less than half its present number, surely now they would be able to expel them from America altogether. The attack was to be begun by General Hull, governor of Michigan Territory, and commander of the north-western army, as it was termed. His force consisted of between five hundred and a thousand regulars, and some two thousand militia from Ohio. With these, the army of the centre, consisting of about two thousand regulars and over two thousand militia, was to coöperate on the Niagara frontier; and it was confidently expected, that they would be able to sweep every thing before them, and in a short time plant the standard of the Union on the walls of Montreal. Had General Hull been the right man, and had he been properly furnished and supported by executive ability at Washington, this expectation of the country at large might have been gratified.

About the middle of June, Hull left Dayton in Ohio, with the forces under his command, Colonels M'Arthur, Cass, and Findlay being at the head of the three regiments of Ohio volunteers. Passing through Stanton and Urbanna, the army were compelled, in traversing the uncultivated regions between the latter place and the Rapids of the Maumee, (about a hundred and fifty miles,) to remove obstructions, and make their own road. Having built four block-houses, and garrisoned them with the disabled, they reached the Rapids on the 30th of June. On the 26th, four days previous, General Hull had received by express, a letter from Dr. Eustis, the secretary of war, written on the morning of the day on which the declaration of war was made. By some strange carelessness, this letter merely reiterated former orders, and contained expressions which seemed to show that war would soon be declared. Expecting to be informed, by express, when the declaration actually took place, and not imagining such a thing as that the British could be in 1812.
possession of such important intelligence earlier than himself, Hull, for the purpose of disencumbering his army, and facilitating their march, hired

a vessel, which had sailed as a packet, to convey to Detroit, his sick, his hospital stores, and a considerable part of his baggage. This vessel, which sailed on the 1st of July, fell into the hands of the British near Malden, who had been two or three days in possession of the information that war was declared. With Hull's private baggage, his aid-de-camp unfortunately had placed on board the vessel a trunk of official and confidential papers, by means of which the enemy obtained possession of his correspondence with the government and the returns of his officers, thus having disclosed to them the number and condition of Hull's troops.

The letter from the secretary of war, dated June 18th, containing the important information of the declaration of war, was received on the 2d of July. To our astonishment, we learn that this letter was entrusted to the ordinary course of the mail, as if it were a matter of very small consequence! Hull was on his march at the time, and on the 5th of July, encamped at Spring Wells, opposite Sandwich and within a few miles of Detroit. Three or four days were spent in rest and refreshment, and, having entered Detroit, in considering what next should be done.

The army as a body, were eager to enter upon the work laid out for them, and were confident of success in invading Canada. On the 9th of July, Hull received dispatches from the secretary of war, authorizing him to commence offensive operations if he judged best; upon which, yielding to the wishes of the officers and troops, he crossed the river on the 12th, took possession of the village of Sandwich, and issued a boldly-worded proclamation to the inhabitants of the province. He had come, he told them, to set all who desired liberty, free from the tyranny and injustice of Great Britain, and he would charge himself with their protection; but he would exterminate the British forces, if they employed Indians in the war; his force was sufficient to break down all opposition, and it was but the forerunner of a much larger one. His deeds, however, did not correspond to his words. Now was the moment to push forward to the attack of Malden, or Amherstberg, an important fortress held by the British, on the Detroit River, near its entrance into Lake Erie. It was garrisoned by some six hundred men, under Colonel St. George, and had Hull acted with promptitude and spirit, would no doubt have yielded to the American arms. The commander hesitated, and wavered, and thought it best to wait for the getting his heavy artillery in readiness, and so the precious opportunity slipped away.

Instead of attacking Malden, or liberating Canada, he remained, week after week, in a state of inactivity as mortifying as it was inexplicable, not doing a single thing to justify either the invitations or the menaces of his proclamation; so that whatever ardor had fired his troops was cooled greatly, and distrust and contempt expelled confidence and attachment from the hearts of the Canadians. The enemy meanwhile were not idle. Malden was reinforced; the supplies were almost entirely cut off; and Hull was get-

1812.

ting deeper and deeper into the "slough of despond." News reached him near the end of the month, that Mackinaw had fallen into the hands of the enemy, who were thus put in possession of one of the strongest posts in the country. It had been attacked on the 17th of July, by a party of British and Indians, principally the latter, amounting in the whole to one thousand and twenty-four. Lieutenant Hanks, who commanded at this fort, had only fifty-seven men under his command; nor, though twelve days had elapsed since Hull's arrival at Detroit, had he been informed of the declaration of war. The summons to surrender was the first knowledge given to him that hostilities had broken out. On learning the strength of the enemy, Hanks capitulated, by the unanimous advice of his officers; stipulating, however, that his garrison should march out of the fort with the honors of war.

Hull was panic-stricken at this news, and perceiving that the road was now open for Indian marauding excursions from the north-west, and fearing that he would be overwhelmed if he remained in Canada, he gave orders to retreat, just as the attack on Malden was to be made, and on the 8th of August ingloriously returned to Detroit.

The British were not slow to avail themselves of the opening which Hull's conduct allowed. General Brock took command of the forces at Malden. The agents and others in the employ of the North-West Fur Company, furnished important assistance, especially in rousing the Indian tribes to join against the Americans; and Tecumseh, now a major-general in the British service, was sent to occupy the forest wilderness south of Detroit, and cut off all communication from its garrison.

At the river Raisin, Tecumseh met and stopped a company of Ohio volunteers, under Captain Brush, who were hastening with supplies to join General Hull, whom they expected to find in Canada. Brush contrived to get word to Hull by means of a scout, and Major Vanhorne, with a hundred and fifty or two hundred men, was sent to open the road and escort Brush to Detroit. But falling into an Indian ambush, they were routed by less than half their number, and scarcely a hundred made their way back to the fort, the rest being killed, or dispersed. The Indians also captured Hull's dispatches, which were sent to Brock, and showed him the desponding condition of the American forces.

News soon afterwards reached General Hull, that, in consequence of an armistice for a brief period between Sir George Prevost and General Dearborn, in which, however, Hull was not included, the British commander had an opportunity of directing his whole force against the army of the north-west; and further, that the promised co-operation on the Niagara frontier could not be depended on at all. In this state of affairs, Hull resolved to make another attempt to restore his communications with Ohio, and for that purpose directed Lieutenant-Colonel Miller, with six hundred men, to proceed to the Raisin, and to clear the woods of the savages there. But simultaneously with this movement, General Proctor, on the side of the enemy, had crossed over with all his force, some four or five hundred strong, to press the advantages gained by Tecumseh in that quarter.

At Brown's Town, or Maguaga, about fourteen miles from Detroit, they found the Indians and the British strongly posted; but they gallantly advanced to the attack, and after a severe contest, compelled them to retreat. The **1812.** enemy embarked under cover of their armed vessels, and returned to Malden; and Miller, having lost about eighty men, was soon after recalled to Detroit.

On the 9th of August, Hull sent an order to Captain Heald to evacuate Chicago, where he was in command, and lead his force directly to Detroit. Heald set out on the 15th, with about seventy men, and some fifty friendly Indians, escorting several women and children. They were speedily attacked by the savages, amounting to about five hundred. More than half of his force having been killed, Captain Heald surrendered to Blackbird, a Pottawottamie chief.

Captain Brush having informed General Hull that he should endeavor to reach Detroit by a circuitous route, Colonels Cass and M'Arthur volunteered to go and meet him, in order to insure the safe arrival of the provisions. Taking three hundred and fifty men, they set out on the 13th of August; but, we are sorry to say, they were not successful; for the men lost their way in the trackless forest, and could not contrive either to pass or to round a morass; and therefore, having consumed all their stores, could only go back to Detroit, whither they had been summoned to return, (but the messengers were intercepted by the Indians,) and where they arrived too late to be of any service.

General Brock, who had reached Malden on the 13th of August, recalled the expedition from the Raisin River, and on the 15th, erected batteries on the bank of the river opposite Detroit. The same day, he sent a flag summoning Hull to surrender, to which, answer was sent that the Americans were ready to encounter the foe. Brock immediately opened the batteries upon the town and fort, and did some execution. Hull appears now to have been seized with a terror that completely unmanned him, and his officers were so provoked by his vacillation and timidity, that, had Colonels Cass and M'Arthur been present, he would no doubt have been deprived of his command, and the disgraceful result which followed probably have been prevented.

Early in the morning of the 16th of August, the British landed at Spring Wells, three miles below Detroit, and marched forward to the attack. Hull's force was drawn up in battle-array outside the fort, the artillery was well planted, and the Americans had no fear of meeting the enemy; but when the British were about five hundred yards distant, the astounding command was given for the troops to retire within the fort! The scene which followed beggars description; and poor Hull, anxious only to escape from his present pitiable condition, ordered a white flag to be hung out on the walls of the fort! Not a blow was struck, not a gun was fired, not a word of consultation was had with his officers, not a single stipulation for the honor of his troops; but an unconditional giving up of all to the enemy. The fortress, the garrison, and munitions of war, the detachment under Cass and M'Arthur, and even the soldiers under Captain Brush, were included in the capitulation. Hull's only object seems to have been to escape from the Indian scalping-knife. **1812.** When he had first entered Canada, the British had at Malden but one hundred regular troops, four hundred Canadian militia, and a few hundred Indians. After General Brock's arrival, their whole force was three hundred and thirty regulars, four hundred militia, and six hundred Indians. Including those who were absent, the whole force surrendered by General Hull amounted to two thousand five hundred men, of whom twelve hundred were militia.

Colonels Cass and M'Arthur, with their detachment, arrived in a half-starving condition, just in time to hear of the surrender, and they hoped to escape; but hunger compelled them to accede to the terms of the capitulation. Captain Brush, when he heard the news of the surrender from some Ohio militia, resolved to treat it with contempt; and so he marched his force back again to Ohio.

The amazement and indignation of the whole country, at Hull's surrender, cannot adequately be depicted in words, and charges of not only cowardice and disgraceful inefficiency, but also of treason and collusion with the enemy were freely bestowed upon the unhappy general. His official report, under date of August 26th, was sent to Washington, and puts the best face upon the matter of which it is capable; **1812.** but he was contradicted almost flatly in every thing material by Colonel Cass, in a letter to the secretary of war, under date of September 10th; and the name and reputation of General Hull sunk under the fearful explosion of wrath and disappointment which fell upon his devoted head. Few, if any, thought of the mitigation which existed in his behalf; of the inefficiency of the war department; the cutting off his supplies; the undisciplined troops under his command; the number and savage ferocity of the Indians in the British employ; etc.

In the present connection, we may mention, that General Hull was tried by a court-martial, which assembled in January, and concluded its labors at the close of March, 1814.* Treason, cowardice, neglect of duty and un-officer-like conduct, were the charges against him. Of the first, he was acquitted; but was found guilty of the two latter, and was sentenced to be shot. The court, nevertheless, recommended him to the mercy of the president, in consequence of his advanced age and his revolutionary services. The president listened to this recommendation, and remitted the punishment of

* Hull issued an address to the people of the United States, asking a suspension of judgment till his Vindication could be prepared. This was published in 1824; and in 1848 his grandson gave to the public a large octavo volume, intended as a complete refutation of the charges against him. The reader may consult this volume to advantage, and he will probably come to the conclusion that General Hull was more severely dealt with than, all things considered, he rightly deserved.

death, but at the same time his name was ordered to be stricken from the roll of the army.

The disastrous results of the movements in the north-west, where victory had been counted upon with certainty, were extremely galling to the pride of our countrymen; and they chafed grievously under the prospect of defeat and disgrace in a matter on which the war-party had entered with most confident expectations of glory and distinction. It is worthy of note, as showing the uncertainty of plans for carrying on war, that, from a quarter whence no one looked for it, the most gratifying and most brilliant successes waited upon the American arms. England had always been counted supreme upon the ocean, and her navy had gained so many illustrious victories, that it was thought to be impossible that any reverses could befall her conquering ships of war. Least of all was it supposed, that the United States, who possessed no navy, and who had at best but a few frigates and smaller vessels, would dare to encounter in battle the lordly masters of the sea. But it was speedily demonstrated to England, as well as to the world, that the gallant little navy of the United States was as able as it was willing to meet the enemy, and to teach them some lessons of value and moment.

Early in July, when the British had dispatched a squadron into the American waters, the Nautilus, fourteen, leaving New York for the purpose of cruising in the track of the English Indiamen, fell in with the squadron of Commodore Broke, and was chased,

1812.

her gallant commander, Lieutenant Crane, doing every thing he could to escape, but unavailingly; she therefore struck, without a conflict, to the Shannon; and this was the first vessel of war captured on either side.

The Constitution, forty-four, Captain Hull, had just returned from Europe, where she narrowly escaped an overhauling from the English cruisers, on the pretence of looking for deserters. Proceeding to the north from Annapolis, on the 12th of July, she fell in with the British squadron, and for four days was chased by all the vessels composing it, the Africa, sixty-four, taking the lead. Few such chases have ever occurred in the history of naval warfare, and seldom, if ever, has a vessel escaped from such odds, by dint of seamanship alone. Now towed by boats, and now forced along by hauling at a kedge anchor carried out near half a mile ahead, and let go; using every breath of air that blew fitfully; the Constitution contrived to distance her pursuers, who resorted to the same means, but without coming up to the object of their endeavors. Once and again it seemed as if she must fall into the hands of one or another of her keen enemies; but ever some sudden breeze sprang up, and preserved her. At length, on the fourth day, the wind freshened sufficiently for the American to prove her superior fleetness, and whilst all the five frigates were on the same tack, and under clouds of canvas, from the truck to the water, the Constitution slowly drew ahead of her pursuers; and in fine, a heavy squall in the evening carried her completely out of view.

We may notice in passing, that, on the 13th of August, off the Grand Bank, the Essex, thirty-two, Captain Porter, fell in with the British sloop-of-war the Alert, of twenty guns. The Alert began the attack, but when the Essex opened upon her, in eight minutes she struck, apparently in a panic at mistaking the Essex for a merchantman. This was the first vessel taken from the English in the present war.

On the 19th of August, only three days after the disgrace at Detroit, Captain Hull, in the Constitution, brought unequalled glory upon that name which his uncle had rendered a bye-word in the United States, and proved to the world what the American navy was capable of performing in a fair
1812. fight with their haughty enemy. In the afternoon of the 19th, the Constitution discovered and gave chase to a large English frigate, the Guerriere, thirty-eight, Captain Dacres, who had been extremely desirous of meeting with an American ship of war, and did not doubt that he would obtain an easy victory. Captain Hull gave strict orders not to return the enemy's fire, until they were so near that every shot was certain to take effect. When in the position he desired, Hull opened upon the Guerriere, with broadside following broadside, very rapidly and with tremendous force. In half an hour's time, the Guerriere was little better than a wreck, and Captain Dacres, having lost over a hundred men in killed and wounded, surrendered to the victorious Hull. The loss of the Constitution was only seven killed and seven wounded. As it was impossible to get the Guerriere into port, she was set fire to, and blew up in fifteen minutes.

The exultation caused by this victory was unbounded, and Hull and his gallant crew were greeted with enthusiasm wherever they appeared. Congress, beside a vote of thanks, presented him and his men with $50,000 as a compensation for the loss of the prize.* In England the astonishment which was caused by the news of this battle was indescribable, and mortification and shame fell justly upon those who had boasted so loudly and insolently of their invincibility on the ocean. Every possible reason was searched for to account for Dacres' defeat. The Constitution was said to be a seventy-four in disguise, to have a picked crew of British seamen, and the like. The truth is, beyond doubt, that she was a somewhat larger and heavier ship than the Guerriere, and that the latter had not a full crew; but after making all the allowances which can be claimed, it was felt then, and truly felt, that the invincibility of the British on the ocean was now destroyed. The United States henceforth were to take their place amongst the foremost maritime powers of the world, and the stars and stripes were now to

* "It is not easy," says Mr. Cooper, "at this distant day, to convey to the reader the full force of the moral impression created in America by this victory of one frigate over another. So deep had been the effect produced on the public mind by the constant accounts of the successes of the English over their enemies at sea, that the opinion, already mentioned of their invincibility on that element, generally prevailed; and it had been publicly predicted, that before the contest had continued six months, British sloops-of-war would lie alongside of American frigates with comparative impunity."—"*Naval History*," vol. ii., p. 56.

become known and recognized as floating proudly over vessels not inferior to those of England or any other people who "go down to the sea in ships, and do their business in the great waters."

Other victories followed that of Hull in the Constitution. On the night of the 16th of October, the British sloop-of-war Frolic, eighteen, convoying six merchant ships, fell in with the United States sloop-of-war Wasp, eighteen, Captain Jones. The engagement which ensued was fierce and bloody. The Wasp was much injured in her spars and rigging, but on boarding the Frolic found the deck covered with only the

1812.

dead and wounded. Thirty were killed and fifty wounded. The Wasp had only five killed and five wounded. Lieutenant Biddle lowered the English flag with his own hands, after a contest of forty-three minutes' duration. Both the Frolic and Wasp were, however, taken, a few hours later, by the Poictiers, a seventy-four. On Captain Jones's return to the United States, he was warmly applauded, and Congress voted him and his crew $25,000.

This victory caused greater exultation in the United States than others of more intrinsic importance, because the force on both sides was more nearly equal; and the credit of the success, in consequence, the greater. It did undoubtedly very effectually dissipate the notion of British invincibility at sea; but the most valuable result, perhaps, was the testimony afforded to the superiority of cool and scientific gunnery in naval combat. Sea-fights had been for the most part decided by mere animal courage and brute force. The only science shown had been in the handling of the ships, and the manœuvring of the fleets. Our naval officers, not neglecting this department of strategics, *took aim* when they discharged their guns, and brought these engagements to a speedy decision by not aimlessly squandering their shot. No amount of courage, backed mostly by noise and smoke,—and artillery badly aimed, or not aimed at all, is no more,—could stand against the heavy metal, flying true to its mark, of the American guns. The lesson thus terribly impressed upon the British, we are assured by an English writer, was not thrown away.

Little more than a week later, Commodore Decatur had an opportunity of adding to his well-deserved laurels. He was now in command of the frigate United States, forty-four, and having captured, a few days before, the British packet, Swallow, with a large amount of specie, fell in, on the 25th of October, with the Macedonian, rated at thirty-eight, but carrying forty-nine. A combat at once commenced, the vessels passing and repassing each other for about an hour, when the mizen-mast of the British frigate fell, and the vessel became almost unmanageable, from the fearful injuries she had received. The superior gunnery of the United States told fearfully against her antagonist, and the larger number of her crew gave her the advantage in manœuvring. At this period, the United States stood athwart the bows

1812.

of the Macedonian, and passed out of shot without firing a gun; and her antagonist's crew, supposing she had given up the fight, set a union-jack in the main-rigging, and gave three cheers. But it was only to refill her cartridges, and she soon came back, and took up a raking position across the stern of her defenceless foe;—whereupon the Macedonian struck. She had thirty-six killed and sixty-eight wounded, and had received nearly a hundred shot in her hull; whilst the United States had lost but twelve killed and wounded, and suffered surprisingly little, considering the length of the cannonade. The prize was brought into New London, early in December, and added not a little to the joy and pride of the nation in their gallant navy.

The Argus, sixteen, under Captain Sinclair, which had set out on a cruise, at the same time as the United States, was very successful in making prizes; chased for three days and as many moonlight nights, by a squadron of the enemy; and not only escaped, but actually took and manned a prize during the chase!

One more naval victory belongs to the record of this year. The Constitution, (Captain Hull having given place to Commodore Bainbridge,) on December the 28th, met with the Java, thirty-eight, and maintained with her for about forty minutes a contest, in which seamanship as much as gunnery or courage was conspicuous. The English captain then resolved to attempt to board his antagonist, and ran down on the Constitution's quarter for that purpose. But before this could be
1812. accomplished, the foremast fell with a tremendous crash, the main-top-mast came down, the head of the bowsprit was shot away, and the captain fell, mortally wounded. Lieutenant Chads, who took the command, carried on the fight; but after the American commodore had passed out of the combat, for the purpose of refitting, and returned, he found his vessel a complete wreck, and struck. Finding it impossible to save their prize, after removing the crew, the Java was blown up. A hundred and twenty-four, killed and wounded, were said by the British to have been lost on board the Java; but Bainbridge reckoned their loss as much higher. Thirty-four alone suffered, in both ways, on board the Constitution. The Java had been literally picked to pieces by the fire of the Constitution, spar following spar until there was not one left; while, strange to tell, the American frigate did not lose a single spar. Commodore Bainbridge, landing his prisoners on parole, at San Salvador, left for home, and arrived at Boston on the 27th of February, 1813.

During the autumn of this year, the lakes were witnesses of the gallantry of the small force which our country at the time possessed; and it soon became evident, that important results would depend upon proper preparation to meet the enemy there. Captain Isaac Chauncey was actively engaged in this work for forwarding his country's interests, and captured a schooner with $12,000 in specie on board.

Turning our attention again to operations on the land, we find them carried on in a way that cannot but excite surprise at the large amount of blundering and bungling on the part of most of those in authority, not unmingled with admiration at the spirit and valor of a portion of the troops.

In the north-west, "Hull's treason," as it was termed, was indignantly denounced, and there was a spirit roused, the like to which has hardly, if ever, been witnesed elsewhere. Volunteers offered themselves in large numbers, and Ohio and Kentucky furnished their thousands, who flocked to the standard of General Harrison, ready to march at once to the recovery of what had been lost, and to the defence of the now exposed frontier. General Winchester was appointed by the president to the command in this quarter; but he soon after gave place to General Harrison, who, in the latter part of September, was made commander of the north-western army. Great hopes were entertained of retrieving Hull's disaster before winter; but the spirit of volunteers, though capable of effecting wonders under favorable circumstances, is not to be relied on for patient endurance and necessary discipline. This was shown on several occasions, and prevented the attaining success, where success was plainly within reach.

1812.

The main division of the army, consisting of three thousand men, under Harrison in person, was at this time at the River St. Mary's. Another division, under General Winchester, consisting of two thousand, had penetrated on the road to Detroit, as far as Fort Defiance; but they were in want of provisions, and had sent to Harrison for relief. That general immediately marched with a considerable part of his troops, and on the 3d of October, joined General Winchester at Fort Defiance. He returned the next day to St. Mary's, having previously ordered General Tupper, with one thousand of the Ohio militia, to proceed to the Rapids of the Miami, to dislodge the enemy, and take possession of that place. Want of experience and authority on the part of the officers, and especially of proper subordination on that of the troops, produced a failure in this, and another attempt made by General Tupper; and the British still retained possession of that post.*

Further westward, during September, nearly four thousand men, chiefly mounted riflemen, under command of General Hopkins, gathered at Vincennes, on the Wabash, for the purpose of chastising the Indians on the Illinois and Wabash Rivers. This foray was sanctioned by Governor Shelby of Kentucky, and was in appearance one of the most formidable that had ever entered the Indian country.

Earlier in the month, Captain Zachary Taylor had displayed his ability in defending Fort Harrison on the Wabash. On the 4th of September, the fort was attacked by several hundred Indians with great fury. Captain Taylor's force, though numbering fifty, consisted in fact of only eighteen effective men, the rest being incapable of duty in consequence of sickness; nevertheless, with great intrepidity and steadiness the assault was repelled, and the Indians retired in disgust.

1812.

* For a more full account of General Tupper's movements, see M'Afee's "*History of the Late War in the Western Country*," pp. 147–152.

The army under General Hopkins reached Fort Harrison about the 10th of October, and on the 14th crossed the Wabash, and proceeded on the march against the Kickapoo and Peoria towns; the first about eighty miles distant, the others about one hundred and twenty. Its march lay through open plains covered with the luxuriant prairie grass, which in autumn becomes very dry and combustible. Murmurs and discontents soon began to show themselves in this unwieldy and ill-compacted body, which was kept together by no discipline or authority. Every one consulted his own will; in fact, but little could be expected from this "press of chivalry." The Indians set fire to the prairie grass, which had to be met with a back fire as their only chance of escape. Scarcely four days had they been on their march, when they demanded to be led back; a major, whose name it is unnecessary to remember, rode up to the general, and peremptorily ordered him to return! Of course, after this, nothing could be effected, and the whole force soon turned about and made its way back to Fort Harrison. The same officer, General Hopkins, we may here mention, led another party, in November, with more success, against the towns at the head of the Wabash. On the 11th, he again set out from Fort Harrison, with about one thousand two hundred men; while at the same time, seven boats, under the command of Lieutenant-Colonel Butler, ascended the river with supplies and provisions. On the 19th, he reached the Prophet's town, and immediately dispatched three hundred men to surprise the Winnebago towns on Ponce Passu creek. The party under Colonel Butler came upon the place about day-break, but found it evacuated. This village, together with the Prophet's town, and a large Kickapoo village, containing one hundred and twenty cabins and huts, were destroyed, together with the winter's provision of corn. No Indians were seen until near the end of the month, when a skirmish took place with considerable loss on the part of the white men. The lateness of the season induced the detachment to forego further efforts; and their good conduct under great destitution was in striking contrast with that of the volunteers spoken of above.

Other expeditions were undertaken; one, by Colonel Russel, in October, who, with three hundred regulars and a party of riflemen, destroyed a flourishing Indian town called Pamitaris, and killed a number of the savages; another, by Colonel Campbell, in November, with some six hundred men, with which he marched against the towns on the Mississinewa River, and put the Indians completely to the rout. The result of these and other incursions into the territory occupied by the Indians, was very salutary; and in great measure the frontier was secured against the scalping-knife and the midnight assaults of the savage.*

1812.

Military operations in the north next claim our notice. During the summer and autumn, a number of volunteer companies marched to the borders of

* See M'Afee's "*History of the Late War in the Western Country*," pp. 162–82.

Canada, as also the new recruits, as fast as they could be enlisted, and towards the close of the year, the forces were chiefly concentrated in two bodies; one near Lewistown, consisting of some regulars newly enlisted, and militia, amounting to four thousand men, under General Van Rensselaer, of New York; the other, in the neighborhood of Plattsburg and Greenbush, under the commander-in-chief, General Dearborn. Bodies of regulars were distributed at Black Rock, at Ogdensburgh, and Sackett's Harbor, with officers of experience, for the purpose of drilling the raw troops as they arrived; and it was expected, that an invasion of Canada might be made before cold weather set in. Such officers as Pike, Boyd, and Scott were very diligent in training and disciplining the army; and with a force of between eight and ten thousand men, along the frontier, it was not unreasonable to look for some effective result in the proposed invasion of Canada.

General Van Rensselaer's head-quarters were at Lewiston on the Niagara River, opposite to which stood Queenstown, a fortified British post. Several forays and skirmishes, in which the Americans had been successful, and particularly the cutting out of two English brigs from under the guns of Fort Erie, by Lieutenant Elliot, roused the spirit of the army of the centre, as Van Rensselaer's force was denominated, and they were eager to be led to the fight; indeed, some of the volunteers threatened to return home unless they were gratified directly. The general, nothing loth, determined to make an attack upon Queenstown. From the information he could collect, the enemy's force had been chiefly drawn off for the defence of Malden, as it was supposed, under the command of General Brock, who had left the territory of Michigan under the government of General Proctor, until he could organize a force to return. Could possession be obtained of Queenstown, our troops would be sheltered from the approaching inclemency of the season, and the operations of the western army much facilitated. Accordingly, at four in the morning of the 11th of October, in the midst of a dreadful north-east storm and heavy rain, an attempt was made to pass the river; but, owing to the darkness of the night, and various unforeseen accidents, the passage could not be effected.

This failure served to increase the impatience of the troops, who became almost ungovernable. Orders were dispatched to General Smyth, at Buffalo, to advance with his corps, as another attempt would be made on Queenstown. Every arrangement was rapidly completed; and early on the morning of the 13th, the troops embarked, under cover of the American batteries. **1812.** The force designated to storm the heights, was divided into two columns; one of three hundred militia, under Colonel Solomon Van Rensselaer, the other of three hundred regulars, under Colonel Christie; but, by some mismanagement or carelessness, there were not boats enough to carry them all over at once, and they were forced to cross in detachments. Colonel Fenwick's artillery was to follow, and then the other troops in order.

The British, in the mean while, anticipating this attack, had obtained considerable reinforcements from Fort George, and if necessary, could be still further assisted by General Brock, who, it now appeared, commanded at that place. At daylight, the British opened upon the Americans with a shower of musketry and grape, which did considerable execution, and added to the difficulty of effecting a landing. Colonel Van Rensselaer was amongst the number severely wounded.

Captain Wool, on whom the command devolved at the moment, bravely led his men up the rocks to the right of the fort, though he was himself suffering from a dangerous wound. After several desperate charges, the heights were carried, and the enemy were driven down the hill in every direction. Retreating behind a large storehouse, they kept up their fire; but their batteries, with the exception of one gun, were silenced. Soon after, General Brock arrived at Queenstown, and led the forty-ninth regiment, six hundred strong, against the Americans on the heights. Captain Wool ordered a detachment of one hundred and sixty men to charge. They did so; were driven back; were reinforced, and charged a second time; again were they repulsed, and were about to be driven to the verge of the precipice, when one of the officers, supposing their condition desperate, placed a white handkerchief on the point of a bayonet, in token of submission. Wool indignantly tore it away, and ordered the men to be brought to the charge. They rallied, and drove the British back. General Brock fell, mortally wounded, and the enemy retreated in great disorder.

1812.

At two o'clock, General Wadsworth, of the militia, and Colonels Scott and Mulaney crossed over; and Captain Wool was ordered to retire and have his wounds dressed. The forty-ninth being repulsed, and the British commander having fallen, the victory was thought to be complete; and General Van Rensselaer crossed over, for the purpose of immediately fortifying a camp, to prepare against future attacks, should the enemy be reinforced. But the fortune of the day was not yet decided. At three o'clock, the enemy having rallied, and being reinforced by several hundred Chippewa Indians, again advanced to the attack. At first, our men were disposed to falter, but being animated by such leaders as Colonel Christie and Colonel Scott, marched boldly to the charge, and at the point of the bayonet once more compelled the British, who were now the assailants, to retire. This was the third victory gained since morning, and had the brave men on the Canada shore been properly sustained, complete triumph would undoubtedly have crowned our arms.

General Van Rensselaer, anxious to expedite the embarkation of the troops, recrossed the river for that purpose; but to his dismay, he found that not one of them was willing to go into the fight. Neither commands nor entreaties could prevail on them to move. The number of boats had from the first been insufficient; some of those had been lost or destroyed, and only three or four were left. And a great error had been committed in leaving undisturbed a battery below Queenstown, which enfiladed the ferry. The 1812. militia had seen the wounded; they had seen the Indians; they were panic-struck; and so, fifteen hundred able-bodied men, well armed and equipped, shortly before swelling with prowess and untameable spirit, now "put on the mask of lawfulness to hide their cowardice;" they shamelessly professed to have constitutional objections to invading an enemy's territory!

At four o'clock, the British being reinforced by eight hundred men from Fort George, under General Sheaffe, renewed the engagement with fresh vigor. General Van Rensselaer, perceiving that our men were almost exhausted with fatigue, and their ammunition nearly spent, was compelled, under the most painful sensations, to address a note to General Wadsworth, informing him of the disgraceful conduct of the militia, and leaving it to him to resist or retreat, as he deemed best. "Wadsworth," as Ingersoll states it, "could do neither. Surrender, nearly unconditional, was all he could do or get for his troops, who, from before daybreak in the morning till late in the afternoon, had been constantly engaged. They did not yield at once, without a sharp conflict, however; but panic seized some of the militia, and complete rout soon took place instead of orderly retreat,—a movement beyond the discipline of unpractised troops. Rushing to the shore and finding no boats, many brave men had no alternative but to surrender on the enemy's terms. An armistice of three days, however, was arranged, and the Americans were humanely treated, except in some instances, of what Chrystie, an Englishman, mentions as terrible slaughter by Indians, whom it was impossible to restrain. Of about eleven hundred fighting men who crossed the river, nearly all were killed, wounded, or taken;" and Wadsworth, Scott, Wool, and other brave officers among the prisoners, were paraded through Canada, as trophies of victory.

Van Rensselaer having resigned the command a few days subsequent to the battle of Queenstown Heights, General Alexander Smyth was put in charge of the army of the centre. This gentleman seems to have been fired with an ambitious desire to do something to distinguish himself, and wipe out the disgrace of the numerous failures of the campaign thus far; but forgetting the significant advice, "Let not him that girdeth on his harness boast himself as he that putteth it off," he issued, on the 10th of November, a grandiloquent address to "The Men of New York," assuring them that, in a few days, he should plant the American standard in Canada, and inviting them to "come on" and share 1812. the glory of the enterprise. Another proclamation followed in a similar strain, and several thousand volunteered, probably however, more from their confidence in General Porter, who was to be associated with Smyth, and who was to command the volunteers, than from the effect of that general's inflated appeal. Preparatory to crossing with the army, General Smyth sent two parties, on the night of the

27th of November, one under Colonel Bœrstler, and the other under Captain King, who was accompanied by Lieutenant Angus, of the navy, with a small but valiant band of marines; the whole under the direction of General Winder. The party under Bœrstler, whose object was to destroy a bridge, went several miles down the river, dispersed the enemy, made several prisoners, but returned without having accomplished their object. That under King, who were ordered to attack the batteries opposite Black Rock, performed the service in a most gallant manner. Nine out of twelve of the naval officers who embarked in the affair, and half the seamen, were either killed or wounded. They had dispersed the enemy, rendered useless their artillery, and prepared the way for the safe landing of the army who had been ordered to embark at reveille; but delays occurred, and they were not embarked till noon. General Smyth, at this time, ordered them to disembark to dine. It was then found that there were not sufficient boats to carry over three thousand men at once, as had been the orders of the secretary of war; and the general, amidst the murmurings of the army, called a council of war, and concluded to postpone the invasion for a few days! Most of the brave men who crossed, succeeded in returning; but some were made prisoners, among whom was Captain King. Not finding boats enough to cross over his whole party, he sent all his officers and part of his men, but would not desert the remainder, and was captured with them.

Despite Smyth's pretensions, this whole affair was as clumsily managed by the regular officer as it had been by the militia-men. On the 1st of December, (which was the latest of several days that had been fixed,) the troops received orders to be in readiness to pass the river, and they were all at their posts. The volunteers set out, General Porter in the leading boat, with a flag to indicate his position; fifteen hundred men were found willing to make the attempt, in spite of all the ill omens. But before the other bank could be reached, another council of war was held, and Smyth recalled the expedition, ordered the volunteers to return home, and the regulars to go into winter-quarters. A scene of riot and confusion ensued. Some three or four thousand men, indignant and outraged in feeling, discharged their muskets in every direction, under a keen sense of the indignity which had thus been forced upon them by Smyth's absurd course.

1812.

General Porter posted Smyth in the newspapers as a coward; and this unfortunate general, "never tried but in the public journals and by common opinion, was actually driven away to be no more heard of, mobbed by the militia and the populace, not without strenuous vindication by himself and others in the newspapers, but without favors or further employment."* Porter and Smyth got up a duel out of this newspaper squabble, wherein having

* At the close of 1813, Smyth sent a lengthy petition to Congress, asking for a restoration to his rank, an opportunity to serve the country, etc. The petition was handed over to the secretary of war, which was equivalent to rejecting it with contempt.

fired at one another, their nice sense of honor was soothed; the public were congratulated on the happy issue; Ingersoll dryly says, "the public would have preferred a battle in Canada."

Beside the ill success at Queenstown, and the abortive attempt of Smyth, there were here and there efforts made to do something. In September, a detachment of militia from Ogdensburg, attacked a party of the British, who were moving down the St. Lawrence, and defeated them. They were reinforced, and, in their turn, compelled the militia to retire. In retaliation, the British attempted the destruction of Ogdensburg, on the 2d of October; but they were repulsed by General Brown, the energetic commander at that station.

Colonel Pike, on the 19th of October, made an incursion into Canada, burned a blockhouse, and escaped without loss. On the 22d, Captain Lyon captured forty English at St. Regis, with baggage, dispatches, and a stand of colors; and the enemy, at Salmon River, on the 23d of November, captured two of our officers, with some forty men and four boats.

Thus far, certainly, there is little room for gratulation on account of our land operations. It is bad enough to have to record most of what we have just detailed; but the senile conduct of General Dearborn capped the climax of the military misdeeds of 1812. It was his misfortune, it must be acknowledged, "to have an army to form; an inexperienced, not over ardent executive, a secretary of war constrained to resign; a Senate inclined to distrust the executive; Congress withholding taxes and supplies for near twelve months after war was declared; waiting upon a presidential election; disaffected states,—Dearborn's own state, Massachusetts, at the head of disaffection; a country destitute of military means and men, unaccustomed to restraints, and impatient for exploit."* All this is true enough; but it will not excuse his allowing himself to be deluded into an armistice by Prevost, (p. 159) from which Hull was excluded; neither will it account for his idleness and inactivity, and neglect to avail himself of the plainest advantages within his reach.

1812.

Dearborn had the largest discretion in respect of the *materiel* of war, and had under him more than three thousand regular troops; two thousand Vermont, and one thousand New York militia on Lake Champlain. And opposed to him were, as General Armstrong insists,† not three thousand men altogether, who had to protect nine hundred miles of frontier. After due council of war, Dearborn, on the 20th of November, dispatched General Bloomfield with a large force, to enter Canada, and achieve some deed of daring, in order to redeem the military character of the United States. The "Aurora" announced the fact, and predicted glorious results.

By some means, the British commander, three days before, heard that the invasion was about to take place;

* Ingersoll's "*History of the Second War*," vol. i., p. 99.

† "*Notices of the War of* 1812," vol. i., p. 113.

and on the 20th, in the morning, one of the regiments sent forward to meet them, actually came upon Colonel Pike, leading the advance into Canada. "A confused and incomprehensible skirmish ensued," says Ingersoll, very sharply, "in which each party's object seemed to be to get away from the other, till the Americans, in the dark, mistaking themselves for enemies, began to fire on each other, killed four or five, and wounded as many, of themselves, and then returned, leaving their dead behind, which Indians never would have done. Where Generals Dearborn, Chandler, and Bloomfield were during this wretched foray, did not then appear, nor can be now told; and on no occasion did General Dearborn ever lead his troops into action." Following all this, it is perhaps only a fitting conclusion, that the six thousand men composing this army of the north, should be sent into winter-quarters, to repose after the fatigues of their invasion of Canada.

But, though we have spoken plainly, and even severely, candor compels us to confess, that it is not an easy task to form a just estimate of the campaign of 1812. Our country had been at peace with other nations for many years, and the generation which had grown up since the Revolution was wholly unacquainted with war as a science, and quite unaware of the supreme importance of discipline, steadiness, and prompt obedience. We had not remaining any officers of experience to conduct our armies, and not a single company that had seen actual service. In addition to this, the whole system for the recruiting, feeding, clothing, and maintaining an army, was, as it were, to be created. Many of the necessary munitions of war were to be provided. Platoon, staff, and many of the general officers, were to be selected from the body of the American people, upon conjecture merely as to their merits. It was therefore not unreasonable to expect, that many of them would be found incompetent, and undeserving. Certainly the campaign proved, that our generals needed experience, as much as our officers and soldiers needed discipline; and although it was disastrous, it was not without its consolations. The great body of the army was found to be brave to a fault; and many officers gave earnest of their future glory. Miller, Scott, Christie, Wadsworth, and Wool, gained immortal honor for themselves and their country; and Maguaga and Queenstown will bear comparison with the brave deeds of the heroic age of our country's history.

CHAPTER IX.

1812–1813.

PROGRESS OF THE WAR DURING 1813.

Efforts to arrest the progress of hostilities — Correspondence between Monroe and Warren — Presidential contest — Congress in session — President's message — The principal acts of the present session — Report of the committee of foreign relations — The British manifesto — Special message — Mr. Madison enters on his second term — His Inaugural address — Changes in the cabinet — Opening of the campaign of 1813 — Harrison and Winchester — Disaster at Frenchtown — Proctor's treachery — Massacre of the prisoners — Harrison's movements — Siege and defence of Fort Meigs — Indians taken into the service of the United States — Operations on the northern frontier — Forsyth's incursion into Canada — British attack on Ogdensburgh — Attack on York under General Pike — Death of Pike — Forts George and Erie taken — Prevost attacks Sackett's Harbor — Repulsed — Winder and Chandler at Stony Creek — Result of the expedition — Various skirmishes and expeditions — Dearborn retires from command — English attack on Plattsburg — Course pursued by the enemy on the sea-coast — Disgraceful marauding incursions — Cockburn's exploits — Frenchtown, Havre de Grace, Georgetown and Fredericktown plundered — Attack on Craney Island — Repulsed — Hampton sacked — Cockburn proceeds further south — Blockade at the north under Hardy — Use of the torpedo — Naval affairs — The Hornet captures the Peacock — Lawrence and the Chesapeake — British sentiments — The Shannon's preparations — The battle — Lawrence's death — Effect of the capture of the Chesapeake — The Argus also captured by the British — The Enterprise takes the Boxer — Privateering and its results — The cruise of the Essex under Captain Porter — Its success.

The United States had entered upon this second war with England not without reluctance, and various steps were taken at an early date, to arrest the progress of hostilities, and to hasten the restoration of peace. A proposal was made to the British government, through Mr. Russell, our *chargé d'affaires*, early in July, for an armistice which might lead to an adjustment of

1812.

difficulties, on the single condition, in the event of the orders in council being repealed, that instructions should be issued, suspending the practice of impressment during the armistice. This proposal was soon followed by another, admitting, instead of positive instructions, an informal understanding between the two governments on the subject; and, as an inducement to discontinue the practice of impressment, Mr. Russell was instructed to give assurance, that Congress would pass a law prohibiting the employment of British seamen in American vessels, public or private. Lord Castlereagh, on behalf of his government, rejected these proposals, as wholly inadmissible. England could never consent, under any circumstances, to forego the right of impressment; but he professed that his government was willing to discuss any proposition tending to check abuses in the exercise of this right, etc. Mr. Russell finding his efforts unavailing, returned home in September.

Admiral Warren, who was in command of the British naval force on the

Halifax station, addressed a letter to Mr. Monroe, on the 30th of September, proposing an immediate cessation of hostilities between the two countries. In case this were agreed to, he was authorized to arrange for the repeal of the laws and regulations against British commerce and the entrance of British ships of war into our harbors; but if his propositions were rejected, he informed the secretary of state, that the orders in council, repealed June 23d, would be again revived. Mr. Monroe, who had learned the ill success of Mr. Russell's efforts at London, replied to Admiral Warren on the 27th of October, and expressing the willingness of the American government to take any measures which might lead to peace on conditions honorable to both nations, he avowed his conviction, that, till the subject of impressment was disposed of, a durable peace was hardly to be expected. "The claim of the British government," he remarked in
1812. his letter, "is to take from the merchant vessels of other countries, British subjects. In the practice, the commanders of the British ships of war often take from the merchant vessels of the United States, American citizens. If the United States forbid the employment of British subjects in their service, and enforce the prohibition by suitable regulations and penalties, the motive for the practice is taken away. It is in this mode that the president is willing to accommodate this important controversy with the British government, and it cannot be conceived on what ground the arrangement can be refused. He is willing that Great Britain should be secured against the evils of which she complains; but he seeks, on the other hand, that the citizens of the United States should be protected against a practice, which, while it degrades the nation, deprives them of their rights as freemen, takes them by force from their families and country into a foreign service, to fight the battles of a foreign power, perhaps against their own kindred and country."

The British admiral not being authorized to enter upon this subject in his negotiation, the United States had no alternative but to continue the war, and to prosecute it with vigor. Sincerely desirous, however, of peace, when the emperor of Russia, early in 1813, offered his mediation, it was immediately and cordially accepted by our government; but England peremptorily rejected every thing of the kind.

The presidential contest, in the autumn of 1812, was animated to a high degree, especially in the eastern and middle states. Mr. Madison, having acceded to the views of the war party, (see p. 137,) was nominated for re-election, Mr. Gerry being placed on the same ticket for vice-president. A portion of the democratic party, however, determined to support De Witt Clinton and Jared Ingersoll for president and vice-president; and the federalists, hoping to profit by divisions in the ranks of their opponents, mostly voted for Clinton and Ingersoll. The result of the election was, Mr. Madison received one hundred and twenty-eight votes for president, and Mr. Clinton received eighty-nine for the same high office. For Mr. Gerry, as vice-president, one hundred and thirty-one votes were given, and for Mr. Ingersoll, eighty-six. The federalists, by a skilful use of their present opportunity, managed to elect a number of additional members of Congress to represent their views in the national legislature; so that, although the administration was decidedly in the majority, it was evident, that the minority possessed no little power and influence, and would watch the progress of affairs with unflagging zeal and interest.

Congress assembled again on the first Monday in November, and the next day the president sent in his annual message to both Houses. It is a long and carefully prepared document, calm but decided in tone, and strongly patriotic in its sentiments. "On
1812. our present meeting," he said, "it is my first duty to invite your attention to the Providential favors which our country has experienced in the unusual degree of health dispensed to its inhabitants, and to the rich abundance with which the earth has rewarded the labors bestowed on it. In the successful cultivation of other branches of industry, and in the progress of general improvement favorable to the national prosperity, there is just occasion, also, for our mutual congratulations and thankfulness. With these blessings are necessarily mingled the pressures and vicissitudes incident to the state of war into which the United States have been forced, by the perseverance of a foreign power in its system of injustice and aggression."

The president then enters upon a full account of the various important movements and occurrences of the year; relates Hull's operations and surrender; mentions the refusal of Massachusetts and Connecticut (see note, p. 155) to allow the militia to leave the state; recommends attention to a revision of the militia laws, an enlargement of the navy, the navigation laws, etc. The receipts into the treasury, he states, have been $16,500,000, sufficient to meet all the expenses of the government and to discharge nearly $3,000,000 of the public debt. "We have the inestimable consolation," said Mr. Madison, in conclusion, "of knowing that the war in which we are actually engaged, is a war neither of ambition nor of vain glory; that it is waged, not in violation of the rights of others, but in the maintenance of our own; that it was preceded by a patience without example, under wrongs accumulating without end; and that it was finally not declared, until every hope of averting it was extinguished by the transfer of the British sceptre into new hands, clinging to former counsels, and until declarations were reiterated to the last hour, through the British envoy here, that the hostile edicts against our commercial rights and our maritime independence would not be revoked. . . . It remains only, that, faithful to ourselves, entangled in no connections with the views of other powers, and ever ready to accept peace from the hand of justice, we prosecute the war with united counsels, and with the ample faculties of the nation, until peace be so obtained, and as the only means, under the divine blessing, of speedily obtaining it."

The present session of Congress was

principally occupied in giving attention to the army and navy, and in providing means for carrying on the war. The executive was authorized to raise additional regiments, not exceeding twenty, to appoint six major-generals, and six brigadier-generals, to raise ten companies of rangers, for the defence of the frontiers, etc. The president was also authorized to have constructed, four seventy-four gun ships, six frigates, and six sloops-of-war; so highly had the navy risen in the estimation of the ruling party, who were now as willing to encourage it as they had previously depressed and underrated it. On the 8th of February, 1813, a law was passed, providing for a loan of $16,000,000; and authority was subsequently given, to issue $5,000,000 in treasury notes, making altogether, including the loan of $11,000,000 authorized by the act of March the 14th, 1812, and the $5,000,000 of treasury notes issued by the act of the 30th of June, in the same year, the gross sum of $37,000,000 borrowed by this Congress for the prosecution of hostilities, without providing for the redemption of the debt by the imposition of additional taxes. The loan of $16,000,000, authorized at this session, was promptly taken on the most favorable terms; $7,000,000 were subscribed by Stephen Girard and David Parish, and $2,000,000 by John Jacob Astor; all three of whom were adopted citizens; and the remaining $7,000,000 were taken by banks and individuals, principally in Philadelphia and New York. The federalists, whose animosity to the war was not at all lessened by what had occurred since the commencement of hostilities, spared no efforts to prevent the loan from being taken in the New England states.

1813.

Laws were also enacted for the encouragement of vaccination among the people generally; prohibiting the employment of any seamen on public or private armed vessels, except citizens of the United States; giving the president power of retaliation for violations of the laws and usages of civilized nations, etc. After an animated and protracted discussion, an important bill was passed in respect to the goods imported from Great Britain and Ireland, after the declaration of war, and which had been seized under the non-importation act. By this bill, the secretary of the treasury was directed to remit the fines, forfeitures, penalties, and the like, which the owners of the goods had incurred; or, in other words, to cancel the merchants' bonds, given for those goods. Notwithstanding a most vigorous opposition, this bill passed by the close vote of sixty-four to sixty-one. Messrs. Calhoun, Quincy, and Cheves, were the principal advocates of this measure.

In the latter part of the month of January, the committee of foreign relations made their report to the House. It is an interesting document, prepared evidently under strong feeling, and reviews the course of the British government with great severity. It admits that the "practice of impressment" is the only grievance remaining unsettled, but contends that that is an abundantly sufficient cause for war. "War having been declared, and the case of impressment being necessarily included as one of the most important causes, it is evident, that it must be provided for in the pacification. The omission of it in a treaty of peace would not leave it on its former grounds; it would in effect be an absolute relinquishment, an idea at which the feelings of every American must revolt." In conclusion, expressing the conviction that there is no room for apprehension as to the final result, the report declares: "Our resources are abundant; the people are brave and virtuous, and their spirit unbroken. The gallantry of our infant navy bespeaks our growing greatness on that element; and that of our troops, when led to action, inspires full confidence of what may be expected from them when their organization is complete. Our Union is always most strong when menaced by foreign dangers. The people of America are never so much one family, as when their liberties are invaded."

In contrast with this report, we may refer the reader to the "British Manifesto," under date of January 9th, which was published in the London Gazette, and reached the United States
1813. in the month of February. It is a long and well written paper, and presents the English view of the questions at issue in a clear and forcible manner. The substance of the British complaints was, that the United States had all along manifested a subserviency to France and an aggressive spirit against England: "This complete subserviency to the ruler of France; this hostile temper towards Great Britain; are evident in almost every page of the official correspondence of the American with the French government. Against this course of conduct, the real cause of the present war, the prince-regent solemnly protests;" and, in conclusion, says: "relying on the justice of his cause, and the tried loyalty and firmness of the British nation, his royal highness confidently looks forward to a successful issue of the contest, in which he has thus been compelled most reluctantly to engage."

On the 24th of February, the president sent a special message to Congress, denouncing, in very strong terms, the "demoralizing and disorganizing contrivances," by which the British government was attempting to sever the eastern states from the rest of the Union, in making offers to confine to those states licenses to trade with the West Indies. The message and documents were considered, and bills were introduced and passed in the
House, to prohibit exportations 1813.
and trade by foreign licenses. The Senate, however, refusing to concur, the subject was indefinitely postponed.

Having appointed the fourth Monday in May as the opening of an extra session, the twelfth Congress terminated its labors on the 3d of March, 1813, and Mr. Madison's first term of service was brought to its close.

The next day, the president met the assembled concourse in the capital, to renew his vows of devotion to his country and his resolve to discharge his high duties to the utmost of his ability. His second Inaugural, like his first, was brief, but energetic in tone, and earnest in its defence of the war against England. Claiming to have been actuated by the principles of justice and honor in every thing that had occurred, the address reflects severely upon the enemy: "They have not, it is true, taken into their own hands the hatchet and the knife, devoted to indiscriminate massacre; but they have let loose the savages armed with those cruel instruments; have allured them into their service, and carried them to battle by their sides, eager to glut their savage thirst with the blood of the vanquished, and to finish the work of torture and death on maimed and defenceless captives. And, what was never before seen, British commanders have extorted victory over the unconquerable valor of our troops, by presenting to the sympathy of their chief, captives awaiting massacre from their savage associates. And now we find them, in further contempt of the honorable modes of warfare, supplying the place of a conquering force by attempts to disorganize our political society, to dismember our confederated republic."

The concluding paragraph of the Inaugural is worth quoting. "Our nation," says the president, "is in number more than half that of the British Isles. It is composed of a brave, a free, a virtuous, and an intelligent people. Our country abounds in the necessaries, the arts, and the comforts of life. A general prosperity is visible in the public countenance. The means employed by the British cabinet to undermine it have recoiled on themselves; have given to our national faculties a rapid development; and draining or diverting the precious metals from British circulation and British vaults, have poured them into those of the United States. It is a propitious consideration, that an unavoidable war should have found this seasonable facility for the contributions required to support it. When the public voice called for war, all knew and still know, that without them it could not be carried on through the period it might last; and the patriotism, the good sense, and the manly spirit of our fellow-citizens, are pledges for the cheerfulness with which they will bear each his share of the common burden. To render the war short, and its success sure, animated and systematic exertions alone are necessary; and the success of our arms now, may long preserve our country from the necessity of another resort to them. Already have the gallant exploits of our naval heroes proved to the world our inherent capacity to maintain our rights on one element. If the reputation of our arms has been thrown under clouds on the other, presaging flashes of heroic enterprise assure us, that nothing is wanting to correspondent triumphs there also, but the discipline and habit which are in daily progress."

1813.

The inefficiency of some of the members of the cabinet having become painfully evident, and frequent complaints having been made on that account, they were induced to send in their resignations; which were accepted; and on the 12th of January, 1813, William Jones, of Pennsylvania, was appointed secretary of the navy, in the place of Paul Hamilton; and General Armstrong, late minister to France, succeeded Doctor Eustis, as the head of the war department. The new secretaries had each been engaged in that branch of the service which they were now called to superintend.

The campaign of 1813 was looked to with deep anxiety and concern on the part of the nation at large; and it was hoped, at least, that the mortifying disasters of the previous year would be fully made up by deeds of daring and success in carrying the war into the enemy's country.

1813. General Harrison, as we have related above, (see p. 166,) was in command of the forces in the north-west. Unable to effect any thing of consequence before the end of 1812, with the very beginning of the present year, he put his troops in motion. General Winchester was sent to take possession of the tract about the Rapids of the Miami, or Maumee, which had been vainly attacked by General Tupper two months before. And he effected this, although he had to march through a deep snow; dispersing the Indians who had taken posts there, and making all needful provisions, such as the collection of corn from the Indians' fields near, the erection of a storehouse, etc. Whilst thus engaged, information was brought him from Frenchtown, of the straits to which the inhabitants were reduced by the Canadians and Indians in the British service, who were ready to occupy the place; and they feared a massacre would ensue. A council of officers having been called, it was determined to send a detachment sufficiently strong to defeat the enemy at that place.

Six hundred and sixty men were therefore detached, under the command of Colonels Lewis and Allen, who set out on the morning of the 17th of January. Their movements being quickened by the intelligence that Colonel Elliot was expected from Malden, on his way to attack the camp at the Rapids, they marched partly on the ice of Miami Bay, and the border of Lake Erie, and drove back the Indians, whom they met in the woods. About three o'clock on the next afternoon, they fell upon the enemy, consisting of about five hundred men, four hundred being Indians, and after a sharp engagement, which lasted till it was dark, drove them out of Frenchtown, and pursued them for two miles beyond it; returning then in good order with a loss of twelve killed and fifty-five wounded, they encamped before the town.

Frenchtown was only eighteen miles distant from Malden, from which it could be reached on the ice; this rendered the position of Lewis and Allen one of great danger, and as soon as the tidings of their success reached the Rapids, "a complete ferment" was produced in the camp. "All were anxious to proceed to Frenchtown in support of the advanced corps," says M'Afee; "it was evident that corps was in a critical situation." Every man wished to rush forward and join Lewis, and Winchester, unable to restrain the impetuosity of the volunteers, set out himself, on the evening of the 19th, with two hundred and fifty men, to reinforce Colonel Lewis. That brave officer had posted his force in a place where they were defended by garden pickets, sufficiently close and strong to protect his men against an attack of small arms.

But little precaution was taken to prevent a surprise. The general did hardly any thing to increase the security of the detachment. He named to Colonel Wells, but did not positively order, a breastwork for the protection of his
1813. camp. He established his own quarters in a house on the south side of the river, about three hundred yards from the lines! On the 21st, a place was selected for the whole detachment to encamp in good order, with a determination to fortify it on the next day. About sunset, Colonel Wells solicited and obtained leave to return to the Rapids. Certain information had been received, that the British were preparing to make an attack; and that it would be made as speedily as possible, seemed to be a matter of course. Colonel Wells reached the Rapids that night; at which place, General Harrison,—to whom Winchester, when he started for Frenchtown, had sent for reinforcements, and to inform him of his movements,—had arrived on the 20th of January, and had exerted himself to hasten forward the reinforcements.

After Colonel Wells's departure, a Frenchman from the neighborhood of Malden, came to General Winchester, and informed him that a large force of British and Indians were about to set out from that place. There could be no doubt that Frenchtown was their destination. But, strangely enough, as it seems, knowing their critical position, this information went for nothing; no preparations were made to be in readiness for the enemy; no apprehensions were excited, the most fatal security prevailed; Colonel Lewis and Major Madison alone seem to have been on the alert, and anxious to guard against sudden attack. "Guards were placed out," says M'Afee, "this night as usual; but, as it was extremely cold, no picket guard was placed on the road, on which the enemy was to be expected. The night passed away without any alarm, and the reveille began to beat at daybreak, on the morning of the 22d. A few minutes afterwards, three guns were fired in quick succession by the sentinels. The troops were instantly formed, and the British opened a heavy fire on the camp from several pieces of artillery, loaded with bombs, balls, and grape-shot, at the distance of three hundred yards. This was quickly followed by a charge made by the British regulars, and by a general fire of small arms; and the Indian yell on the right and left. The British had approached in the night with the most profound silence, and stationed their cannon behind a small ravine which ran across the open fields on the right."

The detachment, whose position was left unfortified, as above stated, was driven back, and in spite of the efforts of their officers, of Colonels Lewis and Allen, and of General Winchester, when he reached the field, to rally them, in spite of the assistance of two companies sent from the cover of the pickets, was routed utterly; and after a retreat of three miles, through the deep snow, wholly destroyed or made prisoners. Winchester and Lewis were captured; Colonel Allen was shot by an
Indian whilst he paused, ex- 1813.
hausted by a wound received in a flight

he had used his utmost to prevent; Captain Simpson, a gigantic Kentuckian, six feet six inches in height, was shot and tomahawked at the edge of the woods. The Indians gathered round his body where it lay, to admire its massive proportions.

Proctor, who commanded the British, had suffered very severely in his attack upon the pickets; but when he found that Winchester was a prisoner, he at once, as the writer we have above quoted indignantly states, "basely determined to take advantage of his situation to procure the surrender of the party in the picketing." He assured Winchester, that nothing but an immediate surrender could save the Americans from an indiscriminate massacre by the Indians, and he gave his pledge, that if they would promptly lay down their arms, they should be protected from massacre by the Indians; if this were not done, Proctor declared that he would set fire to the village, and would not be responsible for the conduct of the savages. Winchester, intimidated by this threat, sent an order to the troops under Major Madison, to surrender; which order was reluctantly obeyed, with the distinct understanding, that the lives, persons, and effects of the prisoners should be protected and properly cared for. At this time, the killed, wounded, and missing, of the little army, including those that had been outside of the pickets, amounted to more than three hundred men; those under Madison, who capitulated at Winchester's bidding, numbered thirty-five officers and above four hundred and fifty men.

The shocking barbarities which followed the battle of Frenchtown, are almost incredible. "Scarcely had the Americans surrendered," says a contemporary writer, "under the stipulation of protection from the British officer, when our brave citizens discovered, too late, that they were reserved to be butchered in cold blood. Of the right wing, but a small number escaped; the work of scalping and stripping the dead, and murdering those who could no longer resist, was suffered to go on without restraint. The infernal work was now to begin with those who had so bravely defended themselves. The infamous Proctor and the British officers turned a deaf ear to the just remonstrances of these unhappy men. Contrary to express stipulation, the swords were taken from the sides of the officers; and many of them stripped almost naked, and robbed. The brave dead were stripped and scalped, and their bodies shockingly mutilated. The tomahawk put an end at once to the sufferings of many of the wounded, who could not rise; in allusion to which, some days afterwards, a British officer observed, 'The Indians are excellent doctors.' The prisoners, who now remained, with but a few exceptions, instead of being guarded by British soldiers, were delivered to the charge of the Indians, to be marched in the rear of the army to Malden. This was, in other words, a full permission to indulge their savage thirst for blood; and in this they were not disappointed; for the greater part of these ill-fated men were murdered on the way, through mere wantonness. . . . . . About

1813.

sixty of the wounded, many of them officers of distinction, or individuals of much respectability, had been suffered to take shelter in the houses of the inhabitants, and two of their own surgeons permitted by Proctor to attend them, from whom they also obtained a promise that a guard should be placed to protect them, and that they should be carried to Malden the next morning in sleds. But this affected humanity, was but an aggravation of his cruelty, by awakening a hope which he intended to disappoint. No guard of soldiers was left, and on the next day, instead of sleds to convey them to a place of safety, a party of Indians returned to the field of battle, fell upon these poor wounded men, plundered them of their clothing, and every article of any value which remained, tomahawked the greater part of them, and, to finish the scene, fired the houses, and consumed the dying and the dead!"*

This sad calamity deeply affected the sensibilities of the entire American people. All Kentucky was literally in mourning; for the troops which had been massacred so shamelessly, were of the best families in the state, and many of them were young men of fortune and distinction, with numerous friends and relatives. The indignation of the west was roused to a far higher pitch than it had ever before attained. Winchester was severely censured by many for his advance to the River Raisin; others blamed Harrison for not reinforcing him in time; and some few took occasion, from this unexpected disaster, to reprobate the war altogether.

In the mean time, Harrison, who reached the camp at the Rapids on the 20th of January, as we have said, and who had left orders to his troops at Sandusky to follow him with all speed, when the tidings of the affair at the Raisin reached him, **1813.** fell back behind the Portage River, fearing to be himself attacked. But very soon he advanced again, and constructed a stronghold at the Rapids, on the right bank of the river, which, in honor of the governor of Ohio, he named Fort Meigs. The troops labored with great diligence in strengthening Fort Meigs, Upper Sandusky, and Fort Stephenson; but notwithstanding Harrison's efforts, it was found, by the middle of February, that it was useless to make any attempt against Malden this season. Winchester's movement had deranged Harrison's plan entirely, and he had no alternative but to reorganize his system of operations.

The term of service of the greater part of the militia composing the northwestern army having expired, new levies from Ohio and Kentucky were ordered on to supply their places. But these not arriving in season, the Pennsylvania brigade generously volunteered their services for another month to defend Fort Meigs, which was menaced with an attack. This conduct

* The British "general order," in giving an account of this battle, presented a very different statement, and Proctor was lauded for "his humane and unwearied exertions in rescuing the vanquished from the revenge of the Indian warriors." Beside this, which the Americans looked upon as a gross insult, this same Proctor was at once raised to the rank of a brigadier-general for his gallantry and excellent conduct.

was the more honorable, as this corps had undergone very great hardships during the winter, in dragging the artillery and stores from Sandusky to the Rapids.

Early in April, Harrison received such information as induced him to hasten his return to Fort Meigs, which he reached on the 20th. Immediately on his arrival, General Harrison set about making preparations for the approaching siege. The fort was situated upon a rising ground, at the distance of a few hundred yards from the river, the country on each side of which is chiefly natural meadows. The garrison was well supplied with the means of defence, and Harrison, with unremitted exertions, labored, night and day, to improve its capacity for resisting the siege. On the 28th, the enemy were reported to be in great force about three miles below, and in a day or two the siege commenced in earnest. The British were very active in selecting positions around the fort whence it might be annoyed, and in erecting batteries on the opposite side of the river. The besieged were equally active in keeping up a well-directed fire upon the enemy's works, and impeding their progress in every possible way. On the 1st of May, the British batteries were mounted, and for several days there was an incessant firing of bombs and cannon balls: the besieged, with great bravery and perseverance returned the enemy's fire. Proctor, who professed himself desirous of sparing the effusion of blood, sent a summons to the garrison to surrender, threatening, in case of refusal, to abandon them to the savages. His summons was treated with the contempt it deserved.

1813.

On the 5th of May, news reached Harrison, that General Clay, with twelve hundred Kentucky militia, was but a few miles up the river, descending in boats. An officer was sent to Clay, directing him to detach eight hundred men on the opposite side of the river, for the purpose of forcing the enemy's batteries and spiking their cannon. Colonel Dudley, who was charged with the execution of this movement, performed it in fine style; but his men, elated with their success, continued to pursue the retreating enemy, in spite of Dudley's efforts to the contrary, till they were finally drawn into an ambush, prepared by Tecumseh, and overwhelmed by superior numbers; the greater part of this detachment were killed or taken prisoners. Colonel Dudley was among the killed. While these things were being done on the left bank of the river, Colonel Miller sallied forth from the fort, at the head of three hundred men, assaulted the whole line of their works, manned by three hundred and fifty regulars and five hundred Indians, and after several brilliant charges, drove the enemy from their principal batteries, spiked the cannon, and returned to the fort with forty-two prisoners. The British commander, finding himself disappointed, discontinued hostilities, from the 6th to the 9th of May; arrangements were made for an exchange of prisoners; and the Indians, according to custom, having left their allies, Proctor, in considerable haste, retreated from the contest. The loss of the Americans in the fort, was eighty-one killed and one hundred and eighty-nine wounded. The loss of the enemy was about equal.

After the siege of Fort Meigs, offensive operations in this quarter were, for a considerable time, suspended on both sides. Until the completion of the naval preparations on Lake Erie, which were then in considerable forwardness, the troops were to remain at Fort Meigs, and Upper Sandusky. Without the command of the lake, little of consequence could be effected; the troops would, therefore, continue a great part of the summer in a state of inactivity, awaiting this event. In the mean time, General Harrison, having left General Clay in command at the fort, returned to Franklinton, for the purpose of organizing the forces expected to concentrate at that place. A deputation from all the Indian tribes residing in the state of Ohio, and some in the territories of Indiana and Illinois, made, in June, a tender of their services to follow General Harrison into Canada. Heretofore, the government had declined using the Indians as allies against the British; but, as it was necessary to have them as friends or enemies, and as they thought it an imputation upon them to be asked to remain neutral, it was concluded to be best, on the whole, to accept their aid, on the express condition, that they should spare their prisoners, and not assail defenceless women and children.

1813.

Turning our attention to the operations on the northern frontier, we find, that the war was carried on there with varied success. During the winter, skirmishes were not infrequent, and small detachments were often sent across from Canada for the purpose of apprehending deserters. They found and arrested several, and, being in an enemy's country, committed depredations upon the houses and other property of the inhabitants. In the beginning of February, Major Forsythe, who commanded at Ogdensburgh, resolved to retaliate these incursions. Taking a part of his riflemen, and such volunteers as offered, some of whom were private gentlemen of the neighborhood, in all numbering about two hundred men, he crossed the St. Lawrence, surprised the guard at Elizabethtown, took fifty-two prisoners, among whom were one major, three captains, and two lieutenants; and captured one hundred and twenty muskets, twenty rifles, two casks of fixed ammunition, and other public property. He then returned, without the loss of a single man.

1813.

Soon after, movements in Canada indicated that an attack on Ogdensburgh was intended, and the militia, under Colonel Benedict, were called out to defend it. On the 21st of February, the place was attacked by a force of twelve hundred men, under Colonel M'Donnell. The Americans refused to surrender on being summoned, and notwithstanding they were much inferior in numbers, they fought with great bravery for an hour, when they were compelled to retire, and abandon their artillery and stores to the British. Two schooners, two gunboats, together with the barracks, were committed to the flames. Brackenridge relates, that the British made something of a flourish over this affair; and a message was sent with the news to Colonel M'Feeley, commanding the American garrison at Niagara, informing him that a salute would be fired from Fort George. The American officer expressed his satisfaction at being able to return the compliment, as he had just received intelligence of the capture of his majesty's frigate Java, by an American frigate of equal force (p. 165), and intended to fire a salute from Niagara, at the same time, in honor of this brilliant victory.

General Pike, a brave and energetic officer, was diligently occupied at Sackett's Harbor in disciplining the recruits as they arrived, a work of great difficulty and requiring the utmost patience and perseverance. Great exertions had also been made by Commodore Chauncey to build and equip a squadron on the lake which should enable the Americans there to cope with the British; and in the course of the spring he

1813. had under him two sloops and eleven schooners, manned with crews who doubted not their ability to contend successfully with their enemies. Chauncey was ordered by the navy department to co-operate with General Dearborn in any operations he might direct. Accordingly, on the 25th of April, with sixteen hundred men on board, the flotilla sailed from Sackett's Harbor, for the purpose of making an attack on York (now Toronto) the capital of Upper Canada.

The plan, which had been principally suggested by General Pike, was highly judicious; and, at his particular request, he was entrusted with its execution. On the 27th, at seven o'clock in the morning, the fleet safely reached the place of destination. The debarkation commenced at eight o'clock, and was completed at ten. The British, on discovering the fleet, hastily made the necessary dispositions to oppose the landing of the American forces. General Sheaffe was in command at York, but he could collect only some seven hundred and fifty regulars and about a hundred Indians. With these he endeavored to prevent the landing, but ineffectually. Forsythe, with his riflemen, was first on the shore, and gallantly attacked the enemy. General Pike soon followed, and ably sustained the advance corps. The British were driven back, and took refuge behind the works of York, and our countrymen marched in columns to the assault. They had destroyed one of the enemy's batteries, and were within sixty yards of their main works, when the tremendous explosion of a magazine, at two hundred yards' distance, filled the air in every direction with huge stones and fragments of wood, which falling, caused a dreadful havoc among the troops. One hundred of the Americans and forty of the British were killed. General Pike fell mortally wounded. Whereupon General Sheaffe —for Chauncey had made his way into the harbor—profiting by the confusion, set fire to such of his stores as he could reach, and to a vessel on the stocks, and retreated towards Kingston, with about four hundred regulars, who alone remained unhurt. The militia who were in York capitulated, and the victors seized upon the valuable stores which thus fell into their possession. Property to an immense amount had been destroyed, but there still remained unconsumed to the value of at least half a million of dollars. In his hasty retreat, General Sheaffe abandoned his baggage, containing all his books and papers, which proved a valuable acquisition.* The loss of the British was ninety killed, two hundred wounded, and three hundred made prisoners, beside five hundred militia released on parole.

The American forces evacuated York early in May, and it was determined to attack Fort George and Fort Erie. After visiting Sackett's Harbor, and disposing of the wounded and the prisoners, having taken reinforcements on board, to the number of about five thousand, the fleet sailed for Fort George, on the Niagara River, at the head of the lake. There, under cover of the vessels, the advance, five hundred strong, landed, on the 27th of May, under the command of Colonel Scott and Major Forsythe; and being followed by the brigades of Generals Boyd, Winder, and Chandler, the enemy fled, abandoning their works and laying trains for blowing up their magazines; but Captain Hindman, entering the fort first, was fortunately able to
1813. remove the match, before the fire had reached the powder. In a few hours, Fort George, Fort Erie, and the other fortifications in the vicinity received new masters.

In this affair, it is said that the British lost a hundred and eight killed, and half as many more wounded, while six hundred were made prisoners; of the Americans, one hundred and eight were wounded, and only thirty-nine were killed. Captain Perry, who had volunteered on the 26th, was busily occupied at this date at Presque Isle, preparing the timber for the construction of those vessels, with which he afterwards obtained such imperishable renown, and withal inflicted new and unusual losses on the enemy.

On embarking for York, General Dearborn had left Sackett's Harbor in rather a defenceless state, which induced Sir George Prevost at the head of about seven hundred troops, to combine with Sir James Yeo, whose squadron on Lake Ontario had recently been very considerably reinforced, to put to sea on the 28th of May from Kingston, and attack that American post both by land and water. "The expedition," says Alison, "excited great interest on both sides of the water, (both in Canada and Great Britain,) and the most sanguine hopes were entertained by the British, that it would lead to the destruction of this growing and formidable naval establishment of the enemy. These hopes, however, were disappointed." General Brown, of the New York militia, had the chief command at the Harbor, and on the 29th he detached Colonel Mills with the militia (whom he charged strictly to reserve their fire) and the Albany volunteers to oppose

* Ingersoll mentions, that among the articles taken at the capture of York, was a scalp found suspended over the speaker's chair in the parliament house. "This atrocious ornament" the author cites as one among many evidences of the fact, that the British instigated the Indians to the commission of barbarities of every sort in the war at that date. "*History of the Second War*," vol. i., p. 273.

the landing of the British. Brown had hastily thrown up a slight breastwork at the only place where this could be effected.

At first, although exceeding the attacking force by four or five hundred men, the Americans were seized with a panic from some unexplained cause and were driven back. Colonel Mills lost his life in attempting to rally them. The invaders, thus left in possession of the peninsula, advanced against the loop-holed blockhouses; before which some four hundred regulars, under Colonel Backus, were drawn up. But the resistance made by this small band was so desperate, and the fire from the blockhouses so tremendous, and Brown, having succeeded in rallying about a hundred of the fugitives, made so well-timed an attack upon their rear, that the bravest of the British recoiled. Prevost urged on his men, but notwithstanding all his efforts the strait could not be passed, and a retreat was ordered and hastily made, the wounded being left to the care of the Americans.

During the battle, information having been communicated to Lieutenant Chauncey, that our troops had been defeated, he immediately, according to orders previously received, set fire to the public store houses; and the fire was not extinguished until very great damage had been done. In fact, though the enemy were repulsed, they had accomplished the most important part of their expedition, the destruction of a large part of the supplies which were essential to the success of the campaign. General Brown, whose good conduct was warmly acknowledged, was appointed a brigadier in the regular army. Prevost who, it was expected, would have been successful, was a good deal censured and abused by his countrymen.

1813.

At the time when Forts George, Erie, and the others near them had fallen into the hands of the Americans, Colonel Vincent had retreated to the heights at the head of Burlington Bay, where he occupied a strong position, when he gradually collected from the posts in the vicinity about sixteen hundred troops, one half of which were regular soldiers. The Americans on their side, fully aware of the advantage they had obtained in getting so strong a lodgment in the Canadian territory, determined to drive him out of his stronghold, that they might more securely push on towards the interior, and achieve the conquest of the whole country. Generals Winder and Chandler were, therefore, sent against Vincent, with three thousand infantry, two hundred and fifty horse, and nine guns; and, on the 5th of June, they encamped on the bank of Stony Creek. As soon as the British General was apprised of their approach, he called a council of war, and directly afterwards, dispatched seven hundred and fifty men, under Colonel Harvey, in order to retard the advance of Winder and Chandler. On drawing near the Americans, and finding that they were careless and kept a bad look out, Harvey resolved upon a night attack; which he executed as soon as it was dark, and with considerable success. The sentinels were silently bayonneted; the main guard, who must have been asleep, were passed; but fortunately for our countrymen, the Indians, when they arrived near some fires just abandoned, where the troops had cooked their supper, raised their usual yell, supposing the Americans were sleeping around them. This awoke the troops, who, having slept on their arms, discharged their pieces at the enemy standing in the light of the fires which had deluded them. But they soon retired into the darkness, which was intense; and then no one knew where his enemy was, nor which was friend or foe. Several irregular conflicts took place, in which 1813. some were killed and others wounded. General Chandler, intending to take the head of his artillery, found himself in the midst of a British party, and was made prisoner. A few minutes afterwards, General Winder, under the same mistake, fared no better. Satisfied with the capture of these officers, and about a hundred other prisoners, the enemy made a precipitate retreat, losing however, more than they gained. The English commander, Colonel Vincent, also lost his way in the confusion of the night and wandered some distance off, where he was found next day, without sword or hat.

The American loss was sixteen killed, and thirty-eight wounded; and two brigadiers, one major, three captains, and ninety-four men missing. The loss of the enemy was much more severe, particularly in officers; and one hundred prisoners were taken. The captured generals were much blamed for the result of this encounter, and not without reason. Had the enemy been immediately pursued, there is little doubt they would have been made prisoners; but Colonel Burns, who now commanded, after consultation with the officers, judged it most prudent to fall back on Forty Mile Creek. Here he was joined by Colonel Miller's regiment, which had been sent to guard the boats, and Generals Lewis and Boyd, the former of whom now assumed the command.

A fortnight afterwards, General Dearborn sent out an expedition of six hundred men, under Colonel Boerstler, to dislodge a British picket, which was posted at a place called Beaver Dams, to collect provisions, and to watch such of the Canadians as were friendly to the United States. Whilst on their way through the woods, they were beset by a small body of Indians, and a few of the forty-ninth regiment, not two hundred strong in all. By a skilful *ruse de guerre*, Boerstler and his troops were led to believe, that the force they were fighting with was only an advance corps of a large army near at hand; and so, finding his ammunition nearly exhausted, the American commander surrendered with his whole detachment consisting of five hundred and seventy men, together with two guns and two standards.

Subsequent to this, during the months of June and July, the contest between the British and American armies was little else than a war of posts. On the 8th of July a severe skirmish occurred, without material result to either side. An incident, however, occurred, 1813. which exasperated the Americans to a greater degree than any thing which had transpired during the war in this quarter. Lieutenant Eldridge, a gallant and accomplished youth, with about forty men, was drawn by his impetuosity too far, and was surrounded by British and Indians. The greater part resisted until they were killed; but Lieutenant Eldridge, and ten others, were taken prisoners, and never afterwards heard of. General Boyd, induced by the same considerations which weighed with General Harrison (p. 185) determined to accept the services of the Seneca warriors under Cornplanter, an intelligent and educated chief. The same stipulation, however, in regard to the unresisting and the defenceless was expressly insisted on, and we believe was observed by the Indians during the war.

On the 11th of July, the British made an attack on Black Rock, but were driven back, losing nine of their men and Colonel Bishop their commander. On the 28th of July, an expedition was undertaken against York, which had been re-captured by the enemy after the battle of Stony Creek. Three hundred men, under Colonel Winfield Scott, embarked in Commodore Chauncey's fleet, and suddenly landing at that place, destroyed the public stores and property, released a number of Colonel Boerstler's men, and returned to Sackett's Harbor, with only a trifling loss.

General Dearborn, whose age and increasing infirmities rendered him quite unfit for the arduous duties of his post, retired from the service, in July, by direction of the executive. Much, and we doubt not sincere, regret was expressed by the whole body of the officers at Fort George in consequence of this event. General Boyd now took command of the forces at the Fort; and towards the latter part of August, General Wilkinson was appointed to the command of the army of the centre.

The Americans as well as the English had made diligent efforts to gather a naval force on Lake Champlain. The few armed barges and schooners of the former, early in July, fell in with a superior force of the enemy and were captured. This opened the way for an attack on Plattsburgh, where, on the 31st of July, twelve hundred men landed, and meeting with almost no opposition from the militia hastily collected, proceeded to the destruction of the public buildings, of large amounts of private property, etc., beside carrying off a rich booty. Similar outrage was committed afterwards at Swanton, in Vermont. These acts served only to provoke the inhabitants, and render them better disposed to give the enemy a warm reception at some other period.

1813.

In Europe, the declining power and greatness of Napoleon were already producing their effect, and the state of things was verging to the point which gave England an opportunity to devote more attention to the war in America. The naval victories of the United States had not only mortified British pride, but had also naturally excited a strong desire to punish so audacious a competitor on the ocean. Early in the year it was known, that a British squadron had arrived at Bermuda, with a body of troops on board, and a large supply of bombs and other means of attacking the cities and towns on the sea coast. With the same mistake in judgment which was made in the Revolution, it was determined, to devastate the coast, and lay waste the towns and villages in every accessible direction. The necessary effect in such cases, must be, of course, to rouse the spirit of any people; and in the result, we find, that the outrages of the British under Cockburn, and his willing assistants, stirred up intense indignation, and incited the Americans to deeds of revenge.

Early in February, a squadron appeared in Delaware Bay, which destroyed many vessels and blockaded the Bay. On the 10th of February, Lewiston, in Delaware, was bombarded, because the inhabitants refused to supply the enemy with fresh provisions; and a month later, the militia succeeded in driving away a number of barges which had been sent to obtain water. It was, however, in the Chesapeake principally, that this new and discreditable species of warfare was carried on by the British ships. Admiral Cockburn was in command of the squadron here, and he rendered his name and character notorious, on account of the numerous piratical incursions in which he indulged, the houses he robbed, the families he plundered, the wanton destruction of property he authorized, and the shameful insults and injuries he inflicted upon defenceless women and children. The militia did good service in meeting the invaders whenever possible, but they were not able, of course, to do much in the way of effectual resistance. Frenchtown was assaulted, and plundered; Havre de Grace, early in May, shared the same fate; as did also Georgetown and Fredericktown, a few days later. The details of outrage and injury of every kind are such as excite astonishment and shame, that men calling themselves Englishmen could have sunk so low as to be guilty of conduct to be looked for only in pirates and savages. 1813.

Admiral Warren soon after arrived in the Chesapeake, which increased the enemy's force to seven ships of the line, and twelve frigates, with a proportionate number of smaller vessels. The appearance of this formidable armament created much alarm in the more considerable towns along the neighboring coast. Baltimore, Annapolis, and Norfolk were threatened; and it soon became evident, that the latter of these places was selected to receive the first blow. Commodore Cassin, on the 20th of June, aided by Captain Tarbell with a number of gunboats, made a gallant attack upon a British frigate at Craney Island, but did not succeed in capturing her. On the 22d, it having been determined to open the way to Norfolk, a large British force was detailed against Craney Island. They were bravely met by the Americans, some six hundred in number, partly marines and Virginia volunteers, and after a sharp fight, they were completely defeated, with a loss of over two hundred killed and wounded. Enraged at this unlooked-for result, the British determined to fall upon Hampton and destroy it, so as, if possible, to cut off the communication between Norfolk and the upper part of Virginia. On the 25th of June, Cockburn advanced against the town with 1813.

his barges, and kept up a constant cannonade, while about two thousand men, under Sir Sidney Beckwith, landed below intending to attack the Americans in the rear. The force stationed at Hampton was not more than four hundred, and though they made a gallant resistance, they were compelled to give way, and the enemy took possession of the town. Contemporary accounts are full of details of the shocking and detestable conduct of the lawless and inhuman invaders. Neither age nor sex was spared; and we cannot wonder that the feelings of the people were wrought up almost to frenzy, in the prospect of war to be carried on in this manner by the British commanders.

During the summer, other places, as Washington, Annapolis, Baltimore, etc., were threatened, but with no material result. Cockburn, in July, proceeded further south, and exercised his peculiar ability in marauding expeditions on the coast of North Carolina, where, beside the usual plunder, he inveigled a number of slaves on board his ship, and afterwards sold them in the West Indies.

At the north, attacks on the coast were conducted by the blockading force whenever practicable, but in a manner much more to the credit of the British name. This was due, no doubt, to Commodore Hardy, who was in command north of the Chesapeake, and who was a manly and generous-hearted enemy. The city of New York was strictly blockaded. The frigates United States and Macedonian, and the sloop Hornet, attempted to sail on a cruise from that port about the beginning of May, but finding the force at the Hook much superior to theirs, they put back and passed through Hell Gate, with the intention of getting out by the Sound. In this they were also frustrated; and on the 1st of June, after another attempt, they were chased into New London. Six hundred militia were immediately called in from the **1813.** surrounding country, for the protection of the squadron; and Commodore Decatur, landing some of his guns, mounted a battery on the shore, and at the same time so lightened his vessels, as to enable them to ascend the river out of the reach of the enemy. This town was so well fortified, however, that no attempt was made upon it, although the blockade was kept up for several months.

Incensed by the depredations committed on our coasts by the blockading squadrons, Congress passed an act, by which a reward of half their value was offered for the destruction of ships belonging to the enemy by means other than those of the armed or commissioned vessels of the United States. This measure was intended to encourage the use of *torpedoes*, of which, it will be remembered, Bushnell was the inventor during the Revolution. (See vol. i., p. 518.) On the 18th of July, and during several nights subsequently, attempts were made to blow up the Plantagenet, a British seventy-four, at anchor in Lynnhaven Bay; but without success. The last effort was made on the 24th, when, within a hundred yards of the ship, the torpedo was dropped into the water, and the same moment the sentinel cried "all's well:" the tide swept it towards the vessel, but it exploded a few seconds too soon. A column of water fifty feet in circumference was thrown up thirty or forty feet. Its appearance was a vivid red, tinged with purple at the sides. The summit of the column burst with a tremendous explosion, and fell on the deck of the Plantagenet in torrents, while she rolled into the yawning chasm below, and nearly upset. She however received no material injury. Other attempts of the kind were made in different quarters, the principal result of which was to cause the enemy to be very cautious in approaching our harbors and selecting stations for their ships. The use of this mode of destroying an invading force was strongly condemned by Commodore Hardy, and by a number of our own people, as dishonorable and unmanly; but, as Mr. Hale says, no one was able to show why it was more dishonorable or unfair than the resort to surprizes, ambushes, and mines.

The naval affairs of the year 1813 demand our attention in this place. When Commodore Bainbridge left San Salvador, in January, for home (p. 166) he directed Captain Lawrence, in the Hornet, to blockade the Bonne Citoyenne, a British vessel in that harbor. Lawrence challenged his opponent to meet him outside the port; but his challenge was not accepted. The Hornet continued the blockade until the 24th of January, when the Montague, seventy-four, hove in sight, and compelled her to escape into port. She ran out, however, the same night, and proceeded on a cruise. Her commander first shaped his course to Pernambuco; and on the 4th of February, captured the English brig Resolution, of ten guns, with $23,000 in specie. He then ran down the coast of Maranham, and thence off Surinam, where he cruised for some time; and on the 22d, stood for Demerara. The next day, he discovered an English brig of war lying at anchor outside of the bar, and on beating around the Carabana bank, to come near her, he discovered, at half past three in the afternoon, another sail on his weather quarter, edging down for him. This proved to be a large man-of-war brig, the Peacock, Captain Peake, somewhat superior to the Hornet in force. Lawrence immediately ordered his men to quarters, and had the ship cleared for action. He kept close by the wind, in order, if possible, to get the weather-gage of the Peacock. At ten minutes past five, finding he could not weather the enemy, he hoisted American colors and tacked. About a quarter of an hour after this, the ships passed each other, and exchanged broadsides within half pistol shot. Lawrence, observing the enemy in the act of wearing, bore up, received his starboard broadside, and ran him close on board on the starboard quarter. From this position he kept up a most severe and well-directed fire. So great was its effect, that, in less than fifteen minutes, the British vessel struck. She was almost cut to pieces, and hoisted an ensign, union down, from her fore rigging, as a signal of distress. Shortly after, her mainmast went by the board. The signal of distress was answered with praiseworthy humanity by the brave Americans, and every effort was made by the crews of both vessels to save the disabled ship. But, notwithstanding all their efforts, she went down in a few minutes, with thirteen of her own crew and three of the Hornet's, who were engaged in the noble act of striving to save their enemies. The captain of the Peacock and four men were killed, and thirty-three wounded; whilst there were but one man killed, and two wounded, on board the Hornet. Only one shot fired by the Peacock struck the hull of her adversary; and it did no more damage than that of indenting a plank beneath the cat-head.

The conduct of Captain Lawrence towards his prisoners was such as deserved the highest applause. So sensibly affected were the officers of the Peacock by the treatment they received, that, on their arrival at New York, they made a grateful acknowledgment in the public papers. To use their own expressive phrase, "they ceased to consider themselves prisoners." And the brave tars, emulating the magnanimous spirit of their commander, divided their clothes with the prisoners who were left destitute by the sinking of the Peacock.*

1813.

On the 10th of April, shortly after the return of the Hornet, the Chesapeake arrived at Boston, after a cruise of four months. Her commander, Captain Evans, having been appointed to the New York station, the Chesapeake was assigned to Lawrence. He accepted the post with reluctance, for the Chesapeake was looked upon as an unlucky ship, a circumstance of much moment with sailors, and her crew was ill assorted and in a disaffected and complaining state. He entered with alacrity, however, upon the duties of his post, and, had time been allowed him, he might have rendered the Chesapeake worthy of a better fate than that which befell her and her gallant commander.

The frequent and annoying disasters at sea had impressed the British government with the necessity for the most vigorous efforts, both to retrieve their naval losses, and to prevent the recurrence of mortifying defeat. "Several vessels," as Alison states, "were commenced on the model of the American frigates and sloops, which had been found by experience so swift in sailing, and so formidable in action; and secret instructions were given to the commanders of vessels on the North American station, not to hazard an encounter with an opponent nominally of the same class, unless there was something like a real, as well as an apparent, equality between them. Greater care was, at the same time, taken in the selection of crews; a larger proportion of men was given to the cannon on board; and orders were issued for the frequent exercise of the men in ball practice, both

* The intensely bitter opposition to the war, of a large party in New England, was exhibited in connection with the victory of the Hornet over the Peacock, in a resolution adopted by the Senate of Massachusetts, on the motion of Mr. Quincy, June 15th, 1813, in these words: "*Resolved*, as the sense of the Senate of Massachusetts, that, in a war like the present, waged without a justifiable cause, and prosecuted in a manner that indicates that conquest and ambition are its real motives, it is not becoming a moral and religious people to express any approbation of military or naval exploits which are not immediately connected with the defence of our sea coast and soil."

with small arms and great guns;—a point of vital importance in naval warfare, but one which had hitherto been in an unaccountable manner neglected, with a very few exceptions, in all the departments in the British navy."

The result of these efforts was soon after displayed. Captain Broke, an able officer, commanded the Shannon, a frig-
1813. ate pierced for thirty-eight guns, but really mounting fifty-two; and, contrary to the general practice in the British navy, he had for many years trained the crew, whom, by admirable management, he had brought to the highest state of discipline and subordination, to the practice of ball firing with great guns. In the case of the Chesapeake, however, she was not in a fair condition to meet the Shannon on any thing like equal terms. Her crew were dissatisfied on account of unpaid prize money. She had also an unusual number of landsmen and mercenaries on board; several of her officers were inexperienced, or on the sick list; and altogether, she labored under serious disadvantages in the way of fitness for fighting the Shannon. In the number of guns, the vessels were as nearly equal as was possible. Captain Broke, hearing that the Chesapeake was ready for sea, stood in to the mouth of the harbor, and dispatched to Captain Lawrence a courteous invitation to single combat, "to try the fortunes of their respective flags." But before this *cartel* could be received, the American captain, seeing the British vessel lying close in to the lighthouse, with colors flying, determined to chastise its commander for so daring a defiance, and weighing anchor, on the 1st of June, went gallantly down, with three flags flying, on one of which was inscribed, "Free trade and sailor's right." Numerous barges and pleasure boats, amidst loud cheers, accompanied her some way out, to what they deemed a certain victory.

It was twelve, meridian, when the Chesapeake weighed; and Broke, deeming his challenge accepted, at once stood out to sea. When about thirty miles from the light, at about five, P. M., the Chesapeake signalled the Shannon to heave to, and with three cheers, ran up alongside her, at the distance of about two hundred yards. As she passed not more than a stone's throw off, the Shannon's guns, beginning with her cabin guns, were fired in succession, from aft forward; and as they were heavily loaded, with two round shot, and a hundred and fifty musket balls, or one round and one double-headed shot, in each, they did fearful execution. The Chesapeake did not fire till all
her guns bore, when she deliv- **1813.**
ered a very destructive broadside. Two or three broadsides were then exchanged; and so far as the general effect of the fire was concerned, the Chesapeake had the best of it; but some of her rigging had been shot away, and in attempting to haul her foresail up, she fell on board the Shannon, whose starboard bower anchor locked with her mizzen channels; and she lay exposed to a raking fire from the enemy, who swept her decks with the contents of two thirty-two pounder carronades, beat in her sternposts, and drove the men from their quarters. The boatswain of the Shannon lashed the two

ships together, while the marines exchanged a sharp and galling fire of musketry.

Lawrence was severely wounded before the vessels fouled; and in preparation for that he directed the boarders to be called, but instead of a drummer, there was only a bugleman, a negro, who, as Cooper says, was so much alarmed at the effects of the conflict, that he had concealed himself under the launch, and when found, was so completely paralyzed by fear, as to be totally unable to sound a note. The word was then passed for the boarders to come on deck; but at this very instant, Lawrence fell with a ball through his body. No other officer, higher in rank than a midshipman, remained on the upper deck; and when the boarders came from below, such was the confusion, that they were unarmed; and the enemy was now in possession of the vessel: for the British, on their side, as soon as the vessels were made fast, were prepared to board, and Broke, at the head of the boarding party, leapt upon the Chesapeake's quarter-deck; quickly followed by another party to the forecastle; whilst the sailors of the Shannon's foreyard forced their way into the Chesapeake's tops and cleared them.

This action was one of the most sanguinary that ever occurred. It lasted only fifteen minutes, and yet, in that time, forty-eight were killed and ninety-eight wounded on board the Chesapeake, and twenty-four killed and fifty-nine wounded on board the Shannon. Lawrence's dying words, "DON'T GIVE UP THE SHIP," became consecrated in the eyes of his countrymen, and have many a time since been used to animate the spirits of our brave seamen. Lawrence died a few days after the battle, and was buried in Halifax; but subsequently, his remains were removed to New York, and now repose in Trinity churchyard.

The effect of this capture was wonderful in England, and hardly less so in the United States. The English rejoiced over it with very disproportioned exultation, as if their invincibility were entirely re-established; while the Americans, who had foolishly supposed that they were unconquerable on the ocean, fretted and felt mortified, almost as if they had lost every thing. The truth seems to be, that, under all the circumstances, the victory was nothing more than Broke ought to have gained; and the honors that were heaped upon him for this exploit, were virtual confessions of American superiority on the water, and went a good way towards consoling them for the loss of the Chesapeake.*

Another victory on the side of England followed soon after. The sloop-of-war Argus, having carried out Mr. Crawford, our minister to France, in

* Mr. Ingersoll (vol. i., pp. 395–415) gives in full the proceedings at the trial of Lieutenant Cox, in March, 1814. This gentleman, it appears, assisted in carrying Lawrence below when he was wounded, and did not get back to his station on deck; and to his absence, in part, the loss of the vessel was attributed. It is only due to the character of Cox to state, that the court acquitted him of the charges of cowardice, disobedience of orders, and desertion from his quarters; but convicted him of neglect of duty and unofficerlike conduct in leaving the quarter deck. He was accordingly cashiered, with a perpetua incapacity to serve in the navy of the United States.

PAINTED BY ALONZO CHAPPEL.

DEATH OF CAPTAIN LAWRENCE.

"DON'T GIVE UP THE SHIP"

From the original painting in the possession of the Publishers.

New York, Martin, Johnson & Co. Publishers.

the spring of this year, cruised for some time in the British channel, and was very successful in capturing and destroying British shipping. On the 14th of August, the British sloop-of-war Pelican came in sight of the Argus, and determined to attack her. Finding it impossible to gain the wind of his enemy, Captain Allen of the Argus shortened sail, and a furious conflict began. The captain and first lieutenant fell, *hors de combat*, within a quarter of an hour; and after successfully avoiding one attempt to rake her, she became unmanageable, and the enemy chose his position at pleasure. For a quarter of an hour, the Pelican now maintained a raking fire upon the unfortunate Argus, whilst she could hardly train a gun to bear upon her adversary. She struck, accordingly, and the enemy, at the same moment falling on board, took possession over the bow. Six men were killed, and seventeen wounded, on board the Argus; whilst the victors lost only seven men in all. Captain Allen died in England, and was buried with the honors of war.

1813.

A few weeks later, the American brig Enterprise, Lieutenant Burrows, sailed from Portsmouth on a cruise. On the 4th of September, she fell in with the British brig Boxer, Captain Blythe. The action which ensued lasted forty minutes, when the enemy ceased firing, and cried for quarter; being unable to haul down her flag, as it had been nailed to the mast. The Enterprise had thirteen wounded and one killed, but that one was the lamented Burrows. He fell at the commencement of the action, but refused to quit the deck, and requested that the flag might never be struck. Twenty-five were killed and wounded on board the Boxer, Captain Blythe being among the killed. The two commanders were buried at Portland, with unusual honors and tokens of respect and admiration.

The gallantry of American seamen was displayed in other ways beside those of our ships of war. Contemporary journals are filled with long lists of vessels captured by privateers which were fitted out in large numbers from various ports of the United States. Though many of these were signally successful, yet, as Mr. Hale justly remarks,* the general belief that Providence blesses not wealth so acquired, was strengthened by the quickness with which it vanished, having fixed upon its possessors habits of extravagance, and leaving behind it the love of pleasure which could no longer be gratified. Sometimes, in their search for merchantmen, they met with hostile privateers, or public ships of war, and then they showed themselves worthy of the flag of their country. In August, the American privateer Decatur, mounting seven guns, and manned with one hundred and three men, fell in with the British schooner Dominica, of sixteen guns and eighty-three men. For two hours, the two ships continued manœuvring and firing, the Decatur seeking to board her antagonist, and she to escape. At length the former was placed in such a position, that part

* Hale's "*History of the United States*," vol. ii., p. 187.

of her crew passed, upon the bowsprit, into the stern of the latter. The firing on both sides, from cannon and musketry, was now terrible. In a short time, the two ships came in contact, broadside to broadside, and then the remainder of the Decatur's crew rushed upon her enemy's deck. Fire-arms were thrown aside, and the men fought hand to hand, using cutlasses and throwing shot. Nearly all the officers of the Dominica being killed, her flag was hauled down by the conquerors. Of her crew of eighty-three, sixty were killed or wounded; of that of the Decatur, but nineteen.*

In bringing the present chapter to a close, we cannot pass over the cruise of the Essex, which, for daring and success, may be said to stand first among the naval enterprises of 1813. The

1813.

Essex, under command of Captain Porter, mounted thirty-two guns, and left the United States in October, 1812, with directions to proceed to a station on the coast of South America, where he was to meet Commodore Bainbridge in the Constitution. On the 12th of December, he fell in with and captured the British packet Nocton, with $55,000 in specie on board. Having arrived at the designated station too late to meet Bainbridge, Captain Porter, being at liberty to act according to his own discretion, resolved to take the Essex round Cape Horn, and to try his fortune in defending the American whalers and capturing the British ships that might be found in the Pacific. At Valparaiso, on the 13th of March, he was welcomed as a friend by the new government of Chili; his first exploit was the rescue of two American vessels which had been taken by a Peruvian privateer,—the viceroy having presumed that Spain had declared war against the United States, and granted letters of marque against their shipping. In April, he made three prizes of armed whalers, and one of them he manned and equipped with sixteen guns to sail as consort to his own

1813.

ship. Nine other vessels also fell into his power; making twelve prizes in the course of this year. Three of these he took to Valparaiso for security, and three he sent home with the oil he had taken in the others; two were dismantled, and sent with his paroled prisoners as cartels; the rest he converted into cruisers, or tenders to the Essex, and thus increased his force into a respectable squadron. Four thousand tons of shipping were thus captured by him; and four hundred prisoners made, many of whom consented to serve under him; and but for his presence in those seas, the American whalers would have experienced the same fate, and been taken by the enemy. In the autumn of the present year, hearing that some British vessels had been sent in search of him, he proceeded to the Marquesas, and refitted in the Bay of Nouaheevah, before attempting to make his way back to America.

The story of Porter's adventurous cruise subsequent to this date, we must

* In connection with this topic, we must refer the reader to a volume written *con amore*, entitled, "*History of the American Privateers and Letters of Marque during our war with England, in the years* 1812–1814," By George Coggeshall. It is a volume full of curious information, and will repay perusal.

defer to another chapter. Thus far, he had been uncommonly successful in every thing he undertook, and it was felt every where that he deserved well of his country, the highest praise any of her sons can attain.

CHAPTER X.

1813.

CONCLUSION OF THE CAMPAIGN OF 1813.

Extra session of Congress — The president's message — The mediation of Russia — Commissioners appointed — Financial plans and measures — J. Q. Adams on this topic — Adjournment of Congress in August – The war in the south-west — Tecumseh's efforts among the Creeks — Fort Mimms assaulted — The massacre — Gloom and distress — Arming of the people in Georgia and Tennessee — Floyd and Jackson — Coffee's victory — Jackson's activity — Various battles — The bloody victory at Horse Shoe Bend — Conclusion of the war with the Creeks — Proctor invests Fort Stephenson on the Sandusky — Major Croghan's gallant defence — Commodore Perry on Lake Erie – His famous victory — His dispatch to Harrison — Results of this victory — Proctor's retreat — Harrison in pursuit — Battle of the Thames — Johnson's charge with the mounted volunteers — Tecumseh's death — Chauncey on Lake Ontario — Wilkinson in command of the army of the centre — Hampton at Plattsburg — Delay and hindrances in undertaking the invasion of Canada — Plan of the secretary of war — Wilkinson's advance — The battle at Chrystler's Field, near Williamsburg — Hampton declines forming a junction with Wilkinson — The expedition abandoned — Hampton's movements and plans — Popular censures and complaints in consequence of the failure of the Canada expedition — Assaults on the Niagara frontier — M'Clure burns Newark — Terrible retaliation by the British — Burning and destruction of towns and villages — Close of the year 1813, and its various fortunes.

1813.

ON the 24th of May, the day appointed for an extra session (p. 178), Congress assembled in the Capitol, ready to enter upon the responsible and difficult duties before them. Henry Clay was elected speaker of the House, and Daniel Webster was among the active members in the opposition.* In the Senate, the federalists had several very strong men, as Jeremiah Mason, Rufus King, etc., and although the administration was decidedly in the majority, yet in consequence of the dissatisfaction of De Witt Clinton's friends on account of his defeat, this majority was by no means as effective or reliable, as it would have been under other circumstances.

The president's message was sent in on the following day. It consisted chiefly of a *resumé* of the phases of the war; but it held out hopes of a restoration of peace, and gave an account of the finances of the country that was somewhat reassuring, although probably there was more to be said upon that part of the subject than the president found it expedient, at that time, to express. The receipts into the treasury during the preceding six months, from all sources, loans and treasury

* For the measures which were advocated by this distinguished son of New Hampshire, we must refer the student to his Life and Works, and to the fifth volume of Mr. Benton's "*Abridgement of the Debates of Congress.*"

notes included, were $15,412,000. The expenditure during the same period amounted to $15,920,000. Nevertheless, there were, for the next half year, $1,857,000 in the treasury.

The real difficulty, however, which pressed upon the government had to be stated. So, after a further exposition of the prospects of the year, the president added: "This view of our finances, whilst it shows that due provision has been made for the expenses of the current year, shows at the same time, by the limited amount of the actual revenue, and the dependence on loans, the necessity of providing more adequately for the future supplies of the treasury. This can be best done by a well-digested system of internal revenue, in aid of existing sources; which will have the effect, both of abridging the amount of necessary loans, and on that account, as well as by placing the public credit on a more satisfactory basis, of improving the terms on which loans may be obtained . . . . .

"In recommending to the national legislature this resort to additional taxes, I feel great satisfaction in the assurance, that our constituents, who have already displayed so much zeal and firmness in the cause of their country, will cheerfully give every other proof of their patriotism, which it calls for. Happily, no people, with local and transitory exceptions never to be wholly avoided, are more able than the people of the United States to spare for the public wants a portion of their private means; whether regard be had to the ordinary profits of industry, or the ordinary price of subsistence in our country, compared with those of any other. And in no case could stronger reasons be felt for yielding the requisite contributions. By rendering the public resources certain, and commensurate to the public exigencies, the constituted authorities will be able to prosecute the war the more rapidly to its proper issue; every hostile hope, founded on a calculated failure of our resources, will be cut off; and by adding to the evidences of bravery and skill, in combats on the ocean and the land, an alacrity in supplying the treasure necessary to give them their fullest effects, and demonstrating to the world the public energy which our political institutions combine, with the personal liberty distinguishing them, the best security will be provided against future enterprises on the rights or the peace of the nation."

1813.

Russia, as we have said on a previous page, (p. 175), offered her good offices as a mediator in the existing difficulties between Great Britain and the United States. The president accepted the offer, as made through M. Daschkoff, the Russian minister, and on the 17th of April, appointed John Quincy Adams, then minister to Russia, Albert Gallatin, and James A. Bayard, envoys extraordinary and ministers plenipotentiary to conclude a treaty of peace with England, under the auspices of Russia. Messrs. Gallatin and Bayard proceeded to join Mr. Adams at St. Petersburgh, and the three envoys reached the Baltic in June, ready to enter upon their mission and its work. Great Britain refused, in September, to accede to the mediation; but, early in November, informed the American government that His Majesty was willing to enter upon a direct negotiation for peace. The president accepted this proposition, and it was communicated to Lord Castlereagh that envoys would be immediately sent to Gottenburg, for the purpose of carrying it into effect.

When the names of the gentlemen sent on this mission came before the Senate, Adams and Bayard were confirmed without difficulty; strong opposition, however, was made to Mr. Gallatin, because, as was urged, it was manifestly improper that the office of secretary of the treasury and that of envoy extraordinary should be held by the same person. At first, his nomination was rejected by a vote of eighteen to seventeen; but having subsequently resigned the secretaryship, the Senate approved the nomination. Captain Jones, of the navy department, discharged the duties of secretary of the treasury in connection with those properly devolving on him, till the 9th of February, 1814, when George W. Campbell, of Tennessee, was appointed secretary of the treasury, in the place of Mr. Gallatin. Other nominations made by the president were treated much in the same way by those senators who were warm friends of De Witt Clinton; and the executive was a good deal embarrassed, at times, by the opposition of those who in all other respects were decided friends of democratic measures and principles. Mr. Jonathan Russell, nominated as minister to Sweden, was one of those whom the Senate refused to approve.

During this extra session, Congress was principally occupied in giving attention to measures for relieving the national finances from embarrassment. The presidential question being settled, there was less hesitation in bringing forward certain plans which it was not deemed expedient before this to press. Necessity compelled the adoption of unpopular measures. The existing duties on imports were doubled, and the assessment and collection of direct taxes and internal duties were also provided for.

1813.

This was, in fact, Mr. Gallatin's plan, which had been rejected previously; but now, since there seemed to be no other way practicable, it was proposed to raise an annual revenue sufficient to pay the ordinary expenses of government, and the interest of such sums as it would become necessary to borrow; and to support the war by a series of loans.

Accordingly, acts were passed imposing duties on refined sugars, salt, carriages, auction sales, licenses for distilleries, and for retailing wine, spirit, and foreign goods, with stamp duties on bank notes, bills of exchange, and other notes; (which were expected to produce $2,000,000 yearly;) and a direct tax on houses, lands, and slaves, at their assessed value, amounting to $3,000,000 a year. But the advantages expected from this resumption of the system of internal taxation, which Jefferson had so earnestly denounced, could not be enjoyed before the following year; and for the current year, another loan of $7,500,000 was authorized. The treasury notes, five millions of which had been issued, were, however, at a great discount; and although the former loan had been taken at par, for six per cent. stock, this second loan, apparently taken at the same rate, was all paid in depreciated currency. The finances were, in fact, in a very serious state of embarrassment. The banks had suspended specie payments, excepting a few in New England. The demands upon the treasury had far exceeded what had been anticipated; and when the militia was called out, they all, but particularly those of the middle states, were found insufficiently clothed and equipped in every respect. The regular army, too, was deficient both in blankets and clothing for the soldiers, owing to the prohibition of importations from England, and the incapability of the home manufactures to supply the demand.*

In connection with the important and always difficult topic of the finances during a state of war, Mr. Adams's remarks are worth quoting: "Among the severest trials of the war, was the deficiency of adequate funds to sustain it, and the progressive degradation of the national credit. By an unpropitious combination of rival interests, and of political prejudices, the first Bank of the United States, at the very outset of the war, had been denied the renewal of its charter: (p. 753) a heavier blow of illusive and contracted policy, could scarcely have befallen the Union. The polar star of public credit, and of commercial confidence, was abstracted from the firmament, and the needle of the compass wandered at random to the four quarters of the heavens. From the root of the fallen trunk, sprang up a thicket of perishable suckers—never destined to bear fruit: the offspring of summer vegetation, withering at the touch of the first winter's frost. Yet, upon them was our country doomed to rely: it was her only substitute for the shade and shelter of the parent tree. The currency soon fell into frightful disorder: banks, with fictitious capital, swarmed throughout the land, and spunged the purse of the people, often for the use of their own money, with more than usurious extortion. The solid banks, even of this metropolis, (Boston,) were enabled to maintain their integrity, only by contracting their operations to an extent ruinous to their debtors, and to themselves. A balance of trade, operating like universal fraud, vitiated the channels of intercourse between north and south, and the treasury of the Union was replenished only with countless millions of silken tatters, and unavailable funds; chartered corporations, bankrupt, under the gentle name of suspended specie payments, and without a dollar of capital to pay their debts, sold, at enormous discounts, the very evidence of those debts, and passed off, upon the government of the country, at par, their rags—purchasable, in open market, at depreciations of thirty and forty per cent."*

* Early in July, the legislature of Massachusetts sent in a strong remonstrance to the House, denouncing the war as impolitic and unjust, defending the course of Great Britain, and charging the party in power with blind devotion and even subserviency to France.

* "*Life of James Monroe*," p. 271.

Yet, as Mr. Ingersoll states, in giving the principal causes of the administrative success of the system of 1813, "it may be averred, to the honor of our country, that never were taxes, especially new ones, more promptly or cheerfully paid, nearly the whole amount accruing within the four years, being paid within that period; when the currency was deranged; without National Bank, or other general regulation; and of what was called money, little more than state bank notes, most of which, during the latter part of the war, were not convertible into coin, but mere promises to pay. The cost of collection never exceeded six per cent."*

1813.

Congress adjourned on the 2d of August, 1813, after a session of more order, system, vigor, and advantage, than is usual for the legislature of a country such as ours, where the right of free discussion prevails. The majority of the House, Ingersoll asserts, were unanimous and harmonious. There was some dissidence in the Senate; but hardly any in the House, certainly no dissension, among the supporters of the war, whose pressure suppressed whatever inherent tendency to discord there might and must be in such bodies. The opposition were also united and active; but their efforts were bestowed principally upon questions which affected the mode of carrying on the war rather than in respect to the war itself. There were not many who denied the justice of the war; but the opposition contended, that it should include France as well as England, or should have been put off for fuller preparation.*

During the progress of events at the north and west, as we have related them in preceding chapters, affairs in the south-west were gradually assuming a shape calculated to excite great alarm and anxiety. The southern Indians, under the humane system adopted by Washington, had, many of them, been induced to forsake the savage mode of life, and very great expense was freely incurred to endeavor to win them to the ways in which their white neighbors lived and made advances in wealth and happiness. The Creeks especially had enjoyed every favor at the hand of the United States; their lands had never been encroached upon; and they had, to some considerable extent, intermarried with the whites. Among these, and their neighbors the Choctaws, Chickasaws, and Cherokees, there were not a few who had learned rightly to estimate the arts of civilized life; and who perceived that war with the Americans could not be successful, and might bring destruction upon their nation. These resisted the endeavors of Tecumseh with great energy, and strove to dissuade their fellow tribesmen from joining in his perilous and perfectly hopeless scheme. Nevertheless, his influence amongst the younger and more

* Ingersoll's "*History of the Second War*," vol. i., p. 224.

* At the request of Congress, the president recommended, that the second Thursday in September "be observed by the people of the United States with religious solemnity, and the offering of fervent supplications to Almighty God for the safety and welfare of these states, His blessing on their arms, and the speedy restoration of peace." That day accordingly, we are happy to state, was observed very generally throughout the country.

ardent men, who there, as every where else, were ready for any thing new, was very great, and he did not fail to use it to its fullest extent.

Towards the close of 1812, Tecumseh made his appearance again in the Creek towns, not to tell of impracticable confederacies, and the resumption of old and half-forgotten habits and rites of the Indian races, but to arouse them if he could to war. All the smouldering passions of the savages, who cherished the traditions of the times when as yet no hated pale-faces had trodden the western continent, and who despised the effeminacy of the recreants, whom the fascinations of those pale-faces had won to emulate their mode of life; all the petty feuds which were sure to exist in communities composed as these were; every thing that could be employed by one skilled as he was, was turned by Tecumseh now to this end, that by attacking the United States in the south, whilst he and his allies, the British, attacked them in the north, he should obtain his personal revenge, even though he might never hope to wreak upon these foes of his race the vengeance he had desired to inflict on them for all the wrongs, real and imagined, which they were guilty of in his sight, towards his ancestors, and the forefathers of the other Indian tribes.

The war spirit, naturally enough grew stronger and stronger. The party in favor of peace and civilization did all in their power to make head against the hostile portion; but without success. Murders were committed on the frontiers, and the legislature of Tennessee, in alarm at the prospect, gave authority to the governor to call out ten thousand militia, and make war upon the Creeks, even to extermination, unless the murderers were given up. A state of civil war soon after eventuated, and the opposing parties arranged themselves under their respective leaders. Acts of violence ensued, and several of the friendly chiefs were murdered in cold blood. Gaining strength, they proceeded to new acts of violence; regardless of the legitimate authorities, they deposed and put to death the friends of peace, until the nation was involved in general bloodshed. The war party at length prevailed, and all opposition was summarily crushed by arbitrary force.

Parties of hostile warriors began to assemble in various parts of the Creek nation, with the avowed purpose of commencing hostilities against the white settlements of the Mississippi Territory, and of Georgia, and Tennessee. Emissaries were employed in efforts to induce the Choctaws to unite with them in the general league, Tecumseh having been unsuccessful in his efforts, among the chiefs of that nation. In these efforts, it appears, they failed. Mushulatubbe, and other Choctaw chiefs, succeeded in preserving the nation's loyalty to the United States unsullied.

1813.

Throughout the white settlements on the Tombigbee and Alabama Rivers, the liveliest alarm prevailed; and a brigade of nine hundred volunteers and militia was organized by Governor Holmes, to quiet the apprehensions of the settlers, and at the same time to afford them protection, in case of an attack. The settlers also very generally began to take refuge in the fortifications, if so we may term them, along the Alabama River.

Having obtained an abundant supply of arms and ammunition from Pensacola —furnished, as was charged, by the British—the hostile Creeks determined to venture upon some exploits which should signalize their share in the war. Accordingly, Fort Mimms, on the Alabama, not far from Mobile, was marked out for destruction, in the summer of 1813. This was one of the usual stockaded forts on the river's bank, to which Governor Claiborne had sent Major Beasly, with a hundred and eighty men. The inhabitants of the Tensas settlement were collected there; and subsequently, Claiborne dispatched orders to Beasly, urging him to the utmost vigilance and caution; charging him to complete the block houses, to strengthen the stockades, and to keep a vigilant watch against sudden attack.

Under some unaccountable delusion, Beasly acted as if there was no danger to be feared. Near the end of August, a negro came in, who brought warning that the Indians meant to attack the post. The warning was more than once repeated; but, unhappily, was unheeded. On the night preceding the massacre, the dogs of the garrison, who are said to be able to smell the Indians, gave notice of danger by a peculiar growling. Yet there was no alarm felt; but all were confident of security.

The next day, August 30th, the fatal delusion was dispelled. Towards noon, the Indians advanced through an open field, to within thirty yards of the fort before they were discovered; so well devised, bold, and fortunate, was the plan of the blood thirsty savages! The gate, too, was wide open, and raising their fearful whoop they rushed into the fort. Every man who could fight seized his weapon and hurried to his post. The first struggle took place at the gate, and the slaughter was dreadful. Beasly himself, shot through the body, was one of the first victims. Crowds on crowds of Indians pressed to the attack, driving in by mere numbers the vainly brave garrison, whose immovable security had betrayed them to the enemy. For some hours the fight literally raged. It was a hand to hand combat; bayonet, sword, and clubbed rifle clashing and colliding with tomahawk, scalping knife, and war club. The defences of the white men were fired; they were shot down from without; and encumbered by the women and children, and other non-effectives who had taken refuge in the fort, they were, in spite of the most desperate valor, completely overpowered.

1813.

At length, about five in the afternoon, the few who survived, not one of whom was without a wound, and several had received more than one, gathering the guns of their fallen comrades, and throwing them with the ammunition they could not carry into the flames, resolved to force their way out. The upper part of the block-house, to which some of the women had retreated, was rapidly consuming,—it was certain destruction to remain where they were, —perhaps they might succeed in fighting their way through the swarms of the enemy. Seventeen only, and notwithstanding their wounds, did succeed. Above three hundred and fifty persons —including volunteers and militia, the ordinary garrison, refugees from the neighborhood, (twenty families and more,) friendly Indians, and some hundred of negroes—perished during the fight, or in the flames, or were put to death after all resistance had ceased, with barbarities too revolting to be narrated. The entire number of those who escaped was under thirty. The scene presented to those who came to bury the dead, after the Indians had withdrawn, exceeded all description.

Gloom and consternation took possession of the whole south-western frontier. Every fort was crowded with fugitives, and Mobile, which General Wilkinson had seized in the month of April, was now a most welcome harbor of refuge to multitudes, whom terror at the news of the tragedy at Fort Mimms drove from their homes. The whole region was in a deplorable state, and the distress of the people during the sickly season, in September, was extreme. The number and fierceness of the Indians were frightful, and every station, every block-house, and every fort was assailed by the open foe, or by lurking bands of concealed savages.

In this emergency, it was felt that no help from the government at Washington was to be obtained; the people of the neighboring states must give the requisite assistance, or the whole country must be abandoned by the whites. "The people and government of the contiguous states, Georgia and Tennessee, and of those convenient, South and North Carolina, instantly acted with excellent decision, before it was possible to furnish the means, hardly to give orders, from the seat of government. In war, the well-being of popular government requires that each sovereignty act in its own sphere, and perform the constitutional duty prescribed to it. Irregularities of action betray infirmities which are not inherent in the system. The communities and governments of the states of Georgia and Tennessee faced the emergency with alacrity and energy, similar to what was displayed in Ohio, Kentucky, and Pennsylvania."*

1813.

Amongst other means for reducing the Creeks, now thought of, was the employment of the Choctaws against them. A "Committee of Safety" set forth at length the reasons which appeared to them to call for this measure; the most convincing, in their opinion, being, that if the United States did not secure the co-operation of these Indians, the enemy might do so, and then, instead of being subdued, the Creeks would be reinforced. "In the emphatic language of Major Gibson," says Monette, "the point was narrowed down to this, 'We must engage the Choctaws, or fight them!'"

It was not, however, till the month of November, that the requisite negotiations were completed, and it was the middle of the month before General Claiborne, accompanied by the Choctaw auxiliaries, advanced towards Weatherford's Bluff, on the Alabama, for the

* Ingersoll's "*History of the Second War*," vol. i., p. 333.

purpose of erecting a stockaded dépôt, to receive supplies and military stores for the use of the Tennessee troops, under General Jackson, who were on the march, along the line of the Coosa. Before the close of November, this was done; and Fort Claiborne, with its palisades, block-houses, and half-moon battery, presented a frowning front to all unbidden navigators of the stream.

Georgia and Tennessee very actively seconded the efforts of Mississippi, and had General Flournoy been a more efficient commander, much effusion of blood and waste of property would have been spared. On the western
1813. edge of Georgia, about the middle of October, was stationed General Floyd, at the head of some two thousand five hundred men; and by the beginning of November, he had advanced with nearly a third of them, and four hundred allied Indians, into the Creek country about the Tallapoosa and its tributaries. He very soon made his presence known, as we shall see presently.

But it was from Tennessee that the main body of the forces, relied upon for the effective discharge of the stern duty of repressing the armed Indians, and chastising them for the outrage at Fort Mimms, came. The legislature of that state, then in session, had authorized the governor to call out three thousand five hundred men in addition to those already under arms; and be-
1813. fore many days of October had passed, one column, of two thousand choice volunteers, under General Jackson, set out from Nashville; another column, of about equal strength, advancing from East Tennessee in the same direction under General Cocke.

Mr. Ingersoll, in speaking of this matter, says, that the federal government adopted the men thus raised and in active service, and reimbursed the money, some $200,000, which the legislature of Tennessee had appropriated for the maintenance of the war against the Creeks; and he adds: "Riddance of the country from the savages, theretofore the terror, if not the masters of it, was mainly effected by local popular and state action, consummated by operations of the federal government. The part each one performed, the appropriate function of each, are lessons of that conflict which cannot be too durably impressed on the American mind. While it is one of the most unquestionable and gratifying demonstrations of the war of 1812, that the states saved the United States in several emergencies, it is equally true, that excessive state or popular action embarrassed and endangered the Union; and that it is by the harmonious adjustment of all the elements, popular, state, and federal, that national safety, dignity, and vindication, are accomplished. If obliged to wait the orders, forces, and contributions of the federal government, the Creek war would never have been crushed, as it was, in one victorious campaign. Yet that campaign proved, even without state or popular disaffection, that something more than six months militia and volunteers is indispensable to general safety and welfare."*

Although it is somewhat in advance

* "*History of the Second War*," vol. i., p. 334.

of the progress of our narrative thus far, it will be most convenient, we think, to relate the conclusion of the Creek war, in the present connection. On the 2d of November, General Coffee was detached, with nine hundred men, against Tallushatches, a Creek town, and reached the place about daylight the next morning. The Indians, aware of his approach, were prepared to receive him. Within a short distance of the village they charged upon him with
1813. unexampled boldness; and although repulsed, made a most obstinate resistance. They refused to give or receive quarter, and were slain almost to a man. Nearly two hundred of their warriors were killed in this affair. The women and children were taken prisoners. The loss of the Americans was five killed and forty wounded..

Four days later, having been informed that Lashly's Fort, at the village of Talladega, about thirty miles distant, belonging to the friendly Creeks, was in great danger from the hostile party, Jackson set off with alacrity to relieve the place. At twelve o'clock the same night, he took up his line of march, at the head of twelve hundred men, and arrived within six miles of the fort the next evening. At midnight he again advanced, and by seven o'clock of the following morning was within a mile of the enemy. He now made the most judicious arrangements for surrounding them; and approached, within eighty yards, almost unperceived. The battle commenced on the part of the Indians with great fury. Being repulsed on all sides, they attempted to make their escape, but found themselves enclosed; and had not two companies of militia given way, whereby a space was left open through which a considerable number of the enemy escaped to the mountains, they would all have been taken prisoners or destroyed. In the pursuit many were sabred or shot down. In this action, the American loss was fifteen killed, and eighty wounded. That of the Creeks was not much short of three hundred killed, their whole force exceeding a thousand. "In a very few weeks," wrote General Jackson, "if I had a sufficiency of supplies, I am thoroughly convinced I should be able to put an end to Creek hostilities."

Jackson had ordered General White to join him after Coffee's first success, intending to press forward and crush the Indians before they had time to recover from the panic produced by these blows. White, however, who was subordinate to General Cocke, was detached by him, on the 11th of November, against the hostile towns on the Talapoosa River, where the Hillabees resided. At daylight, on the 1813.
18th, White entered a Hillabee town, and out of about three hundred and sixteen warriors killed some sixty, and took the rest prisoners. Having burnt several villages, which had been deserted by the Indians, he returned on the 23d, without the loss of a single man.

At the close of November, a signal victory was obtained by General Floyd, at the head of the Georgia militia, at Autossee, on the Talapoosa. This was "the Creek metropolis," and the very ground was held to be sacred. It was defended with a spirit animated by every consideration that interest, revenge, and religion could present. Warriors from eight towns were assembled to oppose the invaders there. But the well-directed fire of the artillery, added to the charge of the bayonet, triumphed over all opposition. The Indians lost at least two hundred, among whom were the Autossee king and another, and their wounded were much more numerous. The number of buildings burnt, some of a superior order for the dwellings of savages, and filled with valuable articles, was supposed to be four hundred. The American loss was eleven killed and fifty-four wounded. That of the friendly Indians, who fought with them, and with great intrepidity, was never ascertained.

In the month of December, Claiborne, with the Mississippi volunteers, and a body of Choctaws, advanced into the Creek country; and on the 23d, attacked Ecchanachaca, "Holy Ground," a town on the Alabama, of about two hundred houses, not long built, with many incantations, to serve as

1813.

Weatherford's stronghold, and fancied by the Indians to be impregnable. Weatherford himself, Josiah, Francis, and Sinquister, all of them "prophets," encouraged their followers to display the most furious bravery in defence of the consecrated spot. Thirty only were killed; the chief prophet fled; the town was burned, and all the land round devastated.

The term of service of the Tennessee volunteers having expired, no persuasions of General Jackson were sufficiently strong to induce them to remain longer away from their homes. Becoming mutinous, they were disbanded and ordered to march back to Tennessee. On the 14th of January, however, Jackson was fortunately reinforced by eight hundred volunteers, and soon after by several hundred friendly Indians. Their term of service was only sixty days, and the general determined to employ them at once against the enemy. Having been joined by General Coffee, with a number of officers, Jackson, on the 17th of January, with the view of making a diversion in favor of General Floyd, and at the same time of relieving Fort Armstrong, which was said to be threatened, entered the Indian country, with the determination of penetrating still farther than had yet been attempted. On the evening of the 21st, believing himself, from appearances, in the vicinity of a large body of Indians, he encamped with great precaution, and kept himself in the attitude of defence. At daylight, the next morning, an assault was made on the left flank; which, after being firmly resisted for about half an hour, was successfully repulsed, and a furious charge of the cavalry, under General Coffee, completely routed the Indians, and drove them nearly two miles from the field with great slaughter. Soon afterwards, the camp was attacked on the other flank, but with no better result; the remainder of the enemy's force being routed now, with the loss of forty-five of their warriors.

1814.

The next morning, a retrograde movement was made by General Jackson, under a belief that he had diverted the enemy from their designs against the Georgia troops, and could encounter them best nearer to his dépôt. On the

24th, at the outset of the march, there lay a defile at the crossing of the Enotachopes Creek. Here the Indians, who had followed closely, (and against whom preparations had been made in the night for fear of a sudden attack,) fell upon them, and threw them into disorder for a short time,—some companies taking to flight. Very soon, however, they were rallied and brought into action, and the artillery, which was encumbered in the ford at the moment of attack, took the lead against the swarms of the enemy. The conflict did not last long, and the Indians were routed, and fled in the greatest consternation; leaving twenty-six of their number dead on the field. Jackson's loss, in these fights, was twenty-four killed and seventy-one wounded: the Indians' loss was about two hundred dead on the battle field, beside large numbers wounded.

Notwithstanding these repulses, the Creeks attacked General Floyd at Camp Defiance, early in the morning of the 27th of January, and quite unexpectedly. The sentinels were driven in, and a fierce contest took place within the lines; but Indian valor, weapons, and tactics, here as elsewhere, proved no match for American discipline, grape shot, and the bayonet. Thirty-seven of their warriors were left dead; but it was plain, from the number of head-dresses and war-clubs scattered about, and from the bloody trail they made in their retreat, that this was not the whole of their loss. Seventeen Americans fell, and a hundred and thirty-two were wounded.

Early in March, Jackson was appointed a major-general in the United States service, and was reinforced by the thirty-ninth regiment of United States infantry. Several detachments of militia and volunteers soon afterwards joined him, so that the forces at his command amounted to nearly four thousand men, besides Indian auxiliaries, numbering nearly another thousand. He was now in a condition to bring the war to a close by an attack upon the last stronghold of the Creeks. This was at the bend of the Talapoosa, called by the Indians Tohopeka, and by the whites Horse-shoe Bend. Nature and art had rendered this a place of great security. A breastwork had been erected, from five to eight feet high, across the peninsula, thus enclosing nearly one hundred acres of ground. This could not be approached, without being exposed to a double and cross fire from the Indians who lay behind. About one thousand warriors had collected on this spot. Here General Jackson determined to attack them.

1814.

On the 26th of March, he encamped within six miles of the place, and having learned the shore was lined with canoes, he sent General Coffee to the opposite side of the river to surround the Bend in such a manner that none could escape by crossing the river. With the remainder of his force, he attacked their fortifications in front. A brisk fire was kept up for two hours, when General Coffee crossed to the peninsula to his aid, and commenced a spirited fire upon the enemy, who lay behind the breastwork; but they were still unsubdued. General Jackson determined to storm their fortifications.

The regulars, led on by Colonel Williams and Major Montgomery, advanced to the charge. An obstinate contest ensued, in which the combatants fought through the port-holes, musket to musket. At this time, Major Montgomery, leaping on the wall, called to his men to mount and follow him. Scarcely had he spoken, when a ball struck him on the head, and he fell lifeless to the ground. Yet the Americans obeyed his command, and, following his example, soon gained the opposite side of the works. Though the Creeks fought with a bravery which their desperate situation alone could have inspired, yet they were entirely defeated, and cut to pieces. Five hundred and fifty were killed on the peninsula, and many were drowned or shot in attempting to cross the river. Jackson's loss, including the friendly Indians, was fifty-four killed, and one hundred and fifty-six wounded.

This decisive victory ended in the submission of the remaining warriors, and terminated the Creek war. Among those who threw themselves upon the mercy of their victors, was Weatherford, who was equally distinguished for his talents and cruelty. "I am in your power," said he, "do with me what you please. I have done the white people all the harm I could. I have fought them, and fought them bravely. There was a time when I had a choice. I have none now; every hope is ended. Once I could animate my warriors to battle; but I cannot animate the dead. They can no longer hear my voice; their bones are at Tallushatches, Talladega, Emucfau, and Tohopeka. While there was a chance of success, I never supplicated peace; but my people are gone, and I now ask it for my nation and myself."

During the month of April, General Jackson scoured the country on the Coosa and Talapoosa Rivers. **1814.** A party of the enemy on the latter river, on his approach fled to Pensacola; and a detachment of Carolina militia, under Colonel Pearson, traversed the banks of the Alabama, and received the submission of a great number of Creek warriors and prophets. Finally, the Indians being now completely at the mercy of the conquerors, a treaty of peace was dictated by General Jackson to the Creeks, and signed early in August. The terms were severe, but probably necessarily so, in order to insure future tranquillity. The Creeks agreed to yield a large portion of their country as an indemnity for the expenses of the war; they consented to the opening roads through their country, together with the liberty of navigating their rivers; they engaged to establish trading houses, and to endeavor to bring back the nation to its former state; they also stipulated to hold no intercourse with any British or Spanish post or garrison, and to deliver up the property they had taken from the whites and the friendly Indians. General Jackson, on the part of the United States, undertook to guarantee their remaining territory to them; to restore all their prisoners; and, in consideration of their destitute situation, to furnish them gratuitously with the necessaries of life until they could provide for themselves.

It will be remembered, that during

the early part of the year 1813, great activity had been manifested in the north-west, although no material results had been attained. The spirit of the people was roused to a pitch of enthusiasm, and there was an earnest determination to prosecute hostilities with vigor; but, as we have stated, (p. 185,) without the command of the lake, offensive operations could not be carried on to any great advantage. The utmost exertions, accordingly, were made by Perry to complete his naval armament, and to test the ability of our gallant sailors in a contest with the enemy on Lake Erie.

1813.

Proctor, aware of the spirit and progress of the Americans, which threatened the supremacy which the enemy had acquired and maintained thus far on the lake, determined to strike a blow at Harrison's camp at the Rapids, for the purpose of interrupting his communication with the lake. Unable to induce Clay to quit his lines and risk an engagement, Proctor, on the 1st of August, invested Fort Stephenson, at Lower Sandusky, on the Sandusky River, with five hundred regulars and militia, and above three thousand Indians. Major Croghan, who commanded there, had no more than one gun (a six-pounder) and a hundred and sixty men, and those young and inexperienced. Ingersoll justifiably insists upon the weakness of the place, its bad position, and the perplexing orders left with its commander,—whom Harrison had instructed to fire the fort and retreat, (if he could,) should the enemy approach in force, and with artillery. Proctor demanded a surrender, accompanied with the usual threats of butchery and massacre, if the garrison should hold out; but Croghan, who found that all his companions, full of zeal, like himself, would support him to the last, returned a spirited answer; to the effect that, "when the fort should be taken, there would be none left to massacre; as it would not be given up while a man was able to fight."

A brisk firing was kept up by the enemy during the night; and at an early hour next morning, three six-pounders which had been planted during the night, within two hundred and fifty yards of the pickets, began to play upon the fort, but with little effect. About four in the afternoon, all the enemy's guns were concentrated against the northwestern angle of the fort, for the purpose of making a breach. To counteract the effect of their fire, Major Croghan caused that point to be strengthened by means of bags of flour, sand, and other materials, in such a manner that the picketing sustained little or no injury. But the British, supposing that their fire had sufficiently shattered the pickets, advanced, to the number of five hundred, to storm the place, at the same time making two feints on different points.

1813.

The column which advanced against the northwestern angle, was so completely enveloped in smoke, as not to be discovered until it had approached within eighteen or twenty paces of the lines, but the men being all at their posts, and ready to receive it, commenced so heavy and galling a fire as to throw the column into confusion; but being quickly rallied, Colonel Short, the commander, exclaimed, "come on, my brave fellows, give the Yankee rascals no quarter!" and immediately leapt into the ditch, followed by his troops; as soon as the ditch was entirely filled by the assailants, Major Croghan ordered his one six-pounder, which had been masked in the block house, to be fired. It had been loaded with a double charge of musket balls and slugs. This piece completely raked the ditch from end to end. The first fire levelled the one half in death, Colonel Short being of the number; the second and third either killed or wounded every one except eleven, who were covered by the dead bodies. At the same time, the fire of the small arms was so incessant and destructive, that it was in vain the British officers exerted themselves to lead on the balance of the column; it retired in disorder under a shower of shot, and sought safety in an adjoining wood. The loss of the enemy in killed was about one hundred and fifty, besides a considerable number of their Indian allies. The Americans had but one killed, and seven slightly wounded. Early in the morning of the 3d of August, the enemy retreated down the river, after having abandoned considerable baggage and military stores.

The garrison was composed of regulars, all Kentuckians; a finer company of men was not to be found in the United States. They were as humane as they were courageous. This was proved by their unceasing attention to the wounded enemy after their discomfiture; for during the night they kindly received into the fort, through the fatal port hole of the block house, all those who were able to crawl to it; to those unable to move, they threw canteens filled with water. They even parted with their clothes to alleviate the sufferings of the wounded.

Soon after this gallant exploit, which called forth the admiration of the whole country, Tecumseh, having raised the siege of Fort Meigs, followed Proctor to Detroit; and all hope was given up by the enemy of reducing the American forts, until they could gain entire ascendancy on the lake.

Commodore Perry, in spite of all obstacles and hindrances, pushed forward his preparations, and by the 2d of August, the fleet was equipped; but some time was lost in getting several of the vessels over the bar at the mouth of the harbor of Erie. On the 4th, he sailed in quest of the enemy; but not meeting him, he returned on the 8th. After receiving a reinforcement of sailors brought by Captain Elliot, he again sailed on the 12th, and on the 15th anchored in the Bay of Sandusky. Here he took in about twenty volunteer marines, and again went in search of the enemy; and after cruising off Malden, retired to Put-in Bay, a distance of thirty miles. His fleet consisted of the brig Lawrence, his flag vessel, of twenty guns; the Niagara, Captain Elliot, of twenty; the Caledonian, Lieutenant Turner, of three; the schooner Ariel, of four; the Scorpion, of two; the Somers, of two guns and two swivels; the sloop Trippe, and schooners Tigress and Porcupine, of one gun each; amounting in all to nine vessels, fifty-four guns, and two swivels.

1813.

Commodore Barclay, who had heretofore avoided the encounter, soon after deemed it prudent to meet Perry's fleet and test the question of superiority on this inland sea. Accordingly, very early on the morning of the 10th of September, he bore down upon Perry's squadron; which immediately got under weigh, and stood out to meet him. The Americans had three vessels more than the British; but this advantage was fully counterbalanced by the size, and the number of guns, of those of the enemy. The fleet of the latter consisted of the Detroit, Commodore Barclay, of nineteen guns and two howitzers; the Queen Charlotte, Captain Finnis, of seventeen guns; the schooner Lady Prevost, Lieutenant Buchan, of thirteen guns and two howitzers; the brig Hunter, of ten guns; the sloop Little Belt, of three guns; and the schooner Chippewa, of one gun and two swivels; in all, six vessels, sixty-three guns, four howitzers and two swivels.

About ten o'clock, a change in the wind to the southeast, gave the American squadron the weathergage. Commodore Perry then hoisted his union jack, having for a motto, the dying words of the lamented Lawrence, "Don't give up the ship!" It was received with repeated cheerings by the officers and crews. And now having formed his line he bore for the enemy; who likewise cleared for action and hauled up his courses.

At a quarter before twelve, the enemy's flag ship, and the Queen Charlotte, opened their fire upon the

1813. Lawrence; which she sustained for ten minutes, before she was near enough for her guns, which were carronades, to return it. She continued to bear up, making signals for the other vessels to hasten to her support; and at five minutes before twelve, brought her guns to bear upon the enemy. The tremendous fire to which Perry was exposed, soon rendered the Lawrence unmanageable; she was reduced almost to a wreck; nearly the whole of her crew was either killed or wounded; and the commodore saw that he must make a bold movement or lose the battle.

With a courage and spirit which deserved success, Perry determined to abandon the Lawrence, and hoist his flag on board the Niagara, which was then in the thickest of the fight. Leaving Lieutenant Yarnall in the Lawrence, he hauled down his inspiriting colors, and taking them under his arm, gave orders to be put on board the ship where Elliot was in command. In quitting the Lawrence he gave his pilot choice either to remain on board, or to accompany him; the faithful fellow told him "he'd stick by him to the last," and jumped into the boat. Perry went off from the ship in his usual gallant manner, standing up in the stern of the boat, until absolutely pulled down among the crew. Broadsides were levelled at him, and small arms discharged by the enemy, two of whose vessels were within musket shot, and a third one nearer. His brave shipmates who remained behind, stood watching him, in breathless anxiety; the balls struck around him and flew over his head in every direction; but the same Providence that watched over the heroic commodore throughout this desperate battle, conducted him safely through a shower of shot, and they beheld with exultation his flag hoisted at the mast head of the Niagara. No sooner was he on board, than Captain Elliot volunteered to put off in a boat, and bring into action the schooners which had been kept astern by the lightness of the wind; the gallant offer was accepted, and Elliot left the Niagara to put it in execution.

About this time Perry saw, with great regret, the flag of the Lawrence come down. The event was unavoidable; she had sustained the whole fury of the enemy, and was rendered incapable of defence; any further show of resistance would but have been most uselessly and cruelly to have provoked carnage among the relics of her brave and mangled crew. The enemy, however, were not able to take possession of her, and subsequent circumstances enabled her again to hoist her flag.

Commodore Perry now made signal for close action, and the small vessels got out their sweeps and made all sail. Finding that the Niagara was but little injured, he determined, if possible, to break the enemy's line. He accordingly bore up and passed ahead of the two ships and brig, giving them a raking fire from his starboard guns, and also to a large schooner and sloop from his larboard side, at half pistol

1813.

shot. Having passed the whole squadron, he luffed up and laid his ship alongside the British commodore. The smaller vessels, under the direction of Captain Elliot, having, in the mean time, got within grape and canister distance, and keeping up a well-directed fire, the whole of the enemy struck, excepting the Little Belt and Chippewa, which attempted to escape, but were pursued by two gunboats and taken.

The engagement lasted three hours, and never was a victory more decisive and complete. The carnage was fearful; the Americans having lost twenty-seven killed, and ninety-six wounded; and the British forty-one killed, and ninety-four wounded; Commodore Barclay was among the latter. Perry, who was unhurt, immediately sent a dispatch to General Harrison, which, for its brevity and point, is well worth quoting:—

"U. S. BRIG NIAGARA,
"*September* 10*th*, 1813; 4 P. M.

"DEAR GENERAL:—We have met the enemy, and they are ours; two ships, two brigs, one schooner, and a sloop. Yours, with great respect and esteem,

"OLIVER HAZARD PERRY."

Directly after, he forwarded an equally terse but expressive communication to the secretary of the navy, saying, "It has pleased the Almighty to give to the arms of the United States a signal victory over their enemies on this lake." The next day, he sent a more full account of the battle, in which he spoke, in fitting terms, of the bravery of Captain Elliot, and of the officers and men in general.* Both

* A good deal of very unpleasant discussion and ill humor was subsequently manifested on the question as to the relative merits of Perry and Elliot in obtaining this famous victory. Sides were taken by the partisans

Perry and Elliot subsequently received gold medals from Congress, and suitable rewards were bestowed upon the other brave defenders of their country's rights and honor.

It would be unjust to Perry not to make mention of the fact, that his treatment of the British prisoners was courteous and considerate to the highest degree; and the English commander is said to have declared, that "the conduct of Commodore Perry towards the captain, officers, and men, was sufficient, of itself, to immortalize him."

The results of this victory were instantaneous and of the first consequence. It had been won by a squadron of American vessels over a British squadron, in which it differed materially from other maritime successes achieved during the war. But that was not the chief matter of exultation; the Americans were now masters of Lake Erie, and had it in their power at once to intercept the whole coasting trade, by which Proctor's troops and Indians were supplied with provisions, and to land any force they chose in his rear, and entirely cut him off from Kingston and York. Abandoning, therefore, and destroying all his fortified posts beyond the Grand River, Proctor commenced a retreat at once, accompanied by Tecumseh and his Indians, Tecumseh not deserting his allies, now that victory had turned against them; although almost all the other Indians abruptly left the camp.

As soon as Proctor's attempt upon Sandusky was known, Governor Meigs of Ohio, ordered a levy in mass of the whole militia of the state; so that when Perry's victory had given to the United States the command of Lake Erie, there was an army ready to turn the advantage thus acquired to the best account. Part of the prizes and part of his squadron Perry now employed as transports, and twelve hundred of Harrison's troops were without delay carried over to Canada, where, on the 23d of September, they took possession of Malden, which had been deserted and dismantled. Detroit was next recovered, on the 27th; and there Colonel Johnson's regiment of mounted rifles joined the expedition, which was the more welcome, because Proctor had driven off all the horses of the country, to prevent pursuit.

1813.

Two days sufficed for the restoration of the state authorities and government at the capital of Michigan, and then the Americans hastened to follow the trail of their flying enemy. Perry's squadron now attended the march of the army with supplies, and all needful aid for its rapid advance, while the British, almost starving, toiled through wretched roads and dreary forests. On the 4th of October, Harrison came up with the British rear, and succeeded in capturing nearly all their stores. Unable to retreat farther in any thing like military array, Proctor had now no alternative but to endeavor to check the Americans by a general battle; and for this

of the two commanders; Perry spoke disparagingly of Elliot; Elliot recriminated, and in 1818, challenged Perry, who refused to meet him; etc. The reader who desires to look into the details, must consult the respective lives of Perry and of Elliot, with which may be compared the full and accurate narration, in Cooper's "*Naval History*," vol. ii., pp. 189–199.

purpose he took up a position at the Moravian village on the Thames.*

General Harrison's force was about three thousand men, including the redoubtable marksmen of Kentucky and Ohio. Proctor numbered something over two thousand, of whom twelve to fourteen hundred were Indians. His force too, it is fair to remember, was discouraged and disarranged by a forced retreat; Harrison's flushed with anticipations of victory, and with the excitement of pursuit.†

The British general drew up his forces across a narrow strip of land covered with beech trees, flanked on one side by a swamp, and on the other by the river; their left resting on the river, supported by the larger portion of their artillery, and their right on the swamp. Still further to the right and near another morass, the Indians were placed under Tecumseh. The position was well chosen; but Proctor was guilty of an error in drawing up his troops "in open order," a mode of array badly calculated to resist a charge of cavalry. Harrison drew up his troops in battle order, and, on the 5th of October, the fight commenced, with the enemy delivering their fire upon the advanced corps, about two hundred yards distant. This was the signal for Johnson's mounted rifles to charge, which they did with an impetuosity and fury that were irresistible. They charged completely through the British line, which was broken and routed beyond all possibility of recovery. Proctor ingloriously fled at this point, and though hotly pursued, managed to escape with a few followers.

On the left, the battle was more serious and more warmly contested. The galling fire of Tecumseh and the Indians did not check the advance of the American columns; but the charge was not successful, from the miry character of the soil and the number and closeness of the thickets which covered it. In these circumstances, Colonel Johnson ordered his men to dismount, and leading them up a second time, succeeded, after a desperate contest, in breaking through the line of the Indians and gaining their rear. Notwithstanding this, and the desperate nature of their position, the Indians were unwilling to yield the day; and quickly collecting their principal strength on the right, attempted to penetrate the line of infantry commanded by General Desha. At first they made an impression on it; but they were soon repulsed by the aid of a regiment of Kentucky volunteers led on by the aged Governor Shelby, who had been posted at the angle formed by the front line and Desha's division. The combat now raged with increasing fury, and the Indians, to the number of twelve or fifteen hundred, seemed determined to maintain their ground to the last. The terrible tones of Tecumseh could be distinctly heard, encouraging his warriors; and although beset

1813.

* For a more full and detailed account of the battle of the Thames, see M'Afee's "*History of the Late War in the Western Country*," pp. 380–98.

† Armstrong, who manifests strong dislike towards Harrison, makes some severe remarks on his third campaign, which the reader may find worth looking into. See his "*Notices of the War of* 1812," vol. i., pp. 176–184.

on every side except that of the morass, they fought with a courage and determination worthy of a better cause. Johnson, dashing into the thickest of the fight, was a conspicuous object on his white horse; some authorities state, it was he who killed Tecumseh; but, however this may be, it was not long ere he fell to the ground severely wounded. Though Tecumseh was slain in the *melée*, his devoted followers kept up the struggle for an hour later, but at last gave way on all sides.*

Seventeen of the Americans were killed and thirty wounded; the British lost nineteen killed, fifty wounded, and about six hundred prisoners; and a hundred and twenty Indians were left dead on the field. Among the trophies of the victory, were several cannons originally captured at Saratoga and York from the British, which had been surrendered by Hull, at Detroit, and were, by this good fortune, regained. With a noble spirit of returning good for evil, the prisoners were, without exception, treated humanely and justly, although the memories of the massacre at the River Raisin were vivid, and might have seemed to furnish justification for acts of severity and retaliation.

Colonel Lewis Cass was left at Detroit, shortly afterwards to be governor of the recovered Territory of Michigan; the Kentucky volunteers were dismissed, and Harrison, towards the close of October, finding that he could not make any attempt to recover Mackinaw, hastened his preparations to join in the invasion of Canada from Buffalo; to which place he transported above twelve hundred of his men, to reinforce the army of the centre there.

On the same day that Proctor was defeated on the Thames, six British schooners, having on board two hundred and fifty soldiers, proceeding from York to Kingston, without convoy, were captured by Chauncey, on Lake Ontario. These repeated losses, **1813.** coupled with the alarming intelligence received at the same time of great preparations for a general invasion of Lower Canada, made Sir George Prevost wisely determine it to be impossible to continue any longer the investment of Fort George; and the siege was accordingly raised a few days later. The retreat was conducted in an orderly manner, and the British took post at Burlington Heights, where Proctor, with those who had fled with him, soon after joined them, making the entire force about fifteen hundred. Having been driven from the territory westward of the River Thames, the British were, necessarily, in a great degree, cut off from their Indian allies, with whom they now could maintain no communication, but by the distant and isolated fort of Michilimackinac, or Mackinaw, on Lake Huron; an advantage of no small moment to our countrymen for the future progress of the war.

* Tecumseh's fall broke completely the spirit of resistance on the part of the Indians. He had been in nearly every battle with the whites, since Harmer's defeat in 1791, and was the soul of the opposition to the United States. As he lay stretched in death on the field of battle, the officers and soldiers surveyed his stern and haughty features with great interest, for he was majestic in stature, and terrible even then to look upon. We are sorry to say, that some of the Kentuckians disgraced themselves by committing indignities on his dead body. He was scalped, and otherwise disfigured.

Painted by A. Chappel

Engd. by W. Wellstood

BATTLE OF THE THAMES - DEATH OF TECUMSEH.

From the original picture in the possession of the Publishers.

Johnson Fry & Co. Publishers New York.

General Armstrong, the new secretary of war, (p. 179,) had effected some changes in the military arrangements for carrying forward hostilities against the enemy. General Dearborn, as we have noted, (p. 190,) retired from the service, and General Wilkinson was placed at the head of the army of the centre. This officer, respecting whose character considerable difference of opinion existed, was entrusted by the secretary of war with the important duty of following up the brilliant successes of Perry and Harrison, and though the season was far advanced, it was confidently expected that he would be able to march at once to Montreal, and establish his winter quarters there. The force under his command on the Niagara, amounted to eight thousand regulars, beside the troops under Harrison, which joined him at the close of October. General Hampton was in command of the army of the north, then encamped at Plattsburg, on Lake Champlain, and amounting to about four thousand men. As the season for military operations was rapidly drawing to a close, it was important that no time should be lost, and measures were immediately taken for carrying into effect the projected invasion of Lower Canada. The outline of the plan which had been adopted, was; to descend the St. Lawrence, passing the British posts without attempting their capture; to form a junction with General Hampton, at some designated point on the river; and then, with the united forces to proceed to the Island of Montreal. After which, to use Wilkinson's flowery language, "their artillery, bayonets, and swords, must secure them a triumph, or provide for them honorable graves."

1813.

Such, however, were the difficulties attending the concentration of the troops, such the want of preparation, notwithstanding all that had been said on the subject, that, not till the beginning of November, could Wilkinson get the flotilla, in which his troops were embarked, under way. French Creek was made the general rendezvous for the troops after their entrance into the St. Lawrence, and General Brown was sent forward to take the chief command. On the 2d of November, Commodore Chauncey took position in the St. Lawrence, near French Creek, so as to command the north and south channels. The enemy, who were vigilant and active, attacked the detachment under General Brown; but to no great effect. On the 6th, the army was embarked on the river, and in the evening landed a few miles above the British Fort Prescott. An attempt was made the same night, under cover of the fog and the darkness, to pass the fort with the flotilla unobserved; but a change in the weather exposed General Brown's movement to the enemy. A severe cannonade of three hours was kept up; nevertheless, out of three hundred boats, not one suffered the slightest injury; and before ten o'clock of the next day, they had all safely arrived at the place of destination. A messenger was now dispatched to General Hampton, informing him of the movements of the army, and requiring his co-operation.

The British commander, anticipating

the designs of the Americans, had ordered a corps of observation, from Kingston, to follow the movements of

1813. Wilkinson's army. At every convenient point, parties of the enemy were stationed along the Canadian shore to annoy and hinder the progress of the invading force. On the 7th of November, Colonel Macomb was dispatched with twelve hundred men to remove obstructions to the descent of the army, and disperse the militia of the enemy; and on the 8th, General Brown, with his brigade, reinforced Macomb, and took command of the advance corps. On the 10th, having arrived at a dangerous rapid, called the *Longue Sault*, General Brown continued the advance with caution and vigilance, while General Boyd was sent against the British and Indians, who were harassing the rear of the expedition. General Wilkinson was confined to his boat by severe indisposition.*

The next morning, when the flotilla was about to proceed down the rapid from Williamsburg, alarm was given that the British were advancing in column. The enemy's galleys were at the same time coming down for the purpose of assailing the rear of the flotilla. General Boyd having received orders to attack the foe, now led on his detachment formed in three columns, and directed a part of General Swartwout's brigade to move forward and bring the enemy into action. Colonel Ripley, accordingly, at the head of the twenty-first regiment, passed the wood which skirts the open ground called Chrystler's Field, and drove in several of the enemy's parties. General Covington had, before this, advanced upon the right, where the enemy's artillery was posted; and at the moment that Colonel Ripley had assailed the left flank, he forced the right by a determined onset. Success appeared scarcely doubtful, when, unfortunately, General Covington, whose activity had rendered him conspicuous, became a mark for the sharpshooters which the enemy had stationed in Chrystler's house, and was shot from his horse. Notwithstanding his fall, the action was sustained with great bravery for more than two hours, when, by a movement of the British, the American infantry, who had been left to cover their retreat, were dislodged, and both parties retired from the field, the enemy to their camp, and the Americans to their boats.

According to Wilkinson's official report, the force engaged amounted to about seventeen hundred; the British probably numbered nearly the same, and had the immense advantage of being regular, disciplined troops. The American loss was over a hundred killed, and more than two hundred wounded. The loss on the part of the enemy was probably not much if any less.

The following day, the army proceeded on its route, and joined the advance under General Brown, at the foot of the rapid, near Barnhart. It was here that Wilkinson received, to his "unspeakable 1813.

* Armstrong, (vol. ii., p. 211,) gives the evidence to prove that Wilkinson was frequently intoxicated.

mortification and surprise," as he states, information from General Hampton, that he should not effect the junction which had been ordered to take place at St. Regis. The reason which he gave was, the scantiness of Wilkinson's provisions, and the bad condition of the roads to St. Regis. He intimated, however, that he had determined to open a communication with the St. Lawrence at Caghnawaga, and would join Wilkinson lower down the river.

General Hampton, between whom and General Wilkinson very cordial dislike and perpetual jealousy existed, seems to have thought it best to proceed in his own way, with reference to the contemplated attempt on Montreal. Accordingly, he marched to Chateaugay at the close of September, where he waited for several weeks for further news from Wilkinson, and to the discouragement of the troops under his command. The British general had collected all his force to oppose Hampton's advance. Leaving his encampment on the 20th of October, Hampton crossed the line and proceeded down the Chateaugay River to Ormstown. Here he ascertained that the British, about six hundred strong, occupied a position six miles below him, on his route to Montreal. For the purpose of dispersing the enemy, who had obstructed the road by fallen timbers, and ambuscades of militia and Indians, Colonel Purdy, on the 25th of October, was ordered to cross the river and march down on the opposite side, until he should have passed the enemy, when he was to re-cross and attack him in his rear; whilst the brigade under General Izard was to assail him in front. Purdy accordingly crossed the river, but misled by the guides, he had not marched far, when his orders were countermanded. On his return, he was attacked by the enemy's infantry and Indians, and repelled them, after a short contest, in which they threw his column, for a time, into great confusion. At the same moment they came out of their works in front, and attacked General Izard, but soon after retired behind their defences. General Hampton, now receiving information that the enemy were obtaining accessions continually, resolved, by the advice of his officers, to retreat to the position which he had occupied some days before, at Chateaugay Four Corners, at which place he arrived on the last day of the month.

1813.

Some days later, Hampton, in reply to Wilkinson's call for a junction with him at St. Regis, (which was about twenty-five miles distant,) sent the answer which we have stated above. On the receipt of this communication, a council of the principal officers was called by General Wilkinson, at which it was determined, that the objects of the campaign were no longer attainable. It was therefore resolved, that the army should quit the Canadian side of the St. Lawrence, and retire into winter quarters at French Mills, on Salmon River. General Hampton, with his troops, soon after retired to Plattsburg for the same purpose. He was loudly censured by the popular voice for his share in the failure of the attempt on Montreal, and soon after, on

the plea of indisposition, resigned his commission, General Izard being his
1813. successor at Plattsburg. As for Wilkinson, he fared little better in public estimation, and his course was sharply criticised and condemned.* He was afterwards brought to trial, but acquitted by the court. Probably, had he been in better health, and not so dilatory and slow in his movements; had General Armstrong not interfered by being personally present at Sackett's Harbor, to oversee the operations of the campaign; and had General Hampton promptly obeyed the orders he received; the result of the expedition would have been quite different; and the opponents of the war would not have been able to triumph in pointing to so great a preparation resulting in so disgraceful a conclusion.

The ill consequences of Wilkinson's leaving a large force in the rear, and withdrawing the troops from the Niagara, soon began to be felt. General Harrison reached Buffalo in October, some days after the departure of Wilkinson; and, although directed to follow immediately, he was compelled to wait until some time in November, in consequence of the deficiency of transports. It was not until General Wilkinson had gone into winter quarters that Harrison embarked; orders having previously been sent for him to remain at Buffalo, which unfortunately did not arrive until after his departure. Colonel Scott remained in command at Fort George until the 12th of October, when he left with the regular troops for Sackett's Harbor. General M'Clure then took command, his force consisting entirely of militia, whose term of service had nearly expired. Receiving intelligence that the enemy was approaching him, M'Clure, on the 10th of December, removed his stores, destroyed the fort, and, acting upon the views of the council of war, set fire to the village of Newark, "leaving the wretched inhabitants," says Ingersoll, "including more than four hundred women and children, to the accumulated horrors of famine and a Canadian winter.* Nor was that all. After M'Clure retreated over the river, and took shelter in Fort Niagara, perceiving the enemy in considerable force on the opposite side deprived of a shelter at Fort George, and therefore seeking it at Queenstown, M'Clure had red hot shot fired at that place, to deprive them of shelter there also."

Availing himself of the indignation excited by the destruction of Newark, Colonel Murray, at daylight, on the 19th of December, carried Fort Niagara by surprise; his force consisted of about four hundred 1813.
regulars, militia, and Indians; and the garrison, nearly three hundred in number, and principally on the sick list, was put to the sword. Not more than twenty effected their escape. The com-

* See Armstrong's "*Notices of the War of* 1812," vol. ii., pp. 1–44. See also Ingersoll's "*History of the Second War*," vol. i., pp. 289–310.

* This act was promptly disavowed by the government; but the British not only did not wait a moment, when retaliation was in their reach, but also made the burning of Newark a pretext for subsequent outrage on our towns and cities in every part of the country.

manding officer, Captain Leonard, appears to have been shamefully negligent, so much so as to have been charged with having been bought by the enemy. He was absent at the time, and had used no precautions against an assault. Having possessed themselves of this post, the British soon after increased their force, and began to lay waste the Niagara frontier with fire and sword. Major Bennet made a spirited attempt to defend Lewistown, which was attacked by the British under General Riall; but after maintaining his ground for some time, was at last compelled to retreat. Major Mallory, from Schlosser, with forty Canadian volunteers, made a gallant resistance. But the exertions of a few scattered troops were ineffectual against a large body of British regulars and seven hundred Indians. They laid waste Lewistown, Manchester, and the Tuscarora villages.

General Hall advanced from Batavia with all the forces which he could collect, for the defence of the frontier. On the night of the 29th of December, the British, under General Riall, crossed at Black Rock. Owing to the darkness of the night, the militia were unable to repulse their attacks. General Hall arrived from Buffalo early on the morning of the 30th; at the same time a large division of British and Indians were crossing the river. The Americans poured a destructive fire upon them in their boats, but they repulsed them and effected a landing. They commenced a spirited attack upon the Americans under General Hall, who was driven from his batteries and pursued to Buffalo, a distance of two miles. Here Hall attempted again to face them; when, of two thousand militia, only six hundred could be prevailed upon to stand their ground. They fled to the woods, and many of them were cut off in the pursuit. The villages of Buffalo and Black Rock were set on fire the same day, and the whole frontier, for many miles, exhibited a scene of ruin and devastation.

And thus the year 1813 ended, with some consolations, but more disappointments. Harrison, Perry, Jackson, these had done well for their country's interests; but the failure and disgrace of the attempts on Canada were mortifying in the extreme. Great Britain was angered and almost furious, and the war henceforth promised to be one of savage inroads and ruthless destruction. She was rich, powerful, haughty; the United States were harassed and perplexed in respect to finances, carrying on the contest at a ruinous rate of expense, and learning only by bitter experience how to make head against their overbearing enemy. Yet, our countrymen had no thought of yielding on any but honorable terms, and the spirit of the executive and the legislature was displayed to this effect, when Congress met early in December. But we must defer to our next chapter an account of the doings of Congress at this important juncture in our country's history.*

* Among those who were removed by death during the present year, we may note, Dr. Benjamin Rush, aged sixty-eight, and Robert R. Livingston, aged sixty-six.

CHAPTER XI.

1814.

OPERATIONS IN THE NORTH DURING 1814.

Congress in session, December, 1813 — Substance of the president's message — Embargo laid — Proceedings of Congress — Webster and Calhoun — Proposal to establish a Bank of the United States — Unsuccessful — Opening prospects of the campaign of 1814 — Change of policy on the part of England — Operations on the northern frontier under Wilkinson — The affair at La Colle Mill — Wilkinson suspended from command — Movements on Lake Champlain — Attack on Oswego — British caught in an ambuscade at Sandy Creek — Chauncey on Lake Ontario — British repulsed at the Thames by Captain Holmes — General Brown determines to attack the enemy under General Riall — The battle of Chippewa — Scott and his officers and men — Results of the battle — Brown advances to attack Riall and Drummond — Particulars of the famous battle of Bridgewater, or Lundy's Lane — Scott, Miller, Jessup, and other heroes — Bravery of our troops — The cannon abandoned by Ripley — Brown's vexation — General Gaines in command at Fort Erie — The British assault the fort — Repulsed — Siege and skirmishes — Brilliant sortie against the enemy's batteries — The British on the northern sea coast — Harbors blockaded, property destroyed, etc. — Eastport seized — Attack on Stonington — The British enter the Penobscot — Plattsburg and Lake Champlain — The enemy's movements — Macomb's and M'Donough's victory — Conclusion of the campaign — Operations in the northwest — Croghan at Mackinaw — General Harrison resigns his commission — M'Arthur's victory at the Thames.

The second session of the thirteenth Congress commenced on the 6th day of December, 1813, and the next day the president sent in his annual message. He began with stating his regret at the failure of the efforts to negotiate a peace by the mediation of Russia. He next spoke of the events of the war thus far; of Perry's victory, of Chauncey's activity and zeal, of Harrison's success at the Thames, of Jackson's conduct of the Creek war to a thorough conclusion, and of the necessity of the measures he had taken to retaliate the course pursued by the British in taking our naturalized citizens and arraigning them as traitors.* The report upon the state of the treasury showed $7,000,000 in hand out of the receipts for the preceding year, amounting to above $37,500,000, nearly $24,000,000 of which were the produce of loans. "Further sums to a considerable amount," the president proceeded to say, "will be necessary to be obtained

1813.

* This subject gave rise to animated debate in Congress. It appears, that twenty-three American soldiers, taken at the battle of Queenstown, in 1812, were sent to England to undergo trial for treason. The president ordered a like number of British prisoners to be kept as hostages. Prevost was then ordered by his government to imprison forty-six American commissioned and non-commissioned officers, and sent word to General Wilkinson, in a very haughty tone, that England would take terrible vengeance if any harm befell the British prisoners. The same number of British officers was put in confinement; and soon after, on both sides, *all* the prisoners were closely confined. The result of the debates in Congress was, a determination to maintain the attitude assumed by the president, and to insist upon the rights which belonged to naturalized equally with American born citizens.

in the same way during the ensuing year; and from the increased capital of the country, from the fidelity with which public engagements have been kept and the public credit maintained, it may be expected, on good grounds, that the necessary supplies will not be wanting."

After presenting a summary of the many blessings which the war had not deprived the nation of, and showing that "the calamities of the contest into which they had been compelled to enter" were "mitigated by improvements and advantages of which the contest itself was the source;" that domestic manufactures had received a powerful stimulus; that many objects permanently valuable had been secured by provisions indispensable to present safety; that the maritime power of the United States had been greatly increased; and that the warlike ardor of the people had shown them to be worthy of the respect even of their antagonists; the president concluded as follows: "In fine, the war, with all its vicissitudes, is illustrating the capacity and the destiny of the United States to be a great, a flourishing, and a powerful nation, worthy of the friendship which it is disposed to cultivate in others, and authorized by its own example to require from all an observance of the laws of justice and reciprocity. Beyond these their claims have never extended, and in contending for these we behold a subject for our congratulation in the daily testimony of increasing harmony throughout the nation, and may humbly repose our trust in the smiles of Heaven on so righteous a cause."

On the 19th of January, Henry Clay, nominated on the commission appointed the year before to treat with Great Britain, resigned his post, and a new speaker had in consequence to be chosen.* Felix Grundy was supported by the friends of the administration, and the majority of the democratic members, as his successor; but Langdon Cheves, for whom all the federalists, and the democrats not in favor of a restrictive policy, voted, was elected in his room, by ninety-four votes against fifty-nine received by Grundy, and twelve scattering votes. Early in February, Richard Rush was appointed attorney-general. A month later, Gideon Granger was removed from the office of postmaster-general, and Return J. Meigs was appointed as his successor.

1814.

Early in the session, on the recommendation of the president, the embargo and non-importation system was revived and extended. An embargo was laid on all ships and vessels within the limits or jurisdiction of the United States, to continue till the 1st of January, 1815, unless hostilities should cease at an earlier date. The provisions of the act were very severe, its principal object being to prevent small vessels and boats from supplying the British squadrons on the coast with provisions. We may mention here, however, that the embargo was repealed by Congress, on the 14th of April, 1814.

* Mr. Russell was also added to the commission, and he and Mr. Clay sailed for Europe directly after their appointment.

Laws were passed for the augmentation of the army and navy, and provision was made for the payment of bounties and pensions. Upon the first of these, Daniel Webster, who had made his maiden speech during the extra session, spoke with great ability and force, but in vain, as far as the vote was concerned; for he, with that love for the ocean, which is common in New England, desired the augmentation of the navy, and the extension of commerce, and competition with the great sea ruler upon her own element. John C. Calhoun was amongst the opponents of the young orator.

A loan of $25,000,000, in addition to the former loans, was authorized at this time for the prosecution of the war. There were also ordered to be re-issued $10,000,000 of treasury notes. For the expenditure was estimated at $45,000,000; and the new taxes could not yield more than $3,500,000, while the income derived from the customs and the sale of public lands did not much exceed $6,500,000.

When the bill for the loan was discussed in committee of the whole House, "every question of politics," according to a shrewd and satirical journalist of the day, "that has agitated the United States for fifteen or twenty years past, and every one that may be expected for twenty years to come, appears to have been embodied in the speeches of the members; some of whom,
1814. it is said, spoke for three hours without mentioning the bill at all." The great speech in its favor was made by Calhoun, of which only one brief passage was devoted to the loan, and all the remainder to the question of the justice and expediency of the war. The opposition had resisted the loan, he said, on the ground "that such was the want of capital, or of public credit, that it could not be had, or if at all, only at an extravagant interest." To this, the distinguished advocate of the war replied: "It ceases to be a question whether the loan can be had at this or that interest. *It is necessary; it must be had;* and the rate *per centum* will depend principally on the state of the money market, and not on arguments used here."

As one of the means of infusing additional vigor into the national finances, a scheme was set on foot to establish a Bank of the United States. The proposition on this subject came now from New York, a petition having been presented from the state, on the 4th of January, 1814, to that effect; offering, moreover, to advance on loan half the proposed capital, $30,000,000, to the government, and stating that the means possessed by such a bank of assisting the government would be much greater than those of the state banks.

This petition, which Calhoun moved only to have printed, was, on the motion of its presenter, referred to the committee of ways and means; of which Mr. Jefferson's son-in-law was chairman, and which consisted, "as Mr. Speaker Clay's committees mostly did," says Ingersoll, "of a decided majority of members of his own party." The commercial interest had no representative on that committee, except Mr. M'Kim of Baltimore; and therefore it is not strange that, on the 10th of January, the chairman should, in three curt lines, report its conclusive rejection, on the old allegation of the unconstitutionality of such institutions. But Calhoun was not to be put off in this way. On the 4th of February, at his motion, "the committee of the whole House was discharged from further consideration of the report of the committee of ways and means, on the petition for a national bank; and both report and petition were referred to the committee of ways and means, with instructions to inquire into the expediency of a national bank in the District of Columbia;" thus adroitly escaping the question of constitutionality.

Mr. Taylor, on the 19th of February, reported a bill for the establishment of a national bank in the District of Columbia, with a capital of $30,000,000. The principle of this bill was approved by Mr. Cheves, Mr. Calhoun, and Mr. Grundy; but opposed by Mr. Eppes and Mr. Seybert. There were others too who did not favor it, for the reason that it contained no provision for the establishment of branches in the states. A motion to ingraft this feature upon the bill, made by Mr. Fiske of New York, received but thirty-six votes, after which there was no further action had upon it. But the public credit was daily depreciating; treasury notes were seventeen per cent., and government stocks thirty per cent. below par; and it is not surprising that many of the democratic members were disposed to waive their scruples, and agree to the establishment of a national bank, as expedient, if not constitutional.

1814.

A resolution was, accordingly, introduced by Mr. Grundy, on the 2d of April, authorizing the appointment of a committee to inquire into the expediency of incorporating a Bank of the United States. The federalists, and a number of democratic members, among whom were Mr. Eppes and Mr. Ingersoll, opposed the resolution, and voted in favor of a motion to postpone it indefinitely. The democrats generally voted against the postponement, and a committee was appointed, of which Mr. Grundy was chairman. But within four days after their appointment they were discharged, on motion of Mr. Grundy, from all further consideration of the subject. The reason for this action consisted in the near approach of the end of the session, which was brought to its close on the 18th of April.

The year 1814 opened with no very encouraging prospects. The resources of the country were almost exhausted; the finances were in a very depressed and deranged condition; internal dissensions and party feuds were producing their necessary results, so much so, that the breaking up of the Union was confidently predicted; yet the spirit of the advocates of the war failed not. Volunteers were ever ready for limited periods of service, in the western states especially; and though money was more scarce than ever, and even weapons were sometimes wanting, men to fight the battles of their country could always be found. Great Britain, on her side, was likewise greatly exhausted by the continental war; yet men and money were at her command, and now that Napoleon's career was nearly at its close, she was at liberty to direct her energies to the speedy settlement of the war with the United States. With singular ignorance of the real condition of things, and the unyielding patriotism of the people, England expected to be able to strike a few decisive blows, and reduce the United States to prompt, and even abject submission.

Hence it was, that busily occupied with the affairs of Europe, and probably entertaining a kind of contemptuous feeling towards our country, Great Britain allowed the war to languish during the early part of the year; but, as an English writer says,
1814.
"no sooner was Europe restored to peace, by the dethronement of Bonaparte, than the British government resolved to prosecute the contest with increased vigor, and to obtain in the field a recognition of those maritime rights, which had hitherto been so strenuously resisted in the cabinet. Two distinct modes of prosecuting the war seemed to have been determined on by the British ministry: first, an invasion of the coast of the United States, and, second, after the protection of Canada had been secured, the conquest of so much of the adjoining territory as might, in the event of a future war, effectually guard that province from all danger. The peace of Paris was scarcely ratified, before fourteen thousand of those troops, which had gained so much renown under the Duke of Wellington, were embarked at Bordeaux for Canada; and about the same time a strong naval force, with an adequate number of troops, were collected, and dispatched for invading different parts of the coast of the United States." We shall see, on subsequent pages, what became of these troops in the final battle of the war.

On the northern frontier, during the months of January and February, the army remained in winter quarters, without having undertaken any expedition against the enemy. General Wilkinson proposed various plans, no one of which met the approbation of General Armstrong, the secretary of war, and he was ordered to withdraw from his position at French Mills. Two thousand men were to march under General Brown to Sackett's Harbor; and the residue were to fall back on Plattsburg. The enemy took advantage of this movement of Wilkinson, and at the close of February, made an incursion as far as Malone, and pillaged private property and destroyed public stores to a considerable extent. On the approach of an American force, the enemy precipitately retreated.

Towards the latter end of March, Wilkinson determined to erect a battery at Rouse's Point, where had been discovered a position from which the enemy's fleet, then laid up at St. John's, might be kept in check, and their contemplated movement on Lake Champlain impeded or prevented. 1814.
The breaking up of the ice on the lake at an earlier period of the season than usual, defeated his plan. A body of the enemy, some two thousand in number, on discovering his design, had been collected at La Colle Mill, three miles below Rouse's Point, for the purpose of opposing him. With a

view of dislodging this party, Wilkinson, at the head of between three and four thousand men, crossed the Canada line on the 30th of March. After dispersing several of the enemy's skirmishing parties, he reached La Colle Mill, a large, fortified stone house, situated in the centre of an open piece of ground, and defended by a strong corps of British regulars, under the command of Major Hancock.

Wilkinson disposed his troops so as nearly to encircle the mill, and brought up a howitzer and one twelve-pounder to batter the walls; but after firing a considerable time, it was found little effect was produced. The enemy kept up a galling fire from the loop holes cut in the mill, during the whole time our troops lay before the place, and directed a great portion of it on the two pieces of artillery: the British fire was returned with great coolness and deliberate aim. The enemy made two sallies, and charged the left, commanded by General Smith, but were repulsed with considerable loss. Towards evening, a British regiment arrived, and made a charge on part of a brigade commanded by General Bissel; but they were so warmly received, that they instantly fell back, leaving on the field a number of their dead and wounded.

Finding it not possible, with the artillery he had, to penetrate the stone walls of the mill, Wilkinson abandoned the attempt in which he had engaged, and having lost about a hundred and forty in killed and wounded, he retired in good order, the enemy making no effort to molest him.

The singular and repeated ill success of the general in command on the northern frontier, led to much complaint and censure not lightly expressed. Wilkinson was suspended from the command, and the troops were placed under the charge of General Izard. Subsequently, Wilkinson was brought before a court martial, and after a trial, was acquitted.

Shortly after the affair at La Colle Mill, the greater part of the British force was collected at St. John's and Isle Aux Noix, for the purpose of securing the entrance of their squadron into Lake Champlain, on the breaking up of the ice. This movement was effected early in May. During the autumn and winter preceding, Commodore M'Donough had labored with great industry to provide a naval force on Lake Champlain, equal to that of the British. The flotilla was lying in the Otter River, at Vergennes; and it was the object of the British to destroy it, before it should make its appearance on the lake. Apprized of this, M'Donough caused a battery to be erected at the mouth of the river. On the 12th of May, the British fleet entered the lake, and were repulsed in an attack upon this battery by water. They were also unsuccessful in attempting to gain the rear of the battery by land, being driven off by a detachment of Vermont militia. Thus repulsed, they abandoned their object, and moved down the lake.

1814.

Active preparations were also under way on Lake Ontario. At Kingston, the British built a ship of larger size than ordinary, which led Chauncey to do the same, so as to preserve, if possible, a nearly equal force with that of the enemy. Various attempts were made to destroy these vessels, but without success, and both the British and Americans were kept constantly on the alert. Oswego, which was a dépôt for naval stores, was defended by a fort mounting only five guns, and was garrisoned by about three hundred men under Colonel Mitchell. The British commander determined to attack it, hoping to seize upon the valuable stores, rigging, guns, etc., which Chauncey was collecting there for his new ship, the Superior. On the 5th of May, the British commenced a bombardment of Oswego, while fifteen hundred men,* under General Drummond, attempted to effect a landing. Failing in this, the next day they renewed the attempt with better success. Colonel Mitchell now abandoned the fort, and joining his corps to the marines and seamen, engaged the enemy's front and flanks, and did great execution. Finding further resistance useless, he fell back, formed his troops, and took up his march to the Falls of Oswego, thirteen miles distant, destroying the bridges in his rear. Hither the naval stores had already been removed, and for all the trouble and loss which they had sustained, the British obtained nothing more than the cannon of the fort, a few barrels of provisions and some whiskey. These were purchased with a loss of two hundred and thirty-five men, in killed and wounded. The loss of the Americans was sixty-nine in killed, wounded, and missing; among the first, a promising officer, Lieutenant Blaney. On the morning of the 7th, the enemy evacuated the place.

* British authorities state, that the number was only about three hundred.

Not long after, Major Appling and Captain Woolsey were appointed to convey the naval stores from Oswego to Sackett's Harbor. On the 28th of May, when off Sandy Creek, sixteen miles southwest of Sackett's Harbor, perceiving themselves covered by the British boats, they entered the creek. Here they landed, and formed an ambuscade. The British followed, were completely surprised, and surrendered after an action of twenty minutes. Not one of Major Appling's party was wounded, and the barges soon after arrived at Sackett's Harbor in safety. **1814.**

Chauncey having completed the Superior, which was capable of mounting sixty-four guns, was again master of the lake. He accordingly sailed out, and several times presented himself before Kingston; but Sir James Yeo, the British commander, did not deem it prudent to hazard an engagement until his new ship of a hundred and twelve guns should be completed.

In the west, the enemy had been able to hold possession of Fort Mackinaw, which was looked upon as an important post for their purposes. Several efforts were made to recover Mackinaw, but none of them were crowned with success. At the close of February, Captain Holmes was dispatched from Detroit, by Colonel Butler, with about a hundred and eighty men, against a party of the British who had stationed themselves on the river Thames, some two days march distant. On the 3d of March, when about fifteen miles distant, he received intelligence that three hundred of the enemy were advancing to attack him. Finding himself not in a situation to give battle, from the fatigue which his men had already encountered and his ignorance of the number of the enemy's party, Captain Holmes fell back a few miles, and chose a position, in which he was confident of being able to maintain himself, until he could obtain the necessary information. For this purpose, he dispatched a small body of rangers, which soon returned, pursued by the enemy, but without being able to learn his force. The British, perceiving the strength of Captain Holmes's position, resorted to stratagem for the purpose of drawing him from it. They feigned an attack, and then retreated, taking care not to show more than sixty or seventy men. Captain Holmes pursued, but with caution; and after proceeding about five miles, discovered their main body drawn up to receive him. Immediately returning to his former position, he disposed his troops in the most judicious manner,

1814.

and firmly waited for the enemy; having in front a deep ravine, and the approaches on the other sides being somewhat difficult and also protected by logs hastily thrown together. The attack was commenced at the same moment on every point, with savage yells and the sound of bugles; and was gallantly sustained by the Americans. After an hour's hard fighting, the British retreated, with a loss of sixty-five killed and wounded. Captain Holmes whose loss was only six in killed and wounded, was promoted to the rank of major for this spirited affair.

General Brown, who had not, during the spring, been able to undertake any expedition against Canada, was, nevertheless, not idle. Aided by Scott and Ripley, he had diligently occupied himself in drilling and disciplining his troops for the work which was before them. The first step was to regain possession of Fort Erie, and in June, Brown marched his army, now about three thousand five hundred men, to Buffalo. On the 3d of July, Fort Erie was invested, and the garrison, amounting to one hundred and seventy men, surrendered without firing a shot. Immediate possession was taken, and the prisoners were sent into the interior of New York.

General Brown promptly determined to advance and attack General Riall, who was entrenched at Chippewa, not far from Erie, but above the Falls; and having made arrangements for the defence of the fort and protecting the rear of the army, he ordered General Scott, on the morning of the 4th of July, to advance with his brigade and Towson's artillery. These were followed in the course of the day, by General Ripley, and the field and park artillery under Hindman, together with General Porter's volunteers. The British commander at Chippewa, General Riall, might with no great difficulty, have checked the advance of the Americans by removing the bridge over the Chippewa River, but he omitted this precaution. His force, it is stated by British writers, was inferior to that of the Americans, consisting of some fifteen hundred regulars, and about a thousand militia and Indians.* Within two miles of the enemy Brown halted, and drew up in regular order; and on the following day Riall left his intrenchments and accepted the challenge to battle.

At five in the morning of the 6th of July, the action commenced, the Canadian militia and Indian allies attacking the American volunteers, the redoubted marksmen of Kentucky, who stood their ground so bravely, and dealt such deadly shots into the ranks of the enemy, that not till some of the regulars came up were they driven back.

The first battalion, under Major Leavenworth, took a position on the right; and the second was led to its station by Colonel Campbell, who, on being wounded shortly afterwards, was succeeded by Major M'Neill. Major Jessup, who commanded the third battalion, which was formed on the left, resting in a wood, was ordered to turn the right flank of the British, then steadily advancing upon the American line. The cool intrepidity of the troops was worthy of the highest praise, and showed what advances in discipline had been made under such officers as Scott, Ripley, and others.

The main body of the British now advanced to the attack in column, the Americans receiving them in line, thus reversing, as Alison says, the usual order of the British and French in the peninsular campaigns. The result was the same as what had there so often occurred; the head of the British column was crushed by the discharges of the American line, which stood bravely, and fired with great precision; and though they succeeded in deploying with much steadiness, the loss sustained in doing so was so serious, that General Riall was compelled hastily to retreat, with the loss of one hundred and fifty men killed, three hundred and twenty wounded, and forty-four missing. M'Neill's battalion, with its left wing thrown forward, took the enemy in front and flank at the same time, and did prodigious execution; and the victory was ascribed in no small part to a daring movement,—a bayonet charge,—by Major Jessup, in the midst of a destructive fire from the British troops. The Americans lost three hundred and twenty-eight in killed, wounded, and missing.

1814.

The result of this battle was especially gratifying to the American people, for it served to prove, that nothing but discipline was wanting on land, to give our soldiers the same capability, which had been so gallantly maintained by our sailors, of meeting and conquering the veteran troops of England. The battle was fought manfully on both sides, and, as above shown, was unusually sanguinary.

General Brown, having resolved to dislodge the British, sent forward General Ripley, two days afterwards, to

* According to American contemporary authorities, the British force was not short of three thousand in all; and as only Scott's brigade was actually engaged in battle, it was fought on the American side by less than thirteen hundred men. The reader will note the frequent discrepancies between the accounts of the numbers engaged in contest; it is, in fact, almost impossible to attain exactitude on these points.

THE BATTLE OF CHIPPEWA.

SCOTT ORDERING THE CHARGE OF McNEIL'S BATTALION

open a road, and build a bridge over the Chippewa River for the passage of the troops. Riall endeavored to prevent this, but unsuccessfully, and soon after, withdrew from his entrenchments and fell back upon Queenstown. The next day he retired to Twenty-mile Creek, and General Brown immediately occupied Queenstown. On the 12th of July, General Swift, of the New York volunteers, set out with a party of a hundred and twenty men, to reconnoitre the works at Fort George. Having surprised an outpost, he captured a corporal and his guard. One of these, after having received quarter, treacherously shot Swift in the breast. This excellent officer survived his wound only a short time, but refused to leave his post until an attacking party of the enemy was beaten off. General Brown was now prepared to advance upon Forts Niagara and George, and purposed doing so; but unfortunately, Commodore Chauncey's illness had prevented his co-operating with the land force as was expected,* and hence the British held the mastery of the lakes, and their vessels only were to be seen at Fort George, when the Americans arrived in its vicinity.

The gallant Brown, disappointed thus of the aid he had hoped for from the fleet, withdrew from his advanced position on the Niagara, and determined to follow and attack the British army at Burlington Heights. For this purpose, on the 24th of July, he fell back to the junction of the Chippewa with the Niagara. General Riall, who had been reinforced by the efforts of General Drummond, took post at Queenstown immediately after it was abandoned by the Americans; thence he sent a detachment across the Niagara, for the purpose of threatening the town of Schlosser, where Brown had collected his supplies, and where were also his sick and wounded. Riall at the same time dispatched an advance party on the Niagara road. General Brown, with a view of drawing off the enemy from his attempt on the village across the river, resolved to put his force in motion towards Queenstown. General Scott, accordingly, with the first brigade, Towson's artillery, and all the dragoons and mounted men, over a thousand in number, set out directly on the road leading to Queenstown, with orders to report if the enemy appeared, and to call for assistance if necessary.*

1814.

It was four o'clock in the afternoon of the 25th of July, that Scott led his brigade from the camp, and after proceeding along the Niagara about two miles and a half from the Chippewa, and within a short distance of the cataracts, discovered General Riall on an eminence near Lundy's Lane, a position of great strength, where he had planted a battery of nine pieces of artillery, two of which were brass

1814.

* Ingersoll (vol. ii., p. 93) censures Chauncey's course, and thinks that he ought to have rendered effectual service to Brown in his plans and purposes. See, also, Armstrong's "*Notices of the War of* 1812," vol. ii., pp. 237–44.

* Armstrong's critical remarks on General Brown's movements and plans are worth consulting: '*Notices of the War of* 1812," vol. ii., pp. 113–18.

twenty-four pounders. On reaching a narrow strip of woods which intervened between the American and the British line, Captains Harris and Pentland, whose companies formed a part of the advance, and were first fired on, gallantly engaged the enemy. The latter now retreated for the purpose of drawing the American column to the post at Lundy's Lane. General Scott resolutely pressed forward, after dispatching Major Jones to the commander-in-chief with intelligence that he had come up with the enemy. He had no sooner cleared the wood, and formed in line on a plain finely adapted to military manœuvres, than a tremendous cannonade commenced from the enemy's battery, situated on their right, which was returned by Captain Towson, whose artillery was posted opposite, and on the left of the American line, but without being able to bring his pieces to bear on the eminence. The battle raged for an hour with great fury, and both officers and men were stricken down in large numbers.

The situation of Scott and his brigade was now becoming critical in the extreme. The British commander waited only for reinforcements to crush his brave opponent, and Scott was well aware that unless aid arrived soon, he must give up the contest. Both armies, as if by concert, ceased from the work of death, and for a time, no sound was heard amid the gathering darkness, on that blood-stained field, save the distant roar of the great cataract, mingled with the groans of the wounded and dying.

It was nearly at the same time that the British and the Americans were reinforced, and the battle was renewed. General Ripley, with Major Hindman's artillery, and General Porter's volunteers, on the one side, and General Drummond with fresh troops, on the other, eagerly entered upon the contest, each anxious to sustain the honor of his country's arms. General Ripley, ascertaining the impossibility of doing any thing effective while the enemy's artillery occupied its commanding position, saw at once that they must be driven from it, or defeat must ensue. Turning to the brave Colonel Miller, he asked, "Can you storm that battery?" It was a desperate undertaking, but the gallant soldier, who knew the men under his command, and what they were capable of doing, answered, in words ever to be remembered, "I WILL TRY, SIR." And steadily, unfalteringly, with nerves strung to the fearful task, our countrymen advanced to the assault. Discharge after discharge of the blazing artillery, lightened up the darkness, and made sad inroads upon the noble twenty-first regiment; but, "close up, steady, men!" was the intrepid Miller's command, and onward they continued their march, until they reached the height, and swept the enemy from their very guns.

Meanwhile, Major Jessup, who, at the beginning of the action, had been detached against the British left, succeeded in turning the enemy's flank. Seizing the opportunity in the darkness, he threw his regiment in **1814.**
the rear of the British reserve, and surprising one detachment after another, made so many prisoners, of both officers and men, as in fact, to im-

pede his progress. General Riall was among the prisoners. Feeling his way through the darkness, to the place where the hottest fire was kept up on the brigade to which he belonged, Jessup, about the time that Miller carried the enemy's cannon, drew up his regiment behind a fence, on one side of the Queenstown road, in the rear of a party of British infantry. So destructive was Jessup's fire, that the enemy broke and fled instantly, and, as General Brown said, in his official report, the Major "showed himself again to his own army in a blaze of fire, which defeated or destroyed a very superior force of the enemy."

The height on which the artillery was placed, was now the point where the battle raged, and on the possession of which victory depended. General Drummond, not more astounded than chagrined at the loss of his cannon, determined to recover the height at any cost; while the Americans, with unflinching energy, resolved to keep that which they had so gallantly secured. Silently did they await, in the deep darkness, the approach of the enemy, reserving their fire till it could tell with deadly effect. The British marched up the ascent at a brisk step, until within twenty paces of the summit of the height, when they poured in a rapid fire, and prepared to rush forward with the bayonet. The American line, being directed by the fire of the enemy, returned it with terrible effect, which threw them
1814. into momentary confusion; but being rallied, they returned furiously to the attack. A most tremendous conflict ensued; which, for twenty minutes, continued with violence indescribable. The British line was at last compelled to yield, and to retire down the hill. Yet the American commander knew that the battle was not over. Transporting the wounded to the rear, General Ripley immediately restored his line to order. General Scott's shattered brigade having been consolidated into one battalion, had, during this period, been held in reserve behind the second brigade, under Colonel Leavenworth. It was now ordered to move to Lundy's Lane, and to form with its right towards the Niagara road, and its left in the rear of the artillery.

After the lapse of half an hour, Drummond was heard again advancing to the assault with renovated vigor. The direction at first given by Ripley was again observed. The fire of the Americans was terrible; and the artillery of Major Hindman was served with the greatest skill and coolness, and with most fatal result to the enemy. After the first discharge, the British general threw himself with his entire weight upon the centre of the American line. He was firmly received by the gallant twenty-first regiment; a few platoons only faltering, which were soon restored by General Ripley. Finding that no impression could be made, the whole British line again recoiled, and fell back to the bottom of the hill.

During this second attempt, two gallant charges were led by Scott in person, the first upon the enemy's left, and the second on his right flank, with his consolidated battalion; but having to oppose double lines of infantry, his attempts, which would have been deci- 1814. sive had they proved successful, were unavailing. Although he had most fortunately escaped unhurt thus far, subsequently, in passing to the right, he received two severe wounds: regardless of himself, however, he did not quit the field, until he had directed Colonel Leavenworth to unite his battalion with the twenty-fifth regiment, under the command of the brave Jessup.

Once again, an hour later, the British general mounted that fatal eminence. Our countrymen, worn down with fatigue, and almost fainting with thirst, nerved themselves a third time, to repel the enemy. This last was more terribly contested than the preceding attempts. The British reached the top of the hill, and the struggle was carried on at the point of the bayonet. Friend and foe were intermingled, and for a short time, the issue of the fight was uncertain; but the Americans, with desperate valor, repulsed their furious assailants, and the whole British line broke and fled. No exertions of their officers could restrain them, or bring them back again to the assault.

Generals Brown and Scott being disabled by severe wounds, General Ripley assumed the command, and made some efforts to obtain the means of removing the captured artillery; but the horses having been killed, and no drag- 1814. ropes being at hand, they were still on the place where they had been captured, when orders were sent to Ripley from General Brown, to collect the wounded, and return to the camp, for the refreshment of the troops. The British cannon were therefore left behind, the smaller pieces having first been rolled down the hill. The whole of the troops reached the camp in good order about midnight, after an unmolested march.

This famous battle (known as the battle of Niagara, or of Bridgewater, or of Lundy's Lane) was the most severely contested, and, in proportion to the numbers engaged, the most destructive to human life, of any that has ever been fought in America. The British force numbered something short of five thousand, including militia and Indians. The American army was, in number, less than three thousand;* yet on each side nearly nine hundred men were killed, wounded, and missing. The proportion of officers killed and wounded, was unusually large, and showed clearly that, so far as the American army was concerned, our countrymen were as able as they were willing, to meet even the veteran troops which had gained laurels on the battle fields of the old world.

General Brown, vexed that the cannon had been left behind, ordered Ripley to proceed at sunrise, to the heights of Lundy's Lane, and, after burying the dead, to bring away the trophies of victory; but the enemy had taken possession of the emi- 1814. nence, and Ripley, with not more than sixteen hundred men, and these much worn down by fatigue, found it impossible to execute General Brown's order. He therefore retreated to Fort Erie;

* It is but proper to advise the reader, that the British accounts state, in respect to the numbers engaged, that the American force was much larger than that of their opponents.

and as additional precautions against the enemy, destroyed the bridge over the Chippewa, and threw part of his baggage and stores into the rapids of the Niagara. Both sides claimed the victory; the Americans, because they captured the British guns, and drove the enemy from his position; the British, because they recovered the guns which Ripley had omitted bringing away, and, as Ingersoll says, found a cannon accidentally left by the Americans in their retreat; and also because the American force the next morning, did not attack them, but retired rather rapidly from the field. "Had General Drummond," says Ingersoll, "availed himself of this hasty and ill-judged retreat" on the part of Ripley, who does not seem to have entered heartily into Brown's views and plans,—"not a man of our army could have escaped. Whether it was the purpose of General Ripley to defend Fort Erie, or to cross the Niagara, he should have held the Chippewa, which was a strong fortress in itself. . . . . By leaving the Chippewa, he put the army, its artillery, all its supplies, and the whole Niagara frontier, into the power of the enemy. Fortunately for his reputation, and that of the country, Drummond failed to avail himself of any of the advantages thus offered to him."*

Arrangements for defending Fort Erie were urged forward, and General Brown, not altogether trusting in Ripley, sent orders to General Gaines, at Sackett's Harbor, to repair to Fort Erie and take command of the army. The British, reinforced by General De Watteville, with a thousand men, followed the Americans and laid siege to Fort Erie, on the 3d of August. **1814.** The same day a detachment, under Colonel Tucker, crossed the Niagara, for the purpose of attacking Buffalo and recapturing General Riall. This party, although subsequently increased by reinforcements to twelve hundred men, was repulsed by Major Morgan with a rifle corps of two hundred and forty men.

General Gaines arrived at the fort on the 4th of August, and entered zealously upon his important duties. The defences were in rapid progress, and the enemy were quite as active in preparing to attack the Americans. For a week or more, an incessant cannonade was kept up by the batteries of both besiegers and besieged; and frequent skirmishes took place, in one of which, on the 11th, Major Morgan lost his life. On the 14th, from various indications, it was evident that the enemy were intending to try the fortune of an assault. General Drummond had made his arrangements to assail the works at Fort Erie on the right, centre and left at the same moment; and General Gaines prepared to meet him at all points. Late in the afternoon, one of the enemy's shells lodged in a small magazine, and blew it up with a tremendous noise, which caused a loud shout on the part of the British troops, although the Americans suffered no loss of men by the explosion.

The British commander, hoping to profit by the injury which he supposed

* Ingersoll's "*History of the Second War*," vol. ii., p. 108.

the Americans to have received, determined to assault the fort that night, under cover of the rain and deep darkness which envelopped all surrounding objects. Accordingly, at half past two, in the morning of the 15th of August, he sent forward his right column, thirteen hundred strong, under command of Colonel Fischer. Advancing quickly and steadily, the British assailed Towson's battery with scaling ladders, and the line towards the lake with the bayonet. A tremendous fire from the battery threw them into confusion, but, urged on by Colonel Fischer, they again advanced, and again were compelled to retire. Fischer next endeavored to pass round the abattis, by wading breast deep in the lake; but this attempt also failed, and nearly two hundred of his men were killed or wounded.

Meanwhile, the left and central columns, under Colonels Scott and Drummond, advanced to the assault of the fort. The attack was furiously made, and though gallantly resisted, was partially successful. Drummond and his corps mounted the scaling ladders, gained the parapet, and with the savage cry, "give the Yankees no quarter!" fell upon the brave men there. The bastion was lost; Captain Williams was mortally wounded; Lieutenants Watmough and M'Donough, severely. The latter, no longer able to fight, called for quarter. This was refused by Colonel Drummond, who repeated his instructions to his troops to deny it in every instance. The almost exhausted strength and spirits of M'Donough were roused by the barbarity of this order, and seizing a handspike, with the desperation of madness, he defended himself against the assailants, until he was shot by the infuriate Drummond himself. The latter survived this act only a few minutes; he received a ball in his breast, which terminated his career.

1814.

The enemy held what they had gained until daylight, although they suffered severely. The left column had already been repulsed with great loss. General Gaines ordered up reinforcements, and vigorous efforts were made to drive out the invaders, which were beginning to be successful, when a terrible explosion took place under the platform of the bastion, and carried it away and all who were on it. The contest was now brought to a speedy close, and the enemy, repulsed at all points, retreated to their encampment.

According to the British accounts, their loss was, in killed, wounded, and missing, six hundred and fifty; the American accounts estimate the British loss at about nine hundred men, while their own was only eighty-four.

The next day, General Drummond was reinforced by two regiments; but he did not deem it advisable to renew the assault. The siege, however, was continued, and some apprehensions began to be felt as to its result. General Izard, at Plattsburg, was ordered, on the 12th of August, by the secretary of war, to proceed to the relief of the besieged army, and he accordingly set out, at the close of the month, with five thousand men, for that purpose.*

* Armstrong (vol. ii., pp. 100–108) is particularly caustic in his review of the course pursued by Izard.

The British pushed forward their regular approaches, while the Americans assiduously labored to complete their defences. General Brown, having recovered from his wounds, reassumed the command at Fort Erie, on the 2d of September; and frequent skirmishes occurred, without any material advantage to either side.

On the 17th of September, a brilliant sortie was made against the enemy's batteries, which he had been busily occupied in erecting for a number of days, quite near to the fort; and after an hour's vigorous fighting, the objects of the sortie were accomplished, and the Americans returned to the fort in good order, with many trophies of victory. The enemy's works were carried, the labors of six or seven weeks destroyed, the cannon spiked, and a thousand men placed *hors de combat.* General Brown's official report speaks in glowing terms of the gallantry of both officers and men. On the night of the 21st, General Drummond broke up his camp and retired to his entrenchments behind the Chippewa.

1814.

The northern sea coast, which had thus far experienced little molestation from the enemy, became the object of attack early in the spring. On the 7th of April, a body of sailors and marines, to the number of two hundred, ascending the Connecticut River, landed at Pettipaug Point, about six miles above Saybrook, and destroyed the shipping they found there: thence, proceeding to Brockway's Ferry, they did the same; and, remained there, amusing themselves, unapprehensive of attack, for twenty-four hours. In the mean time, a body of militia, aided by some marines and sailors, under Captain Jones and Lieutenant Biddle, from the neighboring American squadron, endeavored to cut them off from retreat, but unsuccessfully. Some $200,000 worth of shipping was destroyed on this occasion.

About this time, the coasting trade was almost destroyed by a British privateer, the Liverpool Packet, which cruised in Long Island Sound. Commodore Lewis sailed with a detachment of thirteen gunboats, and succeeded in chasing her off. Proceeding to Saybrook, on his arrival there he found upwards of fifty vessels bound eastward, but afraid to venture out. The commodore undertook to convoy them, and sailed for that purpose on the 25th of April. Lewis, with his gunboats, gallantly put himself between the coasting vessels and a British frigate and sloop of war. The coasters escaped to New London, and Lewis attacked the English vessels to considerable effect.

1814.

The harbors of New York, New London and Boston continued to be blockaded, and the whole coast was exposed to incursions of the enemy.* Commodore Hardy, as we have before men

* Ingersoll (vol. ii., p. 55) devotes a page or two to the subject of the "blue lights treason," as he phrases it, which the reader may examine, not without profit. Commodore Decatur, who was shut up in the harbor of New London, was very anxious to get out, in the winter of 1813, but as often as he attempted it, blue light signals, he averred, were displayed at the harbor's mouth, and the blockading squadron put on the alert. Decatur's official letter of the 20th of December, was brought up in the House of Representatives in January, 1814, but no result came of the movement. The vituperative expression, "blue light federalist," took its rise from this quarter.

tioned, (p. 192) endeavored to prevent outrage upon private property and defenceless villages, but occasionally his orders were not obeyed. Wareham, Scituate, Booth's Bay, and other places, suffered from the cupidity and violence of the enemy. On the 11th of July, Hardy, with eight ships and two thousand men, made a descent on Moose Island, in Passamaquoddy Bay, and having taken possession of Eastport, situated on that island, declared all the islands and towns in the bay to appertain to his Britannic majesty, and required the inhabitants to appear within seven days and take the oath of allegiance. About two-thirds of the inhabitants submitted to this indignity, in the hope of benefit from their submission; but to no purpose. Eastport was soon after strongly fortified, and remained in the possession of the British until the conclusion of the war; but they found extreme difficulty in subsisting their troops, and desertions were so frequent that the officers were often compelled to perform the duties of sentinels.

1814.

On the 9th of August, Commodore Hardy sailed with a part of his squadron, for the purpose of attacking Stonington. The appearance of this force before the town excited much alarm, which was increased by a message from Hardy directing them to remove the women and children, as he was about to reduce the town to ashes. Although the means of defence were small, the inhabitants of Stonington determined to make an effort to repel the enemy. Bravely did the volunteers man the battery, and resist the attempt of the British to land from their boats, an attempt which was made in the evening, under cover of a heavy fire from the ships. Purposing to renew the attack next day, the enemy kept up a steady discharge of cannon until midnight. On the morning of the 10th, at dawn, one of the enemy's vessels approached within pistol shot of the battery, and the barges advanced in still greater numbers than the day before: these were again gallantly repulsed, and the vessel was driven from her anchorage. The squadron then renewed the bombardment of the town, but without effect; and on the 12th, the commodore thought proper to retire. The inhabitants of Stonington received, as they deserved, much praise for their resolute defence of their hearths and homes.

On the 1st of September, a squadron of over twenty British vessels entered the mouth of the Penobscot, and took possession of Castine and Belfast. They destroyed all the vessels which they found there, garrisoned the former place, and thence proceeded against other places in the vicinity. All the country east of the Penobscot River, which Great Britain had formerly contended was the true St. Croix, was at the same time claimed as British territory; and, could she have made good her claim, it would have been very valuable to her interests, as being the most convenient route between Canada and Nova Scotia. And thus, as was reproachfully said, "without a blow struck, Massachusetts passed under the British yoke; and so remained, without the least resistance, till restored at the peace. It was the

1814.

only part of the United States under undisputed British dominion." Part of the force employed in this expedition, ascended the river in pursuit of the United States frigate, John Adams, Captain Morris, which had taken refuge at Hampden, on the Penobscot, when chased by the British squadron. They succeeded in driving away the militia who had been summoned to defend the ship, and the vessel was burnt after the conflict. Preparations were thus made for the setting out of a great expedition, which had been arranged for the purpose of retaliating upon the Americans the invasion of Canada.

Plattsburg was at this time almost wholly denuded of troops, who had been ordered (p. 238) to join the expedition under General Brown. Sir George Prevost, on the other hand, had received such reinforcements from the British army abroad, that he had under his command, at this time, not fewer than from twelve to fourteen thousand men. Nine or ten thousand of these,
1814. all of them veterans in arms, with a formidable train of artillery, and commanders of equal experience and skill, were collected on the frontier of Lower Canada. The naval part of the expedition, however, which, as all former attempts had showed, was of first importance for success, by no means corresponded in fitness and extent with these military preparations. A frigate, a brig, two sloops, and twelve gunboats, badly equipped, and manned for the most part with soldiers and militia, commanded too by an officer with whom the few sailors in the flotilla were unacquainted, composed the force on which Prevost relied for co-operation and support in crushing his American opponents, and invading New York.*

On the 3d of September, this formidable army took possession of the village of Champlain, and, from the proclamations and the impressments of wagons and teams in this vicinity, it was soon discovered that the immediate object of attack was Plattsburg. General Macomb lost no time in placing the works in a state of defence. In order to create emulation and zeal among the officers and men, they were divided into detachments, and stationed in the several forts; and the general declared, in his orders, that each detachment was the garrison of its own work, and bound to defend it to the last extremity. At the same time, he called on General Mooers, of the New York militia, and with him adopted measures for calling them out *en masse*.

General Mooers, having collected about seven hundred militia, advanced, on the 4th, seven miles on the Beekmantown road, to watch the motions of the enemy and skirmish with them as they approached, and at the same time to obstruct the road by breaking down the bridges and felling trees. The rifle corps, under Colonel Appling, on the lake road, fell back as
far as Dead Creek, having done **1814.**
every thing in their power to retard the enemy's progress. The next day,

* Such is the British account: American authorities, on the other hand, claim that the enemy's force was superior to that of the Americans; the British numbering ninety-five guns and a thousand men, while the Americans had only eighty-six guns and eight hundred and twenty men.

the British advanced to within a few miles of Colonel Appling's position, but finding it too strong to attack, they halted, and caused a road to be made west into the Beekmantown road. By this opening the light brigade under General Powers advanced, and on the morning of the 6th, about seven o'clock, attacked the militia, under General Mooers, and a small detachment of regulars under Major Wool, about seven miles from Plattsburg. After the first fire, a considerable part of the militia broke and fled in every direction. A few, however, manfully stood their ground, and, with the small corps of Major Wool, bravely contested the field against five times their number, falling back gradually, until they reached the south bank of the Saranac, where they were able to maintain their position against the onslaughts of the enemy. Colonel Appling's rifle corps, and the detachment under Captain Sprowl, retired from their position at Dead Creek, in time to join the militia just before entering the American works, which they did in good order, keeping up a brisk fire until they got under cover.

Plattsburg is situated on the north side of the small river Saranac, near its entrance into Lake Champlain; the American works were on the southern side, directly opposite. As the village was no longer tenable, General Macomb directed the bridge over the Saranac to be destroyed, and the planks were made to serve for erecting breastworks, behind which our troops were able to hinder effectually the advance of the enemy. The British encamped on the ridge west of the town, their right near the river, and occupying an extent of nearly three miles, their left resting on the lake about a mile north of the village.

From the 6th of September until the morning of the 11th, an almost continual skirmishing was kept up between the enemy's pickets and our militia stationed on the river; and in the mean time, both armies were busily engaged; ours in strengthening the works of the forts, and that of the enemy in erecting batteries, collecting ladders, bringing up his heavy ordnance, and making other preparations for attacking the fort. The New York and Vermont militia, who had come in in large numbers, behaved with excellent spirit, and were at work day and night cheerfully, in strengthening the defences and harassing the invaders.

The British commanders, though possessing so large a force, delayed the assault on the American fortifications until the arrival of their flotilla, intending to conquer on land and water at the same time. About eight in the morning of Sunday, the 11th of September, the British fleet, under command of Captain Downie, appeared round Cumberland Head, and at nine o'clock anchored in a line ahead, about three hundred yards distant from Commodore M'Donough's vessels, which were drawn up to receive them.

1814.

M'Donough, on his part, with a courage far from usual among naval men of that day, gathered his officers and crew together early in the morning, and, being himself a member of the Episcopal Church, offered up, fervently and solemnly, the impressive prayers and supplications appointed in the liturgy of that Church. It was truly a scene worthy of note, when, about to engage in deadly conflict, the gallant young officer, on bended knees, set the noble example of calling upon God to defend the cause of right and truth;—"O most powerful and glorious Lord God, the Lord of hosts, that rulest and commandest all things; Thou sittest in the throne judging right, and therefore we make our address to thy Divine Majesty in this our necessity, that thou wouldest take the cause into thine own hand, and judge between us and our enemies. Stir up thy strength, O Lord, and come and help us; for thou givest not alway the battle to the strong, but canst save by many or by few. O let not our sins now cry against us for vengeance; but hear us thy poor servants begging mercy, and imploring thy help, and that thou wouldest be a defence unto us against the face of the enemy. Make it appear that thou art our Saviour and mighty Deliverer, through Jesus Christ our Lord. *Amen.*"

We may be sure, that the man who could thus dare to do what he deemed to be right, and to brave the sneers of the godless and the profane, would enter upon the battle doubly and trebly armed for the fight, as M'Donough was, and as his conduct on this eventful day abundantly proved.*

Long and hotly contested was the battle of Lake Champlain. Captain Downie, in the Confiance, engaged the Saratoga, which was M'Donough's flag ship, and it was confidently expected, that with his superior force he would soon be able to reduce the American commander to submission. For more than two hours the battle raged, both sides suffering greatly. The guns on the starboard side of the Saratoga were by this time nearly all dismounted or unmanageable, and the situation of the enemy was little better. Whichever could succeed in that difficult naval manœuvre, viz., winding his vessel round and bringing a new broadside to bear, seemed to have the best chance of victory. The Confiance essayed it in vain; but the efforts of M'Donough in the Saratoga, enabled him to take the position he wished. The battle was now speedily decided. **1814.** The Confiance and other vessels surrendered. Three of the galleys were sunk; the ten others escaped. By the time this desperate contest was over, there was scarcely a mast in either squadron capable of bearing a sail, and the greater part of the vessels were in a sinking state. There were fifty-five round shot in the hull of the Saratoga, and in the Confiance one hundred and five. The Saratoga was twice set on fire by hot shot. Of the crew of the Confiance, fifty were killed, and sixty wounded; among the former was Captain Downie. On board the Saratoga, there were twenty-eight killed, and twenty-nine wounded. The total loss in the American squadron amounted to fifty-two killed, and fifty-eight

* Ingersoll has some very appropriate remarks on this topic, which do his heart and head both credit. The great changes which have taken place in the religious spirit and tone of the navy, since that memorable Sunday, the 11th of September, 1814, are worthy of note and thankfulness. "*History of the Second War*," vol. ii., pp. 127–33.

wounded. The enemy had eighty-four killed, and one hundred and ten wounded. The action lasted two hours and twenty minutes.

On land, meanwhile, the battle was urged by Prevost with vigor and skill. His batteries poured forth shells and rockets during the whole time, and, confidently counting upon Downie's success on the Lake, he deemed it certain that he should be equally successful in carrying the American works. Three fierce attempts were made by the British to cross the Saranac, and crush the Americans by assault; but they were bravely met, and failed in accomplishing their purposes. When the shouts of our countrymen announced that the British fleet had surrendered, Prevost felt that it was useless to protract the contest. Although the firing was kept up till dark, his plans were completely frustrated. Now that the Americans had the command of Lake Champlain, the possession of their works on the land could not serve him in any further design; and in the mean time, he was exposed to danger which increased with the hourly augmentation of the American force. He determined therefore to raise the siege. Under cover of the night he sent off all the baggage and artillery for which he could obtain means of transportation; and precipitately followed with all his forces, leaving behind him the sick and wounded. Early the next morning, the Americans started in pursuit, but it was not pressed beyond twelve or fourteen miles from Plattsburg. The British loss in killed, wounded, and missing, was estimated at about fifteen hundred; that of the Americans was thirty-seven killed, sixty-two wounded, and twenty missing.* A large quantity of provisions, ammunition, and implements of war was left by the enemy, on their retreat; subsequently, other valuable stores were found hidden in marshes or buried in the ground.

On the 13th of September, the American and British officers who fell in battle, were interred with the honors of war. M'Donough, equally with Perry and other brave defenders of our country's rights, received the due meed of praise for his humanity and kindness to the vanquished foe.

Soon after the brilliant sortie from Fort Erie, on the 17th of September, (p. 239) General Izard arrived, and being the senior officer, took the command, while General Brown was ordered to Sackett's Harbor. The Americans being now strong enough to commence offensive operations, Colonel Hindman was left at Fort Erie with a sufficient garrison, and the army again advanced towards Chippewa; but the British were rather shy in venturing to meet their opponents. Nothing of moment occurred until the 18th of October, when General Bissell was ordered, with a detachment of his brigade, nine hundred in number, to the

1814.

* Alison, in giving an account of this battle, says that the loss of the British was not more than five or six hundred. The same writer states, respecting Prevost's order to retreat, that "such was the indignation which this order excited among the British officers, inured in Spain to a long course of victory, that several of them broke their swords, declaring they would never serve again; and the army, in mournful submission, leisurely wound its way back to the Canadian frontier."

neighborhood of Cook's Mills, at Lyon's Creek, a branch of the Chippewa, for the purpose of destroying the enemy's stores in that quarter. Having driven in the picket guard, and captured its officers, Bissell encamped for the night. The next morning, he was attacked by the Marquis of Tweedale, with not less than twelve hundred men; but the enemy was repulsed and driven back again to their entrenchments, leaving their killed and wounded behind. Bissell having accomplished his design, returned to Black Rock with a loss of twelve killed and fifty-five wounded. The weather growing cold, and the season for military operations drawing to a close, it was determined to destroy Fort Erie, and evacuate Upper Canada. This was accordingly effected; and early in November, the troops were transported to the American side, and distributed in winter quarters at Buffalo, Black Rock, and Batavia.*

During the summer of this year, an expedition was undertaken for the purpose of recovering Mackinaw. A part of the squadron on Lake Erie, had for this object been extended into Lake Huron, under the command of Commodore Sinclair. Colonel Croghan, accompanied by Major Holmes, left Detroit on the 5th of July. Co-operating with Commodore Sinclair, they succeeded in destroying the British establishments at St. Joseph's and the Sault de St. Marie, and then proceeded to Mackinaw. Croghan landed his troops on the 4th of August, but his force was not sufficient to reduce the fortress. The attempt was attended with the loss of many brave officers, among whom was Major Holmes. Two vessels, which were left by the Americans to prevent supplies arriving at the fort, were blown up by the British. Commodore Sinclair, however, succeeded in capturing the last of their vessels on the upper lakes.*

1814.

General Harrison, vexed at the conduct of the secretary of war, who was no friend of his, and who violated the usual military etiquette on various occasions, sent in his resignation of the post of major-general in the army. His letter was written from Cincinnati, under date of May 11th, and he retired to private life.

On the 22d of October, General M'Arthur, who took the command after General Harrison's resignation, left Detroit, with about seven hundred men, and marched in the direction of the River Thames. Having dispersed the British detachments in the vicinity of the Thames, destroyed all their stores, and taken one hundred and fifty prisoners, M'Arthur's detachment, on the 7th of November, returned to Detroit in good order, and with the loss of only one man. The troops were then discharged and returned home.

* Ingersoll (vol. ii., pp. 109–14) has some reflections on the "moral effect" of the war as carried on in the north. The reader will find them worthy his attention.

* M'Afee, in his History, (p. 410–53) gives a full account of the operations in the northwest at this date, with copious quotations from letters, documents, etc.

CHAPTER XII.

1814.

THE INVASION OF WASHINGTON.

The British in the Chesapeake — Barney's flotilla — A heavy blow contemplated by the enemy — Views and plans of the administration for the defence of Washington — General Winder appointed commander — His trials and perplexities — Cochrane's fleet enters the Chesapeake — The force under General Ross landed at Benedict — Advance into the interior — Winder's force and conduct — Stansbury's brigade — Post taken at Bladensburg — The president and secretaries in the camp — Their presence and plans — The battle of Bladensburg — Retreat to the capitol — Thence to Georgetown Heights, and fifteen miles further — Destruction at the navy yard — General Ross enters Washington — The city devoted to destruction — The next morning's work — The British anxious to get away — Their retreat at night — Effect of this invasion — Gordon's success at Alexandria — Parker's misfortune — Attempt on Baltimore — Death of General Ross — Battle at North Point — The British advance but do not attack — Bombardment of Fort M'Henry — Cochrane and the troops retreat — The return of the president to Washington — Congress meet — The message of the president — Measures entered upon — Mr. Jefferson offers his library to Congress — Changes in the cabinet — The measures of this session — Finances, taxation, bank scheme, etc. — Monroe's plan for augmenting the army — Death of the vice-president — Appendix to Chapter XII. The British account of the invasion of Washington.

The British squadron on the coast continued their system of petty plundering and devastating, wherever they found opportunity. Especially was this plan pursued on the waters of the Chesapeake, where Cockburn was in command; and numerous and disgraceful inroads were made under his direction, or with his entire sanction. A flotilla for the defence of the inlets and smaller rivers of the bay, consisting of a cutter, two gunboats, and nine barges, was placed under command of Commodore Barney, who, during the month of June, performed a number of gallant exploits in the discharge of his responsible duties. Every attempt of the enemy to capture the flotilla failed, Barney at times running up small creeks out of reach of the British guns; at other times, silencing them by his superior skill and accuracy in firing.

1814.

Cockburn had menaced Washington during the preceding year; but the secretary of war and others never believed that any attack was seriously contemplated. The defences appeared to be all that was necessary, and it was thought that the British would not dare, with any force at their command, to attempt so hazardous an expedition as that of assaulting the capital of the United States. But England, now that Napoleon was subdued, having abundance of ships and men unoccupied, (see p. 228) determined to strike a blow or two which should tell with tremendous effect, and compel the Americans to sue for peace on any terms.

The president of the United States,

not unaware of the threatened invasion, by news which reached him at the end of June, called a council of the heads of the departments, and suggested the propriety of collecting all the regulars within reach, of forming a camp of at least three thousand men at some point between the Patuxent and the Eastern Branch of the Potomac, and of embodying ten thousand militia at Washington. These views appeared to meet the approbation of all; and there seems no reason to doubt, that could they have been carried into execution, both the cities of Baltimore and Washington might safely have bid defiance to the British arms. Steps were immediately taken in furtherance of the plan suggested. Requisitions were made on the District of Columbia, for her whole quota of militia, amounting to two thousand men; on Maryland for the same, six thousand men; on Pennsylvania, for five thousand men; and on Virginia, for two thousand men; making in the whole, fifteen thousand men; of which, ten thousand, it was confidently thought, would not fail to take the field. It was ascertained, that about a thousand regulars could be depended on; besides a squadron of horse then in Pennsylvania, some additional regulars which were ordered from North Carolina, and Commodore Barney's men, in case it should be found necessary to abandon the flotilla. On paper, this was certainly a highly respectable force; but, it is to be remembered, that the ten or fifteen thousand militia were yet to be called together, and when assembled, they were to be disciplined, and put in some sort of preparation to meet a veteran force like that which was about to invade the country.

The District of Columbia, Maryland, and part of Virginia, was formed into a new military district, and on the 5th of July, the command was bestowed upon General Winder. He entered upon his difficult command with alacrity, but every thing nearly was to be done, fortifications to be erected, troops collected, plans matured, etc. Difficulties of various kinds sprang up in his path. The governor of Maryland called for three thousand militia, but his call brought out about as many hundred. The governor of Pennsylvania had no authority at all to draft men, and could only appeal to the patriotism of the people, with very indifferent success, as may be supposed. Thus Maryland and Pennsylvania failing, nearly half of the fifteen thousand were cut off at once, and of the balance, not more than one third could be relied on. At the beginning of August, Winder had only a thousand regulars collected, and less than two thousand militia. Some troops embodied at Annapolis, and a brigade of Maryland militia from Baltimore, under General Stansbury, were placed at the disposal of the American commander; and it was hoped, that volunteers would flock in and repel the insulting and haughty enemy. But, as is at once evident, with such miserably insufficient preparation, the British general would meet with very little to hinder him from accomplishing his purpose.*

1814.

* Ingersoll (vol. ii., p. 164) gives a graphic account of the position of things at Washington, in view of

On the 16th of August, twenty-one sail of the line, under Admiral Cochrane, arrived in Chesapeake Bay, and effected a junction with Cockburn's squadron. The enemy's force was divided into three parts. One division was sent up the Potomac, under Captain Gordon, for the purpose of bombarding Fort Warburton, and opening the way to the city of Washington; and another, under Sir Peter Parker, was dispatched to threaten Baltimore. The main body ascended the Patuxent, apparently with the intention of destroying Commodore Barney's flotilla, which had taken refuge at the head of that river, but with the real intention, as it was soon discovered, of attacking Washington. In prosecution of this plan, the expedition proceeded to Benedict, the head of frigate navigation, and about forty miles southeast of the capital. Benedict, on the west bank of the Patuxent, was reached on the 19th of August; and on the next day, the debarkation of the land forces, under General Ross, was completed. On the 21st, pursuing the course of the river, the troops moved to Nottingham, and on the 22d, arrived at Upper Marlborough; a flotilla, consisting of launches and barges, under the command of Admiral Cockburn, ascending the river and keeping pace with them. The day following, the flotilla of Commodore Barney, in obedience to the orders of the secretary of the navy, was blown up by men left for the purpose; the commodore having already joined General Winder with his seamen and marines.

The force under General Ross numbered not more than four thousand five hundred men, although rumor and sudden fright expanded his army into at least ten thousand men. The advance was slow; for not only did the total absence of resistance suggest the need of precaution against ambuscades, but the soldiers, long cooped up in the ships, were too much fatigued, by the weight of their accoutrements and provisions, to proceed rapidly. Occasionally, a few of the famous riflemen of the backwoods showed themselves to the invading force; who also caught sight of bodies of American soldiery,—now posted strongly on some rising ground, whence they hastily withdrew as the British advanced,—now rapidly evacuating some town, as the British entered,—and now envelopped in clouds of dust, as they crossed the line of the British march. Later still, at night, the outposts were conscious of the near approach of small parties of Americans, apparently intent on the capture or death of stragglers; and these casualties were so frequent, in consequence of the heat of the weather, and the pe-

1814.

---

the expected incursion of the British. "There were no funds; though the city banks proffered a few hundred thousand dollars of their depreciated, and in a very few days unconvertible paper,—as, with the fall of Washington, all banks south of New England stopped payments in coin. There were no rifles; not flints enough; American gunpowder was inferior to English; there was not a cannon mounted for the defence of the seat of government; not a regular soldier there; not a fortress, breastwork, or military fortification of any kind, within twelve miles. The neighboring militia of Maryland and Virginia were worn down by disastrous and mortifying service, routed and disheartened. The proportion of regular troops, all of them mere recruits, never tried in fire, was like that of coin to paper, in the wretched currency; so small an infusion of precious metal, that there was scarcely any substance to rely upon."

culiarities of the country and climate, that the halting places were never many miles apart. The inhabitants of both country and towns, panic-stricken, seemed to disappear in mass before the face of the truculent invaders.

General Winder's force amounted to about three thousand men at this time, the half of whom were militia, who had never seen as yet an engagement. The Baltimore and Annapolis militia had not arrived, and the Virginia detachment was still delayed. Winder's camp was at Woodyard, about twelve miles from Washington. Early on the morning of Monday, the 22d of August, an advance corps, under Colonel Scott and Major Porter marched on the road to Nottingham, and were, for the first time, brought in sight of the enemy; yet the American commander, though the men were eager for action, would not risk it with raw and undisciplined troops. Thus, General Ross, who had left the shipping with great uneasiness, was allowed, without cavalry, with hardly a piece of cannon, to advance unmolested, through a well-settled country, abounding in defiles, ravines, streams, woods, and the like, of which the Americans took no advantage, but kept retreating without a blow in defence of their homes and firesides. Winder fell back to the Battalion Old Fields, a position about eight miles from Marlborough, and covering Bladensburg, the bridges on the eastern branch of the Potomac, and Fort Warburton.

1814.

On the same evening, General Stansbury arrived with his brigade at Bladensburg, after a very fatiguing march, and was joined the next evening by the fifth Baltimore regiment, under Colonel Sterrett, and a rifle battalion under Major Pinkney, in all about twenty-two hundred men. Monroe, the secretary of state, who had been active in giving his advice and assistance to Winder, reached Stansbury's quarters about midnight, and informing him of the advance of the enemy on General Winder, advised him to fall on the rear of the British immediately; but Stansbury, with his troops fatigued by their recent march, declined doing this, and remained during the night at his post. Determining to move towards Washington, having heard of Winder's retreat, Stansbury, before day, crossed the bridge over the eastern branch of the Potomac, and after securing his rear, halted for a few hours. Early in the morning, he again moved forward, with the view of taking possession of some ground for defence, when orders were received from General Winder to give battle to the enemy at Bladensburg, in case they came that way. Looking upon his tired and raw troops, and considering the number of the enemy, two or three times as great as his own, Stansbury and his officers resolved that it was impossible for them to make head against the invaders; but receiving peremptory orders to meet the enemy at Bladensburg, Stansbury had no alternative, and prepared as best he could, for what was before him.

General Winder's camp and army were encumbered rather than encouraged by the presence of the executive of the United States himself, with his secretaries of state, war, and navy, and attorney-general. Contradictory rumors, and, in general, great alarm prevailed there, and made it a scene of disquiet and disorder, almost surpassing imagination to conceive. "Such," says Ingersoll, "was the laxity of discipline, insubordination, and turbulence, probably unavoidable in a heterogeneous assemblage on a sudden, of citizens armed and unarmed, that an old officer present described the camp as open as a race-field, and noisy as a fair; the militia and sailors, boisterous with mirth or quarrels, the countersign given so loudly by the sentinels, that it might be heard fifty yards."

On the 23d of August, the British, falling in with a strong body of Americans, practised a rather stale trick upon them,—they wheeled off from the main road, and took the direction of Alexandria. Yet the bait took, General Winder abandoned the strong position he had seized on the main road, harassed his troops by a needless march towards that town, and discovered his mistake only time enough to occupy the heights of Bladensburg, just before the enemy came in sight, on the following day. Before this unwise retreat was undertaken, the president reviewed above three thousand men, in Winder's camp, in the hope of raising in the breasts of the disheartened soldiers, a courageous animation which he did not himself appear to possess. New bands of militia and volunteers joined subsequently; but not in such numbers as was expected or hoped for; and the entire force under Winder did not at any time much exceed five thousand men.

1814.

Leaving Winder posted in three lines, on the rising ground above Bladensburg, with twenty-six guns commanding the only bridge by which the narrow ravine and stream in his front could be crossed, we may notice, in passing, the conduct of the executive and the heads of departments. Every man appears to have been willing to contribute whatever he had, towards making a general and an army. Monroe rode over to the field early in the day, and counselled the loan of General Armstrong to the perplexed commander at Bladensburg; the secretary of the treasury, whom the state of the finances had plunged into a state of profound depression, lent his duelling pistols to the president. Madison and his staff of civilians, hearing of the approach of the enemy, and desirous of affording his countenance to General Winder and his men, were very near riding into the ranks of the British, by mistake. He soon found out that he could do little to aid, and at the first onset he returned to Washington, having, after consulting his cabinet officers grouped round him on horseback, released the brave Joshua Barney from the task of blowing up some bridges, and having sent him and his jolly tars with their guns into line, in order to do something for the credit of the American name.

Though excessively fatigued with the heat and oppressiveness of the weather, the British, when commanded to advance, pushed into the village, which the Americans had neglected to occupy. After a short *reconnaissance*, during which the column sheltered itself from the fire of the American guns behind the houses, they

1814.

made a dash at the narrow bridge, where they suffered severely both from the artillery and from Pinkney's riflemen. Covered in their attack by volleys of rockets, they wheeled off to the right and left of the road, and quickly cleared the thicket of the American skirmishers, who, falling back with precipitation upon the first line, threw it into disorder, before it had fired a shot. In a period of time almost incredibly short, and when the British had scarcely shown themselves, the whole of that line, being ordered to retreat by General Winder, gave way, and fled in the utmost confusion.*

For a while, the second line not only stood their ground, but drove back the enemy—who, lightening themselves by throwing away their knapsacks, extended their ranks so as to show an equal front with the Americans—almost to the wooded bank of the river. But now the second brigade of the British had crossed, and having formed, was advancing to the charge in firm array; threatened thus, and their left flank, being turned, the whole American line wavered, and then broke, and rushed from the field in total and indiscriminate flight. Barney and his sailors alone offered any resistance. They were employed as gunners, and not only did they serve their guns with a quickness and precision which astonished their assailants, but they stood till some of them were actually bayonetted, with fusees in their hands; nor was it till the gallant Barney was wounded and taken, and they saw themselves deserted on all sides by the soldiers, that they quitted the field.

Not more than fifty of the Americans were killed, or wounded, upon this memorable occasion; the rest fled in a state of terror and delirium; "the only death on the retreat was said to be that of a captain of the regular army, of approved courage, who, taken with the contagion of unanimous panic, ran with the crowd till he fell, fainted, and expired." The loss on the part of the English was some seven or eight hundred killed, wounded, and missing; including several officers of rank and distinction. The Americans left ten of their guns in the hands of the victors. None of their artillery, except that which the sailors worked, was fired more than twice or thrice. The British were able to bring only one of their guns into action. The conquerors in this extraordinary engagement, (which lasted from one till four o'clock in the afternoon of the 24th of August,) unprovided with cavalry, and completely exhausted with heat and toil, were unable to pursue the flying Americans. Rest was so indispensable to them, that they laid down and slept upon the field of battle; nor could they resume the march till after some two hours' sleep, when, in the cool of the evening, they set out towards Washington.

1814.

The few efforts made by General Winder to methodize the rout, and

* Colonel Williams's recently published "*History of the Invasion and Capture of Washington*," enters into details more fully than we can possibly do: his volume is a well timed contribution to existing works on the subject, and we have little doubt that, in the main, he is right in supposing that the troops have been unduly censured for what took place, and made to bear the blame which rightly belonged elsewhere.

convert it into a retreat, were but partially successful. About two thousand well-armed men—including a Virginia regiment, which, though it came up the preceding evening, could not get supplied with flints, until the last gun was discharged on their side in the battle—were kept together, and halted for a moment about two miles from Washington. "But General Winder," says Ingersoll, "deemed it prudent to order them to fall back, from the position they occupied and reluctantly left, to another nearer the city; where he contemplated making a stand. Arrived and halted there, however, he ordered them again to retire to the capitol, where they were finally to await the enemy. There General Armstrong suggested throwing them into the two wings of that stone, strong building;" but Winder rejected the proposal with some warmth, and Monroe coincided with him in opinion. "The capitol, he feared, might prove a *cul-de-sac*, from which there would be no escape; the only safety was to rally on the Heights of Georgetown, beyond Washington. For the seventh time that day, a retreat, therefore, was once more commanded. In anguish and with loud execrations, some of them in tears, the city troops, with the rest, for the last time turned their backs on the enemy, then fast asleep on the parched earth not more than cannon shot from the capital. To desert their homes, families, and dwellings; to march degraded by their forsaken wives and children, leaving all they had or cherished to the barbarities of an enraged and inhuman invader, was insupportable. Both at their first order to retreat toward the capitol, and their last to retreat from it, and march beyond the city, insubordinate protests, oaths, tears, and bitter complaints broke forth. To preserve order in ranks so demoralized and degraded, was impossible. Broken, scattered, licentious, and tumultuous, they wandered along the central, solitary avenue, which is the great entry of Washington; when arrived at Georgetown, were a mere mob, from whom it was preposterous to suppose that an army could be organized, to make a stand there; and, in nearly as great disorder as the runagates, who preceded them across the fields, without venturing into the city, the remnant of disgraced freemen reached Tenlytown in utter mortification; there to be disturbed and alarmed nearly all night by the conflagration, as they had reason to believe, of every house in Washington, whose lurid flames, with the detonation from the navy yard, were the shocking sights and sounds of all the surrounding country, filled with fugitives of both sexes, all ages, and thousands of them men of courage, sleeping on their arms. Broken, scattered, and disgusted, most wended their way to Montgomery court house, fifteen miles from Georgetown, where their unquestionably brave, but ill-starred and ill-advised commander, stung with poignant sorrow, deplored that he had not at Nottingham, at the old fields at Bladensburg, at Washington, somewhere, if not everywhere, less scrupulous of bloodshed, by freer expenditure of that of his fellow-citizens and neighbors, saved the capital of his country from profanation, and its na-

1814.

tional character from indelible disgrace."*

At the first alarm, the secretary of the navy gave orders to set fire to the new sloop of war Argus, with ten guns, afloat; the new schooner Lynx, five barges, and two gunboats; and to the large frigate Columbia, on the stocks, just ready to be launched; the whole of which, with a vast quantity of stores and machinery, and the buildings containing them, were destroyed. The appearance of the fugitives from Bladensburg was the signal for a panic in the city, quite equal to that which had lost the battle. The president fled, as did also Mrs. Madison, after securing some valuable papers and the full length portrait of Washington which still adorns the White House. Armstrong, furnishing himself with one of Scott's novels, found refuge in a farm house; the other members of the administration shifted as best they could. Some of the most valuable public records were preserved from destruction by the exertions of the clerks in that department. Washington itself, before the arrival of the enemy, was abandoned to outrage and plunder by numbers of escaped slaves and ruffians; and for some time lawlessness and anarchy, fearful to think of, prevailed in the capital of the United States.

1814.

In the midst of this sad state of affairs, General Ross, about eight o'clock in the evening, accompanied by Cockburn, and a body guard of two hundred men, rode slowly into the now deserted city, its eight or ten thousand inhabitants, with rare exceptions, having fled in every direction. As they advanced, a solitary musket was fired by some unknown person, from behind the wall of Mr. Sewall's house, and the general's horse was killed. The house was immediately assaulted, and the work of destruction commenced in earnest. The two wings of the capitol, which were the only parts finished, were gutted by fire, whereby the library of Congress and many valuable public documents perished. The president's official residence, with the offices of the treasury and state departments near it, shared the same fate. Numbers of cannon were destroyed, and others were spiked, had their trunnions knocked off, and were thrown into the river. Quantities of shot, shell, grenades, and cartridges were also cast into the river. Yet, so groundless was the terror, and mistaken the policy, which had led to the destruction at the navy yard, mentioned above, that only two brass pieces were there spiked by the enemy, whose alarm was so great as that, in their hurry, they left several hundred iron cannons uninjured; and also the arsenal, not far off, an important repository, of which their views and orders especially required the demolition, but which escaped both American and British madness.

Whilst the British were drawing nigh Washington there had been indications of an approaching storm. In the course of the night it rolled up, and near morning, for two hours, the city suffered from a furious tornado. The flames of the burning capitol, and

1814.

* Ingersoll's "*History of the Second War*," vol. ii., p. 181.

of the numerous other conflagrations, were paled by incessant flashes of lightning; and the roar of the guns which were used for destroying the buildings and stores, and the explosions of dépôts of gunpowder, were almost drowned by the heavy bursts of thunder.

The next morning the ruthless invaders continued their work. The war office was burned. The printing office of "The National Intelligencer" was sacked, under Cockburn's personal direction, and the letter thrown into the street. The great bridge across the Potomac was set on fire and destroyed. Two rope-walks, near the navy yard, were burnt, and by accident a torch was flung into a dry well in the arsenal at Greenleaf's Point, which had been used as a receptacle for old cartridges, waste powder, and other combustibles. A terrible explosion instantly ensued, the houses and buildings near were shattered and thrown down, and a great number of soldiers lost their lives, or were frightfully mutilated. There was also some injury done to private houses and stores by the invaders, but, principally owing to the interference of General Ross, who seems to have had grace enough to be ashamed of the contemptible work in which he was engaged, the depredations were not so numerous as Cockburn would have made, had he been allowed his own way entirely.*

Notwithstanding the pusillanimous conduct of the Americans, who had abandoned everything to the foe, the British were very uneasy, and very anxious to get back to the cover of their shipping. A renewal of the hurricane of the preceding evening, more furious and destructive than anything the invaders had ever seen, urged them to hasten their departure. Early in the afternoon, the sky grew black; the wind rose in its fury; and amid the flashing lightning and terrific thunder, the roofs were blown from the buildings; houses and chimneys fell to the ground; and for two hours the rain came down in all directions like a deluge. Thirty or forty of the soldiers perished under the ruins of the fallen walls and buildings. No wonder, if they were in a hurry to get away. Leaving the post office and patent office, and everything else marked out for destruction, the invaders, as soon as the darkness of the night admitted, hastily set out on their retreat. The wounded they could hardly undertake to remove; it was hence determined to leave them behind, and the care of them was assigned to Commodore Barney, who, as we have above said, had been wounded and taken at Bladensburg, and who, with the other prisoners, was released upon parole, for this purpose. The watchfires having all been trimmed, in perfect silence the enemy withdrew from the scene of devastation; more wounded were left behind at Bladensburg; at Nottingham, they met with some of their ships; and on the 29th and 30th, the whole expedition re-embarked at Benedict, to undertake other schemes of rapine and outrage.

1814.

But little need be said further, re-

* The value of the public property destroyed at Washington exceeded $2,000,000. We have no estimate of the loss which was sustained by private individuals, in this disgraceful incursion.

specting this Vandal-like inroad upon Washington.* That it should have been permitted by our countrymen must always remain a marvel; yet, where so many are to blame, it is difficult, perhaps impossible, to discriminate, and fix the stigma upon those who rightly deserve it. However the student of history may decide on this point, there can be no doubt, that the British government disgraced itself effectually, by giving orders for such an expedition. More than anything else, it served to justify the heavy accusations of the war party against the British, and to show that, whatever were the feelings with which the United States had commenced hostilities, Great Britain had entered into them with all the truculence of civil war. And this consideration completely bars the praise which otherwise might be claimed for the skill and daring displayed in the invasion of Washington.†

In one respect the incursion was productive of real advantage to the administration. Although the president and his advisers, especially the secretary of war, were severely censured throughout the country; although General Winder was charged with incompetency, and Armstrong was compelled to retire from his post, in consequence of the storm which arose on all sides against him;* yet so deep was the indignation aroused against the savage mode of warfare which England had ordered, that party spirit for a time was quelled; not a dissenting voice was heard; unanimity prevailed; the war became decidedly popular; and everywhere the militia were organized, and vigorous efforts made to place the seaboard cities and towns in a state of defence against invasion and ruthless destruction.

The enemy's ships, under Captain Gordon, (p. 248,) ascended the Potomac, and passed Fort Warburton three days after the capture of Washington. The fort had been abandoned and blown up by Captain Dyson, the commandant, in a most extraordinary manner; probably under the influence of the dreadful panic which generally prevailed. His orders had been to abandon it only in case of an attack by land forces; but, on a mere rumor, and without waiting the enemy's approach, he thought proper to take this measure, for which he was afterwards cashiered from the army. On the 29th, the squadron reached Alexandria; and the inhabitants of that place, being now in the power of the enemy, ingloriously

* In connection with this unpleasant topic, it is only fair to refer the reader to Armstrong's chapter, in which he gives a brief narrative, with remarks respecting the invasion of the capital.—"*Notices of the War of* 1812," vol. ii., pp. 124–154.

† The Rev. G. R. Gleig, in his "*Campaigns of the British Army at Washington and New Orleans, in the years* 1814, 1815," furnishes an interesting narrative of the invasion of Washington, which the reader will find worth perusing. A brief extract or two from this volume will be found in the Appendix at the end of the present chapter.

* General Winder was tried by a court martial, of which General Scott was president, and was honorably acquitted. Armstrong, whom few, if any, liked, was made the scape-goat of the whole disaster. The president advised him to withdraw from public notice, until the storm should have blown over; which he did; but soon after, on the 3d of September, sent in an indignant resignation of his office. Monroe was then appointed secretary of war provisionally, but without giving up his other office.

made terms for the preservation of the town from conflagration and pillage. The insatiable avarice of
1814.
Gordon and his men imposed the hardest conditions: all the merchandise then in the town, as well as all which had been removed thence since the 19th, was required to be put on board the shipping at the wharf, at the expense of the inhabitants, and, together with the shipping, including those vessels which had been sunk on the approach of the enemy, and the public and private naval and ordnance stores, to be delivered up to the enemy. These terms, slightly modified, were complied with; and Captain Gordon moved down the river with a fleet of prize vessels and a rich booty.

Preparations, meanwhile, had been hastily made by Captains Porter and Perry, of the navy, to throw difficulties in the way of the enemy's descent. During the five days of their return, they were greatly harassed and annoyed by cannon planted on the bluffs and hills, fire vessels on the water, and barges, manned by brave sailors and Virginians, day and night at work to impede the British retreat. But Gordon managed to escape with his ill-gotten booty, and reached the fleet on the 9th of September.

Sir Peter Parker, who ascended the Chesapeake, was less fortunate than his fellow invaders. A number of petty inroads were made, and houses and other property burnt. On the 30th of August, near midnight, Parker landed in the neighborhood of Moor's
1814.
Fields, with the view of surprising a party of militia, encamped there under the command of Colonel Reed. In this he was disappointed, for the militia, having heard the approach of the barges, were prepared to receive him. Having landed, Parker moved forward at the head of about two hundred and fifty men, and, on approaching within seventy yards of the Americans, was received with a heavy fire. He endeavored to press forward on the centre of the line; but being foiled in this, he threw himself on the flank, where also he was bravely repulsed. About forty of the enemy were killed or wounded, Sir Peter Parker being among the latter. The British now retreated, and Parker died a few days afterwards, much and justly lamented.

The success of the marauding expedition against the city of Washington, excited British cupidity to a high degree; and it was determined by their leaders, to make a similar attempt upon Baltimore. The inhabitants, meanwhile, set to work vigorously to strengthen the defences of the city. A ditch was opened, and a breastwork thrown up on the high ground to the northeast of the city, to prevent the approach of the enemy in that quarter. The militia came in from the interior of the state, and from Pennsylvania and Virginia; and Commodore Rodgers of the navy, with his marines, took possession of the heavy batteries on the hill just mentioned. A brigade of Virginia volunteers, and the regular troops, were assigned to General Winder; and the city brigade was commanded by General Stricker; the whole under the chief direction of Major-general Smith. The approach to the city by water was defended by Fort M'Henry, and garrisoned by about one thousand men, volunteers and regulars, under Major Armistead. Two batteries upon the Patapsco, to the right of Fort M'Henry, to prevent the enemy from landing during the night in the rear of the town, were manned by a detachment of sailors, and were named Fort Covington and the City Battery. The people of Baltimore were not without strong hope of being able to repulse the enemy from their fair city, and they looked to the defence of Fort M'Henry with the deepest interest.

Admiral Cochrane proceeded up the Chesapeake, and on the 11th of September, appeared at the mouth of the Patapsco, about fourteen miles from Baltimore, with a fleet of some fifty sail. The next day, the troops, numbering about six thousand, were landed at North Point, and, under the command of General Ross, took up their march for the city. While the land forces were advancing along the northern shore of the estuary, several vessels of light draught were ordered to ascend the river, to co-operate with them in the capture of Fort M'Henry, a fortification about two miles from the city.

1814.

The British troops proceeded for several miles without opposition, but about one o'clock came in contact with an advance corps under Major Heath, whom General Stricker had sent forward from his position at Bear Creek, to reconnoitre. In the skirmish which ensued, General Ross, who had rashly pressed forward to the front, was shot through the side, and expired before he could be taken to the boats. Colonel Brooke immediately assuming the command, the light troops advanced, and a spirited action ensued. The artillery on both sides, the rifles of the Americans, and the British rockets, did great execution; but one regiment, the fifty-first, having been seized with a panic, and the British greatly out-numbering the Americans, General Stricker, after a gallant resistance of an hour and twenty minutes, was compelled to retire before the enemy. Falling back to about half a mile in advance of the entrenchments, Stricker was joined by General Winder, who took post on his left. The American loss in killed and wounded amounted to one hundred and sixty-three; that of the British, was two hundred and fifty. Not thinking it advisable to attempt pursuit, the British remained all night on the field of battle.

The next morning, September 13th, the march was resumed, and the British commander soon had a full view of the position occupied by our countrymen. During the morning, by his manœuvres to the right, he seemed to show an intention of coming down by the Harford and York roads; to baffle which design, Generals Winder and Stricker adapted their movements. At noon, the British concentrated their force in front of the American line, approached within a mile of the intrenchments, and seemed to be making arrangements for an attack that evening. General Smith, therefore, immediately drew Generals Winder and Stricker nearer to the right of the enemy, and ordered them to fall upon their flank or rear, in case the attempt should be made.

1814.

The attack on Fort M'Henry meanwhile had been commenced. About sunrise, on the 13th, the British had brought sixteen ships within two miles and a half of the fort, and the assault was begun by five bomb-vessels, which had anchored at the distance of two miles. These, being out of the range of the guns of the fort, maintained an incessant bombardment; yet, despite the bombs and rockets every moment falling in and about the fort, the garrison wavered not; every man stood to his post without shrinking. Some of the enemy's vessels approaching nearer, a tremendous fire was opened upon them, and they hastily retired. During the night, whilst the enemy on land was retreating, and whilst the bombardment was the most severe, two or three rocket-vessels and barges succeeded in getting up the Ferry Branch; but they were soon compelled to retire, by the guns of Fort Covington and the City Battery. These forts also destroyed one of the barges, with all on board.* At seven o'clock the next morning, the bombardment was given over, fifteen hundred shells having been thrown, but with comparatively little injury to the fort and its defenders. Only four were killed and twenty-four wounded in this assault on Fort M'Henry.

Admiral Cochrane and Colonel Brooke agreed that the enterprise could not be prosecuted to advantage. Accordingly, the army commenced its retreat in the night, and, favored by the extreme darkness and steady rain, were enabled to get beyond pursuit before the day dawned. **1814.** The British fleet, on the 15th, made its way down the bay, and Admiral Cochrane, soon after, retired, with all his forces, to the West Indies.

Mr. Madison, who had suffered no little humiliation, and even insult, because of the capture of Washington, returned to the city directly after the British had retreated. The emergency in public affairs required immediate attention, and the president accordingly issued his proclamation for the assembling of Congress on the 19th of September. The next day, the message was sent in and read to both Houses. Moderate in length, but firm, almost defiant in tone, the message reviewed succinctly the existing state of things, and the measures which seemed to be required under the circumstances. The various successes of our arms on land and sea were dilated upon, and the disgraceful mode of warfare which the British had recently adopted, was vigorously denounced. The necessity of filling the ranks of the regular army was adverted to, as more economical than employing the militia to any great extent, the president at the same time,

* It is an interesting circumstance, worthy of mention in connection with the bombardment of Fort M'Henry, that Francis S. Key, having gone on board to the admiral's ship for the purpose of obtaining the release of some friends, was detained there, and was compelled to be a spectator of the fierce assault on the fort. Mr. Key watched his country's flag with patriotic anxiety, as it waved through the day, until the night shut it out from his view; and during the long hours that followed, he sought, by the glare of the bursting shells and rockets, to see if that noble standard was yet in its place. At early dawn, he exultingly beheld it still floating proudly in the breeze; and under the impulse of poetic fervor, he composed the well-known song, "The Star Spangled Banner." See Ingersoll's "*History of the Second War*," vol. ii., p. 214.

strongly urging that the militia be classed and disciplined for more efficient service. The financial statement of the three quarters of a year that had elapsed since the last preceding account, showed $32,000,000 received, all from loans except about $11,000,000, and $34,000,000 disbursed, leaving nearly $5,000,000 in the treasury. But it was added, that "large sums" would be required to meet the demands already authorized by Congress, and those arising from "the extension of the operations of the war."

The president did not attempt to disguise the fact, that the situation of the country called for the most earnest efforts on the part of Congress
1814. and of the people. The power and means at command of the enemy were vast, and well calculated to enable him to effect his object; but, says Mr. Madison, "the American people will face hostility with the undaunted spirit which in their Revolutionary struggle defeated the adversary's unrighteous projects. His threats and his barbarities, instead of dismay, will kindle in every bosom an indignation not to be extinguished but in the disaster and expulsion of such cruel invaders. In providing the means necessary, the national legislature will not distrust the heroic and enlightened patriotism of its constituents. They will cheerfully and proudly bear every burden of every kind, which the safety and honor of the nation demand. We have seen them every where paying their taxes, direct and indirect, with the greatest promptness and alacrity. We see them rushing with enthusiasm to the scenes where danger and duty call. In offering their blood, they give the surest pledge that no other tribute will be withheld." In conclusion, the president forcibly said; "having manifested, on every occasion, and in every proper mode, a sincere desire to arrest the effusion of blood, and meet our enemy on the ground of justice and reconciliation, our beloved country, in still opposing to his persevering hostility all its energies, with an undiminished disposition toward peace and friendship on honorable terms, must carry with it the good wishes of the impartial world, and the best hopes of support from an omnipotent and kind Providence."

Under a keen sense of national disgrace, a resolution was unanimously adopted, appointing a committee to inquire into the causes which led to the capture of Washington. Two days afterwards, the question came up for consideration respecting the place where Congress was to hold its session, and the government of the country be carried on. The patent office, (which was then under the post office roof,) and a few other buildings, saved at the conflagration, had been temporarily prepared for the accommodation of the members and the officers of the government. Happily for our country, we think, the proposal to return to Philadelphia, which at first equally divided the House, was rejected, on the 18th of October, by a vote of eighty-three to seventy-four; and the president himself was understood to be unfavorable to it, and determined to put his veto upon any bill for removing the seat of government from where Washington and Congress had fixed it.

One treasure destroyed by the British was the library. On the 10th of October, the offer of Mr. Jefferson, through a private letter,* to sell Congress his library, as the nucleus of a new one, was accepted by the Senate, and a bill for the purchase of it read three times, and sent to the House, read twice, and referred to a committee of the whole. For two days this purchase was debated in committee, and very instructive and even melancholy were the signs of unquenchable party hatred given by the opponents of the ex-president, in opposition to this measure. It was probably well for Congress and the country alike, that in this instance, the more numerous party could reply to their arguments by their votes; yet the bill passed after all by a majority of fourteen only, in a house of a hundred and eighteen.

1814.

New changes in the cabinet occurred at this date. General Armstrong, as we have noted, (p. 255) threw up his office in disgust at the censure which was freely poured out upon him. Mr. Monroe, on the 27th of September, took charge of the department of war,† and his office of secretary of state being soon afterwards offered to, but not accepted by, Daniel D. Tompkins, Clinton's successful rival for the governorship of New York, he held both posts till March, 1815. Campbell soon gave up the treasury, and was succeeded, on the 7th of October, by Alexander J. Dallas of Pennsylvania. And Benjamin W. Crowninshield became secretary of the navy, December 19th, William Jones having resigned.

In our estimate of the measures of this session, we must not only remember that it was the last of the thirteenth or war Congress, but also that active efforts were in progress for the negotiation of peace, the American commissioners being at Ghent awaiting the arrival of the envoys from England. And further, it deserves to be noted, that at this period the disaffection of the eastern states attained its highest pitch, and the "Hartford Convention," of which we shall speak further on, was the sign, or the menace, of something terrible in the future; possibly even a dissolution of the Union, with its portentous consequences.

1814.

The finances claim our first notice. The report presented at the beginning of the session was deplorable; the loan had failed utterly; of $6,000,000 advertised for in the preceding month, only some $2,500,000 could be obtained, and that at a loss of twenty *per cent.* Mr. Campbell "faintly suggested" increased taxation, and then retired from office. Mr. Dallas was appointed at once, and entered upon its duties with a vigor and skill little expected from his former occupation, for he had been a lawyer only, or from his powdered hair and

* See the letter of Mr. Jefferson, in Ingersoll, vol. ii., p. 266, second series. In connection with this topic, the author has some pertinent remarks on the subject of pensions, gratuities, etc., to those who have served the country in high and responsible stations.

† John Quincy Adams, in his "*Life of James Monroe*," asserts, as his conviction, that had he been appointed to this responsible post six months before, the heaviest and most disgraceful disaster of the war (the capture of Washington) would have been spared as a blotted page in the annals of our Union.

old fashioned and ostentatious dress and deportment.

Dallas did not waste time in suggesting additional taxation, but carried it. The amount of the direct tax was doubled forthwith. The excise duties, the license duties, the assessed taxes, all were raised. New internal duties were devised and imposed. The charge for postage was increased fifty per cent. And beside all this, he strongly recommended a national bank with a capital of $50,000,000, partly subscribed by the government, and placed under its control, under the obligation to advance to the government a loan of $30,000,000, as "the only efficient remedy for the disordered condition of our circulating medium, safe depository for the public treasure, and constant auxiliary to the public credit."

Mr. Eppes, with his committee of ways and means, was quite outdone by the new secretary of the treasury. Dallas's scheme of taxation drove his out of the field. For eleven days

1814.

the bank scheme was debated in the House. Mr. Webster, disdaining the vituperative language of Mr. Cyrus King and other federalists, nevertheless dealt powerful blows against the policy of the administration. "He would not give his vote for the measures proposed, either by way of expressing his approbation of the past, or his expectations for the future. On the past he looked with mixed emotions of indignation and grief; on the future, with fearful forebodings and apprehensions, relieved only by the hope that the immediate adoption of better counsels might lead to better times." Mr. Calhoun exerted his great eloquence in repelling these strictures on the administration, and in endeavoring to arouse a spirit of patriotic devotion to our country's best interests. In spite of the opposition of the federalist members, the taxes were increased, but the bank proposal failed in the secretary's hands, as similar proposals had failed in Calhoun's and Grundy's before.

Another national bank scheme was brought before the House in December, which was discussed, referred, reported on, amended, sent back to the Senate, where it had originated, and finally adopted, on the 7th of January, 1815. On the 21st of the same month, it was sent to the president, who returned the bill on the 30th, with his objections, which did not extend to the constitutionality of a bank of the United States, but to the inefficiency of the one proposed, for reviving the public credit. New debates ensued, and references, and reports, until, amid the glow of the triumph at New Orleans, and the rejoicings at the peace, the bill was postponed by a single vote, on the ground of want of time, and as not requiring attention at this particular moment. One reason for the utter failure of the bank project just now, was the difference between Mr. Dallas and Mr. Calhoun respecting the obligation to pay in specie, which the former would not make imperative, and even provided for the suspension of; whilst the latter regarded it as indispensable. The federalists, by joining with each leader against the other, helped to defeat both.

In the country at large, especially in New England, much greater excitement was occasioned by a project of Mr. Monroe for augmenting the rank and file of the regular army,—by drafts of a certain number from every hundred of the free male population between the ages of eighteen and forty-five,—to one hundred thousand men; which was the force he estimated as needful for the country in the next campaign. This was loudly denounced as a scheme of conscription, more daring than Napoleon, in the plenitude of his power, would have ventured to propose. And it caused the more stir probably, because in the rear of it the secretary of the navy intended to propose the introduction of a similar scheme for the increase of the navy.

Mr. Monroe, who was already understood to be a prominent candidate for the presidency, certainly deserved credit for proposing a plan so little likely to meet with favor from the mass of the people. His plan was rejected; and a bill authorizing the president to call out the militia of any state, if the governor refused to do so, after being carried through the House with great exertions, was lost in the Senate by one vote.

Elbridge Gerry, the vice-president, died suddenly on the 23d of November, 1814, at Washington; and John Gailliard, of South Carolina, was chosen as president of the Senate for the remainder of the session. Gerry died, we are told, honorably poor, and Congress gave him a costly interment at public expense, but refused any allowance to his distressed widow and children, when his salary would have saved them from the humiliation of want.

The further proceedings of Congress during the present session, we shall narrate in our next chapter; in which also, we shall conclude the story of the second war with England, and tell of the welcome return of peace.

APPENDIX TO CHAPTER XII.

THE BRITISH ACCOUNT OF THE INVASION OF WASHINGTON.

Mr. Gleig states, that the British troops under Ross and Cockburn numbered four thousand five hundred; they were without artillery; advanced with extreme care into the interior; were excessively fatigued with the heat and oppressive weather; and reached Bladensburg on the 24th of August. The author's narrative of what followed the battle, and of the blunders of the Americans, we give in his own words.

This battle, by which the fate of the American capital was decided, began about one o'clock in the afternoon, and lasted till four. The loss on the part of the English was severe, since, out of two-thirds of the army, which were engaged, upwards of five hundred men were killed and wounded; and what rendered it doubly severe was, that among these were numbered several officers of rank and distinction. Colonel Thornton, who commanded the light brigade, Lieutenant-Colonel Wood, commanding the eighty-fifth regiment, and Major Brown, who led the advanced guard, were all severely wounded; and General Ross himself had a horse shot under him. On the side of the Americans the slaughter was not so great. Being in possession of a strong position, they were of course less exposed in defending, than the others in storming it; and had they conducted themselves with coolness and resolution, it is not conceivable how the battle could have been won. But the fact is, that, with the exception of a party of sailors from the gun-boats, under the command of Commodore Barney, no troops could behave worse than they did. The skirmishers were driven in as soon as attacked, the first line gave way without offering the slightest resistance, and the left of the main body was broken within half an hour after it was seriously engaged. Of the sailors, however, it would be injustice not to speak in terms which their conduct merits. They were employed as gunners, and not only did they serve their guns with a quickness and precision which astonished their assailants, but they stood till some of them were actually bayoneted, with fuzes in their hands; nor was it till their leader was wounded and taken, and they saw themselves deserted on all sides by the soldiers, that they quitted the field. With respect to the British army, again, on line of distinction can be drawn. All did their duty, and none more gallantly than the rest; and though the brunt of the affair fell upon the light brigade, this was owing chiefly to the circumstance of its being at the head of the column, and perhaps also, in some degree, to its own rash impetuosity. The artillery, indeed, could do little; being unable to show itself in presence of a force so superior; but the six-pounder was nevertheless brought into action, and a corps of rockets proved of striking utility.

Our troops being worn down from fatigue, and of course as ignorant of the country as the Americans were the reverse, the pursuit could not be continued to any distance. Neither was it attended with much slaughter. Diving into the recesses of the forests, and covering themselves with riflemen, the enemy were quickly beyond our reach; and having no cavalry to scour even the high road, ten of the lightest of their guns were carried off in the flight. The defeat, however, was absolute, and the army which had been collected for the defence of Washington was scattered beyond the possibility of, at least, an immediate reunion; and as the distance from Bladensburg to that city does not exceed four miles, there appeared to be no further obstacle in the way to prevent its immediate capture.

An opportunity so favorable was not endangered by any needless delay. While the two brigades which had been engaged remained upon the field to recover their order, the third, which had formed the reserve, and was consequently unbroken, took the lead, and pushed forward at a rapid rate towards Washington.

As it was not the intention of the British government to attempt permanent conquests in this part of America, and as the general was well aware that, with a handful of men, he could not pretend to establish himself, for any length of time, in an enemy's capital, he determined to lay it under contribution, and to return quietly to the shipping. Nor was there anything unworthy of the character of a British officer in this determination. By all the customs of war, whatever public property may chance to be in a captured town, becomes, confessedly, the just spoil of the conqueror; and in thus proposing to accept a certain sum of money in lieu of that property, he was showing mercy rather than severity to the vanquished. It is true that if they chose to reject his terms he and his army would be deprived of their booty, because without some more convenient mode of transporting it than we possessed, even the portable part of the property itself could not be removed. But, on the other hand, there was no difficulty in destroying it; and thus, though we should gain nothing, the American government would lose probably to a much greater amount than if they had agreed to purchase its preservation by the money demanded.

Such being the intention of General Ross, he did not march the troops immediately into the city, but halted them upon a plain in its immediate vicinity, whilst a flag of truce was sent forward with terms. But whatever his proposal might have been, it was not so much as heard; for scarcely had the party bearing the flag entered the street, when it was fired upon from the windows of one of the houses, and the horse of the general himself, who accompanied it, killed. The indignation excited by this act throughout all ranks and classes of men in the army, was such as the nature of the case could not fail to occasion. Every thought of accommodation was instantly laid aside; the troops advanced forthwith into the town, and having first put to the sword all who were found in the house from which the shots were fired, and reduced it to ashes, they proceeded without a moment's delay to burn and destroy everything in the most distant degree connected with the government. In this general devastation were included the senate-house, the president's palace, an extensive dock-yard and arsenal, barracks for two or three thousand men, several large storehouses filled with naval and military stores, some hundreds of cannon of different descriptions, and nearly twenty thousand stand of small-arms. There were also two or three public ropewalks which shared the same fate, a fine frigate pierced for sixty guns, and just ready to be launched, several gun brigs and armed schooners, with a variety of gun-boats and small craft. The powder magazines were set on fire, and exploded with a tremendous crash, throwing down many houses in their vicinity, partly by pieces of the walls striking them, and partly by the concussion of the air; whilst quantities of shot, shell, and hand-grenades, which could not otherwise be rendered useless, were cast into the river. In destroying the cannon a method was adopted which I had never before witnessed, and which, as it was both effectual and expeditious, I cannot avoid relating. One gun of rather a small calibre was pitched upon as the executioner of the rest, and being loaded with ball and turned to the muzzles of the others, it was fired, and thus beat out their breechings. Many, however, not being mounted, could not be thus dealt with; these were spiked, and having their trunnions knocked off, were afterwards cast into the bed of the river.

All this was as it should be, and had the arm of vengeance been extended no further, there would not have been room given for so much as a whisper of disapprobation. But unfortunately it did not stop here; a noble library, several printing-offices, and all the national archives were likewise committed to the flames, which, though no doubt the property of government, might better have been spared. It is not, however, my intention to join the outcry which was raised at the time against what the Americans and their admirers were pleased to term a line of conduct at once barbarous and unprofitable. On the contrary, I conceive that too much praise cannot be given to the forbearance and humanity of the British troops, who, irritated as they had every right to be, spared, as far as possible, all private property, neither plundering nor destroying a single house in the place, except that from which the general's horse had been killed.

Whilst the third brigade was thus employed, the rest of the army, having recalled its stragglers, and removed the wounded into Bladensburg, began its march towards Washington. Though the battle came to a close by four o'clock, the sun had set before the different regiments were in a condition to move, consequently the short journey was performed in the dark. The work of destruction had also begun in the city before they quitted their ground; and the blazing of houses, ships, and stores, the report of exploding magazines, and the crash of falling roofs, informed them, as they proceeded, of what was going forward. It would be difficult to conceive a finer spectacle than that which presented itself as they approached the town. The sky was brilliantly illuminated by the different conflagrations; and a dark red light was thrown upon the road, sufficient to permit each man to view distinctly his comrade's face. Except the burning of St. Sebastian's, I do not recollect to have witnessed at any period of my life a scene more striking or more sublime.

Having advanced as far as the plain, where the reserve had previously paused, the first and second brigades halted; and forming into close column, passed the night in bivouac. At first this was agreeable enough, because the air was mild, and weariness made up for what was wanting in comfort. But towards morning a violent storm of rain, accompanied with thunder and lightning, came on, which disturbed the rest of all who were exposed to it. Yet in spite of the inconvenience arising from the shower, I cannot say that I felt disposed to grumble at the interruption, for it appeared that what I had before considered as superlatively sublime, still wanted this to render it complete. The flashes of lightning vied in brilliancy with the flames which burst from the roofs of burning houses, whilst the thunder drowned for a time the noise of crumbling walls, and was only interrupted by the occasional roar of cannon, and of large dépôts of gunpowder, as they one by one exploded.

I need scarcely observe, that the consternation of the inhabitants was complete, and that to them this was a night of terror. So confident had they been of the success of their troops, that few of them had dreamt of quitting their homes or abandoning the city; nor was it till the fugitives from the battle began to rush in, filling every place as they came with dismay, that the president himself thought of providing for his safety. That gentleman, as I was credibly informed, had gone forth in the morning with the army, and had continued among his troops till the British forces began to make their appearance. Whether the sight of his enemies cooled his courage or not I cannot say, but, according to my informant, no sooner was the glittering of our arms discernible, than he began to discover that his presence was more wanted in the senate than in the field; and having ridden through the ranks, and exhorted every man to do his duty, he hurried back to his own house, that he might prepare a feast for the entertainment of his officers, when they should return victorious. For the truth of these details I will not be answerable; but this much I know, that the feast was actually prepared, though, instead of being devoured by American officers, it went to satisfy the less delicate appetites of a party of English soldiers. When the detachment sent out to destroy Mr. Madison's house, entered his dining parlor, they found a dinner-table spread, and covers laid for forty guests. Several kinds of wine in handsome cut-glass decanters were cooling on the sideboard; plate-holders stood by the fire-place, filled with dishes and plates; knives, forks, and spoons, were arranged for immediate use; everything in short was ready for the entertainment of a ceremonious party. Such were the arrangements in the dining-room, whilst in the kitchen were others answerable to them in every respect. Spits loaded with joints of various sorts turned before the fire; pots, saucepans, and other culinary utensils stood upon the grate; and all the other requisites for an elegant and substantial repast were in the exact state which indicated that they had been lately and precipitately abandoned.

The reader will easily believe that these preparations were beheld, by a party of hungry soldiers, with no indifferent eye. An elegant dinner, even though considerably over-dressed, was a luxury to which few of them, at least for some time back, had been accustomed; and which, after the dangers and fatigues of the day, appeared peculiarly inviting. They sat down to it, therefore, not indeed in the most orderly manner, but with countenances which would not have disgraced a party of aldermen at a civic feast; and having satisfied their appetites with fewer complaints than would have probably escaped their rival gourmands, and partaken pretty freely of the wines, they finished by setting fire to the house which had so liberally entertained them.

I have said that to the inhabitants of Washington this was a night of terror and dismay. From whatever cause the confidence arose, certain it is that they expected anything rather than the arrival among them of a British army; and their consternation was proportionate to their previous feeling of security, when an event, so little anticipated, actually came to pass. The first impulse naturally prompted them to fly, and the streets were speedily crowded with soldiers and senators, men, women, and children, horses, carriages, and carts loaded with household furniture, all hastening towards a wooden bridge which crosses the Potomac. The confusion thus occasioned was terrible, and the crowd upon the bridge was such as to endanger its giving way. But Mr. Madison, as is affirmed, having escaped among the first, was no sooner safe on the opposite bank of the river, than he gave orders that the bridge should be broken down; which being obeyed, the rest were obliged to return, and to trust to the clemency of the victors.

In this manner was the night passed by both parties; and at daybreak next morning, the light brigade moved into the city, whilst the reserve fell back to a height about half a mile in the rear. Little, however, now remained to be done, because everything marked out for destruction was already consumed. Of the senate-house, the president's palace, the barracks, the dockyard, etc., nothing could be seen, except heaps of smoking ruins; and even the bridge, a noble structure upwards of a mile in length, was almost entirely demolished. There was, therefore, no further occasion to scatter the troops, and they were ac-

cordingly kept together as much as possible on the Capitol Hill. . . . .
There is no denying that the fall of Washington ought to be attributed much more to the misconduct of the Americans themselves, than to the skill or enterprise of those who effected it. Had the emergency been contemplated, and in a proper manner provided against, or had the most moderate ingenuity and courage been displayed in retarding the progress of our troops, the design, if formed at all, would have been either abandoned immediately, or must have ended in the total destruction of the invaders.

. . . .

Here, therefore, lay their principal error: had they left all clear, and permitted us to advance as far as Nottingham, then broken up the roads, and covered them with trees, it would have been impossible for us to go a step beyond. As soon as this was effected, they might have skirmished with us in front, and kept our attention alive with part of their troops, till the rest, acquainted as they doubtless were with every inch of the country, had got into our rear, and, by a similar mode of proceeding, cut off our retreat. Thus we should have been taken in a snare, from which it would have been no easy task to extricate ourselves, and might, perhaps, have been obliged in the end to surrender at discretion.

But so obvious and so natural a plan of defence they chose to reject; and determining to trust all to the fate of a battle, they were guilty of a monstrous error again. Bladensburg ought not to have been left unoccupied. The most open village, if resolutely defended, will cost many men before it falls; whereas Bladensburg, being composed of substantial brick houses, might have been maintained for hours against all our efforts. In the next place, they displayed great want of military knowledge in the disposition of both their infantry and artillery. There was not, in the whole space of their position, a single point where an enemy would be exposed to a cross fire. The troops were drawn up in three straight lines, like so many regiments upon a gala parade; whilst the guns were used as connecting links to a chain, being posted in the same order, by ones and twos, at every interval.

In maintaining themselves, likewise, when attacked, they exhibited neither skill nor resolution. Of the personal courage of the Americans there can be no doubt; they are, individually taken, as brave a nation as any in the world. But they are not soldiers; they have not the experience nor the habits of soldiers. It was the height of folly, therefore, to bring them into a situation where nothing except that experience and those habits will avail; and it is on this account that I repeat what I have already said, that the capture of Washington was more owing to the blindness of the Americans themselves than to any other cause.

CHAPTER XIII.

1814, 1815.

THE END OF THE WAR.

Naval operations — Commodore Porter's cruise — Blockaded in Valparaiso — The desperate fight with the Phœbe and Cherub — Result of the battle — The Peacock takes the Epervier — The Wasp captures the Reindeer and other vessels — The fate of the Wasp — Decatur in the President — Loss of the President, in a battle with three English ships — The Constitution captures the Cyane and Levant — The Hornet takes the Penguin — The Peacock and the Nautilus — General Jackson in command at the South — The British ships at Pensacola — Jackson's measures — Plans of the British — Lafitte and the Baratarian pirates — The attack on Fort Bowyer — Jackson marches into Florida — Takes Pensacola — Makes preparations to defend New Orleans — State of the city — Jackson's plans and measures — Arrival of the British fleet — Plans to oppose the enemy's advance to New Orleans — The gun-boats destroyed — Martial law proclaimed — Arrival of troops — The British land under General Keane — Their course — Night attack on the enemy by Jackson — Sir Edward Pakenham arrives with other troops — Jackson's ramparts — Attack by the British on the 27th and 28th of November — The battle on the 8th of January, 1815 — Fierce and bloody contest — The British defeated — Their retreat — Attack on Fort St. Philip — Jackson's difficulties in New Orleans — The state of things in New England — The Hartford Convention — Its purposes and results — How far justifiable — Negotiations for peace — Treaty agreed upon — Proceedings of Congress meanwhile — Arrival of news of peace — The president's message — Its recommendations — Measures adopted for a peace establishment — Conclusion of the fifth book.

THE operations of the present year on the water were, on the whole, gratifying to the pride which the country took in our gallant little navy. Of Commodore Porter's exploits in the Pacific, we have briefly spoken on a previous page (p. 198). We may now conclude the story of his adventures, and their result; and also tell of the various successes and misfortunes which fell to the lot of our brave seamen in contending against the superior force and numbers of British ships of war.

Porter took possession of the Island of Nouaheevah,* in the name of the United States, and called it Madison Island, in honor of the president. He had some difficulty with the native disputes and warfare, especially with the savage Typee, who endeavored to effect the expulsion of Porter and his men; but failed of course in a conflict with the marines and seamen, who burned a number of their villages. During the month of November, 1813, the Essex was thoroughly overhauled and made ready for sea. On the 12th of December, she sailed for the coast of Chili, Porter having first secured the three prizes which had accompanied him, under the guns of a battery erected for then protection, and left them in charge of Lieutenant

* See "*Journal of a Cruise made to the Pacific Ocean, by Captain David Porter, in the United States frigate Essex*," 2 vols., Philadelphia, 1815.

Gamble of the marines, with twenty-one men, and with orders to proceed to Valparaiso after a certain period.

After cruising on the coast of Chili without success, Porter reached Valparaiso, on the 12th of January, and was not without hope of signalizing his career in the Pacific with some brilliant achievement in a contest with an English ship, which, he understood, had been sent in quest of him. While at anchor in the port of Valparaiso, Commodore Hillyar, in the British
1814. frigate Phœbe, arrived, having long been searching in vain for the Essex, and almost despairing of ever meeting with her. Contrary to the expectations of Porter, however, Hillyar, beside his own frigate, was accompanied by the Cherub, sloop of war, strongly armed and manned. These ships, having been sent out expressly to seek for the Essex, were in prime order and equipment, with picked crews, and carried flags bearing the motto, "God and our country, British sailors' rights; traitors offend them." Porter, in reply, hoisted at his mizzen, "God, our country, and liberty; tyrants offend them." On entering the harbor, the Phœbe fell foul of the Essex in such wise, that she lay at the mercy of Porter, who declined taking advantage of the occurrence, although Mr. Cooper thinks that he would have been justified in so doing. While in Valparaiso, a neutral port, the crews and officers frequently interchanged civilities with their respective enemies.

The Phœbe mounted thirty long eighteens, sixteen thirty-two-pound carronades, with one howitzer, and six threes in her tops; and the Cherub mounted twenty-eight guns. The Essex at this time carried forty thirty-two-pound carronades, and six long twelves; her consort mounted twenty guns. The Essex, for several weeks attempted, by manœuvring, to bring the Phœbe into action without the Cherub; but the British captain, acting under orders most probably, was too wary to risk a conflict, in
which he must have been beaten, and he (for his part) endeavored, 1814.
by all means he could devise, to lure the Essex into an engagement with both his vessels. One dark night, Porter, having remarked that the Cherub occupied the same place for several nights before, prepared and sent out a boat expedition to capture her; but it failed; for on reaching the spot, the Cherub was not there, and the sea all round was illuminated with blue lights, so that, without a stroke given or received, the boats returned to their ship.

At length, on the 28th of March, hoping, by the superior sailing qualities of his ship, to escape from their tedious blockade, Porter endeavored to run out of the harbor, between the British vessels and the shore. Unfortunately, in doubling the headland which closes it in, he lost his maintopmast, together with several of his men, who fell into the sea and were drowned. There was no alternative now but to regain the port, or to fight both the enemy's ships, under the additional disadvantage of being crippled. Finding it impossible to get back to the common anchorage, Porter ran close into a small bay about three quarters of a mile to leeward of the battery, on the east of the harbor, and let go his anchor within pistol shot of the shore. Supposing that the British would, as formerly, respect the neutrality of the place, he considered himself secure, and thought only of repairing the damages he had sustained. The menacing approach of the enemy's ships, however, displaying their motto flags and having their jacks at all their masts' heads, soon showed Porter the real danger of his situation. With all possible dispatch, he got his ship ready for action, and endeavored to get a spring on his cable, but had not succeeded, when, a few minutes before four, P. M., the attack was begun.

At first, the Phœbe placed herself nearly astern, and the Cherub lay off Porter's starboard bow; but the latter, finding herself exposed to a hot fire, soon changed her position, and with her consort kept up a raking fire under the Essex's stern. The American frigate, being unable to bring her broadside to bear on the enemy, was obliged to rely for defence against this tremendous attack, on three long twelve-pounders, which were run out of the stern ports. These were worked with such bravery and skill, and so much injury to the enemy, as in half an hour to compel them to haul off and repair. It was evident that Commodore Hillyar meant to risk nothing from the daring courage of our countrymen; all his manœuvres were deliberate
1814. and wary; his antagonist was in his power, and his only concern was to succeed with as little loss to himself as possible. The Essex, though having suffered greatly, showed no disposition to flinch from the contest, unequal and discouraging as it was.

Having speedily repaired damages, the action was renewed; both the Phœbe and the Cherub now availing themselves of their long guns, and firing with great and destructive precision; while scarcely one of Porter's guns could be brought to bear upon them, or thrown so far as the position they had taken; and they cut down the people of the Essex with their plunging fire, and disabled her guns, almost at their pleasure. The carnage was so frightful, that one gun of the American ship saw nearly three entire crews fall round it, in the course of the action. Finding it impossible to contend successfully against his antagonists, Porter now attempted to run his vessel ashore, and set her on fire; but a sudden shift of the wind prevented it, and not only so, but brought her round so as to expose her to a raking fire, worse than she had experienced before. Twice she took fire; part of her powder exploded; she was hulled at almost every shot; until at last, seventy-five men, officers included, were all that remained for duty; and the colors were hauled down.

The Essex lost fifty-eight men killed, and sixty-six wounded; or, including the drowned and the missing, a hundred and fifty-two were lost out of two hundred and fifty-five. The British loss was only five killed, and ten wounded, but their ships were greatly cut up considering the circumstances in which they were placed. The fight lasted for two hours and a half; was witnessed with deep interest by great crowds on the shore; and for desperate valor and fearful carnage was unequalled since the days of the famous Paul Jones.

The Essex Junior was converted into a cartel, and Porter and his surviving companions were sent home on parole. Detained off New York by a British vessel, and declared a prisoner of war, Porter determined to effect his escape, and though thirty miles from land, succeeded in doing so in a whale boat, which landed him on Long Island. He was received in New York and elsewhere with great enthusiasm, as one who had brought honor to the American navy.

At home, the newly built sloops of war began to go to sea as soon as they were ready. On the 20th of April, the Frolic, eighteen, commanded by Captain Bainbridge, soon after she had got out of port, was chased by the British frigate Orpheus, of thirty-six guns; and having thrown most of her guns overboard to lighten herself, after only two shots had been fired, was captured.

1814.

The sloop of war Peacock, eighteen, Captain Warrington, sailed from New York, in March, and proceeded southwardly, cruising along the Florida shore. On the 29th of April, three sail were discovered to windward, one of which proved to be the British brig Epervier, eighteen, Captain Wales. An engagement ensued soon afterwards, and resulted, after forty-two minutes fight, in the capture of the Epervier. The British vessel suffered very greatly, and lost twenty-two men in killed and wounded. On board the Peacock, only two persons were wounded. The sum of $118,000 in specie was found in the Epervier, and some days later, notwithstanding she was chased by two frigates, the prize was brought in safety into Savannah.

The Wasp, eighteen, Captain Blakely, was one of the new sloops of war just spoken of. On the 1st of May, she sailed from Portsmouth, New Hampshire, and running across the Atlantic, appeared off the English Channel, and began to re-enact the part played there by the Argus (p. 197). Very early on the 28th of June, she fell in with the British sloop, Reindeer, eighteen also, and having in addition to her broadside of nine guns, only a shifting carronade. The British captain, nothing loth for the fight, gave chase, and the American, equally ready, hove to, for the purpose of meeting him. Soon after three, P. M., the Reindeer began to fire, and it was nearly a quarter of an hour before the Wasp could bring any guns to bear; but when she did, the spirit and activity of officers and men speedily brought the conflict to an issue. Twice or thrice the British crew attempted to board their antagonist, and were repulsed; and at last the Reindeer, cut to pieces by the heavy metal and terrible precision of the Wasp's fire, with her upper works one entire wreck, was carried by the American boarders. There were twenty-five killed, and forty-two wounded, ten of them dangerously, on board the Reindeer; the Wasp lost only five killed, and twenty-two wounded. It is very properly pointed out by Mr. Cooper, that the advantage in nearly every particular rested with the Wasp; and the bravery of Captain Manners and crew of the Reindeer, elicited well deserved commendation. The Reindeer was burned, and Captain Blakely went into L'Orient on the 8th of July.

Leaving this port at the close of August, Captain Blakely captured two merchantmen, and on the 1st of September, fell in with a fleet of ten sail, under convoy of the Armada, seventy-four, and a bomb-ship. He stood for them, and succeeded in cutting out of the squadron a brig laden with brass and iron cannon, and military stores, from Gibraltar. After taking out the prisoners and setting her on fire, he endeavored to cut out another, but was chased off by the seventy-four. The same evening, Captain Blakely descried two vessels, one on his starboard and one on his larboard bow, and hauled for that which was farthest to windward. At seven, P. M., she was discovered to be a brig of war, making signals with flags which could not be distinguished, owing to the darkness, and at twenty-nine minutes past nine, she was under the lee bow of the Wasp. An action soon after commenced, which lasted until ten o'clock, when Captain Blakely, finding his antagonist to have ceased firing, paused, and asked if he had surrendered. No answer being returned, he commenced firing again; and the enemy returned broadside for broadside for twelve minutes. Perceiving that his last two broadsides were not returned, he hailed again, and was informed that she was sinking, and that her colors were struck. She proved to be, as was subsequently learned, the Avon, eighteen, Captain Arbuthnot, and sank almost immediately afterwards.

1814.

On the 21st of September, the Wasp took the British brig Atalanta, which was put in charge of Mr. Geisenger, one of the midshipmen, and sent to America. The Wasp, at the time, was off the Madeiras, and continued her cruise; but, we are sorry to say, this is the last certain information that was had respecting this favorite vessel and her brave commander. She must have perished suddenly and entirely, in some one of those terrible gales to which vessels are exposed in the southern seas.*

The squadron under Commodore Decatur, in the harbor of New London, found it impossible to escape from the strict blockade maintained by the enemy (p. 239). The United States and Macedonian were accordingly removed up the Thames above New London, and in the month of April were dismantled. Decatur, and his officers and crew, soon after were transferred to the President, then at New York, and the gallant commodore was actively engaged in taking measures to repel an expected attack upon that important commercial city. The enemy not having made any attempt upon New York, but devoted their energies to the invasion of Washington, and to plans of conquest in the south, Decatur was at liberty to carry out the project which had been formed of a cruise in the East Indies, where, it was thought, British trade and commerce offered a fair field for enterprise and valor. The frigate President, the sloops of war, Peacock and Hornet, and two store ships, were formed into a squadron, and De-

1814.

* See Cooper's *Naval History*," vol. ii., pp. 129, 30.

catur only waited for an opportunity to get to sea.

New York being closely blockaded, Decatur determined to get out of the harbor in his flag ship alone, at the earliest moment.* Accordingly, having appointed a place of rendezvous for the other vessels, Decatur, on the 14th of January, 1815, in a severe snow storm, and a strong gale blowing off shore, weighed anchor and stood down the bay. Through a mistake of the pilot, in the darkness the President struck on the bar, where she remained beating heavily for an hour and a half. The wind rendering it impossible to return, she was forced over the bar, and obliged to proceed, notwithstanding the injuries she had received. At early dawn on the 15th, she was espied by the blockading squadron, and the Majestic, fifty-six, the Endymion, forty, and the Pomona, thirty-eight, gave chase. The Tenedos, thirty-eight, joined in the pursuit somewhat later. Decatur lightened his vessel as well as he could, and for fifty miles, along the coast of Long Island, kept ahead of his pursuers.

Late in the afternoon, the Endymion, which had gained rapidly on the President, opened a fire with her bow-chasers, which was vigorously returned by Decatur's ship from her stern guns. Meanwhile, the Majestic and Pomona fell behind out of gunshot. At length

1815. the Endymion gained so much on the President, as to permit her first broadside guns to begin to bear, and a close running fight ensued; the vessels sailing under easy way, within half-musket-shot distance. Commodore Decatur suffered so severely, especially in his rigging, under their fire, that he took the gallant resolution of laying himself alongside the Endymion, and, having scuttled the President, of carrying the enemy, by boarding. But the British captain avoided that risk, with commendable prudence, and yawing his ship, preserved the advantage she had gained by a fire at half gunshot range.

The fight continued for two hours, both vessels being skilfully handled, when the Endymion, reduced almost to a wreck, fell astern, and Decatur had some slight hope of being able to effect his escape in the night, from the other ships of the enemy. Resuming the course he had adopted in order to avoid the squadron, Decatur wished for the darkness to aid him in getting away; but he was disappointed. The clouds blew over, and a bright starlight revealed his ship to the approaching ships.

"We continued this course," says Decatur, in his official letter, under date of the 18th of January, "until eleven o'clock, when two fresh ships of the enemy (the Pomona and Tenedos) had come up. The Pomona had opened her fire on the larboard bow, within musket shot; the other, about two cables length astern, taking a raking position on our quarter; and the rest, with the exception of the Endymion, within gunshot. Thus situated, with about one-fifth of my crew killed and wounded, my ship crippled, and a more than four-fold force opposed to me, without a

* For a more full account of the sailing and loss of the President, see Mackenzie's "*Life of Stephen Decatur*," pp. 207–33.

chance of escape left, I deemed it my duty to surrender.

"It is with emotions of pride I bear testimony to the gallantry and steadiness of every officer and man I had the honor to command on this occasion; and I feel satisfied that the fact of their having beaten a force equal to themselves, in the presence and almost under the guns of so vastly superior a force, when, too, it was almost self-evident, that whatever their exertions might be, they must ultimately be captured, will be taken as evidence of what they would have performed, had the force opposed to them been in any degree equal."

The loss on board the President was twenty-five killed and sixty wounded; the Endymion's loss was only eleven killed and fourteen wounded. The President was carried to Bermuda, and subsequently sent to England, as a show. Decatur returned to New London, on the 21st of February, and, notwithstanding his misfortune, was received by his countrymen with warm and hearty admiration.

The Constitution, "Old Ironsides," Captain Stewart, sailed from Boston on the 17th of December, 1814. Having made some prizes, in the vicinity of Lisbon, Stewart discovered two ships, on the afternoon of February 20th, 1815. One of these bore up for the Constitution, but soon after changed her course to join her consort. The Constitution gave chase to both, and at six, P. M.,

1815. ranged ahead of the sternmost, brought her on the quarter and her consort on the bow, and opened a broadside. The fire was immediately returned; and exchanges of broadsides continued until both ships were envelopped in smoke. When it cleared away, the Constitution finding herself abreast of the headmost ship, Captain Stewart ordered both sides to be manned, and dropped into his former position. The fight continued with great spirit, until the ship on the Constitution's stern fell off, entirely unmanageable. Captain Stewart pursued the former ship, and very soon reduced her so completely that she could not escape. Returning to the other ship, she fired a gun to leeward to signify her surrender; and on sending an officer on board, she proved to be the Cyane, thirty-four, Captain Falcon. Captain Stewart then proceeded in pursuit of the consort of the Cyane, which surrendered after brief resistance, having five feet water in her hold. She proved to be the Levant, eighteen, Captain Douglass. The loss in killed and wounded on the two vessels, was nearly eighty; the Constitution received but little injury, and had only three killed, and twelve wounded.*

Early in March, Captain Stewart carried his prizes into Porto Praya, in the Island of St. Jago; but, on the 11th, observing a British squadron off the harbor, and having no confidence in the security of a neutral port, he got under weigh, and succeeded in bringing

* With this terminated the exploits of the gallant Constitution, or "Old Ironsides," as she was familiarly termed in the navy. Always well commanded and officered, and manned with the very best of crews, she was emphatically a "lucky ship," and performed actions that will ever live in naval story. Mr. Cooper has written a full account of this noble vessel, as a separate contribution to the History of the United States Navy.

the Cyane to the United States. The Levant was recaptured in the Portuguese harbor by the British frigates.

A few days after the capture of the President, the Hornet and the Peacock, who, as we have above stated, were destined to the Indian Ocean, contrived to get out of New York; and without being aware of the fate of Decatur's vessel, made directly for Tristan d'Acunha, the place of rendezvous, without having heard that the war had terminated. On the morning of the 23d of March, when not far to the west of the Cape of Good Hope, the Hornet met the Penguin, a British vessel of equal size and weight of metal, but a little inferior to her in the number of her crew; and after a furious conflict, in which the captain of the Penguin was slain while attempting to board the Hornet, gained a very complete victory, a third of the crew of the British vessel being killed or wounded, and the ship herself so much injured, that a day or two afterwards, she was scuttled by her captors.

1815.

Joining the Peacock, on the 25th of March, they remained at the place of rendezvous for some weeks, according to orders. About the middle of April, they sailed for the Indian seas, and on the 27th, were descried and chased by the Cornwallis, a British seventy-four. The Peacock, being a capital sailer, easily escaped; but the Hornet, having been followed for nearly two days, and receiving several shot, threw overboard every thing that could impede her sailing, and finally escaped with but one gun, and without boat, or anchor, or cable, or any part of her ship's burden that could be cast into the sea. Having made his way to San Salvador, Captain Biddle heard there of the peace, and on the 30th of July, reached New York, and received the due meed of praise for his gallantry and admirable seamanship.

The Peacock continued her cruise, and on the 30th of June, fell in with the British East India Company's cruiser, Nautilus, fourteen. Captain Warrington, having no knowledge of the peace, exchanged broadsides with his adversary, when the Nautilus struck, having had six killed and eight wounded. The next day, the Nautilus was given up, the American captain being informed of the ratification of the treaty of peace, and learning that the period set for the termination of hostilities had passed. This is Mr. Cooper's account of the matter; but it is only fair to state, that English writers accuse Captain Warrington of insisting upon the flag of the Nautilus being hauled down, notwithstanding the British commander assured him that peace had been made, and that when he was not gratified in this, he enforced obedience by a broadside.* However the exact truth may be in regard to the point in dispute, we may note, that this was the last instance

* Alison, who will not, by those who know his work, be accused of any partiality for Americans, speaks of the close of the war in these terms: "Thus terminated at sea this memorable contest, in which the English, for the first time for a century and a half, met with equal antagonists on their own element: and in recounting which, the British historian, at a loss whether to admire most the devoted heroism of his own countrymen, or the gallant bearing of their antagonists, feels almost equally warmed in narrating either side of the strife."

of hostilities between ships of England and the United States.

It was in August, 1814, as we have related on a previous page, (p. 211,) that General Jackson concluded the treaty with the Creek Indians, and directly afterwards transferred his head-quarters to Mobile. He had previously demanded of the governor of Pensacola the surrender of Francis and M'Queen, two Creek chiefs who had escaped into the Spanish territory; but had received an ambiguous and unsatisfactory reply from that functionary; Jackson, who was now in command of the seventh military district, and had
1814. about two thousand men under him at Mobile, determined to take prompt and effective measures in order to prevent the British availing themselves of Spanish help in their projects against the south.

Towards the close of the month, he received information by express, that three British vessels (the Hermes, Orpheus and Charon,) had arrived at Pensacola on the 25th, and disembarked on the following day a large quantity of arms, ammunition, munitions of war and provisions; and that between two and three hundred troops of the enemy had landed from the vessels, and marched into the Spanish fort. The express also brought information that thirteen sail of the line, with transports, having on board ten thousand troops, were daily expected at that place. General Jackson immediately addressed a letter to the governor of Tennessee, requesting him, without delay, to organize, equip, and bring into the field, the whole of the quota of the militia of that state, agreeably to the requisition of the war department of the preceding July, amounting to two thousand five hundred infantry. This request was promptly complied with; and in a short time the state's quota, and many volunteers from Tennessee and Kentucky, proceeded to put themselves under Jackson's immediate command. Several thousand men were thus got together, and with these the enemy were to be met and repulsed.

Notwithstanding the fact that negotiations were in progress for the restoration of peace, the British admiral was busily engaged in preparing to strike a heavy blow upon New Orleans, and by his directions, a system of petty marauding was kept up along the coast, and injuries of every kind inflicted upon the inhabitants and their possessions. Admiral Cochrane even issued a proclamation, in order to excite the slaves to insurrection, and promised them his aid and protection as "persons desirous to emigrate from the United States."

In carrying out his plans, the enemy made an effort to enlist the services of that horde of smugglers and pirates on the Island of Barataria, who, under Lafitte, had rendered themselves notorious for acts of daring and cruelty. But Lafitte spurned the offer of a captaincy in the British service, and refused to join the enemies of the United States in their purpose of inroad and destruction. Shortly afterwards, at the close of September, Commodore Patterson proceeded to Barataria with a sufficient force, and completely broke up the nest of pirates, captured a number of vessels, and nearly a thousand men, and dispersed the remainder.*

Disappointed in respect to the Baratarians, the British force at Pensacola determined to push forward an attack upon Mobile. It happened that a year or two before, there had been raised, at the end of a tongue of land in Mobile Bay, a redoubt, called Fort Bowyer, mounting twenty guns, and garrisoned by one hundred and sixty men. It had been erected with a view to ulterior operations, in the direction of Florida; but had been neglected as insufficient for either attack or defence. Jackson however, on assuming command of the seventh military district, discerned the use that might be made of this exposed station, to delay the advance of a hostile force against Mobile, which was only thirty miles off; and so, he placed the force above stated in it, under command of Major Lawrence.

1814.

On the 15th of September, a squadron of two sloops and two brigs appeared before Fort Bowyer; a body of soldiers, marines, and Indians, was landed to attack the fort in the rear, while the ships bombarded it from the bay. The men, we are told, composing the garrison, were not artillerists, and their means were extremely slender; nevertheless, they not only endured for three hours a bombardment from four ships of war, and a mortar battery on shore, but returned it with such hearty good will, that the enemy was glad to escape with the loss of more than two hundred men, and one of his ships, which having its cable cut by a shot, drifted so close to the fort, that its crew were compelled to desert and burn it. The American loss was only four killed and five wounded; and the effect of this successful defence against such great odds, was most excellent in nerving our countrymen to repel the enemy. Ingersoll, in a sentence which characterizes the iron-willed man of Tennessee, says, of this "campaign which began and ended at Fort Bowyer, General Jackson acted without specific, if indeed any, orders, sometimes almost against orders, performing exploits of warfare and civil administration, which paved his way to the presidency."

Discovering that the British had returned to Pensacola, on their retreat from Fort Bowyer, Jackson without any difficulty came to the conclusion, that he ought to occupy that place. He had already sent several urgent requests to the secretary of war, for permission to do so; and had at last received a reluctant consent. Accordingly, he advanced upon Pensacola with a force of about three thousand five hundred men, including some Choctaw Indians, and having reached it on the 6th of November, immediately sent a flag with a message to Manriquez, the Spanish governor. As the flag advanced, the fort opened its fire and compelled it to return. Encamping, therefore, for the night, and discovering that the place was defended by British, as well as Spanish sol-

1814.

* Two months later, when General Jackson was in want of men, the Baratarians, on a pledge of pardon, enlisted in the service of the United States, and rendered effective aid in the defence of New Orleans. On the 6th of February, 1815, the president proclaimed their full pardon.

diers, Jackson determined to storm it on the next day. On the morrow, deceiving the Spaniards as to the quarter on which he meant to attack them, three thousand men, in three columns, were marched along the beach, so as to avoid the fire of the fort and the shipping. Approaching the town, the advance of the artillery being retarded by deep sand, the middle column was ordered to charge. It advanced briskly to the attack; entering the principal street, a battery of two guns opened its fire upon it; but it was immediately carried by the Americans at the point of the bayonet; and the governor directly afterwards surrendered the town and fort unconditionally. The British, as Jackson says, in his official letter, abandoned a fort at the Barancas, seven miles below Pensacola, on the night after his arrival; and on the day after he captured the town, blew it up.

After occupying Pensacola two days, perceiving that no more annoyance was to be expected from that direction, General Jackson restored the place to the Spaniards, and returned to Mobile. Thence he proceeded westward, to arrange measures for the defence of New Orleans, which seemed to be (as in fact it was) the point against which the attack of the British was next to be directed. "There," says Ingersoll, with one of his occasional poetic outbursts, "there, like the American eagle perched, surveying the vast expanse of sea and shore, forest, morass, rivers, and lakes, of an alluvial region, anxiously watching the approach of the British lion, a Tennessee warrior, who had hardly ever encountered a regular soldier, took post." This was early in December, and the commanding general entered upon his duties with a resolute energy admirably calculated to meet the critical dangers of his position.

There was more than enough to occupy all his care; for the indolence of Flournoy, and the removal of Wilkinson to the north, before his defensive preparations had been half completed, had left the capital city of the south entirely unprotected. The magazines were empty; there was a deficiency of munitions and stores, of clothing and ammunition, and all the requisites of defensive warfare. There were no funds and no credit. The banks paid no coin, of which the rich hoarded what they had. Committees of the legislature and self-constituted committees of safety differed in their projects. All business was at a stand; all confidence was nearly annihilated.

New Orleans itself seemed wholly unable, or disinclined, to take up arms against the threatened invasion. The peculiar character of its population, in part French, in part Spanish, in part Anglo-American, with a large number of slaves; its principal occupation, trade; its wealth, bringing, as inevitable consequences, in a warm climate, wide spread profligacy and luxury;—these things were altogether unfavorable to the existence of a spirit, which would contend to the death, *pro aris et focis*, against an invading foe. Worse than all the hindrances arising from the motley population, with its various tongues, its indolence and cowardice; and from the divided counsels of its public officers, and the few of its private citizens who were not overwhelmed with despondency; there was treachery to contend against. Disaffected persons, foreigners, were in New Orleans, who discouraged the disposition (of itself faint enough) to resist the approach of the enemy; and, according to the account furnished us by one of Jackson's biographers, communicated to the enemy every species of information which could aid the invaders, and be injurious to our country. Add to this, that General Jackson was considerably worn down by disease; the city was without fortifications; military stores could not be obtained readily; the troops had not yet arrived, and might be delayed still longer; and we have something of a glimpse of the trials under which the defence of New Orleans was to be conducted.

Before he left Mobile, Jackson directed Governor Claiborne to close, as well as he could, the communications between the Mississippi and the Lakes Borgne and Ponchartrain. He issued a proclamation, summoning the free people of color, "to embody themselves and arm for the defence of the country, of which," remarks Ingersoll, "though inhabitants, they were not, and never could be, citizens;" and immediately on his arriving at New Orleans, he called, through the governor, for large gangs of slaves, the only workmen to withstand the climate, that he might erect fortifications in the marshes. These were furnished in greater numbers than he required; and gradually, there was infused into the citizens of New Orleans itself, at least, the resolution to oppose the enemy, if not the hope of doing so with success. For, intent upon increasing his forces to the numbers which he deemed necessary for making the stand he had determined on, General Jackson had admitted into his ranks the Baratarian pirates, of whom we have spoken above; and had actually released and embodied the convicts in the prison; from Lafitte, too, he procured enough pistol flints to render the flintless muskets serviceable for a time; and every class of the community received incessant and pressing intimations of what the indefatigable commander expected of it, in aid of his important undertaking.

1814.

It is not necessary here to dwell upon the many and valuable defences with which nature has surrounded New Orleans against an attack from sea; its peculiar situation; the difficult navigation of its large river; the vast lagunes, with their intercommunicating creeks and channels; and the impassable swamps which breed pestilence around it; each of these served as an obstacle to the foe, and enabled Jackson to provide against his approach. The banks of the Mississippi were fortified, so as to prevent the enemy's vessels from ascending, and a battery was erected at the Rigolets, or pass leading from Lake Borgne into Lake Ponchartrain, so as to oppose his passage in that direction. A strong battery and a garrison were placed at the mouth of the bayou St. John, which forms the chief communication from the city into Lake Ponchartrain; and a flotilla, consisting of five gunboats, a schooner, and a sloop, was stationed at the Bay of St. Louis, sixty miles to the northeast of New Orleans.

In the midst of the active preparations to meet the invaders, news reached the city, on the 9th of December, that the British squadron, consisting of thirty-five to forty sail, had appeared off Ship Island, near the Bay of St. Louis. Lieutenant Jones, the commander of
1814. the flotilla, in a day or two found the enemy's force increasing to such a degree as to render it incumbent on him to retire, and endeavor to oppose the entrance of the invaders into Lake Ponchartrain. On the 12th, the schooner Sea Horse, in the Bay of St. Louis, with public stores on board, finding it impossible to escape, was set on fire and blown up. On the morning of the 14th, the gunboats, while becalmed, were attacked, near the west end of the Malheureux Pass, by more than forty barges of the enemy, manned by over a thousand men; and after a very sanguinary contest, they were captured and destroyed. There were now only two public vessels left to dispute the passage of the British up the river; the Louisiana, sixteen, which had been bought, armed, and manned at the last moment, by offers of special bounties, and the Carolina, fourteen, commanded by Captain Patterson, who was the principal naval officer at the port.

Admirable use was made of this advance of the enemy, and his dearly bought victory, in destroying the gunboats. Every measure of defence was pushed on with redoubled speed and energy; thrilling addresses called the brave to arms, and for a season made all who read them courageous; a levy was ordered of the whole civic soldiery of the state, and the governor put himself and his militia entirely at Jackson's disposal; fortifications rose here and there; the general's eye seemed to be on each part of the work, and all moved on rapidly towards completion; even the men of Tennessee and Kentucky, keen of sight, sure of aim, unequalled in combats where the rifle was the weapon employed, were likely to arrive in season to take part in repelling the invaders of the country.

When the news of the destruction of the gunboats first reached the city, no little alarm was excited, and as the way of access to New Orleans was now open to the enemy, there were not a few disposed to temporize, and
even to propose to give up the 1814.
vain attempt to resist the veterans of the peninsula, who were rapidly approaching in such large numbers. But Andrew Jackson was not the man to yield in a crisis of this kind. Finding that the legislature were inert and ineffective, and believing it necessary to the purpose he had in view in defending the city, he proclaimed, on the 16th of December, the city and environs of New Orleans under strict martial law. Its operation, we are told by Ingersoll, a great admirer of Jackson, "was instantly excellent. All the brave and patriotic thronged to Jackson's banner. The whole of Louisiana became at once one vast camp, animated by one superior spirit, controlled by his iron will. The genius and firmness of one man constrained the prejudices and concentrated the energies of the entire chaotic community. From heterogeneous, inert, discordant, and even traitor-

ous materials, a mass of invincible force was combined, which crushed a formidable invasion."

This declaration of martial law, it may well be believed, was, with General Jackson, no empty formality. Disputes with the legislature rose even higher; honorable members could not be made to understand, that, at this particular juncture, the enemy coming every day nearer to the city, "parliamentary eloquence" was *not* the thing needed; but precisely that which Jackson could supply—adequate military skill and daring. Much pressed to inform the Senate what his plans were—he averred, that he would cut the hair off his head, if he thought it had divined his intentions; and added, rather grimly, "you may expect a warm session, if I am driven from my lines into the city!" Domiciliary visitations, in search of arms, and of any thing else that could be used for the defence of the city; the enrolment of all men capable of bearing arms; the prohibiting of any one from going abroad after nine o'clock at night, except by special permission; these measures, and others even more insupportable, did undoubtedly look very much like "despotic severity;" but martial law, it is to be remembered, includes any and every step, which appears to him who proclaims it, requisite for securing the object he has in view; and General Jackson had made up his mind to assume the responsibility, believing that, in the result, he would be held excusable for the steps he had taken in so great an emergency.

On the 23d of December, Generals Coffee and Carroll, with between three and four thousand Tennessee and Kentucky troops, arrived very opportunely, at New Orleans. Detachments of these troops were immediately posted in different directions to guard the defences of the city. On the same day, the first division of the British troops, under General Keane, effected a landing in the midst of a huge wilderness of reeds beside one arm of the Mississippi, and at once advanced towards the city. 1814.
One party of this division succeeded in capturing the whole of the most advanced American piquet, at the mouth of the bayou Bienvenu, and thus they were enabled to move forward without the least impediment. About noontime, having left the swamp for the cultivated region, they surprised another outpost, but one young man managed to escape, and was the first to announce at New Orleans the arrival of the enemy, now only some six or seven miles distant.

British writers have mooted the question, whether they might not have succeeded in capturing the city, which was then almost in sight, had they attacked it immediately. The *prestige* of their victories in the peninsula might have compensated for their want of numbers, and the subsequent course of events, both in England and America, been considerably different. Instead, however, of venturing upon such an attempt, General Keane halted his men within pistol-shot of the river, without the least pretence of concealment; and they piled their arms, and a regular bivouac was formed. Reconnoitring parties sent out in different directions brought back no tidings of an enemy in sight; and the foragers collected from every house they could enter with safety, no end of good cheer, which was partaken of by both officers and men with the greatest satisfaction and even jollity.

About half-past seven in the evening, the first interruption to this scene of careless hilarity occurred; for the momentary appearance of a few horsemen had occasioned them no concern. The watch-fires had just been replenished, and preparations were almost completed for passing the night, as comfortably as circumstances would allow, when a large vessel was observed just anchoring near the opposite bank of the river, and furling her sails very leisurely. At first, the British thought it was one of their own ships, which had made its way so far up the stream; but no answer was returned to their anxious hail. Several musket-shots were discharged at her, but without producing any reply. At length, having made fast all her sails, and brought her broadside round to bear on the foe, the word rang out on the still night, "Give them this for the honor of America!" and a deadly shower of grape was discharged amongst them;—sad premonition of the blood-stained field and mortal conflict which were before them.

Whilst the British, who had discovered that they had no means of returning the fire of the American vessel, were sheltering themselves in the best way they could from its heavy discharges of grape and round shot, on a sudden, through the densely black night, a new terror burst upon them. After no more warning than a scattered fire, at the extreme outposts, they were roused by a fearful yell, and a simultaneous discharge of musketry on almost every landward side of them. General Coffee, with his troops, was on their rear; while General Jackson in person was assailing them in front and on their left. Coffee's men impetuously rushed to the attack, and were seconded with equal ardor by the troops under Jackson. The enemy were taken by surprise, and although they soon extinguished their fires and formed, yet order was not restored before a large number had been killed or wounded. A thick fog, which arose shortly afterward, and a misunderstanding of instructions by one of the principal officers, producing some confusion in the American ranks, General Jackson called off his troops, and lay on the field that night. At four the next morning, he fell back to a position about two miles nearer the city, where the swamp and the Mississippi approached nearest to each other, and where, therefore, his line of defence would be the shortest and most tenable. General Keane reported above three hundred killed, wounded, or missing, in this night attack; the loss on the American side was about two hundred.

1814.

During the course of this conflict, and early in the following day, reinforcements arrived from the ships. There was, however, little fighting on the 24th of December, although the Louisiana had joined her consort, the Carolina, and menaced the invaders with a more destructive cannonade. Before the end of the day, the whole British force had reached the field of battle; yet, impressed with salutary fear of the

Americans, the only care of General Keane was to withdraw his men farther from the river bank, that they might be less exposed to the chance of such casualties as those of the preceding night. Next day, the real commanders of the expedition, Sir Edward Pakenham and General Gibbs, arrived. And having made themselves acquainted with the position of affairs, they suffered the men to enjoy their "merry Christmas" as well as they could, under an incessant fire from the ships; and as soon as night fell, threw up a battery opposite the Carolina, mounting nine field-pieces, two howitzers, and
1814. one mortar. At dawn, on the 27th, the battery was opened upon the Carolina with red-hot shot, and she was soon set on fire and destroyed. The Louisiana was next attacked, but after sustaining a severe fire, succeeded in escaping up the river; so that the way was now clear for an advance upon New Orleans; and the needful stores, artillery, ammunition, etc., were brought up from the ships, that the grand attack might be made without delay.

General Jackson, in the mean time, we may be sure, had not been idle. In these and the immediately following days and nights, sleepless himself, and allowing none around him to sleep, until an available position for defence had been secured, he had constructed a lengthened rampart about four miles below New Orleans, of the most formidable description for his purpose. Beside the earth, which was thrown up out of the deep ditch in front, bales or bags of cotton, brought from the city, were unsparingly used. The line extended from the Mississippi to a low swamp, about a mile off, and the ditch was filled with water nearly to the top. In the river, the Louisiana protected the right flank; and a work, mounting twenty guns, on the opposite bank, added yet more to the strength of the position. The levée, or embankment of the river, also was by Jackson's direction cut through, both above and below the position of the British, thus embarrassing their movements both in front and in the rear.

On the 28th of December, General Pakenham advanced up the levée with the intention of driving the Americans from their entrenchments; and commenced the attack, at the distance of half a mile, with rockets, bombs, and cannon. After some seven hours' fighting, the British, having been very warmly received, were glad to retire. The attempt was renewed on the first day of the new year, but although, with great secrecy, regular breaching batteries had been erected and mounted with heavy cannon, with accompanying preparations such as might have sufficed for a siege; and although, when first opened, the fire of the thirty pieces of artillery threw the Americans into some confusion, no better success attended this than the previous attack. The American loss was less than fifty: it was supposed that the enemy suffered much more severely.

Failing in these attacks, it was next suggested by Admiral Cochrane, that all hands should be 1815.
set to deepen the canal which connected the Mississippi with the bayou Bienve-

THE BATTLE OF NEW ORLEANS.

From the original Picture in the possession of the Publishers.

PAINTED BY D. M. CARTER. — Martin, Johnson & Co. Publishers, New York. — ENGRAVED BY THOS PHILLIBROWN.

nu; by which boats might be brought up to the river, and troops ferried across, to carry the battery on its right bank. This, however, proved a work of such extraordinary labor, that it was not till the evening of the 6th, that the cut was declared passable. The boats were immediately brought up, and secreted near the river, and dispositions for an assault were made at five o'clock on the morning of the 8th of January.

General Jackson, meanwhile, had completed his works on the left bank of the river. His front was a breastwork of nearly a mile long, extending from the river into the swamp, till it became impassable, and for the last two hundred yards taking a turn to the left. The whole was defended by upwards of three thousand infantry and artillerists. The ditch contained five feet water; and the ground in front, having been flooded by water introduced from the river and by frequent rains, was slippery and muddy. Eight distinct batteries were judiciously disposed, mounting in all twelve guns of different calibres. On the opposite side of the river, there was a strong battery of fifteen guns, and the entrenchments which had been erected were occupied by General Morgan, with some Louisiana militia, and a strong detachment of Kentucky troops.

The British general, on the night of the 7th, dispatched Colonel Thornton, at the head of a large force, to cross the river and carry the American works there. Having effected this, he was to give a signal of his success, and then General Gibbs and General Keane were to advance upon Jackson's entrenchments in front. Owing to delays and hindrances, the day had broken before Thornton reached the opposite shore; but bravely pushing forward, he succeeded in his object, and the troops there having fled, this important position fell into the hands of the enemy.

But Pakenham did not wait for Thornton's signal. Fearing every moment's delay, he gave the word to advance to the assault. Silently, but swiftly, through the wintry morning,—the day just beginning to dawn,—the first column advanced against the works. But they were soon perceived by our wakeful countrymen, and a heavy fire was opened upon them, which mowed them down by hundreds. For, incredible almost as the statement appears which is made by an English writer, it was found, whilst they were in the heat of the charge, that both fascines and scaling ladders had been forgotten; and on the very crest of the glacis the attacking column was forced to halt, without the means of crossing the ditch or mounting the parapet; incapable, too, of defending themselves against the storm of shot which was poured on them from those unimpregnable ramparts. A few, indeed, mounting on one another's shoulders, succeeded in entering the works; but it was only to be overpowered by numbers. One small battery, in front of the lines, was carried at the point of the bayonet. But when the captors, with desperate courage, endeavored to force their way across a single plank into the body of the works, they were repulsed with frightful slaughter, and the battery was recaptured. "It was

1815.

in vain," says Mr. Gleig, "that the most obstinate courage was displayed. They fell by the hands of men whom they absolutely did not see; for the Americans, without so much as lifting their faces above the rampart, swung their firelocks by one arm over the wall, and discharged them directly upon their heads. The whole of the guns, likewise, from the opposite bank, kept up a well directed and deadly cannonade upon the flank; and thus were they destroyed without an opportunity being given of displaying their valor, or obtaining so much as revenge."*

No wonder, that the British column, despite its brave and gallant advance, found it impossible to endure such a fire as met them, and slaughtered them by hundreds at a time. Shattered and disordered, they broke and fled. Pakenham, whose personal courage was inferior to that of none of his compeers, passionately endeavored to rally the panic-stricken and disheartened troops. Waving his hat, and calling on them to follow, he reached the edge of the ditch, —but only to fall dead in front of his men. Generals Gibbs and Keane succeeded in bringing the troops a second time to the charge; but the second approach was more fatal than the first. The continued roll of the American fire resembled peals of thunder; it was such as no troops could withstand. The advancing columns again broke; a few platoons reaching the edge of the ditch, only to meet certain destruction. An attempt was made, by their officers, to lead them to the attack a third time, but entirely without success. Generals Gibbs and Keane were carried from the field, the latter severely, the former mortally wounded. The narrow field of strife between the British and the American lines was strewed with the dead. So dreadful a carnage, considering the length of time and the numbers engaged, has seldom been recorded; for there, on that blood-stained field, lay two thousand men in dead and wounded; while of our countrymen, who dealt such terrible destruction to the invaders from behind those ramparts, there were only six killed, and seven wounded.* General Lam-

1815.

* "*The Campaigns of the British Army at Washington and New Orleans*," p. 179. British writers, we may mention, condemn the course of Pakenham as being "a series,—not of mistakes, (for that word implies the possession of some generalship, however defective,)—but of glaring proofs of the absence of every intellectual quality that enters into the composition of a military leader." Truly, hard measure for those who, like the British general, poured out their life's blood in the vain effort to gain possession of the wealth and resources of New Orleans.

* On former occasions, we have called attention to the discrepancies in the accounts of the number of troops engaged, the killed and wounded, etc., in the various battles fought during this second war with England. We have to repeat the same remark in regard to the battle of New Orleans, with the additional perplexity, that the statements made by different writers vary by thousands instead of hundreds. The numbers given in the text appear to us as nearly correct as we can get them; we may mention, in conclusion, however, that the American statement of the loss in the several engagements, is, fifty-five killed, one hundred and eighty-five wounded, and ninety-three missing; making a total of three hundred and thirty-three; the troops engaged in the battle of the 8th of January, numbered four thousand six hundred and ninety-eight. American authorities also state, in regard to the enemy, that on the 6th of January, their forces amounted to nine thousand; after that date, to twelve thousand; and that their loss in killed, wounded, and missing, was over four thousand five hundred. On the other

bert, upon whom the command now devolved, finding that it was impossible to restore the fortunes of the day, withdrew his reserve from the reach of the American artillery, and collected the wreck of the routed army. He also recalled Colonel Thornton from the other side of the river, deeming it impossible to hold that post, after the disasters to which the army had been subjected on the plains of Chalmette.

A flag of truce was dispatched by the British commander, with proposals for the burial of the dead; and a truce of two days was arranged for that purpose. Despairing of success in the object of his expedition, Lambert took immediate measures to effect a retreat from his perilous position. With great secrecy, but keeping up a menacing attitude, meanwhile, the British, during a number of days following the expiration of the truce, sent their sick and wounded on board the vessels, together with baggage and ammunition, such as could safely be spared. In the dark, through the swamps, amongst alligators, and along causeways, well nigh impassable because of the rain, the disheartened invaders shrank away; while the Americans, on their part, kept throwing shot of every kind, by night and day, into the quagmire where the enemy had sheltered himself. The whole of the field artillery, most of the ammunition, and all the stores of the invading force, were carried away on their retreat; except the siege artillery, which was already in part destroyed, and some powder barrels and piles of shot left in the useless batteries. Only eighty of the wounded were left, with an appeal to the humanity of the foe, which appeal, it is hardly necessary to say, was religiously respected by the victors.

While these operations were in progress near New Orleans, the British fleet on the coast was not inactive. It was intended that a squadron should enter the Mississippi, and, reducing the works at Fort St. Philip, ascend the river, and co-operate in the attack on the city. The bombardment of the fort commenced on the 11th of January, and was continued with more or less activity for eight days. At the end of this time, the enemy, finding they had made no serious impression, dropped down the river, and put to sea. The fort was garrisoned and bravely maintained by three hundred and sixty-six men under the command of Major Overton.

When the purpose of the enemy was fully understood, some efforts were made to annoy him on the retreat; but not to any great extent. The British troops, as Alison states, were safely re-embarked on the 27th of January, and soon after were in some degree comforted for their disasters, by the capture of Fort Bowyer, near Mobile, commanding one of the mouths of the Mississippi, before which they had been so signally repulsed, in the preceding September, as we have related, but which yielded, with its garrison of three hundred and sixty men, and twenty-two

1815.

---

hand, British writers assert, that General Jackson must have had at least twelve thousand men under him, while their effective force was less than half that number. They also state, that their total loss in this whole expedition, was four hundred killed, and less than sixteen hundred wounded and missing. These discrepancies are probably irreconcileable.

guns, to a combined attack of the land and sea forces, on the 12th of February. General Winchester was in command at Mobile at the time, and he was much censured in consequence of the loss of this fort.

Our limits do not admit of entering into details respecting the intestine difficulties and trials which followed Jackson's victory at New Orleans. His unyielding enforcement of the martial law; his ordering the French subjects in the city to retire into the interior; his arresting Mr. Louallier, a member of the legislature, as a spy, and then Judge Hall, who ventured to issue a writ of *habeas corpus*, on the charge of aiding, abetting, and exciting mutiny in his camp; his refusing to recognize the peace till officially proclaimed; his conduct when summoned before the court; his being fined and paying a fine of $1,000;* the popular excitement in consequence; these, and the like, are worthy the reader's examination, and will afford him food for profitable reflection. The local histories, and the biography of General Jackson, will furnish the amplest materials for attaining a right judgment respecting the points under consideration.

While these important operations were in progress at the south, the close of the year 1814, in New England, illustrated very forcibly the strength and tenacity of the opposition which had all along been manifested to the war, in that section of our country. As we have stated several times already, the people of New England, as a body looked with no favor upon the war, and were not disposed to yield it any countenance or support. They felt keenly the burden imposed upon them by the ruin of their commerce, the disorganized currency, the destruction of their resources, the inroads of the enemy, and the like; and when Monroe proposed the "conscription" system, as it was denominated, (p. 262,) and the British threatened to carry fire and sword into every town, and village, and hamlet, which was accessible to their ships and boats, it need cause no surprise that a popular excitement arose, and that it was thought necessary for the New England maritime states to consult upon measures absolutely called for, as they thought, by the perilous emergency.

1814.

When the legislature of Massachusetts assembled in the summer of 1814, this subject came up for discussion and action, and it was agreed, that delegates from the several states should be invited to assemble at Hartford, on the 15th day of December following, to take into consideration the state of the country, and to report to the legislatures of their respective states, such measures, as in their judgment, might lead to a redress of grievances. Connecticut and Rhode Island responded heartily to this invitation, and by considerable majorities in their legislatures, deputed delegates to meet those of

* In the year 1843, a movement was made in Congress, for refunding this fine, principal and interest; and it was carried by a vote of twenty-eight to twenty in the Senate, and a hundred and fifty-eight to twenty-eight in the House. See Ingersoll, (who made the motion in the House,) vol. ii., pp. 242–62, second series; and Benton's "*Thirty Years' View*," vol. ii., pp. 499–502.

Massachusetts. New Hampshire and Vermont, by local conventions, also sent delegates to Hartford.

On the day appointed, the members assembled; twelve from Massachusetts, seven from Connecticut, four from Rhode Island, two from New Hampshire, and one from Vermont,—twenty-six in all. George Cabot, Nathan Dane, Roger Sherman, Harrison Gray Otis, and men of the like stamp, were among the delegates. Cabot was chosen president, and Theodore Dwight secretary. For three weeks, with closed doors, the convention was occupied in its work; and the result of their consultations and labors we have in the lengthy report, the resolutions, and the secret journal of the convention, which have been published in a large volume, with much other matter, by Mr. Dwight, the secretary. The manifesto or report is quite too long to be quoted on our pages: the reader who wishes to see in full what were the grievances complained of, the motives and reasons for the resolutions which were passed, and the amendments which were proposed to be made to the Federal Constitution, must consult the documents just named.

In substance, we may mention, the amendments proposed, were such as these: the withdrawal of the right to reckon slaves, in any ratio, amongst the population in the apportionment of Representatives; the restriction of the constitutional power of Congress to admit new states into the Union;

1815.

the limitation of the power of Congress in relation to embargo, and the restriction of commerce; the restriction of the power of Congress to make war; the exclusion of foreigners, hereafter arriving in the United States, from the capacity of holding office under the government; and lastly, the limitation of the presidency to a single constitutional term, and the forbidding the election of president from the same state two terms in succession.

Having made provision for summoning another convention at Boston, if necessary, the present assemblage adjourned, *sine die*, on the 5th of January. Its resolutions, after being discussed by the legislatures of Massachusetts, Connecticut, and Rhode Island, formed the subject of communications to Congress, by commissioners, from the two first-named states. But before these commissioners could accomplish their purpose, tidings of the victory at New Orleans, and of the peace concluded at Ghent, ere that crowning triumph had been achieved, together with the unfavorable reception of them at every place out of New England, discouraged any attempt to carry out the objects of the convention to the letter; and, as it appears, they returned home, to bear the stigma of having undertaken to accomplish ends which no patriot and true American can ever sanction.

Into the question of the measure of censure justly resting upon the Hartford conventionists, it is not material or necessary to enter. Whether they were traitors, and deserved the punishment of traitors, or whether they were high souled and pure patriots, consulting only for the good and prosperity of the Union, we need not discuss. Both views have their advocates, and the student of history, having weighed carefully all the evidence which exists respecting their plans, purposes, and views, as well as their acts, will be able to judge for himself of the rank which this convention ought to hold in the estimation of every citizen of our glorious Union.*

The British government having appointed Lord Gambier, Henry Goulburn and William Adams, commissioners to negotiate a peace with the United States, they proceeded to Ghent, early in August, and entered at once into the subject in hand, with Messrs. 1814. Adams, Clay, Bayard, Gallatin, and Russell. (See pp. 225, 260.) The proceedings were, as is commonly the case, and especially in circumstances like those under which these commissioners met, tedious enough. More than once, the negotiations seemed upon the very verge of being broken off. The demands put forward by the British commissioners were undoubtedly unreasonable and exorbitant, whilst the resistance offered to them by the Americans not unnaturally appeared to the others somewhat presumptuous and vexatious. At every difference which arose between them, the British commissioners were able to consult their government without delay, and to act upon instructions adapted almost to the daily changes in the aspect of affairs; but the Americans, by reason of their remoteness from home, were under the necessity of deciding upon the spot, and on their own responsibility, all the questions which arose. Notwithstanding this great disadvantage, however, the credit of the United States was not diminished by the conduct of their envoys at Ghent; and we owe it to Mr. Clay and his able coadjutors, that the negotiations finally reached the result which was attained.

After long delays and protracted discussions, concessions having been made on both sides, and the subject of impressment having been dropped, the treaty was concluded on the 1814. 24th of December, and immediately transmitted to London and Washington. It was duly ratified and confirmed on the 17th of February, 1815, and the next day was publicly proclaimed by the authority of the president.

In the uncertainty which existed respecting the final result of the negotiations at Ghent, Congress (p. 261,) did not dare to relax its active exertions in providing for the prosecution of the war. Mr. Dallas, secretary of the treasury, presented with the new year, 1815, a sad picture of the financial distress of the Union, and proposed new taxes to supply the increasing deficit of ways and means, which made the payment of so much as the interest of the loans impossible. A new flood of treasury notes was to be emitted on the country, already inundated with that depreciated paper. Yet, the national legislature did not shrink from the measures which seemed to be requisite. Acts were

* For Mr. Ingersoll's sharp and condemnatory account of the "Hartford Convention," the measures taken by the government in sending Colonel Jessup to that city, to watch and report upon its movements, the odium which was cast upon the convention by John Quincy Adams, etc., see "*History of the Second War*," vol. ii., pp. 216–48. See also Holmes's "*Annals*," vol. ii., pp. 467–69.

passed for filling the ranks of the army; authorizing the president to accept the services of volunteers, not exceeding forty thousand men; creating a navy board of three post-captains; authorizing the purchase of twenty vessels from eight to sixteen guns; prohibiting intercourse with the enemy, under the penalty of fine and imprisonment; and the like. Happily, however, our country was spared the necessity of continuing the contest with England, and the war measures were not called into active operation.

Late on Saturday evening, February 11th, the British sloop of war Favorite, under a flag of truce, arrived at New York, and was the bearer of the treaty of peace. The whole city was soon in a state of joyous excitement, and the following Lord's Day gave fitting opportunity to thousands of pious hearts to offer their devout thanksgivings to the Prince of Peace for the happy return of that inestimable blessing. Every where the gladsome words of congratulation were offered one to another; illuminations lightened up the dark hours of the night; expresses rode with unabated speed in every direction; Peace! Peace! was the exulting cry; and the streaming banners floated on the breeze, the cannon roared, and the mirthful song was poured forth, to testify the universal joy which filled the hearts of all men, to know that the war was now at an end.

1815.

On the 20th of February, the president communicated copies of the treaty to Congress, with a message, in which he congratulated the members, and their constituents, upon the event, terminating as it did "a campaign signalized by the most brilliant successes." The peace, as he said, was "peculiarly welcome" just then. He recommended the bestowal of "testimonials of approbation and applause" upon "the gallant men, whose achievements, in every department of the military service, on the land and on the water, had so essentially contributed to the honor of the American name, and to the restoration of peace." A gradual return to a peace establishment was deemed by the president most advisable, and it was suggested, that the wisdom of Congress should "provide for the maintenance of an adequate regular force; for the gradual advancement of the naval establishment; for improving all the means of harbor defence; for adding discipline to the distinguished bravery of the militia; and for cultivating the military art, in its essential branches, under the liberal patronage of government." Commerce and navigation were also recommended to the care of Congress; and the manufactures which had sprung into existence, and had become so greatly matured, during the war, as a source of national independence and wealth, were placed under their prompt and constant guardianship. Having spoken in high terms of the measures which had been adopted for securing the public credit, the president exhorted them to use their best exertions to consolidate not only the peace with Great Britain, but also the harmony of the country; "and while we accord in grateful acknowledgments," he said, in conclusion, "for the

1815.

protection which Providence has bestowed upon us, let us never cease to inculcate obedience to the laws, and fidelity to the Union, as constituting the palladium of the national independence and prosperity."

Congress, in accordance with the president's recommendations, entered zealously upon the work before them. Less than two weeks of the session remained, and the members felt that no time was to be lost. Various acts relating to a state of war were repealed. A loan of $18,500,000 was authorized, for the purpose of retiring the outstanding and depreciated treasury paper; and $25,000,000 of notes, part of which were to be for sums under a hundred dollars, and not to bear interest,—the rest for larger amounts in the old fashion; and both kinds might be paid for taxes, etc., or funded at the option of the holder, those without interest at seven per cent., and the others at six.

Besides these matters, the army and navy had to be reduced to a peace footing. And upon this, as was naturally to be expected, some discrepancy of opinion was expressed, the military committee of the House recommending ten thousand men, as the total of the regular army in peace, which the House itself desired to reduce to six; the Senate, on the other hand, recommending fifteen thousand: and the president being in favor of twenty thousand. A compromise was effected, and ten thousand was the number finally agreed upon.

Provision was made for the progressive increase of the naval force, and a board for the conduct and control of the maritime defences of the Union, under the presidency of the secretary of the navy, was created. The Algerine cruisers, notwithstanding the severe lessons of former years, having renewed their piratical attacks upon our commerce, and made slaves of a number of citizens, war was declared against the dey of Algiers, and the president was authorized to send a squadron into the Mediterranean to chastise afresh these freebooters on the sea. **1815.** The president having been requested to recommend a day of thanksgiving for the return of peace, with its manifold blessings, on the 3d of March, Congress brought its session to a close.

At this point, we bring our narrative of the second war with England to an end; and we conclude this fifth book of our history with the greater satisfaction, inasmuch as the remaining portion of our work will be devoted to the telling of the triumphs of peace, and the progress of national prosperity, and of the increased and increasing blessings which it has pleased God so freely to bestow upon our beloved country.

Book Sixth.

FROM THE

RETURN OF PEACE IN 1815,

TO THE

END OF JOHN QUINCY ADAMS'S ADMINISTRATION.

1815—1829.

HISTORY

OF THE

UNITED STATES OF AMERICA.

CHAPTER I.

1815-1817.

CLOSE OF MADISON'S PRESIDENCY.

Return of peace — Its effect upon the community — Changes consequent upon the peace — The commercial convention and its results — The "Dartmoor massacre" — Renewal of war with Algiers — Tribute paid to the dey — His course towards Americans — The squadron sent to the Mediterranean under Decatur and Bainbridge — Decatur's prompt and efficient measures — The dey agrees to the treaty proposed — Congress in session — The president's message — Its statements and recommendations — Mr. Dallas's financial statements — The tariff arrangements — Letter of Mr. Dallas recommending a national bank — Debate on the question — The bill passed — Features of the new bank — Bill altering the mode of paying the members of Congress — Dissatisfaction — Other acts of the session — Caucus nominates candidates for president and vice-president — Monroe and Tompkins selected — Result of the election — Course adopted by the secretary of the treasury in regard to paying government dues in specie — The Bank of the United States prepares to go into operation — Congress in session — The president's last annual message — Abstract of its contents — Act for paying off the national debt — The subject of internal improvements — Calhoun's views — Bill passed, but vetoed by the president — Other proceedings of Congress — Close of Madison's official career — Remarks on his character and place in American history.

PEACE, which had come unexpectedly, but with universal welcome, was not without its trials as well as its blessings. Its effect upon the different classes of the community was very great and very various. On some it brought speedy ruin, while it raised others at once from gloomy forebodings to wealth and importance. Foreign commodities, during the last year of the war, were scarce and dear; and the great staples, cotton, tobacco, and the principal agricultural products were reduced in price almost to the lowest point. Domestic manufactures had flourished quite largely, and much capital had been invested in them; but, with the return of peace, it became evi-

1815.

dent, that American workshops could not compete with those of England, unless some protection was afforded to home manufactures. The questions which arose in connection with this topic occupied a large share of the attention of Congress and the people, and the best talent of the country was devoted to the discussion of the subject of protection, and the principles on which trade between various nations is to be conducted, in order best to attain the advantage of each and all of them. With that versatility which marks the American character, the moment the way was open, men at once gave their energies to that which promised to be the most profitable. Commerce sprang into active life, and the ocean soon became white with the canvas of our merchant ships. Cotton rose from ten to more than twenty cents the pound. Tobacco, which had no sale at more than two or three dollars the hundred weight, now brought fifteen, twenty, and even twenty-five dollars a hundred. Land increased proportionably in value, and labor was immediately in demand at high prices. Wealth began to flow in; habits of indulgence in conveniences and luxuries began to be formed; and gold, and silk, and wines, took the place, in part, of silver, and cotton, and common spirits; houses were better furnished; means of personal and social enjoyment were considerably increased; a desire for the advancement of architectural and kindred improvements began to be diffused; and, with the exception of a depreciated currency of irredeemable bank paper, the condition of our country was hopeful, promising, and full of courageous animation. We shall see, as we advance, how the results of the future sustained the hopes and aspirations of our countrymen forty years ago.

In connection with the treaty of peace, we may mention here, that Messrs. Gallatin, Clay, and Adams, after a short delay, proceeded to London, where they at once entered upon the arrangement of a commercial convention, which had been proposed, as a supplement to the peace; and that without adopting Mr. Jefferson's advice, to insist first upon the relinquishment of the claim to impress American seamen. The commissioners did, however, attempt to introduce "neutral rights" into this new negotiation; but as the British government refused to treat with them upon that basis, the commercial relations of the two countries alone were dealt with. After a tedious and not altogether pleasant or satisfactory discussion, a convention for four years was signed on the 3d of July. In substance, this convention amounted to the placing of the direct trade between the United States and Great Britain, upon a strictly reciprocal basis. But the trade with the British possessions in the East Indies, was to be carried on in American ships, directly, only with the United States; and the traffic between the United States and the British possessions beyond the Atlantic, was not to be affected by the reciprocity article; "but," as the convention said, "each party was to remain in complete possession of its rights with respect to such

1815

an intercourse,"—the meaning of which was, that the United States was not to be admitted to this branch of trade at all. At the close of the year, the convention was ratified by the president.

The "Dartmoor massacre," occurring, as it did, while the negotiations just spoken of were in progress, may properly be noticed in this place. It will be remembered, that many hundreds of American seamen had been impressed on board British vessels, in former years; when the war broke out, the larger part of these positively refused to serve against their countrymen. The result was, that the British government put them in prison in great numbers. The Dartmoor prison, some seventeen miles inland from Portsmouth, was selected; and in that gloomy place of confinement, subjected to hardships and trials not easy to describe adequately in words, these brave sons of America dragged out the weary days and nights, sustained only by the hope that the period was not far distant, when their country victorious would demand their release. It requires no effort of the imagination to conceive, that the state of feeling between the prisoners and their keepers was as bad as it could well be, and that it increased in acerbity with the progress of time and events. When it became known to the imprisoned Americans, that a treaty of peace had been concluded, and they saw and felt that they were not immediately set free, the greatest excitement prevailed amongst them. Uneasy, restless, angered, they were in a condition ready for outbreak and manifestations of feeling and sentiments not likely to prove agreeable or even tolerable to the men placed as guards over them. More than five thousand men were shut up in this prison, and, suffering many of them from the small-pox, and all of them from the cruel insolence of their keepers, collisions began to occur, and bloodshed could not be unlooked for. The prisoners became exasperated at the delays in their being released; violent language was freely indulged in; and they declared with oaths that they would make their escape by violence ere long. On the 4th of April they received no bread, which led them the next day to break into the depot for provisions, despite the efforts of the guards. On the 6th, the commander of the guards, induced by what he thought to need the summary course he adopted, in order to subdue the exasperated and excited prisoners, gave orders to the soldiers to fire upon them. Again and again was this done, and seven were killed and sixty wounded in this fearful onslaught on a crowd of unarmed men.

1815.

Messrs. Clay and Gallatin, at that time in London, engaged in negotiating the commercial convention, immediately put themselves in communication with Lord Castlereagh on this subject. Mr. Charles King on the part of the American, and Mr. Larpent on the part of the British government, were appointed commissioners to examine into the whole matter; and a complete, if not a very satisfactory, investigation of this sad affair took place. And finally, the Prince Regent communicated to Mr. Monroe his disapprobation of the conduct of the soldiers, and his desire to make a compensation to the widows and families of the sufferers; which proposition the president declined to accept. This was the "Dartmoor massacre," and, though it was not easy to forgive the outrage, we are glad to say that it led to no rupture of peaceful relations between our country and England.

While the people of the United States were rejoicing at the return of peace, with its manifold blessings, their attention was turned to the necessity of warlike measures in order to protect their rights in the Mediterranean, (p. 290.) A word or two of explanation will make it clear, how it happened that the dey of Algiers, despite the knowledge of American prowess, ventured to take measures which demanded summary retribution.

During the administration of Washington, in 1795, a treaty had been concluded with Algiers, (see vol. ii., p. 368,) and the United States had agreed to pay to the dey, as tribute for the privilege of not being molested in the Mediterranean, which he and his fellow marauders on the African coast had the insolence to claim as belonging to them, the value, in maritime stores, of $21,600 annually. Year by year, this tribute had been paid to the entire content of the dey; but in July, 1812, he was induced, not improbably by some outside pressure or influence,* to act in a very different manner. When the Alleghany arrived, loaded with the usual stores, the dey took upon him to complain of the quantity, quality, and worth of the goods sent to him; and in a passion, real or pretended, declared, that he would not receive them. He also ordered the vessel which had brought the stores to quit the port immediately, and the American consul with her, in spite of every attempt made by that officer to explain matters. A new demand was also made, which shows the dey to be an adept in the kind of cunning that enabled him to tyrannize over his own subjects with effect. The year of the Mohammedans, as our readers know, consists of three hundred and fifty-four days only, and therefore there would be a greater number of their years, in any given period, than of years computed in the usual manner. This peremptory Algerine had the assurance to insist, that the years contemplated in the agreement to send an annual tribute, were Mohammedan, not Christian, years; and that there were, in consequence, arrears of half a year's payments due to him, amounting in value to $27,000. The consul, Mr. Lear, was told, that unless he paid this immediately, he should be sent in chains to the galleys, the vessel and the stores in her should be confiscated, every American in Algiers condemned to slavery, and war declared against the United States.

* In Cooper's "*Naval History*," (vol. iii., p. 8,) there are reasons given for the belief, that British agents in Algiers had led the dey to the conviction, that the United States would be unable to maintain themselves against the overwhelming naval power of England, and hence, that he might venture with impunity, upon acts of outrage and oppression. See, also, Mackenzie's "*Life of Decatur*," pp. 260–63.

Finding that by no other means than compliance with this outrageous order he could avert the threatened penalties, the consul was compelled to get the money by borrowing it of a Jew, and by paying for the use of it, for thirty days, $6,750. But so soon as this was done, and ship, cargo, and consul were gone, the dey commenced a piratical warfare against American vessels, and captured all that he could. Mr. Madison, whose hands were filled with greater troubles, attempted, by confidential and friendly negotiation, to ransom the prisoners thus made; but the terms demanded by the insolent barbarian were so preposterous, that nothing could be done; and the war with Great Britain following immediately, the prisoners were reduced to the necessity of waiting the return of peace, before they could hope to be rescued.

When that important event occurred, the president lost no time in giving attention to this subject. He fitted out the most effective squadron that could be got together, and put Bainbridge in command. The Guerriere, Constellation, and Macedonian, all famed in combats on the sea, with six smaller ships of war, were dispatched on the 20th of May, to the Mediterranean, in advance, under Commodore Decatur. In little more than three weeks his squadron was at Gibraltar, and there received intelligence which induced him to proceed at once against the enemy.

1815.

On the 17th of June, he fell in with the Massouda, forty-six, commanded by Rais Hammida, once a Berber chief, now a famous corsair captain, and admiral of the dey's fleet. A running fight of twenty-five minutes ensued, and at the end of it the Algerine struck to the Guerriere. Hammida was cut in two by a chain-shot, at the first broadside; and at the second, the pirates, not relishing such sharp shot, left their quarters and ran below, in fact, abandoning the ship to her fate. Dispatching his prize to Carthagena, Decatur continued his search, and two days afterwards came up with a brig of twenty-two guns, which, after a chase of three hours, ran into shoal water off the Spanish coast, and was there attacked and captured by the Epervier and other small vessels.

On the 28th of June, the squadron proceeded to Algiers, both to intercept the rest of the dey's fleet, and to open communications with him as soon as possible. Taking a position out of reach of their guns, Decatur, by a signal, invited the Swedish consul on board. With him came the captain of the port, and the terms proposed, as the basis of a treaty, were the absolute and unqualified relinquishment of all claims to tribute from the United States. The Algerine rejected this proposal quite scornfully, until he was assured of the destruction of the two ships, and the death of the admiral. When he found, to his amazement, that Decatur was in a condition to enforce whatever terms he pleased, after offering fruitless objections to some of the articles in the draft produced, the negotiation was closed. All the American captives were released, and the treaty was executed in three hours afterwards, to the satisfaction of the dey, as it proved, for another of the Algerine vessels hove in sight during the interval, and a single hour's delay would have been repaid by its capture. "Tribute renounced for ever," says Ingersoll, "prisoners emancipated, compensation for whatever losses were stated, together with stipulations for humanities of international law, were the terms of this treaty, which served as a model to similar conditions, soon afterwards submitted to, unresistingly, by Tunis and Tripoli."

Decatur, with considerate policy, restored to the dey the two captured vessels, and, before proceeding further, determined to dispatch one of the smaller ships to the United States with the news of his success. The Epervier was selected, and she departed, but was never seen or heard of, after passing Gibraltar on the 12th of July. Early this month, Decatur left Algiers, and on the 25th, arrived with his squadron in the Bay of Tunis.

1815.

Having learned that two American prizes, during the late war, had been taken out of that port, and carried off by a British cruiser, in despite of neutral rights and treaty stipulations, and that other injuries to the United States had been allowed, Decatur demanded and procured instant satisfaction for the insults, and full restoration of the property. On the 5th of August, Decatur arrived at Tripoli, the pacha of which had permitted two American vessels to be taken under the guns of his castle, and had refused protection to an American cruiser within his jurisdiction. For these wrongs, in like manner, full compensation was demanded and given, and the chivalrous Decatur had the additional satisfaction at both these places, of being able to effect the liberation of Neapolitan and Danish subjects doomed to hopeless servitude.

Commodore Bainbridge, in the Independence, seventy-four, and with other ships, arrived not long after Decatur's prompt and decisive measures had taken effect; and finding that every thing required by the honor and the interest of the United States had been accomplished, he left part of his force to winter in the Mediterranean, and in October, returned home, where he found Decatur, who had arrived at New York on the 12th of November.

The first session of the fourteenth Congress was begun at Washington, on the 4th of December. The federalists had gained strength in the Senate, but the administration party was active and efficient in carrying forward the plans and purposes of Mr. Madison and his supporters. In the House, the democratic majority was a little increased, and amounted to fifty-two over the federalists; but the absence of any inducement to organize an opposition, owing to the return of peace, was of greater advantage than the numerical strength of the party. Gaillard was once more elected president of the Senate, *pro tempore;* and Henry Clay, by eighty-seven votes against thirty-two, divided amongst four candidates, was placed, for the third time, in the speaker's chair.

The president's message spoke first of the war which had broken out anew with the Algerines; of the treaty of Ghent and the convention on the subject of commerce which appropriately followed it; and of the wars and treaties with the Indians. It next 1815. requested "legislative aid" in "the execution of the act for fixing the military peace establishment;" and thence passed to the satisfactory "revival of the public credit;" although, it must be confessed, the financial statement was sufficiently disheartening.

During the first nine months of the current year, $12,500,000 were received at the treasury from all branches of the revenue; $14,000,000 of treasury notes were issued; and a loan of $9,000,000 (six in cash, and three in treasury paper) was subscribed. In addition to all which, there were $1,500,000 in the treasury to begin with. There had been paid in the same period, "exclusively of the amount of treasury notes subscribed to the loan, and of the amount redeemed in the payment of duties and taxes," $33,500,000; so that there were $3,000,000 in hand. It was also estimated, that "existing ways and means" would sufficiently provide for certain arrearages, interest on the debt, and other expenditures needful before the end of the year. The amount of the debt,—consisting of the unredeemed balance of the former debt, $39,000,000, the funded debt arising from the recent war, $64,000,000, and the unfunded and floating debt, $17,000,000,—might be set down as $120,000,000; which might perhaps be a little increased; but the floating part of which was in process of payment. This would, as the president suggested, point out the chief subject for the deliberation of the session; and "the probable operation of a national bank" was mentioned as one expedient to be considered.

The national defences, the militia, and the navy, were spoken of as requiring the attention of Congress. And "reciprocity" and "protection" were urged as the principles which ought to determine the legislation regarding the tariff. Internal improvement and a national university were also recommended; and the goodness and mercy of God's providence were properly, and in a Christian-like manner, urged upon the notice of Congress and the country at large.

The financial statement of Mr. Dallas, the secretary of the treasury, went over the same ground as the president's message, but more fully and distinctly; recommending definite measures, where the message had only indicated topics for consideration. Especially it counselled the reduction of the direct tax by one half, and the retention of the duty on stamps, and of that on refined sugars; whilst other taxes were marked for abolition or for reduction. Above all, it proposed the establishment of a national bank. 1815.

The able financier, who was at the head of the treasury department, was of opinion, that, whilst inconvenient and unproductive taxes should be repealed, and every impediment removed which might retard the progress of domestic manufactures, a permanent system of internal duties should be set up; and he calculated that an increasing income might be obtained from that source, which at the outset could not be less than some $7,000,000. From imports he reckoned upon receiving nearly $20,000,000 yearly.

Mr. Lowndes, who was chairman of the committee of ways and means, reported strongly in favor of such an arrangement of the revenue system as would provide for the rapid extinction of the public debt. In respect to the sources, the report advised that duties on imports should be principally, but not exclusively, relied on; and that the scale should be regulated so as to discourage no branch of national productiveness, and not to make evasion of payment desirable. Mr. Clay contended, that "in time of peace, we should look to foreign importations as the chief source of revenue; and that in war, when they were cut off, it was time enough to draw deeply on our internal resources." Mr. Calhoun was of opinion, that "the financial resources of the nation would daily become weaker and weaker, instead of growing with its growth, if we did not resort to other objects than our foreign commerce for taxation." The result of the discussion was, the adoption substantially of Mr. Dallas's plan of a moderately productive tariff.

In regard to the proposed national bank, we cannot do better than quote the passage referring to that subject in the secretary's report. "The establishment of a national bank," said Mr. Dallas, "is regarded as the best, and perhaps the only adequate resource, to relieve the country and the government from the present embarrassment. Authorized to issue notes which will be received in all payments to the United States, the circulation of its issues will be co-extensive with the Union; and there will exist a constant demand, leaving a just proportion to the annual amount of the duties and taxes to be collected, independent of the general circulation for commercial and social purposes. A national bank will, therefore, possess the means and the opportunity of supplying a circulating medium, of equal use and value in every state, and in every district of every state. Established by the authority of the United States; accredited by the government to the whole amount of its notes in circulation; and intrusted, as the depository of the government, with all the accumulations of the public treasure; the national bank, independently of its immediate capital, will enjoy every recommendation which can merit and secure the confidence of the public. Organized upon principles of responsibility, but of independence, the national bank will be retained within its legitimate sphere of action, without just apprehension from the misconduct of its directors, or from the encroachments of the government. Eminent in its resources, and in its example, the national bank will conciliate and lead the state banks in all that is necessary for the restoration of credit, public and private. And acting upon a compound capital, partly stock and partly of gold and silver, the national bank will be the ready instrument to enhance the value of the public securities, and to restore the currency of the national coin."

1816.

The proposition of Mr. Dallas was referred to a committee on the currency, of which Mr. Calhoun was chairman; and soon afterwards, early in January, the scheme of the secretary, as contained in an elaborate letter to the committee, was reported by its chairman without change, to the House. The federalists, singularly enough as it seems, opposed the bank scheme, and such men as Pickering and Webster were among its sturdiest opponents. Henry Clay, who, some years before, (see p. 128,) had distinguished himself as an opponent of the bank, now became an advocate for its establishment; and he and John C. Calhoun exerted themselves, with great energy, towards obtaining the approbation of Congress for this important measure.

Our limits do not admit of details in respect to the earnest and able debates on this litigated topic; we must refer the reader to Mr. Benton's carefully prepared volumes, containing an abridgment of the debates in Congress. The various and weighty reasons urged on either and both sides of this question, are well worthy of study, especially in view of what has occurred at a later date in connection with the financial condition and arrangements of the government of our country.

On the 14th of March, the bill passed the House of Representatives, by a vote of eighty to seventy-one; and on the 3d of April, was approved by the Senate, by a vote of twenty-two to twelve. The president, notwithstanding his course on a previous occasion, (see p. 261,) gave his approval to the bill, on the 10th of April; and the Bank of the United States thenceforward entered upon its career, whether for good or evil remains to be seen.

The principal features of the new bank were as follows. Its charter was extended to twenty years. Its capital was fixed at $35,000,000, one fifth of which the government was to subscribe: the rest, in $100 shares, was to consist of gold and silver to the extent of a quarter, and the other three quarters of funded debt. The subscriptions of every kind were made payable in four instalments, and as soon as the first instalment was paid, the bank was to be organized and operations were to be commenced. The location of the bank was to be at Philadelphia, but branches might be established in the states by the directors, to be under the control of thirteen persons appointed by the directors. The management of the institution was vested in a board of twenty-five directors, one fifth appointed by the government, the rest elected yearly by the stockholders, some being changed at each election, on the principle of rotation. The directors were to choose one of their number as president, annually; but resident citizens alone were eligible as directors. Its notes were made receivable in all payments to the United States; and it was to hold the public money, and in return, to transmit and pay the public money without any kind of charge. Specie payments were not to be suspended, unless by the authority of Congress, or of the president of the United States; and $1,500,000 were to be paid in instalments at the end of two, three, and four years, as a bonus for the charter of the bank.

1816.

A bill, altering the mode of paying the members of Congress, was passed near the close of the session, and excited not only unusual interest, but a considerable amount of popular clamor. Instead of the six dollars per day, which they had been receiving, they now voted themselves a salary of $1,500 per annum, whether the session was long or short. We may mention here, that so much dissatisfaction was manifested in the community on account of this proceeding, that at the next session, the law was repealed by a large majority, and eight dollars per day was substituted, as, on the whole, most equitable, and likely to be productive of the best result.

In addition to what we have stated above, respecting the action of Congress during the present session, there were also large appropriations voted for the increase and efficiency of the army and navy, and for coast and harbor defences; for the purchase of custom houses at some of the great ports; for the repair of the Capitol
1816. and public buildings at Washington; for the reward of the crews of some vessels which had fought well in the late war; for the pensioning of invalid soldiers, and the families of those who had fallen in battle, etc. The question of ratifying the commercial convention with England came up, early in the session, and the old dispute was revived, of which we have spoken in giving an account of Mr. Jay's treaty. (See vol. ii., p. 372.) Considerable difference of opinion prevailed between the Senate and the House as to the proper method of giving effect to the reciprocity clause of the convention; the debate was conducted with great ability on both sides; and the matter was finally compromised by passing an act, simply declaring that the discriminating duties were repealed. At the end of December, 1815, the president sent in the long and important correspondence between the Spanish minister and Mr. Monroe, the secretary of state; a month later, papers were communicated respecting the Dartmoor massacre (p. 295); in March, Mr. Randolph obtained the passage of a resolution intended to free the District of Columbia from the disgrace of being a depot for the slave trade of the neighboring states; and on the 30th of April, Congress adjourned.

Before the adjournment of Congress, a caucus of the republican members was held, for the purpose of agreeing upon a candidate for president, it being understood, that Mr. Madison purposed following the example of his predecessor, and retiring to private life. The predominance of Virginia was still evident, and there was no serious opposition to James Monroe being put in nomination for the highest office in the people's gift.* A portion of the democracy, it is true, was desirous of elevating a New York man, Daniel D. Tompkins, to the presidential chair, but, wisely for his interests, withdrew his name, when it was offered to make him the candidate for vice-president. Others of the party, who disliked the rule of the Old Dominion, named Wil-

* Aaron Burr, writing to his son-in-law, Allston, in November, 1815, urged him to anticipate the dictation of Virginia, and to free the states from her tyranny, by securing a nomination for Andrew Jackson, a scheme which Burr regarded as certain of success.

liam H. Crawford, of Georgia, and Simon Snyder, of Pennsylvania, as candidates, in place of Monroe and Tompkins, and the caucus balloted on their respective claims, in spite of a motion to declare such nomination of members of Congress inexpedient. Sixty-five voted for Monroe, and for Crawford only fifty-four; Tompkins received eighty-five votes, Snyder only thirty; Monroe and Tompkins were, therefore, the accredited candidates of the party. The federalists, although there was no hope of their being able to elect their candidate, named Rufus King again, for president, and left the electors to fix upon whom they pleased for vice-president.

The election was held in the autumn, and resulted as follows:—for Monroe and Tompkins, New Hampshire, Vermont, Rhode Island, New York, New Jersey, Pennsylvania, Maryland, Virginia, the Carolinas, Georgia, Louisiana, Tennessee, Kentucky, Ohio, and Indiana, voted entire; and each received a hundred and eighty-three votes. Rufus King received all the votes of Massachusetts, Connecticut, and Delaware—thirty-four. Massachusetts bestowed its twenty-two votes on John E. Howard for the vice-presidency; Connecticut, five of its votes on James Ross, and four on John Marshall; and Delaware, its three upon R. G. Harper. And there were three vacancies in the electoral college of Maryland, and one in that of Delaware.

One of the principal objects of those who favored the establishment of a national bank was, to compel the state banks to resume specie payments, which, it will be remembered, all south of New York had suspended; and a resolution was passed by Congress, directing the secretary of the treasury to adopt such measures as, in his judgment, were necessary to secure the important end had in view. He was to cause all payments to the United States to be made in specie, in treasury notes, or in notes of specie paying banks; and it was declared, that, after the 20th of February, 1817, no payments to the United States ought to be made in any other currency. In July, the
secretary of the treasury gave **1816.**
notice, that, after the first day of October, no bills of any bank which did not pay specie for all notes of five dollars and under, would be received in discharge of government dues; and that, after the 20th of February next, no bills of any bank would be received, which did not pay all its notes in specie on demand. The banks resisted this regulation, and endeavored to put off the resumption of specie payments for another year; but the secretary of the treasury urged forward as rapidly as possible, the putting the United States Bank into operation, so as to furnish a sound circulating medium, and a safe place of deposit for the national treasure.

The books of subscription to the capital stock had been opened early in the spring, and it was found, by the returns received in August, that shares amounting to more than $3,000,000 had not been taken. Stephen Girard, of Philadelphia, immediately filled up the deficient subscription, and it was determined to commence operations, if possible, on the 1st of January, 1817. For immediate use, an agent was sent to England to obtain $5,000,000 in specie, on account of the bank.

The second session of the fourteenth Congress was commenced on the 2d of December, and the next day the president sent in his eighth and last annual message. It is a long and interesting document, and abounds in evidences of the earnest patriotism of the man who, for eight years past, had been called upon to administer the government of our beloved country. He adverts, in the opening of his message, to some unfavorable circumstances, as the partial failure of the crops, the depression of the manufactures of the country, the languishing of navigation, etc. Foreign affairs were generally in a quiet condition, and the Indian tribes were gradually improving in progress towards civilization. The organization of the militia, the establishment of a uniform system of weights and measures, the erection of a national university, an amendment of the law in relation to criminal trials, the prevention of the African slave trade, and a proposal to remodify the federal judiciary, and to add another department to the executive branch of government, were all touched upon in succession.

1816.

In respect to the finances, the president expressed his gratification to find, that even within the short period which had elapsed since the return of peace, the revenue had far exceeded all the current demands upon the treasury; so that an ample fund for the extinction of the debt was afforded, even though, through the vicissitudes of commerce, any diminution should occur in its future annual product. Exclusive of loans and treasury notes, it was calculated that the actual receipts, including the balance in hand at the commencement of the year, amounted to about $47,000,000. The total of actual payments was about $38,000,000; so that there was a surplus of some $9,000,000. The condition of the national currency was pointed out as the main source of the difficulties which obstructed the operations of the treasury. Yet there was hope in that quarter; for the Bank of the United States had been organized under most favorable auspices, and could scarcely fail to be a most important auxiliary. The floating debt, it was expected, would soon be entirely discharged. The funded debt had been estimated at a sum not exceeding $110,000,000. The ordinary annual expenses were reckoned at under $20,000,000; and the permanent revenue, from all sources, at about $25,000,000. For other favorable circumstances connected with the financial position of affairs, reference was made to the statement of the secretary of the treasury.

Conscious that his term of office was now nearly closed, the president alludes, in grateful language, to the confidence reposed in him by his country; eulogizes the Constitution by which our liberties are secured; and, reading in the character of the American people their devotion to true liberty, and their determination to support "a government whose conduct, within and without, shall bespeak the most noble of all ambitions—that of promoting peace on earth and good will to man,"

1816.

he concludes his message by saying; "these contemplations, sweetening the remnant of my days, will animate my prayers for the happiness of my beloved country, and a perpetuity of the institutions under which it is enjoyed."

Congress, sincerely anxious to discharge the weighty duties imposed upon them, seconded the views of the president, and entered zealously upon their work. One act of great moment was passed, as it provided for the paying off of the national debt by annual instalments of $10,000,000. For the debt, in fact, exceeded $120,000,000, and neither could Mr. Madison, nor could any one who had borne a part in the management of affairs when it was contracted, properly leave office without making some provision for its ultimate extinction. But it appears to have been chiefly by the exertions of William Lowndes, chairman of the committee of ways and means, that this act was carried successfully through Congress.

The subject of internal improvements again gave rise to animated debates in Congress. On motion of John C. Calhoun, in December, 1816, a resolution was proposed, directing the appointment of a committee to inquire into the desirableness of setting apart the *bonus* and net annual profits in the form of dividends, of the national bank, as a permanent fund for internal improvements. This being adopted by the House, there resulted, on the 23d, a bill constructed for the purpose of securing that end. It was fully considered in a committee of the whole, early in February, 1817, and slightly amended, mainly by the influence of Mr. Pickering. In the Senate, after it had passed the House, it was further amended, and the amendment was accepted by the House. It passed finally on the 8th of February.

Mr. Calhoun's view of the question was large and clear, and expressed in his most masterly manner. The value of a well-arranged system of internal communications by road and water; the magnitude of some of the most desirable works of both kinds; the facility with which private and state enterprise could harmonize with, and supplement the undertakings of Congress; the addition to the sum of national wealth made by increasing the accessibility of the ports and markets for the producers; the additional tax-paying power of the country in consequence; the tendency to promote the stability of the Union;—were all urged as preliminary considerations to the discussion of the constitutionality of the proposal. And its entire accordance with the charter of our Union, interpreted by "plain good sense," he stoutly and intelligently maintained; urging the purchase of Louisiana, and the construction of the Cumberland road, as precedents for the views he advocated.* Henry Clay's speech in favor of the bill repeated Calhoun's arguments, and urged others which produced their effect upon the House.

The president, however, on the last day of his official career, returned the

* For Calhoun's speech on this topic, see "*American Eloquence*," by Frank Moore, vol. ii., pp. 479–82.

bill to Congress, with his objections to its becoming a law, principally on the ground that there was no *express* power granted by the Constitution to make roads and canals. An attempt was made to pass the bill by the constitutional two-thirds vote, but it failed, and the bill was consequently lost.

1817.

The navigation laws were revised during this short session, and made more conformable to the protective policy which was now in favor in the United States. Acts were passed regulating the territories of the United States, confirming to them the privilege of sending each a delegate to Congress, to take part in the debates of the House, but not to vote; fixing the peace establishment of the marine corps at eight hundred men, including officers; providing for the relief of persons imprisoned for debt; determining the erection of the territory of Alabama; for punishing crimes committed in the Indian lands; and for other important national objects. On the 11th of December, 1816, Indiana, having formed a constitution in conformity to the act of Congress, was admitted into the Union. An act was also passed at this session, authorizing the inhabitants of the western part of Mississippi to form a constitution, preparatory to admission into the Union as a state.

On the 3d of March, the fourteenth Congress reached its termination. On the same day also, James Madison, not unwillingly, laid down the office with which he had been entrusted for the preceding eight eventful years.

1817.

Of his ability and character, the reader has had abundant opportunity of judging from what we have narrated respecting his administration. That he was a man of undoubted patriotism, and sincerely devoted to the best interests of his country, cannot be questioned; but it is not to be denied, on the other hand, that he was not a man of genius or commanding talent, and was hardly at all adapted to the taking the helm of state in the stormy period of war and its attendant trials and commotions. Though censured with being deficient in energy; though no hero; though disposed to yield too much to others on various occasions; though far better fitted for the duties of peace than of war; yet his administration was, to a great extent, successful, and clearly met the approbation of the majority of the people. He enjoyed a large share of the confidence of Americans in the day when he presided over the destinies of our country, and that confidence in his wisdom, integrity, and patriotism has not been diminished by the lapse of time, or the searching investigation to which his life and career have been subjected.*

* The reader who wishes to see what eloquent words have been uttered by an appreciative mind, respecting the fourth president of the United States, may consult to advantage the Eulogy delivered by John Quincy Adams, before the two Houses of Congress, in 1836, soon after Mr. Madison's death.

CHAPTER II.

1817-1819.

MONROE'S FIRST TWO YEARS.

The fifth president enters upon his administration — His Inaugural address — Mr. Monroe's cabinet — Political principles of his administration — The president's tour through the eastern, middle, and western states — First session of the fifteenth Congress — The message of the president — Abstract of its contents — Debates in Congress — Abolition of internal taxes — State of the country — Tariff arrangements — Internal improvements — Discussion of the subject — Measures proposed — Amelia Island and Galveston — M'Gregor and Aury, and their proceedings — Expelled by the United States forces — Mississippi admitted into the Union — Treaties with the Indians — The Seminole war — General Gaines's orders — General Jackson in command — Marches into Florida — Arbuthnot and Ambrister — Their trial and execution —Jackson marches to Pensacola — The Spanish authority abolished — Excitement in consequence of Jackson's course — Congress again in session — The president's message — The Bank of the United States complained of — Committee of inquiry appointed — Result of their investigation — Speculations and frauds — New president and directors appointed — Return of confidence — Action in Congress respecting General Jackson and the Seminole war — Debates and result — Illinois admitted into the Union — Question on admission of Alabama and Missouri— Former admitted, latter not — Calhoun's report on roads, canals, etc. — Treaty with Spain, and cession of Florida to the United States — Claims for indemnity on European governments — Pressed, but evaded and refused.

It was on the 4th day of March, 1817, that James Monroe, with a large concourse of friends and fellow-citizens, proceeded to the capitol, and went through the imposing ceremony of inauguration, as the fifth president of the United States. Mr. Madison graced the scene by his presence, and the judges of the supreme court, foreign ministers, and other dignitaries, were there as spectators and witnesses of the pledges which the new president was about to give of his devotion to his country's interests and welfare. His Inaugural address was unusually long; and we regret that our limits do not admit of quoting it in full. It is a calm, clear, and earnest exposition of the principles on which the new president meant to proceed in the discharge of the duties of his position. A paragraph or two, in conclusion, may not inaptly be quoted.

1817.

"It is particularly gratifying to me, to enter on the discharge of these duties, at a time when the United States are blessed with peace. It is a state most consistent with their prosperity and happiness. It will be my sincere desire to preserve it, so far as depends on the executive, on just principles with all nations, claiming nothing unreasonable of any, and rendering to each what is its due.

"Equally gratifying is it, to witness the increased harmony of opinion which pervades our Union. Discord does not belong to our system. Union is recommended, as well by the free and benign principles of our government, extending its blessings to every individual, as by the other eminent advantages attending it. The American people have encountered together great dangers, and sustained severe trials with success. They constitute one great family with a common interest. Experience has enlightened us on some questions of essential importance to the country. The progress has been slow, dictated by a just reflection, and faithful regard to every interest connected with it. To promote this harmony, in accord with the principles of our republican government, and in a manner to give them the most complete effect, and to advance in all other respects the best interests of our Union, will be the object of my constant and zealous exertions.

"Never did a government commence under auspices so favorable, nor ever was success so complete. If we look to the history of other nations, ancient and modern, we find no example of a growth so rapid, so gigantic; of a people so prosperous and happy. In contemplating what we have still to perform, the heart of every citizen must expand with joy when he reflects how near our government has approached to

1817.

perfection; that in respect to it we have no essential improvement to make; that the great object is to preserve it in the essential principles and features which characterize it, and that is to be done by preserving the virtue and enlightening the minds of the people; and, as a security against foreign dangers, to adopt such arrangements as are indispensable to the support of our independence, our rights, and liberties. If we persevere in the career in which we have advanced so far, and in the path already traced, we cannot fail, by the favor of a gracious Providence, to attain the high destiny which seems to await us.

"In the administration of the illustrious men who have preceded me in this high station, with some of whom I have been connected by the closest ties from early life, examples are presented, which will always be found highly instructive, and useful to their successors.

"From these I shall endeavor to derive all the advantages which they may afford. Of my immediate predecessor, under whom so important a portion of this great and successful experiment has been made, I shall be pardoned for expressing my earnest wishes that he may long enjoy, in his retirement, the affections of a grateful country, the best reward of exalted talents, and the most faithful and meritorious services. Relying on the aid to be derived from the other departments of the government, I enter on the trust to which I have been called by the suffrages of my fellow-citizens, with my fervent prayers to the Almighty, that He will be graciously pleased to continue to us that protection, which He has already so conspicuously displayed in our favor."

The president then took the oath of office, and immediately sent in to the Senate the names of the gentlemen whom he had selected as his cabinet. John Quincy Adams, recalled from his post at London, was made secretary of state. William H. Crawford, who had formerly represented the United States at Paris, took the place left vacant by Mr. Dallas's death. Crowninshield was continued at the head of the navy department, and Meigs as postmaster-general. The office of secretary of war was offered to governor Shelby of Kentucky; but he considered himself too old for its duties, and no appointment was made till the end of the year, when Calhoun accepted it. The attorney-generalship was held by Mr. Rush until December, when William Wirt was appointed as his successor. In these, as well as other appointments, Mr. Monroe had an eye to the republican character and principles of the persons chosen to office. The federalists, of course, had nothing to hope for from the new president; and, notwithstanding General Jackson's letter to Mr. Monroe, urging him to put aside all party feeling and party considerations, and to select men for their character, integrity, and fitness, no matter what might be their political sentiments, he was too astute, and too well aware of the inexpediency of such schemes to make the attempt. His answer to Jackson's letter is quite worthy of perusal in this connection.

1817.

Soon after his inauguration, the president determined to make a tour of inspection and observation through the eastern, middle, and western states. He was desirous of becoming acquainted with the strength of the various fortified places along the Atlantic coast; of removing such works as were constructed in improper situations; of selecting new points for the erection of strong and sufficient batteries against invasion; and of posting the regular forces where they would be able to act, in case of need, speedily and effectively. Nor was he less moved to undertake this journey, by his desire to become acquainted with the people and learn their wants, to ascertain how the machinery of government, remote from the central power, performed its functions, and to inform himself in regard to the resources of the country, and the means necessary to develope them. He also intimated publicly, that a regard to the economical expenditure of the national funds, appropriated by Congress to the construction of the coast defences, induced him to make this tour.

Mr. Monroe passed through Baltimore, Philadelphia, New York, the chief towns in Connecticut, and Rhode Island, and reached Boston on the 2d of July. Thence, traversing a large part of Massachusetts, Maine, New Hampshire, and Vermont, he turned his face westward, and inspecting the works on Lake Ontario, he proceeded to Detroit by way of Lake Erie. From Detroit he travelled through parts of Michigan, Ohio, Pennsylvania, and Maryland, and returned to Washington on the 18th of September, having been absent three months and a half, and having performed a journey of more than two thousand miles. Every where, the president was received with demonstrations of respect and cordiality, and there can be no doubt, we think, that his tour was a wise and judicious movement with reference to the great objects to which he had so recently pledged his vows in the capitol.

1817.

The fifteenth Congress commenced its first session at the usual time, in the beginning of December. The republicans were decidedly in the majority, there being only a few of the more distinguished federalists left, such as Rufus King, and Harison Gray Otis, in the Senate, and Timothy Pitkin, Henry Shaw, and John Sergeant, in the House. Henry Clay was elected speaker by a hundred and forty-four votes out of a hundred and fifty; and John Galliard was chosen president of the Senate, *pro tempore.*

Mr. Monroe's first annual message was sent in on the 2d of December. It began with congratulations upon the general condition of the country, and spoke of the various steps which had been taken in regard to arrangements with the British government, naval armaments on the lakes, the north-eastern boundary, the fisheries, the relations with Spain, etc. The internal concerns of the country were represented as peculiarly gratifying. "After satisfying the appropriations made by law for the support of the civil government, and of the military and naval establishments, embracing suitable provision for fortifications and for the gradual increase of the navy, paying the interest of the public debt, and extinguishing more than $18,000,000 of the principal, within the present year, it is estimated that a balance of more than $6,000,000 will remain in the treasury on the 1st day of January next, applicable to the current expenses of the ensuing year." The receipts for the next year were estimated at $24,500,000 and the outgoings at nearly $22,000,000; so that there would be an excess of revenue beyond expenditure amounting to nearly $2,750,000, exclusive of the balance expected to be in the treasury at the beginning of the year. The financial prospects of the country were, consequently, considered as full of encouragement and promise for the future.

The president went on to make suitable mention of the militia, the army and navy, the Indians, and the public lands. In respect to "internal improvements," he said: "Disregarding early impressions, I have bestowed on the subject all the deliberation which its great importance and a just sense of my duty required, and the result is a settled conviction in my mind, that Congress do not possess the right. It is not contained in any of the specified powers granted to Congress; nor can I consider it incident to, or a necessary means, viewed on the most liberal scale, for carrying into effect any of the powers which are specifically granted." Mr. Monroe, therefore, suggested an amendment to the Constitution; in which he thought might be included the right of Congress to institute "seminaries of learning," as one very important branch of such "improvements."

1817.

Manufactures and machinery, the public buildings at Washington, and "the surviving officers and soldiers of our revolutionary army," all received their due share of attention; and the message concluded with a paragraph on the subject of taxation:—"It appearing in a satisfactory manner, that the revenue arising from imposts and tonnage, and from the public lands, will be fully adequate to the support of the civil government, of the present military and naval establishments, including the annual augmentation of the latter to the extent provided for, to the payment of the interest on the public debt, and to the extinguishment of it at the time authorized, without the aid of the internal taxes, I consider it my duty to recommend to Congress their repeal." The president added, however, a promise to recommend the re-imposition of them, if circumstances should seem to indicate the necessity of such a step.

The debates in Congress during this session were earnest and able: yet, we are happy to say, there was less acerbity and acrimony than on many previous occasions, and the principal measures recommended by the president met the approval of the majority in Congress.

Among the matters to which early attention was given, was the abolition of the internal taxes. The duties on licenses to distillers and others, on sales by auction, pleasure carriages, stamps, and refined sugar, were, by one act, removed. The duty on salt was also marked for repeal; but, prosperous as the finances seemed, apprehension was expressed by the secretary of the treasury, that instead of a surplus

1817. there would be a deficit, if all that the president promised, and the people expected, were given up; this, therefore, was retained. Some of the members thought it prudent to retain a part of these taxes; but, from the difficulty of making a selection which would prove satisfactory, the repeal was carried, early in the session, with only five dissentients.

The debates showed that, in some respects, the view of the state of the country was rather highly colored in the message. The finances did, undoubtedly prosper greatly, and the public funds were at a premium; but commerce had not recovered from the embargoes and other paralyzing acts preceding and accompanying the war, which, without them, would have been sufficiently injurious. Excessive importations had raised the public revenue, but ruined the private trader, it was said; and the most profitable of all departments of mercantile enterprise —the carrying trade—was, by treaty, as good as closed against American ships. Neither were the banks without their share of condemnation; they, it seems, were contracting their credits, and endeavoring to close bad accounts, and to recover their debts,—proceedings never popular amongst those affected by them, and yet held to be indispensable both for the banks and the public in general. With respect to Great Britain and her commercial policy, Congress determined upon various retaliatory measures, which were discussed with earnestness and ability, clearly evincing the general sentiment of the country on this important topic. Of the effect produced by these measures, the reader will be better able to judge as we proceed.

For the purpose of compensating for the loss of the internal duties, the abolition of which made it necessary to provide some means for raising the revenue required for the support of government, and of affording protection to the manufactures of the country, some changes were made in the tariff; a small increase of duty was laid upon some fabrics, such as coarse cotton goods, and the like; but there being great opposition to the tariff from the commercial and other sections of the country, nothing of moment was accomplished at this time for the encouragement of home manufactures.

Notwithstanding Mr. Monroe's opinion on the subject of internal improvements, (p. 310), the question came up and was ably and fully discussed this session. The committee on internal improvements brought in a report, and maintained that Congress possessed the power, under the Constitution, of appro-

1818. priating money for the construction of military roads, post roads, and canals. Henry Clay, Mr. Lowndes, Mr. Tucker, and others, argued strongly in favor of the constitutionality of the proposed system; and Messrs. Claggett, Orr, Johnson, Barbour, and others, with equal zeal and earnestness, took the opposite ground on this confessedly difficult topic. On the question of appropriating the dividends received by the United States from the shares held in the national bank to the objects under discussion, there was a majority in favor of such disposition of the public money; but as it was soon understood, that the president would feel called upon to veto any bill in support of the measure, the whole subject was postponed to a future day.

Early in January, a committee of the House reported respecting Amelia Island, and Galveston, in Texas. It appears, that one Gregor M'Gregor, who gave out that he had received a commission as a general from "the United Provinces of New Granada and Venezuela," in conjunction with Louis Aury, had taken possession of Amelia Island, near the boundary of Georgia, with the avowed intention of renewing the attack upon East Florida from that point. M'Gregor's forces called themselves the *patriots;* but they were principally made up of outlaws from the United States, run-away slaves, smugglers, vagrants picked up by chance in the ports of the Southern states, including a number of English emissaries. M'Gregor's professed object was to liberate the province and obtain its annexation to the United States.

"On the 30th of July, 1813," says Monette, "the Spanish governor entered into a capitulation for the surrender of the province to the patriot forces; thus again excluding the authority of Spain. But with this incongruous mass of reckless adventurers, no permanent government could be sustained. Dissensions arose; and General M'Gregor, having been supplanted by the artful intrigue of Hubbard, and having been induced to believe that his personal security was endangered by his enemies, retired from the command, and accompanied the notorious Captain Woodbine to England. It was not long before Aury, (who claimed to be an 'admiral,' under a commission like M'Gregor's,) lost his influence, and retired also, leaving Hubbard in chief command. The government, under the usurped authority, had but short duration. To prevent the lawless assemblage which concentrated near the frontier of the United States, and interrupted the due operation of the revenue laws, the federal government determined to take forcible possession of the country, until Spain should be able to maintain her authority over it. Accordingly, on the 1st of January, 1818, in obedience to instructions, Major J. Bankhead and Commodore J. D. Henly, with a division of the land and naval forces of the United States, expelled the patriots and took possession of the country."*

1818.

The president, in relation to this movement, was careful to state, that, "in expelling these adventurers from these posts, it was not intended to make any conquest from Spain, or to injure, in any degree, the cause of the colonies." The secretary of state, also, in his official report, justified the procedure, as required by the laws of nations, as well as those of the United States.

Mississippi was admitted into the Union on the 10th of December, 1817, and the initiatory steps for the same purpose were taken by the territories of Illinois and Missouri. During the autumn of the same year, a treaty was concluded by commissioners appointed by the president of the United States and the chiefs of the Wyandot, Delaware, Shawanese, Seneca, Ottowas, Chippewa, and Potowattamie tribes of Indians, by which these tribes ceded to the United States all lands which they claimed within the limits of Ohio. The Indians were, at their option, to remain on the ceded lands subject to the laws of the state and of the United States.

The attention of Congress was also devoted to the question of a bankrupt law; the negotiations with Spain; the Seminole war; the sending a minister to La Plata; and other topics of less moment. Our limits do not admit of details; we can only refer to the debates of Congress, and the lives and works of such men as Henry Clay, Daniel Webster, and John C. Calhoun. On the 20th of April, this busy session of Congress was closed by an adjournment to the third Monday in November.

While the adventurers at Galveston and Amelia Island were occupied in their schemes, a war was begun on the frontier of the United States and Florida. Spain, though she had gained possession of the province in 1783, had never, in fact, reoccupied the country; but it was left almost entirely to outlaws, smugglers, buccaneers, and the like; uncontrolled, except here and there by a small military post. The Seminole Indians, who occupied lands on the confines of the province, partly in Florida and partly in the United States, had been guilty of various acts of outrage. Loud complaints began to be made by the people of Georgia; and General Gaines, who commanded in that quarter, having demanded of the Indians on the Flint River surrender of some persons whom he charged with murder, was met by a decided refusal; on the ground that they were not the

* Previously to this, in the summer of 1816, Louis Aury, mentioned above, had gathered a band of brigands and desperadoes on Snake Island, on the coast of Texas, about one hundred and thirty miles west of the mouth of the Mississippi. Smuggling, piratical depredations on commerce, introduction of slaves in violation of law, and the like, formed the occupation of these self-constituted patriots. Aury, in April, 1817, removed further west, to Matagorda, but remained only a short time. He then joined M'Gregor at Amelia Island.

aggressors. Added to this ground of complaint on both sides, there was soon afterwards some violence em-
1817. ployed in obtaining possession of the territory ceded to the United States by the last Creek treaties; violence for which the Indians took revenge in December, by attacking a boat laden with supplies, on the Appalachicola, and killing above forty persons who were on board, some of them being women and children.

So soon as the attack on the boat was known, the government authorized General Gaines to advance into Florida "if necessary;" but specially instructed him not to attack a fort, if the Indians should take shelter under the guns of any, "but to report the fact." General Jackson, who was the principal officer in the south, at the same time received orders, at the close of December, to put himself at the head of the movement; and he was empowered to call out a militia force from his own state, in addition to that which had been raised in Georgia.

Early in January, General Jackson, at the head of a formidable band of Tennessee volunteers, set out for the seat of war. Before the end of the month, he concluded a treaty with that part of the Creek nation which was friendly to the United States; and secured their assistance against the Seminoles. On the 1st of March,
1818. he reached Fort Scott, on the Appalachicola; having now under his command above four thousand men, a force exceeding in number the whole of the nation he was about to attack, including both women and children. Provisions running short, he hastened southward without delay, employing his Indians to scour the whole country round the line of march, by which means he secured a great number of prisoners from the enemy. On the site of the stronghold which the negroes had held, and been dispossessed in 1816, Jackson built a fort, and named it Fort Gadsden; and this he made use of as a dépôt for supplies.

On the 1st of April, the Creek towns on Mickasukie Lake, and the Ocilla River, were stormed and destroyed, and cattle and corn in abundance was taken. Here, too, was found a red-painted war-pole, from which were suspended a great cluster of scalps; fifty of them, it was said; and, as might have been expected, including those of every sex and age. Beside these, there were some two hundred and fifty others of these horrid trophies found, a circumstance which naturally enough shocked Jackson and his men.

The American commander was not a man easily deterred by difficulties or scruples. Having no doubts in his mind of the complicity of the Spaniards and of their furnishing supplies to the Seminoles, he marched forward, without delay, to St. Mark's, a small Spanish post, with a fort, at the head of Appalachicola Bay. After a feeble resistance, the fort surrendered, and was occupied by American forces.

While here, Jackson took prisoners, a Scotch trader, from New Providence, named Alexander Arbuthnot, and soon after Robert C. Ambrister, a native of the same province. Both were engaged in active trade with the Indians, and were charged with stimulating them to hostilities. To most of persons, the question as to what disposition was to be made of these men, would have caused some hesitation and uncertainty; but Jackson was prompt in his determination, and marked out his course as decisively as if it admitted of not a moment's doubt. On the 20th of April, he detailed a court-martial, consisting of General Gaines as president, and a large number of other officers, for the purpose of investigating the charges against Arbuthnot and Ambrister, and deciding upon their guilt or innocence, and what punishment, if any, should be inflicted.

The charges against Arbuthnot were the following: 1st. "For exciting and stirring up the Creek Indians to war against the United States and her citizens, he being a subject of Great Britain, with whom the United States are at peace." 2d. "For acting as a spy, aiding, abetting, and comforting the enemy, and supplying them with the means of war." 3d. "For exciting the Indians to murder and destroy William Hambly and Edmund Doyle, confiscate their property, and causing their arrest, with a view to their condemnation to death, and the seizure of their property, they being citizens of Spain; on account of their active and zealous exertions to maintain peace between
1818. Spain, the United States, and the Indians." He was found guilty of the first and second charge, omitting the words "acting as a spy," and sentenced to be hung.

The next day, Ambrister's trial was entered upon. The charges against him were: 1st. "Aiding, abetting, and comforting the enemy, and supplying them with the means of war, he being a subject of Great Britain, who was at peace with the United States, and late an officer in the British colonial marines." 2d. "Leading and commanding the Lower Creek Indians, in carrying on war against the United States." The court-martial found him guilty of both charges, and sentenced him to be shot; but, on reconsideration, changed the sentence to fifty lashes and confinement with hard labor for a year. On the 29th of April, General Jackson approved the sentence of the court, in the case of Arbuthnot, and also, the first sentence of the same body, in respect to Ambrister; and ordered them both to be executed the next day.

Victorious in East Florida, where he had slain about sixty of the enemy, and burnt seven hundred huts, shot one Indian trader, hung another, and also two Indians, captured by stratagem, and lost twenty of his allied Creeks, General Jackson now marched against Pensacola; where, as usual, the Indians had been sheltered by the Spanish authorities. The governor of the place protested against the invasion of the province, and declared his determination to resist. But as this did not stay the advance of Jackson, he retired to the fort at the Barancas, and left Pensacola undefended, for the Americans to take possession of without a blow. Three days later, the army marched to the Barancas, raised a breast-work in the night, and bombarded the fortress, which, on the 27th of May, was surrendered to the United States. The Spanish civil and military authorities were transported to Havana, and the province was occupied by the American troops. Colonel King was appointed civil and military governor, the Spanish revenue laws were abolished, and all the necessary officers of the new government appointed. General Jackson then returned to Nashville, leaving General Gaines in command. But early in August, he ordered Gaines to take possession of St. Augustine, on the ground that the Indians had been supplied there with ammunition to carry on the war. Immediately on this order becoming known to the war department, it was countermanded.

The proceedings of General Jackson caused great excitement throughout the country, and severe censures were freely bestowed upon measures which were held to be of the most high-handed character. The meeting of Congress, and the course which the government would pursue in this matter, were looked for with deep interest not unmingled with apprehension.

During the recess of Congress, Mr. Monroe paid a visit to the towns and coasts of Chesapeake Bay, for the purpose of examining the forts and defences in that quarter, and of selecting a site for a naval dépôt. He returned by the interior of Virginia to Washington, about the middle of June; and the national legislature re-assembled on the 16th of November. The message was sent in the next day, and contained a full and interesting summary of affairs for the consideration of Congress. The country was represented as being in a prosperous condition; crops abundant, commerce flourishing, and the revenue steadily increasing. The relations with Spain were unsettled as yet, but with all other powers, there was 1818. peace and amity existing. The receipts into the treasury for the first three quarters of the year, the president stated, had exceeded $17,000,000. On the 1st of January of the next year, more than $2,000,000 would remain in the treasury, and the revenue for the year was estimated at $26,000,000; other topics, relating to home affairs principally, were urged upon the notice of Congress.

The bank of the United States, from the establishment of which great expectations of advantage had been formed, did not accomplish all that the people desired. The consequence was, that loud complaints were made, and charges of mismanagement were freely circulated against the directors of the bank. At the time when Congress assembled, and the president presented his flattering picture of the state of things in the United States generally, the bank was evidently getting into an exceedingly unsatisfactory condition; and the greatest fears were every where entertained in consequence. A commitee of inquiry was appointed, with John C. Spencer at the head, who ascertained some of the immediate causes of this;* and they require the best attention of the reader, as well because of their intrinsic importance, as of the large share

* The committee consisted of Messrs. Spencer, Lowndes, M'Lane, Bryan, and Tyler. Their report, which was very elaborate, was brought in on the 16th of January, 1819.

of public concern which has been bestowed upon the question of a national bank and its advantages and disadvantages.

The actual specie capital possessed by the bank, when first entering upon the transaction of business, was only $2,000,000, a sum entirely insufficient for the purposes of the institution. A special agent accordingly was sent to England, at a salary of $20,000, to contract for specie; and between July, 1817, and December, 1818, upwards of $7,250,000 were obtained and imported into the United States. But the cost at which this was done was enormous, being more than half a million of dollars.

Numerically, as it might, perhaps, have been expected under the then existing circumstances, the speculators who held shares in the bank far

1818. exceeded the capitalists; and the former class having thus gained the direction of its operations, they took care to guide them so as to secure advantages and profit for themselves, without regard either to the legitimate object of the establishment of the bank, or the claims of those whose capital, put into the concern, was its only available means of working or subsisting. The particular way in which they employed their power, was the device and perfection of a scheme of stockjobbing in bank shares, the like to which has not often been attempted in this particular species of gambling. The mode of operations was something after this sort. It was agreed to discount the notes of stockholders for the payment of their instalments, upon the pledge of their stock, without any other security; first, at par, and afterwards for twenty-five per cent. more than the nominal amount; requiring, however, an endorser for the excess. These stock-notes, as they were termed, were received indefinitely, at the pleasure of the stockholders. And as a necessary and foreseen consequence, shares were bought without the advance of a cent. An adventurer would engage a certain number of shares, apply to the directors for a loan on the pledge of the stock engaged, and by what was called a "simultaneous operation," the stock was transferred to him, pledged to the bank, and the discount made, with the avails of which he paid for his stock: a rise in the market would enable him to sell his stock at an advance, pocket the difference, and commence new operations. As a further consequence, the price of shares rose, till, about the beginning of September, 1817, they reached $156.50 a share; and at last, all of a sudden, soon after Congress had begun to inquire respecting the business, and no doubt because of the inquiry, the bubble burst, and they fell from $156.50 to $110, and thence to $90 a share; dissipating hundreds of imaginary fortunes, and changing many shareholders in the bank into bankrupts.

The city of Baltimore was the principal scene of these operations; the management of that branch having fallen almost exclusively into the hands of persons without capital, and without principle. Two or three houses, in which some of the directors had an interest, drew from the bank $1,500,000, and the defalcations in the Baltimore branch alone amounted to $1,700,000; a sum about equal to the aggregate amount of losses at the parent bank and all the other branches.

Nor was this the only way in which the institution was injured by these speculations. One of the chief benefits expected from it, for the Union at large, was the creation of a general currency of uniform value; by which the greater part of the evils affecting the business transactions of the country would have been remedied or prevented. And for this purpose it was requisite that bills issued by any particular branch, and, according to their tenor, payable at that branch only, should be received and paid, both at the parent bank and all its branches. Until July, 1818, this plan was followed; but most of the enormous quantity of paper emitted in the southern and western states, by the regular course of trade found its way to the north, and in self-defence the branches there were at last compelled to refuse payment, and then the bank ordered the payment of bills at the branches issuing them alone, so that this first attempt to get a uniform currency proved fruitless.

One of the worst features in the whole case was this; some of the most prominent of the directors, both those elected by the shareholders and those nominated by the government, were implicated in these schemes and speculations; and the parent bank at Philadelphia itself was induced to imitate the dishonest proceedings at Baltimore, to the injury of New York and Boston.

The committee, named above, entered into a most careful investigation of the whole matter, and in their report set forth the real causes of the embarrassments of the bank; the consequence of which was, that Mr. William Jones, the president, and others of the managers, resigned their posts. **1819.** Stringent measures were recommended by the committee, and several resolutions offered in respect to what were considered violations of the charter of the bank.* A new board of direction was chosen, and Langdon Cheves, whose reputation as a financier stood deservedly high, was appointed president. Under his able and vigilant control matters speedily assumed a brighter aspect. The stock found its way into the hands of real capitalists, and rose again in value to $120 per share. The affairs of the institution were minutely examined, and a careful and trustworthy statement was published, which quite reassured the minds of the shareholders. The most prudent measures, in borrowing specie, curtailing discounts, arranging the relations of the branches, and prosecuting defaulters, were adopted; and not only was bankruptcy averted, but the establishment, after a short season of uncertainty and unpopularity, began to recover from its losses, and to regain and to deserve the confidence of the mercantile world.

The president, not long after the

* A clause in the charter allowed no individual to have more than thirty votes, no matter what the number of his shares in the bank might be. The speculators of Baltimore very adroitly evaded the force of this provision of the charter, by subscribing for single shares in the names of other people, who gave them powers of attorney to vote for them at the meetings, and charged the sum of twelve and a-half cents for the risk entailed by their participation in this gross fraud!

commencement of the session of Congress, communicated to both Houses all the papers relative to the Seminole war. In the Senate they were referred to a committee of five, Messrs. Burrell, Lacock, Eppes, King, and Eaton. The first three concurred in a report censuring in very severe terms the whole conduct of General Jackson in invading Florida, and putting to death Arbuthnot and Ambrister. The other members of the committee justified his proceedings; but, as the report was made near the close of the session, no vote was taken on the subject. In the House, the military committee, to whom the papers had been referred, were divided in opinion in a similar manner with the Senate's committee. Four of the committee denounced Jackson's conduct; three of their number vindicated it throughout, and declared that he deserved the thanks of the country. The debate was begun on the 18th of January, and occupied the House for nearly three weeks. The best talent of the country was enlisted on both sides. The eloquent Henry Clay was astounded at the violence and lawlessness of General Jackson's proceedings. "I hope gentlemen will deliberately survey the awful isthmus on which we stand," he said, in concluding his long and able speech; "they may bear down all opposition; they may even vote the general the public thanks; they may carry him triumphantly through this House; but, if they do, in my humble judgment, it will be a triumph of the principle of insubordination, a triumph of the military over the civil authority, a triumph over the powers of this House, a triumph over the Constitution of the land. And I pray most devoutly to heaven, that it may not prove, in its ultimate effects and consequences, a triumph over the liberties of the people."*

Mr. Cobb, Mr. Hopkinson, Mr. Nelson, and others, joined their voices with Mr. Clay's in condemnation; while Mr. R. M. Johnson, Mr. Holmes, and other men of equal ability and force, defended the measures of Jackson, and claimed that he had added new laurels to those which he had so nobly won at New Orleans. When the vote was taken in the House on the resolutions censuring General Jackson, they were lost by majorities of thirty and forty; which demonstrated, that, whatever may be said of the measures of the American general in the conduct of this war, and however doubtful they may appear on a calm and candid investigation of them, Congress was willing to pass a decided vote of approval, and the people were ready to glorify one whose decision of character, no less than his energy and military ability, possessed the highest attractions for the popular eye. The president and cabinet also, principally, it is said, through the influence of Mr. Adams, expressed their approbation of the conduct of General Jackson.

1819.

Illinois was admitted into the Union by a resolution adopted on the 3d of December, 1818. The southern part of the Missouri Territory took the first step towards becoming a state, by ap-

* See Moore's "*American Eloquence*," vol. ii., pp. 273–86.

plying to Congress to be erected into a territorial government, to be called Arkansas; and the territories of Alabama and Missouri took the second step in February, 1819, of applying to be admitted as states of the Union. Mr. Tallmadge in the House, proposed to fix a limit to the existence of slavery in the new state of Missouri, prohibiting the introduction of slaves, and gradually emancipating those then in bondage. The discussion soon became warm and urgent on both sides of the slavery question; but the proposal of Mr. Tallmadge was carried, and the bill was sent to the Senate. The Senate refused to concur in the clauses against slavery, by a vote of twenty-two to sixteen. The House insisted on retaining the clause prohibiting slavery generally; but neither receding on this point, the bill was lost. The whole subject was consequently laid over till the next Congress, when, as we shall see, the "Missouri Question" gave rise to scenes of excitement and discord hardly to be paralleled in our annals.

As to Alabama, there seemed to be no great difference of opinion in Congress, and it was agreed without difficulty to admit it as a slave state. This was accordingly done on the 14th of December, 1819. Contemporaneously with the action named above in regard to Missouri, the question of restricting the duration of slavery in Arkansas Territory was also discussed and voted down in both Houses, thus affording to the southern men the admission of their opponents, in addition to their own arguments, to be urged on this much litigated question.

Early in January, Mr. Calhoun, the secretary of war, made an able report on roads and canals, with a view to military operations. In this report he said, that he regarded **1819.** a judicious system of roads and canals, constructed for the convenience of commerce, and the transmission of the mail, alone, without reference to military operations, as amongst the most efficient means of defence; since the same roads and canals would, with few exceptions, be required for these operations; and such a system, by consolidating the Union, and increasing its wealth and fiscal capacity, would greatly add to the resources of war. Mr. Calhoun also suggested the employment of the regular troops in the construction of some of the lines of communication which he indicated; and Congress so far adopted the suggestion as to appropriate $10,000 for the increase of the pay of the soldiers who should be so employed. An appropriation of $500,000 was also made towards the construction of the Cumberland Road, a project with which Henry Clay soon after became personally identified.

Towards the close of the month of January, Mr. Lowndes made a full and satisfactory report on the subject of weights and measures; and also on the subject of foreign coins in the United States, their value, etc. The suggestions and statements of the committee are of great interest and value.

Notwithstanding the unpleasant posture of affairs caused by General Jackson's march into Florida, negotiations were pushed forward with the Spanish minister, and a treaty was concluded and signed on the 22d of February, by which Florida was ceded to the United States for $5,000,000. The treaty was not, however, to be promulgated until it was ratified by Spain; and the money was to be paid to the citizens of the United States, on account of spoliations by Spain on citizens of the United States. One of the last acts of the session was a bill authorizing the president to take possession of East and West Florida. The king and court of Spain, however, protracted the matter when it was submitted to them, greatly to the disgust of Mr. Forsyth, the American envoy; and it was not till more than a year had elapsed that his majesty saw fit to ratify the treaty; it was finally ratified on the 24th of October, 1820.

On the 3d of March this busy session terminated, and the fifteenth Congress brought its labors to a close.

Before concluding the present chapter, we must give some attention to another topic, belonging to the present period, and which was of no less interest than moment to a large number of our fellow-citizens. American commerce had suffered so severely from the spoliations of the belligerent powers of Europe, that when peace returned, it was determined to endeavor to obtain as speedy redress as was possible. The treaty of Ghent had settled the question of these claims, as far as Great Britain was concerned; but there still remained those against France, Spain, Naples, Holland, and Denmark—some of them dating from before 1800—to be brought to a settlement.

Mr. William Pinkney was charged by the president, in 1816, with a special mission to Naples, before proceeding to Russia as envoy of the United States to that court. His object was to endeavor to prevail upon the king of Naples to make restitution for the losses sustained by our merchants, in consequence of seizure and confiscation of their property during the reign of Murat. The sovereign now on the throne, however, found it convenient to decline all responsibility for what had happened under his predecessor; and Mr. Pinkney departed from Naples without obtaining any redress whatever. Nor was Eustis more successful at the Hague. There, too, the course adopted by Naples was found equally convenient, and a formal disclaimer was put forth against being held to answer for acts done under the Napoleonic dynasty. With Denmark, likewise, nothing could be accomplished.

1816.

Similar objections to many of the claims made upon the Spanish government also, were urged in the course of the long and tedious negotiations with that court. Neither did an offer, in January, 1818, to accept the cession of Florida as full compensation of these claims, lead to a more satisfactory result; although it was supported by the proposal to be contented with a narrower boundary for Louisiana, on the side next Texas. The Spanish ambassador declined to open negotiations, until that part of Florida, of which, as we have said above (p. 316), the United States had taken possession, was restored. He also complained, and with some show of justice, of the violations of neutrality which had been

1818.

tolerated, though proclaimed against, by the government of the United States; and still more of the privateering, which, it was said, was carried on against Spanish commerce, by citizens of the United States, under the flags of the insurgent colonies of Spain. Although no satisfaction for mercantile losses could be obtained from Spain, the president felt bound, after the representation made by the Spanish ambassador, to secure the passage of an act of Congress against the privateers, which was accordingly done. Subsequently, as above stated, by the treaty with Spain in February, 1819, Florida was ceded to the United States, and $5,000,000 was agreed to be paid as indemnity for the spoliations on American commerce.

France, we are sorry to say, showed as little disposition as any of the European powers just named, to make compensation for the depredations she had committed upon the property of our citizens. Nothing was accomplished at this date, and the whole subject formed a theme of complaint and vexation for many years. Further on, we shall recur to this topic again.

CHAPTER III.

1819-1822.

PROGRESS OF AFFAIRS DURING 1819-1822.

The president visits the southern states — The slavery question — Congress in session — The president's message — The "Missouri Question" — Great excitement — Abstract of the argument on both sides — The great men concerned in the debate — The Compromise — Result of the matter to the north and south — Action of Congress in respect to other matters, bankruptcy law, national currency, revolutionary pensions, public land sales, etc. — Commodore Decatur killed in a duel — The fourth census — Gloomy period of 1819 and 1820 — Congress reassembles in November, 1820—Abstract of the president's message—The Missouri question revived — The battle fought over again — Clay's efforts — Dispute how settled — Result of the presidential election — Financial distress — The Florida treaty — Monroe's second inauguration — Jackson appointed governor of Florida — His proceedings and troubles there — The president's proclamation in regard to the admission of Missouri — The seventeenth Congress—The message of the president—The work of the session, investigating Jackson's conduct, fixing the ratio of representation, refusing further help to domestic manufactures, etc. — Congress adjourns on the 8th of May.

During the summer of 1819, Mr. Monroe, carrying out his plan with reference to personally examining the state of the country, made a short visit to the southern states. Proceeding to Charleston first, and thence to Savannah, Augusta, and other places, he returned through the Cherokee country to Nashville, and so by Louisville and Lexington in Kentucky, to Washington. He reached the seat of government early in August.

The slavery question, as may be supposed from what had occurred in the last Congress, began to assume an importance far beyond what had heretofore been accorded to it; and popular feeling, both at the north and the south, was greatly roused on this subject. Interest as well as principle; prejudice as well as conscientiousness; sectional feuds and jealousies as well as patriotism and love of the Union, moved the minds of men and guided their course of action; and before Congress assembled, it became evident, that the old battle was to be renewed, with circumstances of bitterness and savageness added to the contest. Under such a state of things as this, the whole country looked with no little interest and anxiety to the approaching session of the national legislature.

1819.

The first session of the sixteenth Congress was commenced on the 6th of December, 1819. Mr. Clay was re-elected speaker without opposition, and the president's third annual message was communicated to both Houses on the next day. A large portion of the message was taken up with a *résumé* of the state of affairs as regarded Spain, and the course that government had seen fit to adopt. The commercial convention with Great Britain had not resulted satisfactorily, and the president threw out suggestions as to "prohibitory provisions," in relation to intercourse with the British possessions. The pecuniary embarrassments of the country were spoken of; and Mr. Monroe intimated his willingness to go as far as was possible in consistency with the Constitution, for the purpose of affording relief to the sufferers. He was also quite in favor of giving further encouragement to domestic manufactures, due regard being paid to the other great interests of the nation. One very influential reason for these suggestions was the diminution of the receipts at the treasury, which had followed from the disastrous condition of trade and the currency. There would be no more than $23,000,000 for the year; and the pensions granted to the soldiers of the Revolution had made a larger income than ordinary needful; but a considerable surplus was, nevertheless, expected. Having spoken of coast fortifications, the increase of the navy, measures for suppressing the slave trade, etc., the president closed his message in the following terms:—

"In the execution of the duty imposed by these acts, and of a high trust connected with it, it is with deep regret I have to state the loss which has been sustained by the death of Commodore Perry. His gallantry in a brilliant exploit in the late war, added to the renown of his country. His death is deplored as a national misfortune."

1819.

The "Missouri Question," as was to be expected, formed the engrossing theme of the session, and was entered into at an early day after the assembling of Congress. Great excitement prevailed both in and out of Congress; the subject was discussed in all its details and its manifold ramifications; and the best talent of the national legislature was enlisted in the endeavor to determine upon the great question at issue, viz., whether slavery should be restricted within certain bounds and its progress put an end to, or whether it should be permitted to have free scope and to spread wherever its advocates and supporters could carry it.

The position of things at the time helped on the excitement. The south, jealous of the advancing progress of the free states, had insisted all along that Congress should admit a slave state as often as they admitted a free state; and this practice had been followed. Alabama had been the last admitted, and that was a slave state; so that now the advocates of the other side claimed that Missouri, according to rule, ought to come in as a free state. At this date, there were only ten slave states, whilst the free numbered twelve; another, which was free, was soliciting admission; so that unless Missouri could be secured, the southern members felt that slavery was threatened with extinction by the action of Congress, in opposition, as they averred, to the original compromise of the Constitution. Besides, the following year the census was to be taken, and a new distribution of the Representatives would be made: already there were a hundred and five members from free states, opposed to only eighty from slave states; so that if Missouri were not secured amongst the latter, the opponents of slavery would have so undoubted a majority in both Houses of Congress as to enable them to do what they pleased, whether the south liked it or not. Whilst, to add to this embroilment, the presidential election was approaching, and if Missouri were not admitted, there would be votes lost or gained for some of the candidates.

1819.

It would be impossible within the brief space at our command, to enter at all fully into the arguments adduced by able and eloquent members of Congress on both sides of this vexed question. The most that we can do, is to present a brief abstract of the argument, referring the reader for fuller information to the debates of Congress, and the speeches of such men as Rufus King, Henry Clay, John Randolph, William Pinkney, John Sergeant, and the like. Mr. Benton, in his "Thirty Years' View," devotes a chapter to this subject, which is worth consulting, and comparing with other authorities.

On the side of the south it was urged, that Congress had no right to impose restrictions on this subject; that the Constitution recognized slavery as existing and as entitled to protection; that the slaves, as a class, are contented, happy, and well provided for, far more so than the half-starved laboring population of Ireland and Great Britain; that, even admitting slavery to be an evil, its abolition at the south would be a greater calamity than its continuance; that the addition of Missouri to the Union would not increase the number of slaves, but only diffuse them over a larger space; that the people of that state are entitled to have slaves by the clause in the treaty ceding Louisiana to the United States; that legislation on this topic is a right of which they cannot be deprived, so that if they prefer slavery, they have the power to insist upon it within their own bounds. These and the like arguments were amplified, and pressed with eloquence, earnestness, and zeal; it being evident that on the settlement of the question now, would, in great measure, depend the political strength and efficiency of the several sections of the Union.

The opponents of slavery-extension combated the views of southern members with equal zeal and energy. They urged, that it was plain, from the tendency of things in the United States, slavery was discountenanced and disliked; it was opposed entirely to the genius of free institutions, and could not be looked upon otherwise than as a temporary evil to be got rid of as soon as possible; and however true it might be that the Constitution recognized slavery, that could only be urged with respect to the original thirteen states, respecting which there
1820. was now no point of difference; but to propose to extend the evil of perpetual bondage over a territory of greater dimensions than the original United States, and over unborn millions of the human family, was too revolting to be entertained by freeman for a moment. The northern and western members also held, that Congress certainly possessed the power of legislation on this subject as respects the admission of new states, and could impose restrictions, as they saw fit, upon states formed out of the vast territory which constituted the public domain, and was under the governance of the national legislature. Congress, they held, not only possessed the power, but was bound by every consideration of uprightness and love of freedom, to put a stop to the further extension of slavery. They urged too, with force, that the slave trade would be carried on, and slaves would be smuggled in, despite the law, if the area of human bondage were to be enlarged; and some went so far, in reply to menaces of a dissolution of the Union if the south were not gratified, as to declare, that they would much prefer that to seeing the increase of territory cursed with slavery and its detestable evils.

Thus the battle raged. Our abstract above given can furnish no idea of the intense excitement, the bitterness, the furiousness of declamation and personal abuse that prevailed day after day, and week after week, while this topic engrossed all the thoughts and all the attention of Congress. The Senate, no less than the House, was fully occupied with this exciting question. There, new features were added to the debate by uniting the bill for the admission of Maine to that for the admission of Missouri. Mr. William Pinkney, of Maryland, was the great and truly eloquent advocate on the one side; and Mr. Rufus King, of New York, sustained the views of the north, and ably set forth the principles of the men who like himself desired to see a limit fixed to the progress of slavery.*

After continuing from the opening of Congress till the beginning of March, great fears began to be entertained respecting the possibility of giving independent existence to 1820.
either Maine or Missouri, in time for them to join in the next election. Maine loudly and justly complained, that a matter affecting her so intimately, was

* For the speeches of Mr. King and Mr. Pinkney, on the Missouri Question, the reader may refer to Moore's "*American Eloquence*," vol. ii., pp. 44–51, and 114–129.

made contingent upon another, with which she had not naturally any connection. The spirited appeal which was made to Congress in behalf of Maine, had not, however, any effect, for the opponents of restriction deemed their chances of success greater by insisting upon the consideration of the cases of Maine and Missouri together.

Henry Clay, as a matter of course, took a deep interest in this engrossing subject. He urged the admission of Missouri, but, while holding that the subject of her domestic slavery belonged to her, declared most emphatically his detestation of the system to be so great, that were he a citizen of Missouri, he would never consent to a state constitution which did not provide for its extinction. He plead for conciliation and compromise, believing that the safety of the Union required mutual sacrifices. As Mr. Colton says, in a panegyrical strain, when speaking of Henry Clay's share in the work of effecting a settlement of the question, he was the "one man of truly national feeling; calm, but not indifferent; with lofty, but dignified and not less anxious port, looking down upon the scene, as one of deep and unutterable concern. Often did he rise to hush the tempest, and call back reason to its useful offices. He stood up, a mediator between the conflicting parties, imploring, entreating, beseeching. On one occasion, during these debates, Mr. Clay spoke four hours and a half; pouring forth an uninterrupted and glowing torrent of his thoughts and feelings, with captivating and convincing power."

Wearied with the strife, and alarmed at the prospect before them, other members were willing to join with Mr. Clay in an effort to effect an arrangement which should put an end to the contest. The Senate and the House disagreed in several important particulars, and both seemed disposed to **1820.** insist upon their amendments and propositions. A committee of the two Houses on their disagreement was appointed, and they reported a recommendation to the Senate to recede from their amendments, and also a recommendation to the two Houses to strike out of the bill for the admission of Missouri the clause prohibiting the further increase of slavery in that state, and to substitute for it, that, in all the territory of Louisiana north of 36° 30′, slavery shall be for ever prohibited. This clause as to the dividing line was introduced by Jesse B. Thomas, senator from Illinois. On the Senate's amendment to strike out the restrictive clause, the vote was ninety in favor, to eighty-seven against; and on the question as to the line of 36° 30′, one hundred and thirty-four voted in favor of that line to only forty-two against it.*

The cabinet held grave and earnest deliberation over the proposed "compromise." By it, slavery was "forever" prohibited north of the line determined upon, and the president and his advisers held, that the measure was entirely constitutional; but, as we learn from Mr. Adams's diary, the question

* For some sharp and bitter strictures on Mr. Clay's course, as speaker, in regard to the Missouri Compromise, from the pen of the irate Virginian himself, see Garland's "*Life of John Randolph*," vol. ii., pp. 128–133.

was raised in the cabinet as to whether the prohibition was meant to extend only to the territories, or to the states formed out of the territories in coming years. Some took one view, some another, as well in the cabinet as in the country generally; and it augured but badly for future peace on this subject, that a door of litigation and dispute was thus left open.

It was the 6th of March, 1820, when this bill for the admission of Missouri became a law; the bill admitting Maine was signed three days earlier. Northern writers generally hold, that the victory in this contest was really and substantially on the side of the slaveholding states, and that the north gave way in a spirit of forbearance and with great reluctance. Senator Benton, on the other hand, affirms,* that the Missouri Compromise "was all clear gain to the anti-slavery side of the question, and was done under the lead of the united slave vote in the Senate, the majority of that vote in the House of Representatives, and the undivided sanction of a southern administration. It was a southern measure, and divided free and slave soil far more favorably to the north than the ordinance of 1787. That divided about equally; this of 1820 gave about all to the North. It abolished slavery over an immense extent of territory where it might then legally exist, over nearly the whole of Louisiana, left it only in Florida and Arkansas Territory, and opened no new territory to its existence. It was an immense concession to the non-slaveholding states; but the genius of slavery agitation was not laid." As we shall see, when we come nearer our own day, the Missouri Compromise did not have the effect of settling the vexed question between the north and the south, a question which, at times, seems as though it would ultimately sever the bonds which hold our glorious Union together.

1820.

Notwithstanding the large amount of time consumed in the discussion of the subject of slavery, Congress found opportunity for several important acts of legislation. The tariff of 1816 had not produced the beneficial results which had been looked for by the advocates of protection to domestic manufactures. The disposition to attempt great operations without adequate capital, had led many to venture largely, upon credit alone, and they were, of course, prostrated at the first crisis in financial affairs. The president, as we have intimated on a previous page (p. 323), was inclined to favor legislation on this subject, which was accordingly taken up and discussed with much earnestness and ability, both for and against the policy of protective duties. Separate committees were appointed for trade and manufactures, heretofore intrusted to the watchfulness of one and the same; and the speaker of the House zealously and energetically plead in behalf of the "American system." Mr. Baldwin, the chairman of the committee on manufactures, reported three bills, for the purpose of giving further encouragement to American manufactures: one, revising the tariff, and making it still more decidedly protective,

* Benton's "*Thirty Years' View*," vol. i., p. 5.

another, abolishing credit for duties on imported manufactures; and a third, imposing a heavy duty on auction sales of foreign manufactured goods. Under the influence of Mr. Clay, the first and last passed the House by respectable majorities; the second was negatived; but as the Senate rejected the tariff bill, the auction duty bill was not sent to them; and the whole subject, on the motion of Mr. Baldwin, was postponed to the next session.

Petitions and memorials in great numbers were presented in favor of a uniform bankrupt law. The northern and eastern members generally advocated the passage of such a law, as their constituents had been the principal sufferers during the late derangement in the finances of the country; the southern and western members, however, opposed the adoption of any law of the kind, and so the measure was not carried.

1820.

About the middle of February, Mr. Crawford, secretary of the treasury, presented a report on the subject of the national currency. It was ably written; its statements were carefully digested; and its suggestions seemed to be wise and judicious in the present state of the country. The reader who desires to understand the complicated and difficult subject of the currency, will find it to his advantage to examine this report. The Revolutionary pensioners being larger in number than was expected, some new regulations were made respecting them, and the secretary of the treasury was to judge, on a sworn valuation of their means of support, whether the United States could with propriety continue their pensions. On Mr. Clay's motion, an outfit and salary were voted to enable the president to send a minister or ministers to the newly established governments in South America. There was also voted a new appropriation for the Cumberland Road; and delinquents in the public offices were placed more directly within reach of punishment. Besides these, an act of great importance was passed, by which the plan of credit sales of public lands, which had led to speculations, injurious alike to the pretended purchasers and to the revenue, was abolished after the 1st of July; half-quarter sections were offered for sale, and the price was reduced to $1.25 per acre. By a special law, piracy was not only more strenuously denounced, but the foreign slave-trade was declared to be piracy, and a capital offence. Provisions were also made for the taking of the census, which were far more complete in their arrangements than any that had been acted upon before; and promised a much more useful contribution to the statistics of the Union. And after an active and laborious session, Congress adjourned, on the 15th of May, to meet again in November.

1820.

Previously to the adjournment of Congress, a caucus was held with respect to the candidates for the presidency and vice-presidency; but it was speedily ascertained, that Monroe and Tompkins would obtain the largest amount of suffrages, and they were accordingly named for re-election by unanimous assent.

It seems proper, in this place, to make mention of the lamentable death of Commodore Decatur in a duel, in order that we may give expression to the sentiment, which fills every honorable and manly mind, that this detestable species of murder ought to be marked with the reprobation and scorn which it deserves. Mackenzie, in his "Life of Decatur," gives a full account of the various steps in the dispute which led Barron to send Decatur a challenge. They met on the 22d of March, at Bladensburg, and Decatur was killed. Congress honored his funeral by an adjournment, and the president, with the heads of departments, the foreign ministers, the members of the legislature, and a great concourse of citizens, attended his body to the grave, by this means expressing their sense of the loss, which in him their country had sustained. Strange and shocking to say, no notice was taken of this atrocious murder; though the law was violated openly and without scruple, no motion was made to arrest the guilty; no attempt to vindicate the honor and dignity of the law of the land; but, as if such a mode of settling disputes was quite proper and becoming, the president and all others charged with the due execution and support of the laws, passed the whole transaction over in silence. It is humiliating to think, that one of the bravest and most chivalrous men that our navy has ever produced, should have gone down to the grave with the sad blot on his fair fame, "killed in a duel."

During the summer, the fourth decennial census of the United States was taken, showing the population on the 1st of August, 1820. The number of

white males was, 4,001,064; of white females, 3,871,647; total, 7,872,711. The number of free colored males was, 112,783; of free colored females, 120,783; total, 233,566. **1820.** The number of slaves was, males, 790,965; females, 752,723; total, 1,543,688. The grand total of the population, consequently, was, 9,649,965.

Several additional returns were required by the act of Congress which made arrangements for taking this census. Of foreigners not naturalized, it appeared there were, 53,687, in the United States. The number of persons engaged in commerce, was 72,493; in manufactures, 349,506; and in agriculture, 2,070,646. The numbers engaged in manufactures, will help to account for the attention given to the measures for fostering and encouraging the manufacturing interest.*

Mr. Senator Benton's view of the "gloom and agony" of the years 1819 and 1820 deserves to be quoted in this connection, although probably it is more highly colored than, every thing considered, was necessary. "No money," says he, "either gold or silver: no measure, or standard of value, left remaining. The local banks, (all but those of New England,) after a brief resumption of specie payments, again sank into a state of suspension. The Bank of the United States, created as a remedy for all those evils, now at the head of the evil, prostrate and helpless,

* For some interesting facts and conclusions respecting the population of our country, see Tucker's "*Progress of the United States in Population and Wealth, in Fifty Years, as exhibited by the Decennial Census*," pp. 28–35, etc.

with no power left but that of suing its debtors, and selling their property, and purchasing for itself at its own nominal price. No price for property, or produce. No sales but those of the sheriff and the marshal. No purchasers at execution sales but the creditor, or some hoarder of money. No employment for industry, no demand for labor, no sale for the product of the farm, no sound of the hammer, but that of the auctioneer, knocking down property. Stop laws, property laws, replevin laws, stay laws, loan-office laws, the intervention of the legislator between the creditor and the debtor; this was the business of legislation in three-fourths of the states of the Union—of all south and west of New England. No medium of exchange, but depreciated paper; no change even, but little bits of foul paper, marked so many cents, and signed by some tradesman, barber, or innkeeper; exchanges deranged to the extent of fifty or one hundred per cent. Distress, the universal cry of the people; Relief, the universal demand thundered at the doors of all legislatures, state and federal."

Few countries, as a recent writer has well said, could have struggled through such a crisis as this. Fewer still could have seen it recorded, that, at the very period when the most numerous and clamorous classes were in such a condition as this, precisely then, the wrath and fire of party feeling seemed to have died out, and antagonists who had been opposed as the democrats and the federalists had showed themselves, laid aside their strife, and contended side by side to give stability and energy to "the Washington-Monroe policy." This is one of the noteworthy features in the history of Monroe's administration, and may well deserve the reader's attentive consideration.

On the 13th of November, Congress reassembled, and entered zealously upon the work marked out for the national legislature. Henry Clay, who was compelled to be absent on private business, sent a letter to the House, asking the acceptance of his resignation of the office of speaker, which led to an exciting canvass in order to fill this important post. Three candidates of note were put forward: Smith, of Maryland; Lowndes, of South Carolina; and Taylor, of New York. Sergeant, of Pennsylvania was also nominated, but his supporters were too few to entitle him to more than a bare mention, in connection with this warm contest. For three days the balloting was continued. Five several times was a majority, though not sufficient for the victory, secured by Taylor, on the second day; while Lowndes enjoyed the same fruitless triumph four times, and Smith three times. At length, the northern men united their votes, and carried the New York candidate, at the twenty-second balloting, by a majority of one vote only, over Mr. Lowndes.

The president's message was read to the two Houses on the next day. It is a very interesting document, and presents a view of public affairs much less doleful and discouraging than that which we have quoted above from Senator Benton. There was, according to the president, "much cause to rejoice in the felicity of our

1820.

situation," and this, too, notwithstanding the acknowledged "pressures on certain interests which have been felt," in various sections of the country. Having referred to these in hopeful terms, and spoken of the position of our relations with foreign governments, the president spoke of the "internal concerns" of the Union, somewhat at large. "The revenue," he said, most truly, "depends on the resources of the country; and the facility by which the amount required is raised, is a strong proof of the extent of the resources, and of the efficiency of the government." And then he draws a contrast between the amount of the United States debt on the 30th of September, 1815, and the 30th of September, 1820. At the former date, the entire debt, including all the items, was, $158,713,049; at the latter, it amounted to $91,193,-883; having been reduced during the interval of five years, by payments of $66,879,165; and this was in addition to the discharge of all the other obligations of the government, in respect to the civil, military, and naval establishments. "By the discharge of so large a portion of the public debt," continued the president, "and the execution of such extensive and important operations in so short a time, a just estimate may be formed of the great extent of our national resources. The demonstration is the more complete and gratifying, when it is recollected that the direct tax and excise were repealed soon after the termination of the late war, and that the revenue applied to these purposes has been derived almost wholly from other sources."

The receipts into the treasury had amounted to $16,794,107 66; the loan of $3,000,000 had readily been obtained at five per cent.; and there was due to the treasury for the sale of pub lic lands, nearly $23,000,000. Other topics of interest were noted, as the progress of the coast survey; the military stations in the west; the advance of civilization among the Indians; the efforts of some of the national ships to suppress the slave trade, etc.

On the 16th of November, a copy of the constitution of Missouri was presented to Congress. It had been framed during the recess, and its consideration gave rise to new contests in both Houses. In the Senate, it was referred to a select committee of three, who reported a resolution for the admission of Missouri into the Union. Little difficulty, in all probability, would have been made, respecting the final admission of this state, had not a clause been inserted in its constitution, through Mr. Benton's agency, prohibiting free persons of color from so much as entering the state, "under any pretext whatsoever." This clause revived the discussion with all its former acrimony, and the triumph of the advocates of the compromise seemed in danger of being lost. The committee, indeed, reported in favor of sanctioning the constitution, notwithstanding the objectionable clause; and the Senate, on the 11th of December, after an animated debate, adopted the requisite resolution for admitting Missouri, by a vote of twenty-six to eighteen, with the amendment, that Congress did not hereby give assent to any provision

1820.

in the constitution of Missouri which contravened that clause in the Constitution of the United States, declaring "that the citizens of each state shall be entitled to all the privileges and immunities of the several states."

In the House, however, the question was more sharply contested. The attempt to carry a resolution in favor of the admission of Missouri was rejected by a vote of ninety-three to seventy-nine. The next step was a resolution for admitting Missouri, provided the obnoxious provision in her constitution be expunged. The resolution was, on the 15th of January, 1821, referred to the committee of the whole, as was also the resolution from the Senate. For some weeks the question rested in the House, various amendments having been proposed, and numerous schemes devised to get rid of the difficulty, and if possible harmonize the conflicting views and opinions of members of Congress. Early in February, a resolution was proposed, calling upon Missouri to expunge the objectionable clause, as contrary to the Constitution of the United States, by a certain day, and then to be admitted into the Union. This proposition was, however, rejected; whereupon Henry Clay, who had returned and taken his seat again, rose and endeavored to pour oil upon the troubled waters. He moved the appointment of a select committee of thirteen, to consider the proposal which had just been negatived, and to report thereupon.

1821.

Even Henry Clay's great skill and ability proved hardly equal to the task he had undertaken. Notwithstanding the care with which "he consulted the feelings of both parties," in constructing the resolution which he reported; notwithstanding the feeling and power of his speeches, which not unfrequently "drew tears from the hearts" of his hearers, and the prophetic tone with which he besought the legislators to consider what they owed to their country; the resolution was thrown out by two votings, and when brought up for reconsideration, was again lost. On the 22d of February, a committee was appointed to act jointly with a committee of the Senate; and on the 26th, this committee reported a joint resolution, viz., That Missouri shall be admitted on the fundamental condition that the fourth clause (respecting free negroes) shall never be construed to authorize the passing of any law; and no law shall be passed by which any citizen of any of the states, shall be excluded from the enjoyment of any of the privileges to which he is entitled by the Constitution; provided the legislature, by a solemn public act, shall declare its assent, and transmit it to the president, as in the amendment recommended by the select committee. This amendment required the assent to be transmitted to the president by the fourth Monday in November, when the president was to make proclamation of the fact, and the admission of the new state was then to be considered as complete. The resolution passed by a vote of eighty-seven to eighty-one in the House, and twenty-eight to fourteen in the Senate; and its terms having been complied with on the part of Missouri, she thenceforward took her place in the Union, among the United States of America.

On the 14th of February, the two Houses met in convention to count the votes given for president and vice-president. The Missouri question not then having been settled, some excitement was caused by the difference of view, as to whether the electoral votes offered by Missouri should be accepted and counted or not. A good deal of debate occurred to little purpose, the Senate having withdrawn; and on their return, by special invitation, the duty of counting the votes was proceeded with, and the result was announced, the votes of Missouri not being included. All the electoral votes, (excepting one from Massachusetts, bestowed upon John Quincy Adams,) were given to James Monroe for the presidency. The total number was two hundred and thirty-one. Daniel D. Tompkins received, for the vice-presidency, two hundred and eighteen votes, including those of all the states, except New Hampshire, Massachusetts, Delaware, and Maryland. Massachusetts gave eight of its votes to Stockton; Delaware gave all of its, four in number, to Rodney; Rush received one from New Hampshire; and Harper one from Maryland.

1821.

The financial distress of the country necessarily occupied a large share of the attention of Congress. The treasury became embarrassed, and the loan of the preceding session would not have helped the secretary to the end of the year, had not some of the public creditors been forbearing. A new loan was the first expedient proposed, and one of $5,000,000, on Mr. Crawford's recommendation, was authorized. But this, without retrenchments, was insufficient. The reduction of the salaries of the executive and legislative departments of the government was proposed; but such a sacrifice was greater than could have been expected from the members of Congress; so, of course, all propositions of the kind were rejected. The army could, however, be reduced. The possibility of a renewal of the war with England seems to have lurked still in many ardent minds; and in addition to that, military glory, won so easily at New Orleans, appears to have not a little fascinated the spirits of the people. The officers of the army would, of course, resist the disbanding of it. But whatever the feelings were which had saved the military establishment, want of money made it absolutely necessary to disregard them, and four thousand, out of the ten which had been left when the war was over, were now dismissed to pacific and productive labor. Several of the officers resigned, and no more were retained than the actual strength of the regiments required. In addition to these measures, half the annual appropriation for the maintenance of the navy was withdrawn; and the sums devoted to the construction and armament of fortifications was similarly reduced.

On the motion of Mr. Clay, an appropriation was made for sending a minister to one of the new states of South America, which clearly indicated the sentiments of Congress and the people in favor of recognizing the independence of those states. The necessary steps were also taken for carrying into effect the treaty by which Florida had been added to the possessions of the United States; $100,000 were appropriated, and a board of three commissioners was appointed to settle existing claims under the treaty. Measures of relief for the public land debtors were adopted, as the president had suggested; by which $23,000,000, owing to the government, were extinguished, or in good part sacrificed; but the sales for the future were rendered *bonâ fide*, and fresh inducements were provided for both settlers and speculators of the honorable sort. A motion in the Senate to declare the sedition law of 1798 unconstitutional, and to repay the fines incurred under it, was lost; Congress thus affirming the authority of the federal courts, in respect to their decisions under this law. Propositions to establish a national system of education, by means of the revenue arising from the land sales; and for prohibiting the payment of government demands in bills of state banks, which issued notes of less than five dollars, were also rejected, and by decisive majorities.

1821.

On the 3d of March, the sixteenth Congress terminated its second session, and at the same time Mr. Monroe's first term of service expired. The great unanimity with which he had been reelected demonstrates, that the people generally were satisfied with his efforts, and devotion to the best interests of our country; and his prudence and discretion gave promise of his being equally successful in discharging the high and important duties again entrusted to his care.

The 4th of March falling on a Sunday this year, the president's inauguration took place the next day. The usual ceremonies were observed in the presence of an august assemblage, and Mr. Monroe delivered his second Inaugural address to a numerous company of friends and countrymen. It is a very long document, quite unostentatious, and, in a business-like way, recites the principal incidents of his first administration, and indicates the resources of the country. The fortification of the sea-coast, and the augmentation of the navy; neutrality with regard to the new states in South America and their contests with foreign powers; negotiations with Great Britain, France, and other European nations; the removal of the Indian tribes westward; the brilliant prospects of our country in the future; these and the like formed the staple of Mr. Monroe's address, and were not only adapted to the occasion but were received with approbation throughout the Union.

1821.

Among the earliest acts of the president after his inauguration, was the appointment, on the 10th of March, of General Jackson to be the governor of the newly-acquired territory of Florida. He was vested with "all the powers and authorities hitherto exercised by the governor and captain-general and intendant of Cuba, and by the governors of East and West Florida." Elijius Fromentin was appointed chief justice of the territory. About the middle of June, General Jackson arrived in Florida, and proceeded to take formal possession, in the name of the United States.

Fixing his head-quarters at Pensacola, he issued proclamations and ordinances for the government under his charge; but he speedily discovered, that the Spanish authorities were very reluctant to retire from their position, and were determined to embarrass him in every possible way. "Apprehending," says Monette, "a renewal of the evasions and artifices practised by the Spanish authorities, relative to the surrender of the Natchez District, in 1798, and relative to the factitious land-titles of Louisiana, Governor Jackson determined, by prompt measures, to suppress any such attempt. Having been informed that the ex-governor, Calleva, was about to transmit to Havana certain documents and archives pertaining to land titles, in violation of the second article of the treaty of cession, he made a peremptory demand for their surrender, as the property of the United States. The ex-governor refusing to obey the demand, Governor Jackson issued an order for his arrest and confinement in the calaboose, and the documents were seized and taken from his house, where they had been boxed up for shipment. The ex-governor was then released." Calleva, in the meantime, had obtained a writ of *habeas corpus* from Judge Fromentin, for his release; but General Jackson treated the writ very unceremoniously, and summoned the judge before him to answer for his conduct in the matter. Fromentin plead indisposition and did not appear, and after much altercation between the governor and the judge, the subject was dropped, and the respective parties—Jackson, Fromentin, and Calleva — published their statements and appeals in the newspapers.

1821.

The summary proceedings of General Jackson touched the Castilian pride to the quick, and some seven of the Spanish officers published in the Pensacola newspaper, a remonstrance against the governor's acts with regard to Calleva. Jackson, considering it an unwarrantable interference with his authority, and highly offensive in language, issued an order for their immediate departure from the country, on pain of imprisonment. Twelve of them were accordingly compelled to sail for Havana, with but little time allowed for settling up their affairs and disposing of their property.

A similar controversy occurred with the governor of East Florida, in relation to the archives of that province, and it was settled by Colonel Worthington, in October, in the same summary mode. The papers were seized and secured, and the Spaniards had no alternative but to submit to evident necessity. We may mention in this connection, that General Jackson retained his position till the following year, when the American population having increased so greatly as to include five thousand males, Florida was organized as a territory, in the first grade of territorial government.*

The president, on the 18th of Au-

* Three years later, in 1825, it was entitled to enter on the second grade. The white settlements were for the most part clustered round Pensacola, St. Mark's, Tallahassee, (which had been selected as the seat of government,) and St. Augustine; but the greater part of the country was still occupied by the native tribes of Indians.

gust, in conformity with the joint resolution for the admission of Missouri, issued his proclamation, announcing the fact, that that state had complied with the terms prescribed in the resolution, and declaring the admission of Missouri to be now complete. The vexatious controversy connected with the question of Missouri, and the progress of slavery, was held to be settled on a permanent basis; but there were men of thought and perspicacity who even then doubted the soundness and value of the "compromise." Subsequent events in our history demonstrate, that the real question at issue has not been settled; and there are those who entertain the opinion, that it never will be settled on mutually satisfactory terms.

On the 3d of December, the seventeenth Congress commenced its first session. In the Senate, now appeared for the first time, Samuel L. Southard, of New Jersey; Martin Van Buren, of New York; Thomas H. Benton, of Missouri; and Cæsar A. Rodney, of Delaware. In the House, the republican members were among the most distinguished of their party, such as Taylor, Sergeant, Randolph, Barbour, Cambreling, Walworth, Lowndes, etc. Henry Clay was not a member of this Congress; and Barbour was elected speaker by a small majority.

The president's fifth annual message was sent in the same day, and entered fully into the various questions requiring the attention of Congress.

1821. Its view of public affairs, abroad and at home, was encouraging, showing that there was a surplus in hand, by the help of the $5,000,000 loan; but, convinced that an increase of revenue would be necessary, the president recommended a moderate additional duty on certain articles.*

Early in the session, a resolution was adopted calling upon the president for information relative to General Jackson's course in Florida and his disputes with Judge Fromentin, etc. The president's answer, with the documents, was sent in at the close of January, 1822, and after considerable debate, it was settled, that the House would not enter into any investigation, or cast censure upon General Jackson. The apportionment of Representatives under the fourth census came up in February, and after much time was wasted in fixing the ratio, it was finally determined that there should be one member for every forty thousand of the people; this increased the number of members to two hundred and thirteen. **1822.**

A general bankrupt law was again proposed, and warmly urged on various grounds; but being opposed by the southern and western members it was lost by a vote of ninety-nine to seventy-two. The tariff question gave rise to much discussion, and the standing committee on manufactures reported against the expediency of further protection to home manufactures. Provision was made for receiving subscriptions to a loan of $26,000,000, at five per cent.,

* Among the distinguished men who were removed by death at this date, we may make mention of Elias Boudinot, who died in 1821, aged eighty-two; and of William Pinkney, aged fifty-seven; William Lowndes, aged forty-two; and General Stark, aged ninety-four; who died in 1822.

for the purpose of meeting the public debt at six and seven per cent., then falling due. In accordance with public sentiment, Congress, early in March, almost unanimously agreed to appropriate $100,000 to defray the expenses of missions to the South American republics. A bill for the preservation and repair of the Cumberland Road passed both Houses, the vote being, in the House of Representatives, eighty-three to seventy-one. The president, however, early in May, declined giving his sanction to the bill, and sent to Congress a very long and able document arguing against the constitutional power of the national legislature to make appropriations for internal improvements. The vote on the reconsideration of the bill with the president's objections, was sixty-eight in favor to seventy-two against it.

On the 8th of May, Congress adjourned to meet again on the first Monday in December.

CHAPTER IV.

1822-1825.

END OF MONROE'S ADMINISTRATION.

New political combinations — Candidates for the presidency — Convention with France — Relations with England — Congress in session — The message of the president — Acts of the session — "The A. B. plot" — Vice-president Tompkin's accounts — Decoudray's expedition against Porto Rico — Piracies in the West India seas — Porter's measures, and results — Eighteenth Congress — President's message — South American republics — "The Monroe doctrine" — J. Q. Adams its author — Amendments to the Constitution — Schemes and plans of politicians — Roads and canals, bankrupt law, etc. — Revision of the tariff — Long debate — Sympathy with the Greeks — The caucus system — Crawford nominated by a caucus — General Lafayette visits the United States — Enthusiastic reception — His progress through the country — Honors every where paid to him — Action of Congress in his behalf — The presidential contest — The result of the votes for Andrew Jackson, J. Q. Adams, W. H. Crawford, and Henry Clay — Second session of the eighteenth Congress — Position of matters as to the approaching election of president — Clay gives his influence in favor of Adams — Charges against him — Adams elected president by the House of Representatives — The Beaumarchais claim — Congress adjourns — Retrospect of James Monroe's administration — Extract from J. Q. Adams's Eulogy on Monroe.

During the session of Congress which had just closed, it became evident, that new political combinations were gradually forming in the United States. The question of protection divided
1822. the politicians of the Union by new lines; and it was the same with the right of Congress to superintend internal improvements; and since the greater number of the federalists had been absorbed into the democratic body, it was only by division in this body that new parties could be formed. The prospect of another presidential election, remote as it was, had called forth no fewer than six candidates. John Quincy Adams, who was the "successor," according to precedent, in the cases of Madison and Monroe; Andrew Jackson, whose undoubted democracy, added to

the triumph of New Orleans, made him the popular candidate, though at first his nomination excited much ridicule; Henry Clay, whose high standing as a diplomatist, and in Congress, justified his claims to the first office in the nation; William H. Crawford, William Lowndes, (who died in this year, 1822,) and John C. Calhoun, who represented sectional feelings, and personal or local politics, rather than party preference, or national renown. Adams, by virtue of his name alone, and Clay, by reason of his course, and as an opponent of the new democratic party, received the support of the federalists, or of those who had been federalists. Jackson received that of the democrats universally. It was also observed, that New England rallied round Adams, not unnaturally; the south mostly affected Crawford and Calhoun; while Jackson and Clay divided the supremacy of the western states. All of the candidates, it is worth noting, belonged to the old republican party.

In the month of June, a commercial convention was entered into with France. Its terms were considered favorable, and it was to continue for two years. The American and British commissioners under an article of the treaty of Ghent, ran the northern boundary line between the United States and the British possessions. The retaliatory course pursued in reference to the West India trade was loudly complained of by the British islands, and the English government felt compelled finally to agree to a reciprocal trade between its colonies in America and the United States. The president issued a proclamation on this subject on the 24th of August.

On the 2d of December, Congress reassembled, and the president's message was sent in on the following day. Various and important topics were spoken of in the message, **1822.** and a promising aspect of foreign and domestic affairs was presented; but no measure of special moment was recommended, none probably being deemed necessary, in the then position of the country. The receipts into the treasury for the first three quarters of the year had been more than $14,745,000. The payments during the same period had exceeded $12,279,000, leaving in the treasury $4,128,000. The gross amount of duties for the whole year was estimated at $23,000,000.

Few acts of note were passed during the present session, nor was any stirring political question obtruded upon the attention of the legislature. Government proceeded with the tranquility which characterizes a period of general prosperity, or one in which the energies of the people are not roused by any exciting topic. No increase of the duty on woolen goods could be effected; nor could imprisonment for debt be abolished; neither were the proposals to survey various canal routes (chiefly in the north) received; but an appropriation for the repair of the Cumberland Road passed, and received Monroe's signature, as he had intimated his willingness to co-operate to this extent in the cause of internal improvements—the right of exercising jurisdiction and sovereignty over the route not being assumed by the federal government.

An attempt was made to effect a settlement on the Pacific at the mouth of the Columbia River, Mr. Floyd, of Virginia, being very active in the matter; but the majority of the members of Con-
1823. gress deemed it visionary to pay attention to a region so distant and so inaccessible. An additional force was authorized for the suppression of piracy; the state of Ohio had certain grants of land made to it for aiding in constructing a road from the rapids of the Miami to the western boundary of the Connecticut reserve; an act was passed relative to the mode of doing business in the custom-houses, etc. Charges were made against Mr. Crawford, secretary of the treasury, of having mismanaged the public funds, violated the law, and the like; but after a full and thorough investigation, he was honorably and entirely acquitted. The accusations against Mr. Crawford having come from Ninian Edwards, who used the signature A. B., in a Washington newspaper, this affair was stigmatized as "the A. B. plot."

A rather singular question came before Congress at this session, viz., respecting the state of Vice-president Tompkins's accounts. In accordance with a bill passed in the preceding session, the payment of his salary was suspended, as it appeared that he was in arrear, in respect of the payments due by him to the treasury. He had in fact become involved in his private affairs, in consequence of advances he had made for the defence of New York in the late war, and of default in the payment of public moneys by his subordinate agents. In the trial before the circuit court, however, he claimed to be in advance, in his account with government, to the amount of nearly $136,800; and a committee of the House of Representatives, who investigated the circumstances of the case, reported a sum of $35,190 actually due to him; the payment of his salary was, therefore, resumed, and the arrears due to him, paid. "He had performed," said the committee, "all that was required, and more than was promised or expected. The protection of the city of New York, and the successful issue of the campaign of 1814, on the frontier, was owing in a great measure to his exertions."

This being the short session, the seventeenth Congress finished its career on the 3d of March, 1823.

An expedition under Decoudray, a Swiss adventurer, was illegally fitted out in New York, during 1822, for the purpose of seizing upon Porto Rico. It failed, however, entirely, and was soon forgotten. But the system of privateering, which was extensively carried on in the West India seas, compelled attention and called loudly for redress. During the contest between Spain and her revolted provinces, in consequence of the weakness and poverty of both sides, every species of atrocity was resorted to, and piracy, under the name of privateering, was eagerly pursued. The northern coast of Cuba was the chief haunt of the buccaneers, and Congress caused a part of the fleet to be stationed in those seas, for the
protection of American com- **1823.**
merce, which had suffered greatly from the attacks of these corsairs. In 1823,

Commodore Porter, once of the Essex — whose exploits in the Pacific we have narrated in a previous chapter—was appointed to the command of this squadron. His vigorous measures speedily freed the navigation of those seas from such dangers; but it was at a great sacrifice of life, principally in consequence of yellow fever.

Porter at last, having barely escaped death from yellow fever himself, returned home; and as he had received no orders to do so, was ordered back immediately. Returning to his post in October, 1824, he acted with such imprudent energy against Foxardo, a town of Porto Rico, where one of his officers, who had gone on an unauthorized errand, had been insulted, that he was superseded; and being tried by a court-martial, was suspended for six months. Upon which he entered the Mexican service, although it was illegal, as to his own government, to do so, and was made commander-in-chief of the naval forces of Mexico, with a salary of $25,000 a year. In his new capacity, he treated the United States and their neutrality very curtly and unceremoniously.* Captain Warrington was appointed to the command in the West Indies, and actively watched the interests of American commerce in that quarter.

The eighteenth Congress assembled on the first day of December, 1823. The approaching contest for the presidency exercised, as was to be expected, considerable influence in the elections to the House of Representatives; for it was believed by many, that in consequence of the number of candidates, that branch of the legislature would in the end be charged with the choice of the executive, and the friends of the various aspirants exerted themselves to the utmost to secure a return favorable to their hopes.

Rufus King, Southard, Van Buren, W. R. King, Macon, and others, were still in the Senate; and Hayne, of South Carolina, and Andrew Jackson, of Tennessee, were among the new appointments. In the House, Henry Clay was returned for Kentucky **1823** once more; Daniel Webster took his seat again, but it was for Massachusetts now; and there were also sent for the first time to this Congress, Samuel A. Foot, John Forsyth, William C. Rives, and Edward Livingston. As was customary, the first trial of strength took place on the election of a speaker; and the predominant influence of Clay was manifest, when he was returned at the first ballot, by a majority of nearly a hundred, over Philip P. Barbour.

The seventh annual message of the president was sent in the next day. It represented the finances as in a highly favorable condition—promising a surplus of $9,000,000 by the end of the year; and advised a revision of the tariff, for the especial purpose of protecting American manufactures, and as a means of increasing the national prosperity. It also recommended the construction of a canal to connect the Chesapeake and the Ohio, as a great

* Porter remained in the Mexican service, until 1829, when he returned to the United States. He was subsequently consul-general at Algiers, and minister to the Turkish court. He died at Pera, on the 28th of March, 1843.

national work, provided the jurisdiction were left in the hands of the states through which the canal should pass.

The chief interest, however, connected with the message, was in relation to foreign powers and their course of policy as respected the continent of America. Naturally, the United States took a deep interest in the condition and progress of the people of South America, and, as we have seen, there was an earnest desire manifested for their success in their struggles for liberty, and in their steadfast determination to throw off the yoke of foreign masters and rulers. European powers, on the other hand, viewed this matter with very different feelings; and Spain made urgent application to the allied sovereigns to assist her in subduing her rebellious colonies, promising extensive and valuable commercial privileges in return. Probably, they would have interfered in behalf of Spain, had not Great Britain opposed, in part at least, any such course of action. The president, in his message, states, that amicable negotiations were in progress with Russia and England, to settle their respective rights and interests on the north-west coast. "In the discussions to which this interest has given rise," he adds, "and in the arrangements by which they may terminate, the occasion has been judged proper for asserting, as a principle in which the rights and interests of the United States are involved, that the American continents, by the free and independent condition which they have assumed and maintain, are henceforth not to be considered as subjects of future colonization by any European powers."

Towards the close of the message, beside expressing warm sympathy with the heroic struggles of the Greeks, the president adverts to the efforts which had been made in Spain and Portugal, to improve the condition of the people of those nations, and **1823.** goes on to say, in words which deserve to be weighed carefully by the student of history; "Of events in that quarter of the globe, with which we have so much intercourse and from which we derive our origin, we have always been anxious and interested spectators. The citizens of the United States cherish sentiments the most friendly in favor of the liberty and happiness of their fellow-men on that side of the Atlantic. In the wars of the European powers, in matters relating to themselves, we have never taken any part, nor does it comport with our policy so to do. It is only when our rights are invaded or seriously menaced, that we resent injuries or make preparation for our defence. With the movements in this hemisphere we are of necessity more immediately connected, and by causes which must be obvious to all enlightened and impartial observers. The political system of the allied powers is essentially different in this respect from that of America. This difference proceeds from that which exists in their respective governments. And to the defence of our own, which has been achieved by the loss of so much blood and treasure, and matured by the wisdom of their most enlightened citizens, and under which we have enjoyed unexampled felicity, this whole nation is devoted. We owe it, therefore, to candor, and to the amicable relations existing between the United States and those powers, to declare, that we should consider any attempt on their part to extend their system to any portion of this hemisphere as dangerous to our peace and safety. With the existing colonies or dependencies of any European power we have not interfered, and shall not interfere. But with the governments who have declared their independence, and maintained it, and whose independence we have, on great consideration, and on just principles, acknowledged, we could not view any interposition for the purpose of oppressing them, or controlling in any other manner their destiny, by any European power, in any other light than as the manifestation of an unfriendly disposition toward the United States. In the war between those new governments and Spain, we declared our neutrality at the time of their recognition, and to this we have adhered, and shall continue to adhere, provided no change shall occur which, in the judgment of competent authorities of this government, shall make a corresponding change on the part of the United States indispensable to their security.

"The late events in Spain and Portugal show that Europe is still unsettled. Of this important fact no stronger proof can be adduced, than that the allied powers should have thought it proper, on a principle satisfactory to themselves, to have interposed by force in the internal concerns of Spain. To what extent such interposition may be carried, on the same principle, is a question to which all independent powers, whose governments differ from theirs, are interested; even those most remote, and surely none more so than the United States. Our policy in regard to Europe, which was adopted at an early stage of the wars which have so long agitated that quarter of the globe, nevertheless remains the same, which is, not to interfere in the internal concerns of any of its powers; to consider the government, *de facto*, as the legitimate government for us; to cultivate friendly relations with it, and to preserve those relations by a frank, firm, and manly policy; meeting, in all instances, the just claims of every power, submitting to injuries from none. But in regard to these continents, circumstances are eminently and conspicuously different. It is impossible that the allied powers should extend their political system to any portion of either continent without endangering our peace and happiness; nor can any one believe that our southern brethren, if left to themselves, would adopt it of their own accord. It is equally impossible, therefore, that we should behold such interposition, in any form, with indifference. If we look to the comparative strength and resources of Spain and those new governments, and their distance from each other, it must be obvious that she can never subdue them. It is still the true policy of the United States to leave the parties to themselves, in the hope that other powers will pursue the same course."

1823.

We have quoted these paragraphs in full, in order that the reader might see exactly what is meant by the "Monroe doctrine." It was a bold announcement on the president's part, although justice requires that the merit of it, if merit there be in it, should be attributed to John Quincy Adams, who originated the view, and from whom Mr. Monroe adopted it. However questionable it might be considered for the president to avow so openly and fully sentiments like these, committing the United States to a policy as novel as it was bold, the people of the Union adopted them at once; and though foreign powers were startled somewhat, and a little disposed to complain, the line of policy then marked out has ever since been that by which our government has regulated its conduct on this important subject.

Various amendments to the Constitution were proposed and advocated warmly, all of them, however, having reference, more or less direct, to the approaching presidential contest; but no one of the proposed amendments found sufficient favor to be adopted. The attention of members of Congress was greatly engrossed by schemes, and plans, and hopes, and fears, with regard to the man who was to be the next president. Manœuvres and intrigues of all kinds were put in practice, and every man gave in his adhesion to Adams, Jackson, Clay, Crawford, or Calhoun. The attack on Mr.
1824. Crawford was renewed, but to no purpose (see p. 339); and the other candidates were exposed to an ordeal more or less severe, in the way of personal attacks and imputations on character, which, however groundless, answered the object of political rivals and aspirants.

A long debate was had again on the subject of roads and canals, and $30,000 were appropriated for surveys, plans, and estimates of such roads and canals as the president might deem of national importance. Another attempt was made to establish a general bankruptcy law; and also to abolish imprisonment for debt; but both failed of meeting the approval of Congress.

In accordance with the president's recommendation on this subject, a very large share of attention was devoted to the revision of the tariff. The subject was fully discussed, Henry Clay being the great advocate on the one side, and Daniel Webster displaying his superior ability on the other. The agricultural and manufacturing interests in the east and the west were united in support of the principle of a protective tariff; and constituted a small majority in both Houses. The commercial and navigating interests of the north, joined with the large planters of the south, constituted a powerful, intelligent, and persevering minority, opposed to any tariff except for purposes of revenue. This sectional division, we may mention, helped not a little in determining one of the new parties, which were now germinating,—the national republicans, or whigs, as they were subsequently termed. For some ten weeks was this question debated; and at last, on the 16th of April, the bill passed
the House by a majority of five, **1824.**
which might have been less, for two members were absent; and the Senate accepted it, but amended its details considerably, the majority there being but four. It passed the Senate on the

15th of May, and, after a conference with the House, was finally adopted, and approved by the president.

Carrying out Mr. Monroe's suggestion, and going much beyond it, Daniel Webster prepared a resolution to the effect, that the president be authorized to send an agent or commissioner to Greece, whenever he might see fit. The speech of the great orator on this occasion, (January 19th), was one of the most eloquent which he ever made; and throughout the country the spirit of the people responded to the glowing sentiments of Webster. Meetings were held; subscriptions liberally made; money, clothing, provisions, arms, and the like, were shipped to Greece; and many an American citizen went and joined the patriots who were striving to do for their native land, what our fathers had accomplished in the western world. Mr. Clay and Mr. Poinsett advocated a resolution of sympathy with the Greeks in their struggles for independence; John Randolph opposed it with all his might, and the resolution was negatived on the ground of inexpediency.*

The adjournment did not occur (although it was not the longest session that had been held) till the 27th of May, so protracted were the debates.

1824. But it is worth noting, no session before it had ever been so fruitful in legislation; two hundred and twelve measures having passed through all stages to their completion.

The caucus system, which had been practiced a good deal in former contests, was now sharply discussed, and it began to be felt, that it would operate very injuriously to some of the candidates and aspirants for the highest office in the gift of the people. The system was denounced by the press, and efforts were made to induce the state legislatures to condemn them. Early in the session it was ascertained, that a decided plurality of the members of Congress were in favor of W. H. Crawford, the secretary of the treasury, who had nearly defeated Monroe in the caucus held in 1816; and great was the manœuvring and intriguing which followed. The partisans of the other candidates finally resolved, under something like a tacit understanding, that they would not hold any caucus in favor of their nominees; but the friends of Crawford held one, which, though attended by no more than sixty-six members, obtained for him only sixty-four votes. Afterwards two were given to Adams, one to Macon, and one to Andrew Jackson. The sixty-four were, however, nearly all the leading politicians of the old republican party, and they declared him to be duly nominated as the candidate of their party. And it was to this meeting that Crawford's failure was afterwards attributed; although it was also assigned to the failure of his health, which made his supporters question if he could discharge the duties of the president's office, in case he were elected. Gallatin was nominated for the vice-presidency by the same caucus, but he declined the honor. No other caucus was held in behalf of any of the competitors, but

* See Garland's "*Life of John Randolph*," vol. ii., pp. 196–200.

the canvass was actively pursued, and the partisans of each strenuously exerted themselves.

Notwithstanding the zeal and activity of political partisans, and the vigorous contest which was going on, the summer of 1824 was rendered memorable by the visit of the illustrious Lafayette, "the hero of two worlds." Some three years before, this noble patriot had expressed a wish to look upon the scenes of his early exploits again, and to press the hands of the few survivors of the armies and the actors of the Revolution; and Congress had, by a formal resolution, placed a government vessel at his disposal to convey him to America. Declining this honor, Lafayette embarked at Havre in the packet ship Cadmus, Captain Allen, accompanied by his son, who bore the revered name of Washington, and arrived at New York on the 15th of August.

It needs not that we tell of the celebrations, processions, dinners, illuminations, bonfires, parties, balls, serenades, and rejoicings of every description, which attended his way, from the moment he set foot on the American soil, until his embarkation to return to his native France; how his tour through the Union was one perpetual ovation, and his reception by the inhabitants *en masse* of one city and town after another, was marked by demonstrations of unbounded popular enthusiasm; and how in his gratitude and delight at all this, he saw nothing any where but prosperity and insured security, public and private; good order, the appendage of true freedom, and a national good sense, the final arbiter of all difficulties; and a glorious demonstration, to the most timid and prejudiced minds, of the superiority, over degrading aristocracy or despotism, of popular institutions founded on the plain rights of men. These have been fully detailed by the affectionate pen of his secretary, M. Levasseur.

We may, however, put on record, that Lafayette, leaving New York, proceeded to Boston, thence to Portsmouth in New Hampshire, and returning to New York, visited the towns along the Hudson, including Albany and Troy. Thence, he passed through New Jersey, visited Philadelphia, Baltimore, Washington, Yorktown and Richmond, and returned to the seat of government early in the session, where Congress united with their constituents in paying him honor. In February, 1825, he proceeded to the South, travelling through the Carolinas, Georgia, Alabama and Mississippi, to New Orleans; thence up the Mississippi to St. Louis; and passing through Kentucky, Ohio, Pennsylvania and New York, he arrived in Boston again to take part in the ceremony of laying the corner-stone of the Bunker Hill monument. Lafayette next visited Portland in Maine, passed through New Hampshire and Vermont, and returned to New York, where he shared in celebrating the 4th of July. Having gone again to Washington, and paid the sad tribute of shedding tears at the tomb of the great father of his **1825.** country, Lafayette, on the 7th of September, 1825, in the large hall of the capitol, amidst a vast concourse of all ranks, received the solemn words of farewell from President Adams, speaking in behalf of the whole people of the United States.

Congress, desirous of showing the nation's appreciation of Lafayette's sacrifices and exertions for the United States, voted him $200,000 in money, and a township of land in Florida. A new frigate, named in honor of him, Brandywine, was provided for his return to France; and so "the nation's guest" was sped on his way by the prayers and the love of admiring millions.

The contest for the presidency was actively carried on during the summer and autumn of 1824, and the friends and supporters of each candidate were not without hopes of ultimate success. Jackson, Adams, Crawford and Clay, were now before the people, and the result of the electoral vote was as follows:—for Andrew Jackson for president, all the votes of New Jersey, Pennsylvania, the Carolinas, Alabama, Mississippi, Tennessee, Indiana, with one from New York, seven from Maryland, three from Louisiana, and two from Illinois, ninety-nine in all;—for John Quincy Adams, all the votes of Maine, New Hampshire, Vermont, Massachusetts, Rhode

1824. Island, and Connecticut, with twenty-six from New York, one from Delaware, three from Maryland, two from Louisiana, and one from Illinois, in all eighty-four;—for William H. Crawford, all the votes of Virginia and Georgia, with five from New York, two from Delaware, and one from Maryland, in all forty-one;—and for Henry Clay, all the votes of Kentucky, Ohio, and Missouri, with four from New York, thirty-seven in all. There were two hundred and sixty-one votes to be given, and therefore an absolute majority would have been one hundred and thirty-one, which none of the candidates received; consequently, in accordance with the constitutional provision, the election devolved upon the House of Representatives.

Before this expected result was certainly known, the eighteenth Congress commenced its second session, on the 6th of December. The message of the president, being his last, was principally occupied in eulogizing the happy circumstances in which our country is placed, and the wide-spread prosperity which every where has marked our agriculture, commerce, and manufactures. The public debt, he stated, had been reduced to $86,000,000, and the current revenue was amply sufficient to meet all the liabilities of the government, besides discharging some $11,500,000 of the principal of the debt, and leaving a balance in the treasury of more than $3,000,000. After alluding to the position of Indian affairs; making especial mention of the visit of Lafayette; expressing his sympathy with the Greeks and with the South American states; he concluded his message in grateful and graceful terms of acknowledgment for the uniform confidence and steady support of his fellow-citizens, during his long career of public life.

Very little business of moment was transacted at this session of the national legislature. On the 9th of December, Lafayette was received by the

Senate, and the next day, by **1824.**

the House. In both cases, the profound respect and admiration for the man were evidenced by the distinguished honor which was paid to his presence in the hall of Congress. Not long after the commencement of the session, the result of the voting in the electoral colleges was known, and then the canvassing of members began; every body looking forward with no little excitement to the 9th of the following February, when the real choice was to be made. In this state of things, little regular business could be done; attention was given to the post-office affairs; the drawback on goods re-exported was arranged; the punishment of certain crimes against the United States was determined; and the appropriations required for carrying on the government, and extending the Cumberland Road, were made. Johnson could not succeed in carrying his bill for abolishing imprisonment for debt; nor could Rufus King persuade the Senate to adopt his plan, by which, after the payment of the national debt, the proceeds of the public lands were to be applied to the emancipation of slaves, and the removal of free persons of color to some territory beyond the limits of the United States.

The canvass in the House was marked by the usual electioneering devices, into the details of which we need not enter; but we may state here, that Henry Clay, finding his own election impossible, and considering his prospects at the next vacancy to be better served by the return of Adams now, followed his previously expressed determination, and exerted all his influence in favor of that experienced statesman. In consequence of this, an accusation of corruption was brought forward in a newspaper against Henry Clay, which he (unwisely, as it appeared to most of his friends,) raised into importance, by taking notice of in the House. Eventually the matter was dropped, but only to be resumed in a more serious manner on a future opportunity.*

On the 9th of February, the House proceeded to make a choice between the three highest candidates on the list, and on the first ballot, John Quincy Adams received the votes of thirteen states; Andrew Jackson, the votes of seven states, and William H. Crawford, the votes of four states. Mr. Adams, consequently, having **1825.** obtained a majority of the whole number, was declared duly elected president of the United States. John C. Calhoun, who had received one hundred and eighty-two votes in the electoral college for the second office in the gift of the people, now became vice-president of the United States.

The Beaumarchais claim, respecting which we have spoken in connection with our Revolutionary annals, (see vol. i., p. 528,) was again brought up

* No event in the political life of Mr. Clay was so injurious to his prospects of being made president, as his acceptance of the office of secretary of state, which was soon after urged upon him. Had he followed his own judgment in this matter, he would not have committed the mistake which proved fatal to his future advancement; but he was over persuaded, and though probably few, if any, believed the story of bargain and corruption, yet it was too convenient and too popular a mode of injuring an opponent, to expect the political press and stump orators to abstain from using it on nearly every occasion, when Henry Clay's name was before the people.

for investigation, and was fully discussed in the House. The particulars we need not enter into here; the claim was again refused to be entertained, although strong reasons were presented in its behalf. The matter, however, was finally settled in the treaty negotiated by Mr. Rives, in 1835.*

On the 3d of March, 1825, the eighteenth Congress came to a close. At the same date, Mr. Monroe's second term of office ended, and he retired from the high dignity of president of the United States to private life, with the respect and esteem of his fellow-citizens, and with a consciousness that he had deserved well of his country.

1825.

In a retrospect of the administration of James Monroe, it must be admitted, that it was unusually successful, so much so as to be termed "the era of good feeling." Monroe himself, as his immediate successor testified, possessed "a mind anxious and unwearied in the pursuit of truth and right; patient of inquiry; patient of contradiction; courteous, even in the collision of sentiment; sound in its ultimate judgments; and firm in its final conclusions." There was nothing brilliant about him; he was not a man of genius evidently; his ability was certainly not above the average of men of his day; he was courteous, discreet, peace-loving, not fond of bold measures, and sincerely desirous that the hand of government should be seen and felt as little as was possible in public affairs. His foreign policy, as conducted mainly through his able secretary of state, was dignified, firm, and acceptable to the people; while at home, his administration was memorable for the acquisition of Florida, and for the steady advance of the country, despite all financial embarrassments, in its progress towards national prosperity and greatness. We may, in conclusion, quote the words of John Quincy Adams's eulogy on the fifth president of the United States, as expressing the devout admiration of one who knew, and was able thoroughly to appreciate, his virtues and his excellence:* "Let us join in humble supplication to the Founder of empires and the Creator of all worlds, that he would continue to your posterity, the smiles by which his favor has been bestowed upon you; and since 'it is not in man that walketh to direct his steps,' that he would enlighten and lead the advancing generation in the way they should go. That in all the perils and all the mischances which may threaten or befall our United Republic, in after times, he would raise up from among your sons, deliverers to enlighten her councils, to defend her freedom, and if need be to lead her armies to victory. And should the gloom of the year of Independence ever again overspread the sky, or the

* For some interesting remarks in connection with this subject, and the man whose name occurs a number of times in our history, we refer the reader to M. De Loménie's "*Beaumarchais and His Times*," or, Sketches of French Society in the Eighteenth Century, from unpublished documents. Translated from the French. New York, 1857

* This Eulogy was delivered before the Corporation of Boston, in 1831.

John Quincy Adams.

The last Portrait taken from life

metropolis of your empire be once more destined to smart under the scourge of an invader's hand, that there never may be found wanting among the children of your country a warrior to bleed, a statesman to counsel, a chief to direct and govern, inspired with all the virtues, and endowed with all the faculties, which have been so signally displayed in the life of James Monroe."

CHAPTER V.

1825-1829.

JOHN QUINCY ADAMS'S ADMINISTRATION.

Inauguration of John Quincy Adams — Extract from his Inaugural Address — The cabinet of the new president — Treaty with the Creeks — Difficulties of the subject — Other Indian treaties — Jackson nominated by the legislature of Tennessee — Opposition organized against the administration — The Erie canal — The nineteenth Congress — Abstract of the president's message — The American Congress at Panama — Attacked by the opposition — Result — Amendments to the Constitution — Political objects in view — The Creek treaty — Movements for increase of the judges — Congress favors internal improvements — The deaths of Thomas Jefferson and John Adams — Extract from Daniel Webster's eulogy — Congress in session — The message of the president — Action of Congress — "The Great Conspiracy" — Its object — How met by Henry Clay — Elections for members of Congress — The twentieth Congress — Full attendance — Abstract of the message — The tariff question — Warm and long contest — How settled — Senator Benton quoted — Retrenchment advocated — Judiciary bill, Revolutionary pensioners' bill, etc. — The presidential contest of 1828 — Fierce and unscrupulous warfare — Congress in session — Mr. Adams's last message — Subject of protection, etc. — Action of Congress — End of the session — Review of John Quincy Adams's administration.

ON the 4th of March, 1825, John Quincy Adams was inaugurated as the sixth president of the United States. The ceremonial was an imposing one, and was attended and watched with deep interest by a large body of the new president's fellow-citizens. Clad in a plain suit of black, wholly of American manufacture, Mr. Adams, at the proper moment, delivered his Inaugural address. It is a well-written document, glowing with patriotism and earnest wishes for the advancement of our country in every thing that is good, and pure, and true. Conciliatory in his tone, anxious to promote concord and unanimity among the people in all parts of the Union, highly lauding the administration of James Monroe, Mr. Adams concludes his Inaugural in terms which deserve to be quoted, as marking out clearly his views on the much disputed question of internal improvements, and as modestly appealing for support and confidence in endeavoring to discharge the responsible duties of his lofty station.

1825.

1825.

"In this brief outline," said Mr. Adams, "of the promise and performance of my immediate predecessor, the line of duty for his successor is clearly delineated. To pursue, to their consummation, those purposes of improvement in our common condition, instituted or recommended by him, will embrace the whole sphere of my obligations. To the topic of internal improvement, emphatically urged by him at his inauguration, I recur with peculiar satisfaction. It is that from which I am convinced that the unborn millions of our posterity, who are, in future ages, to people this continent, will derive their most fervent gratitude to the founders of the Union; that, in which the beneficent action of its government will be most deeply felt and acknowledged. The magnificence and splendor of their public works are among the imperishable glories of the ancient republics. The roads and aqueducts of Rome have been the admiration of all after ages, and have survived thousands of years, after all her conquests have been swallowed up in despotism, or become the spoil of barbarians. Some diversity of opinion has prevailed with regard to the powers of Congress for legislation upon objects of this nature. The most respectful deference is due to doubts originating in pure patriotism, and sustained by venerated authority. But nearly twenty years have passed since the construction of the first national road was commenced. The authority for its construction was then unquestioned. To how many thousands of our countrymen has it proved a benefit? To what single individual has it ever proved an injury? Repeated liberal and candid discussions in the legislature have conciliated the sentiments, and proximated the opinions of enlightened minds, upon the question of constitutional power. I cannot but hope, that by the same process of friendly, patient, and persevering deliberation, all constitutional objections will ultimately be removed. The extent and limitation of the powers of the general government, in relation to this transcendently important interest, will be settled and acknowledged, to the common satisfaction of all, and every speculative scruple will be solved by a practical public blessing.

"Fellow-citizens, you are acquainted with the peculiar circumstances of the recent election, which have resulted in affording me the opportunity of addressing you, at this time. You have heard the exposition of the principles which will direct me in the fulfilment of the high and solemn trust imposed upon me in this station. Less possessed of your confidence in advance, than any of my predecessors, I am deeply conscious of the prospect that I shall stand, more and oftener, in need of your indulgence. Intentions, upright and pure; a heart devoted to the welfare of our country, and the unceasing application of all the faculties allotted to me, to her service, are all the pledges that I can give, for the faithful performance of the arduous duties I am to undertake. To the guidance of the legislative councils; to the assistance of the executive and subordinate departments; to the friendly co-operation of the respective state governments; to the candid and liberal support of the people, so far as it may be deserved by honest industry and zeal, I shall look for whatever success may attend my public service; and knowing that, except the Lord keep the city, the watchman waketh but in vain; with fervent supplications for His favor, to His overruling Providence I commit, with humble but fearless confidence, my own fate, and the future destinies of my country."

The new president then took the oath required by the Constitution, and, having received the congratulations of the assemblage, Monroe and Jackson being of the number, was prepared to enter upon the duties of his office. He immediately sent to the Senate, for their confirmation, the names of the gentlemen he had selected as forming his cabinet. Henry Clay was nominated for secretary of state; Richard Rush, secretary of the treasury; James Barbour, secretary of war; Samuel Southard, secretary of the navy; and William Wirt, attorney-general. The two latter, with Mr. McLean, postmaster-general, had held the same posts under Mr. Monroe. No objection was made to any of these names, except that of Mr. Clay, against whom the charge of bargaining and corruption was made. Twenty-seven voted for Mr. Clay's confirmation; fourteen opposed it, Andrew Jackson being one of these.

One of the earliest subjects brought before the new administration, was the arranging a treaty with the Creek Indians in Georgia, for a cession of their lands, and for their removal west of the Mississippi. It appears that some fifteen millions of acres had been purchased from the Indians, and conveyed to the state of Georgia before the year 1824; about nine millions and a half remained in the possession of the Indians, the larger moiety belonging to the Cherokees, and the remainder to the Creeks. Commissioners were appointed, and efforts were made to induce the Creeks to remove and vacate the lands occupied by them; but whether it was owing to the consideration that the Indians began to appreciate the advantages of civilization, or to some other cause or causes, the nation generally opposed a cession of their lands, and were exceedingly unwilling to remove west of the Mississippi. One of their chiefs, however, M'Intosh, and some others, made a treaty at the Indian Springs, on the 12th of February, and the Senate, on the last day of the session, ratified it on the part of the United States. The Creeks, at least the larger number of them, were not at all pleased with what had been done, and on the 30th of April, they summarily murdered M'Intosh, Tustanuggee, and Hawkins, who had been the principal agents in giving up their lands. The state of Georgia, which was greatly benefited by this treaty, insisted on its being carried into effect, and Governor Troup actually began a survey of the lands, in order to their distribution amongst the people The Creeks, on their part, were resolute in their determination to resist such action of the government by force, and sent a messenger to Washington, claiming the protection of the federal authorities.

1825.

Mr. Adams doubted the validity of the treaty, and sent General Gaines to the Creek country to prevent any outbreak, if possible, and also a commissioner to investigate the affair. On his report, which seemed to prove clearly bad faith and corruption in obtaining the treaty, the president decided that the Creeks should not be interfered with until the next session of Congress. The governor of Georgia was disposed to take matters in his own hands, and used a good deal of lofty language, which was far from respectful to the government; but, on the whole, discretion being the better part of valor, he concluded to wait the result of the action of Congress.

During the summer of the present year, other treaties with Indian tribes were made on equitable terms. The Kansas Indians ceded to the United States all their lands both within and without the limits of Missouri, except a reservation beyond that state on the Kansas River, about thirty miles square, including their villages. In consideration of this cession, the United

1825. States agreed to pay $3,500 a year for twenty years; to furnish the Kansas immediately with three hundred head of cattle, three hundred hogs, five hundred fowls, three yoke of oxen, and two carts, and with such farming utensils as the Indian superintendent may deem necessary; to provide and support a blacksmith for them; and to employ persons to aid and instruct them in their agricultural pursuits, as the president may deem expedient. Of the ceded lands, thirty-six sections on the Big Blue River, were to be laid out under the direction of the president, and sold for the support of schools among the Kansas. Reservations were also made for the benefit of certain half-breeds; and other stipulations mutually satisfactory. It was also agreed, that no private revenge shall be taken by the Indians for the violation of their rights; but that they shall make their complaint to the superintendent or other agent, and receive justice in a due course of law; and it was lastly agreed, that the Kansas nation shall never dispose of their lands without the consent of the United States, and that the United States shall always have the free right of navigation in the waters of the Kansas.

A treaty was also concluded, early in June, with the Great and Little Osages, at St. Louis, Missouri. The general principles of this treaty were the same as those of the treaty with the Kansas. The Indians ceded all their lands in Arkansas and elsewhere, and then reserved a defined territory, west of the Missouri line, fifty miles square; an agent was to be permitted to reside on the reservation, and the United States were to have the right of free navigation in all the waters on the tract. The United States agreed to pay an annuity of $7000 for twenty years; to furnish forthwith six hundred

head of cattle, six hundred hogs, 1825.

one thousand fowls, ten yoke of oxen, six carts, with farming utensils, persons to teach the Indians agriculture, and a blacksmith, and build a commodious dwelling-house for each of the four principal chiefs, at his own village. Reservations were made for the establishment of a fund for the support of schools for the benefit of the Osage children; and provision was made for the benefit of the Harmony missionary establishment. The United States also assumed certain debts due from certain chiefs of the tribes; and agreed to deliver at the Osage villages, as soon as might be, $4000 in merchandise, and $2600 in horses and their equipments.*

In October, the legislature of Tennessee, by a nearly unanimous vote, passed a resolution, nominating General Jackson for the presidency at the next election. This led to Jackson's resignation as Senator, on the ground that candidates for the presidency ought not to be members of Congress. In this connection, we may mention the fact, that immediately on Adams's election, all the friends of the disappointed candidates resolved to unite, so as to prevent his re-election, and bring in Andrew Jackson in his place. Personal differences were speedily reconciled. Benton and Jackson, who had formerly met w'th pistols and dirks in a duel, put their quarrels on one side, in order to work for a common object; and Crawford and Calhoun were also ranged on the side of Jackson, in opposition to the administration. The reader will do well to bear these things in mind, in order to understand some of the difficulties and trials of Mr. Adams's four years of service.†

1825.

During the autumn of the present year, the completion of the Erie canal was effected, and was duly celebrated in the city of New York. It demonstrated the wisdom of that policy which De Witt Clinton advocated with so much perseverance and ability, and the final success of the great undertaking has established on a firm basis, the sagacity and statesmanship of this distinguished son of New York. The ground for the canal was broken on the 4th of July, 1817; and the first boat from Lake Erie, arrived at New York, on the 4th of October, 1825. The length of the canal is three hundred and sixty miles.

The nineteenth Congress began its first session on the 5th of December, and the president's first annual message was sent in the next day. The Senate numbered among its members, Woodbury, Van Buren, Macon, Hayne, Eaton, Harrison, etc.* In the House were, Edward Everett, Daniel Webster, C. C. Cambreling, James K. Polk, J. W. Taylor, and others of more or less note. Mr. Taylor was elected speaker on the second ballot.

1825.

The president's message was unusually long, but ably and clearly written, and containing suggestions and views which demanded attention. There was presented in it a favorable picture of the general concerns of the nation, both foreign and domestic. Yet several questions, arising out of the foreign relations of the Union, were spoken of as unsettled. It recommended the entire abolition of discriminating duties

* Holmes's "*Annals*," vol. ii., pp. 512, 13.

† De Witt Clinton was offered the mission to England, but declined it; Mr. Poinsett was sent as minister to Mexico; and Mr. Everett to Madrid.

* John Randolph entered the Senate at the close of the month of December, having been elected to supply the vacancy caused by Mr. Barbour's acceptance of the post of secretary of war. At the close of the term, in March, 1827, Mr. John Tyler was elected to the Senate, in Mr. Randolph's place, and he was returned again for a seat in the House.

on tonnage, in respect of all nations who were willing to reciprocate the privilege; a revision of the judiciary system; a general bankruptcy law; an extension of the law of patents; internal improvements on an enlarged scale; the establishment of an observatory, a national university, and a uniform standard of weights and measures; and the promotion of voyages of discovery. Mr. Adams also added,—"The Constitution under which you are assembled is a charter of limited powers; after full and solemn deliberation upon all or any of the objects which, urged by an irresistible sense of my own duty, I have recommended to your attention, should you come to the conclusion, that, however desirable in themselves, the enactment of laws for effecting them would transcend the powers committed to you by that venerable instrument, which we are all bound to support, let no consideration induce you to assume the exercise of powers not granted to you by the people."

The state of the finances was pronounced to be very flourishing. There had been a balance, little short of $2,000,000 in the treasury, at the commencement of the year; and the receipts, to the end of September, were estimated at $16,500,000, while those of the current quarter were expected to exceed $5,000,000. And this was without reckoning the loan of $5,000,000 which had been authorized by Congress. The expenditure of the year, it was said, would not exceed the receipts by more than $2,000,000; but in it was included the extinction of $8,000,000 of the public debt. The revenue for the coming year was calculated at $24,000,000, which would exceed the whole expenditure of the year. The entire amount of public debt, remaining due on the last day of the current year, was stated to be less than $81,000,000. The president, in conclusion, thus expressed himself: "Finally, fellow-citizens, I shall await with cheering hope, and faithful co-operation, the result of your deliberations; assured that, without encroaching upon the powers reserved to the authorities of the respective states, or to the people, you will, with a due sense of your obligations to your country, and of the high responsibilities weighing upon yourselves, give efficacy to the means committed to you for the common good. And may He, who searches the hearts of the children of men, prosper your exertions to secure the blessings of peace, and promote the highest welfare of our country."*

1825.

The president's views in regard to the American Congress at Panama, afforded a fair ground of attack to the opposition. It appears, that in 1823, Bolivar, at that time president of Columbia, invited the governments of the provinces which had thrown off the Spanish yoke, to join in a general Congress at Panama; and some steps were taken to effect it, but without success. At the

* This copious and conciliatory message was commented on by the political press, and by numerous opponents of the administration, with great severity; and as the president had expressed himself with much freedom on the subject of internal improvements, and had termed observatories, by a rather unusual conceit, "light-houses of the sky," ridicule and argument were both brought to bear, for the purpose of rendering the administration unpopular, and thus the better prepare for the success of Andrew Jackson.

end of the next year, the invitation was renewed, and all the governments accepted it, excepting Buenos Ayres. Next spring, the government of the United States was invited to send representatives to Panama, and John Quincy Adams replied, that, although the United States would take no part in the war with Spain, or in deliberating on the manner or means of carrying it on, he believed that such a Congress might be serviceable, by giving authority to some important principles of public law, arranging matters of great interest to the whole of the New World, and promoting a friendly intercourse between the various republican governments which had become established in America. In his message, the president thus spoke of his reception of Bolivar's proposal; "The invitation has been accepted, and ministers on the part of the United States will be commissioned to attend those deliberations, and to take part in them, so far as may be compatible with that neutrality, from which it is neither our intention, nor the desire of the other

1825.

American states, that we should depart." This announcement was followed by the nomination of Richard C. Anderson and John Sergeant, as commissioners to the Congress, and William B. Rochester, as secretary. The Senate, after a long and violent discussion of the expediency of taking part in this Congress, in the course of which the members of the opposition attacked the administration with unsparing severity, approved the nomination of the commissioners. This was at the close of March, 1826. In the House of Representatives, also, the subject was fully discussed; and, what is not usual, with less violence on the part of the opposition.* In the end, however, the necessary appropriation was voted, the arguments and oratory of Daniel Webster proving unanswerable.

1826.

It was quite evident, that the great heat and excitement of the dispute on this subject was due rather to political factiousness, than because there was any danger arising from this mission to the interests of the United States; but, so far as appears by the result, neither side gained or lost anything of moment from the discussion on this question. It is worth noticing, in this connection, that no representative from the United States ever appeared at the Panama Congress. For the debates in the House of Representatives were so protracted, that it was impossible for Sergeant to reach Panama in time for the meeting; although it had been postponed from October, 1825, to midsummer, in the year following. Anderson, who was minister at Columbia, as soon as he received instructions, set out for Panama; but on reaching Carthagena, he was attacked by a malignant fever,

* It was in the course of John Randolph's furious diatribe on this topic, that he used the expressions, "I was defeated, horse, foot, and dragoons—cut up, and clean broke down, by the coalition of Blifil and Black George—by the combination, unheard of till then, of the puritan with the black-leg." Mr. Clay, deeming himself insulted by this language and its vile imputations, challenged Randolph to the field. They met on Saturday, the 8th of April, on the Virginia side of the Potomac; Clay missed Randolph, and Randolph fired into the air. No murderous result, consequently followed; but the insult was considered as wiped out, and the parties renewed their former friendly relations.

and died. Poinsett, the ambassador at Mexico, was then appointed in his place, and he, with Sergeant, immediately prepared to be present, when the Congress should reassemble, in February, 1827, at Tacubaya. It did not, however, meet at the appointed time; and Sergeant, therefore, returned to the United States. This project was never afterwards revived, principally because the intestine dissensions of South America rendered it impossible to effect anything of importance, and also because no further political capital could well be made out of it.*

Early in the session, on the 20th of December, 1825, the House called on the president for information, respecting the convention between England and the United States for the suppression of the slave trade. On the 27th, the president sent in the correspondence between Mr. Clay and Mr. Addington, the English *chargé d'affaires*, from which it appeared, that there was no immediate prospect of a harmonising of the views held by the two governments.

As helping to keep alive the spirit of opposition to the administration, various amendments to the Constitution were proposed, in order to do away, if possible, with the intervention of the House of Representatives in electing the president, it being asserted that Mr. Adams, though elected in the constitutional way, was not the choice of the people. In the Senate, Mr. Benton took the lead, with a resolution, declaring for what, in rather fantastic phraseology, he terms "the *demos-krateo* principle;" by which was meant the direct vote of the people. Mr. Benton's bill providing for the proposed change in the Constitution, was laid on the table on the 9th of May. In the House, Mr. M'Duffie, of South Carolina, proposed the establishment of a uniform mode of electing the executive officers by districts, instead of leaving it to the state legislatures, who were capable, it was thought, of doing very unhandsome things for unjust and party purposes. He also introduced a declaration, in favor of preventing the election from ever devolving upon Congress. Other amendments, one of them prohibiting the re-election of a president for more than a second term of office, were also introduced. There were, in fact, nearly a dozen different resolutions upon this subject before Congress at the same time, and they were all referred by the House to a committee of twenty-four; which, after much discussion, and many efforts to reach some practical conclusion, found it impossible to agree in favor of any scheme, and begged to be discharged. Thus nothing resulted from the movement, unless perhaps an increase to the unpopularity of Mr. Adams's administration.

1826.

At the close of January, another treaty was negotiated with the Creeks, which was ratified by the Senate in April. By this treaty, the lands

* At the close of Mr. Adams's administration, in compliance with a call to that effect, copies of the instructions given to the commissioners to Panama, were supplied to both Houses; and not long after they were made public. These instructions the reader may be interested in examining; we are of opinion that he will discover little, if anything, to justify the favorers of this Congress, or excite the fears of its opponents.

in Georgia were ceded to the United States, and the government agreed to pay them $217,600, to be divided among their chiefs and warriors, and also to pay a perpetual annuity of $20,000. M'Intosh's friends and followers being willing to emigrate, were to do so within two years, and the United States were to defray the expense of their removal. They were also to be paid $100,000, and to be paid for their improvements. The remaining lands of the Creeks in Georgia were afterwards purchased by the United States for $30,000, and the House, by a very large vote, agreed to appropriate $60,000 for the proposed emigration of a part of the Creeks.

Towards the close of the session, Mr. Macon offered a resolution in the Senate, in respect to the expediency of reducing the patronage of the executive. No fewer than six bills were reported by the committee, to which the question was referred, as the foundation of a system to be followed up hereafter. But although unusual means were adopted to excite public opinion upon this subject, the matter remained in its first stage to the end of the session, and expired with the rest of the unfinished business.

1826.

Notwithstanding the vast increase in the population of the west, no modification had been made in the arrangement of the judiciary department, since 1807, when Ohio, Kentucky, and Tennessee, had been formed into a circuit. The result had been of late years to cause great delay in administering justice, and great dissatisfaction to the parties concerned. An attempt was made, in 1819, to correct this state of things, by the introduction of a bill to establish the system of circuit courts throughout the United States; another of the same kind, for increasing the number of judges of the supreme court, was made in the first session of the eighteenth Congress; but nothing had been done. Daniel Webster, therefore, now, as chairman of a committee on the judiciary, introduced a bill, which provided for the creation of three additional associate judges to those at present existing, and an entire re-arrangement of the circuits of the west. Great opposition was made to the passage of this bill. Some opposed it on the ground that it would render the bench of the supreme court too numerous, and thus diminish the responsibility, and impair the usefulness of the several judges. Others objected to the introduction of so many judges, at one time, from the west. The bill finally passed the House by a considerable majority; but having been much modified in the Senate, a difference arose between the two branches of the legislature, and in spite of the efforts made to effect an understanding, the bill was lost.

Congress was now, in general, as it seemed, favorable to measures of internal improvement; and a number of appropriations, having this object in view, were made during the present session. With the details we are not at present concerned; but we may observe, that the execution of several plans was intrusted to the war department. The usual appropriations for carrying on the government, etc., according to the president's programme

1826.

of business, were made; but the opposition contrived to delay a bill, by which provision was to be made for the survivors of the army of the Revolution, until there was not sufficient time for it to become a law. The condition of the finances could not be appealed to, as an objection to this appropriation; and its failure seems to show, that the opposition were resolved to leave no course untried in order to thwart the wishes and measures of the administration.

On the 22d of May, Congress adjourned to meet again on the first Monday in December.

The present year was memorable in our annals, for the removal by death of two of those distinguished men, who had taken part in the glorious struggle for liberty, and had served in the highest office which a grateful country can entrust to any of her sons. And what rendered the event more striking was, that Thomas Jefferson and John Adams, the one by whose pen the Declaration of Independence was prepared, the other by whose powerful voice it was advocated and urged in the Continental Congress, both died on the same day, and that day the fiftieth anniversary of our national independence. The 4th of July, 1826, was indeed a day to be remembered. No wonder that the whole nation was roused, and that the occasion was embraced by the first men of the country, to dilate upon the wonderful events which the last half century had witnessed. Our limits do not admit of details respecting the honors heaped upon the memories of Adams and Jefferson; yet we cannot forbear a brief quotation from the glowing eulogy on these two patriots of our early history, which Daniel Webster delivered at Boston, on the 2d of August, 1826.*

"No men, fellow-citizens," said the eloquent speaker, "ever served their country with more entire exemption from every imputation of selfish and mercenary motives, than those to whose memory we are paying these proofs of respect. A suspicion of any disposition to enrich themselves, or to profit by their public employments, never rested on either. No sordid motive approached them. The inheritance which they have left to their children, is of their character and fame. Fellow-citizens, I will detain you no longer by this faint and feeble tribute to the memory of the illustrious dead. Even in other hands, adequate justice could not be performed, within the limits of this occasion. Their highest, their best praise, is your deep conviction of their merits, your affectionate gratitude for their labors and services. It is not my voice, it is this cessation of ordinary pursuits, this arresting of all attention, these solemn ceremonies, and this crowded house, which speak their eulogy. Their fame, indeed, is safe. That is now treasured up, beyond the reach of accident.

. . . .

"The striking attitude, too, in which we stand to the world around us, a topic to which, I fear, I advert too

* William Wirt also delivered an elaborate and eloquent discourse on the lives and characters of Jefferson and Adams, at the request of the citizens of Washington, in the Hall of Representatives, on the 19th of October, 1826. See Moore's "*American Eloquence*," vol. ii., pp. 443–60.

often, and dwell on too long, cannot be altogether omitted here. Neither individuals nor nations can perform their part well, until they understand and feel its importance, and comprehend and justly appreciate all the duties belonging to it. It is not to inflate national vanity, nor to swell a light and empty feeling of self-importance; but it is that we may judge justly of our situation, and of our duties, that I earnestly urge this consideration of our position, and our character, among the nations of the earth. It cannot be denied, but by those who would dispute against the sun, that with America, and in America, a new era commences in human affairs. This era is distinguished by free representative governments, by entire religious liberty, by improved systems of national intercourse, by a newly awakened and an unconquerable spirit of free inquiry, and by a diffusion of knowledge through the community, such as has been before altogether unknown and unheard of. America, America, our country, fellow-citizens, our own dear and native land, is inseparably connected, fast bound up, in fortune and by fate, with these great interests. If they fall, we fall with them; if they stand, it will be because we have upholden them. Let us contemplate, then, this connection, which binds the prosperity of others to our own; and let us manfully discharge all the duties which it imposes. If we cherish the virtues and the principles of our fathers, Heaven will assist us to carry on the work of human liberty and human happiness. Auspicious omens cheer us. Great examples are before us. Our own firmament now shines brightly upon our path. WASHINGTON is in the clear upper sky. Those other stars have now joined the American constellation; they circle round their centre, and the heavens beam with new light. Beneath this illumination, let us walk the course of life, and at its close devoutly commend our beloved country, the common parent of us all, to the Divine Benignity."

1826.

During the recess of Congress, a convention of amity, commerce, and navigation, was concluded at Washington with Central America, on terms which were regarded as both liberal and reciprocal. The treaty was to continue in force for twelve years, and was ratified by the president on the 28th of October.*

The second session of the nineteenth Congress commenced on the 4th of December, and the second annual message of the president, was transmitted to the House on the same day. Foreign affairs were represented as, on the whole in a favorable condition, as respects France, the Netherlands, Denmark, etc. With Great Britain, however, as well as France, various and important topics were, as yet, unsettled. In regard to the financial affairs of the Union, the president informed Congress, that although the revenue of the preceding year had not equalled the anticipated amount, above $7,000,000 had been

* In the autumn of 1826, the abduction of Morgan took place, and gave rise to the anti-masonic excitement, and the measures resulting therefrom. For some three or four years, the masonic fraternity was freely denounced, and numerous politicians made use of this topic, as a means of advancing ends in which they had an interest.

applied to the reduction of the public debt, and nearly $4,000,000 to the payment of interest thereon; and the balance in the treasury at the close of the year, was expected to be $1,200,000. The prospects for the coming year were represented as more favorable. Amongst the recommendations, which were few in number, and did not include any of those contained in the former message, to which so little attention had been paid, the principal that we find, are a plan for the gradual increase of the navy, and the performance of certain works of internal improvement.

1826.

Another attempt was now made, to introduce a uniform system of bankruptcy, but ineffectually,—the majority asserting, that though such a law would benefit the wealthy merchants of the Atlantic seaports, the rest of the community would receive from it nothing but harm. A bill for the increase of the duties on imported woolen goods, the design of which was to promote American manufactures by the operation of *protection*, was introduced early, and passed the House of Representatives; but it failed in the Senate, being thrown out by the casting vote of the vice-president. Various grants, and appropriations for the promotion of internal improvements, were made in compliance with the president's recommendation. The sum of $500,000 yearly, was also granted for six years, for the gradual improvement of the navy. The proposal to bestow pensions upon the Revolutionary survivors did not meet with the success which it merited. The subject of British colonial trade also occupied the attention of both Houses; and bills were prepared in order to effect a mutually satisfactory arrangement; but no result followed; the matter was left unsettled. The truth seems to have been, that the spirit of party was so strong, that although there was a great deal of talk, there was very little work done. The session closed on the 3d of March, 1827, with a large amount of public business unfinished.*

1827.

Great excitement arose after the adjournment of Congress, in consequence of the story being revived which charged Mr. Clay with corruption and bargaining, in respect to the election of Mr. Adams; and the opposition, now thoroughly organized, used this potent weapon with great force, to the injury of the administration, and the advancing the claims of Andrew Jackson, on whom, as we have previously stated, (p. 353,) the democratic party now united their strength. Into the particulars of this "great conspiracy," as Mr. Clay's friends termed it, we need not now enter. General Jackson was prominent in setting the charge afloat, in a letter which he addressed to Mr. Carter Beverley, of Virginia, and when called on for authority, named Mr. Buchanan, (now, in 1857, president of the United States,) as the "member of Congress, of high respectability," who had approached him with propositions on the subject of Mr. Clay's being made

* Certain charges of corruption against Mr. Calhoun, while he was secretary of war, were investigated by a committee of the House at his request; and Elijah Mix and "the Rip Rap Contract" were disposed of, and the vice-president entirely exculpated from censure.

secretary of state, in case he would give his influence for Jackson's election. When Mr. Buchanan's letter on the subject was published, it soon became evident to all candid men, that Mr. Clay had been belied, and that there was no real foundation for the atrocious charge which had been so freely circulated respecting him. Yet, as falsehood nearly always gets sufficient start of truth to accomplish the purposes of those who are willing to use it, so in this case, the administration suffered grievously from the attacks of those who rang the changes on corruption, bargaining, bribery, and the like, and, as we have before pointed out, Mr. Clay's political prospects were virtually blasted.*

The elections for members of Congress were carried on during the course of this fierce political warfare; and, as might have been expected, the result showed, that the opposition had gained strength in both Houses. In the Senate, at this date, were Webster, Hayne, Woodbury, Tyler, Harrison, Van Buren, Benton, and others; while in the House, we find among its numerous members, such men as Buchanan, Everett, Dwight, Cambreling, Rives, Polk, M'Duffie, Stevenson, Livingston, etc. Under the existing state of things, the prospect for the administration and its measures was by no means encouraging.

1827.

The twentieth Congress began its first session on the 3d of December, 1827. Two hundred and seven members of the House answered to their names, and only six were absent; while in the Senate, every member, excepting two, was in his place; such was the excitement which attended this renewed struggle between the contending parties. The first contest arose about the speakership; and Stevenson, of Virginia, was elected by a small majority over Mr. Taylor, which was looked upon as a decided gain for the opposition.

The next day, the president sent in his third annual message, which, like his others, was very long and very full on all those points which he deemed it proper to bring before the national legislature. A large portion of the message was devoted to the foreign relations of the Union, which, on the whole, were amicable and encouraging. The state of the revenue was said to be highly favorable, although there was a small excess of expenditure over the receipts; because upwards of $6,000,000, out of the $22,300,000, for the year's expenses, had been applied to the reduction of the public debt. The balance which was expected to be in the treasury at the end of the year, was nearly $5,500,000. Next came a notice of disturbances among the Indians on the north-western frontier, which had been happily suppressed. Various schemes for internal improvements were then spoken of; and these formed a prominent feature in the recommendations to Congress. The increase of the navy, and the formation of a naval school, were also recommended; the necessity of attending to the public lands was urged;

1827.

* Mr. Clay published a pamphlet on this subject, in the course of the summer, in which he presented a mass of unimpeachable testimony, in order to show his entire innocence of any unworthy or unbecoming conduct in the course he had adopted.

"the debt, rather of justice than gratitude, to the surviving warriors of the Revolutionary War," was again pressed upon the attention of the members of both Houses; together with other points relating to the judiciary, the militia system, etc.

During the present session, much and earnest attention was devoted to the tariff question, and the friends and opponents of protection exerted their best abilities in defence and in condemnation of the whole "American system." Conventions were held on the subject during the summer; at Harrisburg, by the friends of Mr. Clay and the necessity of the tariff to the interests of the country; and at Columbia, in South Carolina, by those who opposed and denounced protective duties as beneficial to the capitalists at the north, but "a grievance not to be patiently submitted to, and but too well calculated to bring on the dangerous inquiry, in what manner are the southern states benefited by the Union?" This engrossing topic occupied the House almost exclusively, from the 1st of February to the 22d of April, when a bill passed, much altered from that reported by the committee, but by no means conformable to the wishes of the advocates of the protective system; ayes, one hundred and five; noes, ninety-four. In the Senate, it passed on the 13th of May; ayes, twenty-six; noes, twenty-one; with various amendments, not essentially altering its general character, which were concurred in by the House. All the southern states voted against the bill, as did Maine and New Hampshire, Massachusetts, with Connecticut and Rhode Island, being divided. By this act, as Mr. Pitkin says, the minimum system was extended generally to woolens; different qualities of woolen fabrics being charged *ad valorem* duties of forty-five or fifty per cent., upon the minimum of their estimated value. Unmanufactured wool was also subjected to a duty of four cents per pound, and forty per cent. *ad valorem*. Additional duties were also laid upon iron, hemp, flax, and molasses; and the minimum price of cottons was raised to thirty-five cents the square yard. The policy of this act was questioned by many of the merchants of this country, and its constitutionality by most of the people of the southern states. Unfortunately, it was a compound made up by its enemies as well as its friends, and was not satisfactory to either.

1828.

Mr. Benton, in his "Thirty Years' View," has a chapter devoted to the subject of a revision of the tariff. Speaking of it as a measure concocted by manufacturing capitalists and politicians, and as freshly recurring about the time of every presidential election, Mr. Benton goes on to remark: "the south believed itself impoverished to enrich the north by this system; and certainly a singular and unexpected result had been seen in these two sections. In the colonial state, the southern were the rich part of the colonies, and expected to do well in a state of independence. They had the exports, and felt secure of their prosperity: not so the north, whose agricultural resources were few, and who expected privations from the loss of British favor. But in the first half century after independence, this expectation was reversed. The wealth of the north was enormously aggrandized; that of the south had declined. Northern towns had become great cities: southern cities had decayed, or become stationary; and Charleston, the principal port of the south, was less considerable than before the Revolution. The north became a money-lender to the south, and southern citizens made pilgrimages to northern cities, to raise money upon the hypothecation of their patrimonial estates. And this in the face of a southern export since the Revolution, to the value of $800,000,000! —a sum equal to the product of the Mexican mines since the days of Cortez! and twice or thrice the amount of their product in the same fifty years. The southern states attributed this result to the action of the federal government—its double action of levying revenue upon the industry of one section of the Union, and expending it in another—and especially to its protective tariffs. To some degree this attribution was just, but not to the degree assumed; which is evident from the fact, that the protective system had then only been in force for a short time—since the year 1816; and the reversed condition of the two sections of the Union had commenced before that time. Other causes must have had some effect; but for the present, we look to the protective system; and, without admitting it to have done all the mischief of which the south complained, it had yet done enough to cause it to be condemned by every friend to equal justice among the states, —by every friend to the harmony and stability of the Union,—by all who detested sectional legislation,—by every enemy to the mischievous combination of partisan politics with national legislation. And this was the feeling with the mass of the democratic members, who voted for the tariff of 1828, and who were determined to act upon that feeling upon the overthrow of the political party which advocated the protective system; and which overthrow they believed to be certain at the ensuing presidential election."

Another topic which occupied a good deal of the time and attention of Congress, was that of retrenchment, a favorite topic of aspiring politicians, and one which will always attract the notice of the people. Mr. Chilton, of Kentucky, moved first in the business, and a committee was appointed on the subject. Much time was spent in the investigation, and the majority of the committee brought in a report adverse to the economical and prudent conduct of affairs by the administration. On the other hand, Messrs. Everett and Sergeant, a minority of the committee, and the only two on it who were friendly to the government, brought in a counter report, which, of course, took an opposite view of the subject, and claimed that the financial affairs of the nation had been managed with economy and sound judgment. The whole movement was almost purely political, the object of the opposition being to bring discredit upon, and to annoy the administration, and the design of the friends of the government being to demonstrate the economy with which public affairs were carried on.

1828.

With a view to remedy certain difficulties in the mode of proceeding in the federal courts, in the states which had been admitted into the Union since 1789, a bill, after much discussion, passed the Senate, and with little amendment (the exception of Louisiana being the chief alteration made,) was accepted by the House, and finally became law. Among the appropriations, one was at last made for the pensions of the Revolutionary veterans;* and another for carrying on the Cumberland Road. The principle and constitutionality of internal improvements were, as usual, copiously discussed; but, it must be confessed, that the honorable members seemed to have in view their standing with their constituents, and the political effect of what they might say and do, far more than the endeavoring to fix upon some wise and judicious measures for the settlement of this important topic.

Other subjects which came before Congress, we need not enter into; as the question of the navigation of the St Lawrence; the north-eastern boundary; the claims of American citizens for spoliations by the French on our commerce; etc. The session was brought to a close on the 26th of May, and the members dispersed to their several sections of the country, to enter into the fierce contest which was already begun with reference to the presidency.†

1828.

It was a battle of unprecedented excitement, in which every engine known to political warfare was vigorously set in motion, and in which the shameless abuse of private character, and the slanderous imputations of every thing unworthy and disgraceful, were enough to disgust all candid truth-loving minds, and make them almost tremble for the result of unscrupulous party movements and measures. The result was what the democratic party confidently expected; General Jackson received one hundred and seventy-eight of the two hundred and sixty-one electoral votes; and John Quincy Adams received only eighty-three, less than half the number of those which were given to his successful competitor. Mr. Calhoun was again elected vice-president.

The second session of the twentieth Congress began on the 1st of December, 1828, and the president's message was received on the same day. Like his former messages, this, which was his last, was long and full of details on all those points which it was the duty of the executive to bring to the notice of Congress. Foreign affairs were spoken

* It was on this topic, in April, 1828, that Daniel Webster made one of his most effective speeches. It will well repay the reader who may not yet have made himself acquainted with its contents.

† General Brown, who held the position of commander-in-chief, died on the 24th of February, 1828. General Scott and General Gaines, who had received their commissions on the same day, had equal claims to succeed General Brown; but the government, unwilling to decide between the two, appointed General Macomb, the senior brigadier, to this honorable post. Attempts were made to abolish the office of major-general; the bill passed the House, but failed in the Senate. General Scott resented the course of the war department, claiming that he was not justly treated; and refusing to obey orders from General Macomb, he was suspended. During his suspension, he visited France, where he saw Lafayette, and soon after, by his advice, resumed his position in the army. On General Macomb's death, in 1841, Scott became commander-in-chief of the army of the United States.

of at large in the first half of the message. The war which had broken out between Russia and Turkey was mentioned; hopes were expressed that the French government would yield to the claims of justice in regard to the spoliations on American commerce; the king of the Netherlands had been selected as umpire on the subject of the north-eastern boundary; commercial relations with Great Britain had not yet been satisfactorily arranged; but with other powers there was a good state of feeling and sentiment existing on these and kindred points. A very favorable account was given of the condition and prospects of the revenue; the receipts of the year were $2,000,000 more than had been estimated, but the expenditure had exceeded them by about $1,500,000; above $9,000,000 of the public debt had been paid off; and more than $5,000,000 were expected to be in the treasury at the end of the current year. At the end of the year, he stated, the public debt would not much exceed $58,000,000.

The former messages of the president had been complained of by his own friends, and not a little wondered at by his opponents, because they contained no reference to the tariff, or its protective principle. He compensated on this final occasion for his former silence respecting them. Holding up the commercial policy, pursued at that time by Great Britain, as an example, he laid it down as the duty of the government to act upon the principle sanctioned by the tariff act of the preceding session, and he expressed the hope, that to it—one of the principles, "upon which the Constitution itself was formed"—he hoped and trusted the authorities of the Union would adhere. The remainder of the message was taken up with the condition of the Indians dwelling within the territories of the United States; the need for fortifying the sea coast, and increasing the navy; the desirableness of educating the officers of the army, for the purpose of increasing the usefulness of that arm of the service; and the necessity for making provision for taking the fourth census of the country, and of obtaining more complete and specific returns of the ages of the population. And, in conclusion, the president assured Congress of his continued earnest desire for the adoption of the measures he had before recommended; and of his cordial concurrence in every constitutional provision which might receive their sanction during the session, and which tended to the general welfare. But he made no allusion to the fact, although it was then fully known, that this was the last time he should be called upon to address them in the capacity of president of the United States.

1828.

This being the short session, and the present administration being also near its close, hardly any thing more was done than was absolutely requisite to carry on the government. Bills encouraging the shipping interest, by allowing certain drawbacks on exported goods, passed both Houses, and became law. A tonnage bill, proposing to repeal that duty on all American vessels, and on those of other nations placed by treaty on the same footing, was rejected in the Senate. Liberal appro-

priations were made for the promotion of internal improvements of various kinds; and the principle was once more largely debated, and at length affirmed by considerable majorities, both in the Senate and in the House of Representatives. The continuation of the Cumberland Road, and the conditional cession of it to the states through whose boundaries it passed, occupied
1829. much of the time devoted to this section of public business. These are the principal matters which engaged the attention of Congress now; other bills, and amongst them some originating with the retrenchment committee, expired with the session, not having been able to get through all the stages necessary to constitute them laws.

On the 3d of March, 1829, the twentieth Congress expired, and at the same date John Quincy Adams's administration reached its close. Owing to a rather unpleasant correspondence with some of the principal men of Boston, growing out of the course pursued by Mr. Adams, when he thought that he perceived an intention on the part of the federalists to attempt a dissolution of the Union, (see p. 108), the ex-president preferred to remain in the capital, which was his home for some time afterwards.

In briefly reviewing the administration of the sixth president, it is to be borne in mind, that, attempting to do without a party, and to rise above mere party, it was assailed by its opponents with more vigor and activity than any one which had preceded it. In the House, the majority was against it, and nearly one half of the Senate 1829.
arrayed themselves in opposition to its measures. Whatever may have been its faults and failings, it certainly was conducted with purity and uprightness; and in respect to ability, it compared favorably with those which had gone before. Mr. Adams himself was above reproach, in the blamelessness of his life and the patriotic devotion of his best energies to the good of his country. But he did not, at any time, possess the popular favor; he was not a man of the stamp to win popular applause; his learning, his talents, his ability, his glowing patriotism, never produced the effect which it might be supposed they would upon the community; and it need excite no surprise, that, when the contest came between him and a man such as Andrew Jackson was, with every thing nearly to attract the mass of the people, and to lead them to admire his dashing boldness, his unflinching energy, his prompt decision, and the like, John Quincy Adams should fail of receiving votes sufficient to re-elect him to the office he had held during the past four years. The future years of Mr. Adams demonstrated the purity of his principles, and his willingness to serve his country in any position for which they deemed him worthy; and we believe that it may be asserted now, without fear of dissent, that he was one of the noble band of patriots of whom the United States may justly be proud, and may hold up to the admiration of succeeding generations.

Book Seventh.

FROM THE

INAUGURATION OF ANDREW JACKSON,

TO THE

ADMINISTRATION OF JAMES BUCHANAN.

1829—1857.

Andrew Jackson

HISTORY

OF THE

UNITED STATES OF AMERICA.

CHAPTER I.

1829-1832.

JACKSON'S ADMINISTRATION: FIRST THREE YEARS.

Inauguration of Andrew Jackson — His address — The new cabinet — Prospects of the administration — "Retrenchment and reform" — Removals from office — Extent and character of these removals — Mr. Benton's views — The twenty-first Congress — The president's message — Measures recommended — His views on various topics — The public lands question — Mr. Foot's resolution in the Senate — Debate upon it — Speeches made — Hayne's and Webster's efforts — Revision of the tariff — The Senate's action on the president's appointments — Retrenchment attempted — Removal of the Indians to the west of the Mississippi — Proceedings on the subject of the United States Bank adverse to the president's views — The fifth census — Congress in session — The message — Action in relation to internal improvements — Measures of the session — Correspondence between Calhoun and Jackson — Troubles in the cabinet — New cabinet appointed — The twenty-second Congress — Contents of the message — The Senate refuse to confirm Van Buren's appointment as minister to England — The apportionment under the new census — The great bank controversy — Both the Senate and the House pass bills to renew the charter of the bank — Jackson's bank veto — Other questions, as the public lands, the tariff, etc.

THE inauguration of the seventh president of the United States was attended with all those ceremonies which add interest to so important an event in our national history. Having arrived at Washington about a month previously, and all the arrangements having been completed, Andrew Jackson, on the 4th of March, in the presence of a large concourse, gathered at the eastern portico of the capitol, stood up before his fellow-citizens to deliver his Inaugural address. It was brief, plainly expressed, and sufficiently indicative of the president's views and opinions on the great questions of policy and government, which would be likely to require the attention of the executive.

1829.

Two or three paragraphs are all that we have room to quote.

"*Fellow-citizens:* About to undertake the arduous duties that I have been appointed to perform by the choice of a free people, I avail myself of this customary and solemn occasion, to express the gratitude which their confidence inspires, and to acknowledge the accountability which my situation enjoins. While the magnitude of their interests convinces me that no thanks can be adequate to the honor they have conferred, it admonishes me that the best return I can make, is the zealous dedication of my humble abilities to their service and their good.

. . . .

"In such measures as I may be called on to pursue, in regard to the rights of the separate states, I hope to be animated by a proper respect for those sovereign members of our Union; taking care not to confound the powers they have reserved to themselves with those they have granted to the confederacy.

"The management of the public revenue—that searching operation in all governments—is among the most delicate and important trusts in ours; and it will, of course, demand no inconsiderable share of my official solicitude. Under every aspect in which it can be considered, it would appear that advantage must result from the observance of a strict and faithful economy. This I shall aim at the more anxiously, both because it will facilitate the extinguishment of the national debt—the unnecessary duration of which is incompatible with real independence—and because it will counteract that tendency to public and private profligacy which a profuse expenditure of money by the government, is but too apt to engender. Powerful auxiliaries to the attainment of this desirable end, are to be found in the regulations provided by the wisdom of Congress, for the specific appropriation of public money, and the prompt accountability of public officers.

. . . .

"The recent demonstration of public sentiment inscribes, on the list of executive duties, in characters too legible to be overlooked, the task of REFORM; which will require, particularly, the correction of those abuses, that have brought the patronage of the federal government into conflict with the freedom of elections, and the counteraction of those causes which have disturbed the rightful course of appointment, and have placed, or continued, power in unfaithful or incompetent hands.

"In the performance of a task thus generally delineated, I shall endeavor to select men whose diligence and talents will ensure, in their respective stations, able and faithful co-operation—depending, for the advancement of the public service, more on the integrity and zeal of the public officers, than on their numbers.

"A diffidence, perhaps too just, in my own qualifications, will teach me to look with reverence to the examples of public virtue left by my illustrious predecessors, and with veneration to the lights that flow from the mind that founded, and the mind that reformed our system. The same diffidence induces me to hope for instruction and aid from the co-ordinate

1829.

branches of the government, and for the indulgence and support of my fellow-citizens generally. And a firm reliance on the goodness of that Power whose providence mercifully protected our national infancy, and has since upheld our liberties in various vicissitudes, encourages me to offer up my ardent supplications, that He will continue to make our beloved country the object of his Divine care and gracious benediction."

After concluding this address, the oath of office was administered to the new president by the venerable Chief Justice Marshall, who had discharged the same duty on many previous occasions. The Senate being in session, Jackson sent in the names of those whom he had selected to form his cabinet. They were: Martin Van Buren, (at the time governor of New York,) secretary of state; Samuel D. Ingham, of Pennsylvania, secretary of the treasury; John H. Eaton, of Tennessee, secretary of war; John Branch, of North Carolina, secretary of the navy; John M. Berrien, of Georgia, attorney-general; and William T. Barry, of Kentucky, postmaster-general. This last office was held by Mr. M'Lean, (appointed by Mr. Monroe) who was understood to be a supporter of the new administration; a vacancy, however, having occurred in the supreme court, by the death of Mr. Justice Trimble,* Mr. M'Lean was nominated to fill his place, and was confirmed by the Senate on the 7th of March. That body, having acted on all the nominations presented to them, closed their extra session on the 18th of the same month.

The new administration came into power under favorable auspices. General Jackson had been very little in public life, was not committed to any particular line of policy, and was known to have counselled Monroe, (p. 309,) to discard party lines and distinctions, and to act in all respects as the president of the *whole* United States. He was consequently at liberty to mark out a truly national policy, and to conduct the government on principles which recognized the rights and privileges of both majority and minority among the people. "Retrenchment and reform," were the rallying cries of the party during the election, and retrenchment and reform the president was bound, of course, to see carried into effect wherever it was necessary. The only question to be settled was, what was meant by these terms; whether, on the one hand, the introducing of economy, prudence, simplicity, and such like, into the management and conduct of public affairs, with the utmost and stringent responsibility of public officers; or, on the other, the removing of honest, capable men, who were *not* political adherents, and the appointing of others in their places, who *were* political adherents and supporters. It may well be believed, that the holders of office, and the seekers of office, looked with no little anxiety for the practical

1829.

* Justice Trimble died in August, 1828. At the opening of the session, in December of that year, Mr. Adams nominated Mr. Crittenden, of Kentucky, to fill the vacancy. The opposition, who were in the majority in the Senate, refused to allow the nomination to be acted upon.

settlement of this question of reform, of which Jackson had spoken in his Inaugural address.

The president did not leave the country long in doubt, as to what he and the democracy understood by the needed "reform." It consisted in an extensive removal of officers who were, politically considered, known, or believed, to be friends and supporters of Mr. Adams at the last election, and the appointment of others in their places who had been active in securing the election of General Jackson; thus opening the door to the conviction, that office under the government is to be the reward of partizanship, that "to the victors belong the spoils," and that from the highest office in the state, down to the very humblest and most insignificant, no man can be deemed qualified except he be, out and out, a member and supporter of the dominant party. In carrying out his views on this subject, the president reached the following result, before the meeting of Congress in the present year. Four new ministers plenipotentiary had been appointed, two new *chargés d'affaires*, and four new secretaries of legation; the marshals and district-attorneys had been changed in sixteen states, forty-eight collectors, surveyors, naval officers, and appraisers had been removed, to make way for other men, and twenty-six receivers and registers in western land offices; twenty-one new consuls had been appointed; and in the department at Washington alone, forty-six changes had been made. Altogether, in the course of the nine months of the recess, a hundred and sixty-seven removals and re-appointments, in which the Senate could have no voice, had taken place.

The postmaster-general, having now become a member of the cabinet, the pruning knife of "reform" was very vigorously applied in that department. Within the year that the work was begun, four hundred and ninety postmasters had been displaced, and others appointed in their room. And to show how the discrimination was made, we may mention, that in eleven states or territories which had voted for Adams, there were three hundred and nineteen removals; while in seventeen states or territories which had supported Jackson, there were only a hundred and sixty-one removals. Thus, during the first year of the new administration, nearly seven hundred changes in government officers were brought about in this wise; and it became tolerably plain, what was meant by the president, and the party who placed him in his lofty position, by "retrenchment and reform."*

In thus narrating this matter, our object is to give a simple statement of *fact*. We are well aware, that the course of the president was held to be defensible, and was energetically defended by the democratic press; and

* In contrast with this procedure on the part of Jackson, it deserves to be noted, that, although Mr. Jefferson began the system which has since been carried out so fully, (see pp. 16–18 of the present volume,) he removed only thirty-nine in the course of eight years; John Adams, during his four years, removed ten; Washington removed nine; Madison, five; Monroe, nine; and John Quincy Adams, two; making the sum total of removals by six presidents, only seventy-four, and most of these for sufficient cause.

we know, that the views of all parties, as parties, now are, that changes of the most thorough and complete description should be made in the officials of all kinds, when a new administration succeeds to power. Nevertheless,
1829. we are bound to say, that, in the judgment of impartial men, great mischief was set on foot when the plan of the seventh president was carried out, and when he furnished an example which later presidents have been only too ready to follow.

This is acknowledged, in substance, by Senator Benton, who undertakes an elaborate defence of the course and policy of Andrew Jackson in this particular. In justice to the president, whose advocate he is, we may quote briefly from Mr. Benton's chapter on this topic, in his "Thirty Years' View."

Having stated, that notwithstanding the extent to which removals had been effected, General Jackson left many thousands, who were in his power, untouched, Mr. Benton goes on to say of the president; "He came into office under circumstances well calculated to excite him to make removals. In the first place, none of his political friends, though constituting a great majority of the people of the United States, had been appointed to office during the preceding administration; and such an exclusion could not be justified on any consideration. His election was, in some degree, a revolution of parties, or rather a re-establishment of parties on the old line of federal and democratic. It was a change of administration, in which a change of government functionaries, to some extent, became a right and a duty; but still, the removals actually made, when political, were not merely for opinions, but for conduct under these opinions; and unhappily there was conduct enough, in too many officials, to justify their removal." Mr. Benton further states, that the subordinate officers of the government, following the leading of Henry Clay, were active during the presidential canvass, and so lost their true position. "Rightly considered," he says, "they were non-combatants. By engaging in the election they became combatants, and subjected themselves to the law of victory and defeat; reward and promotion in one case, loss of place in the other. General Jackson, then, on his accession
to the presidency, was in a new 1829.
situation with respect to parties, different from that of any president since the time of Mr. Jefferson, whom he took for his model, and whose rule he followed. He made many removals and for cause, but not so many as not to leave a majority in office against him—even in the executive departments in Washington city."

Such is the defence of General Jackson which Mr. Benton urges, and it is probably the best that can be offered; yet he himself is by no means blind to the effect of the system of removals on the scale on which it has ever since been put into operation. "The practice of removals for opinion's sake is becoming too common, and is reducing our presidential elections to what Mr. Jefferson deprecated, 'a contest of office instead of principle'; and converting the victories of each party, so far as office is concerned, into the political extermination of the other. . . . . I consider 'sweeping' removals, as now practised by both parties, a great political evil in our country, injurious to individuals, to the public service, to the purity of elections, and to the harmony and union of the people. . . . . It converts elections into scrambles for office, and degrades the government into an office for rewards and punishments; and divides the people of the Union into two adverse parties—each in its turn, and as it becomes dominant, to strip and proscribe the other. . . . I deprecate the effect of such sweeping removals at each revolution of parties, and believe it is having a deplorable effect both upon the purity of election and the distribution of office, and taking both out of the hands of the people, and throwing the management of one and the enjoyment of the other, into most unfit hands."*

The twenty-first Congress assembled for its first session on the 7th of December, 1829. There was a large gathering of the members of both Houses, and the strength of the new administration was shown by the re-election of Andrew Stevenson, as speaker of the House, by a hundred and fifty-two votes, against twenty-one given to William D. Martin, and eighteen scattering. On

1829.

the next day, the first annual message of President Jackson was received and read to the two Houses. It was very long, drawn up evidently with much care, and gave an elaborate view of the foreign relations and domestic concerns of the United States. Among the principal measures recommended were; an amendment of the Constitution on the subject of electing the president, in order that it might be done by the people, without the intervention of electors, and that he should be ineligible for a second term;* a review and alteration of the judiciary law, so as to extend the circuit court to all the states; a discontinuance of building ships of the larger classes, and the collecting and storing of materials instead; a gradual reduction of duties on articles of general consumption, which are not the production of the country; the re-organizing the department of state; etc. A few extracts from this elaborate message, in which Jackson's policy is clearly shadowed forth, may serve to put before the reader the views of the president on the various great questions at issue at that date.

In connection with his proposed amendment to the Constitution, Jackson set forth his views on the subject just spoken of, and which had excited considerable noise already, we mean his extensive removals from office. "There are, perhaps, few men who can for any great length of time enjoy office and power, without being more or less under the influence of feelings unfavorable to the faithful discharge of their public duties. Their integrity may be proof against improper considerations, immediately

---

* Benton's "*Thirty Years' View*," vol. i., pp. 159–163. For some interesting remarks, which Mr. Benton criticizes, see M. De Tocqueville's "*Democracy in America*," vol. i., chapters viii. and xvii.

* Andrew Jackson, however, like Thomas Jefferson, whose sentiments on this point he reiterates, was prevailed upon to consent to be elected for a second term.

addressed to themselves; but they are apt to acquire a habit of looking with indifference upon the public interests, and of tolerating conduct from which an unpractised man would revolt. Office is considered as a species of property; and government rather as a means of promoting individual interests, than as an instrument created solely
1829.
for the service of the people. Corruption in some, and in others a perversion of correct feelings and principles, divert government from its legitimate ends, and make it an engine for the support of the few, at the expense of the many. The duties of all public officers are, or, at least, admit of being made so plain and simple, that men of intelligence may readily qualify themselves for their performance; and I cannot but believe, that more is lost by the long continuance of men in office, than is generally to be gained by their experience. I submit therefore to your consideration, whether the efficiency of the government would not be promoted, and official industry and integrity better secured, by a general extension of the law which limits appointments to four years.

"In a country where offices are created solely for the benefit of the people, no one man has any more intrinsic right to official station than another. Offices were not established to give support to particular men, at the public expense. No individual wrong is therefore done by removal, since neither appointment, nor continuance in office, is matter of right. The incumbent became an officer with a view to public benefits; and when these require his removal, they are not to be sacrificed to private interests. It is the people, and they alone, who have a right to complain, when a bad officer is substituted for a good one. He who is removed has the same means of obtaining a living, that are enjoyed by the millions who never held office. The proposed limitation would destroy the idea of property, now so generally connected with official station; and although individual distress may be sometimes produced, it would, by promoting that rotation which constitutes a leading principle in the republican creed give healthful action to the system."

In speaking of the tariff, the president stated, that its operation thus far had not proved so injurious to agriculture and commerce, or as beneficial to manufactures, as had been anticipated; that foreign importations had not diminished, while domestic competition, under an illusive excitement, had increased the production much beyond the demand for home consumption; and that consequently, there had ensued "low prices, temporary embarrassment, and partial loss." In discussing this topic, the president urgently recommended the laying aside local prejudices and the like, and the dealing with it on a truly national scale, under "the patriotic determination to promote the great interests of the whole."

The balance in the treasury, on the 1st of January, 1829, was stated to be nearly $6,000,000. The receipts of the year were estimated at above $24,600,000, while the expenditures, it was thought, would amount to more than $26,000,000; so that the **1829.**

balance in the treasury, at the end of the current year, would be a little less than $4,500,000. During the year, $12,405,000 had been paid on account of the public debt; which amounted now to $48,565,406. "The sudden withdrawal from the banks in which it had been deposited, at a time of unusual pressure in the money market," said the president, of so large a sum as nearly $9,000,000, which was paid off on the 1st of July, it was feared "might cause much injury to the interests dependent on bank accommodations. But this evil was wholly averted by an early anticipation of it at the treasury, aided by the judicious arrangements of the officers of the Bank of the United States."

In anticipation of the time, when, by the payment of the debt, the demand upon the federal treasury should be greatly diminished; while by the progress of commerce the revenue should be largely increased; it was suggested, that the surplus should be apportioned among the several states, "according to their ratio of representation." In the same connection, the president urged, that there be no resort to strained constructions of the Constitution, but an appeal to the people, to amend the national charter in all matters requiring it. "The scheme has worked well," he remarked. "It has exceeded the hopes of those who devised it, and become an object of admiration to the world. We are responsible to our country, and to the glorious cause of self-government, for the preservation of so great a good. The great mass of legislation, relating to our internal affairs, was intended to be left, where the federal convention found it, in the state governments. . . . I cannot therefore too strongly or earnestly, for my own sense of its importance, warn you against all encroachments upon the legitimate sphere of state sovereignty. Sustained by its healthful and invigorating influence, the federal system can never fall."

Many suggestions relating to the treasury department were next offered. They bore upon the method of collecting the revenue; the large amount of public money outstanding; the release of debts to the government, "where the conduct of the debtor is wholly exempt from the imputation of fraud;" and the numerous frauds committed on the treasury, which had necessitated several prosecutions. "And," continued the president, "in connection with this subject, I invite the attention of Congress to general and minute inquiry into the condition of the government, with a view to ascertain what offices can be dispensed with, what expenses retrenched, and what improvements may be made in the organization of its various parts, to secure the proper responsibility of public agents, and promote efficiency and justice in all its operations."

1829.

Beside the topics already noticed, the president warmly commended the academy at West Point, urged the extending the benefits of the pension law to all the surviving Revolutionary veterans, and spoke of the removal of the Indian tribes, as called for by every consideration of policy and propriety. At the close of his message, the president gave his views on the subject of the United States Bank, which, as marking out his determination in regard to that institution, and as closely connected with the excitement which subsequently arose on the subject, we quote in full: "The charter of the Bank of the United States expires in 1836, and its stockholders will most probably apply for a renewal of their privileges. In order to avoid the evils resulting from precipitancy in a measure involving such important principles, and such deep pecuniary interests, I feel that I cannot, in justice to the parties interested, too soon present it to the deliberate consideration of the legislature and the people. Both the constitutionality and the expediency of the law creating this bank, are well questioned by a large portion of our fellow-citizens; and it must be admitted by all, that it has failed in the great end of establishing a uniform and sound currency.

"Under these circumstances, if such an institution is deemed essential to the fiscal operations of the government, I submit to the wisdom of the legislature whether a national one, founded upon the credit of the government, and its revenue, might not be devised, which would avoid all constitutional difficulties; and, at the same time, secure all the advantage to the government and country, that were expected to result from the present bank."

The question of the public lands, always an interesting one, came before Congress early in the session, and gave rise to a very ardent and very important discussion. It is to be borne in mind, that, owing to the failure of many purchases made by speculators, and the inability of other buyers to pay when the full sum was due, so much public money on the land account was outstanding after some years, that a measure for the relief of insolvent purchasers was passed by Congress, and the upset price per acre was reduced from two dollars to one and a quarter, on condition that the payment should be immediate. The practice of selling at the minimum price, the lands not sold by public auction, failed, however, as is not surprising, to bring purchasers for the less valuable tracts, and the state governments, not unnaturally, looked upon the general government and its land system, as hostile to the progress of their sovereignties in population and prosperity.

1829.

This was the feeling of the western states especially, and in 1826, Senator Benton, who was virtually the representative of that section of the country, proposed a system of prices, graduated according to the actual value of the unsold lands, so as to secure a more evenly dispersed population; he also recommended the donation of small tracts to settlers, for the purpose of attracting such as were unable to migrate westward, in consequence of poverty. The views of Mr. Benton were warmly supported by the western states, who were disposed to claim entire and exclusive sovereignty over the lands within their boundaries, as was clearly shown by a vote of the General Assembly of Indiana, in January, 1829.

Some steps on the part of the general government seemed to be plainly required; and accordingly Mr. Foot, of Connecticut, on the 29th of December, submitted to the Senate a resolution, which, after amendment, was expressed in the following terms: "*Resolved*, That the committee on public lands be instructed to inquire and report the quantity of public lands remaining unsold, within each state or territory; and whether it be expedient to limit, for a certain period, the sales of the public lands to such lands only as have heretofore been offered for sale, and are subject to entry at the minimum price; and also, whether the office of surveyor-general, and some of the land offices, may not be abolished without detriment to the public interest; or whether it be expedient to adopt measures to hasten the sales, and extend more rapidly the surveys of the public lands."

Mr. Foot's design in proposing this resolution seemed to be manifest enough. The average annual sales of public lands amounted to a million of acres, and there were nearly a hundred millions of acres of the national domain, already surveyed, unsold; which he thought would supply the market, were the annual sales to experience a far more remarkable rise than was at all probable, for more than the life-time of one generation; so that, if his suggestions were adopted, a considerable retrenchment of the public expenditure might be effected, without any diminution of the revenue from that source, or any actual hindrance to the settlement of the west.

The usual course, when a resolution proposing an inquiry was presented, was to postpone the discussion till the committee should report something which required the action of Congress. On the present occasion, however, this course was not pursued; for Senator Benton at once resisted the resolution, on the ground that its effect would be to check emigration to the new states in the west, and to deliver up large portions of them to the dominion of wild beasts.

Mr. Benton made his speech on the 18th of January, and as the presiding officer, Mr. Calhoun, among other fantastic notions, held, that he had no power to preserve order in the debates in the Senate, the energetic member from Missouri took the largest liberty of saying whatever he thought best on this topic. On the 19th, Mr. Hayne, of South Carolina, adopting Mr. Benton's views, branched out still more widely, and gave utterance to heavy and sharp invectives against the eastern states especially, and advocated the doctrine of state rights in terms which startled sober-minded men. On the 20th, Mr. Webster, although he had not intended to speak at all, took the floor in reply, and delivered the first of his great speeches on this subject.

1830.

Our limits do not admit of entering into details respecting the speakers and speeches in this celebrated debate. Both Mr. Benton and Mr. Hayne undertook to reply to Mr. Webster, Mr. Hayne doing so under great excitement, and reiterating his charges against New England, and enlarging upon his views of state sovereignty and independence with much energy and boldness. Daniel Webster, whose great abilities and power as an orator were well known, and from whom a defence of the Constitution was universally looked for, did not refuse to meet the impulsive South Carolinian, and on the 26th of January,

1830. he uttered that memorable oration, which every man, woman, and child in our country has heard of, and which was then, and has ever since been considered, not only a conclusive refutation of the charge of hostility on the part of the east towards the west, but also an unanswerable defence and exposition of the Constitution. It would be impossible to do justice to the scene, and the power of the orator, in any space at our command; and we shall not attempt it. It is sufficient to know, that the sentiments of Mr. Webster struck a responsive chord in the bosoms of millions, and the odious doctrine of nullification and disunion found no favor with our countrymen. So may it ever be! "Liberty and union, now and for ever, one and inseparable!"

The issue of this protracted discussion was the passage of the bill brought forward in the Senate by Mr. Benton early in the session; but it was taken to the House of Representatives too near the day of adjournment, to allow time for consideration, and it was ordered, with others in the same circumstances, "to lie upon the table."

Next in importance to this debate, and the effect of Webster's great speech upon the internal affairs and relations of the Union, may be reckoned the revision of the tariff law.* The principal discussion arose respecting a bill reported on the 27th of January, by Mr Mallory, the chairman of the committee on manufactures, to regulate the entry of woolen importations; but it was renewed and extended by the introduction of other bills, and of amendments, the relevancy whereof to their original motions is not always obvious; and the entire effect was certainly not in favor of the policy advocated (in this instance) by the southern party. Separate bills were introduced, providing for a reduction of duties on salt and molasses, tea and coffee, etc., which were passed by considerable majorities. The tonnage duties, and the whole question of a reciprocal policy, which, according to Mr. Benton, is the true commercial policy of the Union, were also largely discussed on this occasion. But the most instructive, and at the same time the most painful part of the business, was the disclosure of frauds on the revenue, amounting, it was said, to some $3,000,000 a year.

The appointments to office made during the recess, were not immediately submitted to the Senate for its approbation. A month expired before the commencement of the long list was presented, and more than two months had elapsed before the last name was sent in. This delay, which was attributed to the disagreement between the friends of the vice-president and of Mr. Van Buren, the secretary of state, although it no doubt helped to consolidate the strength of the administration, did not produce a general confirmation of the appointments. However widely opinions differed with regard to the necessity of that kind of "reform" which

* In Mr. Hayne's speech on Mr. Foot's resolution, he sharply censured Daniel Webster, for apparent inconsistency and contradiction in opposing the tariff in 1824, and supporting it in 1828. For Mr. Webster's defence and reply, the reader must consult his great speech spoken of above.

General Jackson had attempted, by removing so many persons from office, there was not much difference of sentiment as to the impropriety of his using the opportunities thus created for rewarding the electioneering services of his partisans. And in consequence, several of the nominations were rejected, and in some instances the vote rejecting them was so large as to convey a decided censure upon the course adopted by the executive.

In regard to the other point, of which the dominant party had said a good deal, that of retrenchment, considerable activity was manifested. No fewer than ten bills were brought forward in the House; but to very little purpose; and nothing of moment resulted from this movement. Bills for reforming the mode of publishing the laws, the appointment of postmasters, the displacement of defaulters, etc., introduced by Mr. Benton in the Senate, met with no better success. So too a resolution upon General Jackson's recommendation to amend the constitutional mode of electing the president and vice-president, did not meet the approbation of Congress. Whereat the opposition sarcastically said; "These subjects of excitement had subserved the purposes for which they were intended, and the object of the agitation being answered in the triumph of their party, the instruments by which they had accomplished their ends were laid aside as no longer necessary."

The question respecting the Indians in the south-west, (p. 356,) and their removal beyond the Mississippi, again came before Congress. Georgia, in particular, was determined to have possession of the Indian lands, and to effect the removal of the Indian tribes within her borders. The poor aborigines memorialized Congress, and hoped for protection and justice; but in general, the legislature and the executive were opposed to their wishes, and emigration seemed to be the only thing left to them. In June, the governor of Georgia issued a proclamation, declaring that the laws of the state were in force over the Indian territory, and threatening penalties for any violation of them. Congress also passed an act for the purchase of a region west of the Mississippi, beyond the limits of the states and organized territories, to which the Indians were to be removed within a year, and where they were to be protected against other tribes in the vicinity. The sum of $500,000 was appropriated for carrying this act into effect. The troubles that grew out of this Indian question, occupied the attention of Congress and the people for several years subsequently.

That portion of the president's message which we have quoted respecting the Bank of the United States, was referred, in the House, to the committee of ways and means. The movement of the executive was looked upon as rather surprising, seeing that **1830.** the charter of the bank had some seven years yet to run, and seeing also that it had made no application for a renewal of its charter. Strictly speaking, it was difficult to perceive what Congress had to do with the question in its present position. However, as the president had seen fit to speak of it in the manner which he did in his message, the supporters of his administration could not well pass over the subject in silence. The committee of ways and means, accordingly, through Mr. M'Duffie, their chairman, in an able report, took ground against the president's view; claimed that the bank had faithfully performed its duties; that it was essential to the correct management of the national finances, etc. And as to General Jackson's suggestion of a government national bank, to be furnished with capital from the treasury, the report declared, that it could hardly furnish a currency without branches; whilst "with branches it would be still more objectionable, as it invested the federal government with patronage of most extensive influence, and embracing the control of all the bank accommodations to the standing amount of $50,000,000. Such a control would introduce more corruption in the government than all the patronage now belonging to it. It was a desperate financial experiment, without parallel in the history of the world." To the same effect, though not so much in detail, Mr. Smith, of Maryland, in behalf of the committee of finance, in the Senate, reported against the suggestions of the president;—circumstances which might have shaken the resolution of any ordinary man. But Andrew Jackson was *not* an ordinary man, and having set his mind upon a certain view of this matter, he was not to be driven from it by any doubts or hesitation, as to whether he might not possibly be wrong, in a question wherein the learning, and experience, and ability of statesmen and financiers, of his own party, too, were, with scarce an exception, arrayed against him.

After the performance of a great deal of business, notwithstanding the long and ardent debates, this busy session of Congress was terminated on the 31st of May, 1830.*

The fifth decennial census of the United States was taken this year, with the following results. Of free whites, there were, under twenty years of age, males, 2,996,405; females, 2,907,347;—between twenty and forty, males, 1,548,697; females, 1,473,648;—between forty and sixty, males, 597,009; females, 579,456;—above sixty, males, 210,967; females, 209,803; in all, according to Mr. Tucker, 10,537,378. The number of free colored persons amounted to 319,599; and there were 2,009,043 slaves. The grand total of the population, consequently, as given by the tables in Mr. Tucker's work on this subject, was, 12,866,020.

1830.

The increase of the population, when compared with the numbers ascertained in 1820, was just thirty-three and a quarter per cent.; but, compared with those in 1790, the increase was above three hundred and twenty-seven per cent. The decennial increase in the Atlantic states, in 1830, was above twenty-nine and three quarters per

* General Jackson, it was noted, used the veto power of his office four times during the session; whereas, looking back, it was found, that Washington used this power only twice, during his eight years; John Adams and Jefferson, not at all; Madison, four times; Monroe, once; and John Quincy Adams, not at all. From all which it became tolerably evident, that executive power, in Jackson's hands, was a *real* thing, which he meant to exercise as he judged best.

cent., and in the western states, above sixty-three and a half; whilst in the free states it was above thirty-five and three quarters, and in the slave-holding states under thirty per cent.

During the recess, a sort of quarrel among the members of the cabinet and the president, made considerable progress, and it became evident, that the friendly political relations existing between Mr. Calhoun and General Jackson were about to be ruptured. Mr. Van Buren was charged with fomenting this quarrel, having perceived that his political advancement would be promoted by it. But we do not pretend, in our limited space, to enter into any discussion of the secret history of the times.

The second session of the twenty-first Congress began on the 6th of December. The message, which was sent in the next day, spoke of the bills which the president had retained at the close of the last session, on the ground that he had not had time to consider them properly, and which were now returned without his approval.

1830.

The necessity of amending the Constitution, in relation to the election of president and vice-president, was again urged. "I cannot," said he, "too earnestly invite your attention to the propriety of promoting such an amendment of the Constitution, as will render him ineligible after one term of service."

The Indian question was next spoken of, and the progress of the removal scheme; and then came the tariff. The effects of the existing law, said the message, were "doubtless overrated, both in its evils and in its advantages." "To make this great question," the president remarked, "which unhappily so much divides and excites the public mind, subservient to the short-sighted views of faction, must destroy all hope of settling it satisfactorily to the great body of the people, and for the general interest. I cannot, therefore, too earnestly for my own feelings of the common good, warn you against the blighting consequences of such a course."

The financial report was in every respect most favorable. The receipts for the year were expected to exceed $24,160,000, being about $300,000 more than had been reckoned upon when the last annual report was presented. The expenditure amounted to over $13,742,000, beside payments on account of the public debt, falling little short of $11,500,000. And the balance in the treasury at the end of the year, was expected to be above $4,819,000.

First in importance of the legislative business of the session prescribed by the message, were the measures for the promotion of internal improvement, which, in complete neglect of the president's scruples, were passed by Congress. Nor was this practical resistance to Jackson's views offered without consideration; a committee sat upon the objections by which he had justified his vetoes, and the report presented by it, through one of the supporters of the administration, strongly and pointedly condemned his opinions, and concluded by a resolution, affirming the expediency of continuing the prosecution of internal improvements by appropriations of money, and by subscriptions for stock, in companies incorporated in the

Lew Cass

From an original Portrait taken expressly for this work.

Johnson, Fry & Co. Publishers, N.Y.

states wherein the improvements might be effected, on the part of the general government.

So decisive were the majorities in both branches of the legislature, by which the bills with this object in view were passed, that "the president and his cabinet found themselves compelled to yield to public opinion," and approve them, in spite of the decided disapprobation which they had expressed, for measures of precisely the same character and intention. And it was considered that this course of policy was now established as that of the nation, nothing being required to carry it most beneficially into effect, but prudence and harmony on the part of the different sections of the government.

1831.

The other measures of the session deserving mention, were,—an act to amend the laws of copy-right, extending the term to twenty-eight years; and for fourteen years, if the author, etc., should be living, or have left widow or child living, at the conclusion of that term;—one for the relief of certain insolvent debtors of the United States;—another for finally adjusting and settling the claims of James Monroe, the late president, against the United States;* and various appropriations for internal improvement, as that for carrying on the Cumberland Road, and that for improving the navigation of the Ohio. The session closed on the 3d of March, 1831.

Soon after the breaking up of Congress, a rather tart correspondence was published, in which both writers, the president and vice-president, clearly manifested that a schism had taken place in the party, and that several political changes must result from this dispute. The details are not important in this place. A great deal was said in public and private on the subject, and charges and countercharges were freely made on both sides. The president, finding that he could not bring the members of the cabinet to his view on certain questions of etiquette and propriety, in matters of social intercourse, was, naturally enough, displeased, and as he was not a man who bore opposition very meekly, the gentlemen associated with him as constitutional advisers found it expedient to resign, which they did in the month of April.* General Jackson, accordingly, set about a reorganization of his cabinet; and during the summer, he completed it as follows: Edward Livingston, of Louisiana, was made secretary of state; Louis M'Lane, of Delaware, secretary of the treasury; Lewis Cass, of Ohio, secretary of war; Levi Woodbury, of New Hampshire, secretary of the navy; Roger B. Taney, of Maryland, attorney-general.

1831.

A strong opposition to General Jackson's re-election began gradually to acquire head; and using the designation of "national republican," it was determined to support Henry Clay as its candidate for the presidency.

* Mr. Monroe, we may note here, died on the 4th of July, 1831, in the seventy-second year of his age.

* Mr. Van Buren, who had resigned the post of secretary of state, was appointed by the president minister to England; and embarked for London, in August, 1831.

The twenty-second Congress began its first session on the 5th of December, 1831. Stevenson was elected speaker by a bare majority; and the president's message was read to both Houses on the following day. This document was largely occupied with an account of foreign affairs at that date. The relation of the administration to the Indian tribes was also fully discussed. "It is confidently believed," said the president, "that perseverance for a few years in the present policy of the government, will extinguish the Indian title to all lands lying within the states composing our Federal Union, and remove beyond their limits, every Indian who is not willing to submit to their laws."

The amount of the revenue was anticipated as not less than $27,700,000; whilst the total expenditure was no more than $14,700,000. More than $16,500,000 had been applied to the reduction of the public debt, and the payment of interest upon it. So that in the three years that Jackson had been at the head of affairs, nearly $40,000,000 had been applied to this important object; certainly a just cause for gratulation.

Few recommendations were offered to Congress; but amongst them we find renewed those for "a modification of the tariff," justice to the interests of the merchant being observed, as well as to those of the manufacturer; "a more liberal policy towards unfortunate debtors to the government;" the amendment of the Constitution, in the article regulating the mode of electing the

1831. president and vice-president; and further and careful attention to the position of the Bank of the United States. New ones were presented respecting the complications of the system of keeping the public accounts; the reorganization of the District of Columbia; and correction of anomalies in the distribution of the circuit courts.

The president's appointments, made during the recess, were sent in to the Senate early in December, and after considerable discussion, were confirmed on the 13th of January, 1832, excepting that of Mr. Van Buren, minister to England. This was laid on the table by the casting vote of the vice-president, and was finally rejected by the same vote. How much mere party considerations had to do with this result, we stop not to inquire; but certainly, the opponents of the administration made a great mistake in not leaving Mr. Van Buren where he was, instead of forcing his return, and giving him a claim to further advance-

ment in the ranks of the demo- **1832.**

cratic party. The consequence was, that the late secretary of state was placed on the same ticket with Andrew Jackson, for vice-president; was secure of being elected to that office; and had also every reason to hope for the honor of being made his successor.

The apportionment of Representatives under the census of 1830, was warmly debated in Congress. The committee, early in January, through Mr. Polk, suggested forty-eight thousand as the ratio. After a large number of conflicting propositions by way of amendment, the numbers suggested varying from sixty thousand to forty-four; and several motions having had the hard fate of being carried one day, and rescinded the next; forty-seven thousand seven hundred was finally settled upon in May; and the Senate took the subject into immediate consideration. That body undertook to fix the total of the House at two hundred and fifty-one members, leaving the ratio of apportionment to be fixed in accordance therewith. But the House disagreeing, the Senate receded from its amendment, and the arrangement settled by the House was finally adopted.

The president having, in each of his three annual messages to Congress announced, with tolerable distinctness, his hostility to the Bank of the United States, that institution thought it best, at an early day, to apply for a renewal of its charter; and so the great bank controversy began. A memorial was presented in the Senate by Mr. Dallas, on the 9th of January, and referred to a select committee for consideration. The opponents of the bank wished to postpone the subject, but were unsuccessful. On the 13th of March, the committee reported in favor of renewing the charter for fifteen years, with certain modifications, by which it would seem, every reasonable objection would have been obviated. And a bill was brought in, conformable with the report; but in order to secure the harmonious action of Congress, it was not pushed through, because the committee of inquiry appointed by the House had not yet reported.

1832.

Mr. M'Duffie, of South Carolina, presented the memorial of the bank to the House of Representatives, and it was referred to the committee of ways and means. On the 10th of February, this committee reported in favor of a renewal of the charter; the minority, however, presented a counter report. A motion was then made for a committee of inquiry into the affairs of the bank. The majority of this committee was hostile to the bank, and so, having entered into an examination of the whole affairs of the institution, a report was presented, recommending the postponement of the consideration of the renewal of the charter, till the public debt was paid, and the revenue adjusted to the expenditure of the government. The minority also reported (John Quincy Adams sending in a report in his own name alone,) in vindication of the management of the bank, and recommended the renewal of the charter.

The conflict was now removed to the Senate, where, in committee of the whole, various amendments to the bill before them were proposed by the friends and by the opponents of the bank. But after a hot debate of three weeks, the bill, without many alterations, passed, on the 11th of June, by a vote of twenty-eight to twenty.* The bill was sent to the House, and taken up there on the 30th of June. Mr. M'Duffie proposed an amendment, to the effect that the provision limiting the number of branches in the several states, should not inter-

1832.

* Mr. Benton's statements and remarks on this subject are well worthy the reader's examination. He was one of the most active, energetic, and uncompromising opponents of the bank, which have at any time been in public life. See his "*Thirty Years' View*," vol. i., pp. 158–9, 187–205, 220–265.

fere with existing branches; and others proposed other amendments, and a short but sharp contest ensued, ending in the adoption of M'Duffie's amendment, with which the Senate also concurred, and the rejection of all the others; and the bill finally passed by a majority of a hundred and seven against eighty-five. This was on the 3d of July; for the session had been unusually protracted; but Congress arranged its adjournment so as to leave ten clear days after the bill was put into the hands of the president, lest it should be retained till the next session, as other bills had been.

Andrew Jackson was not unready to meet the question. The bill was presented to him on the 4th of July, and on the 10th he returned it with his veto, a document of great length, in which the question is argued in full. The last paragraph is all that we have room to quote.

"I have now done my duty to my country. If sustained by my fellow-citizens, I shall be grateful and happy; if not, I shall find in the motives which impel me, ample grounds for contentment and peace. In the difficulties which surround us, and the dangers which threaten our institutions, there is cause for neither dismay nor alarm. For relief and deliverance let us firmly rely on that kind Providence which, I am sure, watches with peculiar care over the destinies of our republic, and on the intelligence and wisdom of our countrymen. Through *His* abundant goodness, and *their* patriotic devotion, our liberty and union will be preserved."

Mr. Webster and Mr. Clay addressed the Senate earnestly on this subject, when the bill was returned with the veto of the president; and the question of renewing the charter of the bank was again discussed; but the bill not receiving a two-thirds vote, it was of course rejected.

The public lands occupied considerable attention in Congress; but, owing to the lateness of the time when they were under discussion, nothing of moment was accomplished. Internal improvements were warmly agitated, and several large appropriations were made and sanctioned by the president, having this object in view. The harbor bill, however, was kept back by the president, and was thus prevented from becoming a law. **1832.** The tariff also came under the attention of Congress, being distinctly recommended by the president, and the progress of the anti-tariff feeling in the south requiring it. The subject was taken up by the two committees of the House on ways and means, and on manufactures; and reports and bills were presented by both. That from the first committee, of which M'Duffie was chairman, (although it originated with the secretary of the treasury, and so was a government measure,) was negatived, on the 1st of June; that of the other, of which John Quincy Adams was chairman and reporter, after some discussion, and a few amendments, was carried by a vote of one hundred and thirty-two to sixty-five, some of the opponents of protection even voting for it. The principle of protection was maintained by this bill, but the duties on many protected articles of domestic manufactures were considerably reduced, and it was received as a concession to the free-trade party, and with the hope (a most delusive one, as it proved,) that it would allay the existing excitement in South Carolina.

This unusually long session of Congress was closed on the 14th of July, 1832.

CHAPTER II.

1832-1837.

JACKSON'S ADMINISTRATION: CONCLUDED.

The ch lera and its ravages — Indian war in the north-west — Black Hawk — Movements in South Carolina against the tariff law — Congress in session — Abstract of the president's message — Action in Congress on the tariff question — The enforcing bill — Calhoun's speech — Clayton's resolution — Henry Clay's "compromise tariff" bill — The land bill — Question on the deposits of the public money — Jackson's second inauguration — His northern tour — The president determines to remove the deposits — Duane refuses to give the necessary order — Taney appointed secretary of the treasury — Deposits removed — Excitement in the community — Congress in session — Its proceedings — Resolution condemning the president for removing the deposits — Jackson's protest — Stormy debate — Commercial distress and embarrassments — Action of the House on re-chartering the bank, etc. — Debate in the Senate — Taney's nomination rejected — The "whig" opposition — Congress in session — Not much accomplished — Claims on France — Jackson determines to have a settlement — The result — Other claims on European powers settled — Texas and its affairs — Democratic convention at Baltimore — Van Buren nominated — The twenty-fourth Congress — The message — Proceedings of Congress in regard to the deposits in the state banks — Distribution of the surplus revenue — Effect of this course — Speculation, gambling, fraud, etc. — Slavery discussion — The "specie circular" — Effect upon the country — Van Buren elected president — Johnson elected vice-president by the Senate — Jackson's last message to Congress — The "expunging resolution" — Attempt to rescind the specie circular unsuccessful — Close of Andrew Jackson's administration.

DURING the summer of 1832, the whole country was greatly alarmed and excited by the appearance of that terrible scourge, as it proved, the Asiatic cholera. About the close of June, it began its ravages; and partly in consequence of terror and fright, and partly from ignorance of the nature and mode of the treatment of the disease, it was extensively fatal in its effect. Over three thousand died in New York city,
between the 4th of July and the
1832. 1st of October. In Philadelphia, nearly a thousand died; in Baltimore, about six hundred; in Washington, nearly two hundred; and other towns and cities suffered in about the same proportion. But in New Orleans the cholera proved very malignant; for between the 28th of October and the 11th of November, sixteen hundred and sixty-eight deaths occurred. The nature and peculiarities of this fearful visitation excited universal attention, and gave rise to various contributions to medical literature, by eminent members of the faculty. Among these, Dr. Francis's letter is especially worthy of

note; a brief quotation will not be out of place in the present connection. "Whether the materies morbi of cholera claims a siderial or telluric origin, the atmosphere is the medium through which it operates. It prevails in all climates, and at all seasons; it exists in every variety of soils; on mountains and in valleys, in marshes and on rocks, in dryness, and in humidity. Unlike influenza, and some other specific diseases, its ravages are independent of winds and currents; neither the analysis of the gases of the atmosphere, nor barometrical or thermometrical investigation, solve the difficulty of its birth, and we are baffled in reviewing its progress, to ascertain the peculiar influence of localities in producing it. . . . . . When this formidable disease shall have disappeared from among us, and its history be recorded by the faithful historian, the skill and humane exertions of the medical profession, the munificence of the affluent, and the disinterested benevolence of all classes, will not be forgotten."*

In the north-west fresh troubles broke out in the spring of the present year. The Sacs and Foxes, who, by treaty had agreed to remove, showed much reluctance in doing so, and the governor of Illinois was disposed to hasten their departure. He accordingly ordered the militia to use compulsion in carrying out the measure. Black Hawk was leader of the Indians at the time, and he at once resorted to the only practicable means of revenge—predatory and hostile ravages in the frontier settlements; whilst he prepared for a more formidable retaliation. In March, 1832, he assembled his own tribes, the Sacs and Foxes, with Winnebagoes, to the number of about a thousand in all, and crossed the Mississippi into Illinois. All was dismay; the settlers nearest the point of invasion fled, and a brigade of militia, ordered out for their protection, by no means appeased the alarm. By June, however, the United States troops there, together with about three thousand mounted volunteers, took the field, and Black Hawk withdrew his warriors into the swamps, which were their fortresses, and trenches, and ambuscades, at the same time; and he extended his murderous incursions over the whole of the most advanced north-western settlements.

General Scott was thereupon ordered to lead eleven companies of infantry and nine companies of artillery against the savages; and with the utmost promptitude, undeterred by distance, and although his force suffered severely from cholera, he marched to Chicago. The same spirit actuated the army already in the field; for, finding that they could not be reinforced by Scott's troops, they penetrated into the lurking-places of the Indians, on the 21st of
July, inflicted a decisive defeat 1832.
on them on the banks of the Wisconsin, followed them up, and once more, and yet more disastrously, routed them, near the mouth of the Iowa, on the left bank of the Mississippi, on the 2d of August; and Black Hawk and his small band

* "*Letter on the Cholera Asphyxia*, now prevailing in the city of New York; addressed to Dr. Read, of Savannah." By John W. Francis, M. D. New York, 1832. Pp. 35.

of survivors having surrendered, on the 15th and 21st of September, treaties were concluded with the Winnebagoes, and the Sacs and Foxes, by which they agreed to the cession of the remainder of their territory, and the federal government to pay $10,000 annually, for twenty-seven years to the Winnebagoes, and $20,000 for thirty years, to the Sacs and Foxes, and to provide them with the means of improvement and civilization. And thus was peace restored again in the north-west.

Directly after the passage of the tariff act, mentioned on a previous page, (p. 386,) the representatives of South Carolina addressed their constituents on the subject, and urged upon them to sustain the sovereign rights of that state, which, they said, were invaded by the recent action of Congress. Meetings were accordingly held in South Carolina, and much excitement was manifested against the general government. The legislature was convened by Governor Hamilton, at Columbia, on the 22d of October, and the tariff question was warmly discussed. The result was, the calling of a state convention, which met on the 19th of November, at the same place. This convention proceeded to the length of recommending nullification, in the completest sense of the term. The legislature, which met on the 27th, passed ordinances to carry into effect the recommendations of the state convention, and South Carolina became thus arrayed in opposition to the laws of the United States, refusing to allow the revenue to be collected, and determining to resist by force every attempt to compel obedience. This, of course, brought the question to an issue, and it remained to be seen, whether the executive would take care to have the laws of the United States enforced, and whether South Carolina would be reduced to her proper place as one of the members of the Union.

The twenty-second Congress commenced its second session on the 4th of December, 1832. Hugh L. White, Senator from Tennessee, was elected president *pro tempore;* on the 28th, Mr. Calhoun resigned his post as vice-president of the United States, and was immediately elected a Senator from South Carolina, in place of Mr. Hayne, who had been chosen governor of the state. **1832.**

In the message of the president, among other things, he pressed upon Congress the necessity for revising the tariff; both for the purpose of adapting the revenue to the expenditure, and to limit the protection afforded by the imposts to the counteraction of the protective laws of other nations, and the securing of "a supply of those articles of manufacture essential to the national independence and safety in time of war." He insisted, that perpetual protection, secured by a tariff of high duties imposed for that object specially, had entered into the minds of but few American statesmen. "The most they have anticipated is a temporary and generally incidental protection, which they maintain has the effect to reduce the price, by domestic competition, below that of the foreign article. Experience, however, our best guide on this as on other subjects, makes it doubtful whether the advantages of this system are not counterbalanced by many evils, and whether it does not tend to beget, in the minds of a large portion of our countrymen, a spirit of discontent and jealousy dangerous to the stability of the Union."

While speaking of the tariff, "nullification" came under the president's notice; and he quietly but resolutely intimated his belief "that the laws themselves were fully adequate to the suppression of such attempts as might immediately be made" to carry out the views of those who favored absolute state sovereignty. "Should the exigency arise," he continued, "rendering the execution of the existing laws impracticable from any cause whatever, prompt notice of it will be given to Congress, with the suggestion of such views and measures as may be deemed necessary to meet it."

In regard to the United States Bank, Jackson showed himself equally uncompromising. He now recommended that "provision should be made to dispose of all stocks then held (by the general government,) in corporations, whether created by the general or state governments, and to place the proceeds in the treasury." He also brought against the bank the definitive charge of effecting "an arrangement with a portion of the holders of the three per cent stock;" by which, said he, "a surrender of the certificates of this stock may be postponed until October, 1833; and thus the liability of the government, after its ability to discharge the debts, may be continued by the failure of the bank to perform its duties." And then it was recommended, that Congress should seriously investigate this question,—"whether the public deposits in that institution may be regarded as entirely safe." The president also recommended a reduction of the price of the public lands, so as to prevent their becoming a source of revenue, and an amendment of the Constitution, so as to limit and define the power of the general government over internal improvement. The policy of the government in relation to the Indians was applauded; and an extension of the judiciary system to the new western states was again recommended.

1832.

South Carolina having proceeded to the lengths mentioned above, General Jackson manifested his usual decision in meeting the emergency. He gave orders to the military force at his disposal, to be ready to sustain and protect the federal officers at Charleston; and on the 10th of December, a long and energetic proclamation was issued, denouncing the movements of the nullifiers as palpable treason, and calling upon the South Carolinians to return to their loyalty to the Union.

The House of Representatives, at an early day, applied itself to the subject of the tariff, referring to the committee of ways and means the consideration of the president's suggestion concerning it. In the Senate a resolution was carried, calling upon the secretary of the treasury, who had in his annual report urged the reduction of duties to the revenue standard, for a draught of a bill embodying his views, or rather those of the administration. On the

27th of December, the committee of ways and means reported, by Mr. Verplanck, of New York; and a bill proposing a diminution of the duties on all protected articles, but leaving from fifteen to twenty per cent. for protective purposes, and to take effect immediately, with a further reduction to follow, was laid before the House; and this seems to have been in effect the reply to the resolution of the Senate.

At the commencement of the new year, 1833, the discussion of this scheme was entered upon; but it had gone on only a week, when the president, on January the 16th, by a message, communicated information respecting the ordinance and nullifying laws of South Carolina, and his own proclamation thereupon, accompanied by his views of what Congress should do; and on the 21st of the month, a bill to enforce the collection of the revenue according to the law was reported by the judiciary committee of the Senate. Thus there were two bills of primary importance on the same subject, but looking in precisely opposite directions, under discussion in the Houses of Congress at the same time,—this enforcing or force bill in the Senate, to compel South Carolina to submit to the tariff of 1828, and the new tariff bill in the House of Representatives, to abolish that very tariff which the enforcing bill was to uphold.

1833.

The enforcing bill, which had, with great judgment, been drawn in a general form, so as not to wear an invidiously hostile aspect towards the nullifying state, made slow progress in the Senate. But the tariff bill in the House seemed like to perish in a perfect flood of amendments and debates. The excitement in the country was intense, for the state legislatures were almost all in session, and each felt bound to deliver itself upon the question of the day. New England called to mind the Hartford Convention, and what was said then; whilst the south was anxious to see the tariff lowered to the revenue scale, anxious to see the supremacy of state sovereignty demonstrated, yet anxious for the maintenance of the Union; for, however much talk may have been indulged in on this subject, neither at the south nor anywhere else has there ever been wanting a conviction, that the dissolution of the Union would prove fatal to the state which should bring about such a result.

Mr. Calhoun, for the purpose (as he observed) of testing the principles of the "force" bill, proposed a series of resolutions to the Senate, which were no more than expansions of the old view of the state-sovereignty principle, and yet they involved the whole principle of "nullification." Starting from the definition of the Constitution, as a "compact" uniting "the people of the several states;" and of the Union, as "a union between the states" which ratified "the constitutional compact;" he proceeded to the assertions, that whilst "certain definite powers" were delegated to the general government, "to be executed jointly," each state reserved to itself "the residuary mass of powers to be exercised by its own separate government;" and that in the assumption by the general government of powers not delegated to it, its acts are "unauthorized, void, and of no effect," each state having "an equal right to judge for itself, as well of the infraction as of the mode and measure of redress," all being "sovereign parties, without any common judge." Lastly, he distinctly denied the opposite allegations, that the Union was based on a social compact of the people, "taken collectively, as individuals," and "that they have not the right of judging, in the last resort, as to the extent of powers reserved, and, of consequence, of those delegated;" because the tendency of those opinions was to "subvert the sovereignty of the states, to destroy the federal character of the Union, and to rear on its ruins a consolidated government, without constitutional check or limitation, and which must necessarily terminate in the loss of liberty itself."

1833.

Mr. Grundy, on behalf of the administration, offered a series of counter resolutions, asserting the power of the United States to lay duties on imports, and denying that any state has the right to attempt to obstruct the execution of any acts of Congress. Mr. Clayton, one of the opposition Senators, declaring that these resolutions "tacitly yielded the whole doctrine of nullification;" submitted an additional resolution, setting forth the real reply to Calhoun's statement. It was to this effect,—"That the people of these United States are, for the purposes enumerated in their Constitution, one people and a single nation;" "that while the Constitution does provide for the interest and safety of all the states, it does not secure all the rights of independent sovereignty to any;" "that the Supreme Court of the United States is the proper and only tribunal in the last resort for the decision of all cases in law and equity, arising under the Constitution, the laws of the United States, and treaties made under their authority;" and further, that the Senate "would not fail in the faithful discharge of its most solemn duty to support the executive in the just administration of the government, and clothe it with all constitutional power necessary to the faithful execution of the laws and the preservation of the Union."

Matters were making but slow progress, notwithstanding the session was drawing to its close. South Carolina hesitated to proceed to actual resistance, and the government was reluctant to press its determination further than could be helped. At this point Mr. Clay again stood forward as the supporter of some measure of compromise, which should enable both parties to agree upon steps whereby a collision might be prevented, and conflicting claims and theories be allowed to rest. On the 11th of February, Mr. Clay rose and gave notice, that he should ask leave of the Senate to introduce a bill to modify the acts imposing duties on imports. Next day he did ask leave, and after a brief discussion obtained it. This was the "Compromise Tariff" bill; it provided that, at the end of the year then current, all *ad valorem* duties of more than twenty per cent. should be reduced one-tenth, and at the end of each alternate year afterwards till 1839, an equal reduction; and that at the end of 1841,

1833.

and half a year after that term, the residue of the excess should be taken off in two equal portions, leaving a maximum of twenty per cent. It also provided for the abolition of credit for duties, and the assessment of the value of imports at the ports of entry, or home valuation, after the 30th of June, 1842. Thus he thought, that the protective tariff would be preserved for a sufficient length of time, whilst the country would be tranquillized and good feeling restored.*

After a full discussion, in the course of which Mr. Calhoun expressed his approbation of the measure, it reached a third reading; and then it was stated by Mr. Clay, that a bill of precisely the same character had passed the House, and would most probably be presented at once, for the approval of the Senate. In effect, the administration measure was shelved, Robert P. Letcher, of Kentucky, moving its recommittal, with instructions to the committee to report Mr. Clay's bill in its place; which was done, and it was accepted by a majority of a hundred and nineteen against eighty-five. This was on the 26th of February; on the next day it was sent to the Senate, passed that body on the 1st of March, twenty-nine voting for it, and sixteen against; and on the following day (which this year was the last in the session,) received the approval of the president.

The enforcing bill passed the Senate on the 20th of February; thirty-two voting for it, and only one, John Tyler, afterwards president, in opposition to it. On the 28th, it passed the House, by a majority of a hundred and fifty against thirty-five; and received the president's approval at the same time as the tariff bill.*

In close connection with the compromise tariff was Mr. Clay's land bill, which was re-introduced by him early in December. Discussed at intervals during the three months of the session, but with no accession of light respecting any of its obscure points, it passed the Senate near the end of January, by a majority of four. The House took it up only on the 1st of March, but passed it then by ninety-six against forty, with some trifling amendment, which the Senate agreed to by a vote of twenty-three against five, and it was sent to the president. The lateness of the day on which it was sent gave the executive good opportunity to decline to return it, which was the course he pursued, and the bill was accordingly defeated. **1833.**

The president, as we have noted, threw out doubts in his message, respecting the safety of the deposits of public money which were in the keeping of the United States Bank, and recommended to sell the stock in the hands of the government. The committee of ways and means reported through Mr. James K. Polk, the desirableness of the latter step; but the meas-

---

* For Senator Benton's "secret history of the compromise of 1833," see his "*Thirty Years' View*," vol. i., pp. 342–44.

* Mr. Webster's position on the subject of the tariff and the federal revenue, according to Mr. Benton, accorded very nearly with the standard recommended by General Jackson in his message at the opening of the session.

ure was immediately rejected, though by a small majority, a hundred and two against ninety-one. The same committee soon afterwards, by Mr. Verplanck, presented a resolution to the House, to the effect that the public deposits were quite safe whilst in the bank, and it was adopted by the large vote of a hundred and nine to forty-six. An agent, appointed by the secretary of the treasury, had previously reported, that the bank had an excess of funds of more than $7,000,000 over its liabilities, besides its capital of $35,000,000.

The twenty-second Congress expired on the 2d of March, (the 3d being Sunday,) and at the same time, General Jackson's first term of service reached its close. He had been re-elected by a large vote, in the preceding autumn, and Mr. Van Buren, had also, by the same vote, been elevated to the vice-president's chair. Jackson received two hundred and nineteen votes, and Van Buren one hundred and eighty-nine. Henry Clay and John Sergeant received only forty-nine votes each; which clearly demonstrated the strength of the democracy, in their support of the views and measures of Andrew Jackson.*

On Monday, the 4th of March, the ceremonies connected with the inauguration of the president, were again gone through with, and Andrew Jackson delivered his second Inaugural,

1833.

and a second time took the oath of office. Political excitements seemed to have quieted down, in great measure, and the president, deeming it a favorable opportunity, determined to make a tour through the middle and eastern states during the summer. He was every where received as the chief magistrate of the Union, and was greatly gratified by the evident marks of affectionate confidence manifested by so many thousands towards his person and principles.*

Notwithstanding the decisive expression of sentiment on the part of Congress, General Jackson did not recede from his determination on the subject of removing the deposits from the United States Bank. Mr. Livingston having been sent as minister to France, Mr. M'Lane, at the end of May, was appointed secretary of state, in his place, and in the treasury, vacated by him, William J. Duane was placed. The president probably expected that this gentleman would proceed, without hesitation, to carry out the views and purposes of the executive. But he had mistaken the man. Duane was not willing to act without authority from Congress, and only assented at length to the commissioning of Amos Kendall, to inquire into the terms upon which the state banks would take the money upon the basis of mutual guarantee.

The president having made up his mind to assume the responsibility, called his cabinet together on the 18th of

* In the latter part of June, 1830, John Randolph sailed for Europe, as minister to Russia. In the autumn of 1831, he returned to the United States; and died in Philadelphia, on the 24th of June, 1833.

* In the autumn of this same year, 1833, Mr. Clay went over pretty much the same ground, and was received with even greater enthusiasm and marks of personal attachment, than had been bestowed upon the president.

September, and laid before it a statement of his views on the question at issue. Not much impression appears to have been produced by the elaborate document which was then read
1833.
to the gentlemen present, and Senator Benton admits, that "the major part of them dissented from his design."* Mr. Duane agreed to remove the deposits, if Congress directed him to do so; but the president insisted upon his right to act without the intervention of Congress. Accordingly, on the secretary's refusal to do as the president directed, he removed him from his post, and on the 23d of September, appointed Roger B. Taney, then attorney-general, in his room. The new secretary had no scruples on the subject, and on the 1st of October, the deposits were removed, and placed in certain selected banks in different parts of the country.

It would require much larger space than we have at command, to give anything of an adequate description of the commercial excitement and distress which ensued upon the course adopted by General Jackson. At the time, the business of the country was unusually active. The capitalists, and the merchants, and mechanics, had unlimited confidence in each other, and all the moneyed institutions in the country had extended their loans to the utmost bounds of their ability. At such a juncture, great and rigid retrenchment, attended with want of confidence, was necessarily productive of ominous consequences; private credit was deeply affected; the business of the country was interrupted; and, in short, a complete and terrible panic was produced, which seemed to be at its height when Congress met, but which was destined to last, with many fluctuations in its symptoms and violence, for some ten years.

The first session of the twenty-third Congress commenced on the 2d of December, 1833. Mr. Stevenson was re-elected speaker of the House by a large majority, and Mr. Van Buren took his seat as presiding officer in the Senate. The administration, however, though so strong in the 1833.
House, were in a minority in the Senate.

The president's message was a long and carefully prepared document, setting forth the views of the executive quite at large on the various topics then agitating the community. Its recommendations received due attention from Congress, and many of them gave rise to long and animated debates. The principal business of the session was, necessarily, the removal of the deposits; and the opposition derived no little

* A day or two afterwards, this paper was printed in the "Globe," and is well worth the reader's examination. General Jackson concludes in the following words:—"The president again repeats, that he begs his cabinet to consider the proposed measure as his own, in support of which, he shall require no one of them to make a sacrifice of opinion or principle. Its responsibility has been assumed, after the most mature deliberation and reflection, as necessary to preserve the morals of the people, the freedom of the press, and the purity of the elective franchise; without which all will unite in saying, that the blood and treasure expended by our forefathers, in the establishment of our happy system of government, will have been vain and fruitless. Under these convictions, he feels that a measure so important to the American people cannot be commenced too soon; and he therefore names the first day of October next, as a period proper for the change of the deposits, or sooner, provided the necessary arrangements with the state banks can be made."

strength from the energy with which they pressed their attacks upon the administration on account of it. The power of the administration as a party, however, grew all the greater by means of these very attacks; the deed done remaining irreversible, and the proceedings of the bank, and the universal distress, afforded to the supporters of the president a full and satisfactory justification of it.

The Senate, at an early day, called for the report of the secretary of the treasury, which, when presented, was not found to contain much in the way of argument or explanation, that was new. Not considering this report as sufficient to enable it to discuss the subject properly, the Senate, on the 11th of December, respectfully called on the president, to communicate the paper read to the cabinet on the 18th of September, and published in the newspapers immediately afterwards. But General Jackson declined compliance with the request; leaving the Senate to interpret his refusal as it pleased, and Henry Clay's friends to denounce the whole proceeding as a "usurpation" consciously made, on the functions and prerogatives of Congress.

In the assault upon the administration, it was but natural that Henry Clay should take the lead. On the 26th of December, he offered the following resolution, which gave rise to long and earnest debates: "*Resolved*, That the president, in the late executive proceedings in relation to the public revenue, has assumed upon himself authority and power not conferred by the Constitution and laws, but in derogation of both." The resolution was adopted on the 28th of March, by a vote of twenty-six to twenty, which led to the president's preparing and sending in, about the middle of April, **1834.** a long argumentative protest, denying the right of the Senate to censure his proceedings, and "respectfully requesting, that this message and protest might be entered at length on the journal of the Senate." Much excitement was caused by reading this protest in the Senate, and it was immediately moved, that it be not received. Mr. Benton seized the opportunity to deliver the speech he had already prepared, moving (but without any expectation of carrying it at this time,) a resolution, to expunge the condemnation from the record of the Senate's proceedings.

For some three weeks the new storm raged, until, on the 7th of May, by a vote of twenty-seven against sixteen, the following modified resolutions were passed: "That the protest communicated to the Senate on the 17th (of April,) by the president of the United States, asserts powers as belonging to the president, which are inconsistent with the just authority of the two Houses of Congress, and inconsistent with the Constitution of the United States; and that the aforesaid protest is a breach of the privileges of the Senate, and that it be not entered on the journal."

Mr. Calhoun exerted his great powers of argument and of illustration, in opposition to the course of the president; and Daniel Webster uttered one of his great speeches, in which he combatted the assumptions of the protest, and denounced the evident tendency on Jackson's part, towards high-handed exercise of executive power and patronage.

Whilst this contest was going on in the national legislature, the people in all the great cities and towns throughout the Union, and in many of less note, held meetings, and dispatched petitions to Congress, and committees to wait in person on the president, for the purpose of representing their distress, and begging him to recommend some measure of relief. As the session advanced, this popular action on the executive and Congress grew in intensity, both as to the numbers and urgency of the applications. The petitioners for relief were told, that the government could provide neither remedy nor relief; it was all in the hands of the bank, or the banks, and themselves; for "they who traded on borrowed capital ought to break."

1834. The Senate willingly received the petitions which complained of distress, and implored relief; but in the House of Representatives, where the majority supported the president, they met with little countenance. Nevertheless, all the session long, these proofs of commercial embarrassment and popular excitement continued to pour into Washington; nor was it possible for any, quite to shut out the conviction, that the country had to pay dearly for the accomplishment of the president's design.

In the House of Representatives, a line of operations, wholly distinct, and indeed opposed to that we have seen proceeding in the Senate, was being carried on. There, the message, the secretary's report, the bank memorial, and the other documents relating to the matter, were all referred to the committee of ways and means; and Mr. Polk, the chairman, on the 4th of March, reported four resolutions, which were carried on the 4th of April, to this effect:—That the bank ought not to be rechartered; that the deposits ought not to be replaced; that state banks ought to be used as places of deposit, but that Congress (and here they implicitly blamed the president, and that with some severity,) ought to prescribe the mode of selecting them, the securities, the terms, and the manner of employing them; and that a complete investigation of the affairs of the Bank of the United States should be made, for the purpose of ascertaining "the cause of the commercial embarrassment and distress, complained of by numerous citizens of the United States."*

These resolutions were yet under discussion in the House, when, at the beginning of February, several incidents occurred, which mark the onward movement of the struggle. On the 4th, the president sent a message to both Houses of Congress, in which he censured the bank for refusing to deliver to him the books, papers, and funds, connected with the pension to the surviving sol-

* According to a report presented in the Senate, at the close of April, "in relation to the memorials for and against the removal of the public deposits," it appeared, that the number of signatures attached to memorials against the removal, and for the replacement of the deposits in the national bank, was a hundred and fourteen thousand nine hundred and eighteen; while those in favor of the proceeding of the president, amounted to eight thousand seven hundred and twenty-one.

diers of the Revolution. A censure which the judiciary committee of the Senate, on the 17th of the month, reported as undeserved; which decision was affirmed by the Senate, after much debate, near the end of May. Many speeches were made by Mr. Clay, Mr. Webster, and others; and it was in one of these that Henry Clay made his well-known apostrophe to Mr. Van Buren, calling upon him to go to the president, and tell him of the distress of the country, and of the obligation resting upon him to afford relief. "Tell him," said the eloquent Kentuckian, "that in his bosom alone, under actual circumstances, does the power abide to relieve the country; and that unless he opens it to conviction, and corrects the errors of his administration, no human imagination can conceive, and no human tongue can express, the awful consequences which may follow. Entreat him to pause, and reflect that there is a point beyond which human endurance cannot go; and let him not drive this brave, generous, and patriotic people to madness and despair."

The Senate having refused to entertain the president's protest, Mr. Clay proposed two other resolutions, in which he hoped that the House also would join;—to the effect, that the reasons for removing the deposits, offered by the secretary, were unsatisfactory and insufficient, and that the public money ought to be placed in the Bank of the United States again. After a long debate, in which no argument of novelty enough to deserve attention was advanced, the Senate accepted the resolutions, on the 4th of June, by votes of twenty-eight and twenty-nine to sixteen; and they were sent to the House. There, however, on the motion of Mr. Polk, the resolutions were laid upon the table by a vote of one hundred and fourteen to a hundred and one.

At the beginning of June, Mr. Stevenson, who had been nominated minister to England, resigned his post as speaker; and after a number of ballotings, John Bell, of Tennessee, was elected to fill the vacancy. On the 23d of June, just at the close of the session, the president sent in Mr. Taney's name for confirmation as secretary of the treasury. The Senate rejected the nomination by a vote of twenty-eight to eighteen. The next day, Mr. Stevenson's nomination as minister to England was rejected by a vote of twenty-three to twenty-two. On the 30th, after a long and busy session, Congress brought its labors to a close.* **1834.**

The elections, during 1834, showed, that though General Jackson's course was largely popular with the mass of the people, still, in the commercial states, there was no little dissatisfaction; and the opposition, organized under the name of "whigs," determined to do all

* Just before the close of the session, the news of the death of General Lafayette, on the 20th of May, 1834, reached the United States. Suitable resolutions were adopted in Congress on the 24th of June, and the venerable John Quincy Adams was unanimously requested to deliver an oration on the life and character of the eminent deceased, at the next session. Accordingly, "the old man eloquent," on the 31st of December, before the two Houses, delivered his admirable and touching discourse upon the life and career of the noble-hearted patriot, for whom our country was mourning with deep and unfeigned sorrow.

in their power to effect a change in the administration of public affairs.

Congress reassembled on the 1st of December, for its closing session; and the president's message was read on the following day. Beside a full consideration of foreign affairs, the message dilated upon the subjects then occupying the attention of nearly all our citizens,
1834. viz.: in relation to the currency, the revenue, the United States Bank, the local banks, etc. Other topics, as the army, the navy, Indian affairs, the post-office, defects in the judicial system, and the like, were recommended to the notice and action of Congress. Not much, however, was accomplished during the session. The report of the bank investigation committee was presented, in the Senate, by John Tyler; but nothing new or important was evolved; the subject had already been discussed almost *ad nauseam*. Mr. Benton brought forward his expunging resolution, but obtained only seven votes in its favor. Some appropriations were made to carry on internal improvements;* branches of the mint were established at the gold mines in North Carolina and Georgia, and also at New Orleans. But when the 3d of March arrived, and the twenty-third Congress expired, it left almost all of the important measures of this session, which had been discussed and partly acted upon, unfinished; amongst which was the post-office reform bill, the custom house regulations bill, the judiciary bill, the bill regulating the deposit of the public moneys in the deposit banks, the bill respecting the tenure of office and removals from office, the bill for indemnifying
the claimants for French spoli- 1835.
ations before the year 1800, and the fortification bill.

On several occasions we have spoken of the unwillingness and negligence of France to give proper attention to the subject of indemnity for spoliations on American commerce; and other European powers, emboldened by this conduct on the part of France, were holding back and endeavoring to evade the just demands of the United States. (See pp. 321, 322.) Previous administrations had labored to effect a settlement of this matter with the French government, but without success. General Jackson determined, that, as the executive of the nation, he would not suffer this topic to be continued longer in dispute. He resolved to bring France to terms, and he took his measures accordingly.

Mr. W. C. Rives, of Virginia, who had been appointed minister plenipotentiary and envoy extraordinary to Paris, for the purpose of pressing these claims, succeeded in negotiating, in 1831, with the government of Louis Philippe, the newly established citizen king, a treaty by which twenty-five millions of francs, (less one million and a half on

---

* Mr. Calhoun, indulging in some denunciatory remarks upon the party in power, sharply said, "The only cohesive principle, (a principle as flexible as India-rubber, and as tough too, he said, later in his speech,) which binds together the powerful party rallied under the name of General Jackson, is official patronage. Their object is to get and to hold office; and their leading political maxim, openly avowed on this floor, by one of the former senators from New York, now governor of that state, is, that 'to the victors belong the spoils of victory!'"

account of counter-claims by the royal treasury, or French citizens) were to be paid in six equal annual instalments, to satisfy all demands on the part of American citizens and the government of the United States. Interest at four per cent. was to be paid upon this sum, after the exchange of the ratifications of the treaty. This sum did not amount to one half of the real value of the damages sustained, and there was no allowance of interest before the treaty; yet it was deemed expedient to accept this compromise, and both the president and the people of the United States congratulated themselves that at length this troublesome matter was arranged.

In February, 1832, the ratifications of this treaty were duly exchanged, but neither the king, nor his ministers, nor the chambers, took any steps to carry its stipulations into effect. Congress, for its part, passed the needful laws; and on the 7th of July, 1833, the secretary of the treasury drew a bill of exchange upon the minister of state and finance of the French government, directing the first instalment to be paid to the order of the cashier of the United States Bank. When this bill was forwarded, through the bank, to Paris, it was not accepted; and the French government acted with very vexatious and annoying indifference as to whether the United States took it well or ill.

A bill to provide for this instalment was brought before the French chambers, but it was lost through want of proper attention. Instructions were then given to the American minister to urge a prompt compliance with the treaty upon the government of Louis Philippe; and to add, that the United States would demand indemnity for the refusal to accept the bill for the first instalment. And in his sixth annual message, in December, 1834, the president said,—"It is my conviction, that the United States ought to insist on a prompt execution of the treaty, and in case it be refused, **1834.** or longer delayed, to take redress into their own hands. After the delay on the part of France of a quarter of a century in acknowledging these claims by treaty, it is not to be tolerated that another quarter of a century is to be wasted in negotiating about the payment. The laws of nations provide a remedy for such occasions. It is a well-settled principle of the international code, that when one nation owes another a liquidated debt, which it refuses or neglects to pay, the aggrieved party may seize on the property belonging to the other, its citizens or subjects, sufficient to pay the debt, without giving just cause of war."

This was looked upon by France as a very summary measure, and was resented with a good deal of spirit. The French minister at Washington was recalled, and Mr. Livingston, at Paris, was offered his passports. In the Senate, a long and able report on this subject was presented by Mr. Clay, disapproving of the president's recommendation to make reprisals; and on the 14th of January, 1835, a resolution unanimously passed the Senate, declaring it inexpedient that there should **1835.** be any more legislation concerning the state of affairs between France and the United States. The House of Representatives took no action upon the suggestion of the president's message.

France, although willing to pay the money, thought that her dignity required some explanations from the American government, and a clause to this effect was introduced in the bill before the chambers to authorize the payments. Any thing of this sort was, of course, out of the question. Neither the president nor the people would demean themselves to make apologies for having insisted upon their just rights. About the middle of January, 1836, the president informed Congress, that the French government had peremptorily refused to execute the treaty, "except on terms incompatible with the honor and independence of the United States," having, in fact, demanded "an official written expression of regrets, and a direct explanation addressed to it," and having intimated that this was a *sine qua non*. The suspension of diplomatic intercourse with France was notified, and Congress was counselled "to retaliate her present refusal to comply with her engagements by prohibiting the introduction of French products, and the entry of French vessels into our ports." It was also recommended, that, as France was preparing a naval armament for the American seas, the navy should be increased, and the coast defences completed.

1836.

Before the committee on foreign relations, to which this communication was referred, could make any report upon it, a new message informed Congress, on the 8th of February, that Great Britain had offered her mediation, and that both he and the government of France had accepted it; and recommended the suspension of retaliatory measures, as well as the vigorous prosecution of the works for permanent national defence. "Within a month from the date of that message," adds Mr. Benton, "the four instalments of the indemnities then due were fully paid; and without waiting for any action on the part of the mediator."

In the present connection, following Senator Benton's summary of General Jackson's "foreign diplomacy," we may properly state the result of the claims for indemnity on other powers. Denmark agreed to indemnify the citizens of the United States for various injuries inflicted during the years 1808 to 1811, to the amount of $650,000; and renounced all the counter-claims it had before advanced. The convention preceded the treaty with France. After the signature of the last-named treaty, Naples also yielded to the demands of justice, and agreed to the payment of two millions one hundred and fifty thousand ducats, for the satisfaction of the claimants. In like manner Spain, which had inflicted much damage upon American commerce, during the time when it was fruitlessly endeavoring to recover its revolted provinces, now consented to pay twelve millions of reals in compensation for it; the president at the same time renouncing all unfounded claims, and pressing those only which were consistent with "the laws of nations." Indemnity for seizures made by Portugal in 1829 and 1830 was also paid, after some delay, in full, in 1837.

We may also mention here, that a

convention assembled at San Felippe, in Texas, in April, 1833, and declared the independence of that state or province. Santa Anna, who had made himself dictator in 1834, marched into Texas in the spring of 1835, in order to compel the submission of the inhabitants to his rule. In March, 1836, a number of delegates assembled at Washington, and a republican government was established, David G. Bûrnet being chosen first president. The victory at San Jacinto was gained by General Houston, April 21st, 1836, and application was made to be annexed to the United States. Houston was elected president of Texas. The Mexican minister at Washington solemnly protested against the proceedings with regard to Texas, and soon after took his departure; but this was looked upon as a matter of no great moment. The question of annexing Texas was only a question of time; it was certain to be accomplished at no distant day. Accordingly, as a preliminary step, in February, 1837, it was resolved by Congress to recognize the independence of Texas, and establish diplomatic relations with it. The population at the time was about twenty thousand; but from that date it rapidly increased.

A national democratic convention having been suggested by General Jackson, in a letter which was published in February, 1835, the suggestion was immediately adopted, and the convention met at Baltimore, in May. Some six hundred delegates were in attendance, and Martin Van Buren was unanimously nominated for president. Richard M. Johnson also received the nomination for vice president. That portion of the party opposed to Mr. Van Buren's elevation, named Hugh L. White as their candidate. The whigs had three candidates in the field, viz.: William Henry Harrison, John M'Lean, and Daniel Webster.*

1835.

On the 7th of December, 1835, the twenty-fourth Congress commenced its first session. James K. Polk was elected speaker of the House, and the next day the president's message was received. Beside the usual narrations in regard to foreign negotiations and affairs, a very flattering account was given of the national finances, and the general prosperity of the country. The public debt had been extinguished, and there was a balance of some $19,000,000 in hand. The president anticipated a surplus of $6,000,000 over and above the necessary appropriations which were to be made. This surplus, it was suggested, might be laid out in navy yards, or new national works, rather than distributed amongst the states, or "reduced faster than would be effected by the existing laws." The receipt of $11,000,000 from the sale of public lands in the current year was announced; and the need of some great changes in the general land office was intimated; together with the abolition of the offices of commissioners of loans and of the sinking fund. Other topics of the message we need not dwell upon, as the army, the navy,

* The venerable Chief-Justice Marshall died, at a ripe old age, on the 6th of July, 1835. In March, of the following year, the Senate confirmed the nomination of Roger B. Taney to fill the vacancy caused by Marshall's decease.

the post-office, etc. For details, the reader must consult the document itself.

Notwithstanding the session was prolonged into the summer of 1836, its proceedings were not of very special interest.* One of the most important acts passed was that for regulating the deposits of the public moneys in the state banks. The majorities in its favor

1836. were unusually large, and it was approved by the president at the close of June, 1836. "That fatal act," as Mr. Ingersoll terms it, gave direction to deposit all the surplus beyond $5,000,000 in the treasury of the United States, on the 1st day of January, 1837, with the states pledging their faith to keep safe, and repay the said moneys, from time to time, whenever required; (in proportion to their several representations in Congress;) pursuant to which act, $37,000,000, so called, that is, credit to that amount, were transferred from the national treasury to commonwealths greedy of gain, and who will never repay. By the same act, Congress required the secretary of the treasury to select and employ such state banks for depositories of the money of the United States, as redeemed their notes in specie on demand, and issued none for less than five dollars. Happily, in one aspect of the matter, the pecuniary difficulties of the government in 1837 prevented the deposit of the fourth instalment with the states, and thus that part of the surplus was preserved to the Union.

The effect of this distribution of the surplus revenue among the states was what was naturally to be expected. New banks sprang suddenly into existence, with nominal capital, and the country was deluged with paper money. Speculations of the wildest character were set on foot; and it seems almost incredible, that infatuation, and folly, and greed of gain, should have seized upon nearly the entire community. No scheme seemed to be too wild or chimerical to receive attention, and so easily deluded were the people, that prodigious frauds were perpetrated without producing that shock to the moral sensibilities which is always felt in a healthy state of the body politic. A calamitous reverse was, of course, ere long to be looked for, and it came with terrible effect within a short time.

The United States Bank, two weeks before the expiration of its charter from Congress, obtained from the legislature of Pennsylvania (at the cost of $2,000,000, in the form of a *bonus*,) a charter, with its original amount of capital, viz., $35,000,000. But it was found, ere long, that its *prestige* was gone, and that it could never, in this shape, exercise the vast influence which it formerly possessed.

Internal improvements, the patent laws, the admission of Arkansas and Michigan, as independent and sovereign states, into the Union, and the military academy, (against which Frank-

lin Pierce indulged in a speech, **1836.**
which Benton has quoted in his "Thirty Years' View,") were amongst the sub-

* On the 1st of July, 1836, Congress accepted the trust offered to it by James Smithson, of London, in England, of employing £100,000 in the establishment of "The Smithsonian Institution," at Washington, "for the Increase and Diffusion of Knowledge amongst Men."

jects of minor importance to which Congress devoted its time and labor now. There was one bill *vetoed*, (June 9th;) it fixed the time of meeting and adjournment of Congress, annually, to a day; and when examined by the eyes of General Jackson, disclosed some unconstitutional provision, about adjourning to the second Monday in May, which led him to deny it his sanction.

The subject of slavery came before Congress again, and gave rise to much excitement. It was brought on by the presentation of memorials praying that slavery be abolished in the District of Columbia, over which, it was pleaded, Congress had entire authority. John Quincy Adams took an active share in this whole matter, and planted himself upon the inalienable right of petition; but the southern influence was too strong for the abolitionist memorialists to obtain anything. Congress refused to interfere with slavery in the district, and resolved to lay upon the table, without printing or reference, or taking any action whatever on them, all petitions, etc., "relating in any way to the subject of slavery, or the abolition of slavery."

Congress was also called upon to consider this exciting topic in connection with the admission of Arkansas; and with a change in the boundary line of Missouri, effected through Mr. Benton's exertions, he assures us; which was "accomplished," as he writes, "by the extraordinary process of altering a compromise line, intended to be perpetual, and the reconversion of soil, which had been slave and made free, back again from free to slave." Some further remarks of the Senator from Missouri may not inaptly be here quoted. Speaking of the chapter in which he has set forth his views at large, he goes on to say: "It relates to a period when a new point of departure was taken on the slave question; when the question was carried into Congress, with avowed alternatives of dissolving the Union; and conducted in a way to show that dissolution was an object to be attained, not prevented; and this being the starting point of the slavery agitation, which has since menaced the Union, it is right that every citizen should have a clear view of its origin, progress, and design. From the beginning of the Missouri controversy, up to the year 1835, the author of this View looked to the north as the point of danger from the slavery agitation; since that time, he has looked to the south for that danger, as Mr. Madison did two years earlier. Equally opposed to it in either quarter, he has opposed it in both."*

Congress closed its session on the 4th of July, 1836. On the 11th of the same month, a circular was issued by the secretary of the treasury, "by order of the president," instructing the receivers of public money to take silver and gold alone (with the exception of Virginia land scrip in certain cases) in payment for the public lands. It had been attempted, in April, by means of Mr. Benton, to secure this object by a joint resolution of the two Houses of Congress; but the Senate refusing to entertain the proposal, it was **1836.**

* See Benton's "*Thirty Years' View*," vol. i. p. 623.

left to the president to act on his own responsibility in this matter.

Large purchases of public lands had been made on speculation, principally through the facilities afforded by the state banks; and the immediate effect of this order was necessarily to make specie abundant in the states where the purchasers of public lands were most numerous; and to make it scarce in the older states, where trade and commerce were most active, and specie was most required. It did unquestionably check the operations of the speculators; but at the same time, and in a more disastrous degree, it embarrassed those of the manufacturers and merchants. In several respects, no doubt, it was called for, and was salutary in its operation; but at the same time, it was felt to be a hard and stringent measure, which would not probably have been deemed at any period necessary, had not General Jackson succeeded in breaking down the United States Bank, and had not the consequences which followed upon that success been such as we have noted on previous pages.

During the autumn, the presidential election took place, and resulted as follows: Martin Van Buren received one hundred and seventy votes; General Harrison, seventy-three; Hugh L. White, twenty-six; Daniel Webster, fourteen; and W. P. Mangum, eleven. For the vice presidency, R. M. Johnson received one hundred and forty-seven; Francis Granger, seventy-seven; John Tyler, forty-seven; and William Smith, twenty-three. No election having been made for vice president, when the votes were counted, the Senate proceeded to elect one of the two highest on the roll, and Johnson was accordingly placed in the vacant chair.

The twenty-fourth Congress met for its second session on the 5th of December, 1836, and General Jackson sent in his last annual message on the following day. It gave a very favorable account of the state of affairs, and showed **1836.** that a large surplus — over $41,000,000--would be in the treasury on the 1st of January, 1837. The specie circular was defended; the operation of the local banks as fiscal agents of the government, was highly praised; a number of recommendations on various subjects were made; and the message concluded with the president's thanking his fellow-citizens for their partiality and indulgence, in which he had "found encouragement and support in the many difficult and trying scenes through which it had been his lot to pass during his public career."

Senator Benton's famous "expunging resolution" gave rise to animated debate, but it was carried on the 16th of January, 1837. Nearly three years before (see p. 396) the Senate had condemned General Jackson for removing **1837.** the deposits from the United States Bank; and Mr. Benton, with unabated zeal, had labored to have the record of this condemnation effaced from the journal of the Senate. It was accordingly done, amid no little excitement, and broad black lines were drawn round the offensive resolution, by the secretary of the Senate, and across it these words were written, "expunged by order of the Senate, this 16th day of January, 1837." The vote on the expunging resolution was twenty-four to nineteen.*

A vigorous attempt was made to rescind the treasury circular respecting specie payments for land sales. A resolution to this effect having been referred to the committee on public lands, a bill was reported, purporting the designation and limitation of the funds receivable for the revenues of the United States, and, in fact, providing for the reception of the notes of specie-paying banks, in certain cases. Mr. Benton, the "hard money" man, vehemently opposed it, but it passed by an overwhelming majority—forty-one against five. In the House an attempt was made to amend it, so as to save the specie circular, but it failed; a hundred and forty-three Representatives voted for the bill as it came from the Senate, and only fifty-nine against it. On the last day but one of the session it was sent to the president, who retained it in his possession, thus preventing its becoming a law. His reasons were published in the "Globe" a few days afterwards.

Few acts of general interest having been passed during the session, the twenty-fourth Congress reached its termination on the 3d of March, 1837. At the same time General Jackson finished his eight years of public service, and gave way to his successor. The events of these years are too near the day on which we are writing to be impartially viewed, and calmly judged, as they will be by the future historian of our country. Hence we do not attempt any review of Jackson's administration, being conscious that it would be of no avail. The ardent admirers and partizans of the hero of New Orleans would be satisfied with nothing less than an unqualified laudation; and on the other hand, his political enemies would receive as justly due no sentence short of condemnation of his acts and his principles. Let the reader of these pages judge, from the narrative of facts now before him, and let him meditate upon the life and career of the man whom so many thousands of Americans have regarded with an enthusiastic admiration, unequalled in the annals of our country.

* "The gratification of General Jackson was extreme. He gave a grand dinner to the expungers (as they were called) and their wives; and being too weak to sit at the table, he only met the company, placed the 'head expunger' in his chair, and withdrew to his sick-chamber. That expurgation! it was the 'crowning mercy' of his civil, as New Orleans had been of his military life."—Benton's "*Thirty Years' View*," vol. -., p. 731.

M Van Buren

CHAPTER III.

1837-1841.

VAN BUREN'S ADMINISTRATION.

Inauguration of Martin Van Buren — His Inaugural address — Condition of the country at this date — Failures and distress — Deputation of merchants goes to Washington — Extra session of Congress — The recommendations of the president — The sub-treasury plan proposed — Congress meet in December — The sub-treasury discussed — Acts of the session — The Seminole war in Florida — Resolutions in favor of annexing Texas — Attempted revolution in Canada — Burning of the Caroline — The president's proclamation against the insurgents — Proceedings of the last session of the twenty-fifth Congress — The opposition gain strength — Opening of the twenty-sixth Congress — The case of the New Jersey members — Whig convention at Harrisburg — General Harrison nominated for president — Van Buren nominated by the democratic convention — The president's message on the financial state of affairs — Good advice — The independent treasury established — Its chief provisions — The sixth census — The presidential election — Exciting canvass — Harrison elected — End of Van Buren's administration.

HAVING reached a point in the history of the United States which is too nearly contemporaneous to authorize our treating public affairs with any fulness or critical examination, we shall not undertake more than to present a concise summary of events during the last fifteen or twenty years; leaving the just historical estimate of our era to the historian of a later day, when time shall have set its seal upon the past, and when history can exercise its proper office in describing the progress of our national career.

The inauguration of Martin Van Buren, as the eighth president of the United States, took place on the 4th of March, 1837, with the usual ceremonies; and, after he had delivered his Inaugural address, the oath of office was administered to him by Chief-Justice Taney. His address was

1837.

a well-written paper, and set forth the views and principles by which he expected to be governed in the discharge of his duties. He renewed the pledge which he had given before his election, viz., "I must go into the presidential chair the inflexible and uncompromising opponent of every attempt, on the part of Congress, to abolish slavery in the District of Columbia, against the wishes of the slave-holding states; and also with a determination equally decided to resist the slightest interference with it in the states where it exists." And he closed his address with invoking the choicest of blessings upon our beloved country.

The condition of commercial and business affairs, at the beginning of Mr. Van Buren's presidency, was critical and alarming. The removal of the deposits, the specie circular, and the distribution of the surplus revenue, had, it was believed, brought about this distressing state of things; and mercantile men, in general, gave expression to the opinion, that the only effectual remedy for the evils affecting the currency and commercial exchanges was to be found in the establishment of a national bank. Failures began to occur in every quarter. During the first three weeks in April, two hundred and fifty houses stopped payment in New York. In New Orleans, during two days' time, houses stopped payment, owing an aggate of $27,000,000; and in other cities similar evidences were given of the storm that had burst over the country. The demands upon the banks increased rapidly; they could not keep their notes in circulation; the alarm grew into a panic; and a general run was made upon the banks. On the 10th of May, all the banks in New York stopped specie payments; and on the 16th, the legislature authorized this step on the part of the banks, to last for one year. The banks of other states speedily followed the example of those of New York; and all classes of the community gloomily anticipated widespread ruin and beggary as the result of this distressing state of commercial affairs.

On the 3d of May, a numerous meeting of merchants and bankers in New York, appointed a deputation to proceed to Washington and request the president to rescind the specie circular, to defer commencing suits upon unpaid bonds, and to call an extra session of

1837. Congress; and the committee stated, that, "under a deep impression of the propriety of confining our declarations within moderate limits, we affirm, that the value of our real estate has within the last six months depreciated more than $40,000,000;* . . . that within the same period a decline of $20,000,000, has occurred in our local stocks; . . . that within a few weeks not less than twenty thousand individuals, depending upon their daily labor for their daily bread, have been discharged by their employers because the means of retaining them were exhausted; and that a complete blight has fallen upon a community heretofore so active, enterprising and prosperous."

Other towns and cities followed the lead of New York, and sought relief at the hands of the executive; but Mr. Van Buren declined acting upon their petitions, and only consented, with reluctance, to the calling an extra session of Congress. His proclamation to this effect was issued on the 15th of May, and Congress was summoned to meet on the first Monday in September, on account of "great and weighty matters claiming their consideration." The interval was largely occupied in criminations and recriminations, by the opponents and upholders of the administration, as to where the blame rightly rested for the deplorable state into which the currency and business of the country had fallen.

The extra session was begun on the 4th of September, and it became evident at once, from the tone of the president's message, that no relief was to be looked for from the government. He ascribed the state of things to overtrading speculation, fostered and stim-

* A great and destructive fire occurred in New York in December, 1835, when five hundred and twenty-nine buildings were consumed, and property was destroyed to the amount of more than $20,000,000.

ulated by the banks, and avowed his belief, that all the government could do, or was designed to do, was to take care of itself; and that it could not be expected to legislate with reference to the monetary affairs of the people. The most important recommendation which Mr. Van Buren made, was, that the government should for the future keep its money in its own hands, by the instrumentality of the scheme of a sub-treasury, or, as it was called by its supporters, the independent treasury; so that there should be an entire and total separation of the business and funds of the government from those of the banks.

The finance committee of the Senate presented four bills; one, for suspending the payment of the fourth instalment of the surplus revenue to the states; a second, for authorizing the issue of treasury notes equal to any deficiency which might be felt in the treasury, with an addition of $4,000,000, by way of reserve; another, for the exten-
1837. sion of the indulgence in the payment of revenue bonds; and a fourth, for the organization of the sub-treasury system.

This last proposal caused no little excitement, both in and out of Congress, for it was looked upon as a direct assault upon the entire credit system, and a scheme to destroy all the banks. Yet it passed the Senate by a vote of twenty-six to twenty; but in the House, it was lost by a vote of a hundred and twenty to a hundred and seven. Other matters were debated, but nothing of moment was done, except authorizing the issue of $10,000,000 in treasury notes, for the immediate wants of the government. The session closed very unsatisfactorily, on the 16th of October.

On the 4th of December, Congress again assembled, and the president sent in his first annual message. It contained various matters of public interest and concern; but, as was to be expected, the chief matter which came under discussion, was the sub-treasury scheme. Mr. Calhoun, in the Senate, supported the views of the administration, while on the other hand, Mr. Clay and Mr. Webster exerted their great powers against the plan proposed for a treasury bank. In the progress of the debate the bill was considerably modified, and a clause prohibiting the receipt of bank-paper in payment of government dues was struck out; and thus amended, it passed the Senate, in June, by 1838.
the scanty majority of twenty-seven against twenty-five. No sooner, however, was it presented in the House, than it was met by a motion to lay it on the table, which in the end prevailed, by a vote of a hundred and twenty-five to a hundred and eleven.

Among the acts of the session, we may note here; the granting pre-emption rights to actual settlers; establishing the territory of Iowa; authorizing several works for internal improvements, in the way of light-boats and beacons, the navigating of certain rivers in Florida, and the like; appropriating money for suppressing Indian hostilities; authorizing the printing the Madison papers; etc. The establishment of a national bank was suggested, but not so as to bring on a debate concerning it. And the following resolution, respecting the specie circular, passed the Senate, by a vote of thirty-four to nine, and the other House, by a hundred and fifty-one to twenty-seven:—"*Resolved*, That it shall not be lawful for the secretary of the treasury to make, or continue in force, any general order which shall create any difference between the different branches of revenue, as to the money or medium of payment in which debts or dues accruing to the United States may be paid."

The Florida war was still in progress, and proved a source of great trouble and almost incredible expense. The removal of the Indians was a settled measure, (p. 380,) and when they proved reluctant, collisions naturally followed. The war with the Seminoles, began in December, 1835, and lasted for five years. Some of the ablest men in the army were sent against them, as Scott, Jessup, Taylor, Worth, and others; but led on by such chiefs as Osceola, Jumper, and Tiger-Tail, and with a country abounding in swamps and marshes, extensively fatal to the whites, they resisted every attempt to subdue them. No treaty stipulations were regarded by them, and they seized every occasion to inflict severe blows upon the Americans. More than once they repulsed with great loss superior numbers. In July, 1836, General Jessup officially announced the war at an end, yet next season it was carried on as actively as ever. In March, 1837, the same general proceeded so far as to negotiate a treaty, which stipulated that all hostilities were to cease, and that by the 10th of April, all the Indians were to be at Tampa, with their families, ready to be transported to their new country. But the treaty was not fulfilled, and the war went on. The capture of Osceola, and his death in January, 1838, did not terminate hostilities. In May, 1839, the chiefs agreed to retire below Pease Creek, in Florida, removal being impossible; but in the following July, the Indians broke the treaty, and the war began afresh. Bloodhounds were obtained, at considerable cost, from Cuba, to the disgust of civilized men, every where; but they proved of no avail in hunting Indians. The United States had under arms nearly nine thousand men, and the cost of the war exceeded considerably $15,000,000. It was not till the year 1842, that an entire cessation of troubles in Florida took place.*

In the Senate, Mr. Preston, of South Carolina, introduced resolutions in favor of the annexation of Texas, but they did not receive much attention at the time. The independence of the Texian republic had been recognized in the last year of Jackson's administration, (see p. 402,) and it was the earnest desire of the inhabitants of Texas, as well as of many in the United States, that it should be added to the Union. On the 9th of July, 1838, the twenty-fifth Congress closed its second session.†

An attempt at revolutionizing Can-

* For the particulars in relation to this war, we must refer the reader to Captain J. T. Sprague's "*Origin, Progress, and Conclusion of the Florida War.*" New York, 1848. Pp. 557.

† The United States exploring expedition to the South Seas, under Lieutenant Wilkes, with six vessels and a corps of scientific assistants, set sail in August, 1838.

ada was made in the latter part of 1837, and quite a number of the citizens of the United States sympathized with the movement, and were ready to give it assistance. Mackenzie in Upper, and Papineau in Lower Canada, were the active spirits in this revolt, and
1837. various bodies of Americans joined the rebels, so that it speedily became evident, that collision would ere long take place, in which our country's faith and honor were involved. A party of Americans, some seven hundred strong, under Van Rensselaer of Albany, took possession of Navy Island, in the Niagara River, about two miles above the falls. Colonel M'Nab, with a body of militia, was posted opposite this island, with instructions to watch the insurgents, and not to violate the American territory. Finding that most of the supplies for the island were conveyed by a small steamer, named the "Caroline," from a landing-place on the American side, called Fort Schlosser, M'Nab despatched some of his militia in boats, to take or destroy her. This they accomplished in the middle of the night of the 29th of December, after a short but desperate struggle, in which they killed or drove out of the vessel all the crew, and having set it on fire, let it drift down the rapids and over the Falls of Niagara. But the act, however to be regarded in itself, having been committed on American territory, caused no little excitement in the United States.

On the 5th of January, 1838, the president issued a proclamation against all persons engaged in such unlawful schemes as the invasion of Canada, and exhorted them to abandon their designs or expect to suffer the consequences. General Scott was sent to the frontier to assume command, and the insurgents, on the 14th of January, evacuated Navy Island, giving up the arms, cannon, stores, etc. Van Rensselaer was arrested, but released on bail. 1838.
Other attempts, however, of a similar character, were made at Detroit, Sandusky Bay, and the north-eastern end of Lake Ontario. Various acts of outrage were committed during the year. In November, an attempt was made to take Prescott, in Upper Canada, but failed, and about a hundred and fifty American citizens were captured and taken to Kingston, to be tried by court martial. The British authorities dealt more leniently with them than they deserved, the greater portion of them being pardoned, a very few suffering death.

The concluding session of the twenty-fifth Congress began on the 3d of December, 1838. Few acts, however, of general interest were passed. The Seminole war required new appropriations, and it was found that the expenses far exceeded any previous cal- 1838.
culation on the subject. An act was passed abolishing imprisonment for debt in certain cases; and a sharp discussion took place upon a series of resolutions, forbidding the introduction of the slavery question into Congress. The public lands question was again discussed, as also were propositions for abolishing the salt tax and the fishing bounties. Difficulties respecting the much vexed topic of the north-eastern boundary seeming to require it,

the president had additional powers given him for the defence of the United States. On the 3d of March, 1839, this Congress expired.

The president's course not having been such as to please many of those who were members of the democratic party, the elections began to show a falling off, as respected the administration, and an increased efficiency on the part of the opposition. Vigorous efforts were made on both sides to obtain the majority in Congress, and the result showed, that the democrats had a small majority of members elect, leaving out of view the five or six New Jersey members, whose seats were contested. This question could not but excite much interest in view of the final settlement of it. But there was another, growing out of the alarm and distress still existing in regard to the currency,* which was awaiting the meeting of Congress, from whom some relief was earnestly looked for.

1839.

The twenty-sixth Congress assembled on the 2d of December, 1839; when, in the House, a not very creditable dispute arose, and was protracted for three weeks, as to the right to seats of the New Jersey members. These five gentlemen were whigs, and had certificates of their election under the seal of the state; but it was contended, that they were not elected by majorities of the votes, and so were not duly entitled to seats. On the 16th of December, R. M. T. Hunter was elected speaker, and the House was organized on the 21st. The president's message was received on the 24th. The committee in charge of the New Jersey question made a report in July, 1840, which gave rise to an angry debate. The whigs refused to vote; but the question was decided by the rest of the House in favor of the democratic claimants, which gave the administration a majority, though too late in the session to be of any service.

Early in December, 1839, a whig convention was held at Harrisburg, in Pennsylvania, to select candidates for the coming presidential election. Three names were laid before the convention, Henry Clay, General Harrison, and General Winfield Scott. Daniel Webster had withdrawn from the contest. Appearances at first were all in favor of Mr. Clay, who received a majority of votes (both by heads and by states,) over each of the other candidates, but not a majority of the votes of the convention. But after conferences, public and private, and various ballotings, by a final ballot the post of honor was given to General Harrison, who received a hundred and forty-eight votes, while Clay had but ninety, and Scott sixteen. John Tyler, whom we have seen a candidate for the vice-pres-

1839.

* The New York banks resumed specie payments on the 16th of May, 1838. In March of this year, Mr. Biddle resigned the presidency of the United States Bank of Pennsylvania, which soon after fell into difficulties. On the 9th of October, it suspended specie payments, and its example was followed by the banks south and west of New York, and by those of Rhode Island. Mr. Gallatin, in reviewing the disasters of this time of embarrassment, justly says: "There was a universal disregard of all considerations of prudence on the part of the managers of banks, as regarded the safety and interests of the shareholders, and of the public as recipients and holders of their issues, and of the business community generally, as interested in having the circulating medium of the country maintained in that staple and sound condition so essential to their prosperity."

idency at the last preceding election, was unanimously adopted by the convention for the same honor again.

The democratic convention met at Baltimore, on the 5th of May, 1840, and re-nominated Martin Van Buren for president, leaving the question of the vice-presidency open. Colonel Johnson and Mr. Polk were generally named for support.

The financial aspect of the country occupied the principal part of the president's message. The reader will find it interesting as well as profitable to examine its statements, and weigh the views and opinions of the president. One passage we may quote as containing counsel valuable at all times to our citizens. "Let it be indelibly engraven on our minds," says Mr. Van Buren, "that relief is not to be found in expedients. Indebtedness can not be lessened by borrowing more money, or by changing the form of the debt. The balance of trade is not to be turned in our favor by creating new demands upon us abroad. Our currency can not be improved by the creation of new banks, or more issues from those which now exist. Although these devices sometimes appear to give temporary relief, they almost invariably aggravate the evil in the end. It is only by retrenchment and reform, by curtailing public and private expenditures, by paying our debts, and by reforming our banking system, that we are to expect effectual relief, security for the future, and an enduring prosperity."

The independent treasury system was long and ably discussed during the session, and the prominent speakers and debaters, on both sides, set forth the advantages and disadvantages of the plan with great fulness of detail. The bill passed both Houses by the beginning of July, 1840, and on the 4th of the month received the president's signature and became the law of the land. The chief provisions were, that, after the 30th of June, one-fourth of all payments to the United States were to be made in gold and silver only, and so on, annually from that day, one-fourth more, until after the 30th of June, 1843, the entire amount of the revenues of every description, including payments at the post-office, would be receivable in specie alone. And similarly with regard to payments made by the United States. Four persons were very soon after the passage of the bill appointed receivers-general of the public money, for four years.

1840.

A bankruptcy law was introduced by Mr. Webster, and carried through the Senate, but it was laid upon the table of the other House by a vote of a hundred and one to eighty-nine. The graduation of prices for public lands was again attempted in vain; an issue of $5,000,000 more of treasury notes was authorized; and on the 21st of July, Congress adjourned.*

* Some changes in the cabinet may here be noted. In 1838, James K. Paulding was made secretary of the navy in the place of Mr. Dickerson, who resigned in the same year; Felix Grundy received the attorney-generalship, which had been relinquished by Mr. Butler; and in the following year, on Mr. Grundy's resignation, Henry D. Gilpin was appointed. Amos Kendall, in 1840, gave up the post-office, and John M. Niles received it. Here, too, we may state in passing, that the public debt, which was extinct at Van Buren's accession, and in 1839 exceeded $11,000,000, was reduced to nearly $4,000,000 during the year 1840.

The sixth decennial census was taken during the year, and the result, on the 1st of June, 1840, was as follows:—White males, 7,249,266; white females, 6,939,842; free colored males, 192,550; free colored females, 199,821; slaves, males, 1,240,408; females, 1,240,805; making a grand total of the population of the United States, (including seamen in the national service), 17,069,453.

The presidential election, during the autumn of 1840, gave rise to unprecedented excitement, and more time and attention were bestowed upon politics, and the numerous questions at issue between the two parties, than probably had ever been the case at any previous time. There was hardly a definable limit to the conventions, the speeches, the political pamphlets, the newspaper engineering, on the thousand topics which were brought forward and debated at the time. The democratic party hoped to re-elect Mr. Van Buren; the

1840.

whigs were enthusiastic in their efforts to secure the election of their candidates. The result was, that General Harrison and John Tyler received, each, two hundred and thirty-four votes; Martin Van Buren received sixty-six votes, and Richard M. Johnson forty-eight. Consequently, Harrison and Tyler were elected president and vice-president of the United States.

Congress met on the 7th of December; but the session was not productive of any results of moment. Another issue of treasury notes was authorized; various appropriations were made; and many schemes, which had already been much talked of in Congress, were debated anew. The matter of most interest, especially for the promise it gave of what might be done under the next administration,

1841.

was a resolution proposed by Henry Clay, for the repeal of the sub-treasury law. The Senate, however, rejected the resolution. On the 3d of March, 1841, the session closed, and with it the administration of Martin Van Buren. He came into office by a very large vote; the people denied him a re-election by an equally large vote against him. It remains to be seen whether the hopes of those who effected this change in the administration were to be gratified or not

CHAPTER IV.

1841-1845.

HARRISON'S AND TYLER'S ADMINISTRATION.

General Harrison's inauguration — His cabinet — His death — John Tyler president — His address to the people — Extra session of the twenty-seventh Congress — Tyler's message — The secretary of the treasury recommends the establishment of a national bank — Action in Congress on the subject — The sub-treasury repealed — The fiscal bank established — The bill vetoed by Tyler — Further attempt — The president consulted and his approbation secured — Another veto — The cabinet send in their resignations, except Mr. Webster — Course of the whigs in Congress — Acts of the session — Congress meet in December — The longest session ever held — Large amount of legislation — Other banking schemes — The Washington treaty — Its provisions — Troubles in Rhode Island — The Oregon question brought forward — Further proceedings with respect to it — The elections — Congress in session, December, 1843 — Position of affairs — Mr. Tyler's measures with reference to the annexation of Texas — Action in Congress — The presidential candidates — Result of the contest — Polk and Dallas elected — Last session of Congress — Tyler's message — The joint resolutions for the annexation of Texas — Prospect of future trouble — Close of Tyler's administration.

DURING the month of February, General Harrison reached the city of Washington, and on the 4th of March was inaugurated as the ninth president of the United States. The ceremonies were imposing; unusual enthusiasm prevailed; and high hopes were entertained, that the new president would be able to discharge the duties of his office in such wise, as to meet the wishes and expectations of his countrymen. His Inaugural address was very long, but full of interest nevertheless; and, as became the position in which he was placed, he dwelt at length upon the topics which had been so fully discussed during the canvass, and respecting which he now renewed the pledges which were naturally looked for at his hands.

1841.

The cabinet chosen by General Harrison was an able one, and promised well for the administration of affairs. Daniel Webster was appointed secretary of state; Thomas Ewing, secretary of the treasury; John Bell, secretary of war; George E. Badger, secretary of the navy; Francis Granger, postmaster-general; and John J. Crittenden, attorney-general; the Senate having at once confirmed all the nominations. Other vacancies were filled up without delay. And a proclamation was issued on the 17th of March, summoning Congress together for an extra session, on the 31st of the following May.

And this was all that Harrison was permitted to do. Though advanced in years, his physical ability seemed to give promise of energy and power of endurance; but the harassing toils of the government soon proved too much for his strength. He was beset with office seekers; he was anxious to gratify the numerous friends and supporters who flocked about him; he gave himself incessantly to public business; and at the close of the month, he was lying on a sick bed. On Sunday, the 4th of April, pneumonia having set in, his brief career as president was brought to its close. His last words, spoken after he had ceased to be conscious of immediately surrounding things, as if addressing a successor or associate, were these: "Sir, I wish you to understand the principles of the government. I wish them carried out. I ask nothing more."

This being the first instance of a president dying while in office, it produced a feeling akin to dismay, and wide-spread concern was felt as to what would result from so severe a dispensation of God's providence. To the party who had elected Harrison, it was a terrible blow; for with him at the head of affairs, they were sure of being able to carry on the government to general satisfaction. But, as respected the man who, by constitutional provision, now was to occupy the executive chair, the whig party had grave and not unnatural doubts and perplexities. John Tyler had been placed on the ticket without much thought or care as to his political principles and consistency, or his executive ability, since, in the post of vice-president these were points of comparatively little moment. When, however, by Harrison's death, he was suddenly placed in the presidential chair, with the whole term of four years before him, the dominant party experienced all the pains of uncertainty, as to the course which Tyler would pursue on the many and great questions wherein he would be called upon to take part.

John Tyler arrived at Washington, on the 6th of April, and at once assembling the heads of departments, requested them all to continue in the exercise of the functions they had been charged with by his predecessor. He then, for the sake of preventing all occasion of future trouble, took and subscribed a new oath of office before the chief judge of the circuit court of the District of Columbia, and assumed the presidency. On the 7th, the funeral of General Harrison took place; and was attended by a prodigious concourse of people from every quarter of the Union, who forgot party distinctions, and heartily joined in doing honor to the lamented dead. The 14th of May was recommended by the new president as a day of fasting and prayer, and it was universally observed throughout the country, giving an opportunity for the expression of sorrow for the deceased Harrison, and of the profound sense of the instability of human greatness inspired by his death.

1841.

Two days after this affecting solemnity, Mr. Tyler issued an address to the people of the United States, in which he briefly set forth his views, and gave utterance to sentiments, which, though not very unambiguously expressed, still proved generally satisfactory. It was hoped, by the prominent members of the whig party, that he would co-operate with the majority of Congress, in carrying out the views and desires of those by whom he had been elected.

The twenty-seventh Congress met for an extra session on the 31st of May, and Mr. Tyler's message was sent in the following day. Of the foreign relations of the Union, a very satisfactory account was given. A treaty with Portugal had been duly ratified. The claims upon Spain seemed in a fair way of being settled. The M'Leod business was progressing to a conclusion.* Speaking of domestic affairs, Mr. Tyler said; "We hold out to the people of other countries an invitation to come and settle amongst us, as members of our rapidly growing family; and for the blessings which we offer them, we require them to look upon our country as their country, and to unite with us in the great task of preserving our institutions, and thereby perpetuating our liberties." The allusions to a national bank, and to the inexhaustible subject of internal improvements, contained in the message, were so ambiguous, that from them nothing of the president's real intentions could be divined. The whig party, however, believed him to be with them on those points; notwithstanding there were reasons to doubt, respecting Mr. Tyler's course on the questions at issue at the time.

1841.

The report of the secretary of the treasury, sent with the message, warmly recommended the establishment of a national bank, as likely to "produce the happiest results, and confer lasting and important benefits on the country." The president was understood to be friendly to the plan, and Mr. Ewing, on the invitation of both Houses, reported, about the middle of June, a draft of a bill for the establishment of "The Fiscal Bank of the United States." In its business details this scheme did not differ widely from the old plans; except in two features, which it was understood, were introduced by the president himself, and which were designed to obviate the constitutional objections. They were, the proposal to incorporate the bank in the District of Columbia, where Congress had the power of a state legislature; and to give the bank power to establish branches only in such states as should assent to it by their legislatures. There were, of course, inserted many provisions, by which it was hoped that the abuses and corruptions alleged or proved against the former banks would be prevented.

1841.

This draft was referred, in the Senate, to the select committee on the currency, of which Henry Clay was chairman; and at the end of a week a report was presented, concluding with a bill, agreeing with the secretary's in almost every part; differing from it chiefly on matters of detail, respecting the management of the bank, and its method of doing business; but differing also from it on the subject of the conditions of establishing branches in the several states.

Much debate was had on this point,

* In January, 1841, Alexander M'Leod, of Upper Canada, being in New York on business, was arrested by the authorities at Lockport, on the charge of having been a participator in the burning of the Caroline, (see p. 411.) Much excitement prevailed, and much trouble seemed likely to grow out of the matter. The grand jury found a bill against M'Leod for murder; and his trial took place in October. Fortunately for all concerned, an *alibi* was proved. M'Leod was allowed to return home, and this source of difficulty was removed.

and a compromise was at last effected, by which it was hoped the conflicting opinions might be harmonized, and the question be settled. The bill passed by twenty-six to twenty-three in the Senate, and by a hundred and twenty-eight to ninety-seven in the House; and on the 6th of August was sent for the president's approval. From the 6th to the 16th of August, Mr. Tyler retained the bill, and the excitement through the country was prodigious. The White House was thronged with visitors, of all shades of political opinion, all anxious to know whether the approval would be withheld, all ready to give advice upon the matter. On the 9th of August, the law by which the sub-treasury was established was repealed, by a vote of a hundred and thirty-four to eighty-seven; and the whigs warned and entreated the vacillating occupant of the presidential chair, not to disappoint the expections of the party and the country generally.

On the 16th of August, however, the bill was returned vetoed, for reasons set forth in his message. The whigs were furious; the opposition hoped to gain advantage from the result. The bank question was the main issue, and as it could not be carried without Mr. Tyler's aid, the whigs smothered their mortification, and set to work to arrange a bank on such a basis as the president would not veto it. Two prominent members of Congress, Messrs.

1841. Berrien and Sergeant, waited on Mr. Tyler, and ascertained his wishes, and a bill was prepared, on the 19th of August, which, to make all sure, was submitted to the president through the secretary of state, approved by him, and returned. On the 20th, Mr. Sergeant introduced it into the House, as an amendment to some bill then pending in a committee of the whole; and after due debate, it passed on the 23d, without the alteration of a word, by a vote of a hundred and twenty-five to ninety-four. In proof of the anxiety of Congress to meet the wishes of the president, it may be mentioned, that in this bill the institution was not entitled a bank at all; but "The Fiscal Corporation of the United States." The Senate passed it without amendment, on the 3d of September, by twenty-seven to twenty-two.

John Tyler, having kept the bill six days, though as above stated, he h already approved it, made certain stinging words of Mr. Botts, respecting the "heading of Captain Tyler," and his currying favor with the locofocos, an excuse for changing his mind; and, strange to say, on the 9th of September, he vetoed this bill also. The strength of the party was not sufficient to carry it by a two-third's vote, and so, of course, it was lost.

Two days afterwards the cabinet resigned, with the exception of Mr. Webster,* and on the 13th of September, when the session closed, the whig members of Congress issued an address to the people, giving an account of their action, in terms far from complimentary to Mr. Tyler. Perhaps, for the inter-

* In their places, Mr. Tyler chose Walter Forward, secretary of the treasury; John C. Spencer, secretary of war; Abel P. Upshur, secretary of the navy; C. A. Wickliffe, postmaster-general; and Hugh S. Legare, attorney-general.

ests of the party, it would have been better not to have gone to this length, at this time

Brief as this extra session was, it was one of the most important under the administration of John Tyler. Provision was made for the widow of General Harrison, as a durable testimony of regret at his sudden decease; a loan of $12,000,000 was authorized, for the purpose of covering the deficit under Van Buren's administration; a provisional tariff act laid as much as twenty per cent. on many articles admitted free by the compromise tariff; a uniform system of bankruptcy was established; and an act was passed granting rights of pre-emption as to the public lands, and providing for the distribution of the proceeds from land sales amongst the states, substantially in accordance with Mr. Clay's plan. Seventy-five acts were passed, the veto power was twice exercised.

The elections, during the summer and autumn, resulted on the whole, unfavorably to the whigs, and renewed the hopes of the democrats that Mr. Tyler might advance their views to a greater extent than those of the party which had elevated him to power.

1841.

The second session of the twenty-seventh Congress began on the 6th of December, and continued until the 31st of August, 1842, being the longest session of the national legislature that had ever yet occurred. A very large amount of public business was transacted, there having been passed no fewer than two hundred and ninety-nine acts. Besides these bills and the discussion arising out of them, Congress was occupied in this session by a thousand and ninety-eight reports, and above three hundred other bills, not passed. There were about a hundred private bills ready for final passage in the House, but retained till the next session, because the Senate was so much occupied by the treaty of Washington and other momentous matters. The president put his veto to four bills this session; which of course occasioned much debate and many protests.

Instead of a bank, Mr. Tyler suggested a "board of control," but Congress would not agree to any such plan. The tariff formed the leading topic of discussion, and after the president had vetoed two bills on this subject,* he approved a third, which omitted the provision in the former for distribution of the proceeds of the public lands among the states. This was on the 30th of August, 1842.

Another banking scheme originated with Mr. Tyler, and was called "the exchequer plan." It proposed to assist the operations of the government by establishing a board of exchequer in connection with the treasury department; and it was calculated that its bills would be so eagerly sought for by the public creditors, that the issue would in a short time reach the amount of $15,000,000, which was to be the *maximum;* and that $10,000,000 would thereby be added to the available means of the treasury

1842.

* John Quincy Adams, on this occasion, prepared a report, in which a sharp and deserved rebuke was administered to John Tyler for his having, during the last fifteen months, strangled legislation, "by the five times repeated stricture of the executive cord."

without cost or charge. Favorable reports were made upon this plan in both Houses, and in each a bill to establish such a board was introduced; but the plan was not adopted by Congress.

Before Congress adjourned, the Senate was called upon to ratify a very important treaty, usually known as the treaty of Washington. Daniel Webster was the negotiator on the part of the United States, and in behalf of Great Britain, Lord Ashburton arrived at Washington, as special minister, on the 4th of April, 1842. Besides the boundary question, which had been so long in dispute, there were other matters of no small moment to be discussed, and if possible settled now; one, the indemnification or "atonement" due on the ground of the violation of the United States' territory when the Caroline was destroyed, and for that vessel, if it were not proved that its owner had acted in conjunction with the insurgents on Navy Island; and another, the right of search claimed and enforced by the British cruisers, as to ships suspected of being slavers, which arose near the end of the preceding year.*

When Lord Ashburton undertook the duties of carrying on the negotiations, matters proceeded at a much more rapid rate, and in a far more satisfactory manner than before. The "Caroline" business was soon dispatched. The other points were, the north-eastern boundary, the right of search, mutual extradition of fugitives from justice, and the taking of measures for the more effectual suppression of the slave trade.

On the 9th of August, 1842, four months after the arrival of Lord Ashburton, the labors of the negotiators were brought to a successful conclusion, and the treaty of Washington signed. By this treaty the boundary between the State of Maine and the British provinces was at length definitely settled. On the whole, though more or less objection was made to the final arrangement, it was regarded as fair and just by sensible and reasonable men on both sides the Atlantic. The navigation of the River St. John was declared free; all grants of lands, on whichever side of the boundary line they might be, were to be held valid; and the United States agreed to satisfy the claims of the States of Maine and Massachusetts, out of its share of the "disputed territory" fund.

1842.

By the eighth article, it was stipulated, that Great Britain and America should each maintain on the coast of Africa, a sufficient squadron or naval force, carrying not less than eighty guns, for the purpose of enforcing separately and respectively the laws, rights, and obligations of the two countries for the suppression of the slave trade. Another article of the treaty provided for the reciprocal extradition of the fugitives from justice, an arrangement evidently of importance to the welfare of both countries. The Senate ratified this treaty by a majority of thirty-nine against nine, Senator Benton being one of the minority; and the bill for car-

* This subject had been largely discussed between Mr. Stevenson, the American minister, and Lords Palmerston and Aberdeen. Mr. Stevenson asserted as unquestionable, that the right of search would, in no case, be submitted to by the United States.

rying the treaty into effect passed, in the following session, with the equally emphatic assent of both Houses of Congress.

Rhode Island, having become restive under its ancient charter, granted by Charles II., passed an act, in January, 1841, calling a convention in the following November, in order to frame a state constitution. This had been attempted in 1824 and 1834, without success. The "suffrage party," composed of those who advocated the right of suffrage without regard to the legal right under the old charter (which required possession of a freehold estate, valued at $134), held a meeting at Providence, and framed what was called the "people's constitution," which was duly ratified in the manner provided by it. The other convention met at the time appointed; framed a constitution in February, 1842, which, on being submitted to the people, was rejected by a small majority. The suffrage party, in April, chose Thomas W. Dorr, governor, and elected a legislature. The "law and order party," as it was called, elected Samuel W. King, governor, and resisted the proceedings of Mr. Dorr and his supporters. Great excitement was the consequence, and a bloody struggle seemed to be at hand. Dorr escaped arrest and left the state; but, returning in May, 1843, he entrenched himself, with about seven hundred men, on a hill in Chepachet, with five pieces of artillery. A large force was called out; the insurgents deserted Dorr, who was taken and convicted of treason; a new constitution was duly adopted; and Dorr, who had been sent to state's prison, was released in 1845.

On the 5th of December, the last session of the twenty-seventh Congress commenced. In his message, after congratulations on the completion of the treaty of Washington, Mr. Tyler said: "It would have furnished additional cause for congratulation, if the treaty could have embraced all subjects calculated in future to lead to a misunderstanding between the two governments. The territory of the United States, commonly called the Oregon Territory, lying on the Pacific Ocean, north of the forty-second degree of latitude, to a portion of which Great Britain lays claim, begins to attract the attention of our fellow-citizens; and the tide of population, which has reclaimed what was so lately an unbroken wilderness in more contiguous regions, is preparing to flow over these vast districts, which stretch from the Rocky Mountains to the Pacific Ocean. In advance of the requirement of individual rights to these lands, sound policy dictates that every effort should be resorted to by the two governments, to settle their respective claims." This is the first public notice of the "Oregon question," although for twenty years past it had been more or less before the eyes and in the thoughts of statesmen, at home and abroad.

1842.

A continued deficit of $5,000,000 was announced, in speaking of the finances. The remedying of the defects of the tariff act was urged upon Congress, and it was suggested, that the warehousing system might be advantageously adopted. The exchequer plan was again commended to the notice of the legislature, and expounded at great length; and the embarrassed state of the public credit, which arose from the deficit, from "the utter and disastrous failure of the United States Bank of Pennsylvania," and from the "repudiation" of their debts by several states, was appealed to as a reason for immediate attention to the subject.

The proceedings of this session were not of much moment. Considerable excitement arose out of the question relative to Oregon, and it was attempted to be used largely for the purpose of making political capital. The president informed Congress, that he was about to enter into negotiations with Great Britain for the purpose of terminating the joint occupation, and fixing the boundary on mutually satisfactory terms; yet a bill was brought into the

1843. Senate, and carried by a majority of one, for taking possession of the whole of the disputed territory, the title of the United States to which it declared was certain, and would not be abandoned. The House, however, refused its concurrence. On the 3d of March, 1843, the session closed; having provided the means of future intercourse between the United States and the government of China,* and having also passed an act to test the practicability of establishing a system of electro-magnetic telegraphs.

In May, Mr. Webster, resigned his post, which led to other changes in the cabinet. The elections during the autumn proved generally adverse to the administration, and seemed to presage a return of the tide in favor of the democrats; and when the twenty-eighth Congress assembled, on the 4th of December, although the whigs were in a majority in the Senate, the opposition elected their candidate for speaker by a vote of a hundred and twenty-eight to fifty-nine.* Mr. Tyler, in his message, asserted the American claim, in respect to Oregon, to the paral- **1843.** lel of 54° 40′ north latitude, but stated that no effort would be spared to effect a mutually satisfactory settlement of the question with Great Britain. The position of matters in regard to Texas was discussed at length; the finances were spoken of quite fully; a disquisition on currency in its various ramifications was furnished; and a number of recommendations on subjects of moment were made.

There was not, however, much business of general interest transacted during the session. A number of private and local acts were passed; appropriations were made for carrying on the government, for internal improvements, and the like; laws regulating the management of the territories were enacted, etc.

John Tyler, anxious to distinguish

* Mr. Caleb Cushing was appointed, in May, 1843, commissioner, for the purpose of proceeding to China, and opening negotiations with its government. He did so, and succeeded in arranging and settling with the emperor of China, a very valuable treaty.

* The whig members protested against the right to seats of the members elected from New Hampshire, Georgia, Mississippi, and Missouri, on the ground that they had not been elected in conformity with the act of the last Congress. The majority would not allow the protest to be read, and the members claiming seats took them accordingly.

himself by something of moment to the country, had sought with eagerness to bring about the annexation of Texas; and a treaty to this effect was arranged, in April, 1844, between the secretary of state and the commissioners on the part of the republic of Texas. The Senate, however, rejected this treaty, on the 8th of June, by a vote of thirty-five to sixteen. Mr. Benton, immediately after the rejection of the treaty, introduced into the Senate a bill for the annexation of Texas, provided the consent of Mexico were first obtained; and the president sent a message to the House, announcing the refusal of the Senate to ratify his treaty, in a manner which indicated his desire that some measure would be devised there to accomplish his object. But the House did not gratify him in his wish; and Senator Benton took occasion to express a rather general feeling, when he denounced John Tyler's effort in this wise to grasp at a chance of re-election, as "a fraud," "a base, wicked, miserable presidential intrigue," "originating in the most vicious purpose," and "prosecuted for the most knavish conclusions;" whilst the appeal from the decision of the Senate, involved in Tyler's Message, he regarded as an insulting violation of the Constitution, which deserved impeachment.*

1844.

The national whig convention met at Baltimore on the 1st of May, and with great enthusiasm nominated Henry Clay and Theodore Frelinghuysen for president and vice-president. The democratic convention met at the same place, on the 27th of May, and after a number of ballotings between the names of Van Buren, Cass, Johnson, Calhoun, took a new man, James K. Polk, who received the nomination for the presidency. George M. Dallas was placed on the same ticket for vice-president. The annexation of Texas and the claim to the 54° 40′ parallel for the boundary of Oregon, were among the chief issues presented in connection with the approaching contest. Mr. Tyler was nominated by some friends for re-election; but soon after finding his prospects hopeless, he withdrew, and published an address, which concluded by saying: "I appeal from the vituperation of the present day to the pen of impartial history, in the full confidence that neither my motives nor my acts will bear the interpretation which has, for sinister purposes, been placed upon them."

The canvass was animated and exciting to a high degree, and the result was as follows; Mr. Polk and Mr. Dallas received one hundred and seventy electoral votes; Mr. Clay and Mr. Frelinghuysen, one hundred and five;*

* The rise and progress of that strange abomination, Mormonism, deserves fuller consideration than we can here give it. Joseph Smith, with his band of one thousand two hundred followers, in 1833, in Missouri; with his thousands in Illinois, in 1840; the murder of Smith and his brother in prison by a mob, in July, 1844; and the expulsion of the hated sect from Illinois, and their emigration beyond the Rocky Mountains; where now (1857) they present a front of armed rebellion and resistance suggestive of no light evils in the future; these are points which the reader may look into with advantage. It is a strange thing that a vile imposture like this should prevail in our day.

* The whigs charged, that their defeat was owing to the fact of a large and scandalous amount of illegal voting in various parts of the country by their opponents.

consequently the former were declared duly elected president and vice-president of the United States.

Congress met, for its closing session, on the 2d of December, 1844. The principal topic of the last message of Mr. Tyler was the annexation of Texas, respecting which he said: "a controlling majority of the people, and a large
1845. majority of the states, have declared in favor of immediate annexation. Instructions have thus come up to both branches of Congress, from their respective constituents, in terms the most emphatic. It is the will of both the people and the states, that Texas shall be annexed to the Union promptly and immediately." The financial statement showed a great improvement, it being estimated that a surplus of $7,000,000 would remain in the treasury at the close of the fiscal year. The message closed with some self-congratulatory words on account of his repeated use of the veto power, and the approbation which he believed the people to have manifested in his behalf.

On the 25th of January, 1845, the House of Representatives, by a vote of a hundred and twenty to ninety-eight, passed a series of resolutions, to the effect that Congress consented to the
1845. erection of the territory "included within and rightfully belonging to the Republic of Texas" into a new state; and to the construction of a republican form of government by a convention, according to the usual plan, as we have seen, for the purpose of being admitted into the Union. The usual cessions of public property to the general government were made; and it was provided, that other states might be formed out of the territory, as was customary with areas of considerable extent when first admitted into the Confederation. The Senate, some weeks later, adopted the joint resolutions, by a vote of twenty-seven to twenty-five; and on the 1st of March, they received the approval of the president.

Texas thus became an integral part of the United States, although necessarily the final arrangements, and the settlement of the difficulty growing out of the complaints and menaces of Mexico, were left for future consideration. All diplomatic attempts thus far to induce Mexico quietly to yield to the necessity of the case had failed, and there was room to expect hostilities on the south-western frontier. How the succeeding administration dealt with this whole matter, we shall see in our next chapter.

Other proceedings of the session we need not dwell upon. Various appropriations were made; an act was passed by which Florida was admitted into the Union; a bill (vetoed by Mr. Tyler) forbidding him to build revenue cutters at his discretion, was passed by more than a two-thirds vote, and thus became a law; and an appropriation bill for certain harbors and rivers, sent to the president just at the close of the session was retained by him, and thus disposed of by what was styled a "pocket-veto." On the 3d of March, the twenty-eighth Congress terminated, and Mr. Tyler also retired from the office, which he had attained by one of those contingencies on which all human affairs are more or less dependent. His administration must speak for itself; we have neither time nor space at command to enter into any review of it.

CHAPTER V.

1845-1847.

POLK'S ADMINISTRATION: TWO YEARS.

Inauguration of James K. Polk — His cabinet — John Tyler and Texas matters — Annexation completed — The Oregon question — The point in dispute — Excitement on the subject — The twenty-ninth Congress — Mr. Polk's message — Debate on the Oregon question — Negotiations with England — Settlement of the question — General Taylor on the Rio Grande — Commencement of hostilities — Declaration of war — New tariff bill, etc. — Sub-treasury again established — The "Wilmot proviso" — Other acts of the session — Summary of the acts of the second session of the twenty-ninth Congress — Affairs in Mexico — Plan of the campaign — Taylor at Point Isabel — Battle of Palo Alto — Battle of Resaca de la Palma — Mexicans driven across the Rio Grande — Taylor enters Matamoras — Santa Anna and his proceedings — Trials of Taylor's position — His advance on Monterey — Severe contests — Monterey taken — Armistice agreed upon — General Wool's march — Kearney and the "army of the west" — New Mexico taken possession of — Doniphan's advance to Chihuahua — Fremont and his exploits — California taken — Taylor blamed for suspending hostilities — Santa Anna and his army — New programme of attack on Mexico — Scott's measures — Taylor's army greatly weakened — Mexican force much more numerous — Taylor makes a stand at Buena Vista — The celebrated battle of Buena Vista — Taylor victorious — His return to the United States.

THE inauguration of James K. Polk, the eleventh president of the United States, took place on the 4th of March, 1845, and notwithstanding the day was lowering and rainy, a vast concourse assembled, and the ceremonies were striking and impressive. The Inaugural address was long and interesting, and gave expression to the sentiments and views which were expected from the victorious candidate of the democratic party. The annexation of Texas, and the Oregon question, both of them of deep interest to the welfare of the Union, and our relations with Mexico and Great Britain, were spoken of quite fully, and in terms which commended the president's plans and purposes to the majority of the nation.

1845.

Mr. Polk immediately made choice of his cabinet officers, who were confirmed at once by the Senate. James Buchanan was made secretary of state; Robert J. Walker, secretary of the treasury; William L. Marcy, secretary of war; George Bancroft, secretary of the navy; Cave Johnson, postmaster-general; and John Y. Mason, attorney-general.

Mr. Tyler's anxiety to connect his name with the annexation of Texas, we have mentioned already (p. 423). The matter was hurried forward in the very last days of his administration, and Congress left it to his option whether the annexation should be accomplished by treaty, in the regular manner (which would have given the glory of it to Mr. Polk and the democrats), or should be effected immediately, according to the tenor of the resolutions passed at the close of February (p. 424). John Tyler availed himself at once of the opportunity presented, and on the 3d of March, dispatched a messenger to deliver to Mr. Donelson, chargé d'affaires to Texas, the joint resolutions of Congress for the admission of Texas into the Union, instructing him to communicate to the Texian government, that he, the president, had made choice of the alternative of immediate annexation, instead of negotiating by treaty. As might be expected, Mr. Tyler received any thing but praise from the democratic party, for the course he had pursued.

On the part of Texas, a convention was immediately summoned, and on the 4th of July, 1845, it assented to the joint resolutions, and the country was thus fully incorporated into the Union. The president was requested and authorized to lose no time in establishing a line of frontier posts, and occupying any exposed position along the western border of the new state; and an "army of occupation," under the command of General Zachary Taylor, was despatched for its defence. On the 26th of July, a body of United States troops was landed at Aransas Bay, and on the same day the American flag was first hoisted, by authority, at the south end of St. Joseph's Island, in token that the land was now a part of the great republic of the north.

1845.

General Almonte, the Mexican minister at Washington, had demanded his passports on the 6th of March; and at the beginning of the following month, the Mexican government refused to hold any further communication with the United States minister, on the ground that the annexation of Texas was an act of war against Mexico; and it was distinctly announced, that the rights of Mexico would be maintained by force of arms. Matters remained in this unsettled state until the commencement of hostilities in 1846.

Oregon was the next subject of importance before the administration. It will be remembered, that, in 1818, a convention was arranged between the governments of the United States and Great Britain, for the joint occupation of this region, during the next ten years; and that by a second convention, in 1827, this arrangement was indefinitely prolonged, with the provision, that after the 20th of October, 1828, either of the contracting parties might set aside the arrangement, by giving twelve months' notice to the other.

Mr. Polk had been elected with the understanding that he would insist upon the 54° 40′ parallel as the boundary of Oregon, (p. 423,) and that the United States were to have "the whole or none" of that vast region. Nevertheless, he felt it his duty to renew the propositions of compromise, which had previously been made, by which the forty-ninth parallel was to be the northern boundary of the United States territory. Mr. Buchanan, in July, made a proposition to this effect to Mr. Pakenham the British minister; but it was received in so unsatisfactory a manner, that, in his next communication, after giving a very full and complete *resumé* of the question as viewed by his government, Mr. Buchanan withdrew his proposal; preserving, however, the conciliatory tone of his first statement, and expressing the hopes of the president that the controversy might be soon and safely adjusted.

Our readers, most of them certainly, will remember the intense excitement which sprang up in connection with this subject; and had there not been a strong conservative feeling in the bosoms of a large portion of our countrymen, we might have been engaged again in a bloody strife with England, to the infinite harm of both countries, and to the disgrace of the two foremost civilized Christian nations of the world. Happily, such men as Daniel Webster, were willing to exert their influence to bring about a settlement on terms fair and honorable to both parties, and to repress that spirit, more or less rampant, which would lead us to battle in a cause unworthy of our countrymen.

On the 1st of December, 1845, the twenty-ninth Congress began its first session. Mr. John M. Davis was elected speaker, and the president's message was received the next day. It was very long, and contained a great variety of recommendations on topics of interest and importance, among which Oregon, and the state of our relations with Mexico, occupied a prominent place. Mr. Polk recommended a revision of the tariff laws, for the purpose of reducing the rates of duty, and abolishing the protective system; and the establishment of a constitutional treasury for the custody of the public money,—the employment of state banks as depositories being in effect the conversion of that money into banking capital, and the loaning of it to the banks without interest, to be loaned by them at interest to their borrowers. The employment of steam in the navy was also suggested; and a glowing panegyric was pronounced upon Andrew Jackson, who died on the 8th of June, 1845.

1845.

The question relative to Oregon was discussed in the Senate early in the session, and General Cass made a speech looking plainly to the chances of war with England. In the House, Stephen A. Douglas, and others, advocated similar views and claims in respect to Oregon; and at the same time, a joint resolution of the two Houses, giving the requisite notice to Great Britain for terminating the joint occupation of the territory, as the president had recommended, was pressed forward.

The excitement of the debate, and the vast variety of considerations urged, some pertinent but more wholly irrelevant, we need not attempt to describe. Fierce appeals were made to popular passions, and to judge from what was said on the floor of Congress, there would seem to have been great wrongs and outrage committed by England, which could be atoned for only by blood and by extrusion from the continent of America. Meanwhile negotiations had been recommenced between the secretary of state and the British minister, and were urged forward as rapidly as was consistent with the nature of the subject.

On the 23d of April, 1846, the joint resolution authorizing the president, if he considered it discreet to do so, to give notice to Great Britain for terminating the joint occupation of Oregon, finally passed both Houses by large majorities. But, happily, the question was settled without giving rise to any collision between the two countries. Correspondence was actively carried on through the British minister at Washington, and Mr. M'Lane, the American minister at London; and at length, on the 10th of June, the Senate was called upon to discuss a proposal, in the form of a convention, presented to the secretary of state by Her Majesty's minister, for the adjustment of the Oregon question; on the 12th, the Senate, by a vote of thirty-eight to twelve, advised the acceptance of the proposal; three days later, the convention, duly concluded and signed, was transmitted to the Senate for ratification; and on the 18th of June, the ratification was carried by a vote of forty-one to fourteen.

1846.

By this convention, the forty-ninth parallel of north latitude was adopted as the boundary between the territory of the United States and the British possessions, but Vancouver's Island was given up to Great Britain; the navigation of Fuca's Straits, and of the Columbia River, was declared free to both American and British navigators, and rights of actual possessors of land on both sides of the boundary line were to be respected by both parties. Thus, we may hope, as Mr. M'Lane said to the New York Chamber of Commerce, in September, after his return from England "that the settlement of the Oregon question will soon come to be universally regarded as the knell of those inveterate jealousies and feuds which, it may be apprehended, have so long excited a mischievous influence over the people, if not upon the councils, of both countries."

General Taylor, who commanded the "army of occupation" in Texas, was ordered, early in the year 1846, to march to the Rio Grande, which was claimed as the western boundary of the new state. He set out for this purpose in March, reached Point Isabel on the 25th, and on the 28th encamped on the Rio Grande opposite Matamoras. The Mexicans looked upon this advance of Taylor as an invasion of their territory, and from the indications of their feelings towards the Americans, it became apparent, that a collision must speedily follow. Taylor was waiting, in obedience to orders, for the Mexicans to strike the first blow, which they did towards the latter part of April, by attacking and capturing Captain Thornton with a squadron of dragoons. Intelligence of this rencontre reached Washington on the 9th of May. The subject was immediately taken up, and a bill was passed, by large majorities, declaring, that, "by the act of the republic of Mexico, a state of war exists between that government and the United States,"* and placing the military and naval forces of the

1846.

* As Senator Benton justly states, the truth of history demands, that this assertion be pronounced *untrue*. The annexation of Texas was the *real* cause of the war. See his "*Thirty Years' View*," vol. ii., p. 678.

Z. Taylor

country at the president's disposal to enable him to prosecute the war to a speedy conclusion. On the 13th of May, Mr. Polk gave his approval to the war bill, which provided for the services of fifty thousand volunteers, and appropriated $10,000,000 for the carrying on the war, and which was supported and strengthened by other bills on the same subject, all passed before the end of June.

A new tariff bill, by which *ad valorem* duties were imposed instead of specific imposts, gave rise to much discussion. It was eventually carried by a vote of a hundred and fifteen to ninety-three, in the House, but by a majority of only one in the Senate, (and on one question by the casting vote of the vice-president,) where Mr. Webster vigorously opposed it, for bringing into dangerous competition with domestic produce, in the home market, the manufactures of Europe. Another bill, supplemental in its nature to this, for the warehousing of imports, in public stores, and for limited periods, without payment of duties, until they were required for home consumption or re-exportation, was also passed. Both these acts produced great dissatisfaction in the manufacturing states, particularly in Pennsylvania, where the iron trade was largely affected by them.

1846.

In accordance with the president's recommendation, Congress took up for consideration, and finally established anew, the sub-treasury arrangement. In its main features it resembled the plan adopted during Mr. Van Buren's presidency; but many of the objections to that scheme were obviated in this, and despite the opposition of such men as Daniel Webster, the sub-treasury system has continued in use to the present day.

Near the close of the session, the "Wilmot proviso" was originated. A bill was before the House, authorizing the president to use the sum of $3,000,000, if he deemed it expedient, in negotiating a treaty of peace with Mexico, when David Wilmot, a Representative from Pennsylvania, moved to add this *proviso;* "That there shall be neither slavery nor involuntary servitude in any territory of the continent of America which shall hereafter be acquired by, or annexed to, the United States, by virtue of this appropriation, or in any other manner whatsoever, except for crimes whereof the party shall have been duly convicted; *Provided always*, that any person escaping to such territory, from whom labor or service is lawfully claimed, in any one of the United States, such fugitive may be lawfully reclaimed, and conveyed out of said territory to the person claiming his or her labor or service."

There was not much discussion on this proviso, although deep feeling was aroused; the northern members generally voted in its favor, while those from the south opposed it. On the last day of the session, the bill, as amended, was sent to the Senate; but it was too late to secure its passage there, and so it was lost.

Preliminary acts were passed for admitting Iowa and Wisconsin into the Union; and by special enactments Senators and Representatives from Texas took their seats in Congress. Two bills were vetoed by the president, the river and harbor bill, and the bill for indemnifying the sufferers from French spoliations on American commerce. On the 10th of August, after an unusually long session, Congress adjourned.

1846.

The twenty-ninth Congress assembled for its second session on the 7th of December, 1846. The president's message was principally occupied with the subject of the Mexican war, upon which, from the nature of the case and the progress of our arms, a great deal was to be said.* Mr. Polk announced, that the receipts of the last fiscal year were nearly $29,500,000, while the expenditure exceeded, by a little, $28,000,000. The balance in the treasury was above $9,000,000; the public debt was considerably more than $24,000,000, of which nearly $6,500,000 had been incurred by the present administration; and notice was given that a further loan of $23,000,000 would be required for the prosecution of the war in Mexico.

Most of the measures of this session—the short one before a new election—related to the war; and of these, one alone, ("the three million bill," as it was called,) needs here to be spoken of, because there was appended to it the "Wilmot proviso." The House passed this "proviso" again, but the Senate rejected it; and the Representatives, finding the other branch of the legislature resolutely determined not to allow it, assented to the passage of the bill, without this amendment. A bill making appropriations for the improvement of harbors and rivers again passed both Houses, but did not receive the approval of the president. The session closed on the 3d of March, 1847.

Affairs in Mexico, meanwhile, were becoming more and more serious, and necessarily attracted the attention of the people. The government of Herrera had been overthrown; Paredes had assumed the reins of government; Mr. Slidell, the American commissioner and envoy, had been refused a reception in his diplomatic character; and, as we have stated on a previous page, (p. 428), collision had actually occurred between the Mexicans and a portion of General Taylor's troops. Paredes, at the close of March, having announced that "peace not being compatible with the maintenance of the rights and independence of the nation, he should defend its territory, while the national congress would undertake to declare war against the United States," he gave orders, in April, to that effect; and on the 6th of July, the Mexican congress passed a decree "authorizing the government to use the natural defences of the country to repel aggression committed against many of the departments, and to make known to friendly nations the justifiable causes which obliged the nation to defend its rights by repelling force by force."

1846.

Congress having given its approval to the war, the president and his cabinet proceeded to sketch a plan of operations against Mexico, which helped to

* The scheme of appointing a lieutenant-general, (who was to be Colonel Thomas H. Benton himself,) and various matters connected with it, occupied a good deal of attention this session. See Benton's "*Thirty Years' View*," vol. ii. pp. 678–9.

shadow forth the uses to which it was intended to apply the anticipated results of the contest. By this plan, an "army of the west" was to be raised, and to march, under General Kearney, from its rendezvous at Fort Leavenworth, on the Missouri, against New Mexico, and thence westward to cooperate with the fleet, which was to be reinforced, against California; and an "army of the centre," under General Wool, was to invade Coahuila and Chihuahua; but these were to be subordinate to the main design, (as formed by General Scott,) which was, to penetrate into the interior by the line taken by Taylor, and perhaps from the coast, and to strike hard blows, and to repeat them until Mexico should understand, that her true interest consisted in making peace on such terms as should be agreeable to the United States.

Point Isabel being in danger from the Mexicans, General Taylor left Major Brown in the entrenched camp opposite Matamoras, and marched to the relief of the garrison at the Point. The Mexican commanders, looking upon this retrograde movement as a retreat, crossed the Rio Grande in force, and occupied the road along which Taylor had marched. From the batteries on the right of the river they also commenced a vigorous, but not very hurtful, bombardment of Fort Brown; and at Matamoras they published bombastic bulletins setting forth their prowess in arms, and their determination speedily to crush the northern invaders.

Taylor, having put his dépôt at Point Isabel in a condition to resist any attack that might be made upon it, resolved to force his way through the enemy, and to relieve those whom he left on the Rio Grande. Late on the evening of the 7th of May, he left Point Isabel, with his reinforcements, yet having less than three thousand men of all kinds with him, and being encumbered with a train of three hundred wagons, containing provisions and munitions of war, and of course, in the presence of a stronger force of the enemy, requiring a considerable escort.

At a spot called Palo Alto, General Arista, with double the number of Taylor's army, and twelve pieces of artillery, had posted himself quite across the road, having both flanks covered by thickets of chaparral, and a reserve in his rear. At two in the afternoon, the advancing army came in sight, and the Mexican batteries opened upon them when within seven hundred yards' distance. Taylor's artillery replied with terrible effect upon the enemy's troops. The Mexicans attempted a charge with their calvary, but were thrown into confusion before they got near our men, and retreated; another attempt failed in the same manner. They were equally unsuccessful in endeavoring to turn Taylor's right flank; and an advance of their own right was met by two eighteen-pounders, which were placed so as to enfilade their line, and caused great slaughter. After some two hours' fighting, the prairie having taken fire, the battle was intermitted, and when night fell, both sides withdrew, but neither far from the field. The loss on the side of our countrymen was nine killed and forty-four wounded, and two missing. The gallant Major

1846.

Ringgold was mortally wounded, and died a few days subsequently. The official return of the total Mexican loss was two hundred and fifty-two; but, as Arista abandoned the field of battle, and with it his dead and wounded, there is good reason for believing that it was nearly double that amount.

The Mexican general, virtually defeated, fell back on the road to Matamoras, and the next morning took up a strong position on a ravine called the Resaca de la Palma, where he was reinforced by some two thousand men. As soon as this had been ascertained, General Taylor put his army in motion; in the course of the afternoon of the 9th of May, his skirmishers, advancing through the thick chaparral, came upon the enemy's forces. One battery was brought up to oppose them, and very speedily a charge of cavalry, under Captain May, swept the Mexicans from their guns and broke their line on the other side of the ravine, in spite of one or more gallant attempts to retrieve the fortune of the day; while the infantry, now fighting as skirmishers, and now forming and resorting to the bayonet, drove the enemy before them in total rout. From all parts of the field the discomfited Mexicans rushed to the river, where numbers were drowned in the vain attempt to cross. Their camp fell into the hands of the victors, with all Arista's private papers, and a large supply of arms and ammunition.

Thus, with a force of little more than two thousand men, General Taylor had completely defeated the enemy, although their force was three times as large as his own. Thirty-three were killed and eighty-nine wounded, in this battle; while the Mexican loss in killed and wounded was not short of a thousand men. Very probably, had General Taylor pushed forward, he might have taken Matamoras at once; but he was contented with what was accomplished in having driven the Mexicans over the Rio Grande, and relieved Fort Brown. This fortification had suffered but little from the bombardment spoken of above (p. 431), which was kept up from the 3d till the 9th of May, nor were the losses of the garrison severe, as to number, there being but one killed and nine wounded, of whom one, and he the gallant Major Brown, who commanded the defence, and after whom the fort was named, died subsequently.

The 10th of May was spent by our countrymen in burying the dead, and by the Mexicans in rallying a fraction of their force in Matamoras. **1846.** An exchange of prisoners was also effected. General Taylor next made preparations for passing the river; and took possession of a village on the right bank, some miles lower down. By the 17th every thing was in readiness; and Arista then proposed an armistice for diplomatic action about the boundary question, which Taylor summarily declined, and next day crossed, without encountering any resistance, and entered Matamoras; the Mexicans having finally evacuated the place early in the morning, carrying off eleven guns, the rest being spiked or thrown into the river. Their sufferings on this retreat were very severe, although they were not pursued for more than sixty miles, and were left unmolested after the 19th of May; on the 28th, they halted at Linares, where General Arista was displaced, and the command given to Mejia.

The government at Washington was aware of the fact, that Santa Anna was living as a refugee at Havana, and presuming that, if he were in Mexico again, he would favor the ultimate designs of Mr. Polk and his cabinet, or at least, would prove a serious obstacle in the way of Paredes and his administration, the secretary of the navy, Mr. Bancroft, was directed to give orders for his admission into Mexico so soon as Santa Anna pleased. Accordingly, a brief note was addressed to Commodore Conner, commanding the blockading squadron at Vera Cruz, in which note Mr. Bancroft said, "if Santa Anna endeavors to enter the Mexican ports, you will allow him to pass freely." The Mexican general availed himself right gladly of this opportunity. A *pronunciamento* of his party was fulminated against Paredes at the end of July, and on the 5th of August he was a prisoner. On the 16th, Santa Anna entered Vera Cruz, and regardless of promises on his part, or expectations on the part of the American government, he determined to seek his own aggrandizement, and to put himself at the head of the army, confident that he could drive out the insolent invaders. New offers

1846.

had been made to the provisional government of Mexico to terminate hostilities and enter into negotiations; but, after sufficient delay to put Santa Anna at the head of affairs, the proposal was waived by a reference of the whole matter to the Congress of Mexico, accompanied by such a discussion of the grounds for resorting to hostilities, as showed a complete unwillingness to assent to the terms proposed by the president and the ruling party in the United States.*

It was not till after the middle of July, that any further advance into the territory of Mexico was attempted by the American army of occupation; but General Taylor was not idle. In fact, his task during that period, was more harassing than the conduct of military operations would have proved. So enthusiastically did the country respond to Taylor's requisitions and the call of the government, especially after the tidings of the battles of Palo Alto and Resaca de la Palma, that many more volunteers flocked to his head-quarters in Matamoras than he could easily dispose of. Without equipment, without training, without discipline, it was no light task to receive and organize these recruits. "The quarter-master's department, too, was one of incessant toil and anxiety; because, called unexpectedly and for the first time into active service in the field, it was comparatively unprepared to answer the multitude of requisitions that were daily made upon it by the government, the general officers,

* Mr. Benton remarks with great severity upon the intrigues which brought about the return of such a man as Santa Anna to Mexico. "What must history say of the policy and morality of such doings? The butcher of the American prisoners at Goliad, San Patricio, the Old Mission, and the Alamo; the destroyer of republican government at home; the military dictator aspiring to permanent supreme power; this man to be restored to power by the United States, for the purpose of fulfilling speculating and indemnity calculations on which a war was begun."—"*Thirty Years' View*," vol. ii., p. 682.

and the recruits. The whole material of a campaign was to be rapidly created. Money was to be raised; steamers bought; ships chartered; wagons built and transported; levies brought to the field of action; munitions of war and provisions distributed over the whole vast territory which it was designed to occupy."

On the 19th of July, orders were given to advance. Reynosa, Camargo, Mier, and other important posts along the Rio Grande, and on the road to Monterey, were occupied. On the 8th of August, head-quarters were removed to Camargo, which was made the dépôt, on account of its convenience for the reception of supplies and reinforcements by means of the river; land transport being almost impossible. Eleven days later, the march from Camargo
1846. commenced, and was continued without intermission, till, on September the 13th, at Papagayas, the first appearances of the enemy were discovered. Their outposts retired upon Monterey as the Americans advanced, and Taylor's whole army was concentrated on the Rio San Juan, about twenty-five miles from Monterey, on the 15th; and three days afterwards approached the city.

Seated beneath the elevated ridge of the Sierra Madre, on the San Juan de Monterey, which is but a small stream, and surrounded by a fertile and tolerably well cultivated valley, Monterey (which contained about ten thousand inhabitants) was a place of promise, as an *entrepôt*, or emporium, for the commercial intercourse between the coast and the interior. General Ampudia, whom Santa Anna had invested with the command, was here, with a force of more than ten thousand men, seven thousand of whom belonged to the regular army; and his stores of all kinds were ample. General Taylor, having reconnoitred the country round, as well as the city and the works of the enemy, determined to make a circular march with a part of his force, and cut off the communications of the place with Saltillo and the interior, by a road through a vast chasm in the mountains. This movement was intrusted to General Worth, who, on the 20th, took up a position quite at the foot of the mountains, opposite to a fortified hill called Loma d'Independencia, on the north of the river, and another like it, on the south, called Loma de Federacion. Meanwhile, as a diversion, an attack was made at the eastern end of the town, which, being converted into a real assault, ended in the capture of Fort Teneria, and an ineffectual bombardment of the citadel was attempted. Next morning, the attack commenced in earnest, and was continued during the 21st, 22d, and 23d of September; on the 24th the garrison capitulated.

The battle of the 21st began with a cavalry affair, at the western extremity of the town, near the Saltillo road; being successful in that encounter, and having accomplished his design of cutting off the communications of Monterey with the interior, Worth 1846.
next determined to carry the fortress on the Loma de Federacion, south of the San Juan, which commanded the lower road to Saltillo; and after a severe contest, succeeded in his pur-

pose. During that night, an attack was commenced upon the Loma d'Independencia, which terminated on the evening of the 22d, with the capture of the "key of Monterey." Ampudia attempted the recovery of the hill on the next night, but, having been received very warmly, he gave up his design. On the following day, the 23d, the assailants advanced from both extremities of the town, but "instead of risking life in the street, which was raked from end to end by artillery, or rendered untenable by the hidden marksmen, who shot our men from behind the walls of the house-tops, our forces were thrown into the dwellings, and breaking through walls and enclosures, gradually mined their way towards the plaza, or great square of Monterey."

The Mexicans, sensible that their town was doomed, and fearing the consequences if taken by assault, proposed a capitulation, early on the morning of the 24th of September. After some discussion and dispute as to the terms, Ampudia was allowed to evacuate the town, his troops retaining their small arms, and carrying with them one field battery of six guns, with twenty-one rounds of ammunition, and all the cavalry horses. The victors were to have all the other material of war in the town, and all the public property. Taylor's consent to a suspension of arms and to this capitulation was the more readily given, because Ampudia announced, that he had been officially informed that Santa Anna (whose return and resumption of the conduct of affairs Taylor now first heard of) had agreed to receive commissioners from the United States, and had appointed commissioners on the part of Mexico, to negotiate a peace. Next morning, the evacuation commenced, and, on the 28th of September, the whole town and citadel, together with forty pieces of cannon and a vast quantity of military stores, was given up to our countrymen. General Taylor's loss was one hundred and twenty-eight killed, and three hundred and sixty-eight wounded. The Mexican loss was estimated to be between five hundred and a thousand.

At this point it will be convenient to turn to other portions of the seat of war, which in the present case extended across the continent. Immediately on receiving the news of the commencement of hostilities on the Rio Grande, General Wool was ordered to muster and prepare the volunteers to be raised in accordance with the act of Congress declaring war. At the end of May he set out, and passing by Ohio, Indiana, Illinois, Kentucky, and Tennessee to Mississippi, met the newly-enlisted volunteers at various stations along that route, inspected them, and admitted twelve thousand of them; who, about the middle of July, were directed to join the army. About nine thousand of these were ordered to the Rio Grande, as reinforcements to Taylor's army; the rest rendezvoused at Bexar, in Texas, in readiness to march, under Wool himself, as the "army of the centre," against Chihuahua.

1846.

Setting out from Bexar on the 20th of September, Wool crossed the Rio Grande at Presidis, on the 11th of October, and after a march of twenty days, through mountain passes and deserts, along which in many instances roads had to be formed before his train, (which was immense in proportion to his numbers) could pass, and where the sufferings of the men were often very great, he arrived at Monclova. There he learned from General Taylor that Monterey had been captured, and that he had agreed to an armistice with Ampudia; and was also informed, that the route, by which it was originally intended that he should reach Chihuahua, was impracticable for his train; whilst it was manifest that the conquest of New Leon and Coahuila, effected by Taylor, made the expedition against Chihuahua unnecessary. The forces under General Wool were accordingly posted at Parras, so as to be in communication with the army of occupation.

The command of the "army of the west," which was raised principally in Mississippi, was given to Colonel Kearney, who, about the end of July, with less than two thousand men, was at Bent's Fort, on the Arkansas, ready to march for New Mexico. Taking in convoy the annual "caravan" of Santa Fé traders, he then set forth across the prairie; and, after toils and sufferings on the part of his men quite as great as those endured by the other armies, on August the 18th he entered Santa Fé. The governor, Don Manuel Armijo, had intended to oppose him, but thought better of the matter and abandoned the place. Four days afterwards, Kearney issued a proclamation, in which he announced, that the country now having become a part of the United States, the inhabitants were to consider themselves bound to obey the laws, and submit to the regulations of the new government. The whole of New Mexico having submitted without a stroke, Kearney established a territorial government, and appointing a governor and other officers, set out, on the 25th of September, with less than a thousand men, for California. Having advanced nearly two hundred miles, he was met by an express from Captain Fremont, in California, which led to Kearney's sending back most of his troops to Santa Fé.

Colonel Doniphan, early in December, left Santa Fé with eight hundred men, in three divisions, for the purpose of reinforcing General Wool, who, as was supposed, was advancing upon Chihuahua. Being through unknown regions and attended with peculiar trials, this march of Doniphan's force was hazardous in the extreme. **1846.** His men suffered intensely, but their courage and perseverance did not fail. At Brazitos, on the 21st of December, Doniphan encountered a large body of Mexicans, and defeated them without difficulty. On the 27th, he entered El Paso del Norte, where he was compelled to wait for a month in inactivity, and anxiously looking for news from General Wool. Late in February, 1847, Doniphan left El Paso, and on the 28th, discovered the enemy near the Rancho Sacramento, on the river of the same name. The superior skill and the impetuous bravery of the American troops led to a speedy victory. The enemy left on the field three hundred dead and as many wounded, all their guns, and stores, and forty prisoners; while

J. C. Frémont.

THE EXPLORER OF THE ROCKY MOUNTAINS.

Doniphan lost but one man killed and eight wounded, one of whom afterward died. Chihuahua fell into Doniphan's hands on the 1st of March; and there he rested his toilworn band for six weeks; then, continuing his march, he reached General Taylor's encampment, near Monterey, late in the month of May, 1847.*

Captain Fremont, of the topographical corps, set out in the spring of 1845, with an armed party, for the purpose of crossing the mountains and penetrating to the interior of California. His object was stated to be of a purely scientific character. On the 29th of January, 1846, he arrived in the neighborhood of Monterey, California. Here he sought and obtained permission of De Castro, the Mexican governor, to enter the valley of the San Joaquin, in order to obtain forage for

1846.

his horses, and provisions for the men. Whilst availing himself of this permission, in March, 1846, he was informed by some American settlers, that De Castro was preparing to attack him and his men upon the pretext, that, under the cover of a scientific mission, he was exciting the American settlers to revolt. Fremont then, in self-defence, took a position on a mountain overlooking Monterey, at a distance of about thirty miles, entrenched it, raised the flag of the United States, and with his own men, sixty-two in number, awaited the approach of the Mexican general. Having remained in this position from the 7th to the 10th of March, without molestation from De Castro, Fremont continued his march for Oregon. After entering Oregon, and being attacked by hostile Indians, who, it was alleged, were urged to this by De Castro, and having been informed that the Mexican general intended to crush him and his force, Fremont turned back, and resolved to overthrow the Mexican authority in California and establish an independent government there. Hurrying to the Sacramento, while Lieutenant Gillespie of the marines, (who had joined Fremont early in May), went down the river to secure the co-operation of the fleet, Fremont commenced operations; he captured two hundred horses one day; another day took Sonoma, with all its armament; and another attacked and defeated a squadron of seventy dragoons; he rallied round him, now forty settlers, now ninety, and soon had above two hundred at his command; and finally, on the 5th of July, at Sonoma, he and the American settlers proclaimed the Republic of California, with himself at the head of its affairs.

Commodore Sloat, in command of the squadron of observation, had been ordered at the breaking out of the war, "to take and hold San Francisco;" but before that order reached him, on the 7th of June, he heard of the battles of Palo Alto and Resaca de la Palma, and the next day sailed for Monterey. With proclamations in Spanish and English, on July the 7th, just two days after Fremont's proclamation, Monterey was in his hands; and on the 9th, San Francisco fell, and Sloat announced, "henceforward California will be a por-

* See Mr. Benton's address to the corps under Doniphan, on their return; "*Thirty Years' View*," vol. ii., pp. 684–88.

tion of the United States." Commodore Stockton succeeded Sloat in his command, and Fremont having formed a junction with him, entered Ciudad de los Angelos, on the 12th of August, the Mexicans having fled. Stockton took possession of the country, and appointed Fremont governor. Thus the conquest of California, like that of New Mexico, was effected without the loss of a single life in battle.*

1846.

Turn we now to General Taylor, and the progress of affairs in which he was concerned. On a previous page (p. 435,) we have stated, that a suspension of hostilities had been agreed upon by the commanding general, under the conviction, that Mexico had already been brought to that position, that she would be glad to make peace on terms agreeable to the United States, and that the home government would sanction this proceeding on his part. But "the authorities at home," as Mr. Mayer states, "eager for fresh victories, or pandering to public and political taste, did not approve and confirm an act, for which General Taylor has, nevertheless, received, as he truly merits, the just applause of impartial history." The armistice at Monterey accordingly ceased, and Taylor having been informed, on the 25th of November, that Tampico was occupied by the naval forces of the United States, left Worth and Butler at Monterey and at Saltillo, (which had fallen soon after the capture of Monterey,) and about the middle of December, set out for Victoria, the capital of Tamaulipas, where he designed to concentrate a portion of his army.

While absent on this expedition, General Worth informed Taylor, that Santa Anna was making quite extensive preparations to expel the Americans from Mexico. After a careful calculation of the chances in his favor, he had judged it best to take the lead in that policy which was most popular in Mexico, viz., to resist the aggressions of the United States. Accordingly, at San Louis de Potosi, in the heart of Mexico, and on the high road from Monterey to the capital, he had collected an army of twenty thousand men, all eager for the combat, and confident of victory. The scanty and scattered detachments of the American army could scarcely have stood before a well-planned and resolute movement of such a force; but Wool was summoned from Parras to join Worth at Saltillo, and Taylor, finding that the movement against Saltillo was not likely to take place, ordered General Quitman with the volunteers to march to Victoria, where he himself arrived, on the 4th of January, 1847.

1846.

The administration, meanwhile, had come to the conclusion that a change in the plan of operations against Mexico must be made. Taylor's line of attack was not likely to prove successful; and hence, as our ships had possession of the sea, and an army could be thrown upon any point of the coast which might

* For the account which Mr. Benton gives of the court-martial on Colonel Fremont (early in 1848), and its results, see his "*Thirty Years' View*," vol. ii., pp. 715–19. It is worth the reader's examination, and will help him towards understanding various matters connected with the California business, the Mexican war, etc.

seem most suitable as a base of operations, it was resolved to seize Vera Cruz, and thence to march directly upon the capital. General Scott was, therefore, once more summoned to the councils of the government, and towards the close of November, was invested with the office of "commander-in-chief of the American army in Mexico," for the purpose of carrying out this new programme of attack.

Scott devoted himself energetically to the needful preparations before leaving the United States, and among other measures, wrote immediately to General Taylor, that he should be under the painful necessity of depriving him of the best and most efficient troops under his command. Nearly all the regulars under Worth, Patterson, Twiggs, and Quitman, were ordered to Vera Cruz; and Taylor was left to maintain himself as best he could, against the threatened attack of Santa Anna and the most effective army which Mexico could boast. The entire force which Taylor could bring into the field was four hundred and seventy-six regulars, (consisting exclusively of artillery and cavalry,) and four thousand two hundred and fifteen volunteers. The enemy, according to Santa Anna's "summons," were twenty thousand strong, at the time of the battle of Buena Vista; although, it appears, some three or four thousand had been lost, before the engagement, by death, sickness and desertion; yet, admitting this diminution, the Mexican army was more than three times as numerous as that of General Taylor, and it contained the best soldiers and ablest general the country could furnish.

General Taylor had advanced beyond Saltillo, on the road to San Luis, as far as Agua Nueva; but, when the strength of the enemy was known, he resolved to fall back about thirteen miles, to a pass near the *hacienda* of Buena Vista, called *La Angostura*, or the Straits. The road here passed through a gorge in the mountains, and was defended on the west by a complete network of deep gullies, cut by the torrents from the heights on that side, and almost everywhere impassable, whilst on the east a narrow shelf of table-land between it and the mountains was much intersected by ravines, through which, at certain seasons, rapid streams rushed into the rivulet that meandered through the pass. General Wool had been struck by the capabilities of the spot for such a defence as the American army seemed likely to be called upon to make, when he advanced to Agua Nueva, and Taylor confirmed his opinion by selecting it as the place to make a stand against Santa Anna.

1847.

The Mexican army was found to be near at hand, on the 21st of February, which led to immediate arrangements on the part of our countrymen to meet the enemy. Santa Anna had dispatched two thousand cavalry, under General Miñon, in a very circuitous route, to get into the rear of the Americans. threaten Saltillo, and cut off their retreat; at the same time, also, General Urrea had been sent in a circuit to the west of the road held by our troops, with about a thousand rancheros, to cooperate with Miñon. General Taylor, on his part, placed a battery of eight guns under Captain Washington, and properly supported, so as to command the road through the gorge; on the right of the stream, behind the gullies, he planted two guns under Captain Bragg, with supports of infantry and horse; to the left, on the narrow plateau with its steep ravines, were posted two regiments of infantry, with two guns; and on the skirts of the mountains were riflemen and cavalry. Two guns under Captain Sherman were in reserve, and the principal part of the cavalry still further in the rear. Warren's and Webster's commands were intrusted with the defence of Saltillo and a redoubt near; and one gun, with two companies of riflemen, was left to defend the train and head-quarters. Thus Taylor's small force was reduced still smaller in the numbers that could be employed directly against the enemy, from the wide intervals between the points he had to hold, against the enemy's troops in front, on both flanks, and in his rear.

The Mexican commander divided his army into three columns; one of which was to carry Washington's battery and force the pass; the other two were to combine and turn Taylor's left; and, beside these, he had an excellent force in reserve. He had twenty guns, three of them twenty-four-pounders, three sixteens, and five twelve-pounders, with one seven-inch howitzer. Before commencing the attack, Santa Anna sent a flag of truce to General Taylor, assuring him that he would be crushed if he offered any resistance, and summoning him to an immediate surrender. This, of course, the heroic Taylor peremptorily declined.

The battle began on the afternoon of the 22d of February, in honor of which day the word was, "the memory of Washington," and a desultory fight was kept up till nightfall, when General Taylor departed for Saltillo, fearing for its safety, and Santa Anna endeavored to incite the ardor of his men by martial music. The attack was renewed at daybreak on the 23d of February, and though pressed with zeal and courage, was bravely met and sustained by our countrymen. The details we need not here enter into; we must refer to the historians of the Mexican war for particulars, from which **1847.**
it will be evident, that nothing short of the most determined bravery, and the most unflinching hardihood, could have enabled our troops to make head against, and defeat, an army of the size and capability of that under General Santa Anna. At one time, when the Mexican cavalry had succeeded in turning the left of the American lines, it seemed impossible to retrieve the fortune of the day; but, at this juncture, Taylor returned from Saltillo; his presence infused fresh vigor into the army; the impetuous riflemen of Mississippi drove back the enemy; the tide of victory was turned; and despite disasters of various kinds with the infantry, the artillery was so admirably worked and so effective, that, in fact, by it the Mexican advance was effectually stopped and the battle won. When night came, the field was covered with dead, and many an anxious hour was passed by Taylor and his men, waiting for the morrow, and preparing for a renewal of the fight. But, at dawn of day, on

the 24th of February, it was found that Santa Anna had retreated.

The Mexican retreat was attended with intense and pitiable distresses; the sick, the wounded, the dying, and the dead were abandoned at every step. The Americans were too few in number, and too much exhausted by the conflict, to allow a pursuit; and there were the dead to be buried, and the wounded to be cared for. An interchange of prisoners was arranged with Santa Anna; and Miñon with the *rancheros* under Urrea, whose exploits had not been of a kind to compensate for the defeat, were withdrawn. The total loss, on the part of our countrymen, was, amongst the regulars, eight killed and fifty-three wounded; amongst the volunteers, two hundred and sixty-four killed, three hundred and thirty-five wounded, and six missing; in all, six hundred and sixty-six killed, wounded, and missing. The Mexican loss was about two thousand five hundred, in killed and wounded; whilst in missing, and deaths during the retreat, their own authorities say, that at least ten thousand five hundred more were lost. They captured three guns in the battle; but they were defeated, completely and disastrously. By the middle of March, the American communications were completely restored; and the northern frontier of Mexico was entirely in possession of our troops.

General Taylor having little to do now, in consequence of the new line of operations which had been marked out, in the month of November left General Wool in command, and reached New Orleans on the 1st of December. He was received with the most flattering attentions, and everywhere throughout the country the voice of the people was heard in praise of his bravery and his ability as a general.

There can be no doubt, that the qualities displayed by General Taylor, during his campaigns in Mexico, commended his name to the whig party as a candidate for the presidential chair likely to command a large vote of the people in his favor. His sound good sense, his firmness, his excellent private character, and his political views, added to his brilliant reputation as a brave and victorious general, gave promise of success in the great political contest approaching; and the veteran hero was early applied to on the subject of his being nominated for the presidency. The letters from him in respect to this matter were characterized by his plain, good sense, and his willingness to serve his country in any station to which he might be called by the voice of his fellow-citizens.

CHAPTER VI.

1847-1849.

POLK'S ADMINISTRATION: CONCLUDED.

General Scott at Vera Cruz — Bombardment of the city and castle — Advance into Mexico — Battle of Cerro Gordo —Other successes— Scott and the army at Perote — N. P. Trist's mission —Mexican efforts to defend their capital — Santa Anna's plans — Battle of Contreras — Brilliant affair — Armistice of Tacubaya — Result — Assaults on Molino del Rey and Casa Mata — Chapultepec taken — Entire success of the American arms — Entrance into the city of Mexico — War virtually ended — Colonel Childs at Puebla — Attacked by Santa Anna — Dissensions among Scott and his officers — Negotiations for peace—Substance of the treaty of Guadalupe Hidalgo — Reflections on the Mexican war — Congress in session, December, 1847 — Mr. Polk's message—The work done — John Quincy Adams's death — Party conventions for nominating candidates for president and vice-president — The election—Taylor and Fillmore elected—Second session of the thirtieth congress—Mr. Polk's last message—Abstract of its contents — The gold region discovered — Work of the session — Action in regard to California and New Mexico — Principal acts passed — Convention of southern members of Congress on the subject of slavery—Plans for railroad communication with the Pacific coast—End of Mr. Polk's administration.

At the earliest practicable period after his appointment as commander-in-chief of the army in Mexico, General Scott hastened to take command of the expedition. On his arrival at Tampico, he immediately infused vigor into the operations on foot, and by issuing martial-law orders, put a stop to the disgraceful acts of violence and outrage in which many of the troops had previously been permitted to indulge without punishment. He also, as we have before stated (p. 439), withdrew from General Taylor's command the regulars, and a large portion of the volunteers, in order to increase his own force as much as possible; and, relying upon the support of the government at home, set himself earnestly to work to carry out the campaign in gallant style, as became a warrior of his distinguished reputation.

Lobos, an island to the south of Tampico; and about a hundred and twenty-five miles from Vera Cruz, was the rendezvous appointed for the armament which was to be thrown upon the coast at the nearest point to the capital; and there, in the beginning of March, 1847, were collected above twelve thousand men, and a fleet of a hundred and sixty-three vessels to transport the army, with its guns, stores, and equipage of every kind, to its destination. On the 7th of March, the embarkation was effected; and two days afterwards, the whole force was landed, without the loss of a man, at the island of Sacrificios, in close proximity to Vera Cruz. On the 18th, having, without effect, summoned the city to surrender, Scott broke ground before it; he also gave free permission to the non-combatants, such as women and children,

1847.

Winfield Scott

foreign consuls, etc., to retire from the city; and on the 22d, the investment being completed, and another summons rejected, the bombardment began. Aided by the fleet, which co-operated most effectually with the land forces, Scott maintained for four days, and as many nights, such a terrific rain of fire upon the place, that it was almost converted into a heap of ruins; and the loss of life was fearfully great.

Three thousand shells, weighing ninety pounds each, and as many round shot, chiefly thirty-two pounders, were thrown into the city during this bombardment. The Mexicans, whose garrison in the city was about three thousand, and in the castle of San Juan d'Ulloa, about one thousand, displayed spirit enough in their resistance; but they were unprovided with artillery fit to cope with that of their assailants, and it would have required a considerably larger force than they possessed, fully to man the batteries and the citadel. On the evening of the 24th, a joint note was addressed to the general-in-chief, by the French, Spanish, and British consuls, requesting him to suspend hostilities long enough "to enable their respective compatriots to leave the place with their women and children, as well as the Mexican women and children." General Scott, however, felt compelled to refuse this request, on the ground that the neutrals might have left the place before the bombardment; and as to the Mexican women and children, his summons to the city had been disregarded, and now no truce would be allowed apart from surrender. This, which seemed to be a hard measure, has been severely spoken of by some writers, who have reviewed the Mexican war in its inception and progress. Military authorities, however, deem that Scott was justified in his determination, and is not liable to censure for the course he adopted. Four hundred of the garrison were killed, and six hundred were wounded; four or five hundred of the inhabitants had perished; and after some negotiation, the terms of surrender were arranged, and on the 29th of March, both the city and the far-famed castle of San Juan d'Ulloa, were surrendered to the victorious army. All the public stores, etc., in the city were delivered up, but perfect protection was guaranteed to the inhabitants.

General Worth was appointed temporary governor of Vera Cruz, and discharged the duties of the post during the delay necessary to arrange for advancing into the interior. General Scott, as soon as he had made provision for resuscitating the commerce of the port, and effected the necessary arrangements, took up his line of march, on the 8th of April, for the city of Mexico, and arrived, with the greater part of his army, at Plan del Rio on the 14th. He had learned that Santa Anna, having collected what force he could, had taken up a position in advance of Jalapa, at the pass of Cerro Gordo, with the determination to stop his progress; and he hastened his march that he might prevent delay or a change of route, either of which would certainly prove injurious.

1847.

After several reconnaissances, by which he fully ascertained the strength of the Mexican front, Scott resolved to cut a passage through the thick chaparral on his right, so as to turn the left flank of the enemy, whose care had been confined to obstructing the main road. To mask this movement, General Twiggs was ordered, on the 17th of April, to advance against a fortified position, with a steep ascent, almost directly in front of the main entrenchment. This was carried by Colonel Harney, with the rifles and some detachments of infantry and artillery, and a heavy gun having been dragged with immense toil up to the height, a demonstration was made against another fort in its rear. Early on the next morning, the troops moved forward in columns to make a general attack on the enemy's line. Pillow's brigade assaulted the right, but was compelled to retire; and it was of the less moment, because this was not the key of the position. Twiggs's division stormed the centre, carried the fortifications, and cut them off from support; while Riley's brigade drove the main body of the Mexicans into complete rout, and turned their own guns upon them as they fled. Shields's brigade, in the mean time, assaulted and carried the battery in the rear of the enemy's left, and deprived them of the opportunity of rallying.

The American loss was, sixty-four killed, and three hundred and fifty-three wounded. The loss of the Mexicans, in killed and wounded, was never known, but our countrymen took three thousand prisoners, amongst whom were five generals, four or five thousand stands of arms, and forty-three pieces of artillery. Santa Anna himself with great difficulty escaped to Orizaba, where he exerted himself with great diligence to get together again a force sufficient to make head against Scott's advance upon the capital.

The army advanced, as soon as possible after their victory, on Jalapa and Perote, which were abandoned to them without a blow; the latter on the 22d of April, and with it a vast accumulation of warlike stores. At Amozoque, they were unsuccessfully attacked by Santa Anna; and on the 22d of May, Puebla submitted to General Worth, whilst the Mexican forces retired upon the capital. This failure to retrieve the disaster at Cerro Gordo, kindled anew the flames of revolution in Mexico; and the various parties and factions in that unhappy country could agree upon no one point, except that the northern invaders were to be opposed to the last extremity, and that no peace was to be made while an enemy remained on the soil of Mexico.

1847.

The head-quarters of the army were now fixed at Puebla, where General Scott remained until the beginning of August; in part because of the necessity of recruiting his troops, and in part because the home government renewed their overtures of negotiations to the government of Mexico, as soon as the news of the victory at Cerro Gordo reached Washington. But this long halt grievously tried both the health and the *morale* of the army. The numbers in hospital were unprecedented, when the total strength of the forces are taken into consideration, amounting sometimes to a fifth, and even to a quarter of the whole; and the desertions were more frequent and extensive than, under all the circumstances, could have been conceived. Into the unpleasant differences and disputes between the general-in-chief and the authorities at Washington, growing out of the scheme of superseding Scott, by the appointment of a lieutenant-general, we need not enter; neither is it material to enlarge upon the mission of Mr. N. P. Trist, who was sent by the president as commissioner, with full powers to seize upon the earliest opportunity of negotiating a peace with Mexico. The historians of the war, Ripley, Mansfield, and others, will furnish all the details desired by the reader.

Having at length been well reinforced, although he left behind him eighteen hundred men in hospital, on the 7th of August, General Scott took the road to the capital of Mexico; and in four days the advanced division reached Ayotla, about fifteen miles from the city of the Montezumas. By

1847. this route, however, it was soon discovered that Mexico was inaccessible; a new road was therefore constructed, to the south of that running direct from Vera Cruz; and between the 15th and the 18th of the month, the army had rounded Lakes Chalco and Xochimilco, and reached San Augustin, on the Acapulco road, only eight miles distant from the object of its long journey. Nothing can better show the exhaustion of the military power of the government, than this daring march of less than eleven thousand men, so far into a country peculiarly favorable to guerilla warfare, and in which no amount of contributions which might be levied could compensate for the destruction of its communications with the sea and the fleet. The attempts which were made to annoy and harass the advance of the American army confirm this statement in the most convincing manner.

As might be supposed, the Mexicans made intense efforts to defend their capital city. On every road approaching it were strong earth-works and batteries, and around the city itself was a complete girdle of entrenchments. There was, however, an insufficiency of artillery, and the disposable troops were not above twenty thousand in number; the services of some ten thousand armed citizens might perhaps be reckoned upon, in addition to the army; and although the lines were long, the invading force was too inconsiderable to make this of any great moment. In view of all the circumstances, the plans of Santa Anna (as stated by him after the battle was lost,) appear to have been arranged with greater skill than he had shown before. It was his design to have fallen back before Scott's advance, and given battle on ground he had chosen, and in which his numbers would have told with effect upon the comparatively small army of the invaders. But the gross disobedience of General Valencia disconcerted the whole plan. As if he had determined to seize the first opportunity of attacking the Americans, in entire forgetfulness of the first duty of a subordinate commander, and in spite of the untenable character of the ground about

Contreras, (or Padierna,) he left his position at Coyoacan and San Angel, and advanced to Contreras, and on the heights there entrenched himself, not only without any orders from Santa Anna, but without so much as consulting him respecting the movement. By this means he weakened the force opposed to Scott's direct advance, and at the same time he could not prevent that advance, because the nature of the ground in his front neutralized the menace of his position on Scott's flank.

It was, nevertheless, considered safest to dispose of Valencia's force in the first instance; and, accordingly, Worth was sent with Harney's cavalry to threaten San Antonio, and Pillow's division consisting of Pierce's and Cadwallader's brigades, was despatched against Contreras, on the left, across the Pedregal, an almost impassable lava-tract, over which a party, covered by Twiggs's division, undertook the making of a road.

1847.

On the afternoon of the 19th of August, these two divisions arrived within range of Valencia's guns; and the small field batteries of Magruder and Callender were, with great labor, brought into play against them, while the front was extended to the right in such a manner, that, by the aid of Morgan's regular infantry and Shields's volunteers, (which were sent to reinforce them at sunset,) the *rancho* of Ansaldo was carried, and Valencia's communications threatened. Amid the darkness and rain of the night, which rapidly fell upon the field, and terminated the conflict for a short time, General Persifer F. Smith proposed a plan for the assault of Valencia's camp, which Captain Lee, of the engineers, toiling alone across the perilous intervening space, through the impervious gloom and storm, communicated to General Scott, and obtained his approbation for making trial of it.

About three in the morning of the 20th of August, Riley's brigade, followed by Cadwallader's and Smith's, set out, and toiling through the rain and mud, by sunrise reached an elevation in the rear of the Mexican position, from which they were able to attack the entrenchments with such advantage, that in seventeen minutes they were carried. Scott had sent Twiggs's division against the works in front, to effect a diversion, if it should be required; Smith's brigade discovered and routed a mass of Mexican cavalry, while Shields's not only held other masses in check, but captured great numbers of fugitives from Contreras. The American force engaged in this brilliant action was about four thousand five hundred, whilst the enemy numbered about six thousand, and Santa Anna was sufficiently near, with double that number, to have shared in the fight if he had felt disposed.

1847.

This decisive victory, however, was not all that was accomplished on that day. Whilst the divisions just mentioned were engaged on the left, General Worth, by a skillful and daring movement on the right, had turned and forced the enemy's strong position at San Antonio, and then advanced directly upon a strong, well-built fortification, the *tête du pont* of Cherubusco, the other divisions hastening to the same point from the field of Contreras. Pierce and Shields crossing the Rio de Cherubusco by a bridge on the left, turned the position, and engaged Santa Anna's troops, whilst Twiggs assaulted and carried the works round the church of San Pablo, and Worth's and Pillow's troops were engaged in carrying the tête du pont itself. At every point the contest was most furious; but the Mexicans again proved themselves unable to contend successfully with American soldiers; at every point our countrymen triumphed, and the dragoons chased the scattered and disheartened enemy to the very gates of the capital.

We have no returns by which to estimate with any accuracy the losses of the Mexicans in killed and wounded in these obstinate conflicts; but it must have been very great. Nearly sixteen hundred were taken prisoners, including three generals. Seven field pieces were captured, with great quantities of ammunition, and about a thousand mules and horses. General Scott's loss in the battles of the 19th and 20th of August, in regulars and volunteers, was a hundred and thirty-three killed, and eight hundred and sixty-five wounded. This was the most sanguinary of all the engagements in the whole course of the war; but in its effects, it was certainly one of the most decisive.

At this point, everything seemed favorable for entering upon negotiations for peace, on terms which would be acceptable to the United States. General Scott, at his head-quarters, at Tacubaya, and only three miles from the city of Mexico, arranged an armistice, with a view to a treaty; having enforced the offer by the alternative of an assault, which no one doubted would have been successful. Some pause, too, was desirable for his own men, after so long a march and such severe engagements. And for several days after the 24th of August, the commissioners appointed by the two parties attempted to ascertain the existence of some ground of agreement, whence they might start in drawing up the articles of a final treaty. But beside the fact, that Scott was determined to obtain every thing which his country expected from the war, the Mexicans did not know how to proceed; for they not only wished to have it appear that they were unsubdued, but they were also split up into numerous factions and parties, and could agree upon no line of policy calculated to meet the emergency. Mr. Trist, whose unpleasant quarrel with General Scott, had been put to rest some time previously, endeavored to carry out the instructions of his government; but the result showed, that there was no reliance to be placed on Santa Anna or his real purposes in all this movement; and, in fact, every effort failed to arrange a peace on mutually satisfactory terms. Santa Anna thought that he would make one more trial to meet the victorious invaders on the field of battle.

1847.

The Mexican general, according to common report, had been very diligent in strengthening his fortifications, during the armistice, although he had stipulated not to do so; several huge church bells had been cast into cannon, and the remaining portions of the armies that had been raised were organized for the purpose of once more trying the fate of battle. General Scott, meanwhile, had not been idle nor unobservant; he had employed the time in such drilling and military exercise of his troops as their position rendered possible; and put into serviceable condition the artillery which had been captured, and refilled his exhausted ammunition wagons from the stores which victory had put into his power. He had no need to strengthen his position, for his object (if peace was not negotiated) was not to maintain the ground he occupied, but to take that of the enemy; and we do not hear of his receiving any reinforcements from the coast.

The armistice having now lasted for two weeks, and there appearing no probability of a treaty being arranged, General Scott, on the 6th of September, notified Santa Anna that he was aware of his infractions of the armistice, and demanded satisfaction on account of them before noon on the following day, under pain of declaring the suspension of arms at an end, and proceeding with hostilities forthwith. The reply, which was sent on the 7th, accepted the latter alternative, and announced the resolution to try the fortune of war once more. Before night Scott had fully determined upon his plan of action.

1847.

Having ascertained that the western side of the city seemed to be less strongly fortified than the south side, he resolved to assault it by a flank attack. But there lay directly in the line of operations, on this plan, three strong positions—El Molino del Rey, La Casa Mata, and Chapultepec; the latter a castellated height, which under ordinary circumstances could only have been reduced by a regular siege. Nevertheless, knowing the quality of his own men, and the inefficiency of the enemy, he expected to carry it, as well as the rest, by assault, and gave orders accordingly; the King's Mill—El Molino del Rey—being the first point to be carried.

About four o'clock in the morning of the 8th of September, the different sections of General Worth's division took their posts at the places assigned to them; and as soon as dawn appeared, Huger's twenty-four pounders thundered against the walls of the old mill, preluding the assault on the advanced battery, which was effected in so gallant a style by Major Wright and Captain Smith, that in spite of the grape and canister showered upon the attacking column, in spite of a desperate rally on the part of the Mexicans, and a struggle in which eleven out of fourteen American officers fell, the place was taken, and the guns in it turned upon the fugitives, who rushed in the wildest disorder to the forts. In the mean while, Garland's brigade, sustained by Drum's artillery, assaulted the enemy's left, near the Molino, and after an obstinate contest drove them from their position under the protecting guns of Chapultepec. The American guns, being advanced to the position which had been carried, made dreadful havoc amongst the routed foe.

While these vigorous efforts were being made on the Mexican centre and left, Duncan's battery was blazing away

on the right, and Colonel M'Intosh was ordered to assault that point. But the Casa Mata proved to be a massive stone work surrounded with bastioned entrenchments and deep ditches, whence a deadly fire was delivered, and kept up without intermission upon the advancing troops, until they reached the very slope of the parapet surrounding
1847. the citadel. Here they were fairly mowed down by the guns of the fort, and were forced to withdraw to the left of Duncan's battery, where the remnant of the column reformed in readiness for another assault.

The Mexican cavalry threatened an attack on the American left, but were repulsed by the artillery, and by the mere appearance of the American dragoons; while new efforts were made against the Molino, which soon yielded to a desperate charge, led by Major Buchanan and Captain M'Kenzie on one side, and Captains Anderson and Ayres on the other. All the guns were now brought to bear on the Casa Mata, and the garrison cut off from all support, and exposed to a most destructive cannonade, evacuated it. Two attempts to rally and lead their men on, for the recovery of the positions that had been lost, were made by the Mexican leaders, but they could not stand before the terrible fire of the American artillery, and by nine o'clock in the morning the battle was over.

General Scott did not think it expedient to pursue the victory at the present, although Worth begged to be allowed to do so; the Casa Mata was blown up, and the troops were marched back to Tacubaya to prepare for the contest on a succeeding day. The entire American force engaged in this hard fought battle was only three thousand four hundred and forty-seven, whilst the Mexicans were at least ten thousand strong, and were posted behind strong fortifications. The loss in killed and wounded was very severe, amounting to nearly eight hundred, of whom fifty-nine were officers. The loss on the side of the Mexicans was never ascertained, but it must have been great, and two of their generals were killed.

Although no immediate results followed this battle, General Scott was actively engaged in preparing for the assault on the capital at the earliest practicable moment. Three batteries were constructed on the night of the 11th of September, and in the course of the following day; and General Pillow's troops took possession of Molino del Rey again. Throughout the 12th, the fortress of Chapultepec was briskly bombarded; whilst feigned attacks were directed against the *garitas* San Antonio and Niño Perdido. On the
morning of the 13th, all neces- 1847.
sary measures having been arranged between the general-in-chief and his subordinate commanders, the bombardment was renewed with greater vigor than before, until at eight o'clock the batteries suddenly ceased firing, and Pillow's division rushed from its position, overpowered the resistance offered by the enemy on the ground before the fortress, rapidly climbed the steep sides of the hill on which Chapultepec stood, and rearing their scaling ladders against its walls, poured into the works. Quitman, with Shields and

Smith, at the same time advanced against the south-eastern side of the hill, and though they had difficult ground to pass over, and were much exposed to the enemy's fire, they reached the fortress in time to take part in its capture. Chapultepec was entered on every side; the officers who were to have fired the mines were shot down before they could apply the match; and though the garrison made a stout and prolonged defence, almost at the point of the bayonet, it was all in vain, and the survivors, with their commander, General Bravo, were made prisoners.

Whilst the battle was raging round Chapultepec, General Worth, passing to the north of it, had advanced by the causeway and aqueduct of San Cosmé upon Mexico itself. General Quitman, also, as soon as Chapultepec had fallen, pressed on, with the greater part of his command, against the garita Belen: both detachments driving the fugitives and stragglers from the former field before them into the city. A hot fire from the roofs and windows of the houses in the street of San Cosmé delayed Worth's progress, but he made good the ground he had won when night fell. But Quitman, whose attack was intended as a feint merely, converted it into a real assault, carried the garita in spite of all obstacles, and early in the afternoon established himself under the very guns of the citadel.

The final result was now no longer doubtful, and Santa Anna and his officers held a council that night to determine upon what they should do in the present posture of affairs. Immediate retreat was the almost necessary alternative, and it was commenced without delay. Santa Anna, having liberated the convicts in the city prisons, so as to give all the trouble he could to the conquerors, took the road to Guadalupe Hidalgo. The retreat was begun, as Mr. Mayer states, "at midnight, and not long after a deputation from the Ayuntamiento, or city council, waited upon General Scott with the information, that the federal government and troops had fled from the capital. The haggard visitors demanded terms of capitulation in favor of the church, the citizens, and the municipal authorities. Scott refused the ill-timed request, and promising no terms that were not self-imposed, sent word to Quitman and Worth to advance as soon as possible on the following morning, and guarding carefully against treachery, to occupy the city's strongest and most commanding points. Worth was halted at the Alameda, a few squares west of the Plaza; but Quitman was allowed the honor of advancing to the great square, and hoisting the American flag on the national palace. At nine o'clock on the morning of the 14th of September, the commander-in-chief, attended by his brilliant staff, rode into the vast area in front of the venerable cathedral and palace, amid the shouts of the exulting army, to whose triumphs his prudence and genius had so greatly contributed."

1847.

In gaining these decisive victories, there were one hundred and thirty killed, seven hundred and three wounded, and twenty-nine missing. The Mexicans were hopelessly defeated. General Scott's army, which numbered eleven thousand men when he left Puebla, was now reduced to less than six thousand; and above half the loss had taken place in battle; sickness, desertion, and the necessity of garrisoning some of the captured places, accounted for the rest. But the loss of the Mexicans during the same time had exceeded seven thousand, by battle alone; and besides, there were nearly four thousand prisoners in the hands of the conquerors, who had also taken more than twenty colors and standards, seventy-five guns, and fifty-seven wall-pieces, twenty thousand small arms, and an immense quantity of shot, shells, and powder.

With this crowning victory, the Mexican war was, virtually, ended; although there was some fighting at a few other points, which may briefly be noted in the present connection. In the city of Mexico, as we have stated above, Santa Anna, as a last act, let loose the convicts out of prison, who for two or three days committed murders and outrage to an alarming extent. When the American soldiers dispersed from the great square to seek quarters in the city, they were fired upon by these scoundrels from housetops and windows, and from behind walls,
1847. and every screen which could be used for so nefarious a purpose. The better disposed of the inhabitants willingly joined General Scott in his exertions to suppress this insurrection of brigands, which was more to be dreaded by them than by the Americans; and such vigorous measures were adopted under the proclamation of martial law, as speedily brought it to an end. General Quitman was appointed governor of the city; and under his administration of Scott's general order, the city was more peaceable and safe than it had been for ages. The contribution levied amounted to no more than $150,000, the greatest part of which was devoted to the purchase of blankets and shoes for the common soldiers, and comforts for the sick and wounded.

Colonel Childs was left at Puebla (p. 445) when General Scott marched for the capital, having only four hundred efficient men and nearly eighteen hundred in the hospitals. Order was preserved until, false news of Mexican success at Molino del Rey having reached the city, the masses, joined by about three thousand troops under General Rea, rose upon and besieged the garrison. On the 22d of September, Santa Anna (who, when he fled from Mexico, had summoned the congress to Querétaro, and had resigned the presidency to Chief-Justice Peña y Peña) arrived, and increasing the assailants to nearly eight thousand, made the most vigorous efforts, during the following six days and nights, to dislodge the Americans from the position they had seized. Tidings of their danger were carried to General Lane at Vera Cruz, and Major Lally at Jalapa, and they, fighting their way through the swarms of *guerilleros* which infested every pass, fell upon Santa Anna (who had advanced as far as Huamantla to meet them) on the 9th of October, and, although their force was under a thousand strong, defeated him after a sharp action. On the 13th, they reached Puebla, and at once reversed the aspect of affairs. Rea withdrew to Atlixco, whither Lane pursued him, and carried the place after an hour's cannonade by moonlight, on the night of the 19th of October. The losses of the Americans in these affairs were about a hundred killed and wounded. The guerilleros were also about the same time effectually dispersed, and communications from the sea to the capital were rendered safe and free from annoyance.

The American naval force was occupied in several expeditions principally in the Pacific. Guyamas was seized by Captain Lavallette, on the 20th of October, having been deserted by its garrison and governor, and a demonstration afterwards made against it was easily defeated. Mazatlan was occupied, on the 10th of November, by Commodore Shubrick, who hoped to have made it the terminus of a line of communication with General Scott or General Taylor. San Blas, San José, Mulejé, San Antonio, and Todos Santos were also the scenes of combats and skirmishes, all of them invariably ending in the success of our countrymen's arms.

1847.

Mexico having now been effectually subdued, and all hope of armed resistance having been cut off, it remained only to negotiate the terms on which peace was to be obtained, and the demands of the United States satisfied. Mr. Trist's efforts thus far had not been productive of any fruits, and the armistice of Tacubaya had not resulted as General Scott hoped and had reason to expect. Soon after the capture of the capital, Mr. Trist had sounded Peña y Peña respecting the renewal of peace negotiations; but it was not till the end of October, that that prudent statesman expressed, through his secretary, Don Luis de la Rosa, his profound desire for the cessation of hostilities. When Anaya entered on the presidency, and Peña y Peña was no more than a member of the cabinet, he retained the same feeling, and in the latter part of November, offered to appoint commissioners for the purpose of arranging the terms of peace.

1847.

But in the mean time, the president and cabinet at Washington had been convinced by the result of the armistice of Tacubaya, that Mr. Trist was not likely to arrive at a satisfactory issue; and orders had been sent for his recall. This fact General Scott (who was empowered to act as commissioner) was directed to notify to the Mexican authorities; and at the same time Trist was required to break off any unfinished negotiations, and to take with him to Washington any treaty he might have concluded, when he received his notice of recall; which was reiterated in the next dispatches, his government growing more discontented with his course of action. But, notwithstanding all this, Mr. Trist was anxious to have a share in the glory of effecting a treaty, and he ventured to continue to act as American commissioner to Mexico.

At this stage of affairs, the dissensions and squabbles among the American commanders became matter of public notoriety. General Scott was involved in warm and wordy contests with three of his immediate subordinates, at the same time; and he put two of his opponents, General Pillow, whom Mr. Trist looked upon as a personal enemy, and the cause of his recall, and General Worth, whom newspaper correspondents had praised to an extent which seemed to reflect upon himself, under arrest. Into the merits of these disputes we need not enter; they are too recent to be safely adjudicated upon, even were all the necessary data in our possession.*

Mr. Trist, meanwhile, proceeded with his unauthorized negotiations, and on the 2d of February, 1848, the treaty of Guadalupe Hidalgo was completed. It was signed on that day, in the town so named, by Mr. Trist, on the part of the American government, although he had ceased to represent it; and on the part of the Mexican government—which could scarcely be said to exist at all, so perturbed, and vague, and wanting in
1848. means of all kinds was it—by Don Luis G. Cuevas, Don Bernardo Conto, and Don Miguel Atristain. There were twenty-three articles, and one additional and secret article, stipulating that the ratification by the government of Washington might be deferred four months beyond the term fixed in the open articles of the treaty. And the principal conditions contained in it were,—the restoration of peace; the cession not only of Texas, but of New Mexico and Upper California also, to the United States; the payment, in consideration of this cession of territory, of $15,000,000 by the American government, and of the claims of the citizens of the United States against the government of Mexico, to the extent of $3,250,000; and a compact to restrain the incursions and misconduct of the Indians on the northern frontier.

The treaty was immediately dispatched to Washington, and notwithstanding the irregular way in which it had been negotiated, was at once sent to the Senate by Mr. Polk. It was there debated quite at large, and ratified after a few alterations, on the 10th of March. The treaty was subsequently ratified by the Mexican Congress, on the 30th of May; and during the summer of 1848, our brave troops returned home. Peace was proclaimed by the president on the 4th of July, 1848.*

Mr. Benton, in his "Thirty Years' View," has some interesting remarks upon the Mexican war, and the negotiations which led to the treaty of peace, which are worth the reader's examination. "Certainly," as he says, "those who served the government well in that war with Mexico, fared badly with the administration. Taylor, who had vanquished at Palo Alto, Resaca de la Palma, Monterey, and Buena Vista, was quarrelled with; Scott, who removed the obstacles to peace, and subdued the Mexican mind to peace, was superseded in the command of the army; Fremont,

* Major Ripley devotes a number of pages to this matter, and gives it as his opinion, that the effect of the proceedings of the court (held between March and July, 1849) was to produce "the impression, and truly, that the whole affair of the different quarrels had its origin in unfounded suspicions and jealousy on the part of the general-in-chief, and that the army and the country had been disturbed by a scandalous quarrel without any reasonable cause, to the injury of the reputation of the service."—"*The War in Mexico*," vol. ii., p. 632.

* For the president's proclamation and the treaty of peace with Mexico, see Appendix at the end of the present chapter.

who had snatched California out of the hands of the British, and handed it over to the United States, was court-martialed; and Trist, who made the treaty which secured the objects of the war, and released the administration from its dangers, was recalled and dismissed."*

The Mexican war, however gratifying in its results it may have proved to the national pride of our countrymen, is nevertheless suggestive of many and very grave reflections. Our gallant troops, it is true, displayed the courage and endurance of the bravest of the brave, and the whole career of the army, under its accomplished leaders, was one succession of victories; large accessions of territory were made, and beside Texas, New Mexico and California became integral portions of the United States; and from this date, our country has taken her rank in the forefront of the first-rate powers of the world. But it is only right and proper that we should look steadily at the cost of this war, the cost in money, and what is far more valuable, the cost in human life. As to the former, it is, in one sense, of little moment; $20,000,000 were paid for the newly-acquired territory, and official statistics show, that the grand total of expenditure in the way of army and navy support, of bounties, pensions, and the like, was not much, if at all, short of $150,000,000; yet, great as this amount is, it is not of material importance to a nation of so vast and extensive resources as ours. The cost of the war in human lives is far more worthy of note. The number of regulars who served in Mexico was twenty-seven thousand five hundred, and of volunteers seventy-one thousand three hundred, making a total of ninety-nine thousand; of these, some forty thousand resigned or were discharged, and between four and five thousand deserted. The total loss from battle, disease, and all causes, (as calculated by those familiar with the data,) was certainly not less than twenty-five thousand men! The reader will need no aid from us to see how vast an amount of suffering and misery must have resulted from this fearful destruction of human life; how much domestic affliction, pauperism, starvation, suicide, and other deplorable evils, must have followed in the train of war and bloodshed in Mexico. The result is yet in the future; and it may be the task of the historian in later ages to "point the moral" of this war, and to show how, in the wise dispensations of God, important ends were accomplished by it, for civilization and the progress of the human race.*

After this long digression, we return to the consideration of home affairs. The twenty-ninth Congress expired, as was stated on a previous page, (p. 430,) on the 3d of March, 1847, and soon after the contest, with reference to members of the new House, commenced in earnest. The result of the elections

* Benton's "*Thirty Years' View*," vol. ii., p. 711.

* The venerable Albert Gallatin, while the question of our relations with Mexico was unsettled, issued an interesting pamphlet, entitled "*Peace with Mexico*," which we commend to the attention of the reader. Mr. G. had previously sent forth a pamphlet, under the title of "*War with Mexico*," which is also characterized by the same spirit of moderation, justice, and candor.

showed that the measures of Mr. Polk's
1847. administration had not retained for it the popularity which it enjoyed when he entered upon office. The Mexican war had deprived it of the favor of some of the states; and others had been displeased at the repeal of the protective tariff; and so, when the first session of the thirtieth Congress began, it was plain that, though in the Senate democracy was still dominant, a majority of the other House was in the opposition.

This fact was clearly shown when the House came to the election of speaker, on the 6th of December, 1847; for Robert C. Winthrop, a Massachusetts whig, was chosen, on the third ballot, by a majority of a hundred and ten votes against sixty-four given to Linn Boyd, the principal democratic candidate, forty-one to other democrats, and three to other whigs. The other officers of the House, who had now to be appointed, were, of course, of the same political complexion.

A large portion of Mr. Polk's message was occupied with the Mexican war and the questions connected with it. Interesting information of a diplomatic kind was also furnished in one paragraph, in which—after recommending the establishment of legal tribunals for the punishment of criminals in China, lest the impunity of citizens of the United States guilty of crime there, should lead to any interruption of friendly relations with that important nation—mention was made of "treaties with the Sublime Porte, Tripoli, Tunis, Morocco, and Muscat," all awaiting the sanction of the Senate; and of the commencement of diplomatic intercourse with the Papal States, which required an appropriation to defray the expense to be incurred.

The receipts into the treasury, during the year ending in June, 1847, had been $26,346,790; but the expenditure had reached nearly to the amount of $59,500,000. The entire public debt was said now to be $45,660,000. "Should the war with Mexico be continued," the president remarked, "until the 30th of June, 1849, it is estimated that a further loan of $20,500,000 will be required for the fiscal year ending on that day, in case no duty be imposed on tea and coffee, and the public lands be not reduced and graduated in price, and no military contributions shall be collected in Mexico. If the duty on tea and coffee be imposed, and the lands be reduced and graduated in price as proposed, the loan may be reduced to $17,000,000, and will be subject to be still further reduced by the amount of the military contributions which may be collected in Mexico."

The operation of the tariff was spoken of as decidedly beneficial, and the independent treasury was lauded in terms which may be worth quoting here:—"While the fiscal operations of the government have been conducted with regularity and ease under this system, it has had a salutary effect in checking and preventing an undue inflation of the paper cur- 1847.
rency issued by the banks which exist under the state charters. Requiring, as it does, all dues to the government to be paid in gold and silver, its effect is to restrain excessive issues of bank

paper by the banks, disproportioned to the specie in their vaults, for the reason that they are at all times liable to be called on by the holders of their notes for their redemption, in order to obtain specie for the payment of duty and other public dues. The banks, therefore, must keep their business within prudent limits, and be always in a condition to meet such calls, or run the hazard of being compelled to suspend specie payments, and be thereby discredited."

In addition to these various topics, the mint, the public lands, the government of Oregon Territory, the navy, the steam marine, and the post-office, received due attention in the very lengthy message, which was concluded with a timely reference to the wise counsels of Washington against disunion, and with an invocation of the blessing of Almighty God upon the deliberations of the national legislature.

Not much, we are sorry to say, was accomplished during this session of Congress, principally because of the exciting political questions, arising out of, and connected with, the approaching presidential election. The "Wilmot proviso" was again warmly debated, in connection with the bill providing a territorial government for Oregon Territory. When the bill was passing through the Senate, amongst other amendments, on the motion of Senator Douglas, the Missouri compromise amendment was appended to it; but the House refused to concur in this addition to its bill; and the Senate in consequence receded from this amendment, by a vote of twenty-nine to twenty-five, when the House accepted the others. A loan of $16,000,000 was authorized, and an act was passed giving authority to purchase the papers of Mr. Madison, fourth president of the United States. Congress adjourned on the 14th of August, 1848.

1848.

The venerable ex-president, John Quincy Adams, who, with rare patriotism, was serving his country as a member of the House of Representatives, was stricken with paralysis, while in his seat, on the 21st of February, 1848. The House immediately adjourned, as did also the Senate; Mr. Adams was removed to the speaker's room, giving utterance to his dying words, "this is the last of earth;" and on the 23d, he sank quietly to his rest. As was fitting, honors were bestowed upon his memory by the myriads of his countrymen who deplored his removal from the councils of the nation. "He lingered," says Mr. Benton, "two days, and died on the evening of the 23d—struck the day before, and dying the day after the anniversary of Washington's birth—and attended by every circumstance which he could have chosen to give felicity in death. It was on the field of his labors, in the presence of the national representation, presided over by a son of Massachusetts, (Robert C. Winthrop, Esq.); in the full possession of his faculties, and of their faithful use at octogenarian age—without a pang—hung over, in his last unconscious moments, by her who had been for more than fifty years the worthy partner of his bosom. Such a death was the 'crowning mercy' of a long life of eminent and patriotic ser-

Millard Fillmore

vice, filled with every incident that gives dignity and lustre to human existence."

The democratic party, in the spring of 1848, held a national convention for the nomination of candidates for president and vice-president. The convention met at Baltimore, on the 22d of May, and for several days labored earnestly to fix upon names which should command the confidence of the majority of the people. The "hunkers" and "barnburners" sent delegates from New York, both claiming to represent the democracy of the empire state; both were admitted; but, as this only neutralized the vote of that state, both declined to take their seats, and New York, consequently, had no share in the work of the convention. On the fourth ballot, General Lewis Cass was selected as the candidate of the party for the presidency, and General William O. Butler, of Kentucky, was subsequently chosen as its candidate for the vice-presidency.*

The national convention of the whigs assembled, on the 7th of June, at Philadelphia, and spent two or three days in making a choice out of the number of prominent candidates before them. Daniel Webster and Henry Clay, both statesmen of high rank, were passed over—as was also General Scott; and General Taylor, who had acquired so great distinction by his military services in Mexico, was selected as the candidate for president, (p. 441). Millard Fillmore was placed on the same ticket as candidate for vice-president.

The election took place in November, and resulted as follows. General Taylor and Millard Fillmore received each one hundred and ninety-three votes, and were consequently elected president and vice-president. Generals Cass and Butler, received each one hundred and twenty-seven votes. The "free-soil" candidates did not **1848.** receive any of the electoral votes, as they were given by the states; but the popular vote shows their relative strength, and that of the other two parties, thus:—the votes given for Taylor were, a million three hundred and sixty-two thousand and twenty-four; those for Cass, a million two hundred and twenty-two thousand four hundred and nineteen; and those for Van Buren, two hundred and ninety-one thousand six hundred and seventy-eight; and above five thousand other votes were "scattered" and lost. Hence it is quite possible, that, had the Baltimore Convention given general satisfaction to the democratic party, its candidates might have been elected to the high offices on which their aspirations were fixed. "The result of the election," as Senator Benton well says, "was not without its moral and its instruction. All the long intrigues to govern it had miscarried. None of the architects of annexation, or of war, were elected. A victorious general overshadowed them all; and those who had considered

* That portion of the party who were dissatisfied with this result, held a convention at Utica, and nominated Martin Van Buren for president. The "free-soil party," consisting mainly of the abolitionists, held a convention at Buffalo, in August. Mr. Van Buren was adopted as their candidate for the presidency, and Charles Francis Adams as their candidate for the vice-presidency.

Texas their own game, and made it the staple of incessant plots for five years, saw themselves shut out from that presidency which it had been the object of so many intrigues to gain. Even the slavery agitation failed to govern the election; and a soldier was elected, unknown to political intrigue, and who had never even voted at an election."*

The second session of the thirtieth Congress commenced on the 4th of December, 1848, and the next day Mr. Polk sent in his fourth and last annual message. It proved to be unusually long, and it entered fully into the questions of interest and importance which at that date claimed notice from the executive and the national legislature. In speaking of foreign affairs, the president made mention of "advantageous treaties of commerce" concluded with New Grenada, Peru, the Two Sicilies, Belgium, Hanover, Oldenburg, and Mecklenburg-Schwerin. He praised Great Britain for "pursuing our example," and relaxing her restrictive system; and took occasion to laud, with more than the accustomed warmth of retiring presidents, the institutions of the country. After recording the termination of the war with Mexico, Mr. Polk spoke of the military strength of the United States, and boasted of their possessing "virtually a standing army of two millions of armed citizen soldiers;" he also dilated in glowing terms, upon the navy, and the organization of those branches of the executive which had been charged with the conduct of the war.

* Benton's "*Thirty Years' View*," vol. ii., p. 724.

In reviewing the acquisitions of new regions of country, which had been made during his administration, the president declared that they amounted to more than half as much as the entire territory of the United States at the time of his entrance upon office; and, he added, it would be difficult to calculate the value of these immense additions to the area of the country. He said this, in part, because he had to announce the discovery of the incalculably rich gold mines of California;* and in part, because it afforded so prodigious a field for the expansion of the population of the States, and gave to the Union so commanding a position upon both the great Oceans that extend to both the poles. And with a full sense of the lustre which these events must shed upon his administration, he said,—"The acquisition of California and New Mexico, the settlement of the Oregon boundary, and the annexation of Texas, extending to the Rio Grande, are results which combined are of greater consequence, and will add

1848.

* The first discovery of gold was made (in digging for a saw-mill) in February, 1848, on the grounds of Captain Suter. The rumors of the finding of El Dorado, about which the early adventurers to the western world had dreamed so frequently, immediately excited the attention of the whole community, and from not only the older portions of the United States, but from almost every part of the world, the "gold-diggings" were sought for with an avidity and eagerness which the "auri sacra fames" of the poet can hardly adequately express; within six weeks, during December, 1848, and January, 1849, more than a hundred vessels left the ports of the United States for California; and under the spur of excitement and making haste to get rich, a population was drawn to the Pacific coast with unexampled rapidity, and more various and extraordinary than had ever before gathered together in one region of country.

more to the strength and wealth of the nation, than any which have preceded them since the adoption of the Constitution."

Having expressed himself in favor of the extension of the Missouri compromise line, from the western border of Texas to the Pacific Ocean, which in fact would have been decidedly to the advantage of the south and of those who favored the extension of slave territory, Mr. Polk gave an account of the finances of the government. The last year's receipts, it was stated, had fallen little short of $35,500,000; whilst the expenditure had mounted up to nearly $43,000,000. But the receipts of the next year were estimated at above $57,000,000; and the total expenditures at nearly $3,000,000 less: and hopes were held out that the ordinary peace expenditure would not amount to so much as $29,000,000. After speaking in high terms of the new tariff, the public debt was mentioned, and the amount was stated to be $65,778,450. Other topics received attention, as the post-office, the "American system," the veto power, etc., and the message closed with an invocation of God's blessing upon the deliberations of Congress, that so they might "redound to the happiness, the honor, and the glory of our beloved country."

Notwithstanding this was the short session, considerable public business was transacted. Senator Douglas, of Illinois, at as early a day as prac-

1848. ticable, introduced a bill for the admission of California as a state, without the preliminary passage through the different grades of territorial government. The want of harmony, however, between the Senate and the House on the subject of the "Wilmot proviso," the former being opposed, the latter being decidedly in favor of this proviso, prevented all effective legislation with regard to the new regions of territory belonging to the United States.* Mr. Douglas gave as his reasons for introducing his bill that the population had increased so rapidly, there was no reason to wait for the usual forms of procedure. But though both Louisiana and Texas were cited as precedents, the judiciary committee reported, on the 9th of January, against the scheme; whereupon the Illinois Senator drew a new bill, in accordance with the intimation of the committee, and by it proposed to establish both New Mexico and California as **1849.**
new states at once, and to leave the inhabitants of them to determine whether or not to allow slavery there for themselves; but this plan met with no more favor than the former, or than three other bills, all devised for the solution of the difficulty. On the 2d of February, the motion to take it from the table was negatived by a very decided vote.

There being no probability of passing a bill for the organization of the new territories, Mr. Walker, of Wis-

* On the 13th of December, Senator Benton, whose views on the subject of slavery were well understood, presented a petition from the people of New Mexico, praying for a territorial government, and against the dismemberment of their territory in favor of Texas, and also *against the introduction of domestic slavery.* After considerable debate, the motion to print this petition was carried by a vote of thirty-three to fourteen, Mr. Benton himself being one of the majority.

consin, on the 29th of February, introduced into the Senate an amendment to the civil and diplomatic appropriation bill, providing for the extension of the revenue laws over California and New Mexico, and also the Constitution of the United States, with all general laws applicable to the case; which having been adopted by a small majority, the House further amended the bill, by adding to it the favorite "Wilmot proviso." Fresh debate arose upon this phase of the affair, and the original measure was in imminent hazard of not being carried at all, to the jeopardy of the public service. But at length, at five o'clock on Sunday morning, March the 4th, 1849,—the Senate having been kept from breaking up by the tact and influence of Daniel Webster,—both Houses withdrew their amendments, and the bill passed; the Senate at the same time passing the bill for extending the revenue laws to California, which had already been adopted by the House. Thus everything failed in relation to the establishing a temporary government for California and New Mexico.

Among the principal acts of the session may be mentioned, the establishing a territorial government for Minnesota; the making arrangements for the seventh census; the organization of the department of the interior, and the appointment of an assistant secretary of state; the running and marking off the northern boundary of the state of Iowa; and a resolution authorizing the secretary of war to furnish emigrants to Oregon, California, and New Mexico, with suitable arms and ammunition. We may also note here, that a convention or treaty between the United States and Great Britain, for the improvement of the postal communications between the territories of the two parties, was signed in London on the 15th of December, 1848. The Senate confirmed the treaty on the 5th of January, 1849.

The steady perseverance of those who wished to effect the abolition of slavery in the District of Columbia, rather alarmed the southern members of Congress, and they determined to hold a convention in relation to this topic, so as to discuss and fix upon the course which they ought to adopt in the existing state of affairs. Accordingly, sixty-eight members of Congress assembled in the Senate chamber, on the 23d of December, 1848, and Senator Metcalfe of Kentucky, presided.

A series of resolutions, based on the Virginia resolutions of 1798, were introduced by T. H. Bayley, of Virginia, and referred to a committee; and, on the 15th of January, Mr. Calhoun, in behalf of the committee, reported an "Address of the Southern Delegates to their Constituents," which, after reciting the constitutional provisions respecting slavery, and the alleged violations of the constitutional rights of the slave states by the northern or free states, called upon the south to present a united and immovable front, and to be ready to defend their rights. Nearly ninety members attended this second meeting, and at a third meeting, on January the 22d, a smaller number being present, Mr. Calhoun's address was adopted, in preference to one "to the People of the United States," sub-

1849.

mitted as a substitute for it, by John M. Berrien, of Georgia, and was signed by forty-eight members, forty-six being democrats and only two being whigs.

The discovery and the importance of the gold region on the shores of the Pacific, gave rise to various schemes for establishing railroad communication between the eastern and western territory of our republic. Several plans were brought forward in Congress; but the only one that received attention, was that which contemplated a railroad across the Isthmus of Panama, so as to reduce the distance to California from the Atlantic states, from some seventeen thousand miles (which was the distance by way of Cape Horn), to less than six thousand miles. The bill which Mr. Benton brought forward in the Senate, to accomplish this object, did not receive the support of the majority in that body. The overland route also, though the distance was much less, was not considered at all practicable at this date.

With the 4th of March, 1849, the session of Congress ended; and at the same time Mr. Polk's four years of public service reached their termination. They were stirring and eventful years; and at some future day they will afford wide scope for the historian of our country to do them justice. Senator Benton is of opinion that the faults of Mr. Polk's administration were the faults of his cabinet; the merits of it were all his own. "The Mexican war, under the impulse of speculators, and upon an intrigue of Santa Anna, was the great blot upon his administration; and that was wholly the work of the intriguing part of his cabinet. . . . The acquisition of New Mexico and California were the distinguishing events of his administration—fruits of the war with Mexico; but which would have come to the United States without that war, if the president had been surrounded by a cabinet free from intrigue and selfishness, and wholly intent upon the honor and interest of the country." We shall not, however, in this place undertake any review of the measures of Mr. Polk and his advisers during the four years of his presidency. For reasons which have been already stated, we do not feel called upon here to express any opinion as to the due meed of praise or censure which belongs to him and his acts. We leave him to the judgment of posterity.*

* In this connection, we may refer the reader to the Hon. Lucien B. Chase's "*History of the Polk Administration*," N. Y., 1850, pp. 512. Mr. C. claims to have shown entire impartiality and fairness, and as his volume is full of documentary matter, the reader may consult it to advantage. We also place on record here the death of Mr. Polk, which took place at Nashville, Tennessee, June 15th, 1849.

APPENDIX TO CHAPTER VI.

TREATY OF PEACE WITH MEXICO.

By the President of the United States of America.

A PROCLAMATION.

Whereas a treaty of peace, friendship, limits, and settlement between the United States of America and the Mexican republic, was concluded and signed at the city of Guadaloupe Hidalgo, on the second day of February, one thousand eight hundred and forty-eight, which treaty, as amended by the Senate of the United States, and being in the English and Spanish languages, is word for word as follows:

In the Name of Almighty God:

The United States of America and the United Mexican States, animated by a sincere desire to put an end to the calamities of the war which unhappily exists between the two republics, and to establish upon a solid basis relations of peace and friendship, which shall confer reciprocal benefits upon the citizens of both, and assure the concord, harmony, and mutual confidence wherein the two people should live, as good neighbors, have for that purpose appointed their respective plenipotentiaries—that is to say, the president of the United States has appointed Nicholas P. Trist, a citizen of the United States, and the president of the Mexican republic has appointed Don Luis Gonzago Cuevas, Don Bernardo Conto, and Don Miguel Atristain, citizens of the said republic, who, after a reciprocal communication of their respective full powers, have, under the protection of Almighty God, the author of peace, arranged, agreed upon, and signed the following

Treaty of peace, friendship, limits, and settlement, between the United States of America and the Mexican republic.

ARTICLE I.

There shall be firm and universal peace between the United States of America and the Mexican republic, and between their respective countries, territories, cities, towns, and people, without exception of places or persons.

ARTICLE II.

Immediately upon the signature of this treaty, a convention shall be entered into between a commissioner or commissioners appointed by the general-in-chief of the forces of the United States, and such as may be appointed by the Mexican government, to the end that a provisional suspension of hostilities shall take place, and that, in the places occupied by the said forces, constitutional order may be re-established, as regards the political, administrative, and judicial branches, so far as this shall be permitted by the circumstances of military occupation.

ARTICLE III.

Immediately upon the ratification of the present treaty by the government of the United States, orders shall be transmitted to the commanders of their land and naval forces, requiring the latter (provided this treaty shall then have been ratified by the government of the Mexican republic, and the ratifications exchanged) immediately to desist from blockading any Mexican ports; and requiring the former (under the same condition) to commence, at the earliest moment practicable, withdrawing all troops of the United States then in the interior of the Mexican republic, to points that shall be selected by common agreement, at a distance from the sea-ports not exceeding thirty leagues; and such evacuation of the interior of the republic shall be completed with the least possible delay; the Mexican government hereby binding itself to afford every facility in its power for rendering the same convenient to the troops on their march and in their new positions, and for promoting a good understanding between them and the inhabitants. In like manner, orders shall be dispatched to the persons in charge of the custom-houses at all ports occupied by the forces of the United States, requiring them (under the same conditions) immediately to deliver possession of the same to the persons authorized by the Mexican government to receive it, together with all bonds and evidences of debt for duties on importations and on exportations not yet fallen due. Moreover, a faithful and exact account shall be made out, showing the entire amount of all duties on imports and on exports collected at such custom-houses or elsewhere in Mexico by authority of the United States, from and after the day of ratification of this treaty by the government of the Mexican republic; and also an account of the cost of collection; and such entire amount, deducting only the cost of collection, shall be delivered to the Mexican government, at the city of Mexico, within three months after the exchange of ratifications.

The evacuation of the capital of the Mexican republic by the troops of the United States, in virtue of the above stipulation, shall be completed in one month after the orders there stipulated for shall have been received by the commander of said troops, or sooner if possible.

ARTICLE IV.

Immediately after the exchange of ratifications of the present treaty, all castles, forts, territories, places, and possessions, which have been taken or occupied by the forces of the United States during the present war, within the limits of the Mexican republic, as about to be established by the following article, shall be definitively restored to the said republic, together with all the artillery, arms, apparatus of war, munitions, and other public property, which were in the said castles and forts when captured, and which shall remain there at the time when this treaty shall be duly ratified by the government of the Mexican republic. To this end, immediately upon the signature of this treaty, orders shall be dispatched to the American officers commanding such castles and forts, securing against the removal or destruction of any such artillery, arms, apparatus of war, munitions, or other public property. The city of Mexico, within the inner line of intrenchments surrounding the said city, is comprehended in the above stipulations, as regards the restoration of artillery, apparatus of war, etc.

The final evacuation of the territory of the Mexican republic, by the forces of the United States, shall be completed in three months from the said exchange of ratifications, or sooner if possible; the Mexican government hereby engaging, as in the foregoing article, to use all means in its power for facilitating such evacuation, and rendering it convenient to the troops, and for promoting a good understanding between them and the inhabitants.

If, however, the ratification of this treaty by both parties should not take place in time to allow the embarkation of the troops of the United States to be completed before the commencement of the sickly season at the Mexican ports on the gulf of Mexico, in such case a friendly arrangement shall be entered into between the general-in-chief of the said troops and the Mexican government, whereby healthy and otherwise suitable places at a distance from the ports not exceeding thirty leagues shall be designated for the residence of such troops as may not yet have embarked, until the return of the healthy season. And the space of time here referred to as comprehending the sickly season shall be understood to extend from the first day of May to the first day of November.

All prisoners of war taken on either side, on land or on sea, shall be restored as soon as practicable after the exchange of ratifications of this treaty. It is also agreed, that if any Mexicans should now be held as captives by any savage tribe within the limits of the United States, as about to be established by the following article, the government of the said United States will exact the release of such captives, and cause them to be restored to their country.

ARTICLE V.

The boundary line between the two republics shall commence in the Gulf of Mexico, three leagues from land, opposite the mouth of the Rio Grande, otherwise called Rio Bravo del Norte, or opposite the mouth of its deepest branch, if it should have more than one branch emptying directly into the sea; from thence up the middle of that river, following the deepest channel, where it has more than one, to the point where it strikes the southern boundary of New Mexico; thence, westwardly, along the whole southern boundary of New Mexico (which runs north of the town called *Paso*) to its western termination; thence, northward, along the western line of New Mexico, until it intersects the first branch of the River Gila; (or if it should not intersect any branch of that river, then to the point on the said line nearest to such branch, and thence in a direct line to the same); thence down the middle of the said branch and of the said river, until it empties into the Rio Colorado; thence across the Rio Colorado, following the division line between Upper and Lower California, to the Pacific Ocean.

The southern and western limits of New Mexico, mentioned in this article, are those laid down in the map entitled "*Map of the United Mexican States, as organized and defined by various acts of the Congress of said republic, and constructed according to the best authorities. Revised edition. Published at New York in* 1847, *by J. Disturnell.*" Of which map a copy is added to this treaty, bearing the signatures and seals of the undersigned plenipotentiaries. And, in order to preclude all difficulty in tracing upon the ground the limit separating Upper from Lower California, it is agreed that the said limit shall consist of a straight line drawn from the middle of the Rio Gila, where it unites with the Colorado, to a point on the coast of the Pacific Ocean distant one marine league due south of the southernmost point of the port of San Diego, according to the plan of said port made in the year 1782 by Don Juan Pantoja, second sailing-master of the Spanish fleet, and published at Madrid in the year 1802, in the Atlas to the voyage of the schooners *Sutil* and *Mexicana*, of which plan a copy is hereunto added, signed and sealed by the respective plenipotentiaries.

In order to designate the boundary line with due precision, upon authoritative maps, and to establish upon the ground landmarks which shall show the limits of both republics, as described in the present article, the two governments shall each appoint a commissioner and a surveyor, who, before the expiration of one year from the date of the exchange of ratifications of this treaty, shall meet at the port of San Diego, and proceed to run and mark the said boundary in its whole course to the mouth of the Rio Bravo del Norte. They shall keep journals and mark out plans of their operations; and the result agreed upon by them shall be deemed a part of this treaty, and shall have the same force as if it were inserted therein. The two governments will amicably agree regarding what may be necessary to these persons, and also as to their respective escorts, should such be necessary.

The boundary line established by this article shall be religiously respected by each of the two republics, and no change shall ever be made therein, except by the express and free consent of both nations, lawfully given by the general government of each, in conformity with its own constitution.

ARTICLE VI.

The vessels and citizens of the United States shall, in all time, have a free and uninterrupted passage by the Gulf of California, and by the River Colorado below its confluence with the Gila, to and from their possessions situated north of the boundary line defined in the preceding article; it being understood that this passage is to be by navigating the Gulf of California and the River Colorado, and not by land, without the express consent of the Mexican government.

If, by the examinations which may be made, it should be ascertained to be practicable and advantageous to construct a road, canal, or railway, which should in whole or in part run upon the River Gila, or upon its right or its left bank, within the space of one marine league from either margin of the river, the governments of both republics will form an agreement regarding its construction, in order that it may serve equally for the use and advantage of both countries.

ARTICLE VII.

The River Gila, and the part of the Rio Bravo del Norte lying below the southern boundary of New Mexico, being, agreeably to the fifth article, divided in the middle, between the two republics, the navigation of the Gila and of the Bravo below said boundary shall be free and common to the vessels and citizens of both countries; and neither shall, without the consent of the other, construct any work that may impede or interrupt, in whole or in part, the exercise of this right; not even for the purpose of favoring new methods of navigation. Nor shall any tax or contribution, under any denomination or title, be levied upon vessels or persons navigating the same, or upon merchandise or effects transported thereon.

except in the case of landing upon one of their shores. If, for the purpose of making the said rivers navigable, or for maintaining them in such state, it should be necessary or advantageous to establish any tax or contribution, this shall not be done without the consent of both governments.

The stipulations contained in the present article shall not impair the territorial rights of either republic within its established limits.

ARTICLE VIII.

Mexicans now established in territories previously belonging to Mexico, and which remain for the future within the limits of the United States, as defined by the present treaty, shall be free to continue where they now reside, or to remove at any time to the Mexican republic, retaining the property which they possess in the said territories, or disposing thereof, and removing the proceeds wherever they please, without their being subjected, on this account, to any contribution, tax, or charge whatever.

Those who shall prefer to remain in the said territories, may either retain the title and rights of Mexican citizens, or acquire those of citizens of the United States. But they shall be under the obligation to make their election within one year from the date of the exchange of ratifications of this treaty; and those who shall remain in the said territories after the expiration of that year, without having declared their intention to retain the character of Mexicans, shall be considered to have elected to become citizens of the United States.

In the said territories, property of every kind, now belonging to Mexicans not established there, shall be inviolably respected. The present owners, the heirs of these, and all Mexicans, who may hereafter acquire said property by contract, shall enjoy with respect to it guarantees equally ample, as if the same belonged to citizens of the United States.

ARTICLE IX.

Mexicans who, in the territories aforesaid, shall not preserve the character of citizens of the Mexican republic, conformably with what is stipulated in the preceding article, shall be incorporated into the union of the United States, and be admitted at the proper time (to be judged of by the Congress of the United States) to the enjoyment of all the rights of citizens of the United States, according to the principles of the Constitution; and in the mean time shall be maintained and protected in the enjoyment of their liberty and property, and secured in the free exercise of their religion without restriction.

ARTICLE X.

[Stricken out.]

ARTICLE XI.

Considering that a great part of the territories which, by the present treaty, are to be comprehended for the future within the limits of the United States, is now occupied by savage tribes, who will hereafter be under the exclusive control of the government of the United States, and whose incursions within the territory of Mexico would be prejudicial in the extreme, it is solemnly agreed, that all such incursions shall be forcibly restrained by the government of the United States whensoever this may be necessary; and that when they cannot be prevented, they shall be punished by the said government, and satisfaction for the same shall be exacted—all in the same way, and with equal diligence and energy, as if the same incursions were meditated or committed within its own territory, against its own citizens.

It shall not be lawful, under any pretext whatever, for any inhabitant of the United States to purchase or acquire any Mexican, or any foreigner residing in Mexico, who may have been captured by Indians inhabiting the territory of either of the two republics, nor to purchase or acquire horses, mules, cattle, or property of any kind, stolen within Mexican territory by such Indians.

And in the event of any person or persons, captured within Mexican territory by Indians, being carried into the territory of the United States, the government of the latter engages and binds itself, in the most solemn manner, so soon as it shall know of such captives being within its territory, and shall be able so to do, through the faithful exercise of its influence and power, to rescue them and return them to their country, or deliver them to the agent or representative of the Mexican government. The Mexican authorities will, as far as practicable, give to the government of the United States notice of such captures; and its agent shall pay the expenses incurred in the maintenance and transmission of the rescued captives; who, in the mean time, shall be treated with the utmost hospitality by the American authorities at the place where they may be. But if the government of the United States, before receiving such notice from Mexico, should obtain intelligence, through any other channel, of the existence of Mexican captives within its territory, it will proceed forthwith to effect their release and delivery to the Mexican agent as above stipulated.

For the purpose of giving to these stipulations the fullest possible efficacy, thereby affording the security and redress demanded by their true spirit and intent, the government of the United States will now and hereafter pass, without unnecessary delay, and always vigilantly enforce, such laws as the nature of the subject may require. And finally, the sacredness of this obligation shall never be lost sight of by the said government when providing for the removal of the Indians from any portion of the said territories, or for its being settled by citizens of the United States; but, on the contrary, special care shall then be taken not to place its Indian occupants under the necessity of seeking new homes, by committing those invasions which the United States have solemnly obliged themselves to restrain.

ARTICLE XII.

In consideration of the extension acquired by the boundaries of the United States, as defined in the fifth article of the present treaty, the government of the United States engages to pay to that of the Mexican republic the sum of fifteen millions of dollars.

Immediately after this treaty shall have been duly ratified by the government of the Mexican republic, the sum of three millions of dollars shall be paid to the said government by that of the United States, at the city of Mexico, in the gold or silver coin of Mexico. The remaining twelve millions of dollars shall be paid at the same place, and in the same coin, in annual instalments of three millions of dollars each, together with interest on the same at the rate of six per centum per annum. This interest shall begin to run upon the whole sum of twelve millions from the day of the ratification of the present treaty by the Mexican government, and the first of the instalments shall be paid at the expiration of one year from the same day. Together with each annual instalment, as it falls due, the whole interest accruing on such instalment from the beginning shall also be paid.

ARTICLE XIII.

The United States engage, moreover, to assume and pay to the claimants all the amounts now due them, and those hereafter to become due, by reason of the claims already liquidated and decided against the Mexican republic, under the conventions between the two republics severally concluded on the eleventh day of April, eighteen hundred and thirty-nine, and on the thirtieth day of January, eighteen hundred and forty-three: so that the Mexican republic shall be absolutely exempt, for the future, from all expense whatever on account of the said claims.

ARTICLE XIV.

The United States do furthermore discharge the Mexican republic from all claims of citizens of the United States not heretofore decided against the Mexican government, which may have arisen previously to the date of the signature of this treaty; which discharge shall be final and perpetual, whether the said claims be rejected or be allowed by the board of commissioners provided for in the following article, and whatever shall be the total amount of those allowed.

ARTICLE XV.

The United States, exonerating Mexico from demands on account of the claims of their citizens mentioned in the preceding article, and considering them entirely and forever cancelled, whatever their amount may be, undertake to make satisfaction for the same, to an amount not exceeding three and one quarter millions of dollars. To ascertain the validity and amount of those claims, a board of commissioners shall be established by the government of the United States, whose awards shall be final and conclusive; provided, that in deciding upon the validity of each claim, the board shall be guided and governed by the principles and rules of decision prescribed by the first and fifth articles of the unratified convention, concluded at the city of Mexico on the twentieth day of November, one thousand eight hundred and forty-three; and in no case shall an award be made in favor of any claim not embraced by these principles and rules.

If, in the opinion of the said board of commissioners, or of the claimants, any books, records, or documents in the possession or power of the government of the Mexican republic, shall be deemed necessary to the just decision of any claim, the commissioners, or the claimants through them, shall, within such period as Congress may designate, make an application in writing for the same, addressed to the Mexican minister for foreign affairs, to be transmitted by the secretary of state of the United States; and the Mexican government engages, at the earliest possible moment after the receipt of such demand, to cause any of the books, records, or documents, so specified, which shall be in their possession or power, (or authenticated copies or extracts of the same,) to be transmitted to the said secretary of state, who shall immediately deliver them over to the said board of commissioners: *Provided*, That no such application shall be made by, or at the instance of, any claimant, until the facts which it is expected to prove by such books, records, or documents, shall have been stated under oath or affirmation.

ARTICLE XVI.

Each of the contracting parties reserves to itself the entire right to fortify whatever point within its territory it may judge proper so to fortify for its security.

ARTICLE XVII.

The treaty of amity, commerce, and navigation, concluded at the city of Mexico on the fifth day of April, A. D. 1831, between the United States of America and the United Mexican States, except the additional article, and except so far as the stipulations of the said treaty may be incompatible with any stipulation contained in the present treaty, is hereby revived for the period of eight years from the day of the exchange of ratifications of this treaty, with the same force and virtue as if incorporated therein, it being understood that each of the contracting parties reserves to itself the right, at any time after the said period of eight years shall have expired, to terminate the same by giving one year's notice of such intention to the other party.

ARTICLE XVIII.

All supplies whatever for troops of the United States in Mexico, arriving at ports in the occupation of such troops previous to the final evacuation thereof, although subsequently to the restoration of the custom-houses at such ports, shall be entirely exempt from duties and charges of any kind; the government of the United States hereby engaging and pledging its faith to establish, and vigilantly to enforce, all possible guards for securing the revenue of Mexico, by preventing the importation, under cover of this stipulation, of any articles other than such, both in kind and quantity, as shall really be wanted for the use and consumption of the forces of the United States during the time they may remain in Mexico. To this end it shall be the duty of all officers and agents of the United States to denounce to the Mexican authorities at the respective ports any attempts at a fraudulent abuse of this stipulation which they may know of, or may have reason to suspect, and to give to such authorities all the aid in their power with regard thereto; and every such attempt, when duly proved and established by sentence of a competent tribunal, shall be punished by the confiscation of the property so attempted to be fraudulently introduced.

ARTICLE XIX.

With respect to all merchandise, effects, and property whatsoever, imported into ports of Mexico whilst in the occupation of the forces of the United States, whether by citizens of either republic, or by citizens or subjects of any neutral nation, the following rules shall be observed:

1. All such merchandise, effects, and property, if imported previously to the restoration of the custom-houses to the Mexican authorities, as stipulated for in the third article of this treaty, shall be exempt from confiscation, although the importation of the same be prohibited by the Mexican tariff.

2. The same perfect exemption shall be enjoyed by all such merchandise, effects, and property, imported subsequently to the restoration of the custom-houses, and previously to the sixty days fixed in the following article for the coming into force of the Mexican tariff at such ports respectively; the said merchandise, effects, and property being, however, at the time of their importation, subject to the payment of duties, as provided for in the said following article.

3. All merchandise, effects, and property, described in the two rules foregoing, shall, during their continuance at the place of importation, and upon their leaving such place for the interior, be exempt from all duty, tax, or impost of every kind, under whatsoever title or denomination. Nor shall they be there subjected to any charge whatsoever upon the sale thereof.

4. All merchandise, effects, and property, described in the first and second rules, which shall have been removed to any place in the interior whilst such place was in the occupation of the forces of the United States, shall, during their continuance therein, be exempt from all tax upon the sale or consumption thereof, and from every kind of impost or contribution, under whatsoever title or denomination.

5. But if any merchandise, effects, or property, described in the first and second rules, shall be removed to any place not occupied at the time by the forces of the United States, they shall, upon their introduction into such place, or upon their sale or consumption there, be subject to the same duties which, under the Mexican laws, they would be required to pay in such cases if they had been imported in time of peace, through the maritime custom-houses, and had there paid the duties conformably with the Mexican tariff.

6. The owners of all merchandise, effects, or property, described in the first and second rules, and existing in any port of Mexico, shall have the right to reship the same, exempt from all tax impost, or contribution whatever.

With respect to the metals, or other property, exported from any Mexican port whilst in the occupation of the forces of the United States, and previously to the restoration of the custom-house at such port, no person shall be required by the Mexican authorities, whether general or state, to pay any tax, duty, or contribution upon any such exportation, or in any manner to account for the same to the said authorities.

ARTICLE XX.

Through consideration for the interests of commerce generally, it is agreed, that if less than sixty days should elapse between the date of the signature of this treaty and the restoration of the custom-houses, conformably with the stipulation in the third article, in such case all merchandise, effects, and property whatsoever, arriving at the Mexican ports after the restoration of the said custom-houses, and previously to the expiration of sixty days after the day of the signature of this treaty, shall be admitted to entry; and no other duties shall be levied thereon than the duties established by the tariff found in force at such custom-houses at the time of the restoration of the same. And to all such merchandise, effects, and property, the rules established by the preceding article shall apply.

ARTICLE XXI.

If unhappily any disagreement should hereafter arise between the governments of the two republics, whether with respect to the interpretation of any stipulation in this treaty, or with respect to any other particular concerning the political or commercial relations of the two nations, the said governments, in the name of those nations, do promise to each other that they will endeavor, in the most sincere and earnest manner, to settle the differences so arising, and to preserve the state of peace and friendship in which the two countries are now placing themselves; using, for this end, mutual representations and pacific negotiations. And if, by these means, they should not be enabled to come to an agreement, a resort shall not, on this account, be had to reprisals, aggression, or hostility of any kind, by the one republic against the other, until the government of that which deems itself aggrieved shall have maturely considered, in the spirit of peace and good neighborship, whether it would not be better that such difference should be settled by the arbitration of commissioners appointed on each side, or by that of a friendly nation.

And should such course be proposed by either party, it shall be acceded to by the other, unless deemed by it altogether incompatible with the nature of the difference, or the circumstances of the case.

ARTICLE XXII.

If (which is not to be expected, and which God forbid!) war shall unhappily break out between the two republics, they do now, with a view to such calamity, solemnly pledge themselves to each other and to the world, to observe the following rules: absolutely, where the nature of the subject permits, and as closely as possible in all cases where such absolute observance shall be impossible.

1. The merchants of either republic then residing in the other, shall be allowed to remain twelve months (for those dwelling in the interior), and six months (for those dwelling at the seaports), to collect their debts and settle their affairs; during which periods they shall enjoy the same protection, and be on the same footing, in all respects, as the citizens or subjects of the most friendly nations; and, at the expiration thereof, or at any time before, they shall have full liberty to depart, carrying off all their effects without molestation or hinderance: conforming therein to the same laws which the citizens or subjects of the most friendly nations are required to conform to. Upon the entrance of the armies of either nation into the territories of the other, women and children, ecclesiastics, scholars of every faculty, cultivators of the earth, merchants, artisans, manufacturers, and fishermen, unarmed and inhabiting the unfortified towns, villages, or places, and in general all persons whose occupations are for the common subsistence and benefit of mankind, shall be allowed to continue their respective employments unmolested in their persons. Nor shall their houses or goods be burnt or otherwise destroyed, nor their cattle taken, nor their fields wasted, by the armed force into whose power, by the events of war, they may happen to fall; but if the necessity arise to take any thing from them for the use of such armed force, the same shall be paid for at an equitable price. All churches, hospitals, schools, colleges, libraries, and other establishments, for charitable and beneficent purposes, shall be respected, and all persons connected with the same protected in the discharge of their duties, and the pursuit of their vocations.

2. In order that the fate of prisoners of war may be alleviated, all such practices as those of sending them into distant, inclement, or unwholesome districts, or crowding them into close and noxious places, shall be studiously avoided. They shall not be confined in dungeons, prison-ships, or prisons; nor be put in irons, or bound, or otherwise restrained in the use of their limbs. The officers shall enjoy liberty on their paroles, within convenient districts, and have comfortable quarters; and the common soldiers shall be disposed in cantonments, open and extensive enough for air and exercise, and lodged in barracks as roomy and good as are provided by the party in whose power they are, for its own troops. But if any officer shall break his parole by leaving the district so assigned him, or any other prisoner shall escape from the limits of his cantonment, after they shall have been designated to him, such individual, officer, or other prisoner, shall forfeit so much of the benefit of this article as provides for his liberty on parole or in cantonment. And if any officer so breaking his parole, or any common soldier so escaping from the limits assigned him, shall afterwards be found in arms, previously to his being regularly exchanged, the person so offending shall be dealt with according to the established laws of war. The officers shall be daily furnished by the party in whose power they are, with as many rations, and of the same articles, as are allowed, either in kind or by commutation, to officers of equal rank in its own army; and all others shall be daily furnished with such ration as is allowed to a common soldier in its own service: the value of all which supplies shall, at the close of the war, or at periods to be agreed upon between the respective commanders, be paid by the other party, on a mutual adjustment of accounts for the subsistence of prisoners; and such accounts shall not be mingled with or set off against any others, nor the balance due on them be withheld as a compensation or reprisal for any cause whatever, real or pretended. Each party shall be allowed to keep a commissary of prisoners, appointed by itself, with every cantonment of prisoners in possession of the other; which commissary shall see the prisoners as often

as he pleases; shall be allowed to receive, exempt from all duties or taxes, and to distribute whatever comforts may be sent to them by their friends; and shall be free to transmit his reports in open letters to the party by whom he is employed.

And it is declared that neither the pretence that war dissolves all treaties, nor any other whatever, shall be considered as annulling or suspending the solemn covenant contained in this article. On the contrary, the state of war is precisely that for which it is provided, and during which its stipulations are to be as sacredly observed as the most acknowledged obligations under the law of nature or nations.

ARTICLE XXIII.

This treaty shall be ratified by the president of the United States of America, by and with the advice and consent of the Senate thereof; and by the president of the Mexican republic, with the previous approbation of its general Congress; and the ratification shall be exchanged in the city of Washington, or at the seat of government of Mexico, in four months from the date of the signature hereof, or sooner if practicable.

In faith whereof, we, the respective plenipotentiaries have signed this treaty of peace, friendship, limits, and settlement; and have hereunto affixed our seals respectively. Done in quintuplicate, at the city of Guadaloupe Hidalgo, on the second day of February, in the year of our Lord one thousand eight hundred and forty-eight.

N. P. TRIST, [L. S.]
LUIS G. CUEVAS, [L. S.]
BERNARDO CONTO, [L. S.]
MIGL. ATRISTAIN, [L. S.]

And whereas the said treaty, as amended, has been duly ratified on both parts, and the respective ratifications of the same were exchanged at Queretaro, on the thirtieth day of May last, by Ambrose H. Sevier and Nathan Clifford, commissioners on the part of the government of the United States, and by Señor Don Luis de la Rosa, minister of relations of the Mexican republic on the part of that government:

Now, therefore, be it known, that I, James K. Polk, president of the United States of America, have caused the said treaty to be made public, to the end that the same, and every clause and article thereof, may be observed and fulfilled with good faith by the United States and the citizens thereof.

In witness whereof, I have hereunto set my hand and caused the seal of the United States to be affixed.

Done at the city of Washington, this fourth day of July, one thousand eight hundred [L. S.] and forty-eight, and of the Independence of the United States the seventy-third.

JAMES K. POLK.

By the president:

James Buchanan, Secretary of State.

CHAPTER VII.

1849-1853.

TAYLOR'S AND FILLMORE'S ADMINISTRATION.

Inauguration of Zachary Taylor—Ceremonies connected with it—His Inaugural address—General Taylor's cabinet—State of politics—Dispute as to the boundary between Texas and New Mexico—Steps taken by the president—His health injured—The thirty-first Congress—Contest for the speakership—The president's message—Excitement growing out of the slavery question—Special message on California and New Mexico—Henry Clay's compromise resolutions—Excitement on the subject—Calhoun's speech—His death—Webster's speech—Select committee of thirteen—Henry Clay's report—The "omnibus bill"—Debates and troubles in the south-west—General Taylor's illness and death—Millard Fillmore president—His cabinet—Message on Texas and New Mexico difficulties—The compromise measures carried—Result of this legislation—The seventh census—"Filibustering" expeditions against Cuba—The president's proclamation—Lopez's expeditions and their results—Union meetings—Second session of the thirty-first Congress—Substance of Mr. Fillmore's first message—Discussions in Congress—Bills passed—The Hungarian question—Webster's letter to Chevalier Hulsemann—Kossuth in the United States—State of affairs—The first Grinnell expedition—The Greytown affair—Henry Clay's death—The fishery question—The democratic and whig national conventions—Pierce and King nominated—Scott and Graham nominated—The Garay grant question—Congress adjourns—Daniel Webster's death—The presidential election—The tripartite convention—Extracts from Mr. Everett's letter—Congress in session—Abstract of the message—Action of Congress—Close of Mr. Fillmore's administration.

ON Monday, March 5th, 1849, Zachary Taylor, the war-worn hero, appeared before his fellow-citizens congregated in Washington, for the purpose of giving solemn pledges of his devotion to the duties of the high office to which he had been called by the voice of his countrymen. As usual on these occasions, there was a vast concourse of people, and the civic display was both admirably arranged and thoroughly carried out. About midday, dressed in a plain suit of black, and with befitting gravity and dignity, Zachary Taylor joined the grand procession of Senators and distinguished members of the government, and took his place on the staging erected in front of the great portico of the capitol. There, in the presence of some twenty thousand people, he delivered his Inaugural address, a brief, plain, sensible document, such as might have been expected from the man who had been more accustomed to the sword than the pen, and who had displayed qualities of mind and heart which commended him to the majority of his fellow-citizens as the one whom they preferred at that day to take the helm of state.

1849.

The brevity of General Taylor's Inaugural will authorize our giving it in full, and we are sure that it will be perused with interest by our readers.

"Elected by the American people to the highest office known to our laws, I appear here to take the oath prescribed by the Constitution, and, in compliance with a time-honored custom, to address those who are now assembled.

"The confidence and respect shown by my countrymen, in calling me to be the chief magistrate of a republic holding a high rank among the nations of the earth, have inspired me with feelings of the most profound gratitude; but, when I reflect that the acceptance of the office which their partiality has bestowed imposes the discharge of the most arduous duties, involves the most weighty obligations, I am conscious that the position which I have been called to fill, though sufficient to satisfy the loftiest ambition, is surrounded by fearful responsibilities.

"Happily, however, in the performance of my new duties I shall not be without able co-operation. The legislative and judicial branches of the government present prominent examples of distinguished civil attainments and matured experience, and it shall be my endeavor to call to my assistance, in the executive departments, individuals whose talents, integrity, and purity of character, will furnish ample guarantees for the faithful and honorable performance of the trusts to be committed to their charge. With such aids, and an honest purpose to do whatever is right, I hope to execute diligently, impartially, and for the best interests of the country, the manifold duties devolved upon me.

1849.

"In the discharge of these duties, my guide will be the Constitution which I this day swear to 'preserve, protect, and defend.' For the interpretation of that instrument, I shall look to the decisions of the judicial tribunals established by its authority, and to the practice of the government under the earlier presidents, who had so large a share in its formation. To the example of those illustrious patriots I shall always defer with reverence, and especially to his example who was by so many titles 'the father of his country.'

"To command the army and navy of the United States—with the advice and consent of the Senate to make treaties and to appoint ambassadors and other officers—to give to Congress information of the state of the Union, and recommend such measures as he shall judge to be necessary, and to take care that the laws shall be faithfully executed—these are the most important functions intrusted to the president by the Constitution; and it may be expected that I shall briefly indicate the principles which will control me in their execution.

"Chosen by the body of the people, under the assurance that my administration would be devoted to the welfare of the whole country, and not to the support of any particular section or merely local interest, I this day renew the declaration I have heretofore made, and proclaim my fixed determination to maintain, to the extent of my ability, the government in its original purity, and to adopt as the basis of my public policy, those great republican doctrines which constitute the strength of our national existence.

"In reference to the army and navy, lately employed with so much distinction on active service, care shall be taken to insure the highest condition of efficiency; and, in furtherance of that object, the military and naval schools sustained by the liberality of Congress, shall receive the special attention of the executive.

"As American freemen we can not but sympathize in all efforts to extend the blessings of civil and political liberty, but at the same time we are warned by the admonition of history, and the voice of our own beloved Washington, to abstain from entangling alliances with foreign nations. In all disputes between conflicting governments, it is our interest not less than our duty to remain strictly neutral, while our geographical position, the genius of our institutions and our people, the advancing spirit of civilization, and, above all, the dictates of religion, direct us to the cultivation of peaceful and friendly relations with all

1849. other powers. It is to be hoped that no international question can now arise which a government, confident in its own strength, and resolved to protect its own just rights, may not settle by wise negotiation; and it eminently becomes a government like our own, founded on the morality and intelligence of its citizens, and upheld by their affections, to exhaust every resort of honorable diplomacy before appealing to arms. In the conduct of our foreign relations, I shall conform to these views, as I believe them essential to the best interests and true honor of the country.

"The appointing power vested in the president imposes delicate and onerous duties. So far as it is possible to be informed, I shall make honesty, capacity, and fidelity, indispensable prerequisites to the disposal of office, and the absence of either of these qualities shall be deemed sufficient cause for removal.

"It shall be my study to recommend such constitutional measures to Congress as may be necessary and proper to secure encouragement and protection to the great interests of agriculture, commerce, and manufactures, to improve our rivers and harbors, to provide for the speedy extinguishment of the public debt, to enforce a strict accountability on the part of all officers of the government, and the utmost economy in all public expenditures. But it is for the wisdom of Congress itself, in which all legislative powers are vested by the Constitution, to regulate these and other matters of domestic policy. I shall look with confidence to the enlightened patriotism of that body to adopt such measures of conciliation as may harmonize conflicting interests, and tend to perpetuate that Union, which should be the paramount object of our hopes and affections. In any action calculated to promote an object so near the heart of every one who truly loves his country, I will zealously unite with the coordinate branches of the government.

"In conclusion, I congratulate you, my fellow-citizens, upon the high state of prosperity to which the goodness of Divine Providence has conducted our common country. Let us invoke a continuance of the same protecting care which has led us from small beginnings to the eminence we this day occupy; and let us seek to deserve **1849.** that continuance by prudence and moderation in our councils; by well-directed attempts to assuage the bitterness which too often marks unavoidable differences of opinion; by the promulgation and practice of just and liberal principles, and by an enlarged patriotism which shall acknowledge no limits but those of our own wide-spread republic."

The oath of office was then administered by Chief-Justice Taney, and the twelfth president of the United States retired from the scene, to receive the congratulations of thousands and to enter thenceforward upon the onerous duties of his lofty station. The Senate being in session, the president, on the 6th of March, 1849, sent in the following names of the gentlemen selected as his cabinet, and they were confirmed, without difficulty, the next day. John M. Clayton, was appointed secretary of state; William M. Meredith, secretary of the treasury; George W. Crawford, secretary of war; William B. Preston, secretary of the navy; Thomas Ewing, secretary of the interior; Jacob Collamer, postmaster-general; and Reverdy Johnson, attorney-general. The department of the interior, charged with the care of the land office, Indian affairs, patent office, census office, public buildings, etc., added another member to the cabinet, and was organized, as previously noted (p. 460,) just before the adjournment of the last Congress.* The extra session of the Senate closed on the 21st of March.

Notwithstanding General Taylor's personal popularity, it soon became evident that there was about to be a majority in both Houses of Congress opposed to his administration; and from the tone and temper of the opposition press, as well as the dissatisfaction caused by the removal of democrats from office, and the appointment of whigs in their places, the president and his cabinet had reason to look forward to the approaching meeting of Congress with no little anxiety and concern. The position, also, of California and New Mexico, for which the attempt to provide territorial governments had failed, (p. 459,) and the dispute stirred up by the claim on the part of Texas to jurisdiction over quite a large portion of New Mexico, demanded attention, and caused the administration considerable annoyance and vexation. The president took such steps as seemed to be needed in the emergency; he sent Mr. T. B. King, of Georgia, as bearer of dispatches to California, and certain officers to California and New Mexico; and in the latter he kept a force in order to preserve tranquility until the boundary question between Texas and New Mexico could be settled by action of Congress. General Taylor likewise appointed a governor and other officers for the new territory of Oregon; and measures were taken to complete the coast survey on the Pacific shores of the United States.*

The rapidly increasing importance of

* At this extra session of the Senate, General Shields presented himself as Senator elect from Illinois. His seat was contested on the ground of his not having been a naturalized citizen for the term of nine years. The committee appointed to inquire into his eligibility, reported that the election was void, because General Shields had not been a citizen for the term of years required. The Senate adopted the view of the committee, and the seat was declared vacant. The legislature of Illinois, however, re-elected him, and he took his seat at the opening of the next Congress.

* See Senator Benton's interesting speech on the coast survey, in his "*Thirty Years' View*," vol. ii., pp. 726-29.

California and the gold region, caused a large increase of duty to the president, and anxious consideration on his part how best to protect the emigrants flocking thither, and how to sustain, properly and effectually, the authority of the United States in a region which had no settled government of any kind as yet provided for it. The intense application to public business began to tell upon the president's health, and the effect of the new cares and responsibilities he had assumed, was becoming evident as the summer passed away and the time for the opening of Congress approached.*

The thirty-first Congress began its first session on the 3d of December, 1849, and the contest for the speakership of the House, and the other offices, immediately commenced. Two hundred and twenty-three out of two hundred and thirty-one members of the House answered to their names, and as, according to the list which was given by the newspapers, there were a hundred and twelve democrats, a hundred and five whigs, and thirteen free-soilers, it was evident that there would be a sharp battle before a speaker could be elected. And from that day, day after day for nearly three weeks, the members of the House wasted the time which belonged to the people in balloting and speech-making about filling the vacant chair. Mr. Cobb, of Georgia, and Mr. Winthrop, of Massachusetts, were the respective democratic and whig candidates, and either of them would have proved satisfactory to the country as speaker of the House. At last, on the 22d of December, the question was settled by a resolution that, as Mr. Cobb had received a plurality vote, he should be declared duly elected speaker; and the House was accordingly organized for the discharge of its proper duties.

The president's message was sent in on the 24th of December, and read to both Houses. It proved to be a plain, clearly written paper, and not nearly so long as several of those which issued from General Taylor's predecessors. Its recommendations were characterized by good sense and moderation; and there ran through it a vein of earnest and sincere devotion to the best interests of our country. "For more than half a century," said the president, in conclusion, "during which kingdoms and empires have fallen, this Union has stood unshaken. The patriots who formed it have long since descended into the grave; yet still it remains, the proudest monument to their memory, and the object of affection and admiration with every one worthy to bear the American name. In my judgment, its dissolution would be the greatest of calamities; and to avert that should be the study of every American. Upon its preservation must depend our happiness and that of countless generations to come. Whatever dangers may threaten it, I shall stand by it and maintain it in its integrity to the full extent of the obligations imposed and the power conferred upon me by the Constitution."

1849.

The exciting topics of former years,

* On the 12th of August, 1849, the venerable statesman and financier, Albert Gallatin, died in the village of Astoria, New York. Mr. Gallatin was in the eighty-ninth year of his age.

as the tariff, internal improvements, and the like, having in great measure been put to rest, the attention of the country was devoted almost entirely to the aspects of the slavery question, growing out of the vast increase of territory gained by the Mexican war. The south, naturally enough, rejoiced in the acquisition of Texas,* and the enlargement of the area out of which new slave states might be formed, and it was also sanguine in the expectation that New Mexico and California might be included in the same category. The north, on the other hand, while yielding to the necessity of Texas being under the influence and guidance of slaveholders, was earnest in seeking to prevent the spread of what it deemed a great evil and stain upon our national escutcheon; and as it became more and more probable that slavery would be excluded from California and New Mexico, the north could not but exult in the prospect, and also urge in Congress measures calculated to depress southern power and influence in our Pacific possessions.

On the 21st of January, 1850, the president sent in to the House a special message in relation to California and New Mexico, in which he stated, that

1850. he had advised the people of those regions to form state constitutions, and to apply for admission into the Union. He also spoke of the Texas boundary difficulty, and stated, that the people in the western part of California had formed a constitution, the consideration of which was recommended to Congress.* Senator Foote of Mississippi, a few days previously, (January 16th) had brought forward a bill to provide a territorial government for California, Deseret, and New Mexico, and to enable the people of Jacinto, with the assent of Texas, to provide a constitution and state government, and for the admission of such state into the Union. The subject came up as the order of the day, on the 22d, and gave rise to considerable debate. On the 29th of January, Henry Clay brought forward a series of eight resolutions, by which he hoped to provide a basis of compromise for the firm and lasting settlement of the slavery question. His plan in substance was, to admit California as a state; to form territorial governments in other parts of the territory acquired from Mexico; to fix the boundary of Texas and New Mexico; to propose to Texas to pay off her debt contracted previous to annexation to the United States; to declare it inexpedient to abolish slavery in the District of Columbia, while it exists in Maryland, without the consent of the people of the state and the district, and without compensating the slave-owners in the district; to declare it expedient to prohibit the slave trade in the District of Columbia; to make more effectual provision for the recovery of fugi-

* We may mention here, that Justice Story opposed, in every way consistent with his judicial station, the annexation of Texas, which he considered, says his son, a violation of the Constitution, in spirit at least, and a bold attempt to extend the evils of slavery. See "*Life and Letters of Joseph Story,*" vol. ii., pp. 508–15.

* Deseret was the name adopted by the inhabitants for the new state; it was subsequently organized as a territory under the name of Utah.

H Clay

tive slaves; and to affirm that Congress has no power to hinder the trade in slaves between the slave-holding states.

Mr. Clay, venerable for his years and a long life devoted to public service, undertook, on the 5th of February, an elaborate defence of the plan of compromise which he had wrought out. In earnest and affecting terms, he besought the Senate to listen to his appeals; he denounced secession in vigorous language, and graphically painted the terrible evils which would flow from a dissolution of the Union. His speech excited much attention, and its sentiments were approved by a large portion of the people. On the 13th of February, the president transmitted to Congress the state constitution which had been adopted by the people of California, in a convention held for that purpose; but that youthful and vigorous state did not then, as was hoped, receive admission into the Union. The debate

1850. continued, and the excitement on the points at issue spread more widely and deeply throughout the country.

John C. Calhoun, like his compeer, Henry Clay, advanced in years, but unlike him in other respects, greatly reduced in health and strength, brought into the Senate, on the 14th of March, a carefully prepared written speech, which, as he was too weak to deliver it, was read by Mr. Mason of Virginia. He took entirely opposite ground from that of Mr. Clay, and as was to be expected from him and his well-known views on the subject of southern rights and claims, he advocated the dissolution of the Union, and gave it as his settled opinion, that the course of the north was so aggressive and unjust as fully to authorize this last resort. However undoubted were Mr. Calhoun's integrity and sincerity, his views met with but little favor, even among southern state rights men; and it was impossible that his scheme for settling existing difficulties could be agreed upon by the American people. We may mention here, that the great South Carolina Senator ended his career a few weeks later. His strength sank rapidly from this date, and on the 31st of March he was called away from earth to his final account. Nearly three-score years and ten at the time of his death, Mr. Calhoun had spent the larger part of his life in the service of his country; and however unacceptable a large portion of his views must ever be to the majority of his countrymen, there is no one who can doubt his uprightness, his purity of private life, his vast intellectual force and energy, and his earnest wish to promote the welfare of the United States.*

Daniel Webster also, on the 17th of March, gave utterance to his views on the questions under debate; and in terms which we regret we have not room to quote, he scorned the very name of secession as an act of foul treachery and depravity. Mr. Webster was willing to do any thing that was right in order to mitigate the evils of slavery; but, as he emphatically declared, secession would be, must be,

* The Works of John C. Calhoun have been collected and published in six volumes, which the student of history will find it of value and importance to consult and study.

revolution. Mr. Seward of New York, and other Senators, took part in this exciting debate.

Toward the close of February, Mr. Foote of Mississippi moved, that the subject of territorial governments for California, Utah, and New Mexico, be referred to a select committee of thirteen, with instructions to endeavor to effect a compromise upon all the vexed questions then arising out of the institution of slavery. Mr. Foote's resolution was debated from time to time, but was not disposed of till the 18th of April, when it was adopted by a vote of thirty to twenty-two. The compromise resolutions of Mr. Clay, and also others which had been offered by Mr. Bell, of Tennessee, were referred to this same committee, which was composed of six northern and six southern members, and a thirteenth, the chairman, chosen by the other twelve. Mr. Clay was elected chairman of this committee.

1850.

On the 8th of May, Mr. Clay, in behalf of the select committee, brought in a report of a plan of compromise, which, it was hoped, would allay existing excitement. A series of bills was presented—more generally known as the "omnibus bill"—to admit California as a state, to establish territorial governments for Utah and New Mexico, to pay Texas a sum of money sufficient to satisfy her on the subject of her boundary, to provide for the recovery of fugitive slaves,* and to abolish the slave trade in the District of Columbia.

Long and wearisome debates and disputes followed, for week after week, to little or no purpose, and by the beginning of August it was found, that the omnibus bill could not be carried in its present shape.* Important events meanwhile had transpired. The Nashville convention of the supporters of slavery met, early in June, and notwithstanding at one time it seemed to threaten serious consequences, it eventually dispersed without leading to any difficulty. Its propositions for settling the troubles then agitating the country were neither new nor important. Texas, too, had taken lofty ground, and presumed to enter upon such a course as would lead to a settlement of the boundary question with New Mexico, on terms entirely acceptable to herself. That, however, could not for a moment be thought of, and the president took measures to see that the laws should be faithfully carried out in the section of country in dispute.

1850.

In the midst of this excitement, the national holiday was again observed, and General Taylor participated in it, like every good citizen; but within less than five days he quietly sank to his rest. On the 9th of July, 1850, Zachary Taylor died, in the sixty-sixth year of his age, and before he had had opportunity to develop his plans and purposes as president of the United States. The lamentations for his death were

* Senator Benton delivered himself of an elaborate speech against Mr. Clay's plan of slavery compromise, from which copious extracts are given in the "*Thirty Years' View*," vol. ii., pp. 749–65.

* For a long and able review of the debate on the compromise bills, delivered in the Senate, July 22d, 1850, see "*The Life, Correspondence, and Speeches of Henry Clay*," vol. vi., pp. 529–67.

wide spread and sincerely expressed, and the honors heaped upon his memory demonstrated that, whatever difference of political sentiment may exist among us, no one doubted that General Taylor was an honest, patriotic lover of his country, and one who would have discharged the duties of his lofty station with sincere and earnest zeal and unimpeachable integrity.

Millard Fillmore, on the 10th of July, addressed a brief but touching message to both Houses of Congress, formally announcing the afflictive dispensation which had raised him to the presidential chair, and recommending suitable honors to be paid to the distinguished dead. Mr. Fillmore took the required oath the same day; the funeral was celebrated on the 13th; Mr. W. R. King was chosen president *pro tempore* of the Senate; and the cabinet having resigned, others were immediately appointed in their places, Daniel Webster being secretary of state;* and thus, without disturbance or difficulty, the new president was as firmly seated as if he had been placed in his high office directly by the popular vote.

1850.

On the 6th of August, the president communicated to the House a message respecting the boundary question between Texas and New Mexico. He also sent in a copy of Mr. Webster's reply, on the 5th, to Governor Bell's letter, in which he complained of the course pursued by Colonel Monroe in New Mexico. The letter of Mr. Webster is clear and to the point, and while it disclaims all interference on the part of the United States in matters out of the province of the executive, it still asserts, in the plainest terms, the determination of the president to sustain the laws and rights of New Mexico as well as Texas, until the matter be settled by action of Congress. A brief paragraph of this letter may not inaptly be here quoted: "In one of his last communications to Congress,—that of the 17th of June last,—the late president repeated the declaration that he had no power to decide the question of boundary, and no desire to interfere with it; and that the authority to settle that question resided elsewhere. The object of the executive government has been, as I believe, and as I am authorized to say it certainly now is, to secure the peace of the country; to maintain, as far as practicable, the state of things as it existed at the date of the treaty; and to uphold and preserve the rights of the respective parties as they were under the solemn guarantee of the treaty, until the highly interesting question of boundary should be finally settled by competent authority. This treaty, which is now a supreme law of the land, declares, as before stated, that the inhabitants shall be maintained and protected in the free enjoyment of their liberty and property, and secured in the free exercise of their religion. It will, of course, be the president's duty to see that this law is sustained, and the protection which it guarantees made effectual—and this is

1850.

* Thomas Corwin was appointed secretary of the treasury; C. M. Conrad, secretary of war; W. A. Graham, secretary of the navy; Alexander H. H. Stuart, secretary of the interior; N. K. Hall, postmaster-general; and J. J. Crittenden, attorney-general.

the plain and open path of executive duty, in which he proposes to tread."

During the month of August, the various measures of compromise contained in the "omnibus bill" were carried, separately, through Congress, and received in September the approbation of President Fillmore.* Early in August, the boundary between Texas and New Mexico was finally settled upon, Texas to receive $10,000,000 in consideration of relinquishment of her claims against the United States. On the 13th, the bill to admit California as a state passed the Senate by a vote of thirty-four to eighteen; on the 15th, a bill was passed to establish a territorial government for New Mexico; and on the 18th of September, a fugitive slave bill, and a bill for the suppression of the slave trade in the District of Columbia, also passed the Senate by large majorities. By the constitution of California, slavery was prohibited in that state; in New Mexico and Utah, the question was left open for future decision. Messrs. W. M. Gwinn and J. C. Fremont, Senators elect from California, immediately thereafter appeared and took their seats in the great council of the nation.

In this wise, so far as legislation was concerned, the bitter strife over the Wilmot proviso came to a pause; and it was hoped, by all true lovers of their country, that discord would now end in respect to that interminable, unceasing source of contention—the slavery question. But we are sorry to say, that the strife did not cease, and, so far as human eyes can penetrate the veil of the future, is not likely to cease for many long years to come. "The complex, cumbersome, expensive, annoying, and ineffective bill," as Senator Benton designates the fugitive slave law of 1850, gave satisfaction to neither party. The north was irritated and vexed with the mode pursued in the recovery of fugitive slaves, and with the odiousness of the whole matter, as it was now presented before their eyes; the south, on the other hand, was chagrined and exasperated to find that the difficulty of getting back their slaves was rather increased than otherwise by this new act, and that disturbances were sure to follow, and the law sure to become odious, and, consequently, next to impossible to be executed.* In fact, without claiming any special sagacity, we may assert, that, on this subject, our country has, as yet, hardly reached the beginning of the end.

The other acts of the session were not of material moment to be placed on record here; various appropriations

* Mr. Benton points out the fact that the southern Senators considered the *test* question to be upon the admission of California as a state into the Union. He also gives the protest which ten members signed and wished to have entered on the Journal, together with his remarks upon it, its final rejection, etc.

* Early in 1851, no little excitement was created by the rescue at Boston of a fugitive slave, arrested in accordance with the law recently passed. A mob of persons, mainly colored, rushed into the room where the alleged fugitive was in custody of the officers, and carried him off. Soon after which it was understood he had reached Canada. Intelligence of this affair was telegraphed to Washington, and the president, on the 18th of February, issued a proclamation, announcing his determination to enforce the laws promptly and thoroughly. He also the next day sent a message to the Senate on the same subject, in which the whole matter was fully discussed.

were made; the vessels offered by Mr. Henry Grinnell, of New York, to be sent in search of Sir John Franklin, were accepted and attached to the navy; the rank and file of the army were increased; etc. It was not till the 30th of September, 1850, after a session of over three hundred days, that Congress adjourned. We may note, that this was the longest session of the national legislature which had been held since the organization of the government.

The results of the seventh census, taken this year, were substantially as follows. Total white population, 19,557,271; free colored, 429,710; slaves, 3,204,093. The population of the free states was, 13,434,559. The free population of the slave states was, 6,412,151; showing a *decrease* of 778,568 since 1840; whilst the free states had in the same period increased 3,779,933, i. e., rather more than half the entire population of the slave states. The grand total of the population of the United States, in 1850, was 23,191,074. In the new apportionment of Representatives, the free states gained one, making their number a hundred and forty-three; and the slave states lost one, reducing their number to ninety.

1850.

The position of the beautiful Island of Cuba, and its contiguity to the United States, have naturally caused it to be looked upon with no ordinary interest by our countrymen; and partly from good motives, and partly from the restlessness and cupidity of a large number of Americans, manifold plans and schemes have been talked of, and attempted to be carried out, so as to incorporate Cuba into the possessions of the United States. Spain, on her part, ever jealous of her powerful neighbor, has exercised great rigor in endeavoring to maintain her authority intact, and to prevent the "filibustering" schemes and plots of those who have been ready, in past years, to do all in their power to wrest this fertile island from Spain. Some notice of the piratical expeditions against Cuba, in 1850 and 1851, seems to be necessary in this part of our narrative. We shall give the facts as succinctly as possible.

An impression having got abroad that the Cubans themselves were ready for revolt, efforts began to be made, in 1849, to get materials for an expedition thither, from the ports of the United States. General Taylor, at that time president, issued a proclamation, on the 11th of August, in the following terms: "There is reason to believe, that an armed expedition is about to be fitted out in the United States with an intention to invade the Island of Cuba, or some of the provinces of Mexico. The best information which the executive has been able to obtain, points to the Island of Cuba as the object of this expedition. It is the duty of this government to observe the faith of treaties, and to prevent any aggression by our citizens upon the territories of friendly nations. I have, therefore, thought it necessary and proper to issue this proclamation, to warn all citizens of the United States, who shall connect themselves with an enterprise so grossly in violation of our laws and our treaty obligations, that they will thereby subject themselves to the heavy penalties denounced against them by our acts of Congress; and will forfeit their claim to the protection of their country. No such persons must expect the interference of this government, in any form, in their behalf, no matter to what extremities they may be reduced in consequence of their conduct. An enterprise to invade the territories of a friendly nation, set on foot and prosecuted within the limits of the United States, is, in the highest degree, criminal, as tending to endanger the peace and compromit the honor of this nation; and, therefore, I exhort all good citizens, as they regard our national reputation, as they respect their own laws and the laws of nations, as they value the blessings of peace and the welfare of their country, to discountenance and prevent, by all lawful means, any such enterprise; and I call upon every officer of this government, civil or military, to use all efforts in his power to arrest, for trial or punishment, every such offender against the laws providing for the performance of our sacred obligations to friendly powers."

Preparations, however, for the expedition went on, and a military organization was effected at New Orleans, under a Cuban leader, named Narcisso Lopez. About the middle of

1850.

May, the filibusters set out, under the guise of emigrants, in vessels bound for Chagres. Lopez and his company, about six hundred in number, landed at Cardenas on the 18th of May, where he issued a bombastic proclamation, but met with no encouragement. On the contrary, the people rose against the invaders, and Lopez, after a bloody skirmish, burning the governor's house, seizing some bags of specie, re-embarked in the steamer, Creole. His men insisted on being carried to Key West, where, just as they arrived, the Spanish war steamer Pizarro, overtook them. The Spanish commander demanded the restoration of the stolen money, and the persons of the invaders, but did not obtain either from the American authorities; on his return he took from the Island of Contoy, on the coast of Yucatan, (which was Lopez's place of rendezvous) a hundred men, and carried them to Cuba. The naval force which had been dispatched by the president, unfortunately arrived too late to prevent Lopez's invasion; and the Spanish governor-general was strongly minded to put them all to death as pirates.

Lopez immediately began to plot afresh, and found many to encourage him in his schemes against Cuba. General Quitman and others were indicted at New Orleans, in July, by the grand jury, as concerned in setting on foot an unlawful expedition, and the general was arrested, on the 3d of February, 1851, on this charge; he was not, however, convicted, although by many, believed to be guilty. At a later date, in April, J. O. Sullivan, Captain Rogers of the Cleopatra, and others, were arrested at New York, and the vessel which they had procured was seized by the authorities. On the 25th of April, President Fillmore issued his proclamation, in which he expressed the conviction, that the expedition

1851.

against Cuba was instigated "chiefly by foreigners, who dare to make our shores the scene of their guilty and hostile preparations against a friendly power, and who seek by falsehood and misrepresentation to seduce our citizens, especially the young and inconsiderate, into their wicked schemes." And he goes on to say, that, "whereas such expeditions can only be regarded as adventures for plunder and robbery, and must meet the condemnation of the civilized world, while they are derogatory to the character of our country, in violation of the laws of nations, and expressly prohibited by our own;" he exhorts all good citizens, and all honest men, to discountenance and frown upon every effort of the kind, as a blot upon our good name, and as certain to result in loss and disgrace.

The restless Cuban leader, favored by circumstances, escaped the watchfulness of the government, and on the 3d of August, sailed from New Orleans in the steamer Pampero. His present company numbered more than four hundred men. On the 11th, he arrived off the coast of Cuba, in sight of Havana, and turning westwardly, he advanced a few miles beyond Bahia Honda, where the steamer ran aground on a coral reef. Lopez debarked on the Island of Playtas with all his troops, and advanced inland with three hundred men. Colonel Crittenden, his chief officer, was left with the remainder, and, preparing to join Lopez, was attacked by a large force and routed. With difficulty, he escaped to the coast, and putting out to sea in boats, he and his party of some fifty men, were taken on the 15th, carried into Havana, condemned to die, and on the 16th, were shot. Lopez having advanced inland about ten miles, was attacked at Las Posas by eight hundred Spanish troops under General Enna. A sanguinary contest ensued, in which numbers of the enemy were killed, with severe loss on his own side. Lopez retreated towards the mountains, followed by the Spaniards in force; and **1851.** ere long his men were made prisoners, he was hunted by bloodhounds, and, carried to Havana a prisoner, was garroted as a malefactor, on the 26th of August. The Spanish authorities did not proceed to extremities with the other prisoners; about a hundred were sent to Spain; and in 1852, on the intercession of our government, they were released and allowed to return to the United States.*

During the month of November, large public meetings were held in various parts of the country to give expression to the attachment of the people to the Union, and also to throw the weight of all conservative citizens in favor of the measures of compromise adopted by Congress. Philadelphia, Boston, Cincinnati, Nashville, and other cities and towns, witnessed the efforts of patriotic lovers of their country to induce the people to hold fast by the Union at all hazards; and letters from Clay, Webster, Cass, Poinsett, and others, were published in favor of the same great end. On the other hand, in various parts of the south, the spirit of disunion was rife; and such men as

* During Mr. Polk's administration, an offer was made to purchase the Island of Cuba from Spain, for $100,000,000; but that government refused to entertain any proposition on the subject.

General James Hamilton and others who agreed with him, urged upon South Carolina to bide her time on this subject.

The thirty-first Congress began its second session on the 2d of December, 1850, and received on the same day, the first annual message of President Fillmore. This well-written document commenced with a touching allusion to the afflictive event which had removed General Taylor from his lofty position, and very properly embraced the opportunity to give expression to the views entertained by the executive on the great questions of public policy in our country. In clear, decided terms, Mr. Fillmore avowed his devotion to the Constitution, and his determination to see that the laws be faithfully executed, and declared, that it would be his aim ever to exercise the appointing power with wisdom and impartiality. The foreign relations of the country, he announced, were in a good condition, and the United States were at peace with all the world. The Nicaraugua and Tehuantepec routes to the Pacific Ocean were spoken of, as were also our relations with Chili, Peru, and the Hawaiian Islands. The total receipts into the treasury, for the year ending June 30th, 1850, were $47,422, 000. Total expenditures for the year, a little over $43,000,000. The public debt was reduced nearly $500,000; and about $8,000,000 of the public debt were to be provided for within two years.

1850.

In discussing the tariff question, the president spoke out his opinions with great freedom. "All experience," he said, "has demonstrated the wisdom and policy of raising a large portion of revenue for the support of the government from duties on goods imported. The power to lay these duties is unquestionable, and its chief object, of course, is to replenish the treasury. But if, in doing this, an incidental advantage may be gained by encouraging the industry of our own citizens, it is our duty to avail ourselves of that advantage. . . . . A high tariff never can be permanent. . . . . . All duties should be specific, wherever the nature of the article is such as to admit of it. *Ad valorem* duties fluctuate with the price, and offer strong temptations to fraud and perjury. Specific duties, on the contrary, are equal and uniform in all ports, and at all times, and offer a strong inducement to the importer to bring the best article, as he pays no more duty upon that than upon one of inferior quality." An agricultural bureau was also recommended; and a good deal of space was devoted to Indian affairs, the army and navy, the post-office department, etc. The number of post-offices in the United States was stated to be, 18,417, and the rates of postage were recommended to be reduced. On the question of internal improvements, the president expressed his sentiments without disguise, holding it as certain, that Congress possessed power to make such improvements, and commending various works to their approval.

In speaking of the compromise, which had occupied so large a share of the attention of Congress, the president said: "It was hardly to have been expected that the series of measures passed at your last session, with the view of healing the sectional differences which had sprung from the slavery and territorial questions, should at once have realized their beneficent purpose. All mutual concession in the nature of a compromise must necessarily be unwelcome to men of extreme opinions; and though without such concessions our Constitution could not have been formed, and cannot permanently be sustained, yet we have seen them made the subject of bitter controversy in both sections of the republic. It required many months of discussion and deliberation to secure the concurrence of a majority of Congress in their favor. It would be strange if they had been received with immediate approbation by the people and states prejudiced and heated by the exciting controversies of their Representatives. . . . . The series of measures to which I have alluded are regarded by me as a settlement, in principle and substance—a final settlement—of the dangerous and exciting subjects which they embrace. . . . . . By that adjustment we have been rescued from the wide and boundless agitation that surrounded us, and have a firm, distinct, and legal ground to rest upon. And the occasion, I trust, will justify me in exhorting my countrymen to rally upon and maintain that ground, as the best, if not the only means of restoring peace and quiet to the country, and maintaining inviolate the integrity of the Union." With a manly and Christian-like recognition of the manifold blessings of God showered upon our country, the president concluded his message in these words: "While deeply penetrated with gratitude for the past, let us hope that His all-wise providence will so guide our counsels as that they shall result in giving satisfaction to our constituents, securing the peace of the country, and adding new strength to the united government under which we live."

1850.

The annual reports of the heads of the departments were transmitted to Congress along with the president's message. They contain elaborate and carefully digested statements of the condition and wants of the various branches of the public service, and are well worthy the examination of the student of our civil and political history. The secretary of war reported the entire army enrolled, officers and men, as twelve thousand three hundred and twenty-six. The secretary of the navy stated, that there were seven ships of the line, one razee, twelve frigates, twenty-one sloops of war, four brigs, two schooners, six steam-frigates, nine other steamers, and five store ships, besides a number of ships on the stocks. The secretary of the interior presented a large variety of very interesting matter connected with the public land sales, bounty lands, etc.; he also recommended the establishment of an agricultural bureau, and urged the necessity of a highway to the Pacific, either railway or turnpike, as careful investigation of the country might show to be most advisable.

The present session of Congress was occupied in discussing various topics of interest and inportance; but so much time was wasted in this way, that many important bills, which were matured by the committees of the two Houses, remained to be acted upon during the last few weeks of the session. A number of measures of interest to the public failed, some through want of time and pressure of business, some through violent opposition of a sectional character. The majority of the House passed a bill making appropriations on a liberal scale for the improvement of rivers and harbors; but it was defeated in the Senate by a party trick, on the very last night of the session. The democratic party mostly followed the views set forth by Mr. Polk in his veto message on this subject, (Dec., 1847). A joint resolution, creating the grade of lieutenant-general in the army, intended as a deserved honor for General Scott, also failed of obtaining the approbation of Congress.

1850.

The more important bills passed, were, the civil and diplomatic appropriation bill; the army and navy appropriation bill; a bill for erecting light-houses; an act reducing postage on letters to three cents on any distance under three thousand miles; etc. Acts were also passed respecting private land claims in California; establishing a military asylum; appointing the regents of the Smithsonian Institution; authorizing the president to send a government vessel to bring Kossuth and other Hungarian exiles to the United States; etc.*

1851.

It was during the presidency of General Taylor, while the Hungarian contest was pending, that Mr. A. Dudley Mann was dispatched to Vienna, with instructions to watch the progress of the struggle, and in case of its success, to recognize the Hungarian Republic. The Austrian chargé d'affaires, at Washington, Chevalier Hulsemann, on this becoming known to his government, was instructed to protest against the course pursued by the United States, as unwarrantable interference in Austrian concerns. Mr. Hulsemann did so, under date of September 30th, and took occasion to lecture the secretary of state in pretty severe terms. Mr. Webster's reply was delayed from various causes until the 21st of December, when he entered upon the subject with hearty good will, and sent the Austrian chargé such an answer as he was not likely soon to forget. We wish that our limits admitted of quoting this admirable letter in full; we can only give an extract or two as specimens of the tone and temper of the United States government on the topic under consideration.

1850.

"The government and people of the United States, like other intelligent governments and communities, take a lively interest in the movements and the events of this remarkable

* Public necessity having demanded additional accommodations at Washington, an appropriation was made at this session to extend the capitol according to such plan as might be approved by the president. Having adopted a plan by which the original building would be more than doubled in size, by the addition of two extensive wings, the work was immediately commenced. The corner-stone was laid by the president, on the 4th of July, amid a large concourse of citizens, and Daniel Webster gave utterance on the occasion to some noble and patriotic thoughts worthy of his great name and the country he had so long served. See Webster's "*Life and Works*," vol. ii., pp. 595–620.

age, in whatever part of the world they may be exhibited. But the interest taken by the United States in those events has not proceeded from any disposition to depart from that neutrality towards foreign powers which is among the deepest principles and the most cherished traditions of the political history of the Union. It has been the necessary effect of the unexampled character of the events themselves, which could not fail to arrest the attention of the contemporary world, as they will doubtless fill a memorable page in history. But the undersigned goes further, and freely admits, that in proportion as these extraordinary events appeared to have their origin in those
1850. great ideas of responsible and popular governments on which the American constitutions themselves are wholly founded, they could not but command the warm sympathy of the people of this country. Well-known circumstances in their history—indeed their whole history—have made them the representatives of purely popular principles of government. In this light they now stand before the world. They could not, if they would, conceal their character, their condition, or their destiny. They could not, if they so desired, shut out from the view of mankind the causes which have placed them, in so short a national career, in the station which they now hold among the civilized states of the world. They could not, if they desired it, suppress either the thoughts or the hopes which arise in men's minds, in other countries, from contemplating their successful example of free government. . . . .

The power of this republic at the present moment is spread over a region one of the richest and most fertile on the globe, and of an extent in comparison with which the possessions of the house of Hapsburg are but as a patch on the earth's surface. Its population — already twenty-five millions — will exceed that of the Austrian empire within the period during which it may be hoped that Mr. Hulsemann may yet remain in the honorable discharge of his duties to his government. Its navigation and commerce are hardly exceeded by the oldest and most commercial nations; its maritime means and its maritime power may be seen by Austria herself in all seas where she has ports, as well as it may be seen, also, in all other quarters of the globe. Life, liberty, property, and all personal rights, are amply secured to all citizens, and protected by just and stable laws; and credit, public and private, is as well established as in any government of continental Europe. And the country, in all its interests and concerns, partakes most largely in all the improvements and progress which distinguish the age. Certainly the United States may be pardoned, even by those who profess adherence to the principles of absolute governments, if they entertain an ardent affection for those popular forms of political organization which have so rapidly ad- 1850.
vanced their own prosperity and happiness, and enabled them in so short a period to bring their country and the hemisphere to which it belongs to the notice and respectful regard—not to say the admiration—of the civilized

world. Nevertheless, the United States have abstained at all times from acts of interference with the political changes of Europe. They cannot, however, fail to cherish always a lively interest in the fortunes of nations struggling for institutions like their own. But this sympathy, so far from being necessarily a hostile feeling towards any of the parties to these great national struggles, is quite consistent with amicable relations with them all. The Hungarian people are three or four times as numerous as the inhabitants of these United States were when the American Revolution broke out. They possess, in a distinct language, and in other respects, important elements of a separate nationality, which the Anglo-Saxon race in this country did not possess. And if the United States wish success to countries contending for popular constitutions and national independence, it is only because they regard such constitutions and such national independence not as imaginary, but as real blessings. They claim no right, however, to take part in the struggles of foreign powers in order to promote these ends. It is only in defence of his own government and its principles and character that the undersigned has now expressed himself on this subject. But when the United States behold the people of foreign countries, without any such interference, spontaneously moving towards the adoption of institutions like their own, it surely cannot be expected of them to remain wholly indifferent spectators.

. . . . . .

Towards the conclusion of his note, Mr. Hulsemann remarks, that 'if the government of the United States were to think it proper to take an indirect part in the political movements of Europe, American policy would be exposed to acts of retaliation, and to certain inconveniences, which would not fail to affect the commerce and the industry of the two hemispheres.' As to this possible fortune, this hypothetical retaliation, the government and people of the United States are quite willing to take their chances, and abide their destiny. Taking neither a direct nor an indirect part in the domestic or intestine movements of Europe, they have no fear of events of the nature alluded to by Mr. Hulsemann. It would be idle now to discuss with Mr. Hulsemann those acts of retaliation which he imagines may possibly take place at some indefinite time hereafter. Those questions will be discussed when they arise; and Mr. Hulsemann and the cabinet at Vienna may rest assured that, in the meantime, while performing with strict and exact fidelity all their neutral duties, nothing will deter either the government or the people of the United States from exercising, at their own discretion, the rights belonging to them as an independent nation, and of forming and expressing their own opinions, freely and at all times, upon the great political events which may transpire among the civilized nations of the earth."

1850.

In connection with this able letter of Daniel Webster, we may mention, that at the close of the following year, 1851, Louis Kossuth, the famous Magyar chief, arrived in the United States.

The popular voice was loudly raised in his favor; the people every where listened to his impassioned appeals, with strong feelings of sympathy; 1851. he was received with public and civic honors in the cities and towns through which he passed; liberal subscriptions in money were made in support of the cause which he represented; and so far as the expression of general interest went in behalf of the struggling Hungarians, our countrymen seemed to be all in readiness to march at once to the aid of the oppressed and to set them free from the iron rule of Austria; but, as Kossuth was compelled to learn, these were the free and unrestrained outpourings of the people's sympathy and good-will; they were not indicative of the course which the government felt bound to pursue. However warmly, as individual citizens, the president and his advisers,* as well as the members of Congress, were moved to sympathize in behalf of Hungary and her efforts to gain her independence, they could not, as administering the government, take any part whatever in Kossuth's movements. The uniform policy of the United States has been, to form no "entangling alliances" with European states or people; and hence Kossuth was obliged to make the best use he could of what was really in his reach, and to give up all expectation of aid from the government of our country. Having had contributed towards the Hungarian cause about $100,000, Kossuth left the United States for England, in May, 1852.

During the summer of 1851, state conventions were held, and measures were taken by the respective parties to influence the coming elections; the results in the autumn showed a considerable gain to the democratic side, but did not afford much indication as to the presidential struggle of the next year.* The journals of the day pointed out the alarming increase of crime, and attributed it, no doubt correctly, to the fact that a very large number of emigrants had come to our shores during the past year. The proportion of native offenders to those of foreign birth was not one-fifth; and the alms-house statistics presented a similar large increase of foreigners, which had been dispatched to the United States from England and Ireland principally. 1851. The accounts from California, however, threw every thing else into the shade. There, it became a war to the knife between the citizens and organized gangs of desperadoes and villains; and for a period anarchy prevailed, and the "committee of vigilance" took the law and the settlement of matters into their own hands.†

* Mr. Hulsemann undertook to complain of Mr. Webster's having attended at a dinner given to Kossuth in Washington, and having also expressed his warm sympathy with Hungary in her struggles for liberty; and soon after left the United States. The secretary of state, in June, 1852, addressed a letter to Mr. M'Curdy, the American minister to Austria, in which he set forth rather fully the petulant and improper conduct of the bellicose Chevalier.

* The historian of the American navy, and a writer of great and varied powers, J. Fenimore Cooper, died on the 14th of September, 1851.

† As a matter of curious interest, it may be mentioned here, that, from February, 1848, to May, 1852, eleven thousand nine hundred and fifty-three Chinese emigrants arrived at San Francisco; seven only of this number were women.

Early in August, a treaty was arranged and signed with the Sioux Indians, who agreed to cede to the United States twenty millions of acres in Minnesota, reserving to themselves a tract in Upper Minnesota, about a hundred by twenty miles in extent. They were to receive some $300,000 after their removal to their reservation, and an annual payment of $68,000 for the term of fifty years.

In October, the vessels under command of Lieutenant De Haven, of the navy, furnished by the munificence of Mr. Henry Grinnell, of New York, (p. 481,) to aid in the search for the missing Sir John Franklin, arrived in safety at New York. They had been gone a year and a half, and had earnestly prosecuted the object of their mission, but we regret to say, with no satisfactory result.* Dr. E. K. Kane, who accompanied the expedition as surgeon, was not willing to give up all hopes, and principally through his exertions and his noble spirit of courage and enthusiasm, a new expedition was afterwards set on foot to proceed to the Arctic regions. On a subsequent page we shall speak of the issue of this last undertaking.

In November, 1851, an unpleasant event occurred, which might have led to serious consequences between the United States and England. It appears, that the American steamer Prometheus, the property of the "American Atlantic and Pacific Ship Canal Company," having on board some five hundred passengers, being about to leave the harbor of San Juan de Nicaragua, or Greytown, was boarded by a police force, and served with a process of attachment on the ship and captain, for certain charges claimed as port dues, which the captain refused to pay. Immediately upon this, the English brig of war Express, lying in the harbor, got under weigh, made sail for the steamer, and when within a quarter of a mile of her, fired a shot over her forecastle, and a few minutes afterwards, another over her stern, which passed in close proximity to the steamer. On being asked the cause of this remarkable course, the captain of the brig replied, that it was to protect the authorities of Greytown in their demands; that, if the steamer did not immediately anchor, he would fire a bombshell into her; and he ordered his guns to be loaded with grape and canister shot. The steamer then proceeded to the anchorage and anchored, the brig taking a place near by. The captain of the Prometheus paid the dues, under protest, and was allowed to proceed on his way. Happily for the good understanding of both parties, the British government promptly disavowed the proceeding of the commander of the Express, as an act of violence, and in direct contravention of existing treaty engagements.

The first session of the thirty-second Congress was commenced on the 1st of December, and Mr. Linn Boyd, of Kentucky, was elected speaker. The president's message was received the next day, and presented a clear and detailed

* See "*The U. S. Grinnell Expedition in search of Sir John Franklin.*" A Personal Narrative. By Elisha Kent Kane, M. D. New York, pp. 552, 8vo.

account of public affairs. Mr. Fillmore avowed his determination to enforce the laws of the United States, in all cases, and not to allow of interference in the concerns of foreign nations, so as to endanger the peace of the
1851. country. The receipts into the treasury during the year, amounted to $52,312,979. The expenditures had been, $48,600,000. About $7,500,000 had been paid on account of the public debt, which, on the 20th of November, was $62,500,000. The estimated receipts for the next fiscal year, were, $51,800,000; and the estimated expenditures were, $43,000,000. Various important recommendations, on the subject of the tariff, internal improvements, protection of the frontiers, an agricultural bureau, etc., were urged upon Congress; and Mr. Fillmore again gave it as his settled opinion, that the compromise measures of 1850 ought to be adhered to by all good citizens.

On the 17th of December, Henry Clay addressed a letter to the General Assembly of Kentucky, resigning his seat in the Senate, to take effect in September, 1852. His health was manifestly failing, and the aged servant of his country felt, that it was time to retire and prepare for the final event which could not be far distant. As in the case of Calhoun, he died at his post. A severe and protracted illness had resulted, as all perceived that it must result; and Henry Clay, with the devotion of a Christian, and trusting to the hopes and promises of the
1852. Gospel, peacefully expired on Tuesday, June 29th, 1852. It needs not here, that we should tell of the public honors heaped upon his memory by an affectionate and weeping country. His name is indelibly written upon the pages of his native land's history, and so long as the republic lasts, the warm-hearted, the noble-spirited, the patriotic Henry Clay, will be held up to the admiration and love of our countrymen.

Certain difficulties having sprung up on the subject of the fisheries off the coast of British America, the president felt it his duty to take prompt measures to see that the rights of our hardy seamen, engaged in this branch of industry, were not infringed upon. The British foreign secretary, Sir John Pakington, gave certain directions to the naval forces on the station, which materially restricted the privileges heretofore enjoyed by our fishermen, and which it was held in the United States were in contravention of the terms of the treaty. The subject excited considerable discussion in the Senate, in July, and the president was called upon for the correspondence, papers, etc., relative to the whole matter. Mr. Webster's great and varied ability was employed on this subject, and a voluminous correspondence ensued, the result of which has been, the arranging a reciprocity treaty with the British colonies in North America, (in 1854,) and a mutually satisfactory adjustment of the fishery question.

On the 1st of June, the democratic national convention assembled at Baltimore, to make choice of candidates for the presidency and vice-presidency. The names of General Cass, Mr. Buchanan, Mr. Douglas, Mr. Marcy, and others, were before the convention; nearly three hundred delegates were present; a vehement struggle ensued; the balloting was kept up for four days; which resulted finally, on the forty-ninth ballot, in the nomination of Franklin Pierce, of New Hampshire, and W. R. King, of Alabama, as the democratic candidates for the two highest offices in the gift of the people. A series of resolutions was adopted, denouncing all attempts at renewing the agitation of the slavery question, and setting forth the determination to "abide by, and adhere to, a faithful execution of the acts known as the compromise measures, settled by the last Congress,—the act reclaiming fugitives from service or labor included."

On the 16th of June, the delegates of the whig national convention met in Baltimore, to the number of some three hundred. Beside the name of Mr. Fillmore, there were those of General Scott and Daniel Webster before the members of the convention; and no wonder it was hard to select the man whom the party and the country would most fully approve. Resolutions defining the views of the whig party on the various great questions at issue, assenting entirely to the compromise measures, including the fugitive slave law, and deprecating all renewal of agitation on this latter topic, were

1852. adopted by a large vote; and the balloting began. On the fifty-third ballot, General Winfield Scott, was nominated for president; and William A. Graham, of North Carolina, was placed on the same ticket for vice-president.

"The free-soilers" held a convention at Pittsburg, in August, and had also several candidates; but with little division of sentiment, they nominated John P. Hale, of New Hampshire, for president, and George W. Julian, of Indiana, for vice-president.

Congress, after an unusually long session, adjourned on the 31st of August. On the day before the adjournment, Mr. Mason, of Virginia, in the Senate, made a report on the subject of the Garay grant, for the right of way across the Isthmus of Tehuantepec. This grant was made to Don José de Garay, in March, 1842, by Santa Anna, and confirmed, at different times, by others in authority. Garay sold out his right, in 1846, to two Englishmen; and the grant, in 1848, was assigned to Mr. Hargous, a citizen of the United States. Work was commenced on the route across the isthmus; but the Mexican government forbad further steps, in 1851. The question now was, what course ought the United States to pursue; and the report went into the question very fully. Senator Benton, in 1852, wrote a letter, reviewing this subject, and condemning any action on the part of the government in favor of enforcing this grant. The letter is well worth reading.

A considerable amount of public business was transacted during the session, the more important of which we have already indicated. Other acts of the session were, the voting an amendment to the deficiency bill, making an additional appropriation of $25,000 for each trip to the Collins's line of steamers; considerably reducing the rates of postage on printed matter; making

Daniel Webster

large appropriations for the improvement of rivers and harbors in various sections of the country; granting aid to the state of Michigan in constructing a ship canal around the Sault St. Marie; etc. The French spoliation bill, and other measures of importance, were postponed until the next session.

Before entering upon the active and earnestly contested election, the people were again called upon to mourn for the removal of the great and noble compatriot of Henry Clay. It was in the summer of 1852, that Mr. Webster left Washington, being far from well at the time, and betook himself to the retirement and repose of his farm at Marshfield. Unfortunately, he soon after met with a severe injury by being thrown from a wagon. His health continued to fail more and more perceptibly, until, on the 21st of October, his illness was seen to be very dangerous, and the sad conviction forced itself upon his friends and the whole country, that he was on his death-bed. On Sunday morning, October 24th, a little before three o'clock, his mortal career reached its close. Like the father of his country—like the illustrious patriot who, only a few months before, had preceded him to the grave—Daniel Webster was not afraid to die, for his last hours were illumined by the light which the Gospel of our Blessed Saviour has cast upon the tomb, and he was, as we believe, enabled to lay fast hold upon the consolations and hopes of the humble, penitent, and faithful Christian. Words of eulogy we need not utter. His fame is imperishable. His renown, as the greatest of American orators, and among the greatest of American statesmen, is graven in broad characters upon the history of the United States; and we are confident, that his is a name which will grow brighter, and be loved more and more, as years roll on, and as it becomes more plainly evident what a life-time of service he gave to the highest and best interests of our common country.*

1852.

The presidential election, in November, called forth the most earnest and active efforts of both parties; sanguine hopes of success were entertained by the whigs as well as the democrats; but the result proved the strength and efficiency of the organization of the democratic party, and Franklin Pierce was elected president by an unusually large majority, whether counted by the the popular or the electoral votes.

Some months before Mr. Webster's death, the ministers of England and France had been directed to invite the government of the United States, to become party to a tripartite convention, in virtue of which the three powers should severally and collectively disclaim, now and for the future, all intention to obtain possession of the Island of Cuba, as well as to discountenance all attempts of a similar kind by any power whatever. In July, Mr. Crampton addressed a letter to Mr. Webster on the subject, urging the views of his government as to this matter; and the Comte de Sartiges, in

1852.

* For an eloquent and worthy tribute to the departed statesman and patriot, see the Hon. Rufus Choate's "Discourse delivered before the Faculty, Students, and Alumni of Dartmouth College, on the 27th of July, 1853, commemorative of DANIEL WEBSTER."

behalf of France, entirely accorded with the sentiments of Mr. Crampton's letter. "This will, it is hoped, facilitate the adoption by the government of the United States of the project, and enable the government of the United States, by associating themselves with those of Great Britain and France in this important declaration, to secure the future tranquility of the commerce of the world in those seas, to discourage illegal enterprises against Cuba, and to draw closer the bonds of amity which bind the United States to Great Britain, as well as to France and Spain."

Mr. Webster's failing health prevented his giving due attention to this communication, and his death occurring not long after, the president asked Mr. Edward Everett to undertake the duties of secretary of state, which he did. Under date of the 1st of December, Mr. Everett addressed to the Comte de Sartiges a long and very able letter, setting forth the views entertained by our government in respect to this difficult and delicate topic. An extract or two from this letter may properly here be presented.

"The president fully concurs with his predecessors, who have on more than one occasion authorized the declaration referred to by M. de Turgot and Lord Malmesbury, that the United States could not see with indifference the Island of Cuba fall into the possession of any other European government than Spain; not, however, because we should be dissatisfied with any natural
1852. increase of territory and power on the part of France or England. France has, within twenty years, acquired a vast domain on the northern coast of Africa, with a fair prospect of indefinite extension. England, within half a century, has added very extensively to her empire. These acquisitions have created no uneasiness on the part of the United States. In like manner, the United States have, within the same period, greatly increased their territory. The largest addition was that of Louisiana, which was purchased from France. These accessions of territory have probably caused no uneasiness to the great European powers, as they have been brought about by the operation of natural causes, and without any disturbance of the international relations of the principal states. They have been followed, also, by a great increase of mutually beneficial commercial intercourse between the United States and Europe. But the case would be different in reference to the transfer of Cuba from Spain to any other European power. That event could not take place without a serious derangement of the international system now existing; and it would indicate designs in reference to this hemisphere, which could not but awaken alarm in the United States.

. . . .

But the president has a graver objection to entering into the proposed convention. He has no wish to disguise the feeling that the compact, although equal in its terms, would be very unequal in substance. France and England, by entering into it, would disable themselves from obtaining possession of an island remote fom their seats of government, belonging to another European power, whose natural right to possess it must always be as good as their own—a distant island in another hemisphere, and one which by no ordinary or peaceful course of things could ever belong to either of them. If 1852. the present balance of power in Europe should be broken up, if Spain should become unable to maintain the island in her possession, and France and England should be engaged in a death struggle with each other, Cuba might then be the prize of the victor. Till these events all take place, the president does not see how Cuba can belong to any European power but Spain. The United States, on the other hand, would, by the proposed convention, disable themselves from making an acquisition which might take place without any disturbance of existing foreign relations, and in the natural order of things. The Island of Cuba lies at our doors. It commands the approach to the Gulf of Mexico, which washes the shores of five of our states. It bars the entrance of that great river which drains half the North American continent, and with its tributaries forms the largest system of internal water communication in the world. It keeps watch at the doorway of our intercourse with California by the Isthmus route. If an island like Cuba, belonging to the Spanish crown, guarded the entrance of the Thames and the Seine, and the United States should propose a convention like this to France and England, those powers would assuredly feel that the disability assumed by ourselves was far less serious than that which we asked them to assume. The opinions of American statesmen at different times, and under varying circumstances, have differed as to the desirableness of the acquisition of Cuba by the United States. Territorially and commercially it would, in our hands, be an extremely valuable possession. Under certain contingencies it might be almost 1852. essential to our safety. Still, for domestic reasons, on which, in a communication of this kind, it might not be proper to dwell, the president thinks that the incorporation of the island into the Union at the present time, although effected with the consent of Spain, would be a hazardous measure; and he would consider its acquisition by force, except in a just war with Spain, (should an event so greatly to be deprecated take place,) as a disgrace to the civilization of the age.

. . . .

Spain, meantime, has retained of her extensive dominions in this hemisphere, but the two Islands of Cuba and Porto Rico. A respectful sympathy for the fortunes of an ancient ally and a gallant people, with whom the United States have ever maintained the most friendly relations, would, if no other reason existed, make it our duty to leave her in the undisturbed possession of this little remnant of her mighty transatlantic empire. The president desires to do so; no word or deed of his will ever question her title, or shake her possession. But can it be expected to last very long? Can it resist this mighty current in the fortunes of the world? Is it desirable that it should do so? Can it be for the interest of Spain to cling to a possession that can only be maintained by a garrison of twenty-five or thirty thousand troops, a powerful naval force, and an annual expenditure for both arms of the service of at least $12,000,000? Cuba, at this moment, costs more to Spain, than the entire naval and military establishment of the United States costs the federal government. So far from being really injured by the loss of this island, there is no doubt that, were it peacefully transferred to the United States, a prosperous commerce between Cuba and Spain, resulting from ancient associations and common language and tastes, would be far more productive than the best contrived system of colonial taxation. Such, notoriously, has been the result to Great Britain of the establishment of the independence of the United States. The decline of Spain from the position which she held in the time of Charles V. is coeval with the foundation of her colonial system; while within twenty-five years, and since the loss of most of her colonies, she has entered upon a course of rapid improvement unknown since the abdication of that emperor.

1852.

. . . .

No administration of this government, however strong in the public confidence in other respects, could stand a day under the odium of having stipulated with the great powers of Europe, that in no future time, under no change of circumstances, by no amicable arrangement with Spain, by no act of lawful war, (should that calamity unfortunately occur,) by no consent of the inhabitants of the island, should they, like the possessions of Spain on the American continent, succeed in rendering themselves independent, in fine, by no overruling necessity of self-preservation, should the United States ever make the acquisition of Cuba.

1852.

For these reasons, which the president has thought it advisable, considering the importance of the subject, to direct me to unfold at some length, he feels constrained to decline respectfully the invitation of France and England to become parties to the proposed convention. He is persuaded, that these friendly powers will not attribute this refusal to any insensibility on his part to the advantages of the utmost harmony between the great maritime states on a subject of such importance. As little will Spain draw any unfavorable inference from this refusal; the rather, as the emphatic disclaimer of any designs against Cuba on the part of this government, contained in the present note, affords all the assurance which the president can constitutionally, or to any useful purpose, give of a practical concurrence with France and England in the wish not to disturb the possession of that island by Spain."

On Monday, the 6th of December, the second session of the thirty-second Congress commenced, and President Fillmore's last annual message was sent in on the same day. In brief but clearly expressed terms, the president laid before the two Houses a statement of the condition of the country, and gave his views of the principal topics of moment, on which he felt bound to speak. With evident propriety, Mr. Fillmore acknowledged, in behalf of our country, the blessings of God's providence during the past year; he alluded, with great feeling, to the lamented decease of Daniel Webster; and proceeded to give the present position of the fishery question between the United States and England. The condition of affairs in regard to Cuba was next spoken of, and the proposition of England and France, for a tripartite convention fully detailed. Having stated, that he had declined becoming a party to this convention, the president went on to say; "Were this island comparatively destitute of inhabitants, or occupied by a kindred race, I should regard it, if voluntarily ceded by Spain, as a most desirable acquisition. But under existing circumstances, I should look upon its incorporation into our Union, as a very hazardous measure. It would bring into the confederacy a population of a different national stock, speaking a different language, and not likely to harmonize with the other members. It would probably affect in a prejudicial manner the industrial interests of the south; and it might revive those conflicts of opinion between the different sections of the country which lately shook the Union to its centre, and which have been so happily compromised."

The subject of the Tehuantepec route (see p. 492); the relations of the United States to various South American powers; the settlement of the question as to the claim of Peru in regard to the Lobos Islands; and the steps taken with reference to the endeavoring to obtain a change in the policy of Japan towards other nations; were succinctly set forth. Having spoken of the burdens imposed upon the department of state, Mr. Fillmore laid before Congress the present condition of the treasury. The receipts for the year were, $49,728,386; the expenditures were, $46,008,000; the balance in the treasury was, $14,632,135. The value of foreign imports during the year was estimated at $207,240,000; the aggregate exports were, $167,066,000, besides $42,507,285 in specie. The subject of the tariff, the Mexican boundary commission, the Indian tribes, etc., were also brought before the two Houses, and the president renewed his recommendations on the various topics of river and harbor improvements, fortifications, and the like.

Having congratulated the national legislature and the country on the success of our policy of non-interference in foreign affairs, and on the manifold blessings which we enjoy, Mr. Fillmore closed his message with modestly claiming, that he had discharged the duties of his responsible post, to the best of his ability, and with a single eye to the public good.

The proceedings of Congress during this, the concluding session, were not of very material moment. In the Senate, there was much animated debate on the whole subject of the foreign policy of the United States. The Clayton-Bulwer treaty (1850) **1852.** was brought up; General Cass had a great deal to say on the subject of the "Monroe doctrine"; Messrs. Seward, Chase, Butler, Mason, Soulé, and others, took part in the discussion; and the country generally was deeply interested in the important questions involved in dispute. Various matters of business occupied the attention of the House, and a number of acts of local interest were passed, together with a great variety of private bills. On the 11th of February, Mr. Mason, from the committee on foreign affairs, submitted a report in regard to the question of the treaty stipulations with Great Britain concerning Central America, in

1853.

which the opinion was expressed in favor of existing British colonial establishments in Central America, but decidedly against her establishing new ones. The Mexican Garay grant was again brought up, but no action was had on the subject. The plan of a railroad from the Mississippi to the Pacific was repeatedly discussed in the Senate, and an amendment was finally adopted to the appropriation bill, authorizing the president to use $150,000 for the expenses of surveys, explorations of the route, etc. A bill was also passed, erecting a new territorial government out of part of Oregon, to be called the Territory of Washington.

On the 3d of March, the session ended, and the thirty-second Congress closed its career. At the same date, the administration of Millard Fillmore was brought to an end, and he retired from the lofty station which he had well and worthily filled for nearly three years. They were years of importance in our history, and we think that it will be admitted by all candid observers, who may have noted the progress of affairs under Mr. Fillmore's presidency, that he maintained the national honor and dignity in intercourse with foreign powers; he was ever the advocate of measures calculated to promote peace, harmony, concord, and attachment to the Union; and in every section of our vast country he received the meed of praise which was justly his due.

CHAPTER VIII.

1853-1857.

FRANKLIN PIERCE'S ADMINISTRATION.

Inauguration of Franklin Pierce — His Inaugural address, cabinet, etc. — Death of Vice-president King — The Mesilla Valley — Dr. Kane's second expedition — Other expeditions — Lord John Russell's reply to Mr. Everett's letter — Case of Kostza — The thirty-third Congress — Substance of the president's message — Senator Douglas's bill — Kansas and Nebraska — Debate in the Senate — The House's course and debate — The Gadsden treaty — Commodore Perry and the Japan expedition — Political movements — Congress in session — Mr. Pierce's vetoes — Colonel Kinney and emigration to the Mosquito coast — Other acts of the session — The Ostend conference — The "American" party — Efforts in New York to suppress intemperance — The Sound dues question — Dr. Kane's return from the Arctic regions — His death — The Resolute sent to England — Apprehension of difficulties with Great Britain — The thirty-fourth Congress — Long contest for the speakership — Substance of the president's message — The Kansas question — Proceedings in the territory — Outbreaks, etc. — Walker and Central America — Some details — Further troubles in Kansas — Efforts of parties there — Disgraceful attack on Mr. Sumner by P. S. Brooks — The democratic, republican, and whig conventions — Candidates nominated — Buchanan and Breckenridge elected president and vice-president — Congress in session — Mr. Pierce's last message — Mr. Benton's review of it — Business of the session, the tariff, etc. — The Dred Scott case — Excitement — Congress adjourns — End of Franklin Pierce's administration. Appendix to Chapter VIII.—Senator Benton's views on the Missouri Compromise, etc. — II. Opinion of the Supreme Court.

The ceremonies connected with the inauguration of the fourteenth president of the United States, were such as are usual on those occasions, and need not to be again specially described. Franklin Pierce, on the 4th of March, 1853, stood up in the presence of a large concourse of his fellow-citizens, and with much dignity and propriety delivered his Inaugural address. It was

1853.

expressed in clear terms, and gave a cheering outline of the spirit and proposed policy of the new administration. It was not too long, and dealt with such topics as are appropriate to the day and the audience. "The policy of my administration," said Mr. Pierce, "will not be controlled by any timid forebodings of evil from expansion. Indeed, it is not to be disguised, that our attitude as a nation, and our position on the globe, render the acquisition of certain possessions, not within our jurisdiction, eminently important for our protection, if not, in the future, essential for our preservation of the rights of commerce and the peace of the world. Should they be obtained, it will be through no grasping spirit, but with a view to obvious national interest and security, and in a manner entirely consistent with the strictest observance of national faith." The new president also took occasion to reiterate, that "the rights, security, and repose of this confederacy, reject the idea of interference or colonization, on this side of the ocean, by any foreign power, beyond present jurisdiction, as utterly inadmissible." In speaking of domestic affairs, Mr. Pierce gave his views on various points, such as, offices held under the government, the grounds of appointment and removal, and the integrity and economy expected of public men by the people; the respective rights and privileges of the federal government and the state governments, in regard to the many difficult and delicate questions which are liable to disturb the harmony and concord of the Union; the compromise measures of 1850, which are regarded as constitutional and unhesitatingly to be carried into effect; etc.

The Inaugural was well received, and seemed to indicate that the new administration was to be conducted on truly national grounds, and to be guided by principles which would commend it and its acts to the consideration and support of the whole country. The oath of office was administered to Mr. Pierce, and he retired from the presence of the crowd with the good wishes of thousands, and with high hopes of a prosperous and successful career.

On the 7th of March, the president sent in to the Senate, then in extra session, the names of the gentlemen whom he had selected for his cabinet. His nominations were immediately con-
1853. firmed. William L. Marcy was made secretary of state; James Guthrie, secretary of the treasury; Robert McClelland, secretary of the interior; Jefferson Davis, secretary of war; James C. Dobbin, secretary of the navy; James Campbell, postmaster-general; Caleb Cushing, attorney-general.

Before the adjournment of the extra session, the Senate entered upon an animated debate respecting Central American affairs (see p. 498). Mr. Clayton, secretary of state under General Taylor, had returned to the Senate, and he immediately undertook an elaborate vindication of the treaty concluded by himself and Mr. Bulwer. He also discussed the Monroe doctrine, and affirmed, that it had never received the sanction of the United States government in any form. This was on the 9th of March; on the 14th, Mr. Mason made a reply, and was followed by Mr. Douglas on the same side. Mr. Clayton, next day, rejoined, and Mr. Douglas took occasion to deliver a long speech on the subject. On the 21st, Mr. Everett eloquently expressed the views which he entertained on the points at issue, and urged peace and forbearance as the true policy of our country, and as the best means of attaining wide spread prosperity and power.

The vice-president, William R. King, who was suffering from a pulmonary disease at the time of his election, went to Havana, in hopes that the genial climate of Cuba might afford him relief. The oath of office was administered to him there, by the United States consul, in accordance with a special act passed for the purpose. Finding no benefit from his visit, Mr. 1853.
King returned to the United States early in April, and died at his plantation in Alabama, on the 18th of April. Mr. Atchison, of Missouri, who had been elected president *pro tempore* of the Senate, was henceforth charged with the duties belonging to the vice-president's office.

A large number of diplomatic appointments was made at an early day. James Buchanan was sent to England; T. H. Seymour, to Russia; Pierre A. Soulé, to Spain;* P. D. Vroom, to Prussia; H. R. Jackson, to Austria; Solon Borland, to Central America; James Gadsden, to Mexico; etc. The mission to France was not filled so speedily as the others; John Y. Mason was, however, sent out in the course of the year.

The Mexican boundary commission, early in the year, assigned the Mesilla Valley (about one hundred and seventy-five miles long by forty broad), to Mexico; whereupon, Governor Lane, of New Mexico, holding that this allotment was wholly wrong, issued a proclamation, and took possession, until the question of boundary should be settled between the United States and Mexico.

1853.

He also called for the aid of the United States troops; but it was not given. The Mexican governor of Chihuahua, published a counter-proclamation, and resisted the action of Governor Lane to the extent of his power. Santa Anna, who was at the time in authority in Mexico, entertained very inimical feelings towards our country; and for a time, serious difficulty seemed likely to grow out of this matter.

On the last day of May, the second expedition under the auspices of Mr. Grinnell (p. 490), to proceed in the search after Sir John Franklin and his party, set sail from New York. It consisted of a single vessel, the Advance, with a company of only seventeen persons, under the command of Dr. Kane. They were supplied with provisions calculated for two years, independent of what they might gain by hunting. Their immediate destination was Smith's Sound, the farthest point to the north that had been reached. Thence, if the ice permitted, they were to push their way into regions hitherto unexplored. If the northern passages were blocked up, they intended to have recourse to dogs, using their boats as sledges, in order to make a thorough exploration of the region, in search of traces of the lost navigators. The result of this adventurous expedition, under the guidance of the noble-hearted commander, we shall take occasion to narrate further on.

1853.

In the present connection, we may mention, that four other expeditions were fitted out, in accordance with the provisions of Congress, (p. 498), for prosecuting explorations and selecting the best route for railroad communication between the Atlantic and Pacific. The first, under Major Stevens, was to proceed from St. Paul, Minnesota, to the Great Bend of the Missouri River, thence to the most available pass in the Rocky Mountains, from the forty-ninth parallel to the head-waters of the Missouri. The second, under Lieutenant Whipple, was to proceed from the Mississippi, along the head waters of the Canadian, across the Rio Peco, entering the valley of the Rio del Norte near Albuquerque, thence through Walker's

* Mr. Soulé, when on his way to Spain, in the autumn, passed through New York. While there, he was waited upon by a number of Cuban exiles, who congratulated him on his appointment. Mr. Soulé replied to their address in strong language, and avowed his determination to do everything in his power which became the interests and dignity of the United States.

Pass in the Rocky Mountains to the Pacific, some where on the coast of southern California. The third, under Captain Gunnison, was to pass through the Rocky Mountains near the head waters of the Rio del Norte, thence westwardly along the Nicollet River of the Great Basin, thence north to the Lake Utah. The fourth was to operate in California, in the region west of the Colorado to the Pacific, examining the passes of the Sierra Nevada, and endeavoring to ascertain the best route between Walker's Pass and the mouth of the Gila, and from that point to the Pacific at San Diego.

The importance of these expeditions the reader need not be told, was very great, and very valuable results were to be expected from the efforts of the parties sent out, in respect to the geography, the soil, the productions, etc., of the vast western possessions of the United States.

As a matter worthy of record, we may state, that the opening of the Industrial Exhibition in the Crystal Palace, New York, took place on the 14th of July. It was attended by the president of the United States, and several members of his cabinet; by the Earl of Ellesmere, Sir Charles Lyell, and other English gentlemen of eminence; and by a large concourse of citizens and visitors. The opening services were impressive and appropriate to the occasion, and the happiest results were looked for from the effects of this exhibition, not only upon our own countrymen, but also upon foreign nations and people.

1853.

On a previous page (p. 493), we have given an account of the tripartite convention proposed by England and France to the United States, with reference to the guaranteeing Cuba to Spain for ever; we have also quoted some passages from Mr. Everett's letter on this subject, in which the reasons are given at length for declining to enter into the proposed convention. In the course of the summer, a letter from Lord John Russell, dated February 16th, 1853, was published in the United States. It was addressed to Mr. Crampton, the British minister at Washington, and begins by saying, that the object of the argument introduced by Mr. Everett with so much preparation, and urged with so much ability, is clearly to procure the admission of a doctrine, that the United States have an interest in Cuba, to which Great Britain and France can not pretend. If, it was urged, the object of the United States is simply to prevent Cuba from falling into the hands of any European power, the convention proposed would secure that end. But if it is intended to maintain that Great Britain and France have no interest in the maintenance of the present *status* of Cuba, and that the United States alone have a right to a voice in that matter, the British government at once refuses to admit such a claim. Her possessions in the West Indies, to say nothing of the interests of Mexico and other friendly states, give Great Britain an interest in the question which she can not forego: and France has similar interests which she will doubtless urge at the proper time. His lordship expended much ability in controverting the arguments of Mr.

Everett, and closed his dispatch by saying, that, while fully admitting the right of the United States to reject the proposal, Great Britain must at once resume her entire liberty, and upon any occasion that may call for it, be free to act singly, or in conjunction with other powers, as to her may seem fit.

This dispatch, with a similar one from the French government was read, on the 16th of April, to Mr. Marcy, the secretary of state, who promised to lay them before the president, though he intimated, that probably no further continuance of the discussion would be deemed called for. The publication of this letter called out Mr. Everett again, and in writing to Lord John Russell, he vindicated the positions he had previously taken, and replied to his lordship's objections. His reply was, as might be expected, very ably written, and attracted the attention of the people at large. We regret that our limits do not admit of quoting from this last letter of the able statesman just named.

1853.

The case of Kostza, a Hungarian refugee, and the course pursued by Captain Ingraham in rescuing him from Austrian power, excited considerable attention at this date. Kostza, it appears, had taken the preliminary steps to become an American citizen, but was seized by the Austrian consul-general at Smyrna, as a refugee. His release was demanded by our consul, and Captain Ingraham threatened, that unless he were given up, he should fire into the Austrian brig where Kostza was confined. Mr. Marcy, in reply to Mr. Hulsemann's note, demanding satisfaction for the outrage on Austria, entered fully into the question, set forth the grounds on which the United States government is prepared to act in all similar cases, demonstrated that Austria had no cause of complaint, and justified the course of Captain Ingraham as eminently proper under the circumstances. The reply of Mr. Marcy was considered conclusive, and was received every where with approbation.

On Monday, the 5th of December, the thirty-third Congress commenced its first session. Senator Atchison took his seat as presiding officer in the Senate; and the Hon. Linn Boyd, of Kentucky, was chosen speaker of the House. The president's message was sent in the next day, and was read to both Houses. It was an elaborate production, and was full of matter for the consideration of the national legislature. The foreign relations of the United States were fully considered; such as, the position of questions yet unsettled with Great Britain; the state of our affairs as respected Cuba and Spain; the case of Kostza and the conduct of our officers abroad in regard to that individual; the dispute with Mexico as to the boundary line; the various matters in progress with other South American states; etc. The president also spoke of the efforts making by our commissioner to China to advance American interests, and gave intelligence of the arrival of Commodore Perry in Japan, without being able to state any particular results yet arrived at.

1853.

The president's view of domestic matters was, on the whole, very cheering, and he was of opinion, that the graver controversies as well as their causes were passing away.* In regard to the finances, it was stated, that the balance in the treasury, June 30th, 1853, was, $14,632,136. The amount received during the year was, $61,337,574; amount expended, $43,554,262; leaving a balance of $32,425,447 of receipts above expenditures. Since the 4th of March, there had been paid on the public debt, $12,703,329, leaving unpaid, $56,486,708. Beside recommending a reduction of the tariff, Mr. Pierce took up the subject of internal improvements, and gave his views upon the matter, which were substantially in accordance with those entertained by the leading men in the democratic ranks. Referring to the compromise measures of 1850, as having set at rest many litigated questions, and giving some good advice as to cultivating a fraternal spirit among the people, and practicing rigid economy and frugality in the administration of public affairs, the president closed his message with announcing the death of the vice-president on the 18th of the preceding April.

The reports of the heads of the various departments were transmitted with the message, and were full of valuable information in regard to the treasury, the navy, the army, the post-office, etc. Many and important suggestions were made by the several secretaries for the consideration of Congress.

The principal work of the session may be summed up in brief space, so far as our present purpose is concerned.* At the beginning of the year 1854, Mr. Douglas, in the Senate, from the committee on territories, reported a bill for the territorial government of Nebraska, in one section of which it was provided, that whenever the said territory should be admitted into the Union as a state or states, it should be with or without slavery, as the constitution at the time of admission may prescribe. **1854.** Another section extended the provisions of the existing laws for the surrender of fugitive slaves over the territory. Towards the close of the month, the same Senator reported a substitute for the bill, providing for the establishment of two territories, one to be called Nebraska and the other Kansas, and extending over both the Constitution, and all laws of the United States, except the eighth section of the act for the admission of Missouri into the Union, passed in 1820, which section was declared to have been "superseded by the principles of the legislation of 1850, commonly called the compromise measures," and was consequently inoperative.

An animated debate, as a matter of course sprang up upon the old question of slavery extension and limits, and the

* "Mr. Pierce," says Senator Benton, "found the country in the most happy and tranquil state; peace and prosperity at home and abroad, and slavery agitation *stone-dead.* Felicitating himself upon this delightful state of the country, he made it a topic of national congratulation in his first annual message, and dilated upon the happy auspices which saluted his nascent administration."—See Appendix to Benton's "*Examination of the Dred Scott Case,*" p. 156.

* According to the newspapers of the day, there were in the Senate, thirty-five democrats and twenty-two whigs, with five vacancies. The House was composed of one hundred and fifty-nine democrats, seventy-one whigs, and four free-soilers.

various members of the Senate arrayed themselves on that side of the question which their convictions or their interests seemed to dictate. On the 7th of February, Mr. Douglas moved the striking out the amendment he had before reported, and substituting a clause instead, declaring that the Missouri compromise act being "inconsistent with the principles of non-intervention by Congress with slavery in the states and territories as recognized by the legislation of 1850, commonly called the compromise measures, is hereby declared inoperative and void, it being the true interest and meaning of this act, not to legislate slavery into any territory or state, nor to exclude it therefrom, but to leave the people thereof perfectly free to form and regulate their domestic institutions in their own way, subject only to the Constitution of the United States." In favor of the bill, Messrs. Dixon, Badger, Pettit, Butler, Cass, Norris, and others, urged the arguments which appeared to them to demand the action proposed; while in opposition to it, Messrs. Everett, Wade, Houston, Sumner, Seward, Bell, and others, gave expression to the earnest convictions on their minds of the unfairness and impropriety of the course marked out by Mr. Douglas, especially urging that the repeal of the Missouri compromise would be a breach of faith on the part of the southern states. On the 14th of February, however, the amendment offered by Mr. Douglas, which declared the Missouri compromise inoperative and void, was adopted by a vote of thirty-five to nine. The discussion continued to be carried on vigorously during the rest of the month; numerous amendments were offered, one of which, excluding aliens from voting, was concurred in by a vote of twenty-two to twenty; and on the 3d of March, after a considerable amount of speechifying and personal bickerings, the bill was passed by a vote of thirty-seven to fourteen.

On the last day of January, a bill for organizing the territories of Nebraska and Kansas, similar to the one before the Senate, was reported to the House, and gave rise to some debate, but without any action at the time. About the middle of March, on motion of Mr. Cutting, of New York, the Nebraska bill was taken up, and after some warm opposition was referred to the committee of the whole by a small majority. But little further attention was given to it for a month subsequently; but, on the 25th of April, Mr. Benton, who, since leaving the Senate, had entered the House as a Representative from Missouri, delivered an energetic speech against the bill. Protesting, in no measured terms, against the practice of bringing up in the legislature the opinions of the president, and denouncing vehemently the newspapers employed to do the public printing, for daring to dictate to Congress, the veteran statesman went on to resist the proposition to repeal the Missouri compromise, on the ground that it was one of the three great measures by which the Union had been formed and its harmony preserved—the first being the ordinance of 1787, and the second the Federal Constitution. Mr. Benton said, he came into public life on the Missouri

1854.

compromise, and he intended always to stand upon it, even if he should stand alone. It partook of the nature of a contract, and could not be repealed now without a violation of good faith. It had given peace and harmony to the country, and its repeal would inevitably involve us in useless and mischievous agitations. Not a petition for its repeal had come into Congress from any quarter. The slave states had nothing to gain by passing it; the pretence that it was necessary in order to carry out the principle of non-intervention, was utterly fallacious; and on every account the bill ought not to be suffered to pass. Early in May, the bill was referred to the committee of the whole, and by a vote took precedence of all other business. Amendment after amendment was offered; interminable discussions and disputes took place; the bill was reported again and again to the House, and again to the committee of the whole; all sorts of engineering processes were put into operation; and finally, on the 22d of May, the bill, as passed by the Senate, was adopted by a vote of one hundred and thirteeen to one hundred, the clause excluding aliens from voting being omitted. A few days afterwards, the Senate took up the bill, as amended, and after considerable debate, it was agreed to, and passed by a vote of thirty-five to thirteen.*

Early in the year, a treaty was concluded with Mexico by General Gadsden, and sent to the Senate for confirmation. It there underwent important modifications, and was finally arranged to the satisfaction of the respective governments. A part of the first article, respecting the limits between the two republics was as follows: "beginning in the Gulf of Mexico, three leagues from land, opposite the mouth of the Rio Grande, as provided in the fifth article of the treaty of Guadalupe-Hidalgo (p. 463); thence, as defined in the said article, up the middle of that river, to the point where the parallel of 31° 47′ north latitude crosses the same; thence due west one hundred miles; thence south to the parallel of 31° 20′ north latitude; thence along the said parallel of 31° 20′ to the 111th meridian of longitude west of Greenwich; thence in a straight line to a point on the Colorado River twenty English miles below the junction of the Gila and Colorado Rivers; thence up the middle of the said River Colorado, until it intersects the present line between the United States and Mexico." In consideration of being released from the obligation to protect the Mexican frontier against the Indians (see p. 465) and as compensation for the territory ceded by Mexico, the United States agreed to pay $10,000,000. The grant for a railroad route across the Isthmus of Tehuantepec was expressly confirmed, and various other privileges were secured to our countrymen. A good deal of debate was had upon this treaty;

1854.

* A letter from ex-senator Clemens, of Alabama, vindicating his course in opposition to the Nebraska bill, was published, and excited considerable attention. He gave it as his opinion, that the passage of this bill would end in decided ultimate injury to the south; that the compromise of 1850 did not repeal that of 1820; and that by this course of conduct the south was involved in a flagrant breach of faith.

but finally, near the end of the session, the House, by a vote of one hundred and two to sixty-three, and the Senate, by a vote of thirty-four to six, passed the bill making the appropriation of $10,000,000 for carrying the treaty into effect.*

Other topics of interest, to which we can now only allude, were—the manner in which the steamer Black Warrior was treated by the Cuban officials, and the spirit roused by it in the United States; the discussion upon building six first-class steam frigates, and the final passage of the bill by a large vote; the president's veto of the bill appropriating ten millions of acres of public lands to the several states for the relief of the indigent insane within their limits; the holding a convention at Charleston, in April, to consider how best to set forward the interests of the southern states; the various inklings and movements towards annexing the Sandwich Islands; the issuing of a proclamation by the president, on the 31st of May, denouncing the filibustering attempts again about to be made upon Cuba; etc. A considerable amount of public business was left unfinished, and Congress adjourned on the 7th of August.

1854.

Commodore M. C. Perry, who had urged upon the government the importance of effecting a treaty with Japan, succeeded, after many and vexatious delays, in getting an expedition for this important object under way. He sailed from New York on the 24th of November, 1852, in the steamer Mississippi, other vessels in the East being ordered to join him. The Cape of Good Hope was doubled during the latter part of February, 1853; Singapore was reached on the 25th of March; and Shanghai on the 4th of May. Here the commodore transferred his flag to the Susquehanna, and had now a fleet of four vessels, with two others to join him soon after. The Lew-Chew Islands were visited, and early in July, Commodore Perry directed his course to Japan. On the 7th of July, he reached the Bay of Yedo, and caused no little surprise and apprehension by steaming directly into the bay, and insisting upon carrying out the measures for which he had come so far. By his judicious firmness, the commodore succeeded in accomplishing the object of his mission; the letter of the president to the emperor was delivered; negotiations were entered into; and finally, on the 31st of March, 1854, a treaty was agreed upon and signed. Commodore Perry returned home, reaching New York early in 1855, and the treaty with Japan was duly ratified by the Senate.*

* At the close of 1856, the inhabitants of the newly acquired territory, sent a delegate to Washington, requesting that this portion of New Mexico might be erected into a territory, under the name of Arizonia. The committee of the House reported adversely to their petition, mainly on account of the paucity of the population.

* For a full and very interesting account of the whole voyage and its valuable results, see the "*Narrative of the Expedition of an American Squadron to the China Seas and Japan*, 1852–1854." By Commodore M. C. Perry, U. S. N. New York, 1857, pp. 624. This attractive volume was arranged and prepared from the documents, journals, etc., at the request of Commodore Perry, by the Rev. F. L. Hawks, D. D., of New York.

During the summer and autumn, political conventions were held in various parts of the country, and the usual elections excited active interest. The discussions and contrariety of opinions on the subject of the Missouri compromise repeal, and the passage of the bill respecting Nebraska and Kansas, seemed to indicate changes about to take place in some of the old party lines and combinations; and from this date, we may note the increase of a disposition on the part of a portion of our countrymen to form a native American party, as opposed to aliens, and especially Roman Catholic Irish and German naturalized citizens. What will ultimately grow out of the "Know Nothing" movements and operations, it is not easy, perhaps not possible, to predict; but, in the opinion of many, there are grave and serious questions yet to be settled, as to the respective rights and privileges of native born and adopted citizens of the United States.

The second and short session of the thirty-third Congress commenced on the 4th of December, and President Pierce sent in his message on the same day. It contained the usual summary of the state of foreign and domestic affairs, and made a number of suggestions on various points of interest and importance for the consideration of Congress. The balance in the treasury, June 30th, was $21,942,-892; amount received, $73,549,705; making the total available resources, nearly $95,500,000. The expenditures of the year were, $51,018,249; payments on the public debt, $24,336,380; leaving a balance in the treasury of $20,137,967. The public debt remaining unpaid was, nearly, $45,000,000, redeemable at different periods within fourteen years. The reports of the various heads of the departments, and other documents, accompanying the president's message, were elaborate papers containing full statements on all the points necessary to guide Congress in carrying forward wise, appropriate, and economical legislation.

1854.

At the beginning of the year 1855, President Pierce sent in a message, in which he presented an elaborate argument against the policy of internal improvements to be carried on by the general government, and in which he also vindicated his action in having vetoed the bill for this purpose, passed at the last session. The merits of this whole subject have already been pretty fully set forth on previous pages of our history; hence we need not go over the ground again in this place. President Pierce certainly added nothing of moment to the settlement of the question, which is an open one among his own party, and which, we may say, always will be open to difference of sentiment.

General Cass, a few days later, made a speech on the subject of obeying the instructions of the legislature of his state; the substance of which seemed to be that, as the legislature was of different political views from his own, he could not conscientiously obey their instructions; if they agreed with him, as was the case when he came into the Senate, he was ready to obey their directions, but in the present instance he felt bound to decline. So the general refused to do as he was

1855.

told, viz., to endeavor to procure the passage of a law prohibiting slavery from the territories of Kansas and Nebraska.

The emigrating expedition under Colonel Kinney attracted considerable attention at this date. It appears, that the intention of the colonel and his company was, to colonize and settle certain portions of the territory on the Mosquito coast, under a grant which, it was alleged, had been made to Sheppard and Haly, two British subjects, by the late king of the Mosquito country. The government of Nicaragua protested against this expedition, as an invasion of its territory; to which Mr. Marcy replied, that so far as he could learn, there was no intention to do otherwise than peacefully settle upon and improve the lands to which the company were about to proceed. The Nicaraguan minister, Mr. Marcoleta, addressed the secretary of state a long, argumentative letter, urging upon the United States not to allow any movements which should favor British pretensions on the Mosquito coast, or encourage the invasion of the rights of Nicaragua. Colonel Kinney pushed forward his movements, and about the middle of July, reached San Juan del Norte, after experiencing trials of shipwreck and delay. Sanguine of success in obtaining and holding possession of the Sheppard grant of thirty-five millions of acres of land on the Mosquito coast, every step to this end was taken with promptitude. Early in September, a public meeting was held, Colonel Kinney was elected civil and military governor, and a council of five appointed to aid him in the discharge of his duties. During the autumn and winter, the colony seemed to be advancing in prosperity, and a number of emigrants from the United States cast in their lot with those already on the ground. The government of Nicaragua, however, early in 1856, announced its claim to the Mosquito territory, refusing to recognize the validity of the land claims of Colonel Kinney.

A bill having passed both Houses, authorizing the establishment of a commission to investigate and pay the losses sustained by American citizens from French spoliations on American commerce, the president, on the 17th of February, sent in another veto message. An attempt was made to pass the bill in spite of the veto, but it failed of obtaining a two-thirds vote. Another bill, increasing the annual appropriation to the Collins line of steamers from $385,000 to $850,000, for mail service, was passed by both the House and the Senate by a rather close vote. On the 3d of March, President Pierce vetoed this bill likewise, and gave various cogent reasons for his refusal to sign it. On motion of Mr. Seward, in the Senate, the bill just vetoed was added to the naval appropriation bill, omitting the repeal of that clause in the existing contract, which gives Congress the right to discontinue the extra allowance on giving six month's notice. This amendment was unanimously agreed to by the Senate, and the House, finding that it could not obtain a two-thirds vote in favor of the bill, agreed to pass it as received from the Senate. This was done, and the bill thus became a law.

1855.

Various other bills made successful progress through the two Houses. A retired list for the navy was provided; $7,750,000 were appropriated to meet the claims of the creditors of Texas who may hold bonds for the payment of which the revenues of the state were pledged; a bill to protect emigrant passengers was adopted; $25,000 were appropriated for statuary to be executed by Hiram Powers; etc. A joint reso-
1855. lution, approved on the 15th of February, authorized the president to confer the title of lieutenant-general by brevet, in a single instance, for eminent services. General Scott was the recipient of this well-merited and distinguished honor.*

Just at the close of the session President Pierce communicated to Congress a voluminous collection of diplomatic correspondence respecting the Ostend Conference, held in October of the preceding year. The substance of this meeting of the American ministers to England, France, and Spain, at the city of Ostend, may be briefly summed up. The point of it consisted in the value of Cuba to the United States, the almost necessity of getting possession of it, the taking measures to this end openly and fairly, the offering Spain $120,000,000 for the island, etc. Franklin Pierce hesitating about following the course suggested by the minister to Spain, Mr. Soulé, on the 17th of December, 1854, sent a letter resigning his post, under the impression that, unless his plans were to be carried out, he was of no further use in Spain. On the 3d of March, the thirty-third Congress closed its labors, and the members dispersed to their several homes and summer occupations.*

In various portions of the country, the elections of the present season indicated the progress of the "American" party, and to a large extent they were certainly unfavorable to Pierce's administration. Feelings of
mutual dislike seemed to be 1855.
growing in the community between "natives" and "foreigners," and riots and disturbances occurred here and there, indicating a very unhealthy state of a considerable part of the public mind on this topic. As we have hinted on a previous page (p. 508) the final settlement of so difficult and perplexing a dispute as this which has sprung up among us, in regard to native born and naturalized citizens, is yet in the future, and very naturally causes anxiety to those who desire peace and concord to prevail throughout our beloved country. It also deserves to be noted,

* During the months of January, February, and March, 1854, the Darien exploring expedition, consisting of twenty-seven men, under command of Lieut. Isaac Strain of the navy, attempted to ascertain the practicability of a route for a ship canal across the Isthmus. It was attended with dangers, and difficulties, and sufferings, almost passing belief. For a very interesting article, prepared from the journal of Lieut. Strain and from other sources, by Mr. J. T. Headley, see "Harper's Magazine" for the months of March, April, and May, 1855.

* President Pierce visited the White Sulphur Springs, in Virginia, on the 21st of August, where he was received by a committee, at the head of which was ex-president Tyler, who addressed the president, welcoming him to the state, and congratulating him on the prosperous condition of the country. The president, in reply, complimented Mr. Tyler for what he had done while in the executive chair, and made some seasonable remarks on the dangers threatening the peace of the country, especially in the growin spirit of resistance to law and order.

that there was a strong disposition in several quarters to organize a new political party, upon the principle of restoring the Missouri compromise, and resisting what the northern states held to be the aggressions of the slave-holding sections of the Union. The whigs, it was said, favored this movement to a considerable extent.

The legislature of New York, earnestly desirous to place an effectual barrier against the further progress of intemperance, pauperism and crime, passed, at its present session, a very stringent law on the subject of
1855. selling intoxicating liquors. A long and animated debate was had in the legislature, and the whole subject, in all its details, was thoroughly discussed, the intention being to put a stop to the sale of ardent spirits for any purposes except medicinal or other legitimate ends. Penalties of a severe kind were incurred by violations of the law, which was to go into effect on the 4th of July. Considering the good intent of the legislature, and the importance of vigorous action to restrain the tempters to pauperism and crime, who expose for sale intoxicating drinks, and urge forward to speedy ruin thousands upon thousands every year; considering how hundreds of families are reduced to beggary and destitution, how many murders are committed, how large a portion of the community are degraded by drink, physically, morally, socially; we may, without impropriety, express here deep regret, that this effort to break down a monster evil has failed almost entirely. The law, so far as the city of New York is concerned, was never carried out, and probably while things exist as they were two years ago, and are now (in 1857), such a law it will be found impossible to execute in the metropolis of the United States. It is a grave question, a very grave question, what shall be done? and we venture to submit it to the reader as one in which he has a vital interest, both as a philanthropist, a patriot, and a Christian.

In the spring of the present year, the president gave notice to the Danish government, in respect to the 1855.
dues levied on all vessels passing the Sound, that the treaty of commerce which recognized the right to levy these dues, would be terminated at the expiration of a year; and also, that the right would no longer be recognized by the United States. The Danish government, in reply to this notification, complained that so sudden a notice should be given, and that the termination of the treaty would take away the revenues of which, in the present condition of Europe, Denmark professed to feel greatly in need.

On a previous page (p. 490) we have spoken of the expedition undertaken for the purpose of searching for Sir John Franklin and his missing company. Dr. Kane, who had gone with the first expedition, and who was loth to believe that Franklin and all his men had perished, was placed, through the liberality of Mr. Grinnell and the favor of the government, in command of a second expedition to proceed upon the same almost hopeless search. On the 30th of May, 1853, Dr. Kane, with seventeen hardy and brave men under his command, sailed from New York in the Advance, a strongly built hermaphrodite brig of 144 tons burden, and well provided with every thing which experience or judgment could suggest. On the 10th of September they were frozen in on the coast of Greenland, at the most northerly point ever reached. Here the party passed their first Arctic winter. The following summer was spent in exploring in every direction that was practicable, in endeavors to ascertain something through the Esquimaux, in hunting, etc. The second winter, that of 1854–55, was intensely severe and trying, and their stock of fuel became quite exhausted. The search having been prosecuted two years, with no result, and Dr. Kane deeming it impossible to spend a third winter amid the ice, the Advance was reluctantly abandoned, on the 20th of May, 1855. With sledges and in open boats, this brave party set out on their return home; and having gone through sufferings of the most bitter and severe character, they reached the Danish settlements at Upernavik at the beginning of August, completely worn down with a journey of one thousand three hundred miles in eighty-one days. Apprehensions had some time previously begun to be entertained respecting the fate of Dr. Kane and his party; and acting upon these, Lieutenant Hartstene was dispatched in May, 1855, with the bark Release and the steamer Arctic, to seek for Dr. Kane and the Advance. Early in July they reached Upernavik, and fortunately not long after fell in with the brave Arctic explorers, i. e., all who survived, three of the number having died; they were gladly received on board, at Disco, about the middle of September, and on the 11th of October the expedition was welcomed back again to New York.*

1855.

The still youthful navigator (for he was born in February, 1820) made his official report to the secretary of the navy, and it was hoped that he might live to render many years of service to the interests of humanity and for the honor of his country; but the rigors of the Arctic winter had taxed his health and strength with unwonted severity, and he himself was called upon ere long to follow his three lost companions to the grave. Every thing that affectionate solicitude of friends and relatives could suggest was done; but his health sank beyond possibility of arresting the inroads of the fell destroyer; and on the 16th of February, 1857, at Havana, in the Island of Cuba, the spirit of Elisha Kent Kane passed away from earth to his final account. Dr. Wm. Elder, we may here state, has since published a biography of Dr. Kane, in which the reader will find various matters of interest respecting the early life and training of our distinguished countryman.

In connection with the loss of Sir John Franklin and his party, we may mention, that an overland exploring party, dispatched by the Hudson's Bay Company, discovered on Montreal Is-

* For volumes of unsurpassed interest and attractiveness, we may refer the reader to the "*Arctic Explorations; the Second Grinnell Expedition in search of Sir John Franklin, 1853, 4, 5.*" By Elisha Kent Kane, M. D., U. S. N. 2 vols. Philadelphia, 1857.

land, a snow shoe of English make, a part of a ship's boat, with the word *Terror* distinctly visible on it, and other articles of less moment. Fresh interest was excited in this subject also, by the interesting circumstance that at the close of 1855, a New London whaler lighted upon the British relief bark *Resolute*, which had been abandoned in the Arctic ice by Captain Kellett, of the expedition under Sir Edward Belcher. The Resolute, with her armament and stores complete, as at the time when she was abandoned, had drifted a thousand miles from the place where she had been frozen in; and the hardy whalemen of New London took her in charge, and brought her safely into port. Congress subsequently voted $40,000 for the purchase and refitting of the Resolute, and on the 12th of December, 1856, she arrived at Spithead. Lieutenant Harstene was in command, and he was charged with the duty of presenting the Resolute to the English government. We may well believe, that the queen and the people of England received this mark of American good feeling and courtesy with especial satisfaction.

During the autumn, apprehensions began to be felt of approaching difficulties with England. Some of the London journals, it appears, talked in a very belligerent tone, and it was said that the English government had sent several vessels of war to reinforce the West India squadron, with a view to restrain "filibustering" and privateering expeditions from the ports of the United States. Probably, in part, this exhibition of hostility was due to the fact, that the proceedings of various British consuls in enlisting recruits for the Crimean war were severely reprobated in the instructions written by Mr. Cushing, the attorney-general, to the district attorney at Philadelphia, concerning the trials had in that city for violations of the United States neutrality laws. We are glad, however, to be able to say, that the British government disavowed all hostile intentions in the course they were pursuing; and so the threatened difficulty, as on many another occasion, passed away without further notice.*

1855.

On the 3d of December, the thirty-fourth Congress began its first session. In the House, on the question of who should be the speaker, a contest immediately sprang up. Messrs. Banks, Richardson, Campbell, and two or three others, were prominent candidates. Ballot after ballot was had, day after day, and it was not till two months of the public time had been wasted, and the plurality rule had been adopted, that Mr. N. P. Banks, on the 2d of February, 1856, received one hundred and three votes for speaker, while one hundred were cast for Mr. Aiken, of South Carolina,

1855.

* Late in August, some of the directors of the New York, Newfoundland, and London Submarine Telegraph Company, went out to witness the laying down the telegraphic cable between Cape Ray and Cape North, a distance of sixty miles. One end of the cable was fastened on the shore at Cape Ray, and the paying out began; it was continued successfully for more than thirty hours, when the weather became too stormy to proceed further in the attempt, and the cable was reluctantly cut off, after some forty miles length had been sunk in the sea. The party returned to New York, on the 5th of September, purposing to renew the undertaking at as early a day as practicable.

and eleven were scattering. President Pierce, wearied out with waiting for the organization of the House, adopted an unusual course, and, on the 31st of December, sent his message to the Senate. In this document the president brought to the notice of the legislature the various questions of interest and importance which at the time required their attentive consideration. He spoke of the views of the British government as to the interpretation of the treaty of 1850, in regard to Central American affairs; the recruiting for the Crimean war carried on by English agents in the United States; the question of the Danish Sound dues; our relations with Spain; etc. In regard to finances, it was stated, that the balance in the treasury, July 1st, was $18,931,976; estimated receipts for the year, $67,-918,073; making available resources of nearly $87,000,000. Expenditures for the year were estimated at a little over $71,000,000, which would leave a balance in the treasury, July 1st, 1856, of nearly $16,000,000. The recommendations in the message were principally on the subject of the army and the navy, the appointing a commissioner to survey the line between Washington territory and the British possessions, etc. The president devoted considerable space to the existing difficulties in Kansas; the state-rights question, with particular reference to the fugitive slave law; the history of this topic; and such like; and gave it as his opinion, that the south had not "persistently asserted claims and obtained advantages over the north in the practical administration of the general government." He also defended the principles of the Kansas-Nebraska bill.

This Kansas question, a very vexatious one as it has proved, we may properly notice here. From the nature of the case, difficulty was likely to spring out of the position of affairs, when the Missouri compromise had been repealed; and almost immediately it became a matter of contest, whether the influence of southern or northern men should predominate in forming and moulding the institutions and principles of the territory, and the state soon to grow up and demand admission into the Union. In March, an election was held for members of the territorial legislature, and the candidates in favor of introducing slavery into the territory received a decided majority. It was alleged, however, on the other side, that **1855.** the election was carried by illegal voters having come into the territory from Missouri, and interfered with those who had a right to vote, viz., the *bona fide* residents. Governor Reeder, not long after, was on a visit to the eastern states, and in a speech which he made he said, "Kansas had been invaded, conquered, subjugated, by an armed force from beyond her borders, led on by a fanatical spirit, trampling under foot the principle of the Kansas bill and the right of suffrage."

The violence of party spirit increased, and riot and even blood-shed were the consequences. The settlers opposed to slavery-introduction complained, in a memorial to Congress, of the Missourians having entered the territory and deprived them of their rights; the pro-slavery men denounced any attempt to exclude it. On the 22d of May, the election for the first legislature took place, and the slavery ticket was carried. The legislature met, on the 2d of July, at Pawnee, under the summons of the governor, the Council consisting of sixteen, and the House of Representatives of twenty-six members. A good deal of work was done, which we need not particularize here, except that from the first the legislature showed its hostility to Governor Reeder and his views. The governor was written to by the secretary of state respecting certain charges against his official integrity, to which he replied, but not satisfactorily to President Pierce. At the close of July he was removed from his post, and Daniel Woodson, secretary of the territory, succeeded to the discharge of the governor's duties.

The legislature seemed disposed to make thorough work of the matter in hand, and effectually to put down all anti-slavery sentiment and power in the territory. A number of stringent measures to this effect were carried. One act gave the right of voting to any man, without regard to residence, on payment of one dollar and taking certain oaths, viz., to support the Kansas bill, and enforce the fugitive slave law. Acts were passed which forbade the teaching of negroes to read, and the holding of religious meetings of negroes, unless a sheriff, constable, or county justice should be present. Another act forbade any person who was conscientiously opposed to holding slaves, or who did not admit the right to hold slaves in the territory, from acting as a juror in any case connected with slavery; and still another prescribed the penalty of death for inciting rebellion among the slaves, by speaking, writing, or printing; or for enticing or assisting any slave to escape from his master. Following upon legislation of this kind, there were several cases of "lynching" persons on suspicion of holding anti-slavery opinions.

1855.

On the 14th of August, a large convention of settlers was held at Lawrence, attended by over six hundred persons, at which the present alarming condition of the territory was taken into serious consideration. Resolutions were adopted, declaring that they would utterly repudiate the action of the legislature, which had been imposed upon them by the people of Missouri, and calling a convention of representatives of the people of the territory for the 5th of September. The convention met, on the day appointed, at Big Springs. Vigorous resolutions were adopted, declaring that the true interests of Kansas consisted in her being a free state, repudiating the action of the legislature, and calling upon the people to prepare for resistance to usurpation, even by force of arms, if necessary. Ex-governor Reeder was nominated for delegate to Congress, and the election was to take place early in October. Reeder was voted for by the free-soilers on the 9th of October, and it was claimed that he received a larger vote than had been given for Whitfield, who obtained two thousand seven hundred and sixty suffrages from the pro-slavery men, on the 1st of October, the day fixed by the

legislature for the election. This state of things, of course, put the matter in such shape that the House of Representatives, at the next session, would be compelled to decide on the claims of the respective contestants, Reeder and Whitfield. The free-soil party called a convention, which met at Topeka, on the 27th of October, and closed its session on the 11th of November, after having formed a state constitution, which was to be submitted to the people on the 15th of December following, and the principal feature in which was, that slavery was not to exist in the territory after the 4th of July, 1857. The opponents of the free-soilers held what was termed a "law and order" convention at Leavenworth, on the 14th of November. Governor Shannon was appointed president, and the main business which occupied the
1855. convention was, the expressing decided disapprobation of the course pursued by the anti-slavery men, and declaring that, if it were persisted in and sanctioned by Congress, it would lead to civil war.

The movements of Colonel or General Walker in Central America require some notice in this place, although the results of his "filibustering" efforts have not been as favorable as he and his advisers and supporters hoped and expected. At the close of the month of August, Walker landed with his party at San Juan del Sur. On the 3d of September, his force, numbering one
1855. hundred and fifty, was attacked at Virgin Bay by some four hundred government troops. After a brief but fierce contest, Walker defeated his opponents. Granada, the capital, was attacked in October; taken by surprise, but little resistance was made; General Corral surrendered; and a treaty of peace was signed. Walker was elected president of the republic, but declined in favor of General Rivas; Corral, tried by court martial, was condemned and shot; and Colonel Wheeler, the American minister, formally recognized the government as now constituted.

Reinforcements flowed in, principally from California, and the Rivas and Walker government seemed to be gaining strength, early in 1856. Colonel P. H. French was dispatched as minister to the United States; but our government refused to receive him in that capacity. The other states of Central America determined to put Walker down, and joined together for that purpose. In March, Costa Rica formally declared war against Nicaragua, to which Walker replied, by announcing his purpose to carry the war into the enemy's country. Several battles ensued. Colonel Schlessinger, with three hundred men, was totally defeated at Santa Rosa. The Costa Ricans marched into the territory of Nicaragua, some three or four thousand in number; the city of Rivas fell into their hands; and on the 11th of April a bloody battle took place, in which Walker claimed a decisive victory. Much exasperation of feeling followed upon 1856.
Walker's mode of endeavoring to recruit his languishing finances; the Costa Ricans retreated; and the action of the other states was hesitating and uncertain. Troubles soon after sprang up

between Rivas and Walker, owing apparently to jealousy on the part of the former against the Americans. Walker was elected president in June, and inaugurated on the 12th of July, and as the autumn approached, he had to make provision to meet, as best he could, the army by which the confederated states purposed to crush him or drive him out of the country. The further progress of Walker and his party we need not dwell upon here; his affairs grew worse and worse as the year advanced to its close; and finally, in April, 1857, he capitulated, in a state of great destitution, to Captain Davis of the sloop-of-war St. Marys, and was conveyed, together with a part of his company, to the United States.

Towards the close of 1855, the troubles in Kansas were on the increase. A quarrel took place between two men on opposite sides of the slavery question, which resulted in the death of one of them. Great excitement was produced, and the neighboring Missourians prepared to sustain the cause of the pro-slavery men. They entered Kansas in considerable numbers, and encamped near Lawrence, as if about to attack it. Governor Shannon exerted himself to prevent armed collision; and after a time the Missourians returned home again. A free-state convention was held at Lawrence, on the 22d of December, to nominate candidates for state affairs under the constitution. Some eighty delegates were present and took part in the business of the convention.

The president, on the 24th of January, 1856, sent a message to the Senate, in respect to the existing state of affairs in Kansas; he censured the late Governor Reeder for having neglected his duty; he recognized the territorial legislature as, for all practical purposes, a lawful body; he disapproved entirely of the movement which led to the convention and forming a free-state constitution; and he recommended various measures in view of the present and the future of Kansas. On the 11th of February, the president issued a proclamation, stating that combinations had been formed in the territory to resist the execution of the laws; that persons outside the territory were contemplating armed interference; and declaring that he had taken the proper steps to repress all outbreaks and maintain the peace of the country. **1856.**

The Kansas question, as a matter of course, occupied a considerable share of the attention of Congress. Mr. Whitfield and Mr. Reeder were the delegates elected to Congress by the two parties, and the committee on elections reported on the seat, which was claimed by each gentleman. The majority of the committee took ground against Mr. Whitfield and the authority of the territorial legislature, and asked to be empowered to send for persons and papers; the minority brought in a report of a different complexion, and thought it best to dispatch a commission to Kansas to take testimony, rather than send for persons and papers. After a long and tedious debate, the proposition of the majority was adopted by the House. In the Senate, Mr. Douglas, in behalf of the majority of the committee on territories, brought in a report, **1856.**

claiming that the course pursued by the territorial legislature was legal and to be sustained, and recommended, that when the population of Kansas shall amount to ninety-three thousand three hundred and forty, the number requisite to entitle her to a Representative in Congress, they be authorized to hold a convention and form a state government. The report also denounced the free-state convention at Topeka, and sharply censured the measures of the Emigrant Aid Societies. Mr. Collamer presented a minority report, taking the opposite ground, and recommending, as the easiest way to settle the difficulties, that Kansas be at once received into the Union with the present constitution.*

The state legislature (free-soil) met at Topeka, on the 14th of March, and subsequently adjourned to Lawrence. A memorial from this body was presented by Mr. Cass in the Senate, which gave rise to a protracted debate. It

1856. was finally referred to the committee on territories. An unusually caustic correspondence between Mr. Douglas and Mr. Lane (Senator elect from Kansas) grew out of this paper, and certain statements which were made respecting it. In the territory itself, during April and May, difficulties increased, and a state of almost civil war existed. The excesses to which the controversy between the advocates and the opponents of slavery led, filled the journals of the day, and gave rise to serious apprehension as to what might be the final issue. One disgraceful occurrence in Congress, we cannot fail to put on record here.

The debates in the Senate had increased in acerbity, as was not unnatural. Mr. Douglas, Mr. Butler, Mr. Mason, and other Senators, had said much respecting Kansas and kindred matters. Mr. Sumner, of Massachusetts, on the 19th of May, delivered an elaborate speech on "the Crime against Kansas," in which he did not spare Mr. Butler and others, but, with a keenness of invective rarely excelled, poured upon them the well-filled vials of his indignation and contempt for the course they had pursued. Tart retorts followed, and an equally tart rejoinder came from Mr. Sumner. On the morning of the 22d, the Senate having adjourned, and while Mr. Sumner was seated at his desk, Mr. P. S. Brooks, a nephew of Mr. Butler, and a member of the House from South Carolina, came up to the Senator from Massachusetts, and pronouncing him a libeller of South Carolina, and a slanderer of his aged relative, said that he was going to chastise him. Immediately on this, he struck Mr. Sumner over the head with a gutta percha cane, and repeated the blows till he had nearly killed him. Considerable noise was made in Congress by this unmanly attack, and it was attempted to punish Mr. Brooks by expulsion; but those who felt the disgrace of a course of conduct such as his had been, and desired to purge our national legislature of all those persons who are willing to resort to these means of venting their

* On the 9th of April, Senator Seward, of New York, delivered an able speech in favor of the immediate admission of Kansas as a state. We commend it to the careful examination of the reader.

anger or overcoming their opponents, were not strong enough to accomplish this good end; and so Mr. Brooks and his coadjutors, Messrs. Keitt and Edmonson, remained at their posts. Mr. Keitt was censured by the House, and Mr. Brooks was fined three hundred dollars, by the criminal court at Washington, for his assault on Mr. Sumner.

The Kansas investigation committee presented an elaborate report to the House, in which they entered into full details respecting the various matters submitted to them for examination. The committee believed, from the evidence before them, that the Missourians had illegally interfered in Kansas affairs, and they thought that Kansas would be a free state, if the will of the legal voters could be carried out. The committee also reported against admitting either Whitfield or Reeder to a seat as delegate, in the House; and that steps be taken to secure a free and fair election in the territory. Messrs. Howard and Sherman, a majority of the committee, signed the report; Mr. Oliver declined giving his signature, and soon after brought in a minority report. The committee on territories in the House, reported a

1856.

bill for the immediate admission of Kansas as a state, with the Topeka constitution. It was rejected, June 30th, by a vote of one hundred and six to one hundred and five. The next day, the vote was reconsidered, and on the 3d of July, the bill was passed by a vote of ninety-nine to ninety seven. In the Senate, a bill was passed, after discussion and amendment, for the purpose of securing a fair expression of the will of the people of Kansas, and allowing the formation of a state constitution, preparatory to admission into the Union.

Governor Shannon was removed by the president, and Mr. J. W. Geary appointed in his place. Mr. Geary reached the field of his labors early in September, and found his hands full of work at once; for the territory was in a state of virtual civil war, and no one could see what the end was to be. His energetic measures, however, seemed, in the course of a month or so, to promise somewhat of a respite from further outbreaks, and a restoration of peace and order.

On the 2d of June, the national democratic convention assembled at Cincinnati, and after adopting various resolutions setting forth the views and principles of the party, proceeded to nominate candidates

1856.

for the presidency and vice-presidency. Messrs. Douglas, Pierce and Buchanan were prominent before the convention; on the seventeenth ballot James Buchanan received all the votes, and thus became the candidate of the democrats for the highest office in our country. J. C. Breckenridge, on the second ballot, received the nomination for the vice-presidency. Two weeks later, the republican convention, at Pittsburg, nominated John C. Fremont for president, and W. L. Dayton for vice-president. Mr. Fillmore was also nominated by the American party, and accepted the nomination. The whig national convention, in September, cordially approved his nomination. The other gentlemen just named wrote letters of acceptance, and avowed their sentiments on the various topics then agitating the public mind.

Congress, after a long session, and one in which the legislature was called upon to act in many very important matters, adjourned on the 18th of August. The members dispersed to their respective homes, and the grand contest for the presidency occupied them, and nearly every body else, for some months afterwards; for the monster gatherings, the political speechifying, the interminable war of words in the newspapers, the public places, and the like, gave an opportunity for both sides, and all sides, to get their candidates elected, if they could.

The result, announced early in December, we may here put on record: James Buchanan and J. C. Breckenridge received the votes of nineteen states, i. e., one hundred and seventy-four electoral votes; J. C. Fremont and W. L. Dayton received the votes of eleven states, i. e., one hundred and fourteen votes; and Messrs. Fillmore and Donelson received the vote of one state (Maryland) or eight electoral votes; making in all two hundred and ninety-six votes cast. Buchanan and Breckenridge having received a majority of the votes were, of course, president elect and vice-president elect. The popular vote for the respective candidates was, for the democratic candidate, one million eight hundred and fifty-nine thousand three hundred and thirty-seven; for the republican candidate, one million three hundred and forty-one thousand eight hundred and twelve; for the American, eight hundred and eighty-eight thousand and fifty-five.

On the 1st of December, the second session of the thirty-fourth Congress was begun, and President Pierce's last annual message was received and read on the following day. It possessed more than ordinary interest from the fact, that the president entered at large into the exciting questions on which the north and the south were arrayed in hostile opposition. Mr. Pierce exerted himself to defend the views and principles on which he and his administration had proceeded with respect to the abrogating the Missouri compromise, and also with respect to the whole slavery question; **1856.** and he did not scruple to lay all the blame upon the northern men, and those who, while adhering to the compact not to disturb slavery where it lawfully existed, were determined to resist its further expansion. Our limits do not admit of quoting the president's language, which the reader will do well to examine with care and attention. We say this, because we wish also to call his attention to a very searching review of this message, so far as it relates to the abrogation of the Missouri compromise act, published at the close of 1857, by the veteran Senator, Thomas H. Benton, in which, he says, are "exposed and corrected the errors of fact and law" in the president's message.

The concluding paragraph of Mr. Benton's review deserves to be well considered. He is speaking of "the present slavery agitation," and goes on to say; "Up to Mr. Pierce's administration the plan had been defensive—

Thomas H. Benton

that is to say, to make the secession of the south a measure of self defence against the abolition encroachments, aggressions, and crusades of the north; in the time of Mr. Pierce, the plan became offensive—that is to say, to commence the expansion of slavery, and the acquisition of territory to spread it over, so as to overpower the north with new slave states, and drive them out of the Union. In this change of tactics originated the abrogation of the Missouri compromise, the attempt to purchase one half of Mexico, and the actual purchase of a large part; the design to take Cuba; the encouragement to Kinney and to Walker in Central America; the quarrels with Great Britain for outlandish coasts and islands; the designs upon the Tehuantepec, the Nicaragua, the Panama, and the Darien routes; and the scheme to get a foothold in the Island of San Domingo. The rising in the free states in consequence of the abrogation of the Missouri compromise, checked these schemes, and limited the success of the disunionists to the revival of the agitation which enables them to wield the south against the north in all the federal elections and federal legislation. Accidents and events have given this party a strange pre-eminence. Under Jackson's administration, proclaimed for treason; since, at the head of the government and of the democratic party. The death of Harrison, and the accession of Tyler, was their first great lift; the election of Mr. Pierce was their culminating point. It not only gave them the government, but power to pass themselves for the Union party, and for democrats; and to stigmatize all who refused to go with them, as disunionists, and abolitionists. And to keep up this classification, is the object of the eleven pages of the message which calls for this review—unhappily assisted in that object by the conduct of a few real abolitionists, (not five per centum of the population of the free states,) but made to stand, in the eyes of the south, for the whole."*

The president's message stated, that the revenues of the current year had amounted to nearly $74,000,000; the expenditures had amounted to not quite $73,000,000, including $3,000,000 paid to Mexico, and some $13,000,000 of the public debt. This debt amounted, at the present date, to $30,737,129; all of which, if necessary, could be paid within a year. The average expenditure, according to Mr. Pierce, during the preceding five years, had been $48,000,000; and, thinking that this sum would be sufficient for the next five years, a reduction of the tariff was recommended so as to bring the revenue from this source to about $50,000,000.*

1856.

The details of public business transacted by Congress, we need not now enter into; it will be sufficient for our present purpose to state, that the recommendations of the executive, and of the several heads of the departments, re-

* Appendix to Benton's "*Examination of the Dred Scott Case*," pp. 184–5.

* On the subject of steam navigation for the public service, and the importance of the government giving wise and liberal assistance thereto, we refer the reader to a valuable work, entitled "*Ocean Steam Navigation and the Ocean Post*," by Thomas Rainey. 8vo., pp. 224. N. Y. 1858.

ceived due attention, and a number of acts were passed by both Houses and obtained the approval of Mr. Pierce. For the civil and diplomatic expenses of the year were appropriated nearly $17,000,000; which, added to the other necessary appropriations for carrying on the government, as the army, the navy, the post-office, etc., made the total of appropriations, about $70,000,000. The tariff, after amendment and compromise between the views of the House and the Senate, was arranged in accordance with the president's recommendation. The bill passed the Senate by a vote of thirty-three to eight, and the House by a vote of one hundred and twenty-four to seventy-one. It was to go into effect on the 2d of July, 1857, and it was estimated, that the result would be a reduction in the revenue of about $20,000,000. The Atlantic Telegraph bill, as finally passed, provided that the sum to be paid the company should not exceed $70,000 per annum, until the net profits reached six per cent., and after that it should not exceed $50,000; that the tariff of prices should be fixed by the secretary of the treasury and Great Britain; that the citizens of America and England should be placed on an equal footing; and that Congress might end the contract at the expiration of ten years, by giving one year's notice.* Acts were also passed on the subject of promoting the efficiency of the navy, (p. 510); appropriating about $500,000 for constructing wagon-roads from Fort Kearney, by way of the South Pass of the Rocky Mountains and Great Salt Lake Valley, to California; authorizing the people of Minnesota to form a constitution and state government, preparatory to admission into the Union; granting lands in Minnesota, Alabama, etc., to aid in constructing certain railroads; providing for the punishment of certain crimes against the United States; together with the usual number of private acts.

1857.

At the December term, 1856, of the Supreme Court, an important case came before that learned body for decision, which has become well known throughout the country as the "Dred Scott Case." It excited unusual attention in every part of the United States, and the opinions of the chief-justice and the associate justices were submitted to criticism and examination far more than ordinarily keen and searching. Scott and his wife, it will be remembered, were slaves, belonging to Dr. Emerson, a surgeon in the United States army; they were taken into and resided in Illinois, and at Fort Snelling, in the territory in which, by the ordinance of 1787, slavery was forever prohibited; in 1838, Scott and his wife were taken into Missouri, where two children were born, and where they have ever since been held as slaves. They claimed freedom on the ground that, by the act of their master, they had been brought into free territory. The court decided against their claim, and ruled that negroes, slaves or free, are not, by the

* In August, 1857, an attempt was made to lay the cable for the Atlantic Telegraph Company. Unfortunately the cable gave way, when some three hundred miles of length had been paid out; and the great work of connecting the old world with the new by this means had to be postponed.

Constitution, citizens of the United States. The *political* aspects of the question, and the points argued by the court, and the views expressed, respecting the Missouri compromise, and the self-extension of the Constitution to territories, carrying slavery along with it, gave the Dred Scott case an interest which every citizen was able to appreciate; and the decision of the court did not have the effect of quieting agitation on the slavery question, but rather added fuel to that agitation.

1857. We quote, in the Appendix, a part of the chief-justice's opinion, and refer the reader to the official "Report of the Decision of the Supreme Court of the United States, and the opinion of the Judges thereof, in the case of Dred Scott, *versus* John A. Sandford," prepared by B. C. Howard, Reporter.

If the reader be desirous to look into this question under the light thrown upon it by Chief-Justice Taney and the six associate justices who agreed with him, and also under that which is furnished by the opinions of the two dissenting associate justices, he will study this volume, and endeavor to weigh well the force of the arguments on the two sides of that question which *must* be met, whether we wish it or not. Probably, too, the conviction will be forced upon his mind, that the sooner this question is amicably settled, on broad national grounds, on grounds which respect equally the rights of both the north and the south, the better it will be for all concerned; the sooner all the excitement, agitation, disputes, denunciations, threats, and the like, in regard to slavery and the claims of slavery, are put to rest, the better it will be for the country at large, and for the south in particular.* For, as Professor Tucker forcibly remarks—and his words deserve to be well noted, coming, as they do, from a southern man—"causes, not now foreseen, may prolong or abridge the existence of this institution (i. e., slavery) in the United States, but none of them seem capable of averting its ultimate destiny. We may say of it, as of man; the doom of its death, though we know not the time or the mode, *is certain and irrevocable.*"†

Governor Geary, (p. 519,) who had labored very diligently in his efforts to promote peace and order in Kansas, did not meet with all the success which he hoped for; so that, finding his health giving way, and the spirit of opposition still active against him and his proceedings, he judged it best to resign his post. His resignation was made in March, and Mr. Pierce's successor appointed, about the close of the month, Mr. Robert J. Walker governor, and Mr. F. P. Stanton secretary. The free-state convention, and the supporters of the views which led to that convention, continued to maintain their attitude of resistance to the legislative assembly and its acts. The prospect of further difficulties was not lessened, but rather

* In connection with this topic, we beg leave to refer the reader to Senator Benton's "*Examination of the Dred Scott Case.*" It is a vigorous production, and takes strong ground against the decision of the Supreme Court. For some extracts from this volume, see Appendix at the end of the present chapter.

† See the chapter on "The Future Progress of Slavery," in Tucker's "*Progress of the United States in Population and Wealth in Fifty Years.*" New York, 1843.

increased, as the year 1857 advanced in its course. The future of Kansas, and the various issues connected with the settlement of the question relating to it and its constitution, are beyond our present limits. We leave the story here incomplete, hoping that right and truth will prevail.

On the 3d of March, 1857, the thirty-fourth Congress reached its termination. At the same date, Franklin Pierce was released from the burdensome duties of president of the United States, and made way for his successor. Of his administration we need say but little. In most respects, it greatly disappointed the country; and the promises which seemed to be held out at the beginning of his term of office, (p. 500), failed, long before his four years expired, of satisfying the just demands of the people. Mr. Pierce came into office with some considerable *prestige*, as the democratic candidate and the exponent of democratic principles and purposes; he retired from his lofty position with a general feeling that he had not met the expectations of the party, and with, on their part, an ill-concealed sense, that it was high time to place the vessel of state under other guidance, if the party hoped to maintain its ascendency, and carry out its views to their completion. Of course, we are speaking simply of the retiring president's political career; for, in all other respects, as a man, a Christian gentleman, a lover and supporter of truth and order, Mr. Pierce deserves honorable mention. We cheerfully accord him all this; but, so far as the judgment of the country has, at this date, been expressed, Franklin Pierce's administration must be pronounced, to all intents and purposes, little short of a failure.

1857.

APPENDIX TO CHAPTER VIII.

SENATOR BENTON'S VIEWS ON ABROGATING THE MISSOURI COMPROMISE, AND ON THE SELF-EXTENSION OF THE CONSTITUTION.

In assuming to decide these questions—(constitutionality of the Missouri compromise, and the self-extension of the Constitution to territories)—it is believed the Supreme Court committed two great errors; first, in the assumption to try such questions; secondly, in deciding them as they did. And it is certain, that the decisions are contrary to the uniform action of all the departments of the government—one of them for thirty-six years; and the other for seventy years; and in their effects upon each are equivalent to an alteration of the Constitution, by inserting new clauses in it, which could not have been put in at the time that instrument was made, nor at any time since, nor now.

The Missouri compromise was a "*political enactment*," made by the political power, for reasons founded in national policy, enlarged and liberal, of which it was the proper judge; and which was not to be reversed afterwards by judicial interpretation of words and phrases.

Doubtless the court was actuated by the most laudable motives in undertaking, while settling an individual controversy, to pass from the private rights of an individual to the public rights of the whole body of the people; and in endeavoring to settle, by a judicial decision, a political question which engrosses and distracts the country; but the undertaking was beyond its competency, both legally and potentially. It had no right to decide; no means to enforce the decision; no machinery to carry it into effect; no penalties of fines or jails to enforce it; and the event has corresponded with these inabilities. Far from settling the question, the opinion itself has become a new question, more virulent than the former; has become the very watchword of parties; has gone into party creeds and platforms—bringing the court itself into the political field—and condemning all future appointments of federal judges (and the elections of those who make the appointments, and of those who can multiply judges by creating new districts and circuits) to the test of these decisions. This being the case, and the evil now actually upon us, there is no resource but to face it—to face this new question—examine its foundations—show its errors—and rely upon reason and intelligence to work out a safe deliverance for the country.

. . . .

This is the exposition of the first great error of the court, as I hold it, in the part of its opinion which I propose to examine; the error of assuming without right, and without necessity, to decide upon the constitutionality of the Missouri compromise act, and the self-extension of the Constitution to territories. The second great error is in the decision itself upon these questions.

. . . .

The novelty and strangeness of this proposition (self-extension of the Constitution) called up Mr. Webster (1849) who repulsed, as an absurdity and as an impossibility, the scheme of extending the Constitution to territories. His words were; "let me say, that in this general sense, there is no such thing as extending the Constitution. The Constitution is extended over the United States, and nothing else. It cannot be extended over any thing, except the old states and the new states that shall come in hereafter, when they do come in. There is a want of accuracy of ideas in this respect that is quite remarkable, among eminent gentlemen, and especially professional and judicial gentlemen. It seems to be taken for granted, that the right of trial by jury, the *habeas corpus*, and every principle designed to protect personal liberty, is extended, by force of the Constitution itself over every new territory. That proposition cannot be maintained at all. How do you arrive at it by any reasoning or deduction? It can only be arrived at by the loosest of all possible constructions. It is said that this must be so, or else the right of *habeas corpus* would be lost. Undoubtedly, these rights must be conferred by law before they can be enjoyed in a territory." . . . .
Mr. Calhoun replied, contending that the Constitution could be so extended, and, being the supreme law of the land, would carry along with it protection to persons and property, *to wit*, the owner and his slaves; and would override and control all laws opposed to that protection. He boldly avowed his intent to carry slavery into the territories under the wing of the Constitution, and denounced as enemies to the south all who opposed it.

. . . .

It was in the year 1820 that this great compromise was effected. Twenty-five years afterwards it received a re-enactment, and under circumstances the most impressive. It was in the year 1845, and on the occasion of the legislative admission of the state of Texas into the Union. In the previous year, annexation by treaty had been refused; legislation was held by many to be the indispensable basis to any incorporation; and, accordingly, that mode of annexation prevailed. Early in the session, 1844–45, the last of Tyler's administration, a joint resolution was brought into the House of Representatives for the admission of that republic as a state into the Union. . . . . . This brings down the sanctions of the Missouri compromise to the year 1845—being twenty-five years after its first enactment—ample time, it might be supposed, for its constitutionality to be questioned, if there was ground for it; and ample time for it to have been found out, if such was the fact, that its enactment worked an inequality of the states, and involved degradation and injury to a part of them. . . . . . The year 1850 presents the last instance to be given of southern sanction of the Missouri compromise line—a date sufficiently recent to avoid the statute of limitations, if any date can be late enough to prevent the running of that statute against mutable politicians. Mr. Calhoun was then dead; Mr. Davis, of Mississippi, seemed to succeed to the head of his party; and in the discussion of Mr. Clay's compromise scheme, reported from the committee of thirteen, demanded the extension of the Missouri line to the Pacific Ocean, and the recognition of slavery on the south side of that line; and declared these terms to be the least he would take. . . . . . The understanding was, that Congress had power to legislate upon slavery in the territories, and to abolish it therein when it saw fit, and that such legislation worked no inequality in the states; and in the particular case of the Missouri compromise act, the partition of the province of Louisiana between free and slave states was a continuation of the policy which divided the territory east of the Mississippi, between the same classes of states; and as necessary then to save the Union as the ordinance of 1787 had been to save it.

. . . .

Those who suppose that there was no object in view in this abrogation of the Missouri compromise, but merely to make Kansas a free state, are far behind the state of the facts, and can have had but little opportunity of knowing the intentions of the prime movers of that measure—those who ruled the council that commanded it. Certainly that was one of the objects; but there were others far beyond it, far transcending it in importance, and of which the establishment of Kansas as a slave state was only an introduction, and a means of attainment. To form the slave states into a unit, for federal elections and legislation, by the revival of the slavery question, was one object, counting upon the federal patronage to gain as much help from the free states as would give the slave states the majority. Vast acquisitions of free territory to the southward, to be made slave (besides Cuba) was another object; and for this purpose, the principles of the Kansas-Nebraska bill were doubly contrived; first, to carry slavery into these free territories by the Constitution; next, to establish it by the inhabitants of the states, enough southern people going in to dominate over the feeble and ignorant natives. Separation of the slave states, or domination over the free states, driving out of the Union the north Atlantic states, was to be the consequence of this consolidation of the slave states and vast acquisition of slave territory.

. . . .

The prohibition of slavery in a territory is assumed to work an inequality in the states, allowing one part to carry its property with it, the other, not. This is a mistake—a great error of fact—the source of great errors of deduction. The citizens of all the states, free and slave, are precisely equal in their capacity to carry their property with them into territories. Each may carry whatever is property by the laws of nature; neither can carry that which is only property by statute law, and the reason is. because he cannot carry with him the law which makes it property. Either may carry the thing which is the subject of this local property, but neither can carry the law which makes it so. The Virginian may carry his man slave; but he cannot carry the Virginian law which makes him a slave. The citizen of Massachusetts may carry the pile of money which, under a state law, constitutes a bank; but he cannot carry the law or charter which makes it a bank; and his treasure is only a pile of money; and besides being impossible, it would be absurd, and confusion confounded to be otherwise. For, if the citizen of one state might carry his slave state law with him into a territory, the citizens of every other slave state might do the same; and then what Babylonish confusion, not merely of tongues, but of laws, would be found there! Fifteen different codes, as the slave states now number, and more to come. For every slave slate has a servile code of its own, differing from others in some respects—and in some, radically; as much so as land, in the eye of the law, differs from cattle. Thus, in some states, as in Virginia, and others, slaves are only chattels; in others, as in Kentucky and Louisiana, they are real estate. How would all these codes work together in a territory under the wing of the Constitution, protecting all equally?

. . . .

Mr. Calhoun (1848) declared; "I deny that the laws of Mexico can have the effect attributed to them (that of keeping slavery out of New Mexico and California.) As soon as the treaty between the two countries is ratified, the sovereignty and authority of Mexico in the territory acquired by it becomes extinct, and that of the

United States is substituted in its place, conveying the Constitution, with its overriding control over all the laws and institutions of Mexico inconsistent with it." This is the declared effect of the transmigration of the Constitution to free territory by the author of the doctrine; and great is the extent of country, either acquired or to be acquired, in which the doctrine is to have application. All New Mexico and California, at the time it was broached—all the territories now held, wherever situated, and as much as can be added to them—these additions have already been considerable, and vast and varied accessions are still expected. Arizonia has been acquired; fifty millions were offered to Mexico for her northern half, to include Monterey and Saltillo; a vast sum is now offered for Sonora and Sinaloa, down to Guyamas; Tehuantepec, Nicaragua, Panama, Darien, the Spanish part of San Domingo, Cuba! with islands on both sides of the tropical continent. Nor do we stop at the two Americas, their coasts and islands, extensive as they are; but circumvolving the terraqueous globe, we look wistfully at the Sandwich Islands, and on some gem in the Polynesian group; and, plunging to the Antipodes, pounce down upon Formosa in the Chinese Sea. Such were the schemes of the last administration, and must continue, if its policy should continue. Over all these provinces, isthmuses, islands, and ports, now free, our Constitution must spread, (if we acquire them, and the decision of the Supreme Court stands) overriding and overruling anti-slavery law in their respective limits, and planting African slavery in its place, beyond the power of Congress or the people there to prevent it.

II. OPINION OF THE COURT

AS DELIVERED BY MR. CHIEF-JUSTICE TANEY.

It becomes our duty to decide whether the facts stated in the plea, are or are not sufficient to show that the plaintiff is not entitled to sue as a citizen in a court of the United States.

This is certainly a very serious question, and one that now for the first time has been brought for decision before this court. But it is brought here by those who have a right to bring it, and it is our duty to meet it and decide it.

The question is simply this: Can a negro, whose ancestors were imported into this country, and sold as slaves, become a member of the political community formed and brought into existence by the Constitution of the United States, and as such become entitled to all the rights, and privileges, and immunities, guaranteed by that instrument to the citizen? One of which rights is the privilege of suing in a court of the United States in the cases specified in the Constitution.

It will be observed, that the plea applies to that class of persons only, whose ancestors were negroes of the African race, and imported into this country, and sold and held as slaves. The only matter in issue before the court, therefore, is, whether the descendants of such slaves, when they shall be emancipated, or who are born of parents who had become free before their birth, are citizens of a state, in the sense in which the word citizen is used in the Constitution of the United States. And this being the only matter in dispute on the pleadings, the court must be understood as speaking in this opinion of that class only, that is, of those persons who are the descendants of Africans who were imported into this country, and sold as slaves.

The situation of this population was altogether unlike that of the Indian race. The latter, it is true, formed no part of the colonial communities, and never amalgamated with them in social connections or in government. But although they were uncivilized, they were yet a free and independent people, associated together in nations or tribes, and governed by their own laws. Many of these political communities were situated in territories to which the white race claimed the ultimate right of dominion. But that claim was acknowledged to be subject to the right of the Indians to occupy it as long as they thought proper, and neither the English nor colonial governments claimed or exercised any dominion over the tribe or nation by whom it was occupied, nor claimed the right to the possession of the territory, until the tribe or nation consented to cede it. These Indian governments were regarded and treated as foreign governments, as much so as if an ocean had separated the red man from the white; and their freedom has constantly been acknowledged, from the time of the first emigration to the English colonies to the present day, by the different governments which succeeded each other. Treaties have been negotiated with them, and their alliance sought for in war; and the people who compose these Indian political communities have always been treated as foreigners not living under our government. It is true that the course of events has brought the Indian tribes within the limits of the United States under subjection to the white race; and it has been found necessary, for their sake as well as our own, to regard them as in a state of pupilage, and to legislate to a certain extent over them and the territory they occupy. But they may, without doubt, like the subjects of any other foreign government, be naturalized by the authority of Congress, and become citizens of a state, and of the United States; and if an individual should leave his nation or tribe, and take up his abode among the white population, he would be entitled to all the rights and privileges which would belong to an emigrant from any other foreign people.

. . . .

It becomes necessary, therefore, to determine who were citizens of the several states when the Constitution was adopted. And in order to do this, we must recur to the governments and institutions of the thirteen colonies, when they separated from Great Britain and formed new sovereignties, and took their place in the family of independent nations. We must inquire who, at that time, were recognized as the people or citizens of a state, whose rights and liberties had been outraged by the English government; and who declared their independence, and assumed the powers of government to defend their rights by force of arms.

In the opinion of the court, the legislation and histories of the times, and the language used in the Declaration of Independence, show, that neither the class of persons who had been imported as slaves, nor their descendants, whether they had become free or not, were then acknowledged as a part of the people, nor intended to be included in the general words used in that memorable instrument.

It is difficult at this day to realize the state of public opinion in relation to that unfortunate race, which prevailed in the civilized and enlightened portions of the world at the time of the Declaration of Independence, and when the Constitution of the United States was framed and adopted. But the public history of every European nation displays it in a manner too plain to be mistaken.

They had for more than a century before been regarded as beings of an inferior order, and altogether unfit to associate with the white race, either in social or political relations; and so far inferior, that they had no rights which the white man was bound to respect; and that the negro might justly and lawfully be reduced to slavery for his benefit. He was bought and sold, and treated as an ordinary article of merchandise and traffic, whenever a profit could be made by it. This opinion was at that time fixed and universal in the civilized portion of the white race. It was regarded as an axiom in morals as well as in politics, which no one thought of disputing, or supposed to be open to dispute; and men in every grade and position in society, daily and habitually acted upon it in their private pursuits, as well as in matters of public concern, without doubting for a moment the correctness of this opinion.

And in no nation was this opinion more firmly fixed or more uniformly acted upon, than by the English government and English people. They not only seized them on the coast of Africa, and sold them or held them in slavery for their own use; but they took them as ordinary articles of merchandise, to every country where they could make a profit on them, and were far more extensively engaged in this commerce than any other nation in the world.

The opinion thus entertained and acted upon in England, was naturally impressed upon the colonies they founded on this side of the Atlantic. And, accordingly, a negro of the African race was regarded by them as an article of property, and held, and bought and sold as such, in every one of the thirteen colonies which united in the Declaration of Independence, and afterwards formed the Constitution of the United States. The slaves were more or less numerous in the different colonies, as slave labor was found more or less profitable. But no one seems to have doubted the correctness of the prevailing opinion of the time.

. . . .

The language of the Declaration of Independence is equally conclusive:

It begins by declaring that, "when in the course of human events it becomes necessary for one people to dissolve the political bands which have connected them with another, and to assume among the powers of the earth the separate and equal station to which the laws of nature and nature's God entitle them, a decent respect for the opinions of mankind requires that they should declare the causes which impel them to the separation."

It then proceeds to say: "We hold these truths to be self-evident: that all men are created equal; that they are endowed by their Creator with certain unalienable rights; that among them is life, liberty, and the pursuit of happiness; that to secure these rights, governments are instituted, deriving their just powers from the consent of the governed."

The general words above quoted would seem to embrace the whole human family, and if they were used in a similar instrument at this day would be so understood. But it is too clear for dispute, that the enslaved African race were not intended to be included, and formed no part of the people who framed and adopted this declaration; for if the language, as understood in that day, would embrace them, the conduct of the distinguished men who framed the Declaration of Independence would have been utterly and flagrantly inconsistent with the principles they asserted; and instead of the sympathy of mankind, to which they so confidently appealed, they would have deserved and received universal rebuke and reprobation.

. . . .

This brings us to examine by what provision of the Constitution the present federal government, under its delegated and restricted powers, is authorized to acquire territory outside of the original limits of the United States, and what powers it may exercise therein over the person or property of a citizen of the United States, while it remains a territory, and until it shall be admitted as one of the states of the Union.

There is certainly no power given by the Constitution to the federal government to establish or maintain colonies bordering on the United States or at a distance, to be ruled and governed at its own pleasure; nor to enlarge its territorial limits in any way, except by the admission of new states. That power is plainly given; and if a new state is admitted, it needs no further legislation by Congress, because the Constitution itself defines the relative rights and powers, and duties of the state, and the citizens of the state, and the federal government. But no power is given to acquire a territory to be held and governed permanently in that character.

And indeed the power exercised by Congress to acquire territory and establish a government there, according to its own unlimited discretion, was viewed with great jealousy by the leading statesmen of the day. And in the Federalist, (No. 38,) written by Mr. Madison, he speaks of the acquisition of the Northwestern Territory by the confederated states, by the cession from Virginia, and the establishment of a government there, as an exercise of power not warranted by the Articles of Confederation, and dangerous to the liberties of the people. And he urges the adoption of the Constitution as a security and safeguard against such an exercise of power.

We do not mean, however, to question the power of Congress in this respect. The power to expand the territory of the United States by the admission of new states is plainly given; and in the construction of this power by all the departments of the government, it has been held to authorize the acquisition of territory, not fit for admission at the time, but to be admitted as soon as its population and situation would entitle it to admission. It is acquired to become a state, and not to be held as a colony and governed by Congress with absolute authority; and as the propriety of admitting a new state is committed to the sound discretion of Congress, the power to acquire territory for that purpose, to be held by the United States until it is in a suitable condition to become a state upon an equal footing with the other states, must rest upon the same discretion. It is a question for the political department of the government, and not the judicial; and whatever the political department of the government shall recognize as within the limits of the United States, the judicial department is also bound to recognize, and to administer in it the laws of the United States, so far as they apply, and to maintain in the territory the authority and rights of the government, and also the personal rights and rights of property of individual citizens, as secured by the Constitution. All we mean to say on this point is, that, as there is no express regulation in the Constitution defining the power which the general government may exercise over the person or property of a citizen in a territory thus acquired, the court must necessarily look to the provisions and principles of the Constitution, and its distribution of powers, for the rules and principles by which its decision must be governed.

Taking this rule to guide us, it may be safely assumed that citizens of the United States who migrate to a territory belonging to the people of the United States, cannot be ruled as mere colonists, dependent upon the will of the general government, and to be governed by any laws it may think proper to impose. The principle upon which our government rests, and upon which alone they continue to exist, is the union of states, sovereign and independent within their own limits in their internal and domestic concerns, and bound together as one people by a general government, possessing certain enumerated and restricted powers, delegated to it by the people of the several states, and exercising supreme authority within the scope of the powers granted to it, throughout the dominion of the United States. A power, therefore, in the general government to obtain and hold colonies and dependent territories, over which they might legislate without restriction, would be inconsistent with its own existence in its present form. Whatever it acquires, it acquires for the benefit of the people of the several states who created it. It is their trustee acting for them, and charged with the duty of promoting the interests of the whole people of the Union in the exercise of the powers specifically granted.

At the time when the territory in question was obtained by cession from France it contained no population fit to be associated together and admitted as a state; and it therefore was absolutely necessary to hold possession of it, as a territory belonging to the United States, until it was settled and inhabited by a civilized community capable of self-government, and in a condition to be admitted on equal terms with the other states as a member of the Union. But, as we have before said, it was acquired by the general government, as the representative and trustee of the people of the United States, and it must therefore be held in that character for their common and equal benefit; for it was the people of the several states, acting through their agent and representative, the federal government, who in fact acquired the territory in question, and the government holds it for their common use until it shall be associated with the other states as a member of the Union.

But until that time arrives, it is undoubtedly necessary that some government should be established, in order to organize society, and to protect the inhabitants in their persons and property; and as the people of the United States could act in this matter only through the government which represented them, and through which they spoke and acted when the territory was obtained, it was not only within the scope of its powers, but it was its duty to pass such laws and establish such a government as would enable those by whose authority they acted to reap the advantages anticipated from its acquisition, and to gather there a population which would enable it to assume the position to which it was destined among the states of the Union. The power to acquire necessarily carries with it the power to preserve and apply to the purposes for which it was acquired. The form of government to be established necessarily rested in the discretion of Congress. It was their duty to establish the one that would be best suited for the protection and security of the citizens of the United States, and other inhabitants who might be authorized to take up their abode there, and that must always depend upon the existing condition of the territory, as to the number and character of its inhabitants, and their situation in the territory. In some cases a government, consisting of persons appointed by the federal government, would best subserve the interests of the territory, when the inhabitants were few and scattered, and new to one another. In other instances, it would be more advisable to commit the powers of self-government to the people who had settled in the territory, as being the most competent to determine what was best for their own interests. But some form of civil authority would be absolutely necessary to organize and preserve civilized society, and prepare it to become a state; and what is the best form must always depend on the condition of the territory at the time, and the choice of the mode must depend upon the exercise of a discretionary power by Congress, acting within the scope of its constitutional authority, and not infringing upon the rights of person or rights of property of the citizen who might go there to reside, or for any other lawful purpose. It was acquired by the exercise of this discretion, and it must be held and governed in like manner, until it is fitted to be a state.

But the power of Congress over the person or property of a citizen can never be a mere discretionary power under our Constitution and form of government. The powers of the government and the rights and privileges of the citizen are regulated and plainly defined by the Constitution itself. And when the territory becomes a part of the United States, the federal government enters into possession in the character impressed upon it by those who created it. It enters upon it with its powers over the citizen strictly defined, and limited by the Constitution, from which it derives its own existence, and by virtue of which alone it continues to exist and act as a government and sovereignty. It has no power of any kind beyond it; and it cannot, when it enters a territory of the United States, put off its character, and assume discretionary or despotic powers which the Constitution has denied to it. It cannot create for itself a new character separated from the citizens of the United States, and the duties it owes them under the provisions of the Constitution. The territory being a part of the United States, the government and the citizen both enter it under the authority of the Constitution, with their respective rights defined and marked out; and the federal government can exercise no power over his person or property, beyond what that instrument confers, nor lawfully deny any right which it has reserved.

A reference to a few of the provisions of the Constitution will illustrate this proposition.

For example, no one, we presume, will contend that Congress can make any law in a territory respecting the establishment of religion, or the free exercise thereof, or abridging the freedom of speech or of the press, or the right of the people of the territory peaceably to assemble, and to petition the government for the redress of grievances.

Nor can Congress deny to the people the right to keep and bear arms, nor the right to trial by jury, nor compel any one to be a witness against himself in a criminal proceeding.

These powers, and others, in relation to rights of person, which it is not necessary here to enumerate, are, in express and positive terms, denied to the general government; and the rights of private property have been guarded with equal care. Thus the rights of property are united with the rights of person, and placed on the same ground by the fifth amendment to the Constitution, which provides that no person shall be deprived of life, liberty, and property, without due process of law. And an act of Congress which deprives a citizen of the United States of his liberty or property, merely because he came himself or brought his property into a particular territory of the United States, and who had committed no offence against the laws, could hardly be dignified with the name of due process of law.

So, too, it will hardly be contended that Congress could by law quarter a soldier in a house in a territory without the consent of the owner, in time of peace; nor in time of war, but in a manner prescribed by law. Nor could they by law forfeit the property of a citizen in a territory, who was convicted of treason, for a longer period than the life of the person convicted; nor take private property for public use without just compensation.

The powers over person and property of which we speak are not only not granted to Congress, but are in express terms denied, and they are forbidden to exercise them. And this prohibition is not confined to the states, but the words are general, and extend to the whole territory over which the Constitution gives it power to legislate, including those portions of it remaining under territorial government, as well as that covered by states. It is a total absence of power everywhere within the dominion of the United States, and places the citizens of a territory, so far as these rights are concerned, on the same footing with the citizens of the states, and guards them as firmly and plainly against any inroads which the general government might attempt, under the plea of implied or incidental powers. And if Congress itself cannot do this—if it is beyond the powers conferred on the federal government—it will be admitted, we presume, that it could not authorize a territorial government to exercise them. It could confer no power on any local government, established by its authority, to violate the provisions of the Constitution.

It seems, however, to be supposed, that there is a difference between a property in a slave and other property, and that different rules may be applied to it in expounding the Constitution of the United States. And the laws and usages of nations, and the writings of eminent jurists upon the relation of master and slave and their mutual rights and duties, and the powers which governments may exercise over it, have been dwelt upon in the argument.

But in considering the question before us, it must be borne in mind that there is no law of nations standing between the people of the United States and their government, and interfering with their relation to each other. The powers of the government, and the rights of the citizen under it, are positive and practical regulations plainly written down. The people of the United States have delegated to it certain enumerated powers, and forbidden it to exercise others. It has no power over the person or property of a citizen but what the citizens of the United States have granted. And no laws or usages of other nations, or reasoning of statesmen or jurists upon the relations of master and slave, can enlarge the powers of the government, or take from the citizens the rights they have reserved. And if the Constitution recognizes the right of property of the master in a slave, and makes no distinction between that description of property and other property owned by a citizen, no tribunal, acting under the authority of the United States, whether it be legislative, executive, or judicial, has a right to draw such a distinction, or deny to it the benefit of the provisions and guarantees which have been provided for the protection of private property against the encroachments of the government.

Now, as we have already said in an earlier part of this opinion, upon a different point, the right of property in a slave is distinctly and expressly affirmed in the Constitution. The right to traffic in it, like an ordinary article of merchandise and property, was guaranteed to the citizens of the United States, in every state that might desire it, for twenty years. And the government, in express terms, is pledged to protect it in all future time, if the slave escape from his owner. This is done in plain words—too plain to be misunderstood. And no word can be found in the Constitution which gives Congress a greater power over slave property, or which entitles property of that kind to less protection than property of any other description. The only power conferred is the power coupled with the duty of guarding and protecting the owner in his rights.

Upon these considerations, it is the opinion of the court that the act of Congress which prohibited a citizen from holding and owning property of this kind in the territory of the United States north of the line therein mentioned, is not warranted by the Constitution, and is therefore void; and that neither Dred Scott himself, nor any of his family, were made free by being carried into this territory; even if they had been carried there by the owner, with the intention of becoming a permanent resident.

. . . .

Upon the whole, therefore, it is the judgment of this court, that it appears by the record before us, that the plaintiff in error is not a citizen of Missouri, in the sense in which that word is used in the Constitution; and that the Circuit Court of the United States, for that reason, had no jurisdiction in the case, and could give no judgment in it. Its judgment for the defendant must, consequently, be reversed, and a mandate issued, directing the suit to be dismissed for want of jurisdiction.

James Buchanan

CHAPTER IX.

1857.

OPENING OF BUCHANAN'S ADMINISTRATION.

Imposing ceremonies connected with Mr. Buchanan's inauguration — His Inaugural address in full — Takes the oath of office — Opening prospects for the administration of the fifteenth president — Names of the gentlemen chosen as his cabinet — The Senate closes its extra session — Concluding remarks and reflections. APPENDIX TO CHAPTER IX. — Valuable and interesting statistics.

WEDNESDAY, March 4th, 1857, being the day appointed for the commencement of a new administration, was observed at Washington with more than ordinary enthusiasm and display. James Buchanan reached the seat of government early on the 3d of March, and, soon after noon the next day, he made his appearance in the Senate-chamber, where were assembled the

1857.

vice-president, John C. Breckenridge, (who had just taken the oath of office,) the members of the Senate, the Supreme Court judges, the diplomatic corps, and others connected with the government. The retiring president, Mr. Pierce, also graced the inauguration with his presence. At one o'clock, Mr. Buchanan, accompanied by a great crowd of citizens, by the military of the District, civic companies, etc., proceeded to the eastern portico of the capitol, and, following the time-honored custom of those who had preceded him, he delivered his Inaugural address. Its length was moderate, and the sentiments and views of the new president were set forth in the following terms:

"FELLOW-CITIZENS:

"I appear before you this day to take the solemn oath that I will faithfully execute the office of President of the United States, and will, to the best of my ability, preserve, protect, and defend the Constitution of the United States. In entering upon this great office, I most humbly invoke the God of our fathers for wisdom and firmness to execute its high and responsible duties in such a manner as to restore harmony and the ancient friendship among the people of the several states, and to preserve our free institutions throughout many generations. Convinced that I owe my election to the inherent love for the Constitution and the Union which still animates the hearts of the American people, let me earnestly ask their powerful support in sustaining all just measures calculated to perpetuate these, the richest political blessings which Heaven has ever bestowed upon any nation. Having determined not to become a candidate for re-election, I shall have no motive to influence my conduct in administering the government, except the desire ably and faithfully to serve my country, and to live in the grateful memory of my countrymen.

"We have recently passed through a presidential contest in which the passions of our fellow-citizens were excited to the highest degree by questions of deep and vital importance; but when the people proclaimed their will, the tempest at once subsided, and all was calm. The voice of the majority, speaking in the manner prescribed by the Constitution, was heard, and instant submission followed. Our own country could alone have exhibited so grand and striking a spectacle of the capacity of man for self-government. What a happy conception, then, was it for Congress to apply this simple rule, that the will of the majority shall govern to the settlement of the question of domestic slavery in the territories! Congress is
1857. neither to legislate slavery into any territory or state, nor to exclude it therefrom; but to leave the people thereof perfectly free to form and regulate their domestic institutions in their own way, subject only to the Constitution of the United States as a natural consequence. Congress has also prescribed, that when the territory of Kansas shall be admitted as a state, it shall be received into the Union with or without slavery, as their Constitution may prescribe at the time of their admission. A difference of opinion has arisen in regard to the time when the people of a territory shall decide this question for themselves. This is, happily, a matter of but little practical importance, and beside, it is a judicial question, which legitimately belongs to the Supreme Court of the United States, before whom it is now pending, and will, it is understood, be speedily and finally settled. To their decision, in common with all good citizens, I shall cheerfully submit, whatever this may be, though it has been my individual opinion, that under the Nebraska-Kansas act, the appropriate period will be when the number of actual residents in the territories shall justify the formation of a constitution with a view to its admission as a state into the Union. But, be this as it may, it is the imperative and indispensable duty of the government of the United States to secure to every resident inhabitant the free and independent expression of his opinion by his vote. This sacred right of each individual must be preserved. This being accomplished, nothing can be fairer than to leave the people of a territory free from all foreign interference to decide their own destiny for themselves, subject only to the Constitution of the United States. The whole territorial question being thus
settled upon the principle of 1857.
popular sovereignty—a principle as ancient as free government itself—every thing of a practical nature has been decided, and no other question remains for adjustment, because all agree that, under the Constitution, slavery in the states is beyond the reach of any human power, except that of the respective states themselves wherein it exists. May we not, then, hope that the long agitation on this subject is approaching its end, and that the geographical parties to which it has given birth, so much dreaded by the father of his country,

will speedily become extinct? Most happy will it be for the country when the public mind shall be diverted from this question to others of more pressing and practical importance.

"Throughout the whole progress of this agitation, which has scarcely known any intermission for more than twenty years, while it has been productive of no positive good to any human being, it has been the prolific source of great evils to the master, to the slave, and to the whole country; it has alienated and estranged the people of the sister states from each other, and has even seriously endangered the very existence of the Union. Nor has the danger yet entirely ceased. Under our system there is a remedy for all mere political evils in the sound sense and sober judgment of the people. Time is a great corrective. The political subjects which, but a few years ago, exasperated the public mind, have passed away and are now nearly forgotten; but this question of domestic slavery is of far greater importance than any mere political question, because, should the agitation continue, it may eventually endanger the personal safety of a large portion of our countrymen where the institution exists. In that event, no form of government, however productive of material benefits, can compensate for the loss of peace and domestic security around the family altar. Let every Union-loving man, therefore, exert his best influence to suppress this agitation, which, since the recent legislation of Congress, is without any legitimate object.

"It is an evil of the times, that men have undertaken to calculate the mere material value of the Union. Reasoned estimates have been presented of the pecuniary profits and local advantages which would result to different states and sections from its dissolution, and of the comparative injuries which such an event would inflict on other states and sections. Even descending to this low and narrow view of the mighty question, all such calculations are at fault. The bare reference to a single consideration will be conclusive on this point.

"We at present enjoy a free trade throughout our extensive and expansive country, such as the world never witnessed. This trade is conducted on railroads and canals, on noble rivers and arms of the sea, which bind together the North and the South, the East and the West of our confederacy. Annihilate this trade, arrest its free progress by the geographical lines of jealous and hostile states, and you destroy the prosperity and onward march of the whole and every part, and involve all in one common ruin.

"But such considerations, important as they are in themselves, sink into insignificance when we reflect on the terrific evils which would result from disunion to every portion of the confederacy—to the North not more than to the South, to the East not more than to the West. These I shall not attempt to portray, because I feel an humble confidence that the kind Providence which inspired our fathers 1857. with wisdom to frame the most perfect form of government and union ever devised by man, will not suffer it to perish until it shall have been peacefully instrumental, by its example, in the extension of civil and religious liberty throughout the world.

"Next in importance to the maintenance of the Constitution and the Union, is the duty of preserving the government free from the taint or even the suspicion of corruption. Public virtue is the vital spirit of republics; and history proves that when this has decayed, and the love of money has usurped its place, although the forms of free government may remain for a season, the substance has departed forever. Our present financial condition is without a parallel in history. No nation has ever before been embarrassed from too large a surplus in the treasury. This almost necessarily gives birth to extravagant legislation. It produces wild schemes of expenditures, and begets a race of speculators and jobbers, whose ingenuity is exerted in contriving and promoting expedients to obtain the public money. The party, through its official agents, whether rightfully or wrongfully, is suspected, and the character of the government suffers in the estimation of the people. This is, in itself, a very great evil. The natural mode of relief from this embarrassment, is to appropriate the surplus in the treasury to great national objects for which a clear warrant can be found in the Constitution. Among these, I might mention the extinguishment of the public debt, a reasonable increase of the navy, which is at present inadequate to the protection of our vast tonnage afloat—now greater than that of any other nation,—
1857. as well as the defence of our extended sea-coast. It is, beyond all question, the true principle, that no more revenue ought to be collected from the people than the amount necessary to defray the expenses of a wise, economical, and efficient administration of the government. To reach this point, it was necessary to resort to a modification of the tariff, and this has been accomplished in such a manner as to do as little injury as may have been practicable to our domestic manufactures, especially those necessary for the defence of the country. Any discrimination against a particular branch, for the purpose of benefiting favored corporations, individuals, or interests, would have been unjust to the rest of the community, and inconsistent with that spirit of fairness and equality which ought to govern in the adjustment of a revenue tariff—but the squandering of the public money sinks into comparative insignificance, as a temptation to corruption, when compared with the squandering of the public lands.

"No nation in the tide of time has ever been blessed with so rich and noble an inheritance as we enjoy in the public lands. In administering this important trust, while it may be wise to grant portions of them for the improvement of the remainder, yet we should never forget, that it is our cardinal policy to reserve these lands as much as may be for actual settlers, and this, at moderate prices. We shall thus not only best promote the prosperity of the new states, by furnishing them a hardy and independent race of honest and industrious citizens, but shall secure homes for our children and our children's children, as well as for those exiles from foreign shores, who may seek in this country to improve their condition and to enjoy the blessings of civil and religious liberty. Such emigrants have done much to promote the growth and prosperity of the country. They have proved faithful both in peace and in war. After becoming citizens, they are entitled, under the Constitution and laws, to be placed on perfect equality with native-born citizens, and in this character they should ever be kindly recognized.

"The Federal Constitution is a grant from the states to Congress of certain specific powers, and the question whether this grant shall be liberally or strictly construed, has, more or less, divided political parties from the beginning. Without entering into the argument, I desire to state at the commencement of my administration, that long experience and observation have convinced me, that a strict construction of the powers of the government is the only true, as well as the only safe, theory of the Constitution. Whenever, in our past history, doubtful powers have been exercised by Congress, they have never failed to produce injurious and unhappy consequences. Many such instances might be adduced if this were the proper occasion. Neither is it necessary for the public service to strain the language of the Constitution, because all the great and useful powers required for

1857.

a successful administration of the government, both in peace and in war, have been granted, either in express terms or by the plainest implication. While deeply convinced of these truths, I yet consider it clear that, under the war-making power, Congress may appropriate money toward the construction of a military road, when this is absolutely necessary for the defence of any state or territory of the Union against foreign invasion. Under the Constitution, Congress has power to declare war, to raise and support armies, to provide and maintain a navy, and to call forth the militia to repel invasion. Thus, endowed in an ample manner with the war-making power, the corresponding duty is required, that the United States shall protect each of them (the states) against invasion. How is it possible to afford this protection to California and our Pacific possessions, except by means of a military road through the territory of the United States, over which men and munitions of war may be speedily transported from the Atlantic states to meet and repel the invader? In case of a war with a naval power much stronger than our own, we should then have no other available access to the Pacific coast, because such a power would instantly close the route across the Isthmus of Central America. It is impossible to conceive, that while the Constitution has expressly required Congress to defend all the states, it should yet deny to them, by any fair construction, the only possible means by which one of these states can be defended. Beside, the government, ever since its origin, has been in the constant practice of constructing military roads. It might also be wise to consider whether the love for the Union, which now animates our fellow-citizens on the Pacific coast, may not be impaired by our neglect or refusal to provide for them, in their remote and isolated condition, the only means by which the power of the states on this side of the Rocky Mountains can reach them in sufficient time to protect them against invasion.

"I forbear, for the present, from expressing an opinion as to the wisest and most economical mode in which the government can lend its aid in accomplishing this great and necessary work. I believe that many difficulties in the way, which now appear formidable, will, in a great degree, vanish as soon as the nearest and best route shall have been satisfactorily ascertained.

"It may be right that, on this occasion, I should make some brief remarks as to our rights and duties as a member of the great family of nations. In our intercourse with them, there are some plain principles, approved by our own experience, from which we should never depart. We ought to cultivate peace, commerce, and friendship with all nations, and this not merely as the best means of promoting our own national interest, but in a spirit of Christian benevolence toward our fellow-men, wherever their lot may be cast. Our diplomacy should be direct and frank, neither seeking to obtain more nor accepting less than is our due. We ought to cherish a sacred regard for the independence of all nations, and never attempt to interfere in the domestic con-
1857. cerns of any, unless this shall be imperatively required by the great law of self-preservation. To avoid entangling alliances has been a maxim of our policy ever since the days of Washington, and its wisdom no one will attempt to dispute. In short, we ought to do justice, in a kindly spirit, to all nations, and require justice from them in return. It is our glory, that while other nations have extended their dominions by the sword, we have never acquired any territory, except by fair purchase, or, as in the case of Texas, by the voluntary determination of a brave, kindred, and independent people, to blend their destinies with our own. Even our acquisitions from Mexico form no exception. Unwilling to take advantage of the fortune of war against a sister republic, we purchased these possessions, under the treaty of peace, for a sum which was considered at the time a fair equivalent. Our past history forbids that we shall in the future acquire territory unless this be sanctioned by the laws of justice and honor. Acting on this principle, no nation will have a right to interfere or to complain if, in the progress of events, we shall still further extend our possessions. Hitherto, in all our acquisitions, the people under the protection of the American flag have enjoyed civil and religious liberty, as well as equal and just laws, and have been contented, prosperous, and happy. Their trade with the rest of the world has rapidly increased, and thus every commercial nation has shared largely in their successful progress. I shall now proceed to take the oath prescribed by the Constitution, while humbly invoking the blessing of Divine Providence on this great people."

Having concluded the reading of his Inaugural address, and having received the plaudits of the vast crowd in attendance, James Buchanan took the oath of office, which was administered to him by Chief-Justice Taney. The usual festivities followed the inauguration, and the city of Washington presented a gay appearance, in honor of the events of the day.

And thus the fifteenth president of the United States entered upon his high and responsible duties. A long-tried, almost veteran, statesman; an able advocate and defender of the principles of the democratic party, who had raised him to his lofty position; and intimately acquainted with the routine of executive duties; Mr. Buchanan, so far as it was permitted to form an opinion of the future, and what it might bring forth, had every reason to felicitate himself upon a peaceful, prosperous, and satisfactory administration. Time only, which tries every man's work of what sort it is, can make evident whether these anticipations were well or ill founded.

Mr. Buchanan made choice of the following gentlemen to aid him in his duties as members of his cabinet: Lewis Cass, of Michigan, was appointed secretary of state; Howell Cobb, of Georgia, secretary of the treasury; John B. Floyd, of Virginia, secretary of war; Isaac Toucey, of Connecticut, secretary of the navy; Jacob Thompson, of Mississippi, secretary of the interior; Aaron V. Brown, of Tennessee, postmaster-general; and Jeremiah S. Black, of Pennsylvania, attorney-general.

1857. The Senate confirmed these appointments without difficulty; and the session having lasted till the 14th of March, during which several matters of public interest were discussed, the Senate completed its present labors, and adjourned. Diplomatic arrangements in various quarters were made in due time; necessary and expected official changes were promptly effected; and the vessel of state was fairly embarked on her adventurous voyage for four years to come, under her new directors and commanders.

Such were some of the opening scenes and events of Mr. Buchanan's administration. The spring passed on; the summer arrived; public affairs seemed to be proceeding in their usual quiet manner; yet there were occasional mutterings, as if a storm were arising in connection with the Kansas question, and no little trouble seemed to be brewing for the executive and his cabinet advisers. What is to be the end of this *imbroglio*, no human sagacity can venture to pronounce with certainty. By and by, as years roll on, and causes now at work produce their necessary results, it will be seen and known, whether or not James Buchanan acted with that wisdom, prudence, integrity, and patriotism which the people have a right to demand of him whom they may choose to elevate to the chief magistracy of our great country. The story of the future we leave, as perforce we must, to the future. Our present task is completed; our brief narrative of current events is at its close; and with a few plain spoken but earnest words, commended to the reader's consideration, we conclude this third volume of our history.

The origin, rise, and progress of the United States of America, have been succinctly narrated in the pages which are now before the reader. It needs not that we here do more than point to these, as worthy the study, the patient study, of every citizen of our country.

1857. They are full of lessons of encouragement, of instruction, and of warning. They clearly evince, that by the favoring care and guidance of Him who rules in the affairs of men, our country has gone forward with unexampled rapidity, increasing in strength year by year, until now she stands in the very front rank of the great ruling powers of the world. With immense resources; with vast wealth; with a territory stretching from ocean to ocean, a sea-coast of over five thousand miles in length, and an area of country nearly three and a half millions of square miles in extent; with some thirty millions of people, full of spirit, zeal, enterprise, courage, and enthusiasm; what a future seems to be opened for such a nation as ours! Who can predict the extent of its development, the increase of its population, the enlargement of its wealth, the augmentation of its power and greatness? Who can venture to tell what these United States of America are yet to accomplish on this broad continent? Who can say, what shall be the limit of our advances, the extent of our conquests, the terminus of our career?*

To the man who looks upon these things from the point of view which the Christian patriot occupies, the prospect of our country's future causes anxiety no less than exultation. He knows, however men may delude themselves, or be puffed up with the idea that they are acting wholly independently of all control, that there is a "God that judgeth in the earth," and that nations, as well as individuals, are subject to His laws, and are working together to accomplish His purposes. And, consequently, he watches, earnestly and faithfully the course of events; he scans narrowly the principles which are avowed in high places; he notes, with the deepest concern, the tone of public sentiment, the standard of public virtue and honor, and the recognizing, or the refusing to recognize, the overruling providence of Almighty God.

It is hence a very important and very interesting question, what is the mission of our country in the world? Why has God seen fit to favor with His aid the rise and spread of this great western republic? What is the duty of Americans, in view of their 1857.
marked position, and their inestimable advantages? Not, surely, to endeavor to accomplish any merely party ends; not to exult in our advantages and privileges for purely selfish purposes;

* Mr. Guthrie, secretary of the treasury, in his official report, 1856, thus remarks: "A reference to the table of production, taken from the census of 1840, will show, that our agricultural and manufacturing production in that year amounted to $1,006,133,559; and a reference to the like table of production, taken from the census of 1850, will show the agricultural and manufacturing production, for that year, to have been $2,012,520,539. A like ratio of increase, for the five succeeding years, gives $2,602,363,924, as the value for the year 1855. Suppose $1,000,000,000 to be consumed at the places of production, there is left $1,602,363,924 of production as the basis of our foreign and internal trade, and the source from which we derive profitable employment for our registered licensed tonnage and our railroads. Take fifteen per cent. of this for our foreign trade, which is about equal to our exports, and there is left $1,352,009,336 for our internal trade, constituting the commercial ligament that binds us together as one nation and one people."

not to think that we are irresponsible beings, and living without aim and object beyond the present hour. Oh no. Privileges and blessings are not bestowed upon men to use or neglect as their passions or their indolence may dictate; on the contrary, they are like the talents lent unto the Master's servants in the parable; they involve deep responsibility; they must be accounted for; they must yield their fair return; or the Master will certainly pronounce sentence of condemnation. Beyond doubt, our country *has* a mission to fulfil in the history of mankind. God has certainly raised up this people, even as He raised up other nations and peoples, to accomplish His purposes of mercy and goodness, of justice and truth. And if we, acting upon the principles of truth and justice, and endeavoring to promote the spread of those inestimable advantages and blessings which we enjoy as Christian freemen,—if we set ourselves to carry forward every thing that is pure and noble and elevating to our race, we shall accomplish the noblest and highest ends of human existence; we shall work out our "manifest destiny," in the best sense of the words; we shall elevate our species by perpetuating those eternal verities on which rest all our civilization, all our progress, all our hopes here and hereafter.

It is not to be concealed, however, that there is, on every side, much to fill the mind of the patriot and the Christian with anxious forebodings. With all our widely extended national power, with all our millions of population, with all our expanding resources, and our rapid advancement in material wealth and importance, with all that we have in the present, and confidently count upon for the future, there are in our midst elements of evil, and tendencies to discord and ruin, which may, ere long, if unchecked, work out their necessary results. It is hard to say it, it is indeed rather humiliating to have to confess it, but it is nevertheless true, that party spirit is actively at work, from the very presidency down to the lowest office in the country; party spirit, too, in its most pernicious form, in its meanest, most disgusting form,—in office-seeking for the spoils of office, in the scrambling, and shuffling, and scheming on the part of those who are *out* to get *in*, and on the part of those who are *in* to keep all others *out*. Public morality has deteriorated, and public plundering is not, as once, a rare thing; honor and integrity are 1857.
less prized than they were by our fathers; defalcations are not uncommon; swindlers are more unblushingly open in their nefarious operations; men, high in office and position, are not ashamed to be guilty of conduct suitable only to bullies and gamblers, and to avow principles looked for only in infidels and defamers of the truth; robberies, murders, and the fouler sorts of crimes, are more frequent and less horrifying than ought to be the case; human life is valued at a small price; the moral sense is becoming blunted; a large foreign infusion has brought into our country the baser elements of foreign principles and views on social and moral topics; drunkenness is far too common; the mass of current cheap literature, in

the way of newspapers, flash magazines, novels, and the like, foster the most absurd and wicked opinions, the most silly imaginings, the most preposterous expectations, to say nothing of suggesting and inciting to evil deeds and crimes of the deepest dye; greed of gain is on the increase; rash and fatal ventures in business are continually made; extravagance in style of living has grown wonderfully; there is less horror of debt; less sensibility to disgrace, from this source; there is, among the very poor, a harder, sterner, more savage sense, as if they were personally wronged by the rich and the prosperous, and a more ready disposition to yield to the temptation to war against those whom they look upon as their natural enemies.

And so we might go on with this sad and heavy catalogue of tendencies to national debility and decay. We might enlarge upon the dwarfing effects produced by the causes we have alluded to, in lowering the standard of high-toned integrity, manliness, and honor, in the community. We might point out that the same causes substantially are at work here, which in other ages and countries have surely wrought out the degradation and ruin of nations and people; but we forbear. This is not the place to enter upon these topics with the fulness of discussion which they deserve; and we must be content with suggesting them to the reader's serious reflection, as matters in which he and all of us have a direct personal interest.

Let, then, our countrymen, in view of our past history and present condition, cultivate, by every means in their power, a pure, generous, noble love of the Union. Let them set themselves to elevate the standard of public virtue and honor; to purge out the disgraceful corruption which has so extensively crept into the management of
our political affairs; and to place 1857.
the seal of their reprobation upon every dishonest, unworthy public officer, upon every demagogue, upon every seeker for the spoils of party. Let them array themselves on the side of good and upright men for filling the offices in our government, contending for principles, not for party; for truth, not for victory. Let them remember, that liberty can only be sustained by the unceasing vigilance of those who prize liberty and its blessings; the enemies of freedom are never at rest; even so the friends and supporters of freedom and freedom's privileges can never venture to sleep upon their posts. Let our countrymen remember, that what our fathers bequeathed to us can be upheld only by the most earnest and vigorous efforts to promote sound education among the people, sound principles of morality, more general diffusion of religious instruction, more careful training in the sober and healthful ways of truth and godliness, more active efforts to give currency to a vigorous, manly literature, worthy of our country, and of the high destiny of our race. Finally, let it be written on the memories and in the hearts of Americans, as a truth from God Himself, a truth which no nation can safely overlook, that "RIGHTEOUSNESS EXALTETH A NATION; BUT SIN IS A REPROACH TO ANY PEOPLE."

APPENDIX TO CHAPTER IX.

VALUABLE AND INTERESTING STATISTICS.

FOLLOWING the plan adopted at the close of Volume II., we bring together, in an Appendix, a large variety of important statistical matter connected with the history and progress of the United States, from the commencement of Thomas Jefferson's administration, down to the years 1856 and 1857. We are indebted for the materials of the present Appendix to the "American Almanac," Tucker's "Progress of the United States," the "Statesman's Manual," and one or two other volumes.

I. THE CONGRESS OF THE UNITED STATES.

The national legislature consists of a Senate and House of Representatives, and must assemble at least once every year, on the first Monday of December, unless it is otherwise provided by law.

The Senate is composed of two members from each state; and, of course, the regular number is now sixty-two. They are chosen by the legislatures of the several states, for the term of six years, one-third of them being elected biennially.

The vice-president of the United States is the president of the Senate, in which body he has only a casting vote, which is given in case of an equal division of the votes of the Senators. In his absence, a president *pro tempore* is chosen from among the Senators by the Senate.

The House of Representatives is composed of members from the several states, elected by the people, in separate districts composed of contiguous territory, for the term of two years. The Representatives are apportioned amongst the different states, according to population, in the following manner. After each decennial enumeration, the aggregate representative population of the United States is ascertained by the secretary of the interior, by adding to the whole number of free persons in all the states, including those bound to service for a term of years, and excluding Indians not taxed, three-fifths of all other persons. This aggregate is divided by two hundred and thirty-three, and the quotient, rejecting fractions, if any, is the ratio of apportionment among the several states. The representative population of each state is then ascertained in the same manner, and is divided by the above-named ratio, and this quotient gives the apportionment of Representatives to each state. The loss by fractions is compensated for by assigning to as many states having the largest fractions as may be necessary to make the whole number of Representatives two hundred and thirty-three, one additional member each for its fraction. If after the apportionment new states are admitted, Representatives are assigned to such states upon the above basis, in addition to the limited number of two hundred and thirty-three; but such excess continues only until the next apportionment under the succeeding census. When the apportionment is completed, the secretary sends a certificate thereof to the House of Representatives and to the executive of each state a certificate of the number apportioned to such state. The present number of Representatives is two hundred and thirty-four, an additional Representative being temporarily assigned to California. There are, besides, seven delegates, one each from Oregon, Minnesota, Utah, New Mexico, Washington, Kansas, and Nebraska, who have a right to speak, but not to vote.

From March 4th, 1817, to the close of the thirty-third Congress (1855) the pay of members was $8 per day, during the time of their attendance in Congress, and $8 for every twenty miles travel, going to and returning from Washington; the speaker of the House and the president *pro tempore* of the Senate, received each $16 per day. The pay now is, mileage as before, and $6,000 for each Congress, i. e., for the two years. The pay of the speaker, and of the president *pro tempore* of the Senate, is $12,000 for each Congress.

II. THE FEDERAL ADMINISTRATIONS.

3. THE THIRD ADMINISTRATION: 1801 TO 1809, EIGHT YEARS.

President.—Thomas Jefferson, Virginia.

Vice-Presidents.—Aaron Burr, New York; George Clinton, New York.

Secretary of State.—James Madison, of Virginia, March 5, 1801.

Secretaries of the Treasury.—Samuel Dexter (continued in office); Albert Gallatin, of Pennsylvania, January 26, 1802.

Secretary of War.—Henry Dearborn, of Massachusetts, March 5, 1801.

Secretaries of the Navy.—Benjamin Stoddert (continued in office); Robert Smith, of Maryland, January 26, 1802.

Postmasters-General.—Joseph Habersham (continued in office); Gideon Granger, of Connecticut, January 26, 1802.

Attorneys-General.—Levi Lincoln, of Massachusetts, March 5, 1801; John Breckenridge, of Kentucky, December 23, 1805; Cæsar A. Rodney, of Delaware, January 20, 1807.

4. THE FOURTH ADMINISTRATION: 1809 TO 1817, EIGHT YEARS.

President.—James Madison, Virginia.

Vice-Presidents.—George Clinton, New York; Elbridge Gerry, Massachusetts.

Secretaries of State.—Robert Smith, of Maryland, March 6, 1809; James Monroe, of Virginia, November 25, 1811.

Secretaries of the Treasury.—Albert Gallatin (continued in office); George W. Campbell, of Tennessee, February 9, 1814; Alexander J. Dallas, of Pennsylvania, October 6, 1814.

Secretaries of War.—William Eustis, of Massachusetts, March 7, 1809; John Armstrong, of New York, January 13, 1813; James Monroe, of Virginia, September 26, 1814; William H. Crawford, of Georgia, March 2, 1815.

Secretaries of the Navy.—Paul Hamilton, of South Carolina, March 7, 1809; William Jones, of Pennsylvania, January 12, 1813; Benjamin W. Crowninshield, of Massachusetts, Dec. 19, 1814.

Postmasters-General.—Gideon Granger (continued in office); Return J. Meigs, of Ohio, March 17, 1814.

Attorneys-General.—Cæsar A. Rodney (continued in office); William Pinkney, of Maryland, December 11, 1811; Richard Rush, of Pennsylvania, February 10, 1814.

5. THE FIFTH ADMINISTRATION: 1817 TO 1825, EIGHT YEARS.

President.—James Monroe, Virginia.

Vice-President.—Daniel D. Tompkins, New York.

Secretary of State.—John Quincy Adams, of Massachusetts, March 5, 1817.

Secretary of the Treasury.—William H. Crawford, of Georgia, March 5, 1817.

Secretaries of War.—Isaac Shelby, of Kentucky, March 5, 1817; John C. Calhoun, of South Carolina, December 16, 1817.

Secretaries of the Navy.—B. W. Crowninshield (continued in office); Smith Thompson, of New York, November 30, 1818; Samuel L. Southard, of New Jersey, December 9, 1823.

Postmasters-General.—R. J. Meigs (continued in office); John M'Lean, of Ohio, December 9, 1823.

Attorneys-General.—Richard Rush (continued in office); William Wirt, of Virginia, December 16, 1817.

6. THE SIXTH ADMINISTRATION: 1825 TO 1829, FOUR YEARS.

President.—John Quincy Adams, Massachusetts.

Vice-President.—John C. Calhoun, South Carolina.

Secretary of State.—Henry Clay, of Kentucky, March 8, 1825.

Secretary of the Treasury.—Richard Rush, of Pennsylvania, March 7, 1825.

Secretaries of War.—James Barbour, of Virginia, March 7, 1825; Peter B. Porter, of New York, May 26, 1828.

Secretary of the Navy.—Samuel L. Southard (continued in office).

Postmaster-General.—John M'Lean (continued in office).

Attorney-General.—William Wirt (continued in office).

7. THE SEVENTH ADMINISTRATION: 1829 TO 1837, EIGHT YEARS.

President.—Andrew Jackson, Tennessee.

Vice-Presidents.—John C. Calhoun, South Carolina; Martin Van Buren, New York.

Secretaries of State.—Martin Van Buren, of New York, March 6, 1829; Edward Livingston, of Louisiana, 1831; Louis M'Lane, of Delaware, 1833; John Forsyth, of Georgia, 1834.

Secretaries of the Treasury.—Samuel D. Ingham, of Pennsylvania, March 6, 1829; Louis M'Lane of Delaware, 1831; William J. Duane, of Pennsylvania, 1833; Roger B. Taney, of Maryland, 1833; Levi Woodbury, of New Hampshire, 1834.

Secretaries of War.—John H. Eaton, of Tennessee, March 9, 1829; Lewis Cass, of Ohio, 1831.

Secretaries of the Navy.—John Branch, of North Carolina, March 9, 1829; Levi Woodbury, of New Hampshire, 1831; Mahlon Dickerson, of New Jersey, 1834.

Postmasters-General.—William T. Barry, of Kentucky, March 9, 1829; Amos Kendall, of Kentucky, 1835.

Attorneys-General.—John M'Pherson Berrien, of Georgia, March 9, 1829; Roger B. Taney, of Maryland, December, 1831; Benjamin F. Butler, of New York, January, 1834.

8. THE EIGHTH ADMINISTRATION; 1837 TO 1841, FOUR YEARS.

President.—Martin Van Buren, New York.

Vice-President.—Richard M. Johnson, Kentucky.

Secretary of State.—John Forsyth (continued in office).

Secretary of the Treasury.—Levi Woodbury (continued in office).

Secretary of War.—Joel R. Poinsett, of South Carolina, March 7, 1837.

Secretaries of the Navy.—Mahlon Dickerson (continued in office); James K. Paulding, of New York, June 30, 1838.

Postmasters-General.—Amos Kendall (continued in office); John M. Niles, of Connecticut, May 25, 1840.

Attorneys-General.—Felix Grundy, of Tennessee, August, 1838; Henry D. Gilpin, of Pennsylvania, January, 1840.

9. THE NINTH ADMINISTRATION: 1841 TO 1845, FOUR YEARS.

President.—William Henry Harrison, Ohio, (Died April 4, 1841.)

Vice-President.—John Tyler, Virginia.

President.—John Tyler, Virginia, (from April 4, 1841).

Secretaries of State.—Daniel Webster, of Massachusetts, March 5, 1841; Hugh S. Legaré, of South Carolina, May 9, 1843; Abel P. Upshur, of Virginia, June 24, 1843; John C. Calhoun, March 6, 1844.

Secretaries of the Treasury.—Thomas Ewing, of Ohio, March 5, 1841; Walter Forward, of Pennsylvania, September 13, 1841; John C. Spencer, of New York, March, 1843; George M. Bibb, of Kentucky, May, 1844.

Secretaries of War.—John Bell, of Tennessee, March 5, 1841; John C. Spencer, of New York, October 1841; James M. Porter, of Pennsylvania, March, 1843; William Wilkins, of Pennsylvania, February, 1844.

Secretaries of the Navy.—George E. Badger, of North Carolina, March 5, 1841; Abel P. Upshur, of Virginia, September, 1841; David Henshaw, of Massachusetts, July 1843; Thomas W. Gilmer, of Virginia, February, 1844; John Y. Mason, of Virginia, March, 1844.

Postmasters-General.—Francis Granger, of New York, March 6, 1841; Charles A. Wickliffe, of Kentucky, September, 1841.

Attorneys-General.—John J. Crittenden, of Kentucky, March 5, 1841; Hugh S. Legaré, of South Carolina, September, 1841; John Nelson, of Maryland, July, 1843.

10. THE TENTH ADMINISTRATION: 1845 TO 1849, FOUR YEARS.

President.—James K. Polk, Tennessee.

Vice-President.—George M. Dallas, Pennsylvania.

Secretary of State.—James Buchanan, of Pennsylvania, March 5, 1845.

Secretary of the Treasury.—Robert J. Walker, of Mississippi, March 5, 1845.

Secretary of War.—William L. Marcy, of New York, March 5, 1845.

Secretaries of the Navy.—George Bancroft, of Massachusetts, March 5, 1845; John Y. Mason, of Virginia, 1846.

Postmaster-General.—Cave Johnson, of Tennessee, March 5, 1845.

Attorneys-General.—John Y. Mason, of Virginia, March 5, 1845; Nathan Clifford, of Maine, 1846; Isaac Toucey, of Connecticut, 1848.

11. THE ELEVENTH ADMINISTRATION: 1849 TO 1853, FOUR YEARS.

President.—Zachary Taylor, Louisiana. (Died July 9, 1850.)

Vice-President.—Millard Fillmore, New York.

President. — Millard Fillmore, New York, (from July 9, 1850.)

Secretaries of State.—John M. Clayton, of Delaware, March 7, 1849; Daniel Webster, of Massachusetts, July 20, 1850; Edward Everett, of Massachusetts, 1852.

Secretaries of the Treasury.—William M. Meredith, of Pennsylvania, March, 1849; Thomas Corwin, of Ohio, July 20, 1850.

Secretaries of War.—George W. Crawford, of Georgia, March 7, 1849; Charles M. Conrad, of Louisiana, August 15, 1850.

Secretaries of the Navy.—William B. Preston, of Virginia, March 7, 1849; William A. Graham, of North Carolina, July 20, 1850; John P. Kennedy, of Maryland.

Secretaries of the Interior.—Thomas Ewing, of Ohio, March 7, 1849; Alexander H. H. Stuart, September 12, 1850.

Postmasters-General.—Jacob Collamer, of Vermont, March 7, 1849; Nathan K. Hall, of New York, July 20, 1850; Samuel D. Hubbard, of Connecticut.

Attorneys-General.—Reverdy Johnson, of Maryland, March 7, 1849; John J. Crittenden, of Kentucky, July 20, 1850.

12. THE TWELFTH ADMINISTRATION: 1853 TO 1857, FOUR YEARS.

President.—Franklin Pierce, New Hampshire.

Vice-President.—William R. King, Alabama. (Died, April 18, 1853.)

Secretary of State.—William L. Marcy, of New York, March, 1853.

Secretary of the Treasury.—James Guthrie, of Kentucky, March, 1853.

Secretary of War.—Jefferson Davis, of Mississippi, March, 1853.

Secretary of the Navy.—James C. Dobbin, of North Carolina, March, 1853.

Secretary of the Interior.—Robert McClelland, of Michigan, March, 1853.

Postmaster-General.—James Campbell, of Pennsylvania, March, 1853.

Attorney-General.—Caleb Cushing, of Massachusetts, March, 1853.

III. THE SUPREME COURT.

Chief-Justices.—John Marshall, of Virginia; Roger B. Taney, of Maryland, March 15, 1836.

Associate-Justices.—William Johnson, of South Carolina, March 26, 1804; Brockholst Livingston, of New York, January 16, 1807; Thomas Todd, of Virginia; March 3, 1807; Levi Lincoln, of Massachusetts, January 7, 1811; John Quincy Adams, of Massachusetts, February 22, 1811, (declined the appointment); Gabriel Duvall, of Maryland, November 18, 1811; Joseph Story, of Massachusetts, November 18, 1811; Smith Thompson, of New York, December 9, 1823; Robert Trimble, of Kentucky, March 9, 1826; John M'Lean, of Ohio, March 7, 1829; Henry Baldwin, of Pennsylvania, January 6, 1830; James M. Wayne, of Georgia, January, 1835; Philip P. Barbour, of Virginia, March 15, 1836; William Smith, of Alabama, March 8, 1837, (declined the appointment); John Catron, of Tennessee, March 8, 1837; John M'Kinley, of Alabama, September, 1837; Peter V. Daniel, of Virginia, March 3, 1841; Samuel Nelson, of New York, February, 1845; Levi Woodbury, of New Hampshire, January, 1846; Robert C. Grier, of Pennsylvania, 1846; Benjamin R. Curtis, of Massachusetts, 1851; John A. Campbell, of Alabama, 1853.

IV. MINISTERS TO FOREIGN COURTS.

To Great Britain.—Ministers-plenipotentiary, and envoys-extraordinary: James Monroe, of Virginia, April 18, 1803; James Monroe and William Pinkney, jointly and severally, May 12, 1806; William Pinkney, of Maryland, renewed, February 26, 1808; John Quincy Adams, of Massachusetts, February 28, 1815; Richard Rush, of Pennsylvania, December 16, 1817; Rufus King, of New York, May 5, 1825; Albert Gallatin, of Pennsylvania, May 10, 1826; James Barbour, of Virginia, May 23, 1828; Louis M'-Lane, of Delaware, February 10, 1830; Martin Van Buren, of New York, 1831; Aaron Vail, of New York, chargé d'affaires, 1832; Andrew Stevenson, of Virginia, 1836; Edward Everett, of Massachusetts, 1841; Louis M'Lane, of Maryland, 1845; George Bancroft, of Massachusetts, 1846; Abbot Lawrence, of Massachusetts, 1849; Joseph R. Ingersoll, of Pennsylvania, 1852; James Buchanan, of Pennsylvania, 1853; George M. Dallas, of Pennsylvania, 1856.

To France.—Ministers-plenipotentiary and envoys-extraordinary: Robert R. Livingston, of New York, October 2, 1801; John Armstrong, of New York, June 30, 1804; Joel Barlow, of

Connecticut, February 27, 1811; William H. Crawford, of Georgia, April 9, 1813; Albert Gallatin, of Pennsylvania, February 28, 1815; James Brown, of Louisiana, December 9, 1823; William C. Rives, of Virginia, February 10, 1830; Edward Livingston, of Louisiana, 1833; Lewis Cass, of Ohio, 1836; William R. King, of Alabama, 1844; Richard Rush, of Pennsylvania, 1847; William C. Rives, of Virginia, 1849; John Y. Mason, of Virginia, 1853.

To Spain.—Ministers-plenipotentiary: Charles Pinckney, of South Carolina, June 6, 1801; James Monroe, of Virginia, October 14, 1804; James Bowdoin, of Massachusetts, November 22, 1804; George W. Erving, of Massachusetts, August 10, 1814; John Forsyth, of Georgia, February 16, 1819; Hugh Nelson, of Virginia, June 15, 1823; Alexander H. Everett, of Massachusetts, March 9, 1825; Cornelius P. Van Ness, of Vermont, February 10, 1830; William T. Barry, of Kentucky, 1835; John H. Eaton, of Tennessee, 1836; Aaron Vail, of New York, chargé d'affaires, 1840; Washington Irving, of New York, 1842; Daniel M. Barringer, of North Carolina, 1849; Pierre Soulé, of Louisiana, 1853; Augustus C. Dodge, of Iowa, 1855.

To Russia.—Ministers-plenipotentiary: John Quincy Adams, of Massachusetts, June 27, 1809; James A. Bayard, of Delaware, February 28, 1815; William Pinkney, of Maryland, April 26, 1815; George W. Campbell, of Tennessee, April 16, 1818; Henry Middleton, of South Carolina, April 6, 1820; John Randolph, of Virginia, 1830; James Buchanan, of Pennsylvania, 1831; William Wilkins, of Pennsylvania, 1834; John Randolph Clay, of Pennsylvania, chargé d'affaires, 1836; George M. Dallas, of Pennsylvania, 1837; C. C. Cambreling, of New York, 1840; Charles S. Todd, of Kentucky, 1841; Ralph J. Ingersoll, of Connecticut, 1846; Arthur P. Bagby, of Alabama, 1848; Neil S. Brown, of Tennessee, 1849; Thomas H. Seymour, of Connecticut, 1853.

To Prussia.—Ministers-plenipotentiary: Henry Clay, (secretary of state,) with full power to conclude a treaty, April 18, 1828; Henry Wheaton, of Rhode Island, 1837; Andrew J. Donelson, of Tennessee, 1846; Edward A. Hannegan, of Indiana, 1849; Daniel D. Barnard, of New York, 1850; Peter D. Vroom, of New Jersey, 1853.

To Austria.—Ministers-plenipotentiary: Henry A. Muhlenberg, of Pennsylvania, 1838; Daniel Jenifer, of Maryland, 1841; William A. Stiles, of Georgia, chargé d'affaires, 1845; James Watson Webb, of New York, chargé d'affaires, 1849; Charles J. McCurdy, of Connecticut, chargé d'affaires, 1851; Henry R. Jackson, of Georgia, chargé d'affaires, 1853.

To Portugal.—Ministers-plenipotentiary: Thos. Sumpter, of South Carolina, March 7, 1809; John Graham, of Virginia, January 6, 1819; Henry Dearborn, of New Hampshire, May 7, 1822. Chargés d'affaires: Thomas L. L. Brent, of Virginia, March 9, 1825; Edward Kavanagh, of Maine, 1835; Washington Barrow, 1841; Abraham Rencher, of North Carolina, 1843; George W. Hopkins, of Virginia, 1847; James B. Clay, of Kentucky, 1849; Charles B. Haddock, of New Hampshire, 1851; John L. O'Sullivan, of New York, 1853.

To the Netherlands.—William Eustis, of Massachusetts, minister-plenipotentiary, December 10, 1814. Chargés d'affaires: A. H. Everett, of Massachusetts, November 30, 1818; Christopher Hughes, of Maryland, March 9, 1825; W. P. Preble, (minister-plenipotentiary,) February 10, 1830; Auguste Davezac, of Louisiana, 1831; Harmanus Bleecker, 1839; Christopher Hughes, 1842; Auguste Davezac, 1845; George Folsom, of New York, 1850; Auguste Belmont, 1853.

To Sweden.—Jonathan Russell, of Rhode Island, minister-plenipotentiary, January 18, 1814. Chargés d'affaires: Christopher Hughes, Jr., of Maryland, January 21, 1819; W. C. Somerville, of Maryland, March 9, 1825; J. J. Appleton, of Massachusetts, May 2, 1826; Christopher Hughes, March 3, 1830; George W. Lay, of New York, 1842; H. W. Ellsworth, of Indiana, 1845; Francis Schroeder, of Rhode Island, 1849.

To Denmark.—Chargés d'affaires: Henry Wheaton, of New York, March 3, 1827; J. F. Woodside, of Ohio, 1835; W. W. Irwin, of Pennsylvania, 1843; Walter Forward, of Pennsylvania, 1849; Miller Grieve, of Pennsylvania, 1852; Henry Bedinger, of Virginia, 1853.

To Belgium.—Chargés d'affaires: Hugh S. Legaré, 1832; Virgil Maxcy, of Maryland, 1837; H. W. Hilliard, of Alabama, 1842; T. G. Clemson, of Pennsylvania, 1844; R. H. Bayard, of Delaware, 1851; J. J. Seibels, of Alabama, 1853.

To the Two Sicilies.—Chargés d'affaires: John Nelson, of Maryland, 1831; Enos T. Throop, of New York, 1838; William Boulware, of Virginia, 1841; W. H. Polk, of Tennessee, 1845; E. J. Morris, of Pennsylvania, 1850; R. D. Owen, of Indiana, 1853.

To Sardinia.—Chargés d'affaires; H. Y. Rogers, 1840; Ambrose Baber, of Georgia, 1841; Robert Wickliffe, Jr., of Kentucky, 1843; W. B. Kinney, of New Jersey, 1850; J. M. Daniel, of Virginia, 1853.

To Turkey.—David Porter, of Maryland, chargé d'affaires, 1831. Ministers resident: David Porter, 1839; Dabney S. Carr, of Maryland, 1843; George P. Marsh, of Vermont, 1849; Carroll Spence, of Maryland, 1853.

To China.—Commissioners: Caleb Cushing, of Massachusetts, 1843; A. H. Everett, of Massachusetts, 1845; J. W. Davis, of Indiana, 1848; Thomas Nelson, of Tennessee, 1851; H. Marshall, of Kentucky, 1852; Robert McLane, of Maryland, 1853.

To Mexico.—Ministers-plenipotentiary: Andrew Jackson, of Tennessee, January 27, 1823, (declined the appointment); Ninian Edwards, of Illinois, March 4, 1824; J. R. Poinsett, of South Carolina, March 8, 1825; Anthony Butler, of Mississippi, (chargé d'affaires,) March 12, 1830; Powhattan Ellis, of Mississippi, 1837; Waddy Thompson, of South Carolina, 1842; Wilson Shannon, of Ohio, 1844; John Slidell, of Louisiana, 1845; N. P. Trist, of Virginia, (commissioner,) 1847; Nathan Clifford, of Maine, 1848; R. P. Letcher, of Kentucky, 1849; Alfred Conkling, of New York, 1852; James Gadsden, of South Carolina, 1853; John Forsyth, of Georgia, 1856.

To Brazil.—Chargés d'affaires: C. Raquet, of Pennsylvania, March 9, 1825; W. Tudor, 1827; E. A. Brown, of Ohio, 1830; W. Hunter, of Rhode Island, 1834. Ministers-plenipotentiary: W. Hunter, 1841; G. H. Proffit, of Indiana, 1843; H. A. Wise, of Virginia, 1844; David Tod, of Ohio, 1847; Robert C. Schenck, of Ohio, 1851; William Trousdale, of Tennessee, 1853.

To Chili.—Heman Allen, of Vermont, minister-plenipotentiary, January 27, 1823. Chargés d'affaires: S. Larned, of Rhode Island, February 9, 1828; J. Harum, of Ohio, 1830; R. Pollard, of Virginia, 1834; J. S. Pendleton, of Virginia, 1841; W. Crump, of Virginia, 1844; Seth Barton, of Louisiana, 1847. Ministers-plenipotentiary: Bailie Peyton, of Louisiana, 1849; Samuel Medary, of Ohio, 1853.

To Peru.—Chargés d'affaires: J. Cooley, of Ohio, May 2, 1826; S. Larned, December 29, 1828; E. J. West, of Illinois, March 12, 1830; S. Larned, 1831; J. B. Thornton, of New Hampshire, 1836; J. C. Pickett, of Virginia, 1838; A. G. Jewett, of Maine, 1845; J. R. Clay, of Pennsylvania, 1847; the same, minister-plenipotentiary, 1853.

At the present date, (1857,) the United States are represented abroad as follows:

Envoys-extraordinary and Ministers-plenipotentiary, with date of appointment, salary, etc.

G. M. Dallas, Pa., 1856, $17,500; Gt. Britain.
T. H. Seymour, Conn., 1853, $12,000; Russia.
John Y. Mason, Va., 1853, $17,500; France.
A. C. Dodge, Iowa, 1855, $12,000; Spain.
Jos. A. Wright, Ind., 1857, $12,000; Prussia.
John Forsyth, Ga., 1856, $12,000; Mexico.
Richard K. Meade, Va., 1857, $12,000; Brazil.
John Bigler, Cal., 1857, $10,000; Chili.
John R. Clay, Pa., 1853, $10,000; Peru.
William B. Reed, Pa., 1857, $12,000; China.

Ministers Resident.

Carroll Spence, Md., 1853, $7,500; Turkey.
T. S. Fay, Mass., 1853, $7,500; Switzerland.
H. C. Murphy, N. Y., 1857, $7,500; Netherl'ds.
John M. Daniel, Va., 1853, $7,500; Sardinia.
Henry Bedinger, Va., 1853, $7,500; Denmark.
Henry R. Jackson, Ga., 1853, $9,000; Austria.
Vacant . . . . $7,500; Belgium.
Robert D. Owen, Ind., 1853, $7,500; Naples.
B. F. Angel, N. Y., 1857, $7,500; Swed. & Nor.
J. L. O'Sullivan, N. Y., 1854, $7,500; Portugal.
Lewis Cass, Jr., Mich., 1849, $7,500; Rome.
John W. Dana, Me., 1853, $7,500; Bolivia.
Philo White, Wis., 1853, $7,500; Ecuador.
M. B. Lamar, Tex., 1857, $7,500; Argentine C'n.
Vacant . . . . . $7,500; New Granada.
Charles Eames, D. C., 1854, $7,500; Venezuela.
Vacant . . . . $7,500; Guatemala.
Vacant . . . . $7,500; Nicaragua.

Commissioner.

David L. Gregg, Ill., 1853, $7,500; Sandwich Is.

V. THE UNITED STATES ARMY AND NAVY.

1. On the first of January, 1857, the whole number of commissioned officers in the regular army was 1,060; of non-commissioned officers, privates, etc., 11,628; total, 12,688.

The militia force of the United States, as stated in the Army Register, numbers over 50,000 commissioned officers, and some 2,000,000 of non-commissioned officers, musicians, artificers and privates.

2. The United States navy consists of,

Ships of the line	10
Frigates	13
Sloops of war	19
Steamers, (1st, 2d, and 3d classes,)	19
Steam tenders	3
Brigs	3
Schooner	1
Store ships	5
Total	73

Total number of guns, a little over 2,000.

The marine corps, officers and men, numbers about 1,100.

VI. THE PUBLIC LANDS.

The public lands belonging to the general government are situated,—1st. Within the limits of the United States, as defined by the treaty of 1783, and are embraced by the states of Ohio, Indiana, Illinois, Michigan, Wisconsin, and that part of Minnesota east of the Mississippi River, all of which have been formed out of the Northwestern Territory, as conveyed, with certain reservations, to the United States, by New York in 1781, by Virginia in 1784, by Massachusetts in 1785, and by Connecticut in 1786; also the lands within the boundaries of the states of Mississippi and Alabama, north of 31° north latitude, as conveyed to the United States by Georgia in 1802. 2d. Within the territories of Orleans and Louisiana, as acquired from France by the treaty of 1803, including the portion of the states of Alabama and Mississippi, south of 31°; the whole of Louisiana, Arkansas, Missouri, Iowa, and that portion of Minnesota west of the Mississippi River; the Indian territory; Kansas, Nebraska, and Oregon territories. 3d. Within the state of Florida, as obtained from Spain by the treaty of 1819. 4th. In New Mexico and California, as acquired from Mexico by the treaty of 1848.

Within the limits recognized by these treaties and cessions, the public lands covered an estimated area of 1,584,000,000 acres. In this is not included any territory acquired from Mexico by the treaty of 1853. Exclusive of the lands in Oregon, California, New Mexico, Utah, Kansas and Nebraska territories, the entire area of the public domain is stated, after a careful examination, to have been 471,892,439 acres. About one-fourth of this, up to November 30, 1850, had been sold, and $135,339,092 received therefor. The aggregate outlay of every kind upon these lands to the same date, including cost of purchase, of surveying, and of selling, was $74,957,879, leaving as net profit to the government $60,381,-213, or an annual average of nearly $1,000,000 for the last fifty years. If there should be added to this, at the rate of $1.25 per acre, the value of the land granted for bounties, schools, internal improvements, etc., it would amount to nearly double the above sum. The average cost per acre to the government of acquiring title, etc., to the lands is 14.41 cents; of survey, 2.07 cents; of selling and managing, 5.32 cents; in all, 21.80 cents; while it receives $1.25 per acre, or a net profit on each acre sold of $1.032.

For full details of the present condition of the public lands, and of the various grants and donations thereof for purposes of education and of internal improvement, see the American Almanac for 1850, pp. 180–187.

VII. POPULATION OF THE UNITED STATES.

3. CENSUS OF 1810.

States.	Free Whites.	Free Colored.	Slaves.	Total.
Maine	227,736	969	......	228,705
New Hampshire	213,390	970	......	214,360
Vermont	216,963	750	......	217,713
Massachusetts	465,308	6,737	......	472,040
Rhode Island	73,314	3,609	108	77,031
Connecticut	255,279	6,453	310	262,042
New York	918,699	25,333	15,017	959,049
New Jersey	226,861	7,843	10,851	245,555
Pennsylvania	786,804	22,492	795	810,091
Delaware	55,361	13,136	4,177	72,674
Maryland	235,117	33,927	111,502	380,546
Virginia	551,534	30,570	392,518	974,622
North Carolina	376,410	10,266	168,824	550,500
South Carolina	214,196	4,554	196,365	415,115
Georgia	145,414	1,801	105,218	252,433
Kentucky	324,237	1,713	80,561	406,511
Tennessee	215,875	1,317	44,535	261,727
Mississippi	23,024	240	17,088	40,352
Louisiana	34,311	7,585	34,660	76,556
Missouri	17,227	607	3,011	20,845
Ohio	228,861	1,899	......	230,760
Indiana	23,890	393	237	24,520
Illinois	11,501	613	168	12,282
Michigan	4,618	120	24	4,762
District Columbia	16,079	2,549	5,395	24,023
	5,862,004	186,446	1,191,364	7,239,814

4. Census of 1820.

States.	Free Whites.	Free Colored.	Slaves.	Total.
Maine	297,240	995	....	298,335
New Hampshire	242,236	925	....	244,161
Vermont	234,846	918	....	235,764
Massachusetts	516,419	6,868	....	523,287
Rhode Island	79,418	3,598	48	83,059
Connecticut	267,161	7,944	97	275,202
New York	1,332,744	29,980	10,088	1,372,812
New Jersey	257,409	12,609	7,557	277,575
Pennsylvania	1,017,094	32,153	211	1,049,458
Delaware	55,282	12,958	4,509	72,749
Maryland	260,222	39,730	107,398	407,350
Virginia	603,074	37,139	425,153	1,065,366
North Carolina	419,200	14,612	205,017	638,829
South Carolina	237,440	6,826	258,475	502,741
Georgia	189,566	1,767	149,656	340,989
Kentucky	434,644	2,941	126,732	564,317
Tennessee	339,927	2,779	80,107	422,813
Mississippi	42,176	458	32,814	75,448
Louisiana	73,383	10,960	69,064	153,407
Alabama	96,245	633	47,437	144,317
Arkansas	12,579	77	1,617	14,273
Missouri	55,988	376	10,222	66,586
Ohio	576,572	4,862	......	581,434
Indiana	145,758	1,230	190	147,178
Illinois	53,788	506	917	55,211
Michigan	8,591	305	......	8,896
District Columbia	22,614	4,848	6,377	33,039
	7,872,711	238,197	1,543,688	9,654,596

5. Census of 1830.

States.	Free Whites.	Free Colored.	Slaves.	Total.
Maine	398,263	1,190	2	399,455
New Hampshire	268,721	604	3	269,328
Vermont	279,771	881	....	280,652
Massachusetts	603,359	7,048	....	610,408
Rhode Island	93,621	3,561	17	97,199
Connecticut	289,603	8,047	25	297,675
New York	1,873,663	44,870	75	1,918,608
New Jersey	300,266	18,303	2,254	320,823
Pennsylvania	1,309,900	37,930	403	1,348,233
Delaware	57,601	15,855	3,292	76,748
Maryland	291,108	52,938	102,994	447,040
Virginia	694,300	47,348	469,757	1,211,405
North Carolina	472,843	19,543	245,601	737,987
South Carolina	257,863	7,921	315,401	581,185
Georgia	296,806	2,486	217,531	516,823
Alabama	190,406	1,572	117,549	309,527
Mississippi	70,443	519	65,659	136,621
Louisiana	89,441	16,710	109,588	215,739
Tennessee	535,746	4,555	141,603	681,904
Kentucky	517,787	4,917	165,213	687,917
Ohio	928,329	9,568	6	937,903
Indiana	339,399	3,629	3	343,031
Illinois	155,061	1,637	747	157,445
Michigan	31,346	261	32	31,639
Missouri	114,795	569	25,091	140,455
Arkansas	25,671	141	4,576	30,388
Florida	18,385	844	15,011	34,730
District Columbia	27,563	6,152	6,119	39,834
	10,537,378	319,599	2,009,043	12,866,020

6. Census of 1840.

States.	Free Whites.	Free Colored.	Slaves.	Total.
Maine	500,438	1,355	....	501,793
New Hampshire	284,036	537	1	284,574
Vermont	291,218	730	....	291,948
Massachusetts	729,030	8,688	....	737,699
Rhode Island	105,587	3,238	5	108,830
Connecticut	301,856	8,105	17	309,978
New York	2,378,890	50,027	4	2,428,921
New Jersey	351,588	21,044	647	373,306
Pennsylvania	1,676,115	47,854	64	1,724,033
Delaware	58,559	16,919	2,605	78,085
Maryland	318,204	62,078	89,737	470,019
Virginia	740,968	49,842	448,987	1,239,797
North Carolina	484,870	22,732	245,817	753,419
South Carolina	259,084	8,276	327,038	594,398
Georgia	407,695	2,753	280,944	691,392
Florida	27,943	817	25,717	54,477
Alabama	335,185	2,039	253,532	590,756
Mississippi	179,074	1,369	195,211	375,654
Louisiana	158,457	25,502	168,452	352,411
Arkansas	75,574	465	19,935	97,574
Tennessee	640,627	5,524	183,059	829,210
Kentucky	590,253	7,317	182,258	779,828
Missouri	323,888	1,574	58,240	383,702
Ohio	1,502,122	17,342	3	1,519,467
Indiana	678,698	7,165	3	685,866
Illinois	472,254	3,598	331	476,183
Michigan	211,560	707	......	212,267
Wisconsin	30,749	185	11	43,112
Iowa	42,924	172	16	30,945
District Columbia	30,657	8,361	4,694	43,712
	14,189,555	386,848	2,487,355	17,063,353
Add seamen in the United States Service				6,100
Grand Total				17,069,453

7. Census of 1850.

States.	Free Whites.	Free Colored.	Slaves.	Total.
Maine	581,813	1,356	....	583,169
New Hampshire	317,456	520	... ...	317,976
Vermont	313,402	718	....	314,120
Massachusetts	985,450	9,064	....	994,514
Rhode Island	143,875	3,670	....	147,545
Connecticut	363,099	7,693	....	370,792
New York	3,049,457	47,937	....	3,097,394
New Jersey	465,528	23,807	225	489,561
Pennsylvania	2,258,463	53,323	....	2,311,786
Delaware	71,169	18,073	2,290	91,532
Maryland	417,943	74,723	90,368	583,034
Virginia	895,304	53,829	472,528	1,421,661
North Carolina	553,118	27,373	288,412	868,903
South Carolina	274,623	8,900	384,984	668,507
Georgia	521,438	2,880	381,681	905,999
Florida	47,167	925	39,309	87,401
Alabama	426,486	2,293	342,892	771,671
Mississippi	295,758	899	309,898	606,555
Louisiana	255,416	17,537	244,786	517,839
Texas	154,100	331	58,161	212,592
Arkansas	162,068	589	46,982	209,639
Tennessee	756,893	6,271	239,461	1,002,625
Kentucky	761,688	9,763	210,981	982,405
Missouri	592,077	2,544	87,422	682,043
Ohio	1,956,108	24,300	....	1,980,408
Michigan	395,097	2,557	....	397,654
Indiana	977,628	10,788	....	988,416
Illinois	846,104	5,366	....	851,470
Wisconsin	304,565	626	....	305,191
Iowa	191,879	335	....	192,214
California	91,632	965	....	92,597
District Columbia	38,027	9,973	3,687	51,687
Minnesota	6,038	39	....	6,077
New Mexico	61,530	17	....	61,547
Oregon	13,087	206	....	13,293
Utah	11,330	24	26	11,380
	19,557,271	429,710	3,204,093	23,191,074

VIII. COMMERCE OF THE UNITED STATES.

Years.	Imports.	Exports.	Tonnage.
1801	$111,363,511	$94,115,925	1,033,219
1802	76,333,333	72,483,160	892,101
1803	64,666,666	55,800,033	949,147
1804	85,000,000	77,699,074	1,042,404
1805	120,000,000	95,566,021	1,140,369
1806	129,000,000	101,536,963	1,208,735
1807	138,500,000	108,343,150	1,268,548
1808	56,990,000	22,430,960	1,242,595
1809	59,400,000	52,203,231	1,350,281
1810	85,400,000	66,757,974	1,424,783
1811	53,400,000	61,316,831	1,232,502
1812	77,030,000	38,527,236	1,269,997
1818	22,005,000	27,855,997	1,666,628
1814	12,965,000	6,927,441	1,159,209
1815	113,041,274	52,557,753	1,368,127
1816	147,103,000	81,920,452	1,372,218
1817	99,250,000	87,671,569	1,399,912
1818	121,750,000	93,281,133	1,225,184
1819	87,125,000	70,142,521	1,260,751
1820	74,450,000	69,691,669	1,280,166

VIII. COMMERCE OF THE UNITED STATES.
Continued.

Years.	Imports.	Exports.	Tonnage.
1821	$62,585,724	$64,974,382	1,298,958
1822	83,241,541	72,160,281	1,324,699
1823	77,579,267	74,699,030	1,336,566
1824	80,549,007	75,986,657	1,389,163
1825	96,340,075	99,535,388	1,423,112
1826	84,974,477	77,595,322	1,534,191
1827	79,484,068	82,324,827	1,620,608
1828	88,509,824	72,264,686	1,741,392
1829	74,492,527	72,358,671	1,260,798
1830	70,876,920	73,849,508	1,191,776
1831	103,191,124	81,310,583	1,267,847
1832	101,029,266	87,176,943	1,439,450
1833	108,118,311	90,140,433	1,606,151
1834	126,521,332	104,336,973	1,758,907
1835	149,895,742	121,693,577	1,824,940
1836	189,980,035	128,663,040	1,882,103
1837	140,989,217	117,419,376	1,896,686
1838	108,486,616	113,717,404	1,995,640
1839	121,028,416	162,092,132	2,096,380
1840	131,571,950	104,805,891	2,180,764
1841	127,946,177	121,851,803	2,130,744
1842	100,162,087	104,691,534	2,092,391
1843	64,753,799*	84,346,480*	2,158,603
1844	108,435,035†	111,200,046†	2,280,095
1845	117,254,564†	114,646,606†	2,417,002
1846	121,691,797†	113,488,516†	2,562,085
1847	146,545,638†	158,648,622†	2,839,046
1848	154,977,928†	154,036,436†	3,154,042
1849	147,857,439†	145,755,820†	3,334,015
1850	178,138,318†	136,946,912†	3,535,454
1851	216,224,932†	218,388,011†	3,772,439
1852	212,613,282†	209,641,625†	4,138,441
1853	267,978,647	230,976,157	4,407,010
1854	304,562,381	278,241,064	4,802,903
1855	261,468,520	275,156,846	5,212,001
1856	314,639,942	326,964,908	4,871,652

* Only nine months of 1843.
† For the year ending June 30.

IX. INCOME, EXPENDITURES AND DEBT OF THE UNITED STATES.
Payments on Debt not included in Expenditures.

Years.	Income.	Expenditures.	Debt.
1801	$12,500,882	$4,981,669	$83,038,051
1802	13,455,328	3,737,080	80,712,632
1803	10,932,158	4,002,825	77,054,686
1804	11,687,231	4,452,859	86,427,121
1805	13,520,312	6,357,224	82,312,150
1806	15,508,809	6,081,109	75,723,271
1807	16,359,469	4,984,572	69,218,399
1808	17,038,859	6,504,339	65,196,318
1809	7,749,835	7,414,672	57,023,192
1810	9,299,737	5,311,082	53,173,217
1811	14,363,423	5,592,604	48,005,588
1812	9,674,968	17,829,499	45,209,738
1813	14,068,839	28,082,397	55,962,828
1814	11,017,225	30,127,686	81,487,846
1815	15,411,634	26,953,571	99,833,660
1816	47,403,204	23,373,432	127,334,934
1817	32,786,862	15,454,610	123,491,965
1818	21,002,563	13,808,674	103,466,634
1819	23,871,276	16,300,273	95,529,648
1820	16,779,331	13,134,530	91,015,566
1821	14,315,790	10,723,479	89,987,428
1822	19,481,961	9,827,642	93,546,677
1823	20,049,536	9,784,155	90,875,877
1824	18,903,609	15,330,145	90,269,778
1825	21,342,906	11,490,459	83,788,433
1826	24,763,345	13,062,316	81,054,060
1827	21,230,641	12,254,397	73,987,357
1828	24,243,504	12,506,041	67,475,044
1829	24,224,979	12,651,489	58,421,414
1830	24,280,888	13,220,534	48,565,406
1831	27,452,697	13,863,768	39,123,192
1832	31,107,040	16,514,088	24,322,235
1833	33,003,344	22,049,298	7,001,699
1834	21,076,774	18,420,467	4,760,082
1835	34,163,635	17,005,419	37,733
1836	48,288,219	29,655,244	37,513
1837	18,032,846	31,793,587	1,878,221
1838	19,372,984	31,578,785	4,875,660
1839	30,399,043	25,488,547	11,983,738

IX. INCOME, EXPENDITURES, AND DEBT, OF THE UNITED STATES.—*Continued.*

Years.	Income.	Expenditures.	Debt.
1840	$16,993,858	$23,327,772	$ 5,125,073
1841	15,957,512	26,196,840	6,737,398
1842	19,643,967	24,361,336	15,028,486
1843	*8,065,326	10,698,391	26,898,953
1844	28,504,519	19,960,055	26,143,996
1845	29,769,134	21,370,049	16,801,647
1846	29,499,247	26,813,290	24,256,495
1847	26,346,790	55,929,093	45,659,659
1848	35,436,750	42,811,970	65,804,450
1849	31,074,347	57,631,667	64,704,693
1850	43,375,798	43,002,168	64,228,238
1851	52,312,979	48,005,879	62,560,395
1852	49,728,386	46,007,896	67,560,395
1853	61,337,574	43,543,263	56,336,157
1854	73,549,705	51,018,249	44,975,456
1855	65,003,930	56,365,393	39,969,731
1856	73,918,141	60,172,402	30,963,910

* Only 6 months of 1843.

X. IMPORTS AND EXPORTS OF EACH STATE.
During the year ending June 30, 1856.

States.	Value of Exports.	Value of Imports.
Maine	$2,963,641	$1,940,773
New Hampshire	5,275	24,939
Vermont	1,031,450	1,560,118
Massachusetts	29,882,860	43,814,884
Rhode Island	407,374	345,803
Connecticut	800,824	737,401
New York	119,111,500	210,160,454
New Jersey	390	2,788
Pennsylvania	7,232,572	16,590,045
Delaware	76,380	3,053
Maryland	11,121,398	9,119,907
Virginia	5,495,367	692,395
North Carolina	376,174	274,960
South Carolina	17,360,549	1,905,234
Georgia	8,041,688	574,240
Florida	1,976,323	86,014
Alabama	23,734,170	793,514
Louisiana	80,865,080	16,682,392
Ohio	1,045,052	463,473
Michigan	981,028	880,688
Wisconsin	845,493	27,694
Illinois	1,345,223	277,404
Texas	1,940,589	321,834
California	10,718,074	7,298,839
District of Columbia	20,001	55,017
Oregon Territory	6,234	2,724
Washington Territory	91,299	8,955
	$326,964,908	$314,639,942

XI. AMERICAN STATES.
GOVERNMENTS OF NORTH AMERICA.

Governments.		Area in Sq. Miles.	Population.	Capitals.
Danish America, (Greenland)		880,000	9,400	Lichtenfels.
French Possessions, (St. Pierre)		118	200	St. Pierre.
Russian America		894,000	66,000	N. Archangel.
New Britain	British.	1,800,000	180,000	York Factory
Canada West	British.	147,832	999,847	Toronto.
Canada East	British.	201,989	890,261	Quebec.
New Brunswick	British.	27,700	200,000	Frederickton.
Nova Scotia, &c.	British.	18,746	300,000	Halifax.
Prince Edward's Island.	British.	2,134	62,348	Charlotte T'n
Newfoundland	British.	57,000	120,000	St. John's.
Vancouver Is. & British Oregon		213,500	7,500	Ft. Langley.
United States of America		3,306,834	23,191,876	Washington.
United States of Mexico		1,038,865	7,200,000	Mexico.
San Salvador		9,500	450,000	Cojutepeque.
Nicaragua		44,000	400,000	Granada.
Honduras		53,000	380,000	Comagagua.
Guatemala		59,000	1,100,000	N. Guatemala
Costa Rica		25,000	200,000	San José.
Mosquitia			6,000	Blewfields.
Honduras (British colony)			11,066	Balize.
Total		7,779,218	35,774,498	

WEST INDIAN GOVERNMENTS.

Governments.	Area in Sq. Miles.	Population.	Capitals.
Hayti ... } San Domingo, { Em.	11,000	800,000	Cape Hayt'n.
Dominica } { Rep	18,000	200,006	San Domingo.
Cuba............ } Spanish.	42,383	1,007,624	Havana.
Porto Rico	8,865	500,000	San Juan.
Jamaica.......... } British.	5,467	879,690	Spanish Town
Trinidad	2,000	60,319	Puerta d'Esp.
Windward Islands.			
Barbadoes....................	166	135,939	Bridgetown.
Grenada, etc	155	28,923	
St. Vincent	131	27,248	Kingston.
Tobago	187	13,208	Scarboro'.
St. Lucia	225	24,500	Castries.
Leeward Islands.			
Antigua	168	36,178	St. John's.
Montserrat	49	7,365	
St. Christopher and Anguilla ..	103	24,508	Basseterre.
Nevis	30	10,200	Charlestown.
Virgin Islands	187	4,027	
Dominica.........................	291	22,469	Rosseau.
Bahama Islands	5,422	27,519	Nassau.
Turk's Island...................	400	3,400	
Bermuda Islands	47	14,000	Hamilton.
Guadalupe, etc .... } French.	534	134,544	Basseterre.
Martinique........	822	121,145	Port Royal.
St. Martin's, N. Side	21	2,200	
St. Martin's, S. Side.. } Dutch.	11	3,500	
Curaçoa, etc	580	26,311	Wilhemstadt.
Santa Cruz, etc .... } Danish.	81	35,000	Christ'nstadt.
St. Thomas's.......	87	6,000	
St. John's..........	72	3,000	
St. Bartholomew's ....Swedish,	25	9,000	La Carenage.
Total....	91,910	3,669,817	

GOVERNMENTS OF SOUTH AMERICA.

Governments.	Area in Sq. Miles.	Population.	Capitals.
Venezuela, Republic..........	416,600	1,356,000	Caraccas.
New Granada, do.	330,000	2,363,000	Sta Fé de Bog
Ecuador, do.	325,000	665,000	Quito.
Bolivia, do.	374,480	1,650,000	Chuqu.saca.
Peru, do.	580,000	2,400,000	Lima.
Chili, do.	170,000	1,439,000	Santiago.
Argentine Confederation	927,000	800,000	Parana.
Uruguay, Republic............	120,000	250,000	Montevideo.
Buenos Ayres, do.	60,000	350,000	Buenos Ayres
Paraguay, do.	74,000	260,000	Asunçion.
Brazil, Empire of,.............	2,300,000	7,677,800	Rio deJaneiro
Guiana, (British)..............	76,000	127,695	Georgetown.
Guiana, (Dutch)	38,500	64,270	Paramaribo.
Guiana, (French)	21,500	30,000	Cayenne.
Patagonia	380,000	120,000	
Falkland Islands..............	16,000	500	Port Louis.
Total..............	6,553,265	19,553,265	
Grand Total of America.	14,130,208	58,997,580	

XII. POPULATION OF THE GLOBE.

Europe, ...	272,995,393
Asia, (including islands) . . .	626,000,000
Africa, (probably about) . . .	100,000,000
America, (as above).	58,997,580
Australia and Australian group, . .	1,445,000
Polynesia, (about)	1,500,000
Total population of the globe .	1,060,937,973

END OF VOL. III.

www.ingramcontent.com/pod-product-compliance
Lightning Source LLC
LaVergne TN
LVHW021224110826
845150LV00002B/235